Series

$$f(x) = \sum_{n=0}^{\infty} \frac{f^{(n)}(a)}{n!} (x - a)^n \quad \text{(general Taylor series)}$$

$$\frac{(a^n - 1)}{a - 1} = 1 + a + a^2 + a^3 + \cdots + a^{n-1} \quad \text{(geometric series, a} \neq 1)$$

$$\frac{1}{1 - x} = 1 + x + x^2 + x^3 + \cdots = \sum_{n=0}^{\infty} x^n, \quad |x| < 1$$

$$e^x = 1 + x + \frac{x^2}{2!} + \frac{x^3}{3!} + \cdots = \sum_{n=0}^{\infty} \frac{x^n}{n!}$$

$$\cos x = 1 - \frac{x^2}{2!} + \frac{x^4}{4!} - \cdots = \sum_{k=0}^{\infty} \frac{(-1)^k x^{2k}}{(2k)!}$$

$$\sin x = x - \frac{x^3}{3!} + \frac{x^5}{5!} - \cdots = \sum_{k=0}^{\infty} \frac{(-1)^k x^{2k+1}}{(2k + 1)!}$$

$$J_n(x) = \sum_{k=0}^{\infty} \frac{(-1)^k}{k!(k + n)!} \left(\frac{x}{2}\right)^{n+2k}$$

Fourier Series

$$f(x) \sim \frac{a_0}{2} + \sum_{n=1}^{\infty} \left[a_n \cos\left(\frac{n\pi x}{c}\right) + b_n \sin\left(\frac{n\pi x}{c}\right) \right]$$

$$a_n = \frac{1}{c} \int_{-c}^{c} f(x) \cos\left(\frac{n\pi x}{c}\right) dx$$

$$b_n = \frac{1}{c} \int_{-c}^{c} f(x) \sin\left(\frac{n\pi x}{c}\right) dx$$

Fourier Series: Complex Form

$$f(x) \sim \sum_{-\infty}^{\infty} d_n e^{i(n\pi x/c)}$$

$$d_n = \frac{1}{2c} \int_{-c}^{c} f(x) e^{-i(n\pi x/c)} \, dx$$

The Greek Alphabet

A	α	alpha	I	ι	iota	P	ρ	rho
B	β	beta	K	κ	kappa	Σ	σ	sigma
Γ	γ	gamma	Λ	λ	lambda	T	τ	tau
Δ	δ	delta	M	μ	mu	Υ	υ	upsilon
E	ϵ	epsilon	N	ν	nu	Φ	ϕ	phi
Z	ζ	zeta	Ξ	ξ	xi	X	χ	chi
H	η	eta	O	o	omicron	Ψ	ψ	psi
Θ	θ	theta	Π	π	pi	Ω	ω	omega

INTRODUCTION TO
DIFFERENTIAL EQUATIONS

Now consider the nonhomogeneous equation (N).

THEOREM 1.8: PRINCIPLE OF SUPERPOSITION

Let y_p be any particular solution of (N) and let $\{y_1, y_2, \ldots, y_n\}$ be a fundamental set of solutions of (H).   Then a general solution of (N) can be written in the form

$$y = (c_1 y_1 + c_2 y_2 + \ldots + c_n y_n) + y_p,$$

where $c_1, c_2, \ldots, c_n$ are arbitrary constants.

The term $y_c = c_1 y_1 + \ldots + c_n y_n$ is called the **complementary solution.** Hence Theorem 1.8 states that $y = y_c + y_p$. Of course, initial conditions can be specified. These initial conditions will determine the values of the constants c_1, $c_2, \ldots, c_n$.

EXAMPLE 1.9   Find a general solution of

(1.5) $(D^3 - 4D^2 + 5D - 2)y = 4x.$

A particular solution is $y_p = -2x - 5$. (Methods for finding this solution are explained in Section 4.3.) From Example 1.6 we know that

$$y_c = (c_1 + c_2 x)e^x + c_3 e^{2x}.$$

Hence a general solution of (1.5) is

$$y = (c_1 + c_2 x)e^x + c_3 e^{2x} - (2x + 5). \quad \blacksquare$$

EXAMPLE 1.10   A particular solution of

(1.6) $(D^3 + 3D^2 + 3D + 1)y = 3,$

is $y_p = 3$. Find a general solution.
    From Example 1.7 we know that

$$y_c = (c_1 + c_2 x + c_3 x^2)e^{-x}.$$

Hence a general solution of (1.6) is

$$y = (c_1 + c_2 x + c_3 x^2)e^{-x} + 3. \quad \blacksquare$$

PROBLEMS   In Problems 1–4, which equations have constant coefficients and which have variable coefficients over the indicated interval?

1. $3y^{(4)} + y'' - y = 3x - 1,\ -\infty < x < \infty.$

2. $3y^{(3)} + 2y'' + 5y = \sec x, \ -\pi/2 < x < \pi/2.$

3. $3xy''' - 2y' + y = \log x, \ 0 < x < \infty.$

4. $-y^{(4)} + y''' - y = (\tan x)y, \ -\pi/2 < x < \pi/2.$

Review determinants. Make sure that you know how to evaluate 3 by 3 determinants. In Problems 5–11, decide whether or not the solutions given determine a fundamental set for the equation.

5. $y''' - 3y'' + 2y' = 0, \ y_1 = 1, \ y_2 = e^x, \ y_3 = e^{2x}.$

6. $(D^4 - 8D^3 + 24D^2 - 32D + 16)y = 0, \ y_1 = e^{2x}, \ y_2 = xe^{2x}, \ y_3 = x^2e^{2x}, \ y_4 = x^3e^{2x}.$

7. $y''' - 3y'' - y' + 3y = 0, \ y_1 = e^{3x} + e^x + e^{-x}, \ y_2 = 2e^{3x} + 3e^x - e^{-x},$
$y_3 = 3e^{3x} + 4e^x.$

8. $y''' - 3y'' + 2y' = 0, \ y_1 = 1, \ y_2 = 1 + e^x, \ y_3 = 1 + e^x + e^{2x}.$

9. $y''' - 3y'' - y' + 3y = 0, \ y_1 = e^{3x} + e^x, \ y_2 = e^x + e^{-x}, \ y_3 = e^{3x} + e^{-x}.$

10. $y''' - 3y'' - y' + 3y = 0, \ y_1 = e^{3x} + e^x, \ y_2 = e^x - e^{-x}, \ y_3 = e^{3x} + e^{-x}.$

11. $x^2y''' + xy'' - y' = 0, \ y_1 = 1 + x^2, \ y_2 = 2 + x^2, \ y_3 = \log x.$

12. Show that $y_1 = e^x, \ y_2 = e^{-x}, \ y_3 = \cos x,$ and $y_4 = \sin x$ solve the equation $(D^4 - 1)y = 0.$ Show that $y_p = \sin 2x$ is a solution of $(D^4 - 1)y = 15 \sin 2x.$ Solve

$$(D^4 - 1)y = 15 \sin 2x, \qquad y(0) = 1, \ y'(0) = y''(0) = y'''(0) = 0.$$

13. Prove Theorem 1.4. Use mathematical induction and the two relations

$$L(c\varphi_1) = cL\varphi_1, \qquad L(\varphi_1 + \varphi_2) = L\varphi_1 + L\varphi_2.$$

14. (a) Show that if y_p and y are two solutions of $Ly = g,$ then $L(y_p - y) = 0.$

(b) Prove Theorem 1.8.

15. (a) Show that for any real number $\lambda, \ D^k e^{\lambda x} = \lambda^k e^{\lambda x}, \ k = 0, 1, 2, \ldots.$

(b) Show that if $L = D^n + b_{n-1}D^{n-1} + \ldots + b_1D + b_0$ when the b_n are real numbers, then for any real number $\lambda,$

$$L(e^{\lambda x}) = (\lambda^n + b_{n-1}\lambda^{n-1} + \ldots + b_1\lambda + b_0)e^{\lambda x}.$$

16. (a) Recall that $e^{(u+iv)x} = e^{ux}(\cos vx + i \sin vx).$ Show that if $\lambda = u + iv,$ then $D^k(e^{\lambda x}) = \lambda^k e^{\lambda x}, \ k = 0, 1, 2, \ldots.$

(b) Show that if $\lambda = u + iv,$ and $L = D^n + b_{n-1}D^{n-1} + \ldots + b_1D + b_0,$ then $L(e^{\lambda x}) = (\lambda^n + b_{n-1}\lambda^{n-1} + \ldots + b_1\lambda + b_0)e^{\lambda x}.$

4.2 *HOMOGENEOUS EQUATIONS WITH CONSTANT COEFFICIENTS*

We will now study methods of finding solutions of nth-order linear homogeneous differential equations with constant coefficients. These equations have the form

(2.1) $$Ly = (D^n + b_{n-1}D^{n-1} + \ldots + b_1D + b_0)y = 0,$$

where $b_0, b_1, \ldots, b_{n-1}$ are real constants. By analogy with the second-order case we define the **characteristic polynomial** associated with (2.1) by the relation

(2.2) $$p(\lambda) = \lambda^n + b_{n-1}\lambda^{n-1} + \ldots + b_1\lambda + b_0.$$

If $y = e^{\lambda x}$, for any real or complex number λ, then $y' = De^{\lambda x} = \lambda e^{\lambda x}$, $y'' = D^2(e^{\lambda x}) = D[De^{\lambda x}] = D(\lambda e^{\lambda x}) = \lambda D(e^{\lambda x}) = \lambda^2 e^{\lambda x}$, and so on. Hence

$$\begin{aligned} L(e^{\lambda x}) &= D^n e^{\lambda x} + b_{n-1}D^{n-1}e^{\lambda x} + \ldots + b_1 De^{\lambda x} + b_0 e^{\lambda x} \\ &= \lambda^n e^{\lambda x} + b_{n-1}\lambda^{n-1}e^{\lambda x} + \ldots + b_1\lambda e^{\lambda x} + b_0 e^{\lambda x} \\ &= p(\lambda)e^{\lambda x}. \end{aligned}$$

Since $e^{\lambda x} \neq 0$, then $y = e^{\lambda x}$ will solve (2.1) if and only if $p(\lambda) = 0$. Hence $y = e^{\lambda x}$ will solve (2.1) if and only if λ is a zero of (2.2). The **characteristic equation** associated with (2.1) is the equation $p(\lambda) = 0$. The roots of $p(\lambda) = 0$ are called the characteristic roots of (2.1). If (2.2) has n distinct characteristic roots $\{\lambda_1, \lambda_2, \ldots, \lambda_n\}$, then the set $\{y_1 = e^{\lambda_1 x}, y_2 = e^{\lambda_2 x}, \ldots, y_n = e^{\lambda_n x}\}$ is a fundamental set of solutions of (2.1).

EXAMPLE 2.1   The characteristic equation associated with

(2.3) $$y''' - 2y'' - y' + 2y = 0,$$

is $p(\lambda) = \lambda^3 - 2\lambda^2 - \lambda + 2 = (\lambda - 1)(\lambda + 1)(\lambda - 2)$. Hence a fundamental set of solutions is $\{y_1 = e^x, y_2 = e^{-x}, y_3 = e^{2x}\}$. A general solution of (2.3) is

$$y = c_1 e^x + c_2 e^{-x} + c_3 e^{2x}. \quad \blacksquare$$

EXAMPLE 2.2   The characteristic equation associated with

(2.4) $$(D^2 - 1)(D^2 + 4)y = 0$$

is $p(\lambda) = (\lambda^2 - 1)(\lambda^2 + 4) = (\lambda - 1)(\lambda + 1)(\lambda - 2i)(\lambda + 2i) = 0$. A fundamental set of solutions is $\{y_1 = e^x, y_2 = e^{-x}, y_3 = e^{2ix}, y_4 = e^{-2ix}\}$. Notice that y_3 and y_4 are complex-valued solutions. As in the second-order case, they can be replaced by $\cos 2x$ and $\sin 2x$. Hence a *real-valued* fundamental set of solutions of (2.4) is $\{e^x, e^{-x}, \cos 2x, \sin 2x\}$. A general solution is

$$y = c_1 e^x + c_2 e^{-x} + c_3 \cos 2x + c_4 \sin 2x. \quad \blacksquare$$

EXAMPLE 2.3   The characteristic polynomial associated with

$$(D^2 - D - 6)(D^2 - 2D + 3)y = 0$$

is $p(\lambda) = (\lambda^2 - \lambda - 6)(\lambda^2 - 2\lambda + 3) = (\lambda - 3)(\lambda + 2)(\lambda^2 - 2\lambda + 3)$. The characteristic roots are $3, -2, 1 + \sqrt{2}i$, and $1 - \sqrt{2}i$. From $\lambda = 3$ we obtain $y_1 = e^{3x}$, from $\lambda = -2$, $y_2 = e^{-2x}$ and from $\lambda = 1 \pm \sqrt{2}i$, $y = e^x(\cos\sqrt{2}x \pm i\sin\sqrt{2}x)$. The last two solutions are complex valued. They can be replaced by the real-valued solutions

$$y_3 = e^x \cos \sqrt{2}x, \qquad y_4 = e^x \sin \sqrt{2}x.$$

A fundamental set of solutions is $\{e^{3x}, e^{-2x}, e^x \cos \sqrt{2}x, e^x \sin \sqrt{2}x\}$ and a general solution is

$$y = c_1 e^{3x} + c_2 e^{-2x} + c_3 e^x \cos \sqrt{2}x + c_4 e^x \sin \sqrt{2}x. \quad \blacksquare$$

SOLUTION SET: CONSTANT COEFFICIENTS

If λ is a real root of multiplicity $m \geq 1$ of the characteristic equation, then $\{e^{\lambda x}, xe^{\lambda x}, \ldots, x^{m-1}e^{\lambda x}\}$ are m linearly independent solutions. If $\lambda = u \pm iv$ are complex conjugate roots of multiplicity $k \geq 1$, then $\{e^{ux} \cos vx, e^{ux} \sin vx, xe^{ux} \cos vx, \ldots, x^{k-1}e^{ux} \cos vx, x^{k-1}e^{ux} \sin vx\}$ is a set of $2k$ linearly independent solutions. The same procedure is used for each root. The set of all solutions obtained this way is a fundamental set of solutions of the homogeneous equation.

EXAMPLE 2.4   Find a general solution of

$$y''' - y'' - y' + y = (D^3 - D^2 - D + 1)y = 0.$$

Since $\lambda^3 - \lambda^2 - \lambda + 1 = (\lambda - 1)^2(\lambda + 1)$, the roots of the characteristic equation are $\lambda_1 = -1$ with multiplicity 1 and $\lambda_2 = 1$ with multiplicity 2. Hence $\{y_1 = e^{-x}, y_2 = e^x, y_3 = xe^x\}$ is a fundamental set of solutions. A general solution is

$$y = c_1 e^{-x} + c_2 e^x + c_3 xe^x. \quad \blacksquare$$

EXAMPLE 2.5   Find a general solution of

$$y^{(7)} - 2y^{(5)} + y^{(3)} = 0.$$

The characteristic polynomial is $p(\lambda) = \lambda^7 - 2\lambda^5 + \lambda^3 = \lambda^3(\lambda - 1)^2(\lambda + 1)^2$. Hence the roots are $\lambda_1 = 0$ with multiplicity 3 and $\lambda_2 = 1$, $\lambda_3 = -1$ each with multiplicity 2. Since $e^0 = 1$, a general solution is

$$y = (c_1 + c_2 x + c_3 x^2) + (c_4 e^x + c_5 xe^x) + (c_6 e^{-x} + c_7 xe^{-x}). \quad \blacksquare$$

EXAMPLE 2.6   Find a set of real-valued fundamental solutions of

$$y^{(6)} + 12y^{(4)} + 48y^{(2)} + 64y = 0.$$

The equation can be written as $(D^2 + 4)^3 y = 0$. Hence the characteristic roots are $\pm 2i$, each with multiplicity 3. A real-valued fundamental set of solutions is $\{\cos 2x, \sin 2x, x \cos 2x, x \sin 2x, x^2 \cos 2x, x^2 \sin 2x\}$. A general solution is

$$y = c_1 \cos 2x + c_2 \sin 2x + c_3 x \cos 2x + c_4 x \sin 2x$$
$$+ c_5 x^2 \cos 2x + c_6 x^2 \sin 2x.$$

This solution contains six arbitrary constants as required. Note that if d_i is an arbitrary constant for $i = 1, 2, \ldots, 6$, then

$$y = d_1 \sin 2x + d_2 x \sin 2x + d_3 x^2 \sin 2x + d_4 \cos 2x$$
$$+ d_5 x \cos 2x + d_6 x^2 \cos 2x,$$

is also a general solution. These two general solutions are not different in any essential way. Either one is a correct solution. ■

To use the solution technique that was just explained, it is necessary to factor nth-order polynomials. There is no method that will always work. However, there are certain facts which often help. For example, if $p(\lambda)$ is a given polynomial, then $p(\lambda)$ has a factor $(\lambda - \lambda_1)$ if and only if $p(\lambda_1) = 0$. Moreover, if

$$p(\lambda) = b_n \lambda^n + b_{n-1} \lambda^{n-1} + \ldots + b_1 \lambda + b_0,$$

and if $b_0, b_1, \ldots, b_n$ are all integers, any root λ_1 that is a rational number, say $\lambda_1 = r/q$ in lowest terms, must be such that r is a factor of b_0 and q is a factor of b_n.

EXAMPLE 2.7   Find all roots of $p(\lambda) = \lambda^3 + \lambda - 2 = 0$.
    If this equation has any rational root of the form r/q, then $r = \pm 1$ or ± 2 while $q = \pm 1$. Hence any rational root must be among the numbers $-1, 1, -2$, and 2. We see that $p(-1) = -4 \neq 0$. Hence $\lambda + 1$ is not a factor. Next we try 1. Since $p(1) = 0$, then $\lambda - 1$ is a factor; indeed, $p(\lambda) = (\lambda - 1)(\lambda^2 + \lambda + 2)$. By use of the quadratic formula we compute that remaining roots are $(-1 \pm \sqrt{7}i)/2$. ■

An equation of the form $\lambda^n - \alpha = 0$ can be solved exactly. Solving this equation is the same as finding the n different z's that satisfy the equation $z^n = \alpha$. This equation is solved with the help of the complex exponential form. The complex exponential form of a number $w = u + iv$ is essentially the polar form of w:

$$w = u + iv = \sqrt{u^2 + v^2} \left(\frac{u}{\sqrt{u^2 + v^2}} + \frac{iv}{\sqrt{u^2 + v^2}} \right)$$

$$= r(\cos \theta + i \sin \theta)$$

$$= r e^{i\theta}.$$

For example, $3i = 3e^{i\pi/2}$, $-1 = e^{i\pi}$, $1 = e^{2i\pi}$, and $e^{2k\pi i} = 1$ for $k = 0, 1, 2, \ldots$.
    To solve $z^n = \alpha$ let

$$z = x + iy = r e^{i\theta}$$

and

$$\alpha = a + ib = Re^{i\varphi} = Re^{i(\varphi + 2\pi k)}.$$

From $z^n = \alpha$ we see that

$$r^n e^{in\theta} = Re^{i(\varphi + 2\pi k)}.$$

Thus $r^n = R$ and $n\theta = \varphi + 2\pi k$ or

$$r = R^{1/n} \quad \text{and} \quad \theta = \frac{\varphi + 2\pi k}{n} \qquad \text{for } k = 0, 1, 2, \ldots, n - 1.$$

The n distinct roots $z_0, z_1, \ldots, z_{n-1}$ of $\alpha = a + bi = Re^{i\varphi}$ are

$$z_k = R^{1/n} e^{i(\varphi + 2\pi k)/n}, \qquad k = 0, 1, 2, \ldots n - 1.$$

If $\alpha > 0$, then $\alpha = \alpha e^{2\pi k i}$. All of the numbers

$$\lambda_k = \sqrt[n]{\alpha}\, e^{(2k\pi i)/n} \qquad \text{for } k = 0, 1, \ldots, n - 1$$

satisfy $(\lambda_k)^n = \alpha$. If $\alpha < 0$, then $\alpha = |\alpha| e^{(2k+1)\pi i}$ and the numbers

$$\lambda_k = \sqrt[n]{|\alpha|}\, e^{(2k+1)i\pi/n}, \qquad k = 0, 1, \ldots, n - 1$$

satisfy $(\lambda_k)^n = \alpha$.

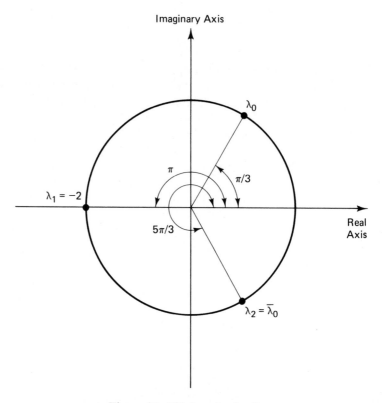

Figure 4.1. Third roots of -8.

EXAMPLE 2.8   Factor $\lambda^3 + 8 = 0$. Then find a general solution of $(D^3 + 8)y = 0$.
The third roots of -8 are

$$\lambda_0 = 2e^{\pi i/3} = 2\left[\cos\left(\frac{\pi}{3}\right) + i\sin\left(\frac{\pi}{3}\right)\right] \qquad (k = 0)$$

$$= 2\left(\frac{1}{2} + \frac{\sqrt{3}\,i}{2}\right) = 1 + \sqrt{3}\,i$$

$$\lambda_1 = 2e^{3\pi i/3} = 2e^{\pi i} = -2 \qquad (k = 1),$$

and

$$\lambda_2 = 2e^{5\pi i/3} = 2\left[\cos\left(\frac{5\pi}{3}\right) + i\sin\left(\frac{5\pi}{3}\right)\right] = 1 - \sqrt{3}\,i \qquad (k = 2).$$

These three roots are shown in Figure 4.1. The three roots lie in the complex plane on the circle with center at the origin and radius 2.

A general solution of $y''' + 8y = 0$ is

$$y = c_1 e^x \cos\sqrt{3}\,x + c_2 e^x \sin\sqrt{3}\,x + c_3 e^{-2x}. \quad\blacksquare$$

EXAMPLE 2.9   Find all roots of $p(\lambda) = \lambda^5 - 7 = 0$.
The zeros of this polynomial are the fifth roots of 7. From $7 = 7e^{2\pi ik}$ we compute

$$\lambda_0 = 7^{1/5}e^{0/5} = 7^{1/5} \qquad (k = 0),$$

$$\lambda_1 = 7^{1/5}e^{2\pi i/5} = 7^{1/5}\left[\cos\left(\frac{2\pi}{5}\right) + i\sin\left(\frac{2\pi}{5}\right)\right] \qquad (k = 1),$$

$$\lambda_2 = 7^{1/5}e^{4\pi i/5} = 7^{1/5}\left[\cos\left(\frac{4\pi}{5}\right) + i\sin\left(\frac{4\pi}{5}\right)\right] \qquad (k = 2),$$

$$\lambda_3 = 7^{1/5}e^{6\pi i/5} = 7^{1/5}\left[\cos\left(\frac{6\pi}{5}\right) + i\sin\left(\frac{6\pi}{5}\right)\right] \qquad (k = 3),$$

and

$$\lambda_4 = 7^{1/5}e^{8\pi i/5} = 7^{1/5}\left[\cos\left(\frac{8\pi}{5}\right) + i\sin\left(\frac{8\pi}{5}\right)\right] \qquad (k = 4).$$

These points are shown in Figure 4.2. They lie on the circle in the complex plane centered at the origin with radius $7^{1/5}$. The roots are equally spaced about this circle.

A calculator will be needed to obtain numerical values for the roots λ_i. For example, $\lambda_0 = 7^{1/5} \cong 1.47577$. Since $\cos(2\pi/5) \cong 0.30902$ and $\sin(2\pi/5) \cong 0.95106$, then

$$\lambda_1 \cong 0.45604 + i1.40354.$$

The remaining roots can be approximated in a similar manner. $\quad\blacksquare$

When factoring do not overlook the obvious. For example, $p(\lambda) = \lambda^5 + 4\lambda^3 + \lambda$ has a factor of λ, $p(\lambda) = (\lambda - 1)(\lambda^3 + 3\lambda + 1)$ has a factor $\lambda - 1$, and $p(\lambda) = (\lambda^2 - 1)(\lambda^3 + 3\lambda + 1)$ has factors $\lambda - 1$ and $\lambda + 1$. In many practical problems it is not possible to factor the given polynomial. In such cases it is often necessary to find roots by using numerical procedures and a digital computer.

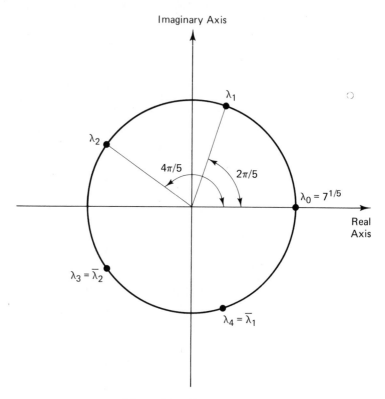

Figure 4.2. Fifth roots of 7.

PROBLEMS

In Problems 1–10, find a real-valued general solution.

1. $y''' - 27y = 0$.

2. $(D^3 - 3D^2 + 3D - 1)y = 0$.

3. $y^{(4)} - 6y^{(2)} + 9y = 0$.

4. $y^{(4)} - 2y''' + 2y'' - 2y' + y = 0$.

5. $y''' - 3y'' + 2y' = 0$.

6. $64y''' + 27y = 0$.

7. $(D - 7)(2D + 1)(D + 2)y = 0$.

8. $(D^2 + 4)(D^2 - 2D + 5)y = 0$.

9. $y^{(5)} + y^{(4)} - 4y' - 4y = 0$.

10. $(8D^3 - 12D^2 + 6D - 1)y = 0$.

In Problems 11–14, find a fundamental set of solutions by using the techniques of this section. Compute the Wronskian at $x = 0$ for the set of solutions that you find.

11. $(D^3 - D^2 + 4D - 4)y = 0$.

12. $(D - 1)^3 y = 0$.

13. $y''' + y'' - 4y' - 4y = 0$.

14. $y''' + 2y'' + 5y' = 0$.

In Problems 15–20, solve the initial value problem.

15. $y''' - y'' + y' - y = 0$, $y(0) = 0$, $y'(0) = 0$, $y''(0) = 1$.

16. $(D - 2)^3 y = 0$, $y(0) = 1$, $y'(0) = -1$, $y''(0) = 0$.

17. $y''' - y'' + y' - y = x$, $y(0) = y'(0) = 0$, $y''(0) = 1$.

Hint: $y_p = -1 - x$ is a particular solution.

18. $\dfrac{d^3 N}{dt^3} - 3\dfrac{d^2 N}{dt^2} + 3\dfrac{dN}{dt} - N = 0$, $N(0) = 1$, $N'(0) = 0$, $N''(0) = 2$.

19. $\dfrac{d^4 B}{ds^4} - B = 0$, $B(0) = 3$, $B'(0) = -1$, $B''(0) = 1$, $B'''(0) = 1$.

20. $\dfrac{d^3 R}{dt^3} + 2\dfrac{d^2 R}{dt^2} + \dfrac{dR}{dt} = t^2 + 4t + 2$, $R(0) = 2$, $R'(0) = -1$, $R''(0) = 1$.

Hint: $R_p = t^3/3$ is a particular solution.

21. Show that if $y = \varphi(x)$ is a solution of

$$Ly = (D^n + q_{n-1}D^{n-1} + \ldots + q_1 D + q_0)y = 0,$$

$$y(0) = c_1, \quad y'(0) = c_2, \quad \ldots, \quad y^{(n-1)}(0) = c_n,$$

then $y = \varphi(x - x_0)$ solves

$$Ly = 0, \qquad y(x_0) = c_1, \quad y'(x_0) = c_2, \quad \ldots, \quad y^{(n-1)}(x_0) = c_n.$$

22. Use Problems 15–21 to find solutions to each initial value problem.

(a) $(D^3 - D^2 + D - 1)y = 0$, $y(1) = 0$, $y'(1) = 0$, $y''(1) = 1$.

(b) $\dfrac{d^3 N}{dt^3} - \dfrac{d^2 N}{dt^2} + \dfrac{dN}{dt} - N = 0$, $N(-1) = 0$, $\dfrac{dN}{dt}(-1) = 0$, $\dfrac{d^2 N}{dt^2}(-1) = 1$.

(c) $(D - 2)^3 R = 0$, $R(\pi) = 1$, $R'(\pi) = -1$, $R''(\pi) = 0$.

(d) $(D^3 - 3D^2 + 3D - 1)y = 0$, $y(5) = 1$, $y'(5) = 0$, $y''(5) = 2$.

(e) $(D^3 - D^2 + D - 1)y = 0$, $y(-2) = 0$, $y'(-2) = 0$, $y''(-2) = 1$.

(f) $(D^4 - 1)y = 0$, $y(-10) = 3$, $y'(-10) = -1$, $y''(-10) = 1$, $y'''(-10) = 1$.

23. Verify that $y_1 = x$, $y_2 = \cos(\sqrt{3}\log x)$, and $y_3 = \sin(\sqrt{3}\log x)$ are solutions of the equation

$$x^3 y''' + 2x^2 y'' + 3xy' - 3y = 0, \qquad 0 < x < \infty.$$

Find a general solution of this equation over the interval $0 < x < \infty$. Find a general solution of this equation over the interval $-\infty < x < 0$.

24. Suppose that $L = D^n + b_{n-1}D^{n-1} + \ldots + b_1 D + b_0$ and $p(\lambda) = \lambda^n + b_{n-1}\lambda^{n-1} + \ldots + b_1\lambda + b_0$.

(a) Show that if y solves $Ly = Ae^{\alpha x}$ for some constants A and α, then $(D - \alpha)Ly = L(D - \alpha)y = 0$.

(b) Show that if y is a solution of $Ly = Ae^{\alpha x}$ and if α is not a root of $p(\lambda) = 0$, then $y = y_c + Be^{\alpha x}$ for some constant B and some function y_c, where $Ly_c = 0$.

(c) Show that if y is a solution $Ly = Ae^{\alpha x}$ and if α is a root of $p(\lambda) = 0$ of multiplicity $m \geq 1$, then $y = y_c + Bx^m e^{\alpha x}$ for some constant B and some function y_c such that $Ly_c = 0$.

25. (a) Show that for any interger $n \geq 0$, any positive α and any real number β,

$$\lim_{x \to \infty} x^n e^{-\alpha x}(\cos \beta x) = 0, \qquad \lim_{x \to \infty} x^n e^{-\alpha x} \sin \beta x = 0.$$

(b) Show that if $Ly = (D^n + b_{n-1}D^{n-1} + \ldots + b_1 D + b_0)y = 0$ and if all characteristic roots are either real and negative or complex with negative real part, then any solution $y = \varphi(x)$ tends to zero as $x \to \infty$.

26. Let $m_1, m_2, \ldots, m_n$ be given real or complex numbers. Define $y_i = e^{m_i x}$ for $i = 1, 2, \ldots, n$.

(a) Show that the Wronskian of $y_1, y_2, \ldots, y_n$ at $x = 0$ is

$$W(y_1, \ldots, y_n)(0) = \begin{vmatrix} 1 & 1 & \cdots & 1 \\ m_1 & m_2 & \cdots & m_n \\ m_1^2 & m_2^2 & \cdots & m_n^2 \\ \vdots & & & m_1^{n-1} \\ m_1^{n-1} & m_2^{n-1} & \cdots & m_n^{n-1} \end{vmatrix}.$$

(b) Show that

$$W(y_1, \ldots, y_n)(0) = \prod_{1 \leq i < j \leq n} (m_j - m_i).$$

(c) Show that $\{y_1, y_2, \ldots, y_n\}$ is a linearly independent set over $-\infty < x < \infty$ if and only if the numbers $m_1, m_2, \ldots, m_n$ are all distinct.

27. Let $y_1 = e^{mx}$, $y_2 = xe^{mx}$, $y_3 = x^2 e^{mx}, \ldots, y_k = x^{k-1} e^{mx}$ for some number m and some positive integer k. Show that the Wronskian of these functions (at $x = 0$) is

$$W(y_1, \ldots, y_k)(0) = \begin{vmatrix} 1 & 0 & 0 & \cdots & 0 \\ m & 1 & 0 & \cdots & 0 \\ m^2 & 2m & 2 & \cdots & 0 \\ \vdots & & & & \\ m^{k-1} & (k-1)m^{k-1} & (k-1)(k-2)m^{k-3} & \cdots & (k-1)! \end{vmatrix}.$$

Compute $W(y_1, \ldots, y_k)(0)$ in terms of m and k. Can it be zero for any choice of m and k?

4.3   *THE METHOD OF UNDETERMINED COEFFICIENTS*

The method of undetermined coefficients, which was explained in Section 3.7, will now be extended to nth-order linear equations of the form

(3.1) $\qquad Ly = y^{(n)} + b_{n-1}y^{(n-1)} + \ldots + b_1 y' + b_0 y = g(x).$

Here $b_0, b_1, \ldots, b_{n-1}$ are real numbers. As before, we require that $g(x)$ be a function that can be written in one of the following ways:

1. $g(x) = q(x)$, where q is a polynomial in x of degree m ($g(x) \equiv$ constant is allowed);
2. $g(x) = e^{\alpha x} q(x)$, where α is a real number and $q(x)$ is a polynomial in x of degree m;
3. $g(x) = e^{\alpha x} q(x) \sin \beta x$, where α and β are real numbers and $q(x)$ is a polynomial in x of degree m; or

4. $g(x) = e^{\alpha x} q(x) \cos \beta x$, where α and β are real numbers and $q(x)$ is a polynomial in x of degree m.

From (3.1) we can find the characteristic polynomial of the corresponding homogeneous equation, namely

(3.2) $$p(\lambda) = \lambda^n + b_{n-1}\lambda^{n-1} + \ldots + b_1\lambda + b_0.$$

There will be exactly n characteristic roots counting multiplicities.

   Case 1. Let $g(x) = q(x)$ Be a Polynomial in x of Degree m.
   Suppose that zero is not a root of $p(\lambda) = 0$. In this case we try to find a particular solution of (3.1) of the form

(3.3) $$y_p = A_0 + A_1 x + \ldots + A_m x^m.$$

The function y_p must be substituted into (3.1) and then like powers of x must be equated. This will determine the numerical values of the constants A_j.
   If $\lambda = 0$ is a zero of the characteristic polynomial (3.2) of multiplicity $r > 0$, the trial solution (3.3) will not work. In this case the trial solution must be of the form

$$y_p = x^r(A_0 + A_1 x + \ldots + A_m x^m).$$

EXAMPLE 3.1   Find a general solution of

(3.4) $$y''' - 2y'' - y' + 2y = x.$$

   The characteristic polynomial is $\lambda^3 - 2\lambda^2 - \lambda + 2 = (\lambda - 1)(\lambda - 2)(\lambda + 1)$. The characteristic roots are $1, 2$, and -1. Since none of these roots are zero, the trial solution should have the form

$$y_p = A_0 + A_1 x.$$

On substituting this into (3.4), we find that

$$-A_1 + 2(A_0 + A_1 x) = x$$

or $-A_1 + 2A_0 = 0$ and $2A_1 = 1$. Hence $A_1 = \frac{1}{2}$, $A_0 = \frac{1}{4}$, and $y_p = \frac{1}{4} + x/2$. A general solution of (3.4) is

$$y = c_1 e^x + c_2 e^{2x} + c_3 e^{-x} + \frac{1}{4} + \frac{x}{2}. \quad \blacksquare$$

EXAMPLE 3.2   Find a general solution of

(3.5) $$y''' + 3y'' = 2 + x^2.$$

   The characteristic polynomial $p(\lambda) = \lambda^3 + 3\lambda^2$ has zeros $0, 0$, and -3. Hence the trial solution must be of the form

$$y_p = x^2(A_0 + A_1 x + A_2 x^2).$$

On substituting y_p into (3.5) and equating coefficients of powers of x, we see that

$$y_p = \tfrac{10}{27}x^2 - \tfrac{1}{27}x^3 + \tfrac{1}{36}x^4.$$

Hence a general solution of (3.5) is

$$y = c_1 + c_2 x + c_3 e^{-3x} + (\tfrac{10}{27}x^2 - \tfrac{1}{27}x^3 + \tfrac{1}{36}x^4). \quad \blacksquare$$

Case 2. Let $g(x) = e^{\alpha x}q(x)$, Where q Is a Polynomial of Degree m.
In this case the trial solution will have the form

$$y_p = (A_0 + A_1 x + \ldots + A_m)e^{\alpha x},$$

when α is not a characteristic root. If α is a characteristic root of multiplicity $r > 0$, the trial solution will have the form

$$y_p = x^r(A_0 + A_1 x + \ldots + A_m x^m)e^{\alpha x}.$$

EXAMPLE 3.3   Find a particular solution of

(3.6) $$y''' - 2y'' - y' + 2y = e^{3x}.$$

The zeros of $p(\lambda) = \lambda^3 - 2\lambda^2 - \lambda + 2$ are 1, 2, and -1. Hence we take $y_p = Ae^{3x}$. On substituting y_p into (3.6) we see that $A = \tfrac{1}{8}$. Hence we have $y_p = e^{3x}/8$. $\blacksquare$

EXAMPLE 3.4   Find a particular solution of $y''' - 2y'' - y' + 2y = xe^x$.
The roots of the characteristic equation are 1, 2, and -1. Hence we take the trial solution

$$y_p = x(A_0 + A_1 x)e^x.$$

On substituting this y_p into the given equation, we find that $A_0 = -\tfrac{1}{4}$, $A_1 = -\tfrac{1}{4}$, and $y_p = (-\tfrac{1}{4})(x + x^2)e^x$. The general solution is

$$y = c_1 e^x + c_2 e^{2x} + c_3 e^{-x} - \tfrac{1}{4}(x + x^2)e^x. \quad \blacksquare$$

Cases 3 and 4. $g(x)$ Is Either $e^{\alpha x}q(x)\sin\beta x$ or $e^{\alpha x}q(x)\cos\beta x$.
In either case, the trial solution will have the form

$$y_p = e^{\alpha x}(A_0 + A_1 x + \ldots + A_m x^m)\cos\beta x$$
$$+ e^{\alpha x}(B_0 + B_1 x + \ldots + B_m x^m)\sin\beta x,$$

when $\alpha + i\beta$ is not a characteristic root of the associated homogeneous equation. If $\alpha + i\beta$ is a characteristic root of multiplicity r, the trial solution will have the form

$$y_p = e^{\alpha x}x^r(A_0 + A_1 x + \cdots + A_m x^m)\cos\beta x$$
$$+ e^{\alpha x}x^r(B_0 + B_1 x + \ldots + B_m x^m)\sin\beta x.$$

EXAMPLE 3.5   Find a particular solution of

(3.7) $$y''' + 8y = \sin x.$$

The characteristic polynomial is $p(\lambda) = \lambda^3 + 8$. Since $p(i) = -i + 8 \neq 0$, then $\lambda = i$ is not a zero of p. Hence we take the trial solution

$$y_p = A_0 \cos x + B_0 \sin x.$$

On substituting this y_p into (3.7), we see that $-B_0 + 8A_0 = 0$ and $A_0 + 8B_0 = 1$. Hence $A_0 = \frac{1}{65}$, $B_0 = \frac{8}{65}$, and

$$y_p = \tfrac{1}{65}(\cos x + 8 \sin x). \quad \blacksquare$$

A general solution of $Ly = g$ will have the form $y = y_c + y_p$, where y_c is a general solution of the corresponding homogeneous equation $Ly = 0$ and y_p is a particular solution. Notice that any forcing function $g(x)$ of the type being considered here will be a particular solution of some homogeneous linear differential equation with constant coefficients, i.e.,

$$(3.8) \qquad\qquad Mg = 0.$$

For example, if $g(x) = q(x)e^{\alpha x}$, then $(D - \alpha)^m g = 0$ and $M = (D - \alpha)^m$. If g is a particular solution of (3.8), then one can apply M to the equation

$$Ly = g$$

to obtain

$$(3.9) \qquad\qquad (ML)y = Mg = 0.$$

Notice that (3.9) is a homogeneous linear equation with constant coefficients. The characteristic roots for (3.9) are the roots for $Ly = 0$ plus the roots for $My = 0$. Thus a general solution of (3.9) contains y_c, i.e., it has the form

$$(3.10) \qquad\qquad y = y_c + y_r.$$

Our solution $y = y_c + y_p$ of (3.1) solves (3.9) and so must be of the form (3.10). Hence y_p has the form y_r. This is why the method of undetermined coefficients works. Equation (3.8) is often restated by saying that the operator M **annihilates** the function g. The technique for finding particular solutions y_p which results from this discussion is called the **method of annihilators.**

To illustrate the technique further, consider the problem

$$(D^2 + 1)^2(D - 2)(D + 1)y = g_i(x).$$

The characteristic roots of the homogeneous problem are $\pm i$ with multiplicity 2 and both 2 and -1 with multiplicities 1. Hence

$$y_c = c_1 \cos x + c_2 \sin x + x(c_3 \cos x + c_4 \sin x) + c_5 e^{2x} + c_6 e^{-x}.$$

If we take

$$g_1(x) = e^x - xe^{-x} + \sin x,$$

then g_1 is a solution of

$$My = (D - 1)(D + 1)^2(D^2 + 1)y = 0.$$

Hence $MLy = 0$ will have the additional roots $\pm i$ and 1 with multiplicities 1 and -1 with multiplicity 2. Thus

$$y_r = c_7 e^x + c_8 x e^{-x} + c_9 x^2 e^{-x} + c_{10} x^2 \cos x + c_{11} x^2 \sin x.$$

From this we see that the trial solution must have the form

$$y_{p1} = A_1 e^x + (A_2 + A_3 x) x e^{-x} + x^2 (A_4 \cos x + A_5 \sin x).$$

On the other hand if $g_2(x) = e^{2x} - x^2 e^{2x}$, then $g_2(x)$ is a solution of

$$My = (D - 2)^3 y = 0,$$

and

$$y_r = c_7 x e^{2x} + c_8 x^2 e^{2x} + c_9 x^3 e^{2x}.$$

Here the trial solution must have the form

$$y_{p2} = A_1 x e^{2x} + A_2 x^2 e^{2x} + A_3 x^3 e^{2x}.$$

Forced linear systems are all around. For example, traditionally, hi-fi components have been designed to be as nearly linear as possible, at least for signals in the range of the human ear. The more nearly "flat," i.e., linear the system, the better the fidelity. Hence analog hi-fi systems can be viewed as forced linear systems, with the forcing being the musical signal from the record, tape, etc., and the output being the audio signal. This design philosophy has changed with digital systems whose design is more nonlinear.

Photo 14. A linear response?

PROBLEMS

In Problems 1–8, determine a general solution.

1. $y''' - 27y = e^x$.

2. $y^{(4)} - 6y'' + 9y = x^2$.

3. $8y''' + y = 2 \sin x$.

4. $y^{(5)} + y^{(4)} - 4y' - 4y = 1 + e^x$.

5. $N''' - N = xe^x$.

6. $y''' - 3y'' + 2y' = 1 - x^2$.

7. $y^{(4)} - y = \cos x$.

8. $\dfrac{d^4 y}{ds^4} - y = e^s$.

In Problems 9 and 10, solve the initial value problem.

9. $y''' + y' = x + 2$, $y(0) = y'(0) = 0$, $y''(0) = 1$.

10. $y''' + y'' = x^2$, $y(0) = y'(0) = y''(0) = 0$.

In Problems 11–18, determine the proper form for a trial solution y_p. *Do not* evaluate the constants.

11. $y^{(4)} - 2y'' + y = e^x + xe^{-x}$.

12. $(D^2 + 4)^3 y = \sin 2x + \cos x$.

13. $(D^2 + 1)^3 y = x^3 e^x + 1$.

14. $\dfrac{d^5 B}{dt^5} + \dfrac{d^4 B}{dt^4} - 4\dfrac{dB}{dt} = 7 \sin \sqrt{2} t + 1$.

15. $27\dfrac{d^3 N}{dx^3} - 8N = xe^{2x} + xe^{-2x}$.

16. $\dfrac{d^3 R}{dt^3} - 3\dfrac{d^2 R}{dt^2} + 2\dfrac{dR}{dt} = 3 - t^3 + e^t \sin t$.

17. $(D - 7)(2D + 1)(D + 2)^2 y = e^{-\pi x} \cos 3x + 5x$.

18. $(D^2 + 1)(D^2 - 2D + 5)y = 3xe^x \sin 2x - e^x \cos 2x$.

19. Show that if $y_p = \varphi(x)$ is a particular solution of

$$Ly = (D^n + b_{n-1}D^{n-1} + \ldots + b_1 D + b_0)y = g(x),$$

then $y = A\varphi(x + B)$ solves $Ly = Ag(x + B)$.

20. Use Problems 1–8 and 19 to find a particular solution of each problem.

(a) $(D^3 - 27)y = -e^{x-1}$.   (b) $y^{(4)} - 6y'' + 9y = x^2 - 4x + 4$.

(c) $(8D^3 + 1)N = 2 \cos x$.   (d) $(8D^3 + 1)N = -4 \sin (x + \sqrt{2})$.

(e) $N''' - N = (x + 1)e^x$.   (f) $(D^4 - 1)y = 3 \sin x$.

21. Let y_{pk} solve

$$Ly = (D^n + b_{n-1}D^{n-1} + \ldots + b_1 D + b_0)y = g_k(x)$$

for $k = 1, 2, 3, \ldots, m$. Show that

$$y_p = d_1 y_{p1} + d_2 y_{p2} + \ldots + d_m y_{pm}$$

is a particular solution of

$$Ly = d_1 g_1(x) + d_2 g_2(x) + \ldots + d_m g_m(x).$$

22. Using Problems 1–8 and 21 as an aid, find a particular solution of each problem.

(a) $(D^4 - 1)y = 1$.   (b) $(D^4 - 1)y = 3e^x + 2 \cos x - 4$.

(c) $(D^4 - 1)y = 5 \cos x - 2e^x + 6$.   (d) $(D^3 - 27)y = e^{-x}$.

(e) $(D^3 - 27)y = 2e^{-x} - 5e^x$.

23. (a) Let

$$Ly = (D^n + b_{n-1}D^{n-1} + \ldots + b_1 D + b_0)y = 0$$

have the solution $y = \varphi(x)$. Show that $w = \varphi(cx)$ is a solution of

$$Mw = (c^n D^n + b_{n-1}c^{n-1}D^{n-1} + \ldots + b_1 cD + b_0)w = 0.$$

(b) If $p(\lambda) = \lambda^n + b_{n-1}\lambda^{n-1} + \ldots + b_1\lambda + b_0$ is the characteristic polynomial for $Ly = 0$, show that $p(\lambda c)$ is the characteristic polynomial for $Mw = 0$.

24. Let

$$L = D^n + b_{n-1}D^{n-1} + \ldots + b_1 D + b_0$$

and let

$$p(\lambda) = \lambda^n + b_{n-1}\lambda^{n-1} + \ldots + b_1\lambda + b_0.$$

Let

$$q(x) = q_0 + q_1 x + \ldots + q_k x^k.$$

(a) If y solves $Ly = q(x)e^{\alpha x}$, show that $(D - \alpha)^k Ly = L(D - \alpha)^k y = 0$.

(b) Show that if $p(\alpha) \neq 0$, then any solution of $Ly = q(x)e^{\alpha x}$ has the form $y = y_c + (Q_0 + Q_1 x + \ldots + Q_k x^k)e^{\alpha x}$, where $Q_0, Q_1, \ldots, Q_k$ are constants and y_c is a function such that $Ly_c = 0$.

(c) Show that if α is a root of $p(\lambda) = 0$ of multiplicity $r > 0$, then any solution y of $Ly = q(x)e^{\alpha x}$ has the form $y = y_c + x^r(Q_0 + Q_1 x + \ldots + Q_k x^k)e^{\alpha x}$, where Q_0, $Q_1, \ldots, Q_k$ are constants and $Ly_c = 0$.

25. Let

$$L = D^n + b_{n-1}D^{n-1} + \ldots + b_1 D + b_0$$

and

$$p(\lambda) = \lambda^n + b_{n-1}\lambda^{n-1} + \ldots + b_1 D + b_0.$$

Let

$$q(x) = (q_0 + q_1 x + \ldots + q_k x^k)$$

and let α and β be real numbers.

(a) Show that

$$[D - (\alpha + i\beta)][D - (\alpha - i\beta)] = D^2 - 2\alpha D + (\alpha^2 + \beta^2).$$

(b) Show that if y solves $Ly = q(x)e^{\alpha x} \cos \beta x$, then

$$(D^2 - 2\alpha D + \alpha^2 + \beta^2)^k Ly = L(D^2 - 2\alpha D + \alpha^2 + \beta^2)^k y = 0.$$

(c) Show that if $\alpha + i\beta$ is a root of $p(\lambda) = 0$ of multiplicity $r \geq 0$, then any solution of $Ly = q(x)e^{\alpha x} \cos \beta x$ has the form

$$y = y_c + (Q_{01} + Q_{11}x + \ldots + Q_{k1}x^k)x^r e^{\alpha x} \cos \beta x$$
$$+ (Q_{02} + Q_{12}x + \ldots + Q_{k2}x^k)x^r e^{\alpha x} \sin \beta x,$$

where $Ly_c = 0$ and $Q_{01}, \ldots, Q_{k2}$ are real constants.

(d) Show that any solution y of $Ly = q(x)e^{\alpha x} \sin \beta x$ also has the form given in part (c).

26. Suppose that all characteristic roots of

$$Ly = (D^n + b_{n-1}D^{n-1} + \ldots + b_1 D + b_0)y = 0$$

are either real and negative or complex with negative real part.

(a) Show that $Ly = A \cos \beta x$ has a solution y_p that is periodic with the same period as the function $\cos \beta x$.

(b) Show that if y is any solution of $Ly = A \cos \beta x$, then

$$\lim_{x \to \infty} [y(x) - y_p(x)] = 0.$$

(c) Repeat parts (a) and (b) for the equation $Ly = A \sin \beta x$.

4.4   VARIATION OF PARAMETERS

The method of variation of parameters can be applied to nth-order equations of the form

$$(4.1) \qquad Ly = y^{(n)} + b_{n-1}(x)y^{(n-1)} + \ldots + b_1(x)y' + b_0(x)y = g(x),$$

whenever a fundamental set of solutions $\{y_1, y_2, \ldots, y_n\}$ of the corresponding homogeneous equation is known. A general solution of the corresponding homogeneous equation is

$$y_c(x) = c_1 y_1(x) + c_2 y_2(x) + \ldots + c_n y_n(x).$$

As in the second-order case we shall replace the constants c_j by functions $v_j(x)$. Hence we use the trial solution

$$y_p = v_1(x)y_1(x) + v_2(x)y_2(x) + \ldots + v_n(x)y_n(x)$$

$$= \sum_{j=1}^{n} v_j(x)y_j(x),$$

and search for functions $v_1, v_2, \ldots, v_n$ such that y_p solves (4.1). We shall impose $(n-1)$ conditions, which make the calculation easier. The remaining condition will be that y_p solves (4.1). First compute

$$y_p' = \sum_{j=1}^{n} v_j y_j' + \sum_{j=1}^{n} v_j' y_j,$$

and imposed the requirement that

$$\sum_{j=1}^{n} v_j' y_j = 0.$$

This means that

$$y_p' = \sum_{j=1}^{n} v_j y_j'.$$

Continuing in this manner, next compute

$$y_p'' = \sum_{j=1}^{n} v_j y_j'' + \sum_{j=1}^{n} v_j' y_j'$$

and require that

$$\sum_{j=1}^{n} v_j' y_j' = 0.$$

This process is continued until we obtain the $(n-1)$ conditions

(4.2) $$\sum_{j=1}^{n} v_j' y_j^{(k)} = 0, \qquad k = 0, 1, \ldots, n-2.$$

This means

$$y_p^{(k)} = \sum_{j=1}^{n} v_j y_j^{(k)} \qquad \text{for } k = 0, 1, \ldots, n-1.$$

In particular, the equation for $y_p^{(n-1)}$ can be differentiated one more time to see that

$$y_p^{(n)} = \sum_{j=1}^{n} (v_j' y_j^{(n-1)} + v_j y_j^{(n)}).$$

The requirement that y_p satisfy (4.1) means

$$g = y_p^{(n)} + b_{n-1}y_p^{(n-1)} + \ldots + b_1 y_p' + b_0 y_p$$

$$= \sum_{j=1}^{n} (v_j' y_j^{(n-1)} + v_j y_j^{(n)}) + b_{n-1} \sum_{j=1}^{n} v_j y_j^{(n-1)}$$

$$+ \ldots + b_1 \sum_{j=1}^{n} v_j y_j' + b_0 \sum_{j=1}^{n} v_j y_j$$

$$= \sum_{j=1}^{n} v_j' y_j^{(n-1)} + \sum_{j=1}^{n} v_j (y_j^{(n)} + b_{n-1}y_j^{(n-1)} + \ldots + b_0 y_j)$$

$$= \sum_{j=1}^{n} v_j' y_j^{(n-1)} + \sum_{j=1}^{n} v_j L y_j.$$

Since $Ly_j = 0$ for $j = 1, 2, \ldots, n,$

(4.3) $$\sum_{j=1}^{n} v_j' y_j^{(n-1)} = g.$$

It is possible to solve (4.2) and (4.3) for $v_1'(x), v_2'(x), \ldots, v_n'(x)$ by using Cramer's rule. Let $W(x) = W(y_1, y_2, \ldots, y_n)(x)$ be the Wronskian of $y_1, y_2, \ldots, y_n,$ that is,

$$W(x) = \begin{vmatrix} y_1 & y_2 & \cdots & y_n \\ y_1' & y_2' & & y_n' \\ \vdots & & & \\ y_1^{(n-1)} & y_2^{(n-1)} & \cdots & y_n^{(n-1)} \end{vmatrix}.$$

Since $\{y_1, y_2, \ldots, y_n\}$ is a fundamental set, then $W(x) \neq 0$ for all x on the interval J. Let $W_k(x)$ be the determinant obtained by replacing the kth column of $W(x)$ by the column which is all zeros except that the last entry is $g(x)$. By Cramer's rule

$$v_k'(x) = \frac{W_k(x)}{W(x)}.$$

Since the constant of integration is not important, v_k can be any integral of v_k'. For example, for any choice of x_0 in J, define

$$v_k(x) = \int_{x_0}^{x} \frac{W_k(s)}{W(s)} \, ds.$$

A particular solution of (4.1) is

$$y_p = \sum_{k=1}^{n} v_k(x)y_k(x) = \sum_{k=1}^{n} y_k(x) \int_{x_0}^{x} \frac{W_k(s)}{W(s)} \, ds.$$

This particular solution can also be written in the form

(4.4) $$y_p(x) = \int_{x_0}^{x} \left\{ \sum_{k=1}^{n} \frac{y_k(x)W_k(s)}{W(s)} \right\} ds.$$

EXAMPLE 4.1   Find a general solution of $y''' + y' = \tan x$.

The characteristic polynomial for the corresponding homogeneous equation is $p(\lambda) = \lambda^3 + \lambda = \lambda(\lambda^2 + 1)$. Hence the characteristic roots are 0, i, and $-i$. Each root has multiplicity 1. A fundamental set of solutions of the corresponding homogeneous equation is $\{1, \cos x, \sin x\}$. Hence

$$W(x) = \begin{vmatrix} 1 & \cos x & \sin x \\ 0 & -\sin x & \cos x \\ 0 & -\cos x & -\sin x \end{vmatrix} = 1,$$

$$W_1(x) = \begin{vmatrix} 0 & \cos x & \sin x \\ 0 & -\sin x & \cos x \\ \tan x & -\cos x & -\sin x \end{vmatrix} = \tan x,$$

$$W_2(x) = \begin{vmatrix} 1 & 0 & \sin x \\ 0 & 0 & \cos x \\ 0 & \tan x & -\sin x \end{vmatrix} = -\sin x,$$

and

$$W_3(x) = \begin{vmatrix} 1 & \cos x & 0 \\ 0 & -\sin x & 0 \\ 0 & -\cos x & \tan x \end{vmatrix} = -\sin x \tan x.$$

Integration gives

$$v_1 = -\log |\cos x| \quad \text{and} \quad v_2 = \cos x.$$

The third integral is a bit more work. Write v_3' as

$$v_3'(x) = -\sin x \left(\frac{\sin x}{\cos x} \right) = \frac{\cos^2 x - 1}{\cos x} = \cos x - \sec x.$$

Hence

$$v_3(x) = \sin x - \log |\tan x + \sec x|.$$

A general solution is

$$y = c_1 + c_2 \cos x + c_3 \sin x - \log |\cos x| + (\cos^2 x + \sin^2 x)$$
$$- \sin x \log |\tan x + \sec x|. \quad \blacksquare$$

PROBLEMS   In Problems 1–3, find a general solution. Use variation of parameters.

1. $y''' - y' = 3x$.   2. $N''' + N' = \sec x$.

3. $x^3 y''' - 3xy' + 3y = x^5$.   *Hint:* Let $x = e^t$.

4. Consider the nth-order nonhomogeneous differential equation

(4.5) $y^{(n)} + a_{n-1} y^{(n-1)} + \ldots + a_1 y' + a_0 y = g(x),$

where $a_0, a_1, \ldots, a_{n-1}$ are constants. Let $Y(x)$ be the solution of the homogeneous version of (4.5) which satisfies the initial conditions $y(0) = y'(0) = \ldots = y^{(n-2)} = 0$ and $y^{(n-1)} = 1$. Show that

(4.6)
$$y_p(x) = \int_{x_0}^{x} Y(x-s)g(s)\,ds,$$

solves (4.5) and the initial conditions $y_p^{(j)}(x_0) = 0$ for $j = 0, 1, \ldots, n-1$.

5. Let $Y(x)$ be the function defined in Problem 4. Compute $Y(x)$ for each equation. Then write down, in integral form, a particular solution of each equation.

(a) $(D^2 + 1)(D - 1)y = g(x)$.

(b) $y^{(4)} - y = g(x)$.

(c) $y''' + 2y'' + 5y' = g(x)$.

6. Write down, in the form (4.6), a particular solution of each equation.

(a) $(D^2 + 1)(D - 1)y = g(x)$, $x_0 = 1$.

(b) $(D^2 + 1)(D - 1)y = g(x_0)$, $x_0 = -3$.

(c) $(D^4 - 1)y = g(x)$, $x_0 = 5\pi$.

(d) $(D^3 + 2D^2 + 5D)y = g(x)$, $x_0 = \sqrt{7}$.

(e) $(D^4 - 1)y = g(x)$, $x_0 = -\sqrt{7}$.

7. (Reduction of order) Suppose that y_1 is a nonzero solution of

$$Ly = y''' + b_2(x)y'' + b_1(x)y' + b_0(x)y = 0.$$

(a) If $y = v(x)y_1(x)$ is a solution of $Ly = g(x)$, show that $v(x)$ must solve

$$Mv = v''' + \left(b_2 + \frac{3y_1'}{y_1}\right)v'' + \left(\frac{3y_1''}{y_1} + \frac{2b_2 y_1'}{y_1} + b_1\right)v' = \frac{g}{y_1}.$$

(b) Use this method to find a general solution of $(D - 1)^3 y = \sqrt{x}e^x$ given that $y_1(x) = e^x$.

CHAPTER REVIEW

A linear nth-order differential equation $Ly = g$ is called **homogeneous** if $g(x) \equiv 0$, and **nonhomogeneous** if $g(x) \neq 0$. A **fundamental set** of solutions of $Ly = 0$ is a linearly independent set $\{y_1, y_2, \ldots, y_n\}$ of solutions. Linear independence can be checked by computing that the **Wronskian** $W(y_1, \ldots, y_n) \neq 0$. It is sufficient to check $W \neq 0$ at one point. Then the principle of superposition implies that $y_c = \sum c_i y_i$ is a general solution. If $Ly = 0$ has **constant coefficients**, then the problem $Ly = 0$ can be solved by the method of characteristic roots.

Solutions of the nonhomogeneous equation have the form $y = y_c + y_p$, where y_c is a solution of the corresponding homogeneous equation and y_p is any particular solution. If the forcing function has one of the special forms listed in Table 3.9, then the **method of undetermined coefficients** can be used to compute y_p. This method is summarized in Table 3.9. The **variation of constants** formula (4.4) can be used to solve *any* nonhomogeneous problem.

CHAPTER REVIEW PROBLEMS

Find a general solution of Problems 1–5.

1. $(D^3 + D^2 - 4D - 4)y = 8x + 12$.

2. $y''' + y'' - 4y' - 4y = 2e^{-x}$.

3. $y''' - y'' + y' - y = 2 + \sin x$.

4. $y''' + 8y' = x$.

5. $y''' + y' = \sec x \tan x$.

CHAPTER FIVE

Series Solutions of Differential Equations

We have seen that the solution of linear differential equations with *constant coefficients* can be accomplished in terms of elementary functions (i.e., sines, cosines, exponentials, and polynomials) and quadratures (i.e., integrations). Linear equations with *variable coefficients* cannot usually be solved so easily. For many differential equations with variable coefficients it is possible to find solutions in terms of series. The purpose of this chapter is to explain how series can be used to solve such equations.

Series methods can be used in the solution of a large number of differential equations that occur in the application of mathematics. Two important and typical examples are the **Hermite equation**

$$(0.1) \qquad y'' - 2xy' + \lambda y = 0,$$

and **Bessel's equation**

$$(0.2) \qquad y'' + \frac{1}{x} y' + \left(1 - \frac{v^2}{x^2}\right) y = 0.$$

The solution of (0.1) is usually needed over the interval $(-\infty, \infty)$ and the solution of (0.2) is usually needed over $(0, \infty)$. Notice that the coefficients of (0.1) are continuous functions of x for all x on the real line, while the coefficients of (0.2) become unbounded as x approaches zero and are not even defined at $x = 0$ (i.e., $x = 0$ is a *singular point* for the equation). Hence the reader may suspect that finding solutions of (0.2) will be more difficult than finding solutions of (0.1). This suspicion turns out to be correct.

The Hermite equation occurs in quantum mechanics. The *Schrödinger wave equation* for a simple harmonic oscillator is

(0.3)
$$\frac{-h^2}{8\pi^2 m}\frac{d^2\psi}{dz^2} + \frac{K}{2}z^2\psi = E\psi$$

where h is Planck's constant, E, K, and m are positive real numbers, and $\psi(x)$ is the *Schrödinger wave function*. The change to dimensionless coordinate $x = \alpha z$ reduces (0.3) to

(0.4)
$$\frac{d^2\psi}{dx^2} + (\lambda + 1 - x^2)\psi = 0$$

where $\alpha^4 = 4\pi^2 m K/h^2$ and $\lambda + 1 = (4\pi E/h)\sqrt{m/K}$. A second change of variables $\psi = ye^{-x^2/2}$ will reduce (0.4) to the Hermite equation (0.1). Many other important differential equations with variable coefficients occur in quantum mechanics. These equations also come up in the solution of partial differential equations. For example, the Bessel equation appears in Chapter 11 when certain partial differential equations, expressed in cylindrical coordinates, are being solved.

5.1 REVIEW OF POWER SERIES

By a power series in $x - x_0$ we mean an infinite series of the form

(1.1)
$$\sum_{n=0}^{\infty} a_n(x - x_0)^n = a_0 + a_1(x - x_0) + a_2(x - x_0)^2 + \ldots.$$

The terms $a_0, a_1, a_2, \ldots$ are given numbers, called the **coefficients** of the power series. The numbers x_0 and x as well as the coefficients a_n can be either real or complex numbers. For our purposes it is usually sufficient to assume that they are real numbers.

In calculus the reader has encountered power series in the form of **Taylor series**. Typical examples are

(1.2)
$$e^x = 1 + x + \frac{x^2}{2!} + \ldots = \sum_{n=0}^{\infty} \frac{x^n}{n!},$$

(1.3)
$$\sin x = x - \frac{x^3}{3!} + \frac{x^5}{5!} - \ldots = \sum_{n=0}^{\infty} (-1)^n \frac{x^{2n+1}}{(2n+1)!},$$

(1.4)
$$\cos x = 1 - \frac{x^2}{2!} + \frac{x^4}{4!} - \ldots = \sum_{n=0}^{\infty} (-1)^n \frac{x^{2n}}{(2n)!}$$

and the **geometric series**

(1.5)
$$(1 - x)^{-1} = 1 + x + x^2 + \ldots = \sum_{n=0}^{\infty} x^n.$$

Of course, any polynomial

(1.6)
$$p(x) = a_0 + a_1 x + a_2 x^2 + \ldots + a_m x^m$$

can be considered as an infinite series if we choose $a_{m+1} = a_{m+2} = \ldots = 0$.

The power series (1.1) is said to **converge** at a point x if the limit

$$\lim_{m \to \infty} \sum_{n=0}^{m} a_n(x - x_0)^n$$

exists and is finite. Otherwise, we say that the series **diverges** at x. A series may converge for some values of x and diverge for other values. For example, the series (1.2)–(1.4) converge for all real (and for all complex) numbers x. The series (1.5) converges for $-1 < x < 1$ and diverges for $|x| \geq 1$. The series (1.6) converges for all x. Series (1.1) **converges absolutely** at x if

$$\sum_{n=0}^{\infty} |a_n| |x - x_0|^n$$

converges. Absolute convergence implies convergence.

Suppose that $\sum a_n(x - x_0)^n$ converges for all x in the interval $|x - x_0| < R_1$ (i.e., the interval $x_0 - R_1 < x < x_0 + R_1$). If we call this sum $f(x)$, then

$$(1.7) \qquad f(x) = \sum_{n=0}^{\infty} a_n(x - x_0)^n, \qquad |x - x_0| < R_1.$$

let $\sum b_n(x - x_0)^n$ be a second series that converges on the same (or a larger) interval to a function $g(x)$, that is,

$$(1.8) \qquad g(x) = \sum_{n=0}^{\infty} b_n(x - x_0)^n, \qquad |x - x_0| < R_2,$$

where $0 < R_1 \leq R_2 \leq +\infty$. We recall from calculus some facts about these two functions and their series representations.

For any constant c, the power series for $cf(x)$ in the interval $|x - x_0| < R_1$ is obtained by multiplying the coefficients of the series for f by c. Thus

$$cf(x) = \sum_{n=0}^{\infty} (ca_n)(x - x_0)^n, \qquad |x - x_0| < R_1.$$

For example,

$$3e^x = \sum_{n=0}^{\infty} \frac{3}{n!} x^n.$$

The two series (1.7) and (1.8) can be added or subtracted term wise. Thus

$$f(x) \pm g(x) = \sum_{n=0}^{\infty} (a_n \pm b_n)(x - x_0)^n, \qquad |x - x_0| < R_1.$$

For example, from (1.5) we see that

$$(1.9) \qquad \frac{1}{1 + x} = \sum_{n=0}^{\infty} (-x)^n = \sum_{n=0}^{\infty} (-1)^n x^n, \qquad |-x| = |x| < 1.$$

Using (1.5) and (1.9), we see that

$$\frac{1}{1-x^2} = \frac{1}{2}\left(\frac{1}{1-x} + \frac{1}{1+x}\right) = \frac{1}{2}\left(\sum_{n=0}^{\infty} x^n + \sum_{n=0}^{\infty} (-1)^n x^n\right)$$

$$= \frac{1}{2}\sum_{n=0}^{\infty} (1 + (-1)^n)x^n = \frac{1}{2}\{2 + 2x^2 + 2x^4 + 2x^6 + \cdots\}$$

$$= 1 + x^2 + x^4 + x^6 + \cdots.$$

Hence

$$\frac{1}{1-x^2} = \sum_{n=0}^{\infty} x^{2n}, \qquad |x| < 1.$$

A second example uses (1.2):

$$\sinh x = \frac{1}{2}(e^x - e^{-x}) = \frac{1}{2}\left\{\sum_{n=0}^{\infty}\frac{1}{n!}x^n - \sum_{n=0}^{\infty}\frac{1}{n!}(-x)^n\right\}$$

$$= \frac{1}{2}\sum_{n=0}^{\infty}\frac{1}{n!}(1 - (-1)^n)x^n = \frac{1}{2}\left\{2x + \frac{2x^3}{3!} + \frac{2x^5}{5!} + \cdots\right\}$$

and thus

$$\sinh x = \sum_{n=0}^{\infty}\frac{x^{2n+1}}{(2n+1)!} \qquad \text{for all } x.$$

DERIVATIVES OF POWER SERIES

Assume that the series (1.7) converges on the interval $|x - x_0| < R$. Then $f(x)$ is continuous and has continuous derivatives of all orders on this interval. These derivatives can be computed by differentiating the series termwise. Thus from (1.7) we see that

$$(1.10) \qquad f'(x) = \sum_{n=0}^{\infty} na_n(x - x_0)^{n-1} = \sum_{n=1}^{\infty} na_n(x - x_0)^{n-1}.$$

The first term of the series can be omitted since it is zero. The series for $f'(x)$ can be written in powers of $(x - x_0)^n$ as follows. Let $m = n - 1$ so that $n = m + 1$ and $m = 0$ when $n = 1$. Using this substitution in the series for $f'(x)$ gives

$$f'(x) = \sum_{n=1}^{\infty} na_n(x - x_0)^{n-1} = \sum_{m=0}^{\infty} (m + 1)a_{m+1}(x - x_0)^m.$$

The name of the variable used in the summation does not matter. Thus

$$\sum_{m=0}^{\infty} (m + 1)a_{m+1}(x - x_0)^m = \sum_{k=0}^{\infty} (k + 1)a_{k+1}(x - x_0)^k$$

$$= \sum_{n=0}^{\infty} (n + 1)a_{n+1}(x - x_0)^n.$$

These are all the same series. Hence

$$f'(x) = \sum_{n=0}^{\infty} (n + 1)a_{n+1}(x - x_0)^n.$$

Further derivatives of $f(x)$ are computed in the same way. From (1.10) we see that

(1.11) $$f''(x) = \sum_{n=0}^{\infty} n(n - 1)a_n(x - x_0)^{n-2} = \sum_{n=2}^{\infty} n(n - 1)a_n(x - x_0)^{n-2}.$$

As before, $f''(x)$ can be written as

$$f''(x) = \sum_{n=2}^{\infty} n(n - 1)a_n(x - x_0)^{n-2}$$

$$= \sum_{m=0}^{\infty} (m + 2)(m + 1)a_{m+2}(x - x_0)^m$$

using the substitution $m = n - 2$. Hence

$$f''(x) = \sum_{n=0}^{\infty} (n + 2)(n + 1)a_{n+2}(x - x_0)^n.$$

For example, the derivative of (1.5) is

$$\frac{1}{(1 - x)^2} = \frac{d}{dx}\left(\frac{1}{1 - x}\right) = \sum_{n=0}^{\infty} nx^{n-1} = 1 + 2x + 3x^2 + 4x^3 + \dots$$

$$= \sum_{n=0}^{\infty} (n + 1)x^n, \qquad |x| < 1.$$

The second derivative is

$$\frac{2}{(1 - x)^3} = \frac{d^2}{dx^2}\left(\frac{1}{1 - x}\right) = \sum_{n=0}^{\infty} n(n - 1)x^{n-2} = 2 + 3 \cdot 2x + 4 \cdot 3x^2 + \dots$$

$$= \sum_{n=0}^{\infty} (n + 2)(n + 1)x^n, \qquad |x| < 1.$$

The Taylor series for $f(x)$ is its power series (1.7). From (1.7) we see that when $x = x_0$, $f(x_0) = a_0$. From (1.10) it follows that $f'(x_0) = a_1$, while (1.11) implies that $f''(x_0) = 2a_2$. Continuing this process gives $f^{(n)}(x_0) = n!a_n$. Thus $a_n = f^{(n)}(x_0)/n!$ and

(1.12) $$f(x) = \sum_{n=0}^{\infty} a_n(x - x_0)^n = \sum_{n=0}^{\infty} \frac{f^{(n)}(x_0)}{n!}(x - x_0)^n, \qquad |x - x_0| < R_1.$$

From (1.12) one can compute the power series of $f(x)$ once f is specified. For example, suppose that $f(x) = (1 + x)^{-1/2}$. Then

$$f(x) = (1 + x)^{-1/2}, \qquad f(0) = 1, \qquad \frac{f(0)}{0!} = 1,$$

$$f'(x) = -\frac{1}{2}(1 + x)^{-3/2}, \qquad f'(0) = -\frac{1}{2}, \qquad \frac{f'(0)}{1!} = -\frac{1}{2},$$

$$f''(x) = \frac{3}{4}(1 + x)^{-5/2}, \qquad f''(0) = \frac{3}{4}, \qquad \frac{f''(0)}{2!} = \frac{3}{4 \cdot 2!},$$

$$f'''(x) = -\frac{3 \cdot 5}{8}(1 + x)^{-7/2}, \qquad f'''(0) = \frac{-3 \cdot 5}{8}, \qquad \frac{f'''(0)}{3!} = \frac{-3 \cdot 5}{2^3 \cdot 3!},$$

and

$$f^{(4)}(0) = +\frac{3 \cdot 5 \cdot 7}{2^4}(1 + x)^{-9/2}, \qquad f^{(4)}(0) = \frac{3 \cdot 5 \cdot 7}{2^4}, \qquad \frac{f^{(4)}(0)}{4!} = \frac{(-1)^4(1 \cdot 3 \cdot 5 \cdot 7)}{2^4 \cdot 4!}.$$

From these calculations one might guess that

(1.13)

$$f^{(n)}(x) = \frac{(-1)^n 1 \cdot 3 \cdot 5 \ldots (2n - 1)}{2^n}(1 + x)^{-n - 1/2},$$

$$\frac{f^{(n)}(0)}{n!} = \frac{(-1)^n 1 \cdot 3 \ldots (2n - 1)}{2^n n!}.$$

This formula is correct. It can be verified using mathematical induction. Hence

(1.14)

$$\frac{1}{\sqrt{1 + x}} = \sum_{n=0}^{\infty} \frac{(-1)^n 1 \cdot 3 \cdot 5 \ldots (2n - 1)}{2^n n!} x^n.$$

We do not yet know in what interval (if any) this series converges. That question will be taken up later.

The power series for the product $f(x)g(x)$ is obtained by multiplying (1.7) times (1.8) and then grouping powers of $x - x_0$. Thus

$$f(x)g(x) = \left\{ \sum_{n=0}^{\infty} a_n(x - x_0)^n \right\} \left\{ \sum_{n=0}^{\infty} b_n(x - x_0)^n \right\}$$

$$= (a_0 b_0) + (a_1 b_0 + a_0 b_1)(x - x_0) + (a_0 b_2 + a_1 b_1 + a_2 b_0)(x - x_0)^2$$
$$+ (a_0 b_3 + a_1 b_2 + a_2 b_1 + a_3 b_0)(x - x_0)^3 + \ldots$$

$$= \sum_{n=0}^{\infty} c_n(x - x_0)^n, \qquad |x - x_0| < R_1,$$

where

$$c_n = a_n b_0 + a_{n-1} b_1 + a_{n-2} b_2 + \ldots + a_0 b_n$$

$$= \sum_{k=0}^{n} a_{n-k} b_k.$$

For example,

$$e^x \sin x = \left\{ 1 + x + \frac{x^2}{2} + \frac{x^3}{6} + \dots \right\} \left\{ x - \frac{x^3}{6} + \frac{x^5}{5!} - \dots \right\}$$

$$= x + x^2 + x^3 \left(\frac{1}{2} - \frac{1}{6} \right) + x^4 \left(-\frac{1}{6} + \frac{1}{6} \right) + x^5 \left(\frac{1}{5!} + \frac{1}{4!} - \frac{1}{3!2} \right) + \dots$$

$$= x + x^2 + \frac{x^3}{3} - \left(\frac{1}{30} \right) x^5 + \dots.$$

For higher powers of x, no pattern is apparent. Hence we must be content to compute the first few terms of the series. If $g(x)$ is a polynomial, the calculations can be done more easily. For example,

$$x^3 e^x = x^3 \sum_{n=0}^{\infty} \frac{x^n}{n!} = \sum_{n=0}^{\infty} \frac{x^{n+3}}{n!}.$$

Let $m = n + 3$ so that $n = m - 3$. Then $m = 3$ when $n = 0$ and

$$x^3 e^x = \sum_{m=3}^{\infty} \frac{x^m}{(m-3)!}.$$

As a second example consider

$$(3 - x^2)e^x = (3 - x^2) \sum_{n=0}^{\infty} \frac{x^n}{n!}$$

$$= \sum_{n=0}^{\infty} \frac{3x^n}{n!} - \sum_{n=0}^{\infty} \frac{x^{n+2}}{n!}$$

$$= \sum_{n=0}^{\infty} \frac{3x^n}{n!} - \sum_{m=2}^{\infty} \frac{x^m}{(m-2)!}$$

$$= \sum_{n=0}^{\infty} \frac{3x^n}{n!} - \sum_{n=2}^{\infty} \frac{x^n}{(n-2)!}$$

$$= 3 + 3x + \sum_{n=2}^{\infty} \left[\frac{3}{n!} - \frac{1}{(n-2)!} \right] x^n.$$

Two series are equal, that is,

$$\sum_{n=0}^{\infty} a_n(x - x_0)^n = \sum_{n=0}^{\infty} b_n(x - x_0)^n, \qquad |x - x_0| < R_1$$

if and only if $a_n = b_n$ for $n = 0, 1, 2, \dots$. For example, suppose that we wish to find a function h,

$$h(x) = \sum_{n=0}^{\infty} c_n x^n$$

such that

$$h(x) = \int_0^x e^{-t^2} \, dt.$$

An equivalent problem is to find $h(x)$ such that $h'(x) = e^{-x^2}$ and $h(0) = 0$. From (1.2) we see that

$$e^{-x^2} = \sum_{n=0}^{\infty} \frac{(-x^2)^n}{n!} = \sum_{n=0}^{\infty} \frac{(-1)^n x^{2n}}{n!}.$$

Since

$$h'(x) = \sum_{n=1}^{\infty} n c_n x^{n-1} = \sum_{m=0}^{\infty} (m+1)c_{m+1}x^m$$

$$= \sum_{n=0}^{\infty} (n+1)c_{n+1}x^n,$$

and since $h(0) = c_0$, then we must find c_m such that $c_0 = 0$ and

$$\sum_{n=0}^{\infty} (n+1)c_{n+1}x^n = \sum_{n=0}^{\infty} \frac{(-1)^n x^{2n}}{n!},$$

that is,

$$(1.15) \qquad c_1 + 2c_2 x + 3c_3 x^2 + 4c_4 x^3 + \ldots = 1 - \frac{x^2}{1!} + \frac{x^4}{2!} - \frac{x^6}{3!} + \ldots$$

The term multiplying x^n on the left in (1.15) must be equal to the corresponding term on the right. Thus we see that $c_0 = c_2 = c_4 = \ldots = 0$ and

$$c_1 = 1, \quad c_3 = \frac{(-1)}{3 \cdot 1!}, \quad c_5 = \frac{(-1)^2}{5 \cdot 2!}, \quad c_7 = \frac{(-1)^3}{7 \cdot 3!}, \quad \ldots$$

and in general

$$c_{2k+1} = \frac{(-1)^k}{(2k+1) \cdot k!}.$$

Thus

$$h(x) = x - \frac{x^3}{3} + \frac{x^5}{5 \cdot 2!} - \ldots = \sum_{n=0}^{\infty} \frac{(-1)^n x^{2n+1}}{(2n+1) \cdot n!}.$$

The **error function,** much used in probability and statistics, is defined to be

$$\text{erf}(x) = \frac{2}{\sqrt{\pi}} \int_0^x e^{-t^2}\, dt.$$

In terms of our function $h(x)$, $\text{erf}(x) = (2/\sqrt{\pi})h(x)$. Hence

$$\text{erf}(x) = \frac{2}{\sqrt{\pi}} \sum_{n=0}^{\infty} \frac{(-1)^n x^{2n+1}}{(2n+1)n!}.$$

We saw earlier that a power series which is absolutely convergent at x is convergent at x. A useful test for absolute convergence is the **ratio test**. This test is stated in the following theorem.

THEOREM 1.1

For any fixed x, if the limit

$$(1.16) \qquad \lim_{n \to \infty} \left| \frac{a_{n+1}(x - x_0)^{n+1}}{a_n(x - x_0)^n} \right| = l$$

exists, then the power series (1.1) converges absolutely when $l < 1$ and diverges when $l > 1$. This test gives no information when $l = 1$.

The ratio test can be restated as follows. Suppose that

$$\lim_{n \to \infty} \left| \frac{a_n}{a_{n+1}} \right| = R$$

exists with $0 \le R \le \infty$. Then

$$\left| \frac{a_{n+1}(x - x_0)^{n+1}}{a_n(x - x_0)^n} \right| = \left| \frac{a_{n+1}}{a_n} \right| |x - x_0| \to \frac{|x - x_0|}{R}.$$

Hence the series (1.1) converges absolutely whenever $|x - x_0| < R$ and diverges when $|x - x_0| > R$. For example, consider the series (1.2) for e^x. Here $a_n = 1/n!$, so that

$$\lim_{n \to \infty} \left| \frac{a_n}{a_{n+1}} \right| = \lim_{n \to \infty} \frac{(n + 1)!}{n!} = \lim_{n \to \infty} (n + 1) = \infty.$$

Hence $R = \infty$; that is, the series (1.2) converges absolutely for all x.

As a second example consider the series (1.5) for $1/(1 - x)$. Here we find that $a_n = 1$ for all n, so that

$$\lim_{n \to \infty} \left| \frac{a_n}{a_{n+1}} \right| = \lim_{n \to \infty} \frac{1}{1} = 1 = R.$$

Hence the series (1.5) converges absolutely when $|x| < 1$ and diverges when $|x| > 1$. As a third example consider the series $\sum n! x^n$. For this series we find that

$$\lim_{n \to \infty} \left| \frac{a_n}{a_{n+1}} \right| = \lim_{n \to \infty} \frac{n!}{(n + 1)!} = 0.$$

Since $R = 0$, the series converges only when $x = 0$.

It is a remarkable fact that every power series has convergence properties similar to one of the three series

$$\sum \frac{x^n}{n!}, \qquad \sum x^n, \qquad \sum n! x^n.$$

Indeed, for every power series (1.1) there is an R, with $0 \le R \le \infty$, called the **radius of convergence** of (1.1), such that the following statements are true.

(a) If $R = 0$, then (1.1) converges only when $x = x_0$.
(b) If $R = \infty$, then (1.1) converges absolutely for all x.
(c) If $0 < R < \infty$, then (1.1) converges absolutely when $|x - x_0| < R$ and diverges when $|x - x_0| > R$.

For example, consider the series (1.14) for $(1 + x)^{-1/2}$. Since

$$\left|\frac{a_n}{a_{n+1}}\right| = \frac{1 \cdot 3 \dots (2n - 1)}{2^n n!} \frac{2^{n+1}(n + 1)!}{1 \cdot 3 \dots (2n - 1)(2n + 1)} = \frac{2(n + 1)}{2n + 1} \to 1$$

as $n \to \infty$, the radius of convergence of this series is $R = 1$.

When the ratio test can be applied, this test will determine the radius of convergence R. When the ratio test does not apply, for example, when $a_n = 0$ for certain arbitrarily large values of n or when $|a_n/a_{n+1}|$ does not have a limit as $n \to \infty$, the computation of the radius of convergence is rather complicated. In some situations where the ratio test does not apply it is possible to estimate the radius of convergence with the help of the **comparison test.** This comparison test can be stated as follows.

THEOREM 1.2

If $|a_n| \leq A_n$ for all $n \geq N$, then $\sum a_n(x - x_0)^n$ is absolutely convergent whenever $\sum A_n(x - x_0)^n$ is absolutely convergent.

In other words, the radius of convergence of $\sum a_n(x - x_0)^n$ is at least as large as the radius of convergence of $\sum A_n(x - x_0)^n$. For example, from (1.2) and (1.3) we see that the radius of convergence of the series for $\sin x$ is at least as large as the radius of convergence of the series for e^x. But the latter radius of convergence is ∞. Hence the radius of convergence of the $\sin$ series is also ∞. By the same argument we see that the radius of convergence of the cosine series (1.4) is ∞.

The radius of convergence can be computed precisely whenever $f(x) = p(x)/q(x)$ is the ratio of two polynomials $p(x)$ and $q(x)$, where p and q have no common factors. Let $z_1, z_2, \dots, z_l$ be the distinct zeros of $q(x)$. Given x_0, let R be the distance from x_0 to the nearest zero of $q(x)$, that is,

$$R = \min \{|x_0 - z_j| : j = 1, 2, \dots, l\}.$$

Then R is the radius of convergence of the power series for $f(x)$.

For example, let $f(x) = 1/(x^4 - 3x^2 - 4)$ and take $x_0 = 0$. Here $p(x) = 1$, while

$$q(x) = x^4 - 3x^2 - 4 = (x^2 + 1)(x^2 - 4) = (x + i)(x - i)(x + 2)(x - 2)$$

has roots $z_1 = i, z_2 = -i, z_3 = -2$, and $z_4 = 2$. The roots ± 2 are distance 2 from $x_0 = 0$, while the roots $\pm i$ are distance 1 from $x_0 = 0$. Hence the power series for $f(x)$ based at $x_0 = 0$ has radius of convergence $R = 1$. Similarly, for the same function $f(x)$ if we choose $x_0 = 5$, then the root z_i nearest $x_0 = 5$ is $z_4 = 2$. Hence $R = 3$.

DEFINITION 1.3: ANALYTIC FUNCTION

A function f defined on an interval I containing x_0 is said to be analytic at x_0 if f can be expanded in a Taylor series $f(x) = \sum a_n(x - x_0)^n$ which has a positive radius of convergence.

It can be shown that whenever $f(x)$ has a Taylor series convergent to $f(x)$ in an interval $|x - a| < R$, then $f(x)$ is analytic at each x_0 in this interval. Hence e^x, $\sin x$, and $\cos x$ are analytic at each point x_0 in the interval $-\infty < x_0 < \infty$. Since $(1 - x)^{-1} = \sum_{n=0}^{\infty} x^n$ for $-1 < x < 1$, then the function $(1 - x)^{-1}$ is analytic at x_0 for at least each x_0 in the interval $-1 < x_0 < 1$.

PROBLEMS

1. Determine the radius of convergence for each power series.

(a) $\displaystyle\sum_{n=0}^{\infty} (x - 2)^n$.

(b) $\displaystyle\sum_{n=0}^{\infty} n^2 x^n$.

(c) $\displaystyle\sum_{n=1}^{\infty} \frac{2^n}{n + 1} x^n$.

(d) $\displaystyle\sum_{n=0}^{\infty} \left(\frac{x - 1}{3}\right)^n$.

(e) $\displaystyle\sum_{n=0}^{\infty} \frac{2^n}{n!} x^n$.

(f) $\displaystyle\sum_{n=1}^{\infty} \frac{\sin n}{n!} (x + 1)^n$.

(g) $\displaystyle\sum_{n=3}^{\infty} n(4x - 1)^n$.

(h) $\displaystyle\sum_{n=0}^{\infty} \sqrt{n!}\, (x + 2)^n$.

(i) $\displaystyle\sum_{n=3}^{17} x^n$.

(j) $\displaystyle\sum_{n=0}^{\infty} \frac{x^n}{(2n + 1)!}$.

(k) $\displaystyle\sum_{n=0}^{\infty} \frac{(\cos n)^n}{(2n)!} x^n$.

2. Each series converges absolutely when $|x| < 1$. At the end points $x = \pm 1$ determine whether the series converges, converges absolutely, or diverges. *Hint:* Get out your calculus book!

(a) $\displaystyle\sum_{n=1}^{\infty} (-1)^n x^n$.

(b) $\displaystyle\sum_{n=0}^{\infty} \frac{x^n}{n}$.

(c) $\displaystyle\sum_{n=1}^{\infty} (-1)^n n x^n$.

(d) $\displaystyle\sum_{n=1}^{\infty} (-1)^n \frac{x^n}{n^2}$.

(e) $\displaystyle\sum_{n=1}^{\infty} (-1)^n \frac{x^n}{n(n + 1)}$.

3. Let f and g be defined by the formulas

$$f(x) = \sum_{n=0}^{\infty} (-1)^n(n+1)x^n, \qquad g(x) = \sum_{n=0}^{\infty} x^n.$$

Compute the power series (at $x_0 = 0$) for each function.

(a) $f(x) + g(x)$.

(b) $g(x) - (1 + x + x^2)$.

(c) $xf(x) - g(x)$.

(d) $xg''(x)$.

(e) $x^2 g'(x)$.

(f) $xg'''(x) + f(x)$.

(g) $\cosh x + g(x^2)$.

(h) $\cos(3x) - 2g(x^2)$.

4. Let $h(x) = \sum_{n=0}^{\infty} c_n x^n$. In each case determine the values of the coefficients c_n that will make the equation true.

(a) $h'(x) = (1 - x)^{-1}$, $h(0) = 1$, and $-1 < x < 1$.

(b) $h''(x) = \sin x$, $h(0) = h'(0) = 0$.

(c) $h(x) = \sinh x - \cosh x$.

(d) $h'(x) = e^x + e^{-x}$, $h(0) = 1$.

(e) $h(x) = \int_0^x \cos t^2 \, dt$.

(f) $h(x) = 3 + \int_0^x \cos t^2 \, dt$.

(g) $h(x) = \int_0^{x^2} e^t \, dt$.

(h) $h(x) = 1 + \int_0^{x^2} e^t \, dt$.

(i) $h(x) = \pi + \int_0^x \operatorname{erf}(t) \, dt$.

5. Write each series in powers of x^n. A model computation for this problem is

$$\sum_{n=1}^{\infty} nx^{n-1} = \sum_{m=0}^{\infty} (m+1)x^m = \sum_{n=0}^{\infty} (n+1)x^n.$$

(a) $\sum_{n=2}^{\infty} n(n-1)x^{n-2}$.

(b) $\sum_{n=2}^{\infty} n(n-1)x^{n-1}$.

(c) $\sum_{n=3}^{\infty} \frac{1}{n^2} x^{n-3}$.

(d) $\frac{1}{x} \sum_{n=1}^{\infty} nx^{n+1}$.

(e) $\sum_{n=3}^{\infty} \frac{n(n-1)(n-2)}{n!} x^{n-3}$.

(f) $x \sum_{n=3}^{\infty} \frac{n(n-1)(n-2)}{2^n} x^{n-3}$.

6. Determine the Taylor series, in powers of $x - x_0$, for each function.

(a) e^{-x^2}, $x_0 = 0$.

(b) e^{3x}, $x_0 = 1$.

(c) $x + 2x^2$, $x_0 = 1$.

(d) $\log x$, $x_0 = 1$.

(e) $(2 - x)^{-1}$, $x_0 = 0$.

(f) $x^2 - 3x + 1$, $x_0 = -1$.

(g) $\sin x$, $x_0 = \pi$.

(h) $(1 + x)^{-1}$, $x_0 = 2$.

(i) $\cos \pi x$, $x_0 = 1$.

(j) x^{-1}, $x_0 = 1$.

(k) $(x - 2)^{-1}$, $x_0 = 0$.

(l) $(x^2 - 2)^{-1}$, $x_0 = 0$.

(m) $\dfrac{x - 1}{x - 2}$, $x_0 = 0$.

7. Let $x = -u^2$ in (1.5) to obtain

$$\frac{1}{1 + u^2} = 1 - u^2 + u^4 - u^6 + \ldots = \sum_{n=0}^{\infty} (-1)^n u^{2n}.$$

(a) Find the radius of convergence of this function.

(b) The integral of this function is arctan u. Compute the power series for arctan u about $x_0 = 0$.

(c) Show that

$$\frac{\pi}{4} = 1 - \frac{1}{3} + \frac{1}{5} - \frac{1}{7} + \dots .$$

8. Suppose that $y(x) = \sum_{n=0}^{\infty} a_n(x - x_0)^n$ for $|x - x_0| < R$. Then in the same interval show that for $j = 0, 1, \dots, k$ and for $k = 1, 2, 3, \dots$

$$x^j y^{(k)}(x) = \sum_{n=k}^{\infty} n(n - 1)(n - 2) \dots (n - k + 1)a_n(x - x_0)^{n-k+j}$$

$$= \sum_{n=j}^{x} (n + k - j)(n + k - j - 1) \dots (n - j + 1)a_{n+k-j}(x - x_0)^n.$$

9. Use mathematical induction to prove that (1.13) is correct for all $n \geq 0$.

In Problems 10–16, find the Taylor series for the given function at $x_0 = 0$. Determine the radius of convergence of each series.

10. $(1 - x)^{-3}$.

11. $(1 + x)^{-2}$.

12. $\log(1 + x)$. *Hint:* The derivative is $(1 + x)^{-1}$.

13. $(1 + x)^{-3/2}$.

14. $(1 - x)^{1/2}$.

15. $(3 - x)^{-1}$.

16. $(1 + x)^{5/2}$.

The functions defined in Problems 17–23 have been found to be useful in applied mathematics. Find their Taylor series at $x_0 = 0$.

17. $\text{Si}(x) = \int_0^x \frac{\sin t}{t} \, dt$.

18. $\int_0^x \frac{\cos t - 1}{t} \, dt$.

19. $\text{Shi}(x) = \int_0^x \frac{\sinh t}{t} \, dt$.

20. $\int_0^x \frac{\cosh t - 1}{t} \, dt$.

21. $\text{erfc}(x) = 1 - \text{erf}(x)$.

22. $C(x) = \int_0^x \cos\left(\frac{\pi t^2}{2}\right) dt$.

23. $S(x) = \int_0^x \sin\left(\frac{\pi t^2}{2}\right) dt$.

In Problems 24–28, compute the first three terms in the Taylor series at $x_0 = 0$.

24. $\log(\cos x)$.

25. $\log(1 + \sin x)$.

26. $e^{\sin x}$.

27. $\tan x$.

28. $(1 + e^x)^{-1}$.

29. *Without computing the Taylor series* determine the radius of convergence of the Taylor series at x_0 for each function.

(a) $\dfrac{1}{x^2 + 4}$, $x_0 = 0$.

(b) $\dfrac{1}{x^2 + 4}$, $x_0 = 1$.

(c) $\dfrac{x}{x^4 + x^2 - 6}$, $x_0 = 0$.

(d) $\dfrac{x}{x^4 + x^2 - 6}$, $x_0 = 4$.

(e) $\dfrac{x^2 + 2}{x^4 - 4x^2 - 5}$, $x_0 = 0$.   (f) $\dfrac{x^3 + 2x}{x^3 - 3x^2 + 3x - 1}$, $x_0 = 0$.

(g) $\dfrac{x^3 + 2x}{x^3 - 3x^2 + 3x - 1}$, $x_0 = -2$.

30. If $z_1 \neq x_0$, then for $u = (x - x_0)/(z_1 - x_0)$ one has $(x - z_1)^{-1} = (x_0 - z_1)^{-1}(1 - u)^{-1}$.

(a) Compute the Taylor series at x_0 for $f(x) = (x - z_1)^{-1}$.

(b) Show that this series has radius of convergence $R = |x_0 - z_1|$.

31. Show that when z_0, z_1, and z_2 are three distinct points, then

$$\frac{z - z_2}{z - z_1} = \frac{z_0 - z_2}{z_0 - z_1} + \sum_{n=1}^{\infty} (z_2 - z_1)(z_1 - z_0)^{-n-1}(z - z_0)^n \qquad \text{for } |z - z_0| < |z_1 - z_0|.$$

5.2 LINEAR EQUATIONS WITH ANALYTIC COEFFICIENTS

In this section we develop a method of solution for linear differential equations whose coefficients are analytic functions on some given interval J. This method consists of assuming that the unknown function y can be expressed as a power series $\sum a_n(x - x_0)^n$. This series is substituted for y in the given differential equation. We then solve for the unknown coefficients a_n. The following two simple examples will illustrate the main features of this method of solution.

EXAMPLE 2.1   Find a general solution of

(2.1) $y' = 2y$.

Use the power series method.

This equation has the form $y' + b_0(x)y = 0$, where $b_0(x) = -2$. Clearly, $b_0(x) = -2$ is an analytic function of x for $-\infty < x < \infty$. A general solution of this equation is $y(x) = ce^{2x}$, where c is an arbitrary constant. We wish to show that this solution can be obtained by the power series method.

Assume a solution of the form

$$y(x) = \sum_{n=0}^{\infty} a_n x^n,$$

where the coefficients a_n are to be determined. On substituting this series into (2.1), we find

$$y'(x) = \sum_{n=1}^{\infty} n a_n x^{n-1} = \sum_{n=0}^{\infty} (n + 1)a_{n+1} x^n$$

and

$$2y(x) = \sum_{n=0}^{\infty} 2a_n x^n.$$

Hence it is required that

$$\text{(2.2)} \qquad \sum_{n=0}^{\infty} (n+1)a_{n+1}x^n = \sum_{n=0}^{\infty} (2a_n)x^n.$$

In order that the two power series be equal, it must be the case that each coefficient on the right in (2.2) is equal to the corresponding coefficient on the left, that is, $(n+1)a_{n+1} = 2a_n$ for $n = 0, 1, 2, \ldots$. This system of equations can be rewritten as the following **recurrence relation:**

$$\text{(2.3)} \qquad a_{n+1} = \frac{2}{n+1} a_n, \qquad n = 0, 1, 2, \ldots.$$

This recurrence relation is used as follows. We have no information about a_0. Hence we set $a_0 = c$, an arbitrary constant. In (2.3) with $n = 0$ we see that $a_1 = 2a_0 = 2c$. We now use (2.3) successively for $n = 1, 2, 3, \ldots$. We find that

$$a_2 = \frac{2}{2} a_1 = 2c, \qquad a_3 = \frac{2}{3} a_2 = \frac{2}{3}\left(\frac{2^2}{2}c\right) = \frac{2^3 c}{3!}, \qquad a_4 = \frac{2}{4} a_3 = \frac{2}{4}\left(\frac{2^3 c}{3!}\right) = \frac{2^4 c}{4!},$$

and so on. Clearly, for any positive integer n we have $a_n = 2^n c/n!$. Thus

$$\text{(2.4)} \qquad y(x) = \sum_{n=0}^{\infty} \frac{2^n c}{n!} x^n = c \sum_{n=0}^{\infty} \frac{(2x)^n}{n!}.$$

We recognize that the last series in (2.4) is the power series for e^{2x}. Hence $y(x) = ce^{2x}$, as required. ∎

If we wish to solve (2.1) together with the initial condition $y(0) = \pi$, we can use this initial condition in the series (2.4). Indeed,

$$y(0) = \left[\sum_{n=0}^{\infty} \frac{c(2x)^n}{n!}\right]_{x=0} = c = \pi.$$

We could also argue in the following way. If $y(x) = \sum_{n=0}^{\infty} a_n x^n$, then $y^{(n)}(0) = n!a_n$. For $n = 0$ we have $y(0) = a_0 = \pi$.

EXAMPLE 2.2 Use the power series method to solve

$$\text{(2.5)} \qquad y'' + y = 0, \qquad y(0) = \alpha, \qquad y'(0) = \beta.$$

Our trial solution will have the form $y(x) = \sum_{n=0}^{\infty} a_n x^n$. Thus

$$y'(x) = \sum_{n=1}^{\infty} na_n x^{n-1},$$

$$y''(x) = \sum_{n=2}^{\infty} n(n-1)a_n x^{n-2} = \sum_{n=0}^{\infty} (n+2)(n+1)a_{n+2}x^n,$$

and (2.5) becomes

$$\sum_{n=0}^{\infty} (n+2)(n+1)a_{n+2}x^n + \sum_{n=0}^{\infty} a_n x^n = 0.$$

Thus $(n + 2)(n + 1)a_{n+2} + a_n = 0$ for $n = 0, 1, 2, \ldots$. The **recurrence relation** for this equation is

(2.6) $$a_{n+2} = \frac{-a_n}{(n + 2)(n + 1)} \qquad \text{for } n = 0, 1, 2, \ldots.$$

The coefficients a_0 and a_1 are unknown and so may be taken to be arbitrary constants. The remaining coefficients a_n for $n \geq 2$ can be found in terms of a_0 and a_1 by using (2.6). This is accomplished as follows. If $n = 0$ in (2.6), we find that $a_2 = -a_0/2 \cdot 1$. If $n = 1$, then $a_3 = -a_1/3 \cdot 2$. Continuing in this way we see that

$$a_4 = \frac{-a_2}{4 \cdot 3} = \frac{-1}{4 \cdot 3}\left(\frac{-a_0}{2 \cdot 1}\right) = \frac{(-1)^2}{4!}\, a_0,$$

$$a_5 = \frac{-a_3}{5 \cdot 4} = \frac{-1}{5 \cdot 4}\left(\frac{-a_1}{3 \cdot 2}\right) = \frac{(-1)^2 a_1}{5!},$$

$$a_6 = \frac{-a_4}{6 \cdot 5} = \frac{-1}{6 \cdot 5}\frac{(-1)^2 a_0}{4!} = \frac{(-1)^3 a_0}{6!},$$

and so on. From the developing pattern we can see that

$$a_{2k} = \frac{(-1)^k a_0}{(2k)!} \quad \text{and} \quad a_{2k+1} = \frac{(-1)^k a_1}{(2k + 1)!}$$

for $k = 0, 1, 2, \ldots$. This means that the solution y has the form

$$y(x) = a_0 + a_1 x - \frac{a_0 x^2}{2!} - \frac{a_1 x^3}{3!} + \frac{a_0 x^4}{4!} + \frac{a_1 x^5}{5!} - \cdots$$

$$= \left\{a_0 - a_0\frac{x^2}{2!} + a_0\frac{x^4}{4!} - \cdots\right\} + \left\{a_1 x - a_1\frac{x^3}{3!} + a_1\frac{x^5}{5!} - \cdots\right\}$$

$$= a_0 \sum_{k=0}^{\infty} \frac{(-1)^k}{(2k)!} x^{2k} + a_1 \sum_{k=0}^{\infty} \frac{(-1)^k}{(2k + 1)} x^{2k+1}.$$

This solution has the form that we would expect given the theory developed in Chapter 3. There are two linearly independent solutions, namely

(2.7) $$y_1(x) = \sum_{k=0}^{\infty} \frac{(-1)^k}{(2k)!} x^{2k} \quad \text{and} \quad y_2(x) = \sum_{k=0}^{\infty} \frac{(-1)^k}{(2k + 1)!} x^{2k+1}.$$

The general solution has the form

$$y(x) = a_0 y_1(x) + a_1 y_2(x),$$

where a_0 and a_1 are two arbitrary constants. These two constants can be determined from the initial conditions, that is,

$$y(0) = a_0 = \alpha, \qquad y'(0) = a_1 = \beta.$$

Formula (2.7) can be compared with (1.3) and (1.4) from Section 5.1 to see that $y_1(x) = \cos x$ and $y_2(x) = \sin x$, as expected. ■

Finding solutions by use of power series works for a large class of equations with variable coefficients. The following theorem, first published in 1866 by L. Fuchs, is true.

THEOREM 2.3: EXISTENCE OF ANALYTIC SOLUTIONS

Suppose that $b_0(x)$ and $b_1(x)$ are analytic at x_0 and suppose that their power series both converge for $|x - x_0| < L$. Then the solution y of the equation

$$(2.8) \quad y'' + b_1(x)y' + b_0(x)y = 0, \qquad y(x_0) = \alpha, \qquad y'(x_0) = \beta,$$

can be expanded in one and only one way as a power series in $(x - x_0)$. This power series has radius of convergence $R \geq L$.

The coefficients of the power series for y can be computed by setting

$$y(x) = \sum_{n=0}^{\infty} a_n(x - x_0)^n,$$

putting $a_0 = \alpha$, $a_1 = \beta$, and then substituting this solution into (2.8). (If initial conditions are not given, then a_0 and a_1 will be arbitrary.)

The reader should be warned that it is not always possible to recognize the general form of the solution of the resulting recurrence relation. When this is so, the best one can do is to compute a finite number of terms and approximate the solution $y(x)$ by the finite sum.

EXAMPLE 2.4   Find a series solution about $x_0 = 0$ for the **Airy equation**

$$(2.9) \qquad\qquad\qquad y'' - xy = 0.$$

We substitute $y = \sum a_n x^n$ into (2.9) as follows. First compute

$$y''(x) = \sum_{n=2}^{\infty} n(n-1)a_n x^{n-2} = \sum_{n=0}^{\infty} (n+2)(n+1)a_{n+2}x^n$$

(use $m = n - 2$) and then compute

$$xy(x) = x \sum_{n=0}^{\infty} a_n x^n = \sum_{n=0}^{\infty} a_n x^{n+1} \qquad (m = n + 1)$$

$$= \sum_{m=1}^{\infty} a_{m-1}x^m = \sum_{n=1}^{\infty} a_{n-1}x^n.$$

On putting these series into (2.9), we see that

$$\sum_{n=0}^{\infty} (n + 2)(n + 1)a_{n+2}x^n - \sum_{n=1}^{\infty} a_{n-1}x^n = 0,$$

or $(n + 2)(n + 1)a_{n+2} - a_{n-1} = 0$ for $n = 1, 2, 3, \ldots$ and $(n + 2)(n + 1)a_{n+2} = 0$ for $n = 0$. Hence $a_2 = 0$ and

$$(2.10) \qquad\qquad a_{n+2} = \frac{a_{n-1}}{(n + 2)(n + 1)}, \qquad n \geq 1.$$

There is no restriction on a_0 and a_1. Hence they are left as arbitrary constants. On solving the recurrence relation (2.10), we see that

$$a_3 = \frac{a_0}{3 \cdot 2} = \frac{a_0}{3!}, \qquad a_4 = \frac{a_1}{4 \cdot 3} = \frac{2a_1}{4!}, \qquad a_5 = \frac{a_2}{5 \cdot 4} = 0,$$

$$a_6 = \frac{a_3}{6 \cdot 5} = \frac{a_0}{6 \cdot 5 \cdot 3!} = \frac{4a_0}{6!}, \qquad a_7 = \frac{a_4}{7 \cdot 6} = \frac{5 \cdot 2a_1}{7!}, \qquad a_8 = \frac{a_5}{8 \cdot 7} = 0,$$

and so on. From the developing pattern it should be clear that

$$a_{3k} = \frac{1 \cdot 4 \cdot 7 \ldots (3k - 2)}{(3k)!} a_0, \qquad a_{3k+1} = \frac{1 \cdot 2 \cdot 5 \ldots (3k - 1)}{(3k + 1)!} a_1, \qquad a_{3k+2} = 0$$

for $k = 1, 2, 3, \ldots$. Hence

$$(2.11) \qquad y(x) = a_0 \left[1 + \sum_{k=1}^{\infty} \frac{1 \cdot 4 \ldots (3k - 2)}{(3k)!} x^{3k} \right]$$

$$+ a_1 \left[x + \sum_{k=1}^{\infty} \frac{1 \cdot 2 \ldots (3k - 1)}{(3k + 1)!} x^{3k+1} \right]$$

or

$$(2.12) \qquad\qquad y(x) = a_0 y_1(x) + a_1 y_2(x),$$

where $y_1(x)$ is defined by the first series and $y_2(x)$ is defined by the second series. This is a general solution with two arbitrary constants a_0 and a_1. Since (2.9) has the form (2.8) with $b_1(x) = 0$ and $b_0(x) = -x$ and since the power series for $b_1(x)$ and $b_0(x)$ have radius of convergence $R = +\infty$, then by Theorem 2.3 the radius of convergence of (2.11) is $R = +\infty$. ∎

We conclude by noting that Theorem 2.3 can be generalized as follows. In that theorem (2.8) can be replaced by a nonhomogeneous equation and the order of (2.8) can be any integer $m \geq 1$. Hence one can consider the equation

$$(2.13) \qquad y^{(m)} + b_{m-1}(x)y^{(m-1)} + \ldots + b_1(x)y' + b_0(x)y = g(x),$$

$$y^{(j)}(x_0) = c_j, \qquad 0 \leq j \leq m - 1.$$

THEOREM 2.5

(Fuchs) Suppose that $b_0(x), b_1(x), \ldots, b_{m-1}(x)$ and $g(x)$ are all analytic at x_0 and each has power series convergent for $|x - x_0| < L$. Then every solution y of (2.13) can be expanded in one and only one way as a power series in $(x - x_0)$. This power series has radius of convergence $R \geq L$. The coefficients of the power series for y can be computed by setting

$$y(x) = \sum_{n=0}^{\infty} a_n(x - x_0)^n,$$

putting $a_n = y^{(n)}(x_0)/n!$ for $n = 0, 1, 2, \ldots, m-1$, and then substituting this series into (2.13).

EXAMPLE 2.6   Solve $y''' + xy' = 2 + x$, $y(0) = 1$, $y'(0) = -2$, $y''(0) = -\pi$.

The trial solution will have the form $y(x) = \sum a_n x^n$. This series will converge for all values of x. We compute the coefficients a_n as follows:

$$y'''(x) = \sum_{n=3}^{\infty} n(n-1)(n-2)a_n x^{n-3} = \sum_{n=0}^{\infty} (n+3)(n+2)(n+1)a_{n+3}x^n,$$

$$xy'(x) = x \sum_{n=0}^{\infty} na_n x^{n-1} = \sum_{n=0}^{\infty} na_n x^n,$$

so

$$\sum_{n=0}^{\infty} (n+3)(n+2)(n+1)a_{n+3}x^n + \sum_{n=0}^{\infty} na_n x^n = 2 + x.$$

Hence $6 \cdot a_3 + 0 \cdot a_0 = 2$, $24 \cdot a_4 + a_1 = 1$ and

$$(n+3)(n+2)(n+1)a_{n+3} + na_n = 0$$

for $n = 2, 3, 4, \ldots$. The recurrence relation is

(2.14)
$$a_{n+3} = \frac{-na_n}{(n+3)(n+2)(n+1)}, \qquad n \geq 2.$$

From the initial conditions it follows that

$$a_0 = y(0) = 1, \qquad a_1 = y'(0) = -2, \qquad a_2 = \frac{y''(0)}{2!} = \frac{-\pi}{2}.$$

From (2.14) we see that

$$a_3 = \frac{-0 \cdot a_0 + 2}{3 \cdot 2 \cdot 1} = \frac{2}{3!}, \qquad a_4 = \frac{-a_1 + 1}{4 \cdot 3 \cdot 2} = \frac{3}{4!}, \qquad a_5 = \frac{-2(-\pi/2)}{5 \cdot 4 \cdot 3} = \frac{2\pi}{5!},$$

$$a_6 = \frac{-3a_3}{6 \cdot 5 \cdot 4} = \frac{-2 \cdot 3}{6!}, \qquad a_7 = \frac{-4a_4}{7 \cdot 6 \cdot 5} = \frac{-4 \cdot 3}{7!}, \qquad a_8 = \frac{-5a_5}{8 \cdot 7 \cdot 6} = \frac{-5(2\pi)}{8!},$$

$$a_9 = \frac{-6a_6}{9 \cdot 8 \cdot 7} = \frac{2(-1)^4 3 \cdot 6}{9!}, \qquad a_{10} = \frac{3(-1)^4 1 \cdot 4 \cdot 7}{10!}, \qquad a_{11} = \frac{\pi(-1)^4 2 \cdot 5 \cdot 8}{11!}.$$

In general, it can be seen that for $k \geq 2$

$$a_{3k} = \frac{2(-1)^{k+1} 3 \cdot 6 \ldots (3k-3)}{(3k)!}, \qquad a_{3k+1} = \frac{3(-1)^{k+1} 1 \cdot 4 \ldots (3k-2)}{(3k+1)!},$$

and

$$a_{3k+2} = \frac{\pi(-1)^{k+1} 2 \cdot 5 \ldots (3k-1)}{(3k+2)!}.$$

Hence

$$y(x) = 1 - 2x - \left(\frac{\pi}{2}\right)x^2 + 2\left\{\frac{x^3}{3!} + \sum_{k=2}^{\infty} \frac{(-1)^{k+1} 3 \cdot 6 \ldots (3k-3)}{(3k)!} x^{3k}\right\}$$

$$+ 3 \sum_{k=1}^{\infty} \frac{(-1)^{k+1} 1 \cdot 4 \ldots (3k-2)}{(3k+1)!} x^{3k+1}$$

$$+ \pi \sum_{k=1}^{\infty} \frac{(-1)^{k+1} 2 \cdot 5 \ldots (3k-1)}{(3k+2)!} x^{3k+2}. \quad \blacksquare$$

PROBLEMS

In Problems 1–9, find a general solution using the method of power series. The series should be in powers of $(x - x_0)$ for the value of x_0 indicated.

1. $y'' - 4y = 0$, $x_0 = 0$.

2. $y'' - xy' - 2y = 0$, $x_0 = 0$.

3. $y'' - xy' + 2y = 0$, $x_0 = 0$.

4. $y'' - xy' + y = 0$, $x_0 = 0$.

5. $y'' - (1-x)y = 0$, $x_0 = 1$.

6. $R'' + (x+1)R' = 0$, $x_0 = -1$.

7. $N' + xN = 0$, $x_0 = 0$.

8. $\dfrac{d^2 S}{dx^2} + (x+1)S = x$, $x_0 = -1$.

9. $y''' + xy = 0$, $x_0 = 0$.

In Problems 10–15, solve the initial value problem using the power series method. The solution should be in powers of $(x - x_0)$, where x_0 is the initial point.

10. $(x^2 + 4)y'' + 5xy' + 3y = 0$, $y(0) = 1$, $y'(0) = -1$.

11. $R'' + (x-1)R = x^2$, $R(1) = 0$, $R'(1) = 0$.

12. $B'' - xB' - B = 0$, $B(0) = 1$, $B'(0) = -2$.

13. $y'' + 2xy' - 4y = 0$, $y(0) = 2$, $y'(0) = 0$.

14. $y'' + 2xy' - 4y = 0$, $y(0) = 0$, $y'(0) = -3$.

15. $\dfrac{d^2 B}{dt^2} - t\dfrac{dB}{dt} + B = 0$, $B(0) = 0$, $B'(0) = \pi$.

The solutions of the equations in Problems 16–19 are called **parabolic cylinder functions.** The term a is constant. Compute the first four nonzero power series coefficients using $x_0 = 0$.

16. $y'' - (x^2/4 + a)y = 0$, $y(0) = 1$, $y'(0) = 0$.

17. $y'' - (x^2/4 + a)y = 0$, $y(0) = 0$, $y'(0) = 1$.

18. $y'' + (x^2/4 - a)y = 0$, $y(0) = 1$, $y'(0) = 0$.

19. $y'' + (x^2/4 - a)y = 0$, $y(0) = 0$, $y'(0) = 1$.

20. Let y be a general solution of $y'' - (x^2/4 + a)y = 0$ and define w by the relation $y = e^{-x^2/4}w$. Find a second-order differential equation that w solves. Then find the power series for w about $x_0 = 0$.

21. Find the first four nonzero terms of the power series for y at $x_0 = 0$.

(a) $y'' + (\sin x)y = 0$, $y(0) = 1$, $y'(0) = -1$.

(b) $e^x y'' - y = 0$, $y(0) = 0$, $y'(0) = 1$.

22. Find the solutions of $(2 - x)y'' - (x - 1)y' + y = 0$ that satisfy the initial conditions:

(a) $y_1(0) = y_1'(0) = 1$.   (b) $y_2(0) = 1$, $y_2'(0) = -1$.

Compute at least four nonzero terms of the resulting series. Using y_1 and y_2, write down a general solution of the equation. Use $x_0 = 0$.

23. According to Theorem 2.3, the power series $\sum a_n x^n$ of any solution of

$$(2 - x)y'' - (x - 1)y' + y = 0$$

will converge for $|x| < L$. What value of L does the theorem predict? Can a solution have radius of convergence larger than the predicted L? (*Hint:* See Problem 22.)

24. According to Theorem 2.3, the power series $\sum a_n x^n$ of any solution of

$$(x^2 + 4)y'' + xy' - 3y = 0$$

will converge for $|x| < L$. What value of L does that theorem predict?

25. (a) (Generalized binomial expansion) Using power series, find a general solution of $(x + 1)y' = ay$, where a is any real, nonzero constant and $x_0 = 0$.

(b) Using separation of variables, show that $y = c(1 + x)^a$ is a solution of the equation.

(c) Find constants b_n such that

$$(1 + x)^a = \sum_{n=0}^{\infty} b_n x^n, \qquad |x| < 1.$$

26. Let $y_1(x)$ and $y_2(x)$ be the solutions of the Airy equation given in (2.12). The **Airy functions** are defined by the relation

$$\text{Ai}(x) = c_1 y_1(x) - c_2 y_2(x), \qquad \text{Bi}(x) = \sqrt{3}\{c_1 y_1(x) + c_2 y_2(x)\}$$

where $c_1 \cong 0.355028$ and $c_2 \cong 0.258819$.

(a) Show that $\text{Ai}(x)$ and $\text{Bi}(x)$ are linearly independent solutions of (2.9).

(b) Determine the radius of convergence for the power series (at $x_0 = 0$) of Ai and Bi.

27. Using (2.6) and mathematical induction, prove that for $k = 0, 1, 2, \ldots$

$$a_{2k} = \frac{(-1)^k a_0}{(2k)!}, \qquad a_{2k+1} = \frac{(-1)^k a_1}{(2k + 1)!}.$$

5.3 POLYNOMIAL SOLUTIONS: THE LEGENDRE EQUATION

The Legendre equation is

(3.1)
$$(1 - x^2)y'' - 2xy' + by = 0,$$

with b constant. By Theorem 2.3 this equation can be solved by a series $y = \sum a_n x^n$ whose radius of convergence is at least 1. From

$$y' = \sum_{n=0}^{\infty} na_n x^{n-1}, \qquad xy' = \sum_{n=0}^{\infty} na_n x^n,$$

$$y'' = \sum_{n=0}^{\infty} n(n-1)a_n x^{n-2} = \sum_{n=0}^{\infty} (n+2)(n+1)a_{n+2}x^n,$$

and

$$x^2 y'' = \sum_{n=0}^{\infty} n(n-1)a_n x^n$$

we see that y will solve (3.1) when

$$(n+2)(n+1)a_{n+2} - n(n-1)a_n - 2na_n + ba_n = 0, \qquad n \geq 0.$$

This equation is equivalent to the recurrence relation

(3.2)
$$a_{n+2} = \frac{n(n+1) - b}{(n+2)(n+1)} a_n, \qquad n \geq 0.$$

The coefficients a_0 and a_1 are arbitrary. If we pick $a_0 = 1$, then from (3.2) we see that

$$a_2 = \frac{-b}{2}, \qquad a_4 = \frac{2 \cdot 3 - b}{4 \cdot 3} a_2 = \frac{6 - b}{4 \cdot 3}\left(\frac{-b}{2}\right) = \frac{-b}{4}\left(1 - \frac{b}{2 \cdot 3}\right),$$

$$a_6 = \frac{5 \cdot 4 - b}{6 \cdot 5} a_4 = \frac{5 \cdot 4 - b}{6 \cdot 5}\left(\frac{-b}{4}\right)\left(1 - \frac{b}{2 \cdot 3}\right) = \frac{-b}{6}\left(1 - \frac{b}{4 \cdot 5}\right)\left(1 - \frac{b}{2 \cdot 3}\right)$$

and in general

(3.3)
$$a_{2k} = \frac{-b}{2k} \prod_{j=1}^{k-1}\left[1 - \frac{b}{2j(2j+1)}\right]$$

$$= \frac{-b}{2k}\left[1 - \frac{b}{2(3)}\right]\left[1 - \frac{b}{4(5)}\right] \cdots \left[1 - \frac{b}{2(k-1)(2k-1)}\right].$$

Similarly, if we take $a_1 = 1$ and use (3.2) we find that

$$a_3 = \frac{1 \cdot 2 - b}{3 \cdot 2} = \frac{1}{3}\left(1 - \frac{b}{2 \cdot 1}\right), \qquad a_5 = \frac{3 \cdot 4 - b}{5 \cdot 4} a_3 = \frac{3 \cdot 4 - b}{5 \cdot 4}\left(\frac{1}{3}\right)\left(1 - \frac{b}{2 \cdot 1}\right)$$

or

$$a_5 = \frac{1}{5}\left(1 - \frac{b}{2 \cdot 1}\right)\left(1 - \frac{b}{3 \cdot 4}\right)$$

and

(3.4)
$$a_{2k+1} = \frac{1}{2k+1} \prod_{j=1}^{k} \left[1 - \frac{b}{2j(2j-1)} \right].$$

A general solution of (3.1) is

$$y(x) = a_0 \left\{ 1 - \frac{b}{2}x^2 - \frac{b}{4}\left(1 - \frac{b}{6}\right)x^4 + \cdots \right\}$$
$$+ a_1 \left\{ x + \frac{1}{3}\left(1 - \frac{b}{2}\right)x^3 + \frac{1}{5}\left(1 - \frac{b}{2}\right)\left(1 - \frac{b}{12}\right)x^5 + \cdots \right\}$$

or

$$y(x) = a_0 y_1(x, b) + a_1 y_2(x, b).$$

An important and useful observation is that for certain special values of b there will be a polynomial solution of (3.1). When $b = n(n + 1)$ for some even integer $n = 0, 2, 4, \ldots$, then (3.3) implies that the $y_1(x, b)$ is an even polynomial of degree n. If $b = n(n + 1)$ for some odd integer $n = 1, 3, 5, \ldots$, then from (3.4) we see that $y_2(x, b)$ is an odd polynomial of degree n. For example, if $b = 0 = 0 \cdot 1$, then $y_1(x, 0) = 1$. If $b = 2 = 1 \cdot 2$, then $y_2(x, 2) = x$. If $b = 6 = 2 \cdot 3$, then $y_1(x, 6) = 1 - 3x^2$, and so on. The polynomials obtained in this way are called **Legendre polynomials.** These useful polynomials arise in several branches of applied mathematics. Of course, if $y_1(x, b)$ (or $y_2(x, b)$) is a polynomial, then so is $a_0 y_1(x, b)$ [or $a_1 y_2(x, b)$]. It is customary to choose the constant a_0 (or a_1) in such a way that the Legendre polynomial of degree n has the form

$$P_n(x) = \frac{(2n)!}{2^n (n!)^2} \left[x^n - \frac{n(n-1)}{2(2n-1)} x^{n-2} + \cdots \right].$$

Table 5.1 contains a list of the first five Legendre polynomials.

TABLE 5.1   Legendre Polynomials

n	$b_n = n(n+1)$	$P_n(x)$
0	0	$P_0(x) = 1$
1	2	$P_1(x) = x$
2	6	$P_2(x) = \frac{3}{2}x^2 - \frac{1}{2}$
3	12	$P_3(x) = \frac{5}{2}x^3 - \frac{3}{2}x$
4	20	$P_4(x) = \frac{35}{8}x^4 - \frac{15}{4}x^2 + \frac{3}{8}$
5	30	$P_5(x) = \frac{63}{8}x^5 - \frac{70}{8}x^3 + \frac{15}{8}x$

In the course of solving certain partial differential equations the following problem occurs. *Find all real numbers b such that the Legendre equation (3.1) has a solution $y(x, b)$ which is bounded on $-1 < x < 1$.* Clearly, when $b = n(n+1)$ the Legendre polynomial $y = P_n(x)$ is such a bounded solution. These polynomials are the only bounded solutions of (3.1). Indeed the following result is true.

THEOREM 3.1

All nonpolynomial solutions of (3.1) become unbounded as $x \to 1^-$ or as $x \to -1^+$ or both.

PROBLEMS

1. **[Chebyshev polynomials $T_n(x)$].** For the equation

$$(1 - x^2)y'' - xy' + by = 0.$$

(a) Find the solution $y_1(x, b)$ and $y_2(x, b)$ such that

   (i) $y_1(0, b) = 1, \ y_1'(0, b) = 0.$

   (ii) $y_2(0, b) = 0, \ y_2'(0, b) = 1.$

(b) Show that $y_1(x, b)$ is a polynomial if and only if $b = n^2$ for some even nonnegative integer n.

(c) Show that $y_2(x, b)$ is a polynomial if and only if $b = n^2$ for some odd positive integer n.

(d) For $n = 0, 1, 2, 3, 4$ compute all polynomial solutions.

2. **[Chebyshev polynomials $U_n(x)$].** Find all values of b such that

$$(1 - x^2)y'' - 3xy' + by = 0$$

has a polynomial solution. Compute all polynomial solutions that have degree zero, one, two, or three.

Problems 3–5 refer to the Legendre equation (3.1) and the Legendre polynomials $P_n(x)$.

3. **(Generating function)** It can be shown that the Legendre polynomials $P_n(x)$ satisfy the relation

$$\frac{1}{(1 - 2xt + t^2)^{1/2}} = P_0(x) + P_1(x)t + P_2(x)t^2 + P_3(x)t^3 + \ldots + P_n(x)t^n + \ldots.$$

Show that this relation is correct through terms of order t^3.

4. **(Orthogonality)** It can be shown that

$$\int_{-1}^{1} P_m(x)P_n(x) \, dx = \begin{cases} 0 & \text{if } m \neq n \\ (n + \tfrac{1}{2})^{-1} & \text{if } m = n. \end{cases}$$

Show that this relation is correct for $0 \leq m, n \leq 3$.

5. It can be shown that for $n = 1, 2, 3, 4, \ldots$

$$(n + 1)P_{n+1}(x) - (2n + 1)xP_n(x) + nP_{n-1}(x) = 0.$$

Use this relation in order to compute $P_6(x)$.

Problems 6–14 refer to the **Hermite equation.**

(3.8) $y'' - 2xy' + by = 0.$

6. Find the solutions of (3.8) that satisfy the following initial conditions.

   (a) $y_1(0) = 1$, $y_1'(0) = 0$. Call this solution $y_1(x, b)$.

   (b) $y_2(0) = 0$, $y_2'(0) = 1$. Call this solution $y_2(x, b)$.

   Determine the radius of convergence of y_1 and of y_2.

7. (a) Show that $y_1(x, b)$ is a polynomial if and only if $b = 2k$ for some even integer k.

   (b) Show that $y_2(x, b)$ is a polynomial if and only if $b = 2k$ for some odd integer k.

   (c) For $b = 2k$, $k = 0, 1, 2, 3$ find that polynomial solution $H_k(x)$ of (3.8) whose leading coefficient is 2^k, that is,

   $$H_k(x) = 2^k x^k + \ldots .$$

   These polynomials are called **Hermite polynomials.**

8. It can be shown that the Hermite polynomials $H_k(x)$ satisfy the relation

   $$\exp\left(-t^2 + 2xt\right) = H_0(x) + H_1(x)t + \frac{H_2(x)t^2}{2!} + \frac{H_3(x)t^3}{3!} + \ldots + \frac{H_k(x)t^k}{k!} + \ldots .$$

   Given your answer from Problem 7, part (c), verify that this relation is correct through terms of order t^3.

9. It can be shown that the Hermite polynomials $H_k(x)$ satisfy the relation

   $$H_{n+1}(x) - 2xH_n(x) + 2nH_{n-1}(x) = 0 \qquad \text{for } n = 1, 2, 3, \ldots .$$

   Use this relation and your answer to Problem 7, part (c) to compute $H_4(x)$.

10. Let y solve the Hermite equation (3.8) and let $w = e^{-x^2/2}y$. Show that w solves the equation

   (3.9) $$w'' + (b + 1 - x^2)w = 0, \qquad -\infty < x < \infty .$$

5.4 *BESSEL FUNCTIONS OF INTEGER ORDER*

An important differential equation that arises in many different branches of applied mathematics is the Bessel equation

(4.1) $$x^2 y'' + xy' + (x^2 - v^2)y = 0,$$

where $v \geq 0$ is a fixed integer. One is usually interested in solutions of (4.1) on an interval which has $x = 0$ as an end point. Since (3.1) can be rewritten in the form

(4.2) $$y'' + \frac{1}{x} y' + \left(1 - \left(\frac{v}{x}\right)^2\right)y = 0,$$

it is clear that the coefficients of this equation are not analytic at $x = 0$. Indeed, they are not even defined there! Hence Theorem 2.3 does not apply. The purpose of this section is to show how the power series method can be modified to obtain solutions of (4.1).

To motivate our method of solution, we consider first the Euler-Cauchy equation

(4.3) $$x^2 y'' + xy' - v^2 y = 0.$$

Comparing (4.1) and (4.3), we see that if x is small, then (4.3) appears to be a good approximation to (4.1). Hence we shall guess that solutions of (4.1) may well be similar to solutions of (4.3)—at least when x is small. The method of Section 3.11 can be used to solve the Euler equation (4.3). A trial solution of the form $y = x^\lambda$ is substituted into (4.3), so that

$$x^2[\lambda(\lambda - 1)x^{\lambda - 2}] + x[\lambda x^{\lambda - 1}] - v^2 x^\lambda = x^\lambda(\lambda(\lambda - 1) + \lambda - v^2) = x^\lambda(\lambda^2 - v^2) = 0.$$

Hence, $\lambda = \pm v$ and $\{y_1 = x^v, y_2 = x^{-v}\}$ is a fundamental set of solutions of (4.3).

Our trial solution of (4.1) will have the form

(4.4) $$y = \sum_{n=0}^{\infty} a_n x^{n+r} = x^r \sum_{n=0}^{\infty} a_n x^n.$$

We expect that r will be $\pm v$ or else will be some number that is close to $+v$ or $-v$. When x is small, the series (4.4) has the form

$$x^r \sum_{n=0}^{\infty} a_n x^n = x^r a_0 + x^r\{a_1 x + a_2 x^2 + \ldots\} = a_0 x^r + \{\text{smaller terms}\}.$$

Hence (4.4) seems to be a reasonable guess.

To substitute (4.4) into (4.1), we first compute

$$xy' = x \sum_{n=0}^{\infty} (n + r)a_n x^{r+n-1} = \sum_{n=0}^{\infty} (n + r)a_n x^{r+n},$$

$$x^2 y'' = x^2 \sum_{n=0}^{\infty} (n + r)(n + r - 1)a_n x^{r+n-2}$$

$$= \sum_{n=0}^{\infty} (n + r)(n + r - 1)a_n x^{r+n},$$

and

$$x^2 y = \sum_{n=0}^{\infty} a_n x^{n+r+2} = \sum_{n=2}^{\infty} a_{n-2} x^{n+r}.$$

Hence (4.4) solves (4.1) if

$$\sum_{n=0}^{\infty} (n + r)(n + r - 1)a_n x^{r+n} + \sum_{n=0}^{\infty} (n + r)a_n x^{r+n}$$

$$+ \sum_{n=2}^{\infty} a_{n-2} x^{n+r} - \sum_{n=0}^{\infty} v^2 a_n x^{r+n} = 0.$$

Thus

(4.5) $$(n + r)(n + r - 1)a_n + (n + r)a_n - v^2 a_n = 0 \qquad (n = 0, 1).$$

and

(4.6) $$(n + r)(n + r - 1)a_n + (n + r)a_n + a_{n-2} - v^2 a_n = 0 \qquad (n \geq 2).$$

From (4.5) we see that

(4.7) $$[r(r - 1) + r - v^2]a_0 = 0, \qquad [(r + 1)r + (r + 1) - v^2]a_1 = 0.$$

These two equations can be satisfied by taking $a_1 = 0$ and letting r be a solution of the **indicial equation**

(4.8) $$r(r - 1) + r - v^2 = r^2 - v^2 = 0.$$

This means that $a_1 = 0$ and $r = \pm v$.

Case 1. $a_1 = 0$ and $r = v \geq 0$

In this case (4.7) is true. We must still deal with (4.6), which we rewrite, using $r = v$, in the form

$$[(n + v)(n + v - 1) + (n + v) - v^2]a_n = -a_{n-2}, \qquad [(n + v)^2 - v^2]a_n = -a_{n-2},$$

or

(4.9) $$a_n = -\frac{a_{n-2}}{(n + v)^2 - v^2} = -\frac{a_{n-2}}{(n + 2v)n}, \qquad n \geq 2.$$

From the recurrence relation (4.9) and the known value $a_1 = 0$, we see that $a_3 = a_5 = a_7 = \ldots = 0$, while

$$a_{2k} = \frac{-a_{2k-2}}{2^2(k + v)k} \qquad \text{for } k = 1, 2, 3, \ldots .$$

Thus

$$a_2 = \frac{-a_0}{2^2 1 \cdot (v + 1)} \qquad (k = 1)$$

$$a_4 = \frac{-a_2}{2^2 \cdot 2 \cdot (v + 2)} = \frac{(-1)^2 a_0}{2^4 2!(v + 1)(v + 2)} \qquad (k = 2)$$

$$a_6 = \frac{-a_4}{2^2 3(v + 3)} = \frac{(-1)^3 a_0}{2^6 3!(v + 1)(v + 2)(v + 3)} \qquad (k = 3)$$

and so on, so that

$$a_{2k} = \frac{(-1)^k a_0}{2^{2k} k!(v + 1)(v + 2) \ldots (v + k)}.$$

Hence the computed solution is

$$y(x) = a_0 x^v \left[1 - \frac{1}{(v + 1)} \frac{x^2}{2^2} + \frac{1}{2!(v + 1)(v + 2)} \frac{x^4}{2^4} - \cdots \right]$$

or

(4.10) $$y(x) = a_0 x^v \sum_{k=0}^{\infty} \frac{(-1)^k (x/2)^{2k}}{k!(v + 1)(v + 2) \ldots (v + k)}.$$

Since we can choose a_0 in any convenient way, it will be chosen in such a way that (4.10) can be written more compactly. Choose $a_0 = (v!2^v)^{-1}$. The resulting solution, labeled $J_v(x)$, is called the **Bessel function of the first kind of order** v. We see that

(4.11)
$$J_v(x) = \frac{1}{v!2^v} x^v \sum_{k=0}^{\infty} \frac{(-1)^k}{k!(v+1)\ldots(v+k)} \left(\frac{x}{2}\right)^{2k}$$

$$= \sum_{k=0}^{\infty} \frac{(-1)^k}{k!\{v!(v+1)\ldots(v+k)\}} \frac{x^v}{2^v} \left(\frac{x}{2}\right)^{2k}$$

and

(4.12)
$$J_v(x) = \sum_{k=0}^{\infty} \frac{(-1)^k}{k!(v+k)!} \left(\frac{x}{2}\right)^{v+2k}$$

Graphs of $J_v(x)$ for some typical values of v are shown in Figure 5.1. Since Bessel functions are very important, they have been studied a great deal and many facts are known. For example, $J_v(x)$ has infinitely many zeros, all of them simple zeros. Between its successive zeros $J_v(x)$ has exactly one relative maximum or one relative minimum. There is exactly one zero of $J_{v+1}(x)$ between any successive pair of zeros of $J_v(x)$. A list of successive zeros of $J_v(x)$ is given in Table 5.2 for several values of v. In many problems it will turn out to be important to know the location of the zeros of $J_v(x)$.

We now return to our computation in hopes of finding a second solution of (4.1) which is linearly independent of $J_v(x)$. As the reader will see, the computation must be done with care if a second solution is to be found.

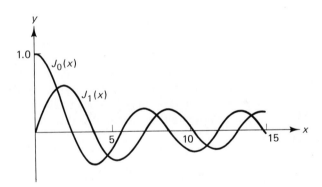

Figure 5.1. Bessel function $J_v(x)$.

TABLE 5.2   Zeros of $J_v(x)$

v	First Zero	Second Zero	Third Zero	Fourth Zero
0	2.40483	5.52008	8.65373	11.79153
1	3.83171	7.01559	10.17347	13.32369
2	5.13562	8.41724	11.61984	14.79595
3	6.38016	9.76102	13.01520	16.22347

Case 2. $a_1 = 0$ and $r = -v \leq 0$

When $v = 0$ this case is the same as Case 1. Nothing new will be found. Hence we assume that $r = -v < 0$. As before, (4.6) and $a_1 = 0$ together imply that $a_3 = a_5 = a_7 = \ldots = 0$. For even integers $n = 2k$ (4.6) takes the form

$$[(2k - v)(2k - v - 1) + (2k - v) - v^2]a_{2k} = -a_{2k-2}$$

or

(4.13) $$(2k)(2k - 2v)a_{2k} = -a_{2k-2}   (k \geq 1).$$

Since $2k - 2v = 0$ when $k = v$, then a_{2v-2} must be zero. From $a_{2v-2} = 0$ and (4.13) we see that $a_{2v-4} = 0$, and so on, so that $a_0 = a_2 = a_4 = \ldots = a_{2v-2} = 0$. This means that the solution

$$y = x^{-v} \sum_{n=0}^{\infty} a_n x^n = x^{-v} \sum_{k=0}^{\infty} a_{2k} x^{2k}$$

$$= x^{-v} \sum_{k=v}^{\infty} a_{2k} x^{2k} = x^{-v} \sum_{k=0}^{\infty} a_{2k+2v} x^{2k} x^{2v}$$

or

$$y = x^v \sum_{j=0}^{\infty} a_{2j+2v} x^{2j}.$$

On comparing this series with (4.12), we see that nothing new will be obtained by continuing the computation. We will only reproduce (4.12) again.

If we go back to (4.7), we see that rather than using $a_1 = 0$ and $r = \pm v$, one could assume instead that $a_0 = 0$ and r solves $(r + 1)^2 - v^2 = 0$. The reader should try working through this computation. The result is that (4.12) is obtained again. If the reader goes back through Chapter 3 in search of help, he or she will notice that (at least in theory) reduction of order can be used to find a general solution of (4.1), since one solution $y_1 = J_v(x)$ is already known. Let us see how well this method will work. The trial solution will have the form

$$y = u(x)J_v(x).$$

Since $y' = u'J_v + uJ'_v$ and $y'' = u''J_v + 2u'J'_v + uJ''_v$, then (4.1) becomes

$$x^2(u''J_v + 2u'J'_v + uJ''_v) + x(u'J_v + uJ'_v) + (x^2 - v^2)uJ_v$$
$$= \{x^2J''_v + xJ'_v + (x^2 - v^2)J_v\}u + x^2J_v u'' + \{2x^2J'_v + xJ_v\}u'$$
$$= \{0\}u + x^2J_v u'' + \{2x^2J'_v + xJ_v\}u' = 0.$$

Let $w = u'$. Then w solves the linear equation

$$w' + \left\{\frac{2J'_v}{J_v} + \frac{1}{x}\right\}w = 0.$$

The equation separates with the result that

$$u' = w = \frac{c_1}{xJ_v(x)^2},$$

and

$$u = c_1 \int_c^x \frac{dt}{tJ_v(t)^2} + c_2.$$

(Since any integral will do, we have used a definite integral with $c > 0$.) Hence

(4.14)
$$y = c_1 J_v(x) \int_c^x \frac{dt}{tJ_v(t)^2} + c_2 J_v(x)$$

is a general solution.

For some purposes the solution (4.14) will suffice. For example, in many applications one requires solutions of (4.1) which are bounded as $x \to 0$. Since $J_v(x) = x^v +$ terms of order $v + 1$ or more, then for x near zero $K_1 x^v \le J_v(x) \le K_2 x^v$ for some positive constants K_1 and K_2. Hence

$$\left| J_v(x) \int_c^x \frac{dt}{tJ_v(t)^2} \right| \ge K_1 x^v \int_c^x \frac{dt}{K_2 t^{2v+1}} \to +\infty$$

as $x \to 0^+$. Thus the solution (4.14) will stay bounded as x tends to zero if and only if $c_1 = 0$, that is, if and only if $y = c_2 J_v(x)$. For appropriate choices of c, c_1, and c_2 the unbounded solution of (4.14) is called a **Bessel function of the second kind** and is written $Y_v(x)$. It can be shown that for $v \ge 1$

$$Y_v(x) = -\left(\frac{2}{x}\right)^v \frac{1}{\pi} \sum_{k=0}^{v-1} \frac{(v-k-1)!}{k!} \left(\frac{x}{2}\right)^{2k} + \frac{2}{\pi} \log\left(\frac{x}{2}\right) J_v(x)$$

$$- \left(\frac{x}{2}\right)^v \frac{1}{\pi} \sum_{k=0}^{\infty} b_k \left(\frac{x}{2}\right)^{2k}.$$

Other normalizations and notations are also used for a second, unbounded solution of (4.1). For example, many physicists and Europeans denote $Y_v(x)$ by $N_v(x)$. If the reader needs to use Bessel functions of the second kind, then proceed with care!

PROBLEMS

1. Using (4.12) show that for any positive integer v

   (a) $\dfrac{d}{dx} \{x^v J_v(x)\} = x^v J_{v-1}(x)$.

   (b) $\dfrac{d}{dx} \{x^{-v} J_v(x)\} = -x^{-v} J_{v+1}(x)$.

2. Show that for any positive integer v

   (a) $J_{v-1}(x) + J_{v+1}(x) = \dfrac{2v}{x} J_v(x)$.

   (b) $J_{v-1}(x) - J_{v+1}(x) = 2J_v'(x)$.

3. Show that

   (a) $J_0'(x) = -J_1(x)$.

   (b) $J_1'(x) = \frac{1}{2}[J_0(x) - J_2(x)]$.

   (c) $J_0''(x) = \frac{1}{2}[J_2(x) - J_0(x)]$.

   (d) $J_0'''(x) = \frac{1}{4}[3J_1(x) - J_3(x)]$.

4. Compute the radius of convergence of the series $x^{-v} J_v(x)$.

5. In (4.7) assume that $a_0 = 0$ while r satisfies $(r + 1)r + (r + 1) - v^2 = 0$.

   (a) Show that $r = -1 \pm v$.

   (b) Show that $a_n = 0$ for all even integers n.

   (c) Show that if $r = -1 + v$, then the solution computed is $y = cJ_v(x)$ for some constant c.

   (d) Show that if $r = -1 - v$, then $a_1 = a_3 = \ldots = a_{2v-1} = 0$. What solutions y does one obtain from this computation?

6. Define $y(x) = (1/\pi) \int_0^\pi \cos(x \sin \theta) \, d\theta$ for all $x \geq 0$.

   (a) Show that $y'(x) = -(x/\pi) \int_0^\pi \cos(x \sin \theta) \cos^2 \theta \, d\theta$. [*Hint:* Compute $y'(x)$ and then integrate the resulting expression by parts.]

   (b) Show that y solves (4.1) when $v = 0$.

   (c) Show that $y(x) = J_0(x)$.

7. Define $y_v(x) = (1/\pi) \int_0^\pi \cos(x \sin \theta - v\theta) \, d\theta$ when $v = 1, 2, 3, \ldots$.

   (a) Show that $\int_0^\pi \cos(x \sin \theta - v\theta)(x \cos \theta - v) \, d\theta = 0$.

   (b) Show that $y_v(x)$ solves (4.1).

8. Let y be a solution of (4.1) and define $w = \sqrt{xy}$ for $x > 0$. Show that w solves the differential equation.

$$(4.15) \qquad \frac{d^2w}{dx^2} + \left[1 + \left(\frac{1}{4} - v^2\right)x^{-2}\right]w = 0, \qquad x > 0.$$

9. It can be shown that for any constants c_1 and c_2 the integral equation

$$(4.16) \qquad w(x) = c_1 \cos x + c_2 \sin x + \int_x^\infty \sin(x - s)(\tfrac{1}{4} - v^2)s^{-2}w(s) \, ds$$

   has a solution $w(x)$ on $1 \leq x < \infty$ which is bounded, that is, $|w(x)| \leq B$ for $1 \leq x < \infty$, where the size of B depends on the choice of c_1 and c_2.

   (a) Show that a bounded solution of (4.16) is also a solution of the differential equation (4.15).

   (b) Show that $\left|\int_x^\infty \sin(x - s)(\tfrac{1}{4} - v^2)s^{-2}w(s) \, ds\right| \leq (\tfrac{1}{4} + v^2)Bx^{-1}$ for $x \geq 1$.

   (c) Show that there are constants A_v, B_v, and θ_v so that

$$\left|J_v(x) - \frac{A_v \cos(x + \theta_v)}{\sqrt{x}}\right| \leq B_v x^{-3/2}, \qquad \text{for all } x \geq 1.$$

5.5   THE GAMMA FUNCTION AND BESSEL FUNCTIONS

The Bessel equation

$$(5.1) \qquad x^2 y'' + xy' + (x^2 - v^2)y = 0$$

makes sense for any real number $v \geq 0$. Moreover, the solution

$$(5.2) \qquad y(x) = a_0 x^v \sum_{k=0}^\infty \frac{(-1)^k}{k!(v + 1)(v + 2) \ldots (v + k)}\left(\frac{x}{2}\right)^{2k},$$

which was computed in (4.10) makes sense for any $v \neq -1, -2, -3, \ldots$. The purpose of this section is to find a general solution of (5.1) when v is not an integer and then to write this solution in convenient notation. To do this, it is useful to introduce the gamma function.

The **gamma function** is a generalization of the factorial function $v!$ to cases where v is not a positive integer. The gamma function is defined by the integral

$$(5.3) \qquad \Gamma(v + 1) = \int_0^\infty t^v e^{-t} \, dt.$$

The improper integral on the right in (5.3) will exist for any real number $v > -1$. Moreover, if $v > 0$, then integration by parts gives

$$\int_a^A t^v e^{-t} \, dt = -t^v e^{-t} \Big|_a^A + v \int_a^A t^{v-1} e^{-t} \, dt.$$

If $a \to 0^+$ and $A \to +\infty$, then

$$[-t^v e^{-t}]_a^A = -A^v e^{-A} + a^v e^{-a} \to 0.$$

Thus we see that

$$(5.4) \qquad \Gamma(v + 1) = v \int_0^\infty t^{v-1} e^{-t} \, dt = v\Gamma(v).$$

This relation suggests the correct way to define $\Gamma(v + 1)$ for $-2 < v < -1$, that is,

$$\Gamma(v) = \frac{\Gamma(v + 1)}{v} \qquad \text{for } -2 < v < -1.$$

Similarly, we define

$$\Gamma(v) = \frac{\Gamma(v + 1)}{v} = \frac{\Gamma(v + 2)}{v(v + 1)} \qquad \text{for } -3 < v < -2,$$

and so on. Hence $\Gamma(v + 1)$ can be defined for all v such that $v \neq -1, -2, -3, \ldots$. Furthermore,

$$\Gamma(1) = \int_0^\infty t^0 e^{-t} \, dt = \lim_{A \to \infty} \int_0^A e^{-t} \, dt = 1.$$

This and (5.4) justify the successive computations

$$\Gamma(2) = 1 \cdot \Gamma(1) = 1, \qquad \Gamma(3) = 2\Gamma(2) = 2,$$
$$\Gamma(4) = 3\Gamma(3) = 3 \cdot 2 = 3!, \qquad \Gamma(5) = 4\Gamma(4) = 4!$$

and in general $\Gamma(n + 1) = n\Gamma(n) = n(n - 1)! = n!$ for any positive integer n. Since $\Gamma(n + 1) = n!$ for $n = 0, 1, 2, \ldots$, $\Gamma(v + 1)$ is sometimes written as $\Gamma(v + 1) = v!$—even when v is not an integer.

With the help of the gamma function (5.2) can be written more compactly. By repeated use of (5.4) we see that for any $v \neq -1, -2, -3, \ldots$ and for any positive integer k

$$\Gamma(v + k + 1) = (v + k)\Gamma(v + k) = (v + k)(v + k - 1)\Gamma(v + k - 1) = \cdots$$
$$= (v + k)(v + k - 1)\ldots(v + 2)(v + 1)\Gamma(v + 1).$$

Hence the kth coefficient in (5.2) can be written as

$$\frac{(-1)^k}{k!(v+1)(v+2)\ldots(v+k)} = \frac{(-1)^k\Gamma(v+1)}{k!\Gamma(v+1)(v+1)\ldots(v+k)} = \frac{(-1)^k\Gamma(v+1)}{k!\Gamma(v+k+1)}$$

and (5.2) takes the form

$$y(x) = a_0\Gamma(v+1)2^v\left\{\left(\frac{x}{2}\right)^v\sum_{k=0}^{\infty}\frac{(-1)^k}{k!\Gamma(v+k+1)}\left(\frac{x}{2}\right)^{2k}\right\}.$$

Take $a_0 = 1/[2^v\Gamma(v+1)]$. The result is the solution

$$(5.5) \qquad J_v(x) = \left(\frac{x}{2}\right)^v\sum_{k=0}^{\infty}\frac{(-1)^k}{k!\Gamma(v+k+1)}\left(\frac{x}{2}\right)^{2k}$$

for $0 < x < \infty$ and for all $v \neq -1, -2, -3, \ldots$. The function $J_v(x)$ so defined is called the **Bessel function of the first kind of order** v. Notice that if v is a positive integer, then (5.5) reduces to the known result (4.12). The student should keep in mind that in (5.5) v can be negative. Hence, if $v > 0$, then $J_{-v}(x)$ is also defined by (5.5) when v is not an integer, that is,

$$J_{-v}(x) = \left(\frac{x}{2}\right)^{-v}\sum_{k=0}^{\infty}\frac{(-1)^k}{k!\Gamma(k-v+1)}\left(\frac{x}{2}\right)^{2k} \qquad (x > 0).$$

If $v > 0$ and $v \neq 1, 2, 3, \ldots$, then $J_v(x)$ and $J_{-v}(x)$ are two linearly independent solutions of (5.1). Hence, if $Y_v(x)$ is defined by

---

TABLE 5.3   Bessel Functions[a]

Type	Order	Formula on $0 < x < \infty$
First kind	$v \neq -1, -2, -3, \ldots$	$J_v(x) = \left(\dfrac{x}{2}\right)^v\sum\limits_{k=0}^{\infty}\dfrac{(-1)^k}{k!\Gamma(v+k+1)}\left(\dfrac{x}{2}\right)^{2k}$
Second kind	$v = 0$	$Y_0(x) = \dfrac{2}{\pi}\left\{\log\left(\dfrac{x}{2}\right) + \gamma\right\}J_0(x)$
		$\qquad + \dfrac{2}{\pi}\left\{\dfrac{1}{(1!)^2}\left(\dfrac{x}{2}\right)^2 - \dfrac{1+\frac{1}{2}}{(2!)^2}\left(\dfrac{x}{2}\right)^4 + \dfrac{1+\frac{1}{2}+\frac{1}{3}}{(3!)^2}\left(\dfrac{x}{2}\right)^6 - \ldots\right\}$
	$v = 1, 2, 3, \ldots$	$Y_v(x) = -\dfrac{1}{\pi}\left(\dfrac{x}{2}\right)^{-v}\sum\limits_{k=0}^{v-1}\dfrac{(v-k-1)!}{k!}\left(\dfrac{x}{2}\right)^{2k} + \dfrac{2}{\pi}\log\left(\dfrac{x}{2}\right)J_v(x)$
		$\qquad -\dfrac{1}{\pi}\left(\dfrac{x}{2}\right)^v\sum\limits_{k=0}^{\infty}\dfrac{\psi(k+1)+\psi(v+k+1)}{k!(v+k)!}(-1)^k\left(\dfrac{x}{2}\right)^{2k}$
	$v \neq$ any integer	$Y_v(x) = \dfrac{J_v(x)\cos(v\pi) - J_{-v}(x)}{\sin(v\pi)}$

[a] γ is the Euler constant (i.e., $\gamma = 0.57721566490153\ldots$; $\psi(1) = -\gamma$, $\psi(m) = -\gamma + \sum\limits_{k=1}^{m-1}k^{-1}$; $\Gamma(v+1) = v!$ when $v = 0, 1, 2, 3, \ldots$.

(5.6) $$Y_v(x) = \frac{J_v(x) \cos(v\pi) - J_{-v}(x)}{\sin(v\pi)}, \qquad v \neq 1, 2, 3, \dots,$$

J_v and Y_v are linearly independent solutions of (5.1). The function $Y_v(x)$ defined by (5.6) is called the **Bessel function of the second kind of order** v. The set $\{J_v(x), Y_v(x)\}$ is a fundamental set of solutions of (5.1) on $0 < x < \infty$. A general solution of (5.1) is

$$y(x) = c_1 J_v(x) + c_2 Y_v(x), \qquad 0 < x < \infty.$$

Table 5.3 summarizes the basic facts for Bessel functions of both integer and noninteger order.

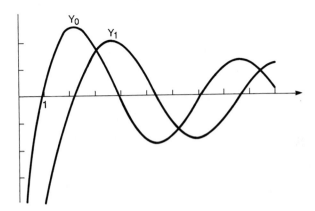

Figure 5.2. Bessel function $Y_v(x)$.

PROBLEMS

1. Given that $\Gamma(\tfrac{1}{2}) = \sqrt{\pi} = 1.77245385\dots$ compute each number in terms of π.

   (a) $\Gamma(-\tfrac{1}{2})$. (b) $\Gamma(-\tfrac{3}{2})$. (c) $\Gamma(-\tfrac{7}{2})$.

   (d) $\Gamma(\tfrac{3}{2})$. (e) $\Gamma(\tfrac{5}{2})$. (f) $\Gamma(\tfrac{11}{2})$.

2. (a) Show that for any positive integer n,

$$\Gamma\left(n + \frac{1}{3}\right) = \frac{1 \cdot 4 \cdot 7 \dots (3n - 2)}{3^n} \Gamma\left(\frac{1}{3}\right).$$

   (b) Given $\Gamma(\tfrac{1}{3}) = 2.6789385\dots$, compute $\Gamma(-\tfrac{2}{3})$ correct to five decimal places.

3. (a) There is a function $h(n)$ such that for any positive integer n,

$$\Gamma(n + \tfrac{1}{4}) = \frac{h(n)\Gamma(\tfrac{1}{4})}{4^n}.$$

   Find $h(n)$.

   (b) Given $\Gamma(\tfrac{1}{4}) = 3.625609908\dots$, compute $\Gamma(-\tfrac{3}{4})$ correct to five decimal places.

4. It is known that $\Gamma(x)\Gamma(1 - x) = \pi \csc(\pi x)$ when x is not an integer. Use this formula to compute (for $m = 1, 2, 3, \dots$) the limit

$$\lim_{u \to -m^+} \frac{1}{\Gamma(u+1)} \quad \text{and} \quad \lim_{u \to -m^-} \frac{1}{\Gamma(u+1)}.$$

5. Use (5.5) to show that for any $x > 0$,

(a) $\dfrac{d}{dx}[x^v J_v(x)] = x^v J_{v-1}(x)$ for $v > 1$.

(b) $\dfrac{d}{dx}[x^{-v} J_v(x)] = -x^{-v} J_{v+1}(x)$ for $v > 0$.

6. Show that for any $x > 0$ and $v > 1$

(a) $J_{v-1}(x) + J_{v+1}(x) = \dfrac{2v}{x} J_v(x)$.   (b) $J_{v-1}(x) - J_{v+1}(x) = 2J_v'(x)$.

7. Let y solve (5.1) and let $u = \sqrt{x}\, y$.

(a) Show that $\dfrac{d^2 u}{dx^2} + \left[1 - \left(\dfrac{1}{4} - v^2\right)x^{-2}\right]u = 0$.

(b) Given $\Gamma(\frac{1}{2}) = \sqrt{\pi}$, find $J_v(x)$ for $v = \frac{1}{2}$ and for $v = -\frac{1}{2}$.

(c) Find $Y_{1/2}(x)$.

8. Compute $Y_{3/2}(x)$. Find a general solution of $x^2 y'' + xy' + (x^2 - \frac{9}{4})y = 0$.

9. Suppose that $v > 0$ and $v \neq 1, 2, 3, \ldots$.

(a) Prove that $\{J_v(x), J_{-v}(x)\}$ are linearly independent on $0 < x < \infty$.

(b) Prove that $\{J_v(x), Y_v(x)\}$ are linearly independent on $0 < x < \infty$.

10. For $v > 0$ compute the radius of convergence of the series in (5.5).

11. Given the differential equation

(5.7) $y'' + (a^2 e^{2x} - v^2)y = 0,$ $0 < x < \infty, a > 0.$

(a) Show that the substitution $y(x) = u(ae^x)$, $ae^x = t$ reduces (5.7) to

$$t^2 \frac{d^2 u}{dt^2} + t \frac{du}{dt} + (t^2 - v^2)u = 0.$$

(b) Find a general solution of $y'' + (3e^{2x} - 2)y = 0$ in terms of Bessel functions.

12. Given the differential equation

(5.8) $x^2 y'' + (a^2 x^2 + \frac{1}{4} - v^2)y = 0,$ $x > 0,$ $a > 0.$

(a) Show that the substitutions $y(x) = \sqrt{x}\, u(ax)$, $t = ax$ reduces (5.8) to

$$t^2 \frac{d^2 u}{dt^2} + t \frac{du}{dt} + (t^2 - v^2)u = 0.$$

(b) Find a general solution of $x^2 y'' + (x^2 - 2)y = 0$ in terms of Bessel functions.

5.6 REGULAR SINGULAR POINTS: RESULTS OF FUCHS

The results concerning generalized series solutions of the Bessel equation can be extended considerably to cover a variety of equations whose coefficients are singular at some point x_0. The purpose of this section and the next is to show how this is done. The theory that we will develop was initiated by the mathematician Lazarius Fuchs in 1866 and completed by G. Frobenius in 1873.

Consider a second-order differential equation

$$(6.1) \qquad a_2(x)y'' + a_1(x)y' + a_0(x)y = 0, \qquad A_1 < x < A_2,$$

where $a_0(x)$, $a_1(x)$, and $a_2(x)$ are analytic functions of x on the interval $J = (A_1, A_2)$. A point x_0 in J is called an **ordinary point** (or **nonsingular point**) if $a_2(x_0) \neq 0$ and is called a **singular point** when $a_2(x_0) = 0$. If x_0 is an ordinary point of (6.1), the coefficients $a_1(x)/a_2(x)$ and $a_0(x)/a_2(x)$ will be analytic at x_0 and (6.1) can be solved using the power series methods developed in Section 5.2. We are now interested in solving (6.1) in a neighborhood of a singular point x_0. It will turn out that some types of singular points are more difficult to deal with than others. Hence we single out a class of singular points x_0 for which solutions of (6.1) can be found using series methods.

DEFINITION 6.1: REGULAR SINGULAR POINT

Suppose that $a_2(x)$, $a_1(x)$, and $a_0(x)$ are analytic at x_0 and that x_0 is a singular point of (6.1). Then x_0 is called a **regular singular point** if the limits

$$\lim_{x \to x_0} \frac{(x - x_0)a_1(x)}{a_2(x)} \quad \text{and} \quad \lim_{x \to x_0} \frac{(x - x_0)^2 a_0(x)}{a_2(x)}$$

both exist and are finite.

EXAMPLE 6.2 Consider an Euler equation $\alpha x^2 y'' + \beta x y' + \gamma y = 0$ where α, β, and γ are constants and $\alpha \neq 0$.

Here $a_2(x) = \alpha x^2$, $a_1(x) = \beta x$, and $a_0(x) = \gamma$ are everywhere analytic. Since $a_2(x) = \alpha x^2 = 0$ if an only if $x = 0$, there is exactly one singular point, $x_0 = 0$. To test whether or not zero is a regular singular point, we form the ratios

$$\frac{(x - x_0)a_1(x)}{a_2(x)} = \frac{x(\beta x)}{\alpha x^2} = \frac{\beta}{\alpha}, \qquad \frac{(x - x_0)^2 a_0(x)}{a_2(x)} = \frac{(x)^2 \gamma}{\alpha x^2} = \frac{\gamma}{\alpha}.$$

Since both ratios are constants, the limits as $x \to x_0 = 0$ certainly exist. These limits are β/α and γ/α. Hence the Euler equation has exactly one singular point, $x_0 = 0$. This singular point is a regular singular point. ∎

EXAMPLE 6.3   Consider the Bessel equation

$$x^2 y'' + xy' + (x^2 - v^2)y = 0.$$

The terms $a_2(x) = x^2$, $a_1(x) = x$, and $a_0(x) = x^2 - v^2$ are everywhere analytic on the real line. Since $a_2(x) = x^2 = 0$ if and only if $x = 0$, the Bessel equation has exactly one singular point, $x_0 = 0$. Since the Bessel equation is the model equation for this whole development, it might be guessed that $x_0 = 0$ is a regular singular point. This is correct. To see this, we form the ratios

$$\frac{(x - x_0)a_1(x)}{a_2(x)} = \frac{(x - 0)x}{x^2} = 1, \qquad \frac{(x - x_0)^2 a_0(x)}{a_2(x)} = \frac{(x - 0)^2(x^2 - v^2)}{x^2} = x^2 - v^2.$$

Since the limits

$$\lim_{x \to 0} 1 = 1 \quad \text{and} \quad \lim_{x \to 0} (x^2 - v^2) = -v^2$$

exist, then $x_0 = 0$ is a regular singular point. ∎

EXAMPLE 6.4   Consider the Legendre equation

$$(1 - x^2)y'' - 2xy' + by = 0,$$

where b is a constant.

Here $a_2(x) = 1 - x^2$, $a_1(x) = -2x$, and $a_0(x) = b$ are everywhere analytic and $a_2(x) = 1 - x^2 = 0$ if and only if $x = 1$ or $x = -1$. Hence the only singular points of the Legendre equation are 1 and -1. At $x_0 = 1$ we compute the limits

$$\frac{(x - 1)a_1(x)}{a_2(x)} = \frac{(x - 1)(-2x)}{1 - x^2} = \frac{(1 - x)(2x)}{(1 - x)(1 + x)} = \frac{2x}{1 + x} \to 1 \qquad (x \to 1)$$

and

$$\frac{(x - 1)^2 a_0(x)}{a_2(x)} = \frac{(x - 1)^2 b}{1 - x^2} = \frac{(x - 1)^2 b}{(1 - x)(1 + x)} = -\frac{(x - 1)b}{1 + x} \to 0 \qquad (x \to 1).$$

Since both limits exist and are finite, then $x = 1$ is a regular singular point of the Legendre equation.

Similarly, at $x_0 = -1$ the limits

$$\lim_{x \to -1} \frac{(x + 1)a_1(x)}{a_2(x)} = \lim_{x \to -1} \frac{(x + 1)(-2x)}{1 - x^2} = 1$$

and

$$\lim_{x \to -1} \frac{(x + 1)^2 a_1(x)}{a_2(x)} = \lim_{x \to -1} \frac{(x + 1)^2 b}{1 - x^2} = 0$$

exist and are finite. Hence $x_0 = -1$ is also a regular singular point. ∎

If x_0 is a regular singular point of (5.1), then $a_2(x_0) = 0$ and we can write $a_2(x) = (x - x_0)^J R(x)$ for some integer $J \geq 1$ and some analytic function $R(x)$ for which $R(x_0) \neq 0$. Since the ratio

$$\frac{(x - x_0)a_1(x)}{a_2(x)} = \frac{(x - x_0)a_1(x)}{(x - x_0)^J R(x)} = \frac{a_1(x)}{(x - x_0)^{J-1}R(x)}$$

has a finite limit as $x \to x_0$, $a_1(x)$ must have a zero at x_0 of order at least $J - 1$. Similarly, since

$$\frac{(x - x_0)^2 a_0(x)}{a_2(x)} = \frac{(x - x_0)^2 a_0(x)}{(x - x_0)^J R(x)} = \frac{a_0(x)}{(x - x_0)^{J-2}R(x)}$$

has a finite limit as $x \to x_0$, then $a_0(x)$ must have a zero at x_0 of order at least $J - 2$. If we divide (6.1) by the term $(x - x_0)^{J-2}R(x)$, the resulting equation has the form

(6.2) $$(x - x_0)^2 y'' + (x - x_0)b(x)y' + c(x)y = 0.$$

We have proved the following result.

THEOREM 6.5: EQUATIONS WITH REGULAR SINGULAR POINTS

Let x_0 be a singular point of (6.1). Then x_0 is a regular singular point if and only if (6.1) can be written in the equivalent form (6.2) where b and c are analytic at x_0.

We wish to solve (6.2) on the interval $x_0 < x < \infty$ using series. To simplify the notation, we shall assume that $x_0 = 0$. [If $x_0 \neq 0$, the change of variable $\bar{x} = x - x_0$ will reduce (6.2) to a new equation whose singularity is at zero.] Hence we wish to solve

(6.3) $$Ly = x^2 y'' + xb(x)y' + c(x)y = 0,$$

where

(6.4) $$b(x) = \sum_{n=0}^{\infty} b_n x^n, \qquad c(x) = \sum_{n=0}^{\infty} c_n x^n, \qquad |x| < L.$$

For $|x|$ small (6.3) is nearly equal to an Euler equation $x^2 y'' + b_0 xy' + c_0 y = 0$. Hence it is natural to try a solution of the form

$$y = x^r \sum_{n=0}^{\infty} a_n x^n = \sum_{n=0}^{\infty} a_n x^{n+r} \qquad (0 < x < L).$$

(For x small this solution is a perturbation of x^r.) Since

$$y' = \sum_{n=0}^{\infty} (n + r)a_n x^{n+r-1}, \qquad y'' = \sum_{n=0}^{\infty} (n + r)(n + r - 1)a_n x^{n+r-2},$$

then

$$x^2 y'' = \sum_{n=0}^{\infty} (n + r)(n + r - 1)a_n x^{n+r} = x^r \sum_{n=0}^{\infty} (n + r)(n + r - 1)a_n x^n$$

and

$$xb(x)y' = x\left(\sum_{n=0}^{\infty} b_n x^n\right)\left(\sum_{n=0}^{\infty} (n+r)a_n x^{n+r-1}\right)$$

$$= x^r\left(\sum_{n=0}^{\infty} b_n x^n\right)\left(\sum_{n=0}^{\infty} (n+r)a_n x^n\right)$$

$$= x^r\left\{\sum_{n=0}^{\infty}\left(\sum_{k=0}^{n} b_{n-k}(k+r)a_k\right)x^n\right\}$$

$$= x^r\{ra_0b_0 + (ra_0b_1 + (r+1)a_1b_0)x + \dots\}$$

and

$$c(x)y = \left(\sum_{n=0}^{\infty} c_n x^n\right)\left(\sum_{n=0}^{\infty} a_n x^{n+r}\right)$$

$$= x^r\sum_{n=0}^{\infty}\left(\sum_{k=0}^{n} c_{n-k}a_k\right)x^n.$$

To solve (6.3), it must be true that

$$x^r\left(\sum_{n=0}^{\infty}\left\{(n+r)(n+r-1)a_n + \sum_{k=0}^{n} b_{n-k}(k+r)a_k + \sum_{k=0}^{n} c_{n-k}a_k\right\}x^n\right) = 0.$$

Hence

(6.5) $$\qquad r(r-1)a_0 + rb_0a_0 + c_0a_0 = 0 \qquad (n=0)$$

and

(6.6) $$\qquad (n+r)(n+r-1)a_n + \sum_{k=0}^{n}\{b_{n-k}(k+r) + c_{n-k}\}a_k = 0 \qquad (n \geq 1).$$

Define $P(r) = r(r-1) + b_0r + c_0$. The equation

(6.7) $$\qquad P(r) = r(r-1) + b_0r + c_0 = r^2 + (b_0-1)r + c_0 = 0$$

is called the **indicial equation** for (6.3). According to (6.5), either $a_0 = 0$ or else $P(r) = 0$; that is, r is a root of the indicial equation. Notice that (6.6) can be written as

$$(n+r)(n+r-1)a_n + \{b_0(n+r) + c_0\}a_n + \sum_{k=0}^{n-1}\{b_{n-k}(k+r) + c_{n-k}\}a_k = 0$$

or

(6.8) $$\qquad P(n+r)a_n + \sum_{k=0}^{n-1}\{b_{n-k}(k+r) + c_{n-k}\}a_k = 0.$$

Hence

(6.9) $$\qquad a_n = -\sum_{k=0}^{n-1}\frac{\{b_{n-k}(k+r) + c_{n-k}\}a_k}{P(n+r)} \qquad (n \geq 1)$$

provided that

(6.10) $$\qquad P(n+r) \neq 0 \qquad \text{for } n = 1, 2, 3, \dots.$$

Fix any constant $a_0 \neq 0$. If (6.10) is true, then use (6.9) to successively determine the coefficients $a_1(r)$, $a_2(r)$, $a_3(r)$, ... [The terms $a_n(r)$ also depend on a_0 but we shall suppress this dependence.] Define

$$(6.11) \qquad \varphi(x, r, a_0) = x^r \sum_{n=0}^{\infty} a_n(r)x^n.$$

According to our computations,

$$(6.12) \qquad L[\varphi(x, r, a_0)] = a_0 P(r)x^r.$$

Let r_1 and r_2 be the roots of the indicial equation (6.7). If r_1 and r_2 are real roots, we shall label these roots in such a way that $r_1 \geq r_2$. Hence (6.10) will always be true for r_1, $\varphi(x, r_1, a_0)$ is always defined for any nonzero constant a_0 and $y_1 = \varphi(x, r_1, a_0)$ is a solution of (6.3) since

$$Ly_1 = L[\varphi(x, r_1, a_0)] = a_0 P(r_1)x^{r_1} = a_0 \cdot 0 \cdot x^r = 0.$$

If $r_1 - r_2$ is not an integer, then (6.10) will also be true for r_2, $\varphi(x, r_2, a_0)$ will be defined and $y_2 = \varphi(x, r_2, a_0)$ will solve (6.3). Both series obtained in this way will converge. Hence y_1 and y_2 represent actual solutions. The convergence of these series is the content of the following result due to Fuchs.

THEOREM 6.6: A RESULT OF FUCHS

Suppose that r_1 and r_2 solve (6.7) and $r_1 - r_2$ is not an integer. Let $a_0 = 1$. If (6.4) is true for $|x| < L$, then (6.11) converges for $|x| < L$ when $r = r_1$ or r_2. The set $\{y_1, y_2\}$ with $y_1 = \varphi(x, r_1, 1)$ and $y_2 = \varphi(x, r_2, 1)$ is a fundamental set of solutions of (6.3) on the interval $0 < x < L$.

EXAMPLE 6.7   Consider the Bessel equation

$$x^2 y'' + xy' + (x^2 - v^2)y = 0.$$

The indicial equation is $r(r - 1) + r - v^2 = r^2 - v^2 = 0$. Hence $r_1 = v$ and $r_2 = -v$. Since $r_1 - r_2 = v - (-v) = 2v$, then $r_1 - r_2$ is not an integer when $v \neq m/2$ for some nonnegative integer m. For $v \neq m/2$ the solutions given by Theorem 6.6 are $y_1 = J_v(x)$ and $y_2 = J_{-v}(x)$. ∎

EXAMPLE 6.8   Find a general solution on an interval $0 < x < L$ of

$$(6.13) \qquad 3x(1 + x)y'' + y' - 6y = 0.$$

We multiply the equation by $x/3(x + 1)$ and rearrange to obtain

$$x^2 y'' + x\left(\frac{1}{3(x + 1)}\right)y' + \left(\frac{-2x}{(x + 1)}\right)y = 0.$$

Hence

$$b(x) = \frac{1}{3(x + 1)} = \frac{1}{3} \sum_{n=0}^{\infty} (-1)^n x^n \qquad \text{for } |x| < 1,$$

and

$$c(x) = \frac{-2x}{1 + x} = -2x \sum_{k=0}^{\infty} (-1)^k x^k = \sum_{n=1}^{\infty} 2(-1)^n x^n, \qquad \text{for } |x| < 1.$$

Hence we expect series methods to determine solutions on $0 < x < 1$ (and perhaps on a larger interval). As $b_0 = \frac{1}{3}$ and $c_0 = 0$, the indicial equation is $r(r - 1) + r/3 + 0 = r(r - \frac{2}{3}) = 0$. The roots are $r_1 = \frac{2}{3}$ and $r_2 = 0$. Since $r_1 - r_2 = \frac{2}{3}$, then Theorem 6.6 applies. Set

$$y = \sum_{n=0}^{\infty} a_n x^{n+r} \qquad (0 < x < 1),$$

so that

$$y' = \sum_{n=0}^{\infty} (n + r)a_n x^{n+r-1} = \sum_{n=-1}^{\infty} (n + r + 1)a_{n+1} x^{n+r},$$

$$y'' = \sum_{n=0}^{\infty} (n + r)(n + r - 1)a_n x^{n+r-2},$$

$$3xy'' = \sum_{n=0}^{\infty} 3(n + r)(n + r - 1)a_n x^{n+r-1} = \sum_{n=-1}^{\infty} 3(n + r + 1)(n + r)a_{n+1} x^{n+r},$$

and

$$3x^2 y'' = \sum_{n=0}^{\infty} 3(n + r)(n + r - 1)a_n x^{n+r}.$$

Substituting these series into (6.13) leads to

$$a_0 x^{r-1}[3r(r - 1) + r] + \sum_{n=0}^{\infty} \{3(n + r + 1)(n + r)a_{n+1} + 3(n + r)(n + r - 1)a_n$$

$$+ (n + r + 1)a_{n+1} - 6a_n\}x^{n+r} = 0.$$

Hence, for $n \geq 0$,

$$a_{n+1} = -\frac{3(n + r)(n + r - 1) - 6}{3(n + r + 1)(n + r) + (n + r + 1)} a_n = -\frac{3(n + r - 2)}{3n + 3r + 1} a_n.$$

For the first solution choose $r = \frac{2}{3}$. Hence, for $n \geq 0$,

$$a_{n+1} = -\frac{3n - 4}{3(n + 1)} a_n.$$

Pick $a_0 = 1$ and compute

$$a_1 = \frac{4}{3}, \qquad a_2 = \frac{1}{6}(\frac{4}{3}) = \frac{2}{9}, \qquad a_3 = -\frac{2}{9}(\frac{2}{9}) = -\frac{4}{81}$$

and in general $a_{n+1} = (-4)(-1)2 \cdot 5 \ldots (3n - 4)/[(-3)^{n+1}(n + 1)!]$. Thus

$$y_1 = x^{2/3}\{1 + \tfrac{4}{3}x + \tfrac{2}{9}x^2 - \tfrac{4}{81}x^3 + \ldots\}, \qquad |x| < 1.$$

For the second solution choose $r = 0$. Hence, for $n \geq 0$,

$$a_{n+1} = -\frac{3(n-2)}{(3n+1)}a_n.$$

Pick $a_0 = 1$ and compute

$$a_1 = 6, \qquad a_2 = \tfrac{3}{4}(6) = \tfrac{9}{2}, \qquad a_3 = 0$$

and $a_n = 0$ for $n \geq 4$. Hence the second solution is

$$y_2 = x^0\{1 + 6x + \tfrac{9}{2}x^2 + 0x^3 + 0x^4 + \ldots\} = 1 + 6x + \tfrac{9}{2}x^2,$$

a polynomial (with infinite radius of convergence). A general solution is

$$y = c_1 x^{2/3}\{1 + \tfrac{4}{3}x + \tfrac{2}{9}x^2 - \tfrac{4}{81}x^3 - \ldots\} + c_2\{1 + 6x + \tfrac{9}{2}x^2\}$$

on $0 < x < 1$. ∎

PROBLEMS

1. Find all singular points of each equation. Decide which points are regular singular points.

   (a) $xy'' + (1 - x)y' + 3y = 0$.

   (b) $(4 - x^2)y'' + xy' + 3y = 0$.

   (c) $(x - 1)^2 x^2 y'' + (x - 1)y' - y = 0$.

   (d) $x(x - 1)y'' + (2 - x)y' + 4y = 0$.

   (e) $(1 - x^2)^2 y'' - (1 - x^2)y' - y = 0$.

   (f) $(x - 3)y'' + \dfrac{3}{x^2}y' + \dfrac{x-4}{x}y = 0$.

2. Find a pair of linearly independent solutions on the interval $x_0 < x < \infty$.

   (a) $x^2 y'' + xy' + (x - 2)y = 0$, $x_0 = 0$.

   (b) $2xy'' + 5y' - 2y = 0$, $x_0 = 0$.

   (c) $xy'' + y' + \left(\dfrac{1-x}{x}\right)y = 0$, $x_0 = 0$.

   (d) $2(x + 2)y'' + 5y' - 2y = 0$, $x_0 = -2$. See part (b)!

   (e) $(x - 4)^2 y'' + (x - 4)y' + (x - 6)y = 0$, $x_0 = 4$. See part (a)!

3. Show that the solutions y_1 and y_2 given in Theorem 6.6 are linearly independent on $0 < x < L$.

4. (a) Show that for any $r > 0$ and any nonnegative integer n,

   $$\frac{d}{dx}|x|^r x^n = (n + r)|x|^r x^{n-1}, \qquad -L < x < 0.$$

   (b) Under the assumptions of Theorem 6.6 let $a_0 = 1$ and $a_n(r)$ be given by (6.9). Show that if the two series

   $$y_1 = |x|^{r_1}\sum_{n=0}^{\infty} a_n(r_1)x^n, \qquad y_2 = |x|^{r_2}\sum_{n=0}^{\infty} a_n(r_2)x^n$$

   converge on $-L < x < 0$, then $\{y_1, y_2\}$ is a fundamental set of solutions of (5.3) on $-L < x < 0$.

5. Find a pair of linearly independent solutions on $-\infty < x < 0$.

    (a) $x^2 y'' + xy' + (x - 2)y = 0$.   (b) $2xy'' + 5y' - 2y = 0$.

    (c) $xy'' + y' + \left(\dfrac{1 - x}{x}\right)y = 0$.

Hint: Use Problems 2 and 4.

6. Suppose that in Theorem 6.6 all terms b_n and c_n are real numbers. Suppose that the roots $(r_1 = \alpha + i\beta$ and $r_2 = \alpha - i\beta)$ of the indicial equation are complex numbers. Let y_1 and y_2 be the solutions determined by Theorem 6.6.

    (a) Show that $y_2 = \bar{y}_1$.

    (b) Show that $w_1 = \operatorname{Re} y_1$ and $w_2 = \operatorname{Im} y_1$ are solutions on $0 < x < L$.

    (c) Show that w_1 and w_2 are linearly independent solutions on $0 < x < L$.

7. Find a real-valued pair of linearly independent solutions of

$$xy'' + y' + \left(\frac{1 - x}{x}\right)y = 0, \qquad 0 < x < \infty.$$

Determine the first three nonzero terms of each series that you use. *Hint:* Use Problems 2, part (c) and 6.

5.7 REGULAR SINGULAR POINTS: THEORY OF FROBENIUS

In Section 5.6 we studied the equation

(7.1) $$Ly = x^2 y'' + xb(x)y' + c(x)y = 0,$$

when the roots r_1 and r_2 of the indicial equation $P(r) = r(r - 1) + b_0 r + c_0 = 0$ do not differ by an integer. We now continue that study in the case where $r_1 - r_2 = m$ is a nonnegative integer. Recall that a series

$$y = \sum_{n=0}^{\infty} a_n x^{n+r}$$

solves $Ly = 0$ if and only if $P(r) = 0$ and

(7.2) $$P(n + r)a_n + \sum_{k=0}^{n-1} \{b_{n-k}(k + r) + c_{n-k}\}a_k = 0.$$

If $P(n + r) \neq 0$ for $n = 1, 2, 3, \ldots$, and if $a_0(r)$ is given, then

(7.3) $$a_n(r) = -\sum_{k=0}^{n-1} \frac{\{b_{n-k}(k + r) + c_{n-k}\}a_k(r)}{P(n + r)}, \qquad n \geq 1.$$

The function φ defined by

(7.4) $$\varphi(x, r, a_0(r)) = x^r \sum_{n=0}^{\infty} a_n(r)x^n$$

solves

(7.5) $$L[\varphi(x, r, a_0(r))] = a_0(r)P(r)x^r.$$

Assume that $r_1 - r_2 = 0$, so that $r_1 = r_2$ and $P(r) = (r - r_1)^2$. Let $a_0 = 1$. Then $P(n + r) \neq 0$ for $n \geq 1$, so that $\varphi(x, r, 1)$ is defined and (7.5) is true for $|r - r_1| < 1$ (with $a_0 = 1$). Take the partial derivative with respect to r in (7.5) and then set $r = r_1$, that is,

$$L\left[\frac{\partial}{\partial r} \varphi(x, r, 1)\right] = \frac{\partial}{\partial r} L[\varphi(x, r, 1)] = P'(r)x^r + P(r)(\log x)x^r$$

and

$$L\left[\frac{\partial}{\partial r} \varphi(x, r, 1)\bigg|_{r=r_1}\right] = P'(r_1)x^{r_1} + P(r_1)(\log x)x^{r_1}$$

$$= 0 \cdot x^{r_1} + 0 \cdot (\log x)x^{r_1} = 0.$$

Hence a second solution is

$$y_2 = \left[\frac{\partial}{\partial r} \varphi(x, r, 1)\right]_{r=r_1} = \sum_{n=1}^{\infty} a_n'(r_1)x^{n+r_1} + \log x \sum_{n=0}^{\infty} a_n(r_1)x^{n+r_1}$$

or

(7.6) $$y_2 = x^{r_1} \sum_{n=1}^{\infty} a_n'(r_1)x^n + (\log x)y_1(x), \qquad 0 < x < L.$$

If $r_1 - r_2 = m$, a positive integer, then a different method of solution is needed. Let $a_0 = r - r_2$. For $r \neq r_2$, $P(n + r) \neq 0$ for $n \geq 1$, so that $\varphi(x, r, r - r_2)$ is defined and (7.5) becomes

(7.7) $$L[\varphi(x, r, r - r_2)] = (r - r_2)P(r)x^r.$$

We wish to compute the limit

$$y(x) = \lim_{r \to r_2} \varphi(x, r, r - r_2).$$

This limit, if it exists, will solve $Ly = 0$. From (7.3) we see that

$$a_1(r) = -\frac{(rb_1 + c_1)a_0}{P(r + 1)} = -\frac{rb_1 + c_1}{P(r + 1)} (r - r_2) = \bar{a}_1(r)(r - r_2).$$

Similarly, $a_2(r)$ has the form

$$a_2(r) = -\frac{(rb_2 + c_2)a_0 - [(r + 1)b_1 + c_1]a_1}{P(r + 2)}$$

$$= -\frac{(rb_2 + c_2) - [(r + 1)b_1 + r_1]\bar{a}_1(r)}{P(r + 2)} (r - r_2) = \bar{a}_2(r)(r - r_2)$$

and so on, up to $a_{m-1}(r) = \bar{a}_{m-1}(r)(r - r_2)$. Since $r_1 - r_2 = m$, then $r_1 - m = r_2$ and $P(m + r_2) = (r + m - r_1)(r + m - r_2) = (r - r_2)(r + m - r_2)$. Hence

$$a_m(r) = -\sum_{k=0}^{m-1} \frac{[(r+k)b_{m-k} + c_{m-k}]a_k(r)}{P(m+r)}$$

$$= -\sum_{k=0}^{m-1} \frac{[(r+k)b_{m-k} + c_{m-k}]\bar{a}_k(r)}{r+m-r_2}.$$

When $r \to r_2$, then $a_n(r) = \bar{a}_n(r)(r - r_2) \to 0$ for $0 \le n \le m-1$ but $a_m(r) \to a_m(r_2) = a$, where

(7.8) $$a = -\sum_{k=0}^{m-1} \frac{[(r_2+k)b_{m-k} + c_{m-k}]\bar{a}_k(r_2)}{m}.$$

For $n > m$, $P(n + r_2) \ne 0$ and $a_n(r) \to a_n(r_2)$ as $r \to r_2$. Hence

$$y(x) = x^{r_2}[0 + 0\cdot x + 0\cdot x^2 + \ldots + 0\cdot x^{m-1} + a_m(r_2)x^m + a_{m+1}(r_2)x^{m+1} + \ldots]$$

$$= x^{r_2+m}\sum_{n=0}^{\infty} a_{n+m}(r_2)x^n = x^{r_1}\sum_{n=0}^{\infty} a_{n+m}(r_2)x^n.$$

From our previous calculations (in Section 5.6) we see that $y(x)$ must be the solution $\varphi(x, r_1, a) = ay_1(x)$, where a is defined by (7.8). Hence $\varphi(x, r, r - r_2)$ is defined for all r and $\varphi(x, r_2, 0) = ay_1(x)$.

Take the derivative of (7.7) with respect to r and then let $r \to r_2$. This gives

$$L\left[\frac{\partial}{\partial r}\varphi(x, r, r - r_2)\right]_{r=r_2} = [P(r)x^r + (r - r_2)P'(r)x^r + (r - r_2)P(r)(\log x)x^r]_{r=r_2}$$

$$= 0.$$

Hence $y_2(x) = [\partial\varphi(x, r, r - r_2)/\partial r]_{r=r_2}$ solves $Ly_2 = 0$. Now

$$\frac{\partial}{\partial r}\varphi(x, r, r - r_2) = \sum_{n=0}^{\infty}[a'_n(r)x^{n+r} + a_n(r)(\log x)x^{n+r}]$$

$$= x^r\sum_{n=0}^{\infty} a'_n(r)x^n + \log x\varphi(x, r, r - r_2),$$

so that

(7.9) $$y_2(x) = x^{r_2}\sum_{n=0}^{\infty} a'_n(r_2)x^n + (\log x)ay_1(x).$$

The series in (7.6) and (7.9) converge. Hence (7.6) and (7.9) represent solutions of $Ly = 0$. This is the content of the next theorem. This theorem, due to Frobenius, includes and extends the result of Fuchs given in Section 5.6.

THEOREM 7.1: A RESULT OF FROBENIUS

Suppose that r_1 and r_2 are the solutions of the indicial equation. If r_1 and r_2 are real numbers, let $r_1 \geq r_2$. Suppose that $b(x)$ and $c(x)$ satisfy (6.4.). Then (7.1) has a solution

$$y_1(x) = x^{r_1} \sum_{n=0}^{\infty} a_n x^n, \qquad 0 < x < L.$$

The coefficients a_n can be determined by substituting y_1 into (7.1). A second, linearly independent solution is obtained as follows:

(a) If $r_1 - r_2$ is not an integer, then

$$y_2(x) = x^{r_2} \sum_{n=0}^{\infty} d_n x^n.$$

The coefficients d_n can be obtained by substituting y_2 into (7.1).

(b) If $r_1 = r_2$, then

$$y_2(x) = x^{r_1} \sum_{n=1}^{\infty} d_n x^n + (\log x)\, y_1(x).$$

The coefficients d_n can be determined, once y_1 is known, by substituting y_2 into (7.1).

(c) If $r_1 - r_2 = m$ is a positive integer, then

$$y_2(x) = x^{r_2} \sum_{n=0}^{\infty} d_n x^n + a(\log x)\, y_1(x).$$

The constant a and the coefficients d_n can be determined, once y_1 is known, by substituting y_2 into (7.1). [The constant a may be zero, in which case no logarithmic term will occur in $y_2(x)$.]

EXAMPLE 7.2   Consider the Bessel equation

$$x^2 y'' + xy' + (x^2 - v^2)y = 0.$$

The indicial equation is $r(r-1) + r - v^2 = r^2 - v^2 = 0$. The roots are $r_1 = v$ and $r_2 = -v$. Note that $r_1 - r_2 = v - (-v) = 2v$. Hence, if $v \geq 0$ and $v \neq m/2$ for some nonnegative integer m, then $y_1 = J_v(x)$ and $y_2 = J_{-v}(x)$, as expected. If $v = 0$, then $y_1 = J_0(x)$, while y_2 has the form

$$y_2 = \sum_{n=1}^{\infty} d_n x^n + (\log x) J_0(x).$$

This form for a second solution was given in Section 5.5. We can now see why it is correct. The last case is $v = m/2$ for some positive integer m. Theorem 7.1 predicts $y_1 = J_v(x)$ and a second solution of the form

$$(7.10) \qquad y_2 = x^{-m/2} \sum_{n=0}^{\infty} d_n x^n + a(\log x) J_{m/2}(x).$$

We compare this with the known answer, for m an odd integer,

$$y_2 = J_{-m/2}(x) = \left(\frac{x}{2}\right)^{-m/2} \sum_{k=0}^{\infty} \frac{(-1)^k}{k! \Gamma(k - m/2 + 1)} \left(\frac{x}{2}\right)^{2k}.$$

Clearly, the constant a in (7.10) must be zero. The terms d_n are given by

$$d_{2k} = \frac{(-1)^k}{k! \Gamma(k - m/2 + 1)} \frac{1}{2^{2k - m/2}}, \qquad d_{2k+1} = 0$$

for $k = 0, 1, 2, \ldots$. When m is an even integer it turns out that $a \neq 0$ (see Table 5.3). ∎

EXAMPLE 7.3   Find two linearly independent solutions of the equation

$$(7.11) \qquad x^2 y'' + x^2 y' - xy = 0, \qquad 0 < x < \infty.$$

This equation can be put in the form (7.1) with $b(x) = x$ and $c(x) = -x$. The indicial equation is $\lambda(\lambda - 1) = 0$. Hence $r_1 = 1$ and $r_2 = 0$. These roots differ by one, an integer. According to Theorem 7.1, there is a solution

$$y_1 = x \sum_{n=0}^{\infty} a_n x^n = \sum_{n=0}^{\infty} a_n x^{n+1}.$$

On substituting this series into (7.11), we find that

$$a_{n+1} = \frac{-na_n}{(n+2)(n+1)}, \qquad n \geq 0.$$

If $a_0 = 1$, then $a_1 = 0$. Hence $a_n = 0$ for all $n \geq 1$ and $y_1 = x$.

The second solution of (7.11) will be of the form

$$y_2 = ax \log x + \sum_{n=0}^{\infty} d_n x^n.$$

Hence

$$-xy_2 = -ax^2 \log x - \sum_{n=1}^{\infty} d_{n-1} x^n,$$

$$x^2 y_2' = x^2 \left[ax\left(\frac{1}{x}\right) + a \log x + \sum_{n=1}^{\infty} n d_n x^{n-1} \right]$$

$$= ax^2 + ax^2 \log x + \sum_{n=2}^{\infty} (n - 1) d_{n-1} x^n,$$

$$x^2 y_2'' = x^2 \left[\frac{a}{x} + \sum_{n=2}^{\infty} n(n - 1) d_n x^{n-2} \right],$$

and y_2 will solve (7.11) provided that

$$0 = \left[ax + \sum_{n=2}^{\infty} n(n-1)d_n x^n \right] + \left[ax^2 + ax^2 \log x + \sum_{n=2}^{\infty} (n-1)d_{n-1} x^n \right]$$

$$- \left[ax^2 \log x + \sum_{n=1}^{\infty} d_{n-1} x^n \right]$$

$$= (a - d_0)x + (2d_2 + d_1 - d_1 + a)x^2$$

$$+ \sum_{n=3}^{\infty} [n(n-1)d_n + (n-1)d_{n-1} - d_{n-1}]x^n.$$

Let $d_0 = 1$.   Then $a = 1$, $d_2 = -a/2 = -\frac{1}{2}$, and $d_n = -(n-2)d_{n-1}/n(n-1)$ for $n \geq 3$.   This gives

$$d_3 = \frac{-1}{3 \cdot 2}\left(-\frac{1}{2}\right) = \frac{(-1)^2}{3!2}, \qquad d_4 = \frac{-2}{4 \cdot 3}\left(\frac{(-1)^2}{3!2}\right) = \frac{(-1)^3}{4!3},$$

$$d_5 = \frac{-3}{5 \cdot 4}\left(\frac{(-1)^3}{4!3}\right) = \frac{(-1)^4}{5!4}, \ldots, d_n = \frac{(-1)^{n-1}}{n!(n-1)}.$$

Notice that the coefficient d_1 is arbitrary. This is so because $y_1 = x$ is a solution of (7.11). Hence we can choose d_1 in any convenient way. Let $d_1 = 0$, so that

$$y_2 = x \log x + \left\{ 1 + \sum_{n=2}^{\infty} \frac{(-1)^{n+1} x^n}{n!(n-1)} \right\}, \qquad 0 < x < \infty. \quad \blacksquare$$

EXAMPLE 7.4   Find two linearly independent solutions on $0 < x < \infty$ of

(7.12) $xy'' + y' + y = 0.$

Notice that $x_0 = 0$ is a regular singular point of (7.12). The indicial equation is $r(r-1) + r + 0 = r^2 = 0$. Hence $r_1 = r_2 = 0$. Set

$$y_1 = \sum_{n=0}^{\infty} a_n x^n,$$

so that

$$y_1' = \sum_{n=1}^{\infty} na_n x^{n-1} = \sum_{n=0}^{\infty} (n+1)a_{n+1} x^n$$

and

$$xy_1'' = x\sum_{n=1}^{\infty} n(n-1)a_n x^{n-2} = \sum_{n=0}^{\infty} (n+1)na_{n+1} x^n.$$

On substituting into (7.12), we see that

$$0 = \sum_{n=0}^{\infty} [(n+1)na_{n+1} + (n+1)a_{n+1} + a_n]x^n = 0.$$

Hence

$$a_{n+1} = \frac{-1}{(n+1)^2} a_n, \qquad n \geq 0.$$

If we take $a_0 = 1$, then $a_n = (-1)^n/(n!)^2$ and

(7.13)
$$y_1 = \sum_{n=0}^{\infty} (-1)^n \frac{x^n}{(n!)^2}.$$

According to Theorem 7.1, part (b), the second solution will be of the form

$$y_2 = y_1(x) \log x + \sum_{n=1}^{\infty} d_n x^n.$$

Thus

$$y_2' = \left[y_1' \log x + \frac{y_1}{x} + \sum_{n=1}^{\infty} nd_n x^{n-1} \right]$$

$$= y_1' \log x + \frac{y_1}{x} + \sum_{n=0}^{\infty} (n+1)d_{n+1} x^n$$

and

$$xy_2'' = x\left[y_1'' \log x + \frac{2y_1'}{x} - \frac{y_1}{x^2} + \sum_{n=0}^{\infty} (n+1)nd_{n+1} x^{n-1} \right]$$

$$= xy_1'' \log x + 2y_1' - \frac{y_1}{x} + \sum_{n=0}^{\infty} (n+1)nd_{n+1} x^n.$$

Substituting into (7.12) gives

$$0 = \left[xy_1'' \log x + 2y_1' - \frac{y_1}{x} \right] + \left[y_1' \log x + \frac{y_1}{x} \right] + y_1 \log x$$

$$+ \sum_{n=0}^{\infty} [(n+1)nd_{n+1} + (n+1)d_{n+1}]x^n + \sum_{n=1}^{\infty} d_n x^n,$$

or

(7.14) $0 = (xy_1'' + y_1' + y_1) \log x + 2y_1' + d_1 + \sum_{n=1}^{\infty} [(n+1)^2 d_{n+1} + d_n]x^n.$

Since y_1 solves (7.12), then the term multiplying $\log x$ is zero. Hence (7.13) and (7.14) give

$$\sum_{n=0}^{\infty} \frac{2(-1)^{n+1} x^n}{(n+1)!n!} + d_1 + \sum_{n=1}^{\infty} [(n+1)^2 d_{n+1} + d_n]x^n = 0.$$

Hence $d_1 = 2$ and $2(-1)^{n+1}/[(n+1)!n!] + (n+1)^2 d_{n+1} + d_n = 0$, that is,

(7.15) $d_{n+1} = \frac{-d_n}{(n+1)^2} + \frac{2(-1)^n}{[(n+1)!]^2(n+1)}, \qquad n \geq 1.$

One cannot easily solve (7.15) for d_n. However, it is easy to compute the first few terms. Thus

$$d_2 = \tfrac{1}{4}(-2 - 1) = -\tfrac{3}{4}, \qquad d_3 = \tfrac{1}{9}(\tfrac{3}{4} + \tfrac{1}{6}) = \tfrac{11}{108},$$

$$d_4 = \tfrac{1}{16}(-\tfrac{11}{108} - \tfrac{1}{72}) = -\tfrac{25}{3456},$$

and

$$y_2 = y_1(x) \log x + \left\{ 2x - \frac{3x^2}{4} + \frac{11x^3}{108} - \frac{25x^4}{3456} + \cdots \right\}. \quad \blacksquare$$

PROBLEMS

In Problems 1–4, find two linearly independent solutions on $0 < x < \infty$. Compute the first four nonzero terms of each series.

1. $xy'' + (1 - x)y' + 2y = 0$.

2. $x^2 y'' - (x^2 - \frac{1}{4})y = 0$.

3. $x^2 y'' + x^2 y' - 2y = 0$.

4. $x^2 y'' + (x^2 - x - 6)y = 0$.

5. Consider the **Laguerre equation** $xy'' + (1 - x)y' + ky = 0$.

(a) Show that $x = 0$ is a regular singular point.

(b) Find all values $k = k_n$ for which the equation has a polynomial solution $y = p_n(x)$ of degree n with $p_n(0) = 1$.

(c) Compute $p_0(x)$, $p_1(x)$, and $p_2(x)$.

(d) For $k = 0$ find two linearly independent solutions on $0 < x < \infty$.

(e) For $k = 1$ find two linearly independent solutions on $0 < x < \infty$.

6. Consider the **Riccati–Bessel equation** $x^2 y'' - (x^2 - k)y = 0$, $-\infty < k < \infty$.

(a) Show that $x_0 = 0$ is a regular singular point.

(b) For what values of k does Theorem 7.1, part (a) apply? What form do y_1 and y_2 take in this case?

(c) For what values of k does Theorem 7.1, part (b) apply? What form do y_1 and y_2 take in this case?

(d) For what values of k does Theorem 7.1, part (c) apply? What form do y_1 and y_2 take in this case?

7. Repeat Problem 6 for the **Coulomb wave equation**

$$x^2 y'' + [x^2 - 2lx - k]y = 0 \qquad (l \text{ fixed}, \; -\infty < k < \infty).$$

8. Repeat Problem 6 for the confluent hypergeometric equation

$$xy'' + (k - x)y' + ly = 0, \qquad (l \text{ fixed}, \; -\infty < k < \infty).$$

9. Consider the equation

$$y'' + B(x)y' + C(x)y = 0,$$

where

$$B(x) = \sum_{n=0}^{\infty} B_n x^{-n}, \qquad C(x) = \sum_{n=0}^{\infty} C_n x^{-n}, \qquad |x| > R.$$

This equation is said to have a **regular singular point at infinity** if the change of variables $t = x^{-1}$ results in an equation with a regular singular point at $t = 0$. Otherwise, it has an **irregular singular point at infinity**. Show that under the change of variables $t = x^{-1}$ the equation becomes

$$t^4 \frac{d^2y}{dt^2} + \left(2t^3 - t^2 B\left(\frac{1}{t}\right)\right)\frac{dy}{dt} + C\left(\frac{1}{t}\right)y = 0.$$

Decide whether the singular point at infinity is regular or irregular in each case.

(a) Equations with constant coefficients, that is, $y'' + By' + Cy = 0$.

(b) The Euler equation $y'' + (B/x)y' + (C/x^2)y = 0$.

(c) The Laguerre equation $xy'' + (1 - x)y' + ky = 0$.

(d) The confluent hypergeometric equation $xy'' + (b - x)y' + ay = 0$.

(e) The hypergeometric equation $x(1 - x)y'' + [c - (a + b + 1)x]y' - aby = 0$.

10. (a) Show that $x(1 - x)y'' + 2(1 - x)y' - \frac{3}{16}y = 0$ has a regular singular point at infinity.

(b) Show that this equation has two linearly independent solutions of the form

$$y = x^{-r} \sum_{n=0}^{\infty} a_n x^{-n}, \qquad x > 1.$$

(c) Compute all possible values for r.

11. (a) Show that $x(1 - x)y'' + (1 - 3x)y' - y = 0$ has a regular singular point at infinity.

(b) This equation has a solution of the form

$$y_1 = x^{-r} \sum_{n=0}^{\infty} a_n x^{-n}, \qquad x > 1.$$

Compute all possible values for r.

(c) If you were to look for a second (linearly independent) solution y_2, what form would you assume for y_2?

CHAPTER REVIEW

Linear second-order equations with analytic coefficients have the form $a_2(x)y'' + a_1(x)y' + a_0(x)y = b(x)$, where $b(x)$ and all $a_i(x)$ are analytic near some point x_0. We say that x_0 is an **ordinary point** if $a_2(x_0) \neq 0$, and a **singular point** if $a_2(x_0) = 0$. A singular point is a **regular singular point** if the expressions $(x - x_0)a_1(x)/a_2(x)$ and $(x - x_0)^2 a_0(x)/a_2(x)$ both have finite limits as $x \to x_0$. If x_0 is a regular point, then power series methods can be used to solve the equation. The Hermite equation $y'' - 2xy' + \lambda y = 0$ is a typical example.

If x_0 is a regular singular point, then one can find solutions of the form $y = \sum_{n=0}^{\infty} a_n(x - x_0)^{n+r}$. The number r will be a root of the indicial equation (6.7). The exact situation is summarized in Theorem 7.1. The **Bessel equation** $x^2 y'' + xy' + (x^2 - v^2)y = 0$ has a regular singular point at $x_0 = 0$.

CHAPTER REVIEW PROBLEMS

Solve Problems 1–4. Find a general solution if no initial conditions are given.

1. $y'' - \alpha^2 xy = 0$.

2. $y'' - 3xy' + (x + 1)y = 0$, $y(0) = 1$, $y'(0) = 0$.

3. $3xy'' + y' + y = 0$.

4. $x^2 y'' + 3y' + 2y = 0$.

CHAPTER SIX

The Laplace Transform and Its Uses

The Laplace transformation originated as a symbolic method for solving differential equations, a method due to the English electrical engineer Oliver Heaviside. The Laplace transformation is particularly useful for obtaining solutions of forced linear ordinary differential equations with constant coefficients. This transform method has two important advantages over competing methods. First, one can directly solve many initial value problems without first finding a fundamental set of solutions of the corresponding homogeneous problem. Second, this transformation provides the easiest method of solution for many nonhomogeneous problems when the nonhomogeneous term is discontinuous or is implusive. Certainly, it is necessary to understand the basic theory of the Laplace transformation and its related terminology in order to follow a modern text on control theory. One cannot even discuss modern methods of design, analysis, or compensation for linear control systems without using the language of Laplace transformation theory. Laplace transforms can also be used to solve many integral equation problems, many problems involving systems of linear differential equations, and many problems in partial differential equations.

In this chapter, we first define the Laplace transformation and develop its basic properties. Next, we show how initial value problems can be solved by using the Laplace transform. We show how to take the Laplace transform of a large class of discontinuous functions and how to solve linear nonhomogeneous differential equations when the nonhomogeneous term is discontinuous. We discuss the unit impulse function, the solution of linear differential equations whose forcing is impulsive, and convolution and its connections to Laplace transforms.

6.1 *DEFINITIONS AND BASIC PROPERTIES*

LAPLACE TRANSFORM

Left $f(t)$ be a given real-valued function. The Laplace transform of $f(t)$, denoted by $L\{f\} = F$, is defined by

(1.1)
$$F(s) = \int_0^\infty e^{-st} f(t)\, dt.$$

We assume for now that s is a real number. Later it will be useful to allow s to be a complex number. The Laplace transform of f is said to *exist at s* if the improper integral (1.1) converges. Otherwise, the transform *does not exist at s*. If $F(s)$ exists at some s_0, it can be shown that $F(s)$ will also exist for all real numbers $s > s_0$. We shall use small letters f, g, h, etc., for functions of t and shall denote their Laplace transforms by $F = L\{f\}$, $G = L\{g\}$, $H = L\{h\}$, etc.

Since the range of integration in (1.1) is infinite, the integral is an improper integral. What is meant in (1.1) is that $f(t)e^{-st}$ is integrable over every finite interval $0 \le t \le T$ and

$$\int_0^\infty e^{-st} f(t)\, dt = \lim_{T \to \infty} \int_0^T e^{-st} f(t)\, dt.$$

EXAMPLE 1.1   Let $f(t) = 1$ for all $t \ge 0$. Then for $s > 0$

$$F(s) = \int_0^\infty e^{-st}\, dt = \lim_{T \to \infty} \int_0^T e^{-st}\, dt$$

$$= \lim_{T \to \infty} \left[\frac{e^{-st}}{-s} \right]_0^T = \frac{1}{s}.$$

Hence, $L\{1\} = 1/s$ exists for all $s > 0$.   ∎

EXAMPLE 1.2   Let $f(t) = e^{at}$ for some real number a. Then for $s > a$

$$F(s) = \int_0^\infty e^{-st} e^{at}\, dt = \lim_{T \to \infty} \int_0^T e^{-(s-a)t}\, dt$$

$$= \lim_{T \to \infty} \left[\frac{e^{-(s-a)t}}{-(s-a)} \right]_0^T = \frac{1}{s-a}.$$

Thus $L\{e^{at}\} = (s-a)^{-1}$ for all $s > a$. For example, $L\{e^{3t}\} = (s-3)^{-1}$ for $s > 3$ and $L\{e^{-3t}\} = (s+3)^{-1}$ for $s > -3$.   ∎

EXAMPLE 1.3   Let $f(t) = \sin t$. The computation of $F(s)$ in this case is more complex than it was in Examples 1.1 and 1.2. One must integrate by parts twice to see that

$$\int_0^T e^{-st} \sin t \, dt = [e^{-st}(-\cos t)]_0^T + \int_0^T (-s)e^{-st} \cos t \, dt$$

$$= [-e^{-st} \cos t - se^{-st} \sin t]_0^T - s^2 \int_0^T e^{-st} \sin t \, dt.$$

A little algebra yields the result that

$$(1 + s^2) \int_0^T e^{-st} \sin t \, dt = [-e^{-st} \cos t - se^{-st} \sin t]_0^T$$

or

$$\int_0^T e^{-st} \sin t \, dt = \frac{1}{s^2 + 1} [-e^{-sT} \cos T - se^{-sT} \sin T + 1].$$

On taking the limit as $T \to \infty$ we see that for $s > 0$

$$L\{\sin t\} = \frac{1}{s^2 + 1}(-0 - 0 + 1) = \frac{1}{s^2 + 1}. \quad \blacksquare$$

We wish to introduce a reasonable class of functions whose Laplace transforms exist. To do this, it is necessary to introduce some terminology. A function f defined over an interval $a \leq t \leq b$ is called **piecewise continuous** on $[a, b]$ if the interval can be divided into a finite number of subintervals $[t_i, t_{i+1}]$ such that on each subinterval f is continuous in (t_i, t_{i+1}) and the one-sided limits

$$\lim_{t \to t_i^+} f(t) \quad \text{and} \quad \lim_{t \to t_{i+1}^-} f(t)$$

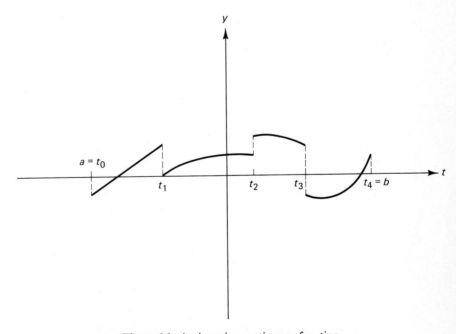

Figure 6.1. A piecewise continuous function.

exist and are finite (see, e.g., Figure 6.1). At the point t_i the two limits

$$\lim_{t \to t_i^-} f(t) \quad \text{and} \quad \lim_{t \to t_i^+} f(t)$$

need not be equal. When they are not equal, f is said to have a **jump discontinuity** at t_i. Notice that it is not required that f be defined at the points t_i.

EXAMPLE 1.4   The function f defined by

(1.2) $$f(t) = \begin{cases} -1 & \text{if } t \le 0 \\ t & \text{if } 0 < t < 1 \\ t^2 & \text{if } t \ge 1 \end{cases}$$

is piecewise continuous on any finite interval $[a, b]$. It has a jump discontinuity at $t = 0$ since

$$\lim_{t \to 0^-} f(t) = -1 \quad \text{and} \quad \lim_{t \to 0^+} f(t) = 0.$$

Since $f(t) \to 1$ as $t \to 1^-$ and as $t \to 1^+$, then f is continuous at $t = 1$. ∎

Notice that if f is continuous on an interval $[a, b]$, then f is automatically piecewise continuous there. Notice also that if f is piecewise continuous on $[a, b]$, then the integral

$$\int_a^b f(t)\, dt$$

can be defined. For example, if $f(t)$ is the function defined by (1.2), then

$$\int_{-1}^2 f(t)\, dt = \int_{-1}^0 f(t)\, dt + \int_0^1 f(t)\, dt + \int_1^2 f(t)\, dt$$

$$= \int_{-1}^0 (-1)\, dt + \int_0^1 t\, dt + \int_1^2 t^2\, dt$$

$$= -1 + \tfrac{1}{2} + \tfrac{7}{3} = \tfrac{11}{6}.$$

A function defined on $[0, \infty)$ is said to be **of exponential order** a if there are real constants M and a such that $M \ge 0$ and such that $|f(t)| \le Me^{at}$ for all $t \ge 0$. A function f is said to be of class Λ if f is defined on $[0, \infty)$, if f is piecewise continuous over $[0, T]$ for each $T > 0$, and if f is of exponential order a for some number a. For example, $f(t) = \sinh t = (e^t - e^{-t})/2$ is continuous, hence piecewise continuous and $|f(t)| \le (e^t + 1)/2 \le e^t$ for all $t \ge 0$. Thus f is of exponential order $a = 1$. Similarly, $g(t) = e^{2t} \sin t$ satisfies $|g(t)| \le e^{2t}$ so $g(t)$ is a continuous function of exponential order $a = 2$.

THEOREM 1.5: EXISTENCE OF LAPLACE TRANSFORMS

If f is of class Λ with $|f(t)| \le Me^{at}$ for all $t \ge 0$, then the Laplace transform $L\{f\} = F(s)$ exists for all $s > a$. Moreover, $|F(s)| \le M(s - a)^{-1}$ for all $s > a$.

Before proving Theorem 1.5, it is necessary to recall a fact about improper integrals. Suppose that $g(t)$ and $h(t)$ are defined on $[0, \infty)$ and $|g(t)| \leq h(t)$ there. Consider the improper integrals

$$I_1 = \int_0^\infty g(t) \, dt \quad \text{and} \quad I_2 = \int_0^\infty h(t) \, dt.$$

If I_2 converges, then I_1 must also converge and $|I_1| \leq I_2$. We shall use this result with $g(t) = f(t)e^{-st}$ and $h(t) = Me^{at}e^{-st}$. Given that $|f(t)| \leq Me^{at}$, then $|g(t)| = |f(t)|e^{-st} \leq h(t)$. Moreover, when $s > a$,

$$\int_0^\infty h(t) \, dt = \int_0^\infty Me^{at}e^{-st} \, dt = M(s - a)^{-1}.$$

Hence $F(s)$ must exist for all $s > a$ and $|F(s)| \leq M(s - a)^{-1}$.

For any fixed number c, the **unit step function** or **Heaviside step function** $u_c(t)$ is defined by

$$u_c(t) = \begin{cases} 0 & \text{if } t < c \\ 1 & \text{if } t \geq c. \end{cases}$$

The graph of $u_c(t)$ is shown in Figure 6.2. Clearly, $u_c(t)$ is piecewise continuous on $[0, T]$ for any $T > 0$. Clearly, $u_c(t)$ is of exponential order a for any $a \geq 0$. Hence u_c is of class Λ. The Laplace transform of u_c is computed as follows:

$$L\{u_c\} = \int_0^\infty e^{-st} u_c(t) \, dt = \int_0^c e^{-st} \cdot 0 \, dt + \int_c^\infty e^{-st} \cdot 1 \, dt$$

$$= \int_c^\infty e^{-st} \, dt = \lim_{T \to \infty} \left[\frac{e^{-st}}{-s} \right]_c^T$$

$$= \frac{e^{-sc}}{s} \qquad \text{for any } s > 0.$$

The Laplace transform L is an **operator,** that is, L is a rule such that given any f in class Λ there is a corresponding function $F = L\{f\}$. The operator L is **linear.** This means that if f_1 and f_2 are of class Λ and c_1 and c_2 are any real numbers, then

$$L\{c_1 f_1 + c_2 f_2\} = c_1 L\{f_1\} + c_2 L\{f_2\}.$$

Similarly, if f_i is of class Λ for $i = 1, 2, \ldots, N$, then for any constants c_i we have $L\{\sum_{i=1}^N c_i f_i\} = \sum_{i=1}^N c_i L\{f_i\}$.

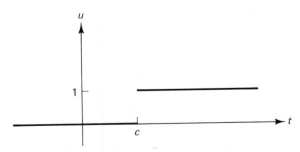

Figure 6.2. Heaviside step function.

EXAMPLE 1.6   Find the Laplace transform of

$$f(t) = 3 - \frac{e^{-t}}{2} + 2u_2(t) - e^{3t}.$$

From previous examples we know that $L\{1\} = s^{-1}$, $L\{e^{at}\} = (s - a)^{-1}$, and $L\{u_c\} = e^{-cs}/s$. Hence

$$L\{f\} = 3\left(\frac{1}{s}\right) - \frac{(s + 1)^{-1}}{2} + 2\left(\frac{e^{-2s}}{s}\right) - (s - 3)^{-1}. \quad \blacksquare$$

THEOREM 1.7: DERIVATIVE OF A TRANSFORM

If f is of class Λ and $F(s) = L\{f\}$ converges when $s > a$, then for $n = 1$, $2, 3, \ldots$

(1.3) $$L\{t^n f(t)\} = (-1)^n \frac{d^n}{ds^n} F(s) \qquad \text{for } s > a.$$

Recall that for $s > a$

(1.4) $$F(s) = \int_0^\infty e^{-st} f(t) \, dt.$$

Take the derivative on each side of (1.4) to see that

$$\frac{d}{ds} F(s) = \int_0^\infty e^{-st} (-t) f(t) \, dt.$$

This is (1.3) for $n = 1$. One can continue taking derivatives of (1.4) to obtain (1.3) for all positive integers n.

EXAMPLE 1.8   Find $L\{t^n\}$ for $n = 1, 2, 3, \ldots$.
         We know that $L\{1\} = s^{-1}$. Apply (1.3) with $f(t) = 1$ and $F(s) = s^{-1}$. This gives

$$L\{t\} = \frac{1}{s^2}, \qquad L\{t^2\} = \frac{2}{s^3}, \qquad L\{t^3\} = \frac{6}{s^4},$$

and so on. In general, one has

$$L\{t^n\} = \frac{n!}{s^{n+1}} \qquad \text{for all } s > 0. \quad \blacksquare$$

THEOREM 1.9: INTEGRAL OF A TRANSFORM

If f is of class Λ and if $f(t)/t$ has a finite limit as $t \to 0^+$, then

(1.5)
$$L\left\{\frac{f(t)}{t}\right\} = \int_s^\infty F(r)\, dr.$$

To see that (1.5) is true, define g by the formula $g(t) = f(t)/t$ for $t > 0$ and

$$g(0) = \lim_{t \to 0^+} \frac{f(t)}{t}.$$

Then g is of class Λ and has a Laplace transform $L\{g\} = G$. Let $F(s) = L\{f\}$. By Theorem 1.7

$$F(s) = L\left\{t\left(\frac{f(t)}{t}\right)\right\} = L\{t(g(t))\} = -\frac{d}{ds}\,G(s).$$

Thus $G'(s) = -F(s)$ or

(1.6)
$$G(s) = A - \int_a^s F(r)\, dr$$

for some constant A and any $a > 0$. Since g is of class Λ, then by Theorem 1.5 $|G(s)| \le M/(s - a)$. Thus $G(s) \to 0$ as $s \to \infty$. Hence if we take the limit in (1.6) as $s \to \infty$, we see that

$$0 = \lim_{s \to \infty} G(s) = \lim_{s \to \infty}\left\{A - \int_a^s F(r)\, dr\right\} = A - \int_a^\infty F(r)\, dr.$$

Hence

$$A = \int_a^\infty F(r)\, dr,$$

and (1.6) becomes

$$G(s) = \int_a^\infty F(r)\, dr - \int_a^s F(r)\, dr = \int_s^\infty F(r)\, dr.$$

EXAMPLE 1.10   Compute $L\{\sin t/t\}$.

We know that $L\{\sin t\} = 1/(s^2 + 1)$ for $s > 0$. Hence

$$L\left\{\frac{\sin t}{t}\right\} = \int_s^\infty \frac{dr}{r^2 + 1} = \frac{\pi}{2} - \arctan s = \arctan\left(\frac{1}{s}\right). \quad\blacksquare$$

EXAMPLE 1.11
The Gamma Function

If $f(t) = t^\alpha$ and α is any nonnegative real number, then f is of class Λ and $L\{f(t)\} = F(s)$ converges for all $s > 0$. Hence for $r = st$ we have

$$L\{t^\alpha\} = \int_0^\infty e^{-st}t^\alpha \, dt = \int_0^\infty e^{-r}\left(\frac{r}{s}\right)^\alpha \frac{dr}{s}$$

$$= \frac{1}{s^{\alpha+1}} \int_0^\infty e^{-r}r^\alpha \, dr = \frac{\Gamma(\alpha+1)}{s^{\alpha+1}}.$$

For example, $L\{t^{1/2}\} = \Gamma(\tfrac{3}{2})/s^{3/2}$ and $L\{t^{4/3}\} = \Gamma(\tfrac{7}{3})/s^{7/3}$. The function Γ, defined by the integral

$$\Gamma(v+1) = \int_0^\infty e^{-r}r^v \, dr,$$

is the **gamma function.** The gamma function was introduced in Chapter 5. It was shown there that $\Gamma(v+1)$ is defined for any real numbers $v > -1$. Moreover, if $v > 0$, then $\Gamma(v+1) = v\Gamma(v)$. Notice that

$$\Gamma(1) = \int_0^\infty e^{-r}r^0 \, dr = \int_0^\infty e^{-r} \, dr = 1.$$

Hence

$$\Gamma(2) = 1 \cdot \Gamma(1) = 1 \cdot 1 = 1!,$$

$$\Gamma(3) = 2\Gamma(2) = 2 \cdot 1 = 2!,$$

$$\Gamma(4) = 3\Gamma(3) = 3 \cdot 2! = 3!,$$

and in general

$$\Gamma(n+1) = n!.$$

Hence the formula

(1.7)
$$L\{t^\alpha\} = \frac{\Gamma(\alpha+1)}{s^{\alpha+1}}, \qquad s > 0$$

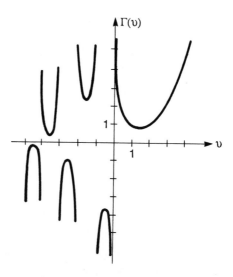

Figure 6.3. Gamma function

reduces to

(1.8) $$L\{t^n\} = \frac{n!}{s^{n+1}}, \qquad s > 0$$

when $\alpha = n$ is a positive integer. Formula (1.7) remains true when $-1 < \alpha < 0$ (see Problem 8).

PROBLEMS

1. Graph each function. In each case decide whether the function given is continuous, piecewise continuous, or neither on the interval $0 \le t \le T$ for all $T > 0$. $u_c(t)$ is the unit step function graphed in Figure 6.2.

(a) $f(t) = \begin{cases} 0 & \text{on } 0 \le t < 1 \\ t & \text{on } 1 \le t < \pi \\ \sin t & \text{on } t \ge \pi. \end{cases}$

(b) $f(t) = \begin{cases} (t - \pi)e^t & \text{on } 0 \le t < \pi \\ \sin t & \text{on } t \ge \pi. \end{cases}$

(c) $f(t) = u_3(t) - 2u_4(t)$.

(d) $f(t) = \begin{cases} 1 & \text{at } t = 0 \\ t^{-1/2} & \text{on } 0 < t < \infty. \end{cases}$

(e) $f(t) = \text{sgn}(\cos 3t)$ on $0 \le t < \infty$.

(f) $f(t) = u_1(t)t^{-1/3} + [1 - u_1(t)]$ for all $t > 0$ and $f(0) = 0$.

(g) $f(t) = 1 - tu_2(t)$ for all $t \ge 0$.

(h) $f(t) = \dfrac{\sin t}{\sqrt{t}}$ for $t > 0$ and $f(0) = 0$.

(i) $f(t) = \dfrac{\cos 2t}{\sqrt{t}}$ for $t > 0$ and $f(0) = 0$.

2. Show that if $f_1(t)$ and $f_2(t)$ are of class Λ and if c_1 and c_2 are any real numbers, then $c_1 f_1(t) + c_2 f_2(t)$ is of class Λ.

3. In Problem 2 show that $L\{c_1 f_1 + c_2 f_2\} = c_1 L\{f_1\} + c_2 L\{f_2\}$.

4. Compute the Laplace transformation of each function.

(a) t^2.

(b) $3t^5 - 2t + 1$.

(c) $2e^{4t}$.

(d) $5e^{-2t} + u_3(t) - 2$.

(e) $3\sin t + t \sin t$.

(f) $\dfrac{3\sin t}{t} - \sin t$.

(g) $t^2 + 2t^3$

(h) $t^5 - \frac{1}{2}\sin t + 4e^{-t}$

(i) $\sinh at$.

(j) $\cosh at$.

5. Use integration by parts to compute the Laplace transform of each function.

(a) $\sin at$.

(b) $\cos at$.

(c) $e^{bt} \sin at$.

(d) $e^{bt} \cos at$.

6. For any constant $a > 0$ compute

(a) $L\left\{\dfrac{\sin at}{t}\right\}$.

(b) $L\left\{\dfrac{\cos at - 1}{t}\right\}$.

(c) $L\left\{e^{bt}\dfrac{\sin at}{t}\right\}$.

Hint: The answers to Problem 5 will be useful.

7. Compute the Laplace transform of each function. Use Theorem 1.7.

(a) te^t.

(b) $t \sin t$.

(c) $t^2 \sin t$.

(d) $t^3 e^{2t}$.

(e) $t^n e^{at}$.

8. Using integration by parts, show that $\Gamma(v + 1) = v\Gamma(v)$ is true for $0 < v < \infty$.

9. (a) Given $\Gamma(v + 1)/s^{v+1} = \int_0^\infty e^{-st}t^v \, dt$, differentiate with respect to v to see that

$$\frac{\Gamma'(v + 1) - (\log s)\Gamma(v + 1)}{s^{v+1}} = \int_0^\infty e^{-st}(\log t)t^v \, dt.$$

(b) Show that $L\{\log t\} = (\Gamma'(1) - \log s)/s$. The constant $\gamma = -\Gamma'(1) = 0.57721566$ ... is called **Euler's constant**.

(c) Show that the improper integral $\int_0^1 e^{-st}t^v \log t \, dt$ converges when $v > -1$.

(d) Compute $L\{t^n \log t\}$, $n = 1, 2, 3$.

10. Let $\chi_{[a,b]}(x) = 1$ if x is in the interval $[a, b]$ and $\chi_{[a,b]}(x) = 0$ if x is not in $[a, b]$. For $0 \le a < b < \infty$ compute

(a) $L\{\chi_{[a,b]}\}$.

(b) $L\{t^n \chi_{[a,b]}\}$, $n = 1, 2, 3$.

   Hint: Show that $\chi_{[a,b]}(t) = u_a(t) - u_b(t)$ if $t \ne b$.

11. Suppose that

$$f(t) = \begin{cases} 1 & \text{on } 0 \le t < 3 \\ -1 & \text{on } 3 \le t < \pi \\ 3\pi & \text{on } \pi \le t < 7 \\ 0 & \text{on } t \ge 7. \end{cases}$$

(a) Verify that $f(t) = 1 - 2u_3(t) + (3\pi + 1)u_\pi(t) - 3\pi u_7(t)$.

(b) Compute $L\{f\}$.

12. Compute $L\{f\}$ when

$$f(t) = \begin{cases} 0 & \text{on } 0 \le t < 2 \\ -1 & \text{on } 2 \le t < 5 \\ 2 & \text{on } t \ge 5. \end{cases}$$

13. (a) Show that $f(t) = t^{-1/2}$ has a Laplace transform when $s > 0$.

(b) $F(s) = L\{t^{-1/2}\} = \Gamma(\tfrac{1}{2})/\sqrt{s}$ does not satisfy $|F(s)| \le M(s - a)^{-1}$ for any number $M > 0$ and $a > 0$. Why does this not violate Theorem 1.5?

14. If one will receive S dollars in m years and if the going annual interest rate is I, then the **present value** of this income is $P = S/(1 + I)^m$. P is the amount that would be invested at the annual interest rate I to yield income S in m years; that is, P takes into account the **time value of money**.

(a) Compute the present value of $300, to be paid in 3 years, if the annual interest rate is 8% (i.e., $I = 0.08$).

(b) Compute the present value of $300, to be paid in 2 years, plus $200 to be paid in 4 years if $I = 0.08$.

15. If the nominal annual interest rate is I and if this rate is compounded N times per year, the actual interest rate is I/N per $1/N$ years.

   (a) Show that the present value of S dollars to be received in t years at nominal annual rate I, compounded N times per year, is

$$P_N = S\left[\left(1 + \frac{I}{N}\right)^{N/I}\right]^{-It}.$$

   (b) If interest is compounded N times per year and if we let $N \to \infty$, the result is **continuous compounding.** Show that the present value of S dollars to be received in t years at nominal annual rate I, with continuous compounding, is

$$P = Se^{-It}.$$

16. (a) If income is received continuously and indefinitely but the rate R of payment varies with time [i.e., $R = f(t)$ dollars per year], and if the nominal annual interest rate is I, show that the present value, continuously compounded, of the income stream $f(t)$ is

$$P = \int_0^\infty f(t)e^{-It}\, dt = L\{f\}(I).$$

   (b) If $f(t) = 100(1 + \sin t)$ dollars per year and if the nominal annual interest rate is 9%, compute the present value of this income stream.

   (c) Repeat part (b) with a nominal annual interest rate of 10%.

   (d) If $f(t) = e^t$, how large must I be in order that P is finite?

6.2   FURTHER PROPERTIES OF L

Suppose that f is any function of class Λ and b is any real number. Then $g(t) = e^{bt}f(t)$ is also a function of class Λ. Hence $G(s) = L\{g\}$ will converge for all s that are sufficiently large. If $F(s) = L\{f\}$, then

$$G(s) = \int_0^\infty e^{-st}\{e^{bt}f(t)\}\, dt = \int_0^\infty e^{-(s-b)t}f(t) = F(s - b).$$

This proves the following result.

THEOREM 2.1: TRANSLATION OF A TRANSFORM

If $f(t)$ has Laplace transform $F(s)$, then for any real number b the function $g(t) = e^{bt}f(t)$ is Laplace transformable and $L\{g\} = F(s - b)$.

EXAMPLE 2.2   Compute $L\{e^{2t}\sin t\}$ and $L\{e^{-t}\sin t\}$. Since $L\{\sin t\} = 1/(s^2 + 1)$, then

$$L\{e^{2t}\sin t\} = \frac{1}{(s - 2)^2 + 1} = (s^2 - 4s + 5)^{-1}$$

and

$$L\{e^{-t}\sin t\} = \frac{1}{(s+1)^2+1} = (s^2+2s+2)^{-1}. \quad \blacksquare$$

EXAMPLE 2.3   Compute $L\{e^{-\pi t}t^3\}$.

Since $L\{t^n\} = n!/s^{n+1}$, then $L\{e^{-\pi t}t^3\} = 3!/(s+\pi)^4$. $\blacksquare$

If f is a continuous function of class Λ whose derivative f' is also of class Λ, then $L\{f'\}$ can be computed in terms of $L\{f\}$. This is accomplished by using integration by parts:

$$\int_0^T e^{-st}f'(t)\,dt = e^{-st}f(t)\Big|_0^T + s\int_0^T e^{-st}f(t)\,dt$$

or

(2.1) $$\int_0^T e^{-st}f'(t)\,dt = s\int_0^T e^{-st}f(t)\,dt - f(0) + e^{-st}f(T).$$

In as much as $e^{-sT}f(T) \to 0$ as $T \to \infty$ (when s is large), then taking the limit as $T \to \infty$ in (2.1) gives

$$L\{f'\} = sL\{f\} - f(0).$$

THEOREM 2.4

If f and f' are both of class Λ, then there is a $b > 0$ such that

(2.2) $$L\{f'\} = sL\{f\} - f(0) \qquad \text{for } s > b.$$

If f'' also exists and is of class Λ, Theorem 2.4 can be applied twice to see that

$$\begin{aligned}
L\{f''\} &= sL\{f'\} - f'(0) \\
&= s[sL\{f\} - f(0)] - f'(0) \\
&= s^2 L\{f\} - sf(0) - f'(0).
\end{aligned}$$

In the same way, if f''' is of class Λ, then

$$\begin{aligned}
L\{f'''\} &= L\{f''\} - f''(0) \\
&= s^3 L\{f\} - s^2 f(0) - sf'(0) - f''(0),
\end{aligned}$$

and so on, for $f^{(n)}$, $n = 4, 5, 6, \ldots$.

THEOREM 2.5: TRANSFORMS OF DERIVATIVES

I₁ $f^{(n)}$ exists and if $f^{(j)}$ is a continuous function of class Λ for $j = 0, 1, 2, \ldots, n$, then

(2.3) $L\{f^{(n)}\} = s^n L\{f\} - s^{n-1} f(0) - s^{n-2} f'(0) - \cdots - f^{(n-1)}(0).$

EXAMPLE 2.6   Given $L\{\sin t\} = (s^2 + 1)^{-1}$, compute $L\{\cos t\}$.
Since $\cos t = (\sin t)'$, then

$$L\{\cos t\} = s\,\frac{1}{s^2 + 1} - \sin 0 = \frac{s}{s^2 + 1}. \quad \blacksquare$$

EXAMPLE 2.7   Compute $Y(s) = L\{y\}$ when $y(t)$ is the solution of the initial value problem

(2.4) $y'' + 3y' + 2y = 1, \qquad y(0) = 1, \qquad y'(0) = -2.$

Taking Laplace transforms of both sides of (2.4), we see that

$$[s^2 Y - sy(0) - y'(0)] + 3[sY - y(0)] + 2Y = \frac{1}{s},$$

$$(s^2 Y - s + 2) + 3(sY - 1) + 2Y = \frac{1}{s},$$

$$(s^2 + 3s + 2)Y = (s + 1) + \frac{1}{s},$$

and so

$$Y(s) = \frac{s + 1}{s^2 + 3s + 2} + \frac{1}{s(s^2 + 3s + 2)}. \quad \blacksquare$$

THEOREM 2.8: TRANSFORM OF AN INTEGRAL

If f is of class Λ and if g is defined by

$$g(t) = \int_0^t f(r)\,dr,$$

then $L\{g\} = L\{f\}/s.$

To see that this is true, we notice that $g' = f$ and $g(0) = 0$. Hence Theorem 2.4 can be applied.

EXAMPLE 2.9   Find the Laplace transform of the sine integral

$$\text{Si}(t) = \int_0^t \frac{\sin r}{r}\, dr.$$

In Section 6.1 it was shown that $L\{\sin t/t\} = \arctan s^{-1}$. Hence

$$L\{\text{Si}\} = \frac{1}{s} \arctan\left(\frac{1}{s}\right). \quad \blacksquare$$

Let f be a given function and let $F(s)$ be its Laplace transform. It is often convenient to define $F(s)$ when s is a *complex number*. To do this, first choose a complex number $s = \sigma + iw$ so that $\sigma = \text{Re } s$ and $w = \text{Im } s$. Since Euler's formula implies that

$$e^{-st} = e^{-(\sigma + iw)t} = e^{-\sigma t}(\cos wt - i \sin wt),$$

then we define

$$F(s) = F(\sigma + iw) = \int_0^\infty e^{-\sigma t} \cos wt\, f(t)\, dt - i \int_0^\infty e^{-\sigma t} \sin wt\, f(t)\, dt.$$

If f is of class Λ, then so are $f(t) \cos wt$ and $f(t) \sin wt$. Hence $F(s) = F(\sigma + iw)$ will converge for Re $s = \sigma$ sufficiently large. All of the formulas and theorems that were derived for real s remain true when s is complex. For example, $L\{t^n\} = n!/s^{n+1}$ is true for all complex numbers s with Re $s > 0$.

EXAMPLE 2.10   Compute $L\{\cos at\}$ and $L\{\sin at\}$.

For any positive numbers s and a we have

$$(2.5) \qquad L\{\cos at\} + iL\{\sin at\} = \int_0^\infty e^{-st}(\cos at + i \sin at)\, dt$$

$$= \int_0^\infty e^{-(s-ia)t}\, dt = \lim_{T \to \infty}\left[\frac{e^{-(s-ia)t}}{-(s-ia)}\right]_0^T$$

$$= \frac{1}{s - ia} \qquad \text{whenever Re } s > 0.$$

Notice that

$$(2.6) \qquad \frac{1}{s - ia} = \frac{s + ia}{s^2 + a^2} = \frac{s}{s^2 + a^2} + i\frac{a}{s^2 + a^2}.$$

Hence the real part of (2.5) equals the real part of (2.6), that is,

$$L\{\cos at\} = \frac{s}{s^2 + a^2}.$$

Similarly, if we equate the imaginary parts of (2.5) and (2.6), it follows that

$$L\{\sin at\} = \frac{a}{s^2 + a^2}.$$

For example, $L\{\cos 3t\} = s/(s^2 + 9)$, $L\{\sin \pi t\} = \pi/(s^2 + \pi^2)$,

$$L\{e^{-t} \sin 2t\} = \frac{2}{(s + 1)^2 + 4},$$

and

$$L\{e^{bt} \cos at\} = \frac{s - b}{(s - b)^2 + a^2}. \quad \blacksquare$$

PROBLEMS

1. Compute the Laplace transform of each function.

   (a) $e^t \sin 2t$.

   (b) $e^{-at} \sin 3t$.

   (c) $e^{2t} \cos bt$.

   (d) $e^{3t} u_2(t)$.

   (e) $e^{-3t} t$.

   (f) $\dfrac{e^{4t} \sin t}{t}$.

   (g) $e^{bt} t^n$.

   (h) $(\sinh bt) \cos 2t$.

   (i) $t^2 \sin bt$.

   (j) $te^{2t} \cos \pi t$.

   (k) $t^2 e^{-t} \sin t$.

2. Compute $L\{y\} = Y(s)$ when $y(t)$ is the solution of the initial value problem given.

   (a) $y'' + 4y = 3$, $y(0) = 1$, $y'(0) = 0$.

   (b) $y'' - 9y = u_3(t)$, $y(0) = 0$, $y'(0) = 2$.

   (c) $y'' - 3y' - 4y = \sin t$, $y(0) = 0$, $y'(0) = 0$.

   (d) $y'' - 3y' - 4y = \sin t$, $y(0) = 2$, $y'(0) = \pi$.

   (e) $y''' - 2y' - y = 1$, $y(0) = 0$, $y'(0) = 1$, $y''(0) = -1$.

   (f) $y^{(4)} - 2y'' + y = 0$, $y(0) = 1$, $y'(0) = 0$, $y''(0) = 0$, $y'''(0) = -1$.

   (g) $y'' + y = t$, $y(0) = 0$, $y'(0) = 0$.

   (h) $y'' - 9y = \int_0^t \dfrac{\sin r}{r} dr$, $y(0) = 0$, $y'(0) = 0$.

   (i) $y' + ay = \cos bt$, $y(0) = c$.

   (j) $y' + ay = \sin bt$, $y(0) = c$.

3. Let $f(t)$ be a piecewise-continuous function that is periodic of period p.

   (a) Show that $f(t)$ is of exponential order α for any $\alpha > 0$.

   (b) Show that for any positive integer k,

   $$\int_{kp}^{(k+1)p} e^{-st} f(t) \, dt = (e^{-sp})^k \int_0^p e^{-st} f(t) \, dt.$$

   (c) Show that for any $s > 0$,

   $$L\{f\}(s) = \frac{1}{1 - e^{-sp}} \int_0^p e^{-st} f(t) \, dt.$$

4. Using Problem 3, find the Laplace transform of each function.

   (a) $f(t) = \max \{0, \sin t\}$.

(b) $f(t) = \max \{0, \sin bt\}$, $b > 0$.

(c) $f(t) = \text{sgn} \{\sin \pi t\}$.

(d) $f(t) = t$ on $0 \le t < 2$, $f(t + 2) = f(t)$ for all $t \ge 0$.

(e) $f(t) = |\sin t|$.

5. Show that if $f(t) = \sin at$ with $a > 0$, then the Laplace transform of f, as computed using Problem 3, part (c), is $a(s^2 + a^2)^{-1}$.

6. For some functions $f(t)$ the Laplace transform can easily be computed from the Taylor series for f. Formally, if

$$f(t) = a_0 + a_1 t + a_2 t^2 + \ldots = \sum_{n=0}^{\infty} a_n t^n.$$

then

$$F(s) = \frac{a_0}{s} + \frac{a_1}{s^2} + \frac{2! a_2}{s^3} + \ldots = \sum_{n=0}^{\infty} \frac{n! a_n}{s^{n+1}}.$$

(a) From $\sin t = \sum_{k=0}^{\infty} (-1)^k t^{2k+1}/(2k + 1)!$, compute $L\{\sin t\}$ by the series method. Show that your result is a series that sums to $(s^2 + 1)^{-1}$.

(b) The Bessel function of the first kind of order 0 is

$$J_0(t) = 1 - \frac{t^2}{2^2} + \frac{t^4}{2^2 \, 4^2} - \frac{t^6}{2^2 \, 4^2 \, 6^2} + \ldots = \sum_{k=0}^{\infty} \frac{(-1)^k}{(k!)^2} \left(\frac{t}{2}\right)^{2k}.$$

Compute $L\{J_0(t)\}$. *Hint:* By the binomial theorem

$$(1 + s^{-2})^{-1/2} = 1 - \frac{1}{2} s^{-2} + \frac{1 \cdot 3}{2 \cdot 4} s^{-4} - \frac{1 \cdot 3 \cdot 5}{2 \cdot 4 \cdot 6} s^{-6} + \ldots.$$

(c) The **error function** erf is defined by

$$\text{erf}(t) = \frac{2}{\sqrt{\pi}} \int_0^t \exp(-u^2) \, du.$$

Compute $L\{\text{erf}(t)\}$ as a series.

(d) Compute $L\{\text{erf}(\sqrt{t})\}$.

(e) Show that $L\{J_0(\sqrt{t})\} = \exp(-\frac{1}{4}s)/s$.

(f) It is known that

$$\frac{2}{\sqrt{\pi}} \int_0^{\infty} \exp(-u^2) \, du = 1.$$

Hence if one defines the complementary error function erfc(t) by the formula

$$\text{erfc}(t) = \frac{2}{\sqrt{\pi}} \int_t^{\infty} \exp(-u^2) \, du,$$

then erf(t) + erfc$(t) = 1$. Use this fact to compute $L\{\text{erfc}(t)\}$.

7. Show that $L\{\text{erf}(t)\} = (1/s)e^{s^2/4} \text{erfc}(s/2)$. *Hint:* Write $L\{\text{erf}(t)\}$ as a double integral and then interchange the order of integration.

8. Let $F(s) = L\{\sin 2t\}$ and $G(s) = L\{\cos 3t\}$. Compute

(a) $F(3i)$ and $F(-3i)$.

(b) $G(2 + i)$ and $G(2 - i)$.

(c) $F(a + ib)$ and $F(a - ib)$.

(d) $G(a + ib)$ and $G(a - ib)$.

9. Let $f(t)$ be a real-valued function of class Λ and let $s = \sigma + i\tau$ be a complex number. The conjugate of s is $\bar{s} = \sigma - i\tau$. Show that $F(\bar{s}) = \overline{F(s)}$ for all complex numbers s such that $L\{f\} = F(s)$ converges.

10. Prove the **initial value theorem:** Let f be a continuous function such that $f'(t)$ is of class Λ and let $F(s) = L\{f\}$. Then the limit

$$\lim_{s \to \infty} sF(s)$$

exists and equals $f(0)$.

11. Compute the Laplace transform of each function.

(a) $\sin (wt + a)$.

(b) $\sin wt \sin ut$.

(c) $\cos wt \sin ut$.

(d) $\cos wt \cos ut$.

12. Consider the system

$$x' = -3x + y, \qquad x(0) = 2$$
$$y' = -x - 3y, \qquad y(0) = -1$$

for the unknowns $x(t)$ and $y(t)$.

(a) Laplace transform both equations and then find $X(s) = L\{x\}$.

(b) Compute $Y(s)$.

13. Using Laplace transforms solve for x and y when

$$x' = -2y, \qquad y' = 2x, \qquad x(0) = 1, \qquad y(0) = 0.$$

14. Use Laplace transforms to solve for $X(s)$ and $Y(s)$ when

$$x' = -x + 10y, \qquad y' = -x + 2y, \qquad x(0) = 0, \qquad y(0) = 2.$$

6.3 SOLUTION OF INITIAL VALUE PROBLEMS

Consider the initial value problem

(3.1) $$y'' - 2y' - 8y = 0, \qquad y(0) = 1, \qquad y'(0) = 3.$$

If we take the Laplace transform of each side of this equation, we find that

(3.2) $$(s^2 Y - s - 3) - 2(sY - 1) - 8Y = 0,$$

so that $(s^2 - 2s - 8)Y = s + 1$ and

(3.3) $$Y(s) = \frac{s + 1}{s^2 - 2s - 8}.$$

If we can recognize the right side of (3.3) as the Laplace transform of a known function, then we can compute the solution $y(t)$ of (3.1). In order to put the right side of (3.3) into a recognizable form, first factor the denominator, that is,

$$Y(s) = \frac{s+1}{(s-4)(s+2)},$$

and then use the method of partial fractions. Thus we seek constants A and B such that

$$\frac{s+1}{(s-4)(s+2)} = \frac{A}{s-4} + \frac{B}{s+2}.$$

Multiply the equation by $(s-4)(s+2)$ to obtain

$$s+1 = A(s+2) + B(s-4).$$

Setting $s = -2$, we see that $-1 = A(0) + B(-6)$ or $B = \frac{1}{6}$. Setting $s = 4$ we see that $5 = A(6)$ or $A = \frac{5}{6}$. Thus

$$Y(s) = \frac{\frac{5}{6}}{s-4} + \frac{\frac{1}{6}}{s+2} = \frac{5}{6} L\{e^{4t}\} + \frac{1}{6} L\{e^{-2t}\}$$

and the solution of (3.1) is

$$y(t) = \tfrac{5}{6}e^{4t} + \tfrac{1}{6}e^{-2t}.$$

This example very nicely illustrates how the Laplace transform may be used to solve initial value problems. The differential equation (3.1) is transformed into the algebraic problem (3.2). The algebraic problem (3.2) is solved for $Y(s)$ and then the solution $Y(s)$ is put into a recognizable form so that $y(t)$ can be found. Notice that the initial values are automatically used when one Laplace transforms the differential equation. The number of initial values in (3.1) is precisely the number needed in order to compute the transform of (3.1).

The difficulty in using the method of Laplace transforms to solve linear differential equations with constant coefficients is the problem of determining the solution $y(t)$ from its transform $Y(s)$. This problem is known as the *inverse problem*. The first question to be settled is whether or not there can be more than one function whose Laplace transform is a given function $Y(s)$. The following theorem is true.

THEOREM 3.1

If $y_1(t)$ and $y_2(t)$ are two functions of class Λ, if y_1 and y_2 are both continuous, and if their Laplace transforms are equal on an interval $s_0 < s < \infty$, then $y_1(t) = y_2(t)$ for all $t \geq 0$.

This theorem is not true for piecewise-continuous functions. For example, for any $a \geq 0$ if

$$y_1(t) = \begin{cases} 1 & \text{for } t \geq a \\ 0 & \text{for } t < a, \end{cases} \qquad y_2(t) = \begin{cases} 1 & \text{for } t > a \\ 0 & \text{for } t \leq a, \end{cases}$$

then y_1 is not identical with y_2 since $y_1(a) \neq y_2(a)$. However, $Y_1(s) = e^{-as}/s = Y_2(s)$ for all $s > 0$. There are other possibilities. For example, if $y_3(t) = 1$ when $t > a$ and $t \neq na$ while $y_3(t) = 0$ when $t < a$ and when $t = na$ for $n = 1, 2, 3, \ldots$, then $Y_3(s) = e^{-as}/a = Y_1(s)$. From the point of view of differential equations, the three functions y_1, y_2, and y_3 are essentially the same function. Their differences are artificial and unimportant. If we disregard such trivial differences, Theorem 3.1 remains true for piecewise-continuous functions.

THEOREM 3.2: UNIQUENESS OF INVERSE TRANSFORMS

If y_1 and y_2 are of class Λ and if $Y_1(s) = Y_2(s)$ on an interval $s_0 < s < \infty$, then $y_1(t) = y_2(t)$ on $0 \leq t < \infty$ except possibly on a set $\{t_n\}$ of isolated points.

Let y be of class Λ and suppose that $L\{y\} = Y$. Then we call y the *inverse Laplace transform* of Y and write $L^{-1}\{Y\} = y$. We shall agree to settle ambiguities in the definition y at points t when y jumps by requiring that y be continuous from the right, that is,

$$y(t) = \lim_{h \to 0^+} y(t + h).$$

Our problem now is to develop methods of computing $y(t)$ given $Y(s)$.

EXAMPLE 3.3　　Use the Laplace transform to solve

(3.4) $$y'' + 4y = e^t, \qquad y(0) = 0, \qquad y'(0) = 0.$$

Taking the Laplace transform of each side of (3.4), we see that

$$\{s^2 Y(s) - s \cdot 0 - 0\} + 4Y(s) = (s - 1)^{-1}$$

or

$$Y(s) = \frac{1}{(s - 1)(s^2 + 4)}.$$

Decompose $Y(s)$ using partial fractions, that is,

$$\frac{1}{(s-1)(s^2+4)} = \frac{A}{s-1} + \frac{Bs+C}{s^2+4}$$

or

$$1 = A(s^2+4) + (Bs+C)(s-1).$$

Setting $s = 1$, we see that $1 = A(1+4) + (B+C)\cdot 0$ or $A = \frac{1}{5}$. Setting $s = 2i$, we see that

$$1 = 0 + (2Bi + C)(2i - 1) = -(C+4B) + i(2C - 2B).$$

The real parts of the equation are equal [i.e., $1 = -(C+4B)$] and the imaginary parts are equal (i.e., $0 = 2C - 2B$). This pair of equations can be solved to see that $B = C = -\frac{1}{5}$. Hence

$$Y(s) = \frac{1}{5}\left(\frac{1}{s-1}\right) - \frac{1}{5}\left(\frac{s+1}{s^2+4}\right)$$

$$= \frac{1}{5}\left(\frac{1}{s-1}\right) - \frac{1}{5}\left(\frac{s}{s^2+4}\right) - \frac{1}{5}\left(\frac{1}{s^2+4}\right).$$

Recall that $L\{e^t\} = (s-1)^{-1}$, $L\{\cos 2t\} = s(s^2+4)^{-1}$, and $L\{\sin 2t\} = 2(s^2+4)^{-1}$. Hence $L^{-1}\{(s-1)^{-1}\} = e^t$, $L^{-1}\{s(s^2+4)^{-1}\} = \cos(2t)$, $L^{-1}\{(s^2+4)^{-1}\} = (\sin 2t)/2$, and

$$y(t) = L^{-1}\{Y(s)\} = \tfrac{1}{5}e^t - \tfrac{1}{5}\cos 2t - \tfrac{1}{10}\sin 2t. \quad \blacksquare$$

EXAMPLE 3.4   Find the inverse Laplace transform of

(3.5)
$$F(s) = \frac{3s+1}{s^2+2s+10}.$$

To find the inverse transform of such a function $F(s)$, we make use of the formulas

(3.6) $$L\{e^{at}\cos bt\} = \frac{s-a}{(s-a)^2+b^2}, \qquad L\{e^{at}\sin bt\} = \frac{b}{(s-a)^2+b^2}.$$

First complete the square in the denominator of (3.5). This gives

$$F(s) = \frac{3s+1}{(s^2+2s+1)+9} = \frac{3s+1}{(s+1)^2+3^2}.$$

With $a = -1$ and $b = 3$ we now try to write $F(s)$ as a linear combination of $L\{e^{-t}\cos 3t\}$ and $L\{e^{-t}\sin 3t\}$, that is,

$$F(s) = \frac{3s+3-2}{(s+1)^2+3^2} = \frac{3(s+1)}{(s+1)^2+3^2} - \frac{2}{(s+1)^2+3^2}$$

$$= 3\frac{s+1}{(s+1)^2+3^2} - \frac{2}{3}\frac{3}{(s+1)^2+3^2}.$$

Hence

$$f(t) = L^{-1}\{F\} = 3e^{-t}\cos 3t - \tfrac{2}{3}e^{-t}\sin 3t. \quad \blacksquare$$

EXAMPLE 3.5   Find the inverse transform of

$$F(s) = \frac{s-1}{(s+1)(s^2-4s+5)}.$$

Decomposing, using partial fractions, we get

$$\frac{s-1}{(s+1)(s^2-4s+5)} = \frac{A}{s+1} + \frac{Bs+C}{s^2-4s+5}$$

or

$$s - 1 = A(s^2 - 4s + 5) + (Bs + C)(s + 1).$$

Setting $s = -1$, we see that $A = -\tfrac{1}{5}$. On substituting $s = 0$, we see that $-1 = (-\tfrac{1}{5})(5) + C$, so $C = 0$. Setting $s = 1$, we get $0 = (-\tfrac{1}{5})(1 - 4 + 5) + (B + 0) \cdot (2)$ or $B = 1/5$. Hence

(3.7) $$F(s) = -\frac{1}{5}\left(\frac{1}{s+1}\right) + \frac{1}{5}\left(\frac{s}{s^2-4s+5}\right).$$

In the second term on the right in (3.7), we complete the square in the denominator and compute

$$\frac{s}{s^2-4s+5} = \frac{s}{(s^2-4s+4)+1} = \frac{s}{(s-2)^2+1} = \frac{s-2}{(s-2)^2+1} + \frac{2}{(s-2)^2+1}.$$

Hence

$$F(s) = -\frac{1}{5}\left(\frac{1}{s+1}\right) + \frac{1}{5}\frac{s-2}{(s-2)^2+1} + \frac{2}{5}\frac{1}{(s-2)^2+1}$$

and

$$f(t) = -\frac{1}{5}e^{-t} + \frac{1}{5}e^{2t}\cos t + \frac{2}{5}\sin t. \quad \blacksquare$$

Decomposition by partial fractions can also be used when the denominator contains repeated factors. The next example illustrates this point.

EXAMPLE 3.6   Find $L^{-1}\{G(s)\}$ when

$$G(s) = \frac{1}{(s+2)^3(s+3)}.$$

The correct partial-fraction decomposition is

(3.8) $$G(s) = \frac{A}{(s+2)^3} + \frac{B}{(s+2)^2} + \frac{C}{s+2} + \frac{D}{s+3}.$$

It is easy to compute that $A = 1$. Indeed, from (3.8) we see that

$$1 = A(s + 3) + B(s + 3)(s + 2) + C(s + 3)(s + 2)^2 + D(s + 2)^3.$$

Setting $s = -2$, we find that $1 = A(-2 + 3)$ or $A = 1$. On subtracting $A(s + 2)^{-3}$ from $G(s)$, we find that

$$G(s) - \frac{1}{(s + 2)^3} = \frac{1}{(s + 2)^3(s + 3)} - \frac{1}{(s + 2)^3} = \frac{-1}{(s + 2)^2(s + 3)}.$$

This and (3.8) gives

$$\frac{-1}{(s + 2)^2(s + 3)} = \frac{B}{(s + 2)^2} + \frac{C}{s + 2} + \frac{D}{s + 3}.$$

It is now easy to compute $B = -1$. Hence

$$\left[G(s) - \frac{1}{(s + 2)^3} \right] + \frac{1}{(s + 2)^2} = \frac{-1}{(s + 2)^2(s + 3)} + \frac{1}{(s + 2)^2}$$

$$= \frac{1}{(s + 2)(s + 3)}.$$

This and (3.8) imply that

$$\frac{1}{(s + 2)(s + 3)} = \frac{C}{s + 2} + \frac{D}{s + 3}$$

or

$$1 = C(s + 3) + D(s + 2).$$

Setting $s = -2$ gives $C = 1$, while $s = -3$ gives the result that $D = -1$. Hence

$$G(s) = \frac{1}{(s + 2)^3} - \frac{1}{(s + 2)^2} + \frac{1}{s + 2} - \frac{1}{s + 3}.$$

Since

$$L^{-1}\{(s + a)^{-n}\} = \frac{t^{n-1}}{(n - 1)!} e^{-at} \qquad \text{for } n = 1, 2, 3, \ldots,$$

then

$$g(t) = \frac{t^2}{2!} e^{-2t} - te^{-2t} + e^{-2t} - e^{-3t}. \quad \blacksquare$$

The technique used in Example 3.6 to decompose $G(s)$ works equally well when the denominator contains a quadratic factor.

EXAMPLE 3.7   Solve the initial value problem

$$(D^2 + 4)(D^2 - 2D + 1)y = 0, \qquad y(0) = y'(0) = 0, \qquad y''(0) = 1, \qquad y'''(0) = 3.$$

Since $(D^2 + 4)(D^2 - 2D + 1) = D^4 - 2D^3 + 5D^2 - 8D + 4$, then

$$(s^4 Y - s - 3) - 2(s^3 Y - 1) + 5s^2 Y - 8sY + 4Y = 0.$$

Hence

$$(s^4 - 2s^3 + 5s^2 - 8s + 4)Y(s) = s + 1$$

or

$$Y(s) = \frac{s + 1}{s^4 - 2s^3 + 5s^2 - 8s + 4} = \frac{s + 1}{(s^2 + 4)(s - 1)^2}.$$

Since $Y(s)$ can be decomposed into

$$Y(s) = \frac{A}{(s - 1)^2} + \frac{B}{s - 1} + \frac{Cs + D}{s^2 + 4},$$

then

$$s + 1 = A(s^2 + 4) + B(s - 1)(s^2 + 4) + (Cs + D)(s - 1)^2.$$

Setting $s = 1$, we find $A = \frac{2}{5}$. We now compute

$$\begin{aligned}
Y(s) - \frac{2}{5}\frac{1}{(s - 1)^2} &= \frac{s + 1}{(s - 1)^2(s^2 + 4)} - \frac{2}{5}\frac{1}{(s - 1)^2} \\
&= \frac{5(s + 1) - 2(s^2 + 4)}{5(s - 1)^2(s^2 + 4)} = -\frac{2s^2 - 5s + 3}{5(s - 1)^2(s^2 + 4)} \\
&= -\frac{(2s - 3)(s - 1)}{5(s - 1)^2(s^2 + 4)} = \frac{3 - 2s}{5(s - 1)(s^2 + 4)}.
\end{aligned}$$

Hence

$$\frac{3 - 2s}{5(s - 1)(s^2 + 4)} = \frac{B}{s - 1} + \frac{Cs + D}{s^2 + 4}.$$

Using the techniques that were explained earlier in this section, one can compute $B = \frac{1}{25}$, $C = -\frac{1}{25}$, and $D = -\frac{11}{25}$. Hence

$$Y(s) = \frac{2}{5}\left(\frac{1}{(s - 1)^2}\right) + \frac{1}{25}\left(\frac{1}{s - 1}\right) - \frac{1}{25}\left(\frac{s + 11}{s^2 + 4}\right),$$

and

$$y(t) = \frac{2}{5}te^t + \frac{1}{25}e^t - \frac{1}{25}\cos 2t - \frac{11}{50}\sin 2t. \quad\blacksquare$$

The method of Laplace transforms can sometimes be used to solve differential equations that have variable coefficients. The important formula to remember is

$$L\{t^n y(t)\} = (-1)^n \frac{d^n}{ds^n} Y(s).$$

The resulting equation for $Y(s)$ will be a differential equation that may be easier (or may be harder) to solve than the original equation.

EXAMPLE 3.8 Find the Laplace transform of the Bessel function $J_0(t)$.
The function $y = J_0(t)$ solves the initial value problem

(3.9) $ty'' + y' + ty = 0,$ $y(0) = 1,$ $y'(0) = 0.$

Laplace transforming (3.9) gives

$$-\frac{d}{ds}(s^2 Y - s - 0) + (sY - 1) - \frac{d}{ds} Y(s) = 0$$

or

$$-2sY - s^2 \frac{dY}{ds} + 1 + sY - 1 - \frac{dY}{ds} = 0.$$

Hence $Y(s)$ solves the first-order linear differential equation

(3.10) $(s^2 + 1)\frac{dY}{ds} + sY = 0.$

Since the equation is first-order linear (or since the variables separate), the solution is easily found to be

$$Y(s) = \frac{K}{\sqrt{s^2 + 1}}$$

for some constant K. By the initial value theorem (see Problem 10 of Section 6.2)

$$J_0(0) = \lim_{s \to \infty} sY(s) = \lim_{s \to \infty} \frac{sK}{\sqrt{s^2 + 1}} = K.$$

However, $J_0(0) = 1$. Hence

$$L\{J_0(t)\} = \frac{1}{\sqrt{s^2 + 1}} \quad \text{or} \quad L^{-1}\left\{\frac{1}{\sqrt{s^2 + 1}}\right\} = J_0(t). \quad \blacksquare$$

Laplace transformation of a differential equation with variable coefficients is not always a useful technique. For example, given the problem

(3.11) $y'' + ty' + t^3 y = 0,$ $y(0) = a_0,$ $y'(0) = a_1,$

one has

$$(s^2 Y - sa_0 - a_1) - \frac{d}{ds}(sY - a_0) - \frac{d^3}{ds^3} Y(s) = 0$$

or

(3.12) $\frac{d^3 Y}{ds^3} + s\frac{dY}{ds} + (1 - s^2)Y = -a_1 - sa_0.$

Since (3.12) is an even harder problem than (3.11), the Laplace transform technique seems to be of no use. For either (3.11) or (3.12), series methods must be used to obtain a solution.

PROBLEMS   In Problems 1–33, use Laplace transforms to solve the initial value problem. (In these problems, $' = d/dt$.)

1. $y'' + y' - 6y = 0$, $y(0) = 1$, $y'(0) = -1$.

2. $y'' - y' - 12y = 0$, $y(0) = 0$, $y'(0) = 1$.

3. $R'' - 4R = 0$, $R(0) = 3$, $R'(0) = 0$.

4. $N'' - N = 0$, $N(0) = 0$, $N'(0) = 2$.

5. $y'' + 9y = 0$, $y(0) = 0$, $y'(0) = -2$.

6. $\dfrac{d^2z}{dt^2} + z = 0$, $z(0) = 2$, $z'(0) = 3$.

7. $y'' + 4y' + 4y = 0$, $y(0) = -1$, $y'(0) = 2$.

8. $y'' + 4y' + 4y = 0$, $y(0) = 1$, $y'(0) = \frac{2}{3}$.

9. $y'' - 4y' - 21y = 2$, $y(0) = 0$, $y'(0) = 0$.

10. $R'' - 4R' - 21R = 2$, $R(0) = -1$, $R'(0) = 2$.

11. $N'' + N' + 12N = t$, $N(0) = 0$, $N'(0) = 0$.

12. $y'' + y' + 12y = t$, $y(0) = 2$, $y'(0) = 0$.

13. $y'' - 4y' - 21y = 3t$, $y(0) = 0$, $y'(0) = 0$.

14. $y'' - 4y' - 21y = 3t$, $y(0) = 0$, $y'(0) = -1$.

15. $y''' - y = e^{-2t}$, $y(0) = 1$, $y'(0) = 0$, $y''(0) = 0$.

16. $y'''' - 4y''' + 6y'' - 4y' + y = 0$, $y(0) = 1$, $y'(0) = 0$, $y''(0) = 0$, $y'''(0) = 0$.

17. $x'' + x' + 4x = 0$, $x(0) = 1$, $x'(0) = -1$.

18. $y'' + y' + 4y = 1$, $y(0) = 0$, $y'(0) = 0$.

19. $y'' - 2y' - y = 0$, $y(0) = -1$, $y'(0) = 0$.

20. $\dfrac{d^2R}{dx^2} - 2\dfrac{dR}{dx} - R = -1$, $R(0) = 0$, $R'(0) = 0$.

21. $y'' - 4y' + 4y = 0$, $y(0) = 1$, $y'(0) = 2$.

22. $y'' + 2y' + y = 0$, $y(0) = -1$, $y'(0) = 3$.

23. $y'' + 9y = \sin t$, $y(0) = 0$, $y'(0) = 1$.

24. $z'' + 4z = \cos 3t$, $z(0) = 0$, $z'(0) = 0$.

25. $y'' - 2y' - 8y = \cos t$, $y(0) = 1$, $y'(0) = 0$.

26. $w'' - 2w' + 2w = \sin t$, $w(0) = 0$, $w'(0) = 0$.

27. $y'' + y = \sin t$, $y(0) = 0$, $y'(0) = 0$. (*Hard!*)

28. $y' - y = t \sin t$, $y(0) = \pi$.

29. $y'' - 4y = e^{-t} \cos t$, $y(0) = 1$, $y'(0) = 0$.

30. $y'' - 4y = \cosh 4t$, $y(0) = 0$, $y'(0) = 0$.

31. $R'' + R = e^{-t} \sinh 2t$, $R(0) = 0$, $R'(0) = 1$.

32. $y'' - y = e^{-t} \sinh 2t$, $y(0) = 1$, $y'(0) = 0$.

33. $y'' + 3y' + 2y = \sin 3t$, $y(0) = 2$, $y'(0) = 0$.

In Problems 34 and 35, compute $Y(s)$.

34. $y'' + ty = 0$, $y(0) = 1$, $y'(0) = 0$.

35. $y'' + y' + ty = 0$, $y(0) = 2$, $y'(0) = 0$.

36. Let f be a Laplace transformable function with $F(s) = L\{f\}$ and let c be any real or complex number.

(a) Suppose that $g'(t) = e^{ct}f(t)$, $g(0) = 0$, and $G = L\{g\}$. Show that $G(s) = F(s - c)/s$.

(b) Show that the function

$$\int_0^t e^{-c(t-r)}f(r)\,dr = e^{-ct}g(t)$$

has Laplace transform $F(s)/(s + c)$.

37. Let f be a Laplace transformable function with $F(s) = L\{f\}$. Using the results of Problem 36, show that for $a > 0$

$$L^{-1}\left\{\frac{F(s)}{s + a}\right\} = \int_0^t e^{-a(t-r)}f(r)\,dr,$$

$$L^{-1}\left\{\frac{F(s)}{s^2 + a^2}\right\} = \frac{1}{a}\int_0^t \sin\left[a(t - r)\right]f(r)\,dr,$$

and
$$L^{-1}\left\{\frac{sF(s)}{s^2 + a^2}\right\} = \int_0^t \cos\left[a(t - r)\right]f(r)\,dr.$$

38. Let $p(s) = a_n s^n + a_{n-1}s^{n-1} + \ldots + a_1 s + a_0$ be a real polynomial of degree n and $q(s) = b_m s^m + b_{m-1}s^{m-1} + \ldots + b_1 s + b_0$ be a real polynomial of degree m, where $m > n$. Suppose that $q(s)$ has m distinct roots $\{s_1, s_2, \ldots, s_m\}$ and that $p(s_j) \neq 0$ for $j = 1, 2, \ldots, m$. Then there are constants c_j such that

$$\frac{p(s)}{q(s)} = \sum_{j=1}^{m} \frac{c_j}{s - s_j}.$$

(a) Show that

$$c_j = \lim_{s \to s_j} (s - s_j)\frac{p(s)}{q(s)}.$$

(b) Show that $c_j = p(s_j)/q'(s_j)$.

39. Use Problem 46 to compute each inverse transform.

(a) $L^{-1}\left\{\dfrac{3s + 4}{s(s + 1)(s - 1)(s - 3)}\right\}.$ (b) $L^{-1}\left\{\dfrac{4 - s^2}{(s + 1)(s - 2)(s - 3)}\right\}.$

(c) $L^{-1}\left\{\dfrac{s^2 + 3s + 2}{s(s - 1)(s + 1)(s + 3)}\right\}.$ (d) $L^{-1}\left\{\dfrac{2s + 3}{s(s^2 + 1)}\right\}.$

(e) $L^{-1}\left\{\dfrac{2s^2 - 4s + 1}{s(s^2 + 4)}\right\}.$ (f) $L^{-1}\left\{\dfrac{s^3 + s}{(s^2 + 4)(s^2 + 1)(s + 3)}\right\}.$

40. Consider the mechanical system depicted in Figure 6.4. The system consists of a point mass M, a linear spring, and a viscous damper. The mass is subjected to an

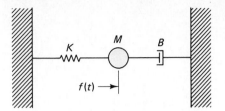

Figure 6.4. Forced mechanical system.

external force $f(t)$. Let x be the deviation of the mass from its equilibrium with positive x to the right. According to Newton's second law,

$$Mx'' + Bx' + Kx = f(t).$$

Here $M > 0$, $K > 0$, and $B \geq 0$. Specification of $x(0) = a_0$ and $x'(0) = a_1$ will complete the description of the motion. Use Laplace transforms to compute $x(t)$ in each case.

(a) $f(t) \equiv 0$, $B^2 - 4MK < 0$.

(b) $f(t) \equiv 0$, $B^2 - 4MK = 0$.

(c) $f(t) \equiv 0$, $B^2 - 4MK > 0$.

(d) $f(t) = F \sin wt$, $M = K = B = 1$, $a_0 = a_1 = 0$.

(e) $f(t) = F \sin wt$, $B = 0$, $a_0 = a_1 = 0$, $K/M \neq w^2$.

6.4 DISCONTINUOUS FUNCTIONS AND THE LAPLACE TRANSFORM

The unit step function (or Heaviside step function) was defined as

$$u_c(t) = \begin{cases} 0 & \text{if } t < c \\ 1 & \text{if } t \geq c, \end{cases}$$

where c is any nonnegative real number. This function is graphed in Figure 6.2. This function will prove very useful for representing discontinuous functions in such a way that their Laplace transforms are easy to compute. For example, given a function $f(t)$ defined on $0 \leq t < \infty$ and given $c \geq 0$, we define the **translated** or **shifted function** for f by the formula

$$g(t) = u_c(t)f(t - c) = \begin{cases} 0 & \text{if } t < c \\ f(t - c) & \text{if } t \geq c. \end{cases}$$

This procedure has the effect of moving the function f along the t-axis so that it starts at $t_0 = c$ and the effect of zeroing out f on the interval $t < c$ (see Figure 6.5). If we think of t as time and $f(t)$ as a signal that changes with time, then $u_c(t)f(t - c)$ is the same signal except that it has been delayed so as to start at time $t_0 = c$ rather than at $t_0 = 0$. It is easy to compute the Laplace transform of a shifted function.

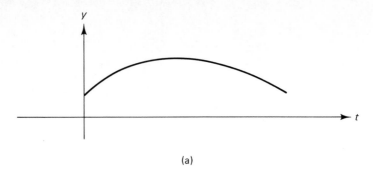

(a)

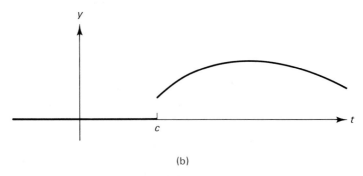

(b)

Figure 6.5. (a) $y = f(t)$,   (b) $y = u_c(t)f(t - c)$.

THEOREM 4.1: TRANSFORM OF A SHIFTED FUNCTION

If f is Laplace transformable and if $F(s) = L\{f\}$ for $s > \alpha$, then for any $c \geq 0$

$$L\{u_c(t)f(t - c)\} = e^{-cs} F(s) \qquad \text{for all } s > \alpha.$$

To prove this result we compute as follows:

$$L\{u_c(t)f(t - c)\} = \int_0^\infty e^{-st} u_c(t)f(t - c)\, dt$$

$$= \int_c^\infty e^{-st} f(t - c)\, dt.$$

Now change variables to $r = t - c$ to see that

$$L\{u_c(t)f(t - c)\} = \int_0^\infty e^{-s(r + c)} f(r)\, dr$$

$$= e^{-cs} \int_0^\infty e^{-sr} f(r)\, dr$$

$$= e^{-cs} L\{f\}.$$

EXAMPLE 4.2   Find $L\{u_1(t)e^{-2(t-1)}\}$.

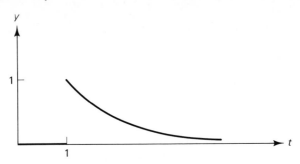

Figure 6.6. $y = u_1(t)e^{-2t+2}$.

The function $u_1(t)e^{-2t+2}$ is graphed in Figure 6.6. Since $L\{e^{-2t}\} = (s+2)^{-1}$, the required Laplace transform is $L\{u_1(t)e^{-2(t-1)}\} = e^{-s}(s+2)^{-1}$.   ∎

EXAMPLE 4.3   Given $f(t) = \cos 2t + 3t^2$, compute $L\{u_3(t)f(t-3)\}$.
Since $L\{f\} = s/(s^2+4) + 6/s^3$, then

$$L\{u_3(t)f(t-3)\} = \frac{e^{-3s}s}{s^2+4} + \frac{6e^{-3s}}{s^3}.$$ ∎

The unit step functions can also be used to represent more complicated functions with several jump discontinuities.

EXAMPLE 4.4   Compute $L\{f\}$ when

$$f(t) = \begin{cases} 0 & \text{on } 0 \le t < 1 \\ 2 & \text{on } 1 \le t < \pi \\ -1 & \text{on } \pi \le t < 2\pi \\ t & \text{on } 2\pi \le t < \infty. \end{cases}$$

First we express $f(t)$ as a sum of shifted functions. To do this we start at $t = 0$ and work to the right. On $0 \le t < \pi$ it is clear that $f(t) = 2u_1(t)$. On $\pi \le t \le 2\pi$ we must subtract 3 from $2u_1(t)$ in order to obtain -1. At the same time we wish to leave $2u_1(t)$ undisturbed on the interval $0 \le t < \pi$. This is accomplished by subtracting $3u_\pi(t)$. Hence $f(t) = 2u_1(t) - 3u_\pi(t)$ over the interval $0 \le t < 2\pi$. For $t \ge 2\pi$ we wish to add $1 + t$ [while leaving f undisturbed on $[0, 2\pi)$]. Hence

$$f(t) = 2u_1(t) - 3u_\pi(t) + (t + 1)u_{2\pi}(t).$$

The first two terms in this sum are shifted functions whose Laplace transforms are known. The third summand can be written as

$$(t + 1)u_{2\pi}(t) = (t - 2\pi)u_{2\pi}(t) + (2\pi + 1)u_{2\pi}(t).$$

Thus

$$f(t) = 2u_1(t) - 3u_\pi(t) + (t - 2\pi)u_{2\pi}(t) + (2\pi + 1)u_{2\pi}(t).$$

Since $L\{1\} = 1/s$, then

$$L\{u_1(t)\} = \frac{e^{-s}}{s}, \qquad L\{u_\pi(t)\} = \frac{e^{-\pi s}}{s}, \quad \text{and} \quad L\{u_{2\pi}(t)\} = \frac{e^{-2\pi s}}{s}.$$

Since $L\{t\} = 1/s^2$, then

$$L\{(t - 2\pi)u_{2\pi}(t)\} = \frac{e^{-2\pi s}}{s^2}.$$

Therefore,

$$L\{f\} = \frac{2e^{-s}}{s} - \frac{3e^{-\pi s}}{s} + \frac{e^{-2\pi s}}{s^2} + \frac{(2\pi + 1)e^{-2\pi s}}{s}. \quad \blacksquare$$

EXAMPLE 4.5   Compute $L\{f\}$ when f is the function defined by the formula

$$f(t) = \begin{cases} 1 & \text{on } 0 \le t < 2 \\ -3 & \text{on } 2 \le t < 3 \\ t^2 & \text{on } 3 \le t < \infty. \end{cases}$$

First it is necessary to write $f(t)$ as a sum of translated functions, that is, a sum of functions having the form $u_c(t)h(t - c)$. As before, we start at $t = 0$ and work to the right. Clearly, $f(t) = 1 = u_0(t)$ on $[0, 2)$. On $[2, 3)$ we wish to subtract 4 from $u_0(t)$ while leaving $u_0(t)$ unchanged on $[0, 2)$. Thus $f(t) = 1 - 4u_2(t)$ on $[0, 3)$. On $t \ge 3$ we must add $3 + t^2$ while leaving $f(t)$ unchanged on $[0, 3)$. Hence

$$f(t) = 1 - 4u_2(t) + (3 + t^2)u_3(t).$$

The term $(3 + t^2)u_3(t)$ can be expressed as a translated function as follows:

$$\begin{aligned} (3 + t^2)u_3(t) &= 3u_3(t) + t^2 u_3(t) \\ &= 3u_3(t) + [(t - 3)^2 u_3(t) + (6t - 9)u_3(t)] \\ &= 3u_3(t) + [(t - 3)^2 u_3(t) + 6(t - 3)u_3(t) + 9u_3(t)] \\ &= \{(t - 3)^2 + 6(t - 3) + 12\}u_3(t). \end{aligned}$$

Therefore,

$$f(t) = 1 - 4u_2(t) + [(t - 3)^2 + 6(t - 3) + 12]u_3(t)$$

and

$$L\{f\} = \frac{1}{s} - \frac{4e^{-2s}}{s} + e^{-3s}\left(\frac{2}{s^3} + \frac{6}{s^2} + \frac{12}{s}\right). \quad \blacksquare$$

It will be necessary to compute the inverse Laplace transform of functions that contain a delay term, that is, of functions of the form $e^{-as}F(s)$. Since every result about Laplace transforms can be stated as a result about inverse Laplace transforms, then $L^{-1}\{e^{-cs}F(s)\}$ is easily computed by using Theorem 4.1. Indeed if $L^{-1}\{F\} = f$, then

$$L^{-1}\{e^{-cs}F(s)\} = u_c(t)f(t - c).$$

EXAMPLE 4.6   Compute the inverse Laplace transform of

$$G(s) = \frac{e^{-\pi s}(2s + 3)}{s^2 + 6s + 15}.$$

It is convenient first to compute $L^{-1}\{F\}$, where

$$F(s) = \frac{2s + 3}{s^2 + 6s + 15}.$$

Complete the square in the denominator and arrange $F(s)$ as follows:

$$F(s) = \frac{2s + 3}{(s^2 + 6s + 9) + 6} = \frac{2(s + 3) - 3}{(s + 3)^2 + 6}$$

$$= 2\frac{s + 3}{(s + 3)^2 + 6} - \frac{3}{\sqrt{6}}\frac{\sqrt{6}}{(s + 3)^2 + 6}.$$

The inverse transform of $F(s)$ is easily computed if one first computes the inverse transform of

$$F_1(s) = 2\frac{s}{s^2 + 6} - \frac{3}{\sqrt{6}}\frac{\sqrt{6}}{s^2 + 6}.$$

Since

$$L^{-1}\{F_1\} = 2\cos\sqrt{6}t - \frac{3}{\sqrt{6}}\sin\sqrt{6}t,$$

then

$$L^{-1}\{F\} = 2e^{-3t}\cos\sqrt{6}t - \frac{3}{\sqrt{6}}e^{-3t}\sin\sqrt{6}t.$$

We can now apply Theorem 4.1 to compute

$$L^{-1}\{e^{-\pi s}F(s)\} = \left[2e^{-3(t - \pi)}\cos\sqrt{6}(t - \pi) - \frac{3}{\sqrt{6}}e^{-3(t - \pi)}\sin\sqrt{6}(t - \pi)\right]u_\pi(t). \quad \blacksquare$$

The Laplace transform can be used quickly and easily to compute the solution of many differential equations that have discontinuous forcing. The computation of these solutions by the methods developed in Chapters 3 and 4 would usually be quite laborious.

EXAMPLE 4.7   Use Laplace transforms to compute $y(t)$ where

(4.1) $y'' + 2y' + 3y = f(t), \qquad y(0) = 1, \qquad y'(0) = -3,$

and where the forcing function $f(t)$ is defined by

$$f(t) = \begin{cases} 1 & \text{on } 0 \le t < 2 \\ 0 & \text{on } t \ge 2. \end{cases}$$

First note that $f(t) = 1 - u_2(t)$. Hence Laplace transforming (4.1) gives

$$[s^2 Y - s + 3] + 2[sY - 1] + 3Y = \frac{1 - e^{-2s}}{s},$$

$$[s^2 + 2s + 3]Y = s - 1 + \frac{1 - e^{-2s}}{s},$$

and

(4.2) $$Y(s) = \frac{s - 1}{s^2 + 2s + 3} + \frac{1 - e^{-2s}}{s(s^2 + 2s + 3)}.$$

We see that Y has the form $Y(s) = F_1(s) + (1 - e^{-2s})F_2(s)$. The first term on the right in (4.2) can be written as

$$F_1(s) = \frac{s - 1}{(s^2 + 2s + 1) + 2} = \frac{s + 1 - 2}{(s + 1)^2 + 2}$$

$$= \frac{s + 1}{(s + 1)^2 + 2} - \sqrt{2}\frac{\sqrt{2}}{(s + 1)^2 + 2}.$$

This term has the inverse Laplace transform

$$f_1(t) = e^{-t}\cos\sqrt{2}t - \sqrt{2}e^{-t}\sin\sqrt{2}t.$$

The term $F_2(s)$ is decomposed using partial functions, that is,

$$F_2(s) = \frac{1}{s(s^2 + 2s + 3)} = \frac{A}{s} + \frac{Bs + C}{s^2 + 2s + 3}.$$

The result is that $A = \frac{1}{3}$, $B = -\frac{1}{3}$, and $C = -\frac{2}{3}$. Hence

$$F_2(s) = \frac{1}{3s} - \frac{1}{3}\frac{s + 2}{s^2 + 2s + 3} = \frac{1}{3s} - \frac{1}{3}\frac{(s + 1) + 1}{(s^2 + 2s + 1) + 2}$$

$$= \frac{1}{3s} - \frac{1}{3}\frac{s + 1}{(s + 1)^2 + 2} - \frac{\sqrt{2}}{6}\frac{\sqrt{2}}{(s + 1)^2 + 2}.$$

The inverse transform of $F_2(s)$ is

$$f_2(t) = \frac{1}{3} - \frac{1}{3}e^{-t}\cos\sqrt{2}t - \frac{\sqrt{2}}{6}e^{-t}\sin\sqrt{2}t.$$

Since $Y(s) = F_1(s) + F_2(s) - e^{-2s}F_2(s)$, then

$$y(t) = f_1(t) + f_2(t) - u_2(t)f_2(t - 2),$$

that is,

$$y(t) = e^{-t}[\cos\sqrt{2}t - \sqrt{2}\sin\sqrt{2}t] + \frac{1}{3} - e^{-t}\left[\frac{1}{3}\cos\sqrt{2}t - \frac{\sqrt{2}}{6}\sin\sqrt{2}t\right]$$

$$- \left\{\frac{1}{3} - e^{-(t-2)}\left[\frac{1}{3}\cos\sqrt{2}(t - 2) - \frac{\sqrt{2}}{6}\sin\sqrt{2}(t - 2)\right]\right\}u_2(t). \quad \blacksquare$$

The technique that was demonstrated in Example 4.7 is not restricted to second-order equations. It can be used for any nth-order linear differential equation with constant coefficients whose forcing is discontinuous.

EXAMPLE 4.8   Solve $y' + 2y = 2u_2(t) + tu_3(t)$, $y(0) = 1$.

The forcing function can be written as a sum of shifted functions as follows:

$$2u_2(t) + tu_3(t) = 2u_2(t) + (t - 3)u_3(t) + 3u_3(t).$$

Hence Laplace transforming the given equation yields

$$[sY(s) - 1] + 2Y(s) = \frac{2}{s}e^{-2s} + \frac{1}{s^2}e^{-3s} + \frac{3}{s}e^{-3s}$$

or

(4.3) $Y(s) = \dfrac{1}{s + 2} + \dfrac{1}{s(s + 2)}[2e^{-2s} + 3e^{-3s}] + \dfrac{1}{s^2(s + 2)}e^{-3s}.$

Using partial fractions, one computes

$$\frac{1}{s(s + 2)} = \frac{A}{s} + \frac{B}{s + 2}$$

or $1 = A(s + 2) + Bs$. On taking $s = 0$ we see that $A = \frac{1}{2}$ while $s = -2$ yields $B = -\frac{1}{2}$. Hence

$$L^{-1}\left\{\frac{1}{s(s + 2)}\right\} = L^{-1}\left\{\frac{1}{2s} - \frac{1}{2(s + 2)}\right\} = \frac{1}{2} - \frac{1}{2}e^{-2t}.$$

A similar computation yields

$$\frac{1}{s^2(s + 2)} = -\frac{1}{4s} + \frac{1}{2s^2} + \frac{1}{4(s + 2)}$$

and

$$L^{-1}\left\{\frac{1}{s^2(s + 1)}\right\} = -\frac{1}{4} + \frac{1}{2}t + \frac{1}{4}e^{-2t}.$$

These computations and (4.3) imply that

$$y(t) = e^{-2t} + 2\left[\frac{1}{2} - \frac{1}{2}e^{-2(t-2)}\right]u_2(t)$$

$$+ 3\left[\frac{1}{2} - \frac{1}{2}e^{-2(t-3)}\right]u_3(t) + \left[-\frac{1}{4} + \frac{t-3}{2} + \frac{e^{-2(t-3)}}{4}\right]u_3(t). \quad \blacksquare$$

PROBLEMS

In Problems 1–8, sketch the graph of the function. Write the function as a sum of shifted functions. Then find the Laplace transform.

1. $f(t) = \begin{cases} 0 & \text{if } 0 \le t < 1 \\ 1 & \text{if } 1 \le t < 3 \\ 2 & \text{if } t \ge 3. \end{cases}$

2. $f(t) = \begin{cases} t & \text{if } 0 \le t < 2 \\ 3 & \text{if } t \ge 2. \end{cases}$

3. $tu_1(t) - t.$

4. $tu_\pi(t) - (t + 1)u_{2\pi}(t).$

5. $u_2(t)e^{3t}.$

6. $t^2[1 - u_3(t)] + 3u_5(t)e^{-t}.$

7. $u_1(t) + u_2(t) + u_3(t) - tu_\pi(t)$.   **8.** $u_\pi(t)te^t - u_5(t)t^2e^t$.

In Problems 9–15, find the inverse Laplace transform of the function.

9. $\dfrac{e^{-s}}{s^2 + 4}$

10. $\dfrac{3!e^{-2s}}{(s-3)^4}$.

11. $\dfrac{1 - e^{-\pi s}}{(s+1)^2 + 5}$.

12. $\dfrac{s - 2e^{-s}}{s^2 - 4s + 7}$.

13. $\dfrac{e^{-s/2}}{s^2 + 4s - 5}$.

14. $\dfrac{2se^{-s} + 3}{s^2 + 1}$.

15. $\dfrac{e^{-2s} + 3}{s(s^2 + 4s + 7)}$.

In Problems 16–27, solve the given initial value problem using Laplace transforms.

16. $y'' + 9y = u_3(t)$, $y(0) = 1$, $y'(0) = 2$.

17. $y'' - 5y' + 4y = \begin{cases} 1 & \text{if } 0 \le t < 5 \\ 0 & \text{if } t \ge 5 \end{cases}$, $y(0) = 0$, $y'(0) = 1$.

18. $y'' + 5y' + 6y = \begin{cases} 0 & \text{if } 0 \le t < 1, \\ 2 & \text{if } 1 \le t < 3, \\ 0 & \text{if } t \ge 3 \end{cases}$ $y(0) = 0$, $y'(0) = 0$.

19. $\dfrac{d^2u}{dx^2} + 2\dfrac{du}{dx} + u = u_5(x)$, $u(0) = 0$, $\dfrac{du}{dx}(0) = 1$.

20. $y'' + y = \sin 2t - u_3(t)\sin 2(t - 3)$, $y(0) = 0$, $y'(0) = 0$.

21. $\dfrac{d^2w}{dt^2} + 2\dfrac{dw}{dt} + 5w = 1 + u_\pi(t)$, $w(0) = 1$, $w'(0) = 0$.

22. $y'' + 2y' + y = u_3(t)e^t$, $y(0) = 0$, $y'(0) = -1$.

23. $\dfrac{dR}{dx} + 2R = \begin{cases} 1 & \text{if } 0 \le x < 1 \\ -1 & \text{if } 1 \le x < 2, \\ 0 & \text{if } x \ge 2 \end{cases}$ $R(0) = 0$.

24. $y'' + y = \begin{cases} t & \text{if } 0 \le t < 1 \\ 0 & \text{if } t \ge 1 \end{cases}$, $y(0) = 0$, $y'(0) = 2$.

25. $y'' + y = \begin{cases} 0 & \text{if } 0 \le t < 1 \\ t & \text{if } t \ge 1 \end{cases}$, $y(0) = 1$, $y'(0) = 0$.

26. $(D - 2)^3y = u_1(t)$, $y(0) = 1$, $y'(0) = 0$, $y''(0) = 0$.

27. $\dfrac{d^4N}{dx^4} + 4\dfrac{d^3N}{dx^3} + 6\dfrac{d^2N}{dx^2} + 4\dfrac{dN}{dx} + N = 1 - u_2(x)$,

$N(0) = 0$, $N'(0) = 0$, $N''(0) = 1$, $N'''(0) = 0$.

28. If $F(s) = L\{f(t)\}$ when $s > \alpha \ge 0$, then

(a) Show that for any positive constant b

$$L\{f(bt)\} = \frac{1}{b}F\left(\frac{s}{b}\right) \qquad \text{for } s > \alpha b.$$

(b) Show that for any positive constant c,

$$L^{-1}\{F(cs)\} = \frac{1}{c}f\left(\frac{t}{c}\right).$$

(c) Show that $L^{-1}\{F(cs + d)\} = c^{-1}\exp(-dt/c)f(t/c)$.

29. If $J_0(t)$ is the Bessel function of the first kind of order 0, compute $L\{J_0(bt)\}$ where b is a positive constant. Use Problem 28.

30. Compute L^{-1} for each function. Use Problem 28.

(a) $\dfrac{1}{(2s-1)^2}$.

(b) $\dfrac{3!}{(4s-3)^4}$.

(c) $\dfrac{e^{-s}}{(2s-1)^2}$.

(d) $\dfrac{e^{-2s}}{(4s-3)^4}$.

(e) $\dfrac{2}{(3s+1)^3}$.

(f) $\dfrac{s+1}{9s^2+2}e^{-\pi s}$.

(g) $\dfrac{se^{-s}}{3s^2+12s+16}$.

(h) $\dfrac{1}{s}\arctan\left(\dfrac{1}{2s+5}\right)$

31. Show that if $y = \varphi(t)$ is the solution of

$$y^{(n)} + b_{n-1}y^{(n-1)} + b_{n-2}y^{(n-2)} + \ldots + b_1y' + b_0y = f(t),$$

$$y(0) = a_0, \quad y'(0) = a_1, \quad \ldots, \quad y^{(n-1)}(0) = a_{n-1},$$

then $y = \varphi(t - c)$ is the solution of

$$y^{(n)} + b_{n-1}y^{(n-1)} + \ldots + b_1y' + b_0y = f(t - c),$$

$$y(c) = a_0, \quad y'(c) = a_1, \quad \ldots, \quad y^{(n-1)}(c) = a_{n-1}.$$

32. Suppose that $y(t)$ solves

$$y'' + ay' + by = u_2(t)f(t - 2), \quad y(2) = 1, \quad y'(2) = -2.$$

(a) Show that $y(t + 2)$ solves

$$y'' + ay' + by = u_0(t)f(t), \quad y(0) = 1, \quad y'(0) = -2.$$

(b) How is the solution of

$$z'' + az' + bz = u_5(t)f(t - 5), \quad z(5) = 1, \quad z'(5) = -2$$

related to $y(t)$?

33. (a) Verify that $y = \exp(-x)^2$ solves

$$y'' + 2y = 4x^2\exp(-x^2), \quad y(0) = 1, \quad y'(0) = 0.$$

(b) Solve

$$w'' + 2w = 4(x-2)^2\exp[-(x-2)^2]u_2(x), \quad w(2) = 1, \quad w'(2) = 0.$$

6.5 IMPULSE EXCITATIONS

In many applications it is necessary to deal with differential equations that are forced impulsively. Figure 6.7 shows a rectangular pulse of time duration a and with height $1/a$. The analytic representation of this pulse is

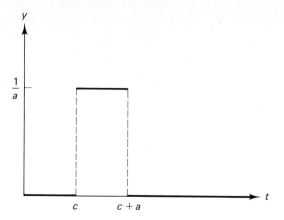

Figure 6.7. Rectangular pulse at c.

(5.1)
$$f_c(t) = \frac{u_c(t) - u_{a+c}(t)}{a},$$

where $u_c(t)$ is the unit step function. This pulse is a *unit* pulse in the sense that the area under the curve is 1. As a decreases, the height increases and the duration decreases in such a way that the area under the curve (i.e., the *strength* of the pulse) remains 1. The limit as $a \to 0^+$ is an idealized pulse that is called the **unit impulse** at $t = c$ and is denoted by $\delta_c(t)$. Clearly, this unit impulse is an idealization. It is, however, an extremely useful idealization.

The Laplace transform of $\delta_c(t)$ is computed using (5.1). From (5.1) we see that

$$L\{f_c(t)\} = L\left\{ \frac{u_c(t) - u_{c+a}(t)}{a} \right\}$$

$$\frac{1}{as}[e^{-cs} - e^{-(c+a)s}] = \frac{1 - e^{-as}}{as} e^{-cs}.$$

In the limit as $a \to 0^+$ one finds that

$$L\{\delta_c(t)\} = \left(\lim_{a \to 0^+} \frac{1 - e^{-as}}{as} \right) e^{-cs} = e^{-cs}.$$

The **delta function** $\delta(t)$ is the unit impulse function $\delta_c(t)$ with $c = 0$. For $c > 0$

$$\delta(t - c) = \lim_{a \to 0^+} \frac{u_0(t - c) - u_a(t - c)}{a}$$

$$= \lim_{a \to 0^+} \frac{u_c(t) - u_{c+a}(t)}{a} = \delta_c(t).$$

Hence $\delta_c(t) = \delta(t - c)$ and

$$L\{\delta(t - c)\} = e^{-cs}, \qquad c \geq 0.$$

The delta function is a **generalized function.** Generalized functions are usually defined by their action in integrals. If $g(t)$ is any continuous function on $0 \le t < \infty$ and if $c \ge 0$, then

$$\int_0^\infty g(t)\delta(t-c)\,dt = \lim_{a \to 0^+} \int_0^\infty g(t)\left[\frac{u_c(t) - u_{c+a}(t)}{a}\right]dt$$

$$= \lim_{a \to 0^+} \frac{1}{a}\int_c^{c+a} g(t)\,dt = g(c).$$

Hence for any continuous function g

(5.2) $$\int_0^\infty g(t)\delta(t-c)\,dt = g(c).$$

For example, for any $v \ge 0$ and $c \ge 0$

$$\int_0^\infty (t^v \sin t)\delta(t-c)\,dt = c^v \sin c$$

while

$$\int_0^\infty e^{-at}\cos bt\,\delta(t-c)\,dt = e^{-ac}\cos bc.$$

Notice that the generalized function $\delta(t-c)$ must be zero for all $t \ne c$ in order for (5.2) to make sense. For example, $e^t\delta(t-c)$ is the same generalized function as $e^c\delta(t-c)$. Indeed, for any continuous function $g(t)$

$$\int_0^\infty g(t)\{e^t\delta(t-c)\}\,dt = \int_0^\infty \{g(t)e^t\}\delta(t-c)\,dt$$

$$= g(c)e^c = \int_0^\infty g(t)e^c\delta(t-c)\,dt.$$

Similarly, for any continuous function $g(t)$ and any $c \ge 0$

$$g(t)\delta(t-c) = g(c)\delta(t-c),$$

and

$$\int_0^\infty f(t)g(t)\delta(t-c)\,dt = f(c)g(c),$$

for all continuous functions f.

Physical systems are sometimes subjected to impulsive inputs. For example, when a gun is fired the bullet is subjected to a force of large magnitude and very short duration. If a steel ball is bounced off a solid wall, then the ball is subjected to a force of large magnitude and short duration. Special hammers, called **impulse hammers** (see Photo 15), are used in mechanics laboratories to provide impulse forces in, for example, beam testing. With such a hammer one can produce an approximate delta function similar to that shown in Figure 6.8. Such a pulse is usually a satisfactory approximation to an idealized pulse $K\delta(t-c)$. The precise shape of the pulse is usually not as important as its strength K and location c. We are particularly interested in those situations where the physical system can be modeled by a linear differential equation with impulsive forcing.

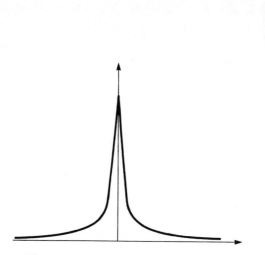

Figure 6.8. An approximate impulse.

Photo 15. An impulse hammer. (Courtesy of Professor Daniel J. Inman, State University of New York at Buffalo.)

EXAMPLE 5.1   Use Laplace transforms to solve

(5.3) $y'' - 2y' + 5y = 2\delta(t - 3), \qquad y(0) = 0, \qquad y'(0) = 1.$

Laplace transforming (5.3) gives

$$[s^2 Y(s) - 1] - 2[s Y(s)] + 5 Y(s) = 2e^{-3s}$$

or

$$Y(s) = \frac{1 + 2e^{-3s}}{s^2 - 2s + 5} = \frac{1 + 2e^{-3s}}{(s - 1)^2 + 4}.$$

Since $L^{-1}\{[(s - 1)^2 + 4]^{-1}\} = \frac{1}{2}e^t \sin 2t$, then

$$L^{-1}\left\{\frac{2e^{-3s}}{(s - 1)^2 + 4}\right\} = u_3(t)e^{t-3} \sin 2(t - 3)$$

and

(5.4) $y(t) = \frac{1}{2}e^t \sin 2t + u_3(t)e^{t-3} \sin (2t - 6).$ ∎

The first term on the right in (5.4) is the complementary solution $y_c(t)$, that is, the solution of

$$y'' - 2y' + 5y = 0, \qquad y(0) = 0, \qquad y'(0) = 1.$$

The second term on the right in (5.4) is the response of the system described by the differential equation to the impulse $2\delta(t - 3)$. This term is zero until $t = 3$ but it affects the solution for all $t \geq 3$. This term is a continuous function of t in spite of the fact that it is the response to the very discontinuous pulse $2\delta(t - 3)$. The first derivative of this term has a jump discontinuity at $t = 3$. This jump is caused by the pulse.

PROBLEMS

In Problems 1–10, find the solution of the initial value problem.

1. $y'' + 3y' + 2y = \delta(t - \pi)$, $y(0) = 0$, $y'(0) = 1$.

2. $y'' - 2y' + 2y = \delta(t - 5)$, $y(0) = 0$, $y'(0) = 0$.

3. $y'' - 4y' + 4y = 2\delta(t - 1) - \delta(t - 2)$, $y(0) = 0$, $y'(0) = 0$.

4. $R'' + 4R = 3\delta(t - 2\pi)$, $R(0) = 1$, $R'(0) = 0$.

5. $\dfrac{d^2N}{dx^2} - N = \pi\delta(x - 2) - \pi\delta(x - 4)$, $N(0) = 0$, $\dfrac{dN}{dx}(0) = 0$.

6. $y'' + 5y' + 6y = 2e^t\delta(t - \pi)$, $y(0) = 1$, $y'(0) = 0$.

7. $w'' + w = (\sin t)\delta\left(t - \dfrac{3\pi}{2}\right)$, $w(0) = 2$, $w'(0) = 0$.

8. $y'' + 4y = e^{3t}\delta(t - \pi)$, $y(0) = 1$, $y'(0) = 1$.

9. $\dfrac{d^2R}{dx^2} + 9R = 3x\delta(x - \pi)$, $R(0) = 0$, $\dfrac{dR}{dx}(0) = 0$.

10. $\dfrac{d^2B}{dx^2} + 2\dfrac{dB}{dx} + B = \delta(x - 1)$, $B(0) = 0$, $\dfrac{dB}{dx}(0) = 1$.

11. From the point of view of Laplace transforms the derivative of $u_c(t)$ is $\delta_c(t)$ when $c > 0$ since

$$L\{u_c'\} = sL\{u_c\} - u_c(0) = e^{-cs} = L\{\delta_c\}.$$

Continue this line of reasoning by computing

(a) $L\{(\delta_c)'\}$.

(b) $L\{(\delta_c)''\}$.

(c) $L\{(u_c(t) - u_d(t))'\}$ with $0 < c < d$.

(d) $L\{[\text{sgn}(\cos t)]'\}$.

12. It is known that $\int_{-\infty}^{\infty} \exp(-x^2)\, dx = \sqrt{\pi}$. We define

$$h_k(x) = \sqrt{\dfrac{k}{\pi}} \exp(-kx^2) \qquad \text{for } k > 0.$$

(a) Compute $\int_{-\infty}^{\infty} h_k(x)\, dx$.

(b) Graph $h_k(x)$ when $k = 1, 5, 10$.

(c) Show that for any bounded and continuous function $f(x)$

$$\lim_{k \to \infty} \int_{-\infty}^{\infty} f(x)h_k(x - c)\, dx = f(c)$$

for any real number c. What is the limit of $h_k(x - c)$ as $k \to \infty$?

13. Define $g(t, a, b) = [u_a(t) - u_b(t)]/(b - a)$, where $a < c < b$ and $c > 0$.

(a) Show that for continuous functions f,

$$\lim_{b \to c^+, a \to c^-} \int_0^{\infty} g(t, a, b)f(t)\, dt = f(c).$$

(b) What is the limit of $g(t, a, b)$ as $a \to c^-$ and $b \to c^+$?

6.6 CONVOLUTION

Suppose that f and g are Laplace transformable functions whose transforms $F(s)$ and $G(s)$ exist for $s > \alpha$. The purpose of this section is to show how $L^{-1}\{F(s)G(s)\}$ is computed in terms of the functions f and g. We put $H(s) = F(s)G(s)$ and $h = L^{-1}\{H(s)\}$. Then

(6.1)
$$H(s) = \int_0^\infty e^{-st}h(t)\, dt = F(s)G(s)$$

$$= \left(\int_0^\infty e^{-st}f(t)\, dt\right)\left(\int_0^\infty e^{-sr}g(r)\, dr\right).$$

Hence $H(s)$ can be written as the iterated integral

$$H(s) = \int_0^\infty \left(\int_0^\infty e^{-s(t+r)}f(t)\, dt\right)g(r)\, dr.$$

In the inside integral we use the change of variables $u = t + r$ and then interchange the order of integration. This gives

$$H(s) = \int_0^\infty \left(\int_r^\infty e^{-su}f(u-r)\, du\right)g(r)\, dr$$

or

(6.2)
$$H(s) = \int_0^\infty \left(\int_0^u f(u-r)g(r)\, dr\right)e^{-su}\, du.$$

When we replace the dummy variable of integration u in (6.2) by the variable t and then compare the result with (6.1), we see that

$$\int_0^\infty e^{-st}h(t)\, dt = \int_0^\infty \left(\int_0^t f(t-r)g(r)\, dr\right)e^{-st}\, dt.$$

This proves the following result.

THEOREM 6.1: TRANSFORM OF CONVOLUTIONS

If f and g are Laplace transformable with $F(s) = L\{f\}$ and $G(s) = L\{g\}$, then

$$L\left\{\int_0^t f(t-r)g(r)\, dr\right\} = F(s)G(s).$$

The function h defined by the formula

(6.3)
$$h(t) = \int_0^t f(t-r)g(r)\, dr$$

is called the **convolution of f and g** and is written $h = f * g$. In this notation the theorem states that

$$L\{f * g\} = L\{f\}L\{g\}.$$

If we change variables in (6.3) to $u = t - r$, then

$$h(t) = \int_t^0 f(u)g(t-u)(-du) = \int_0^t f(u)g(t-u)\, du$$

$$= \int_0^t g(t-u)f(u)\, du = (g * f)(t).$$

Hence we see that convolution is commutative, that is,

$$f * g = g * f.$$

Similarly, it can be shown that convolution is associative,

$$f * (g * k) = (f * g) * k;$$

it is distributive,

$$f * (g + k) = f * g + f * k;$$

and if 0 represents the zero function,

$$f * 0 = 0.$$

Hence we see that the algebraic properties of convolution are much like the algebraic properties of ordinary multiplication of functions. However, in two important ways convolution and ordinary multiplication are quite different. First, it is possible to choose continuous functions $f(t)$ and $g(t)$, neither identically zero, with

$$f(t)g(t) = 0 \qquad \text{for all } t \geq 0.$$

For example, if $f(t) > 0$ for $0 \leq t < 1$ and $f(t) = 0$ for $t \geq 1$ and if $g(t) = 0$ for $0 \leq t \leq 1$ and $g(t) > 0$ for $t > 1$, then neither f nor g is identically zero but $f(t)g(t) \equiv 0$. For convolution this cannot happen. If neither f nor g is identically zero, then $f * g$ cannot be the zero function. The second difference concerns the multiplicative identity. If 1 denotes the function that is identically 1, then

$$f(t) \cdot 1 = f(t) \qquad \text{for all } t \geq 0,$$

that is, 1 is the *multiplicative identity* for ordinary multiplication. However,

$$(f * 1)(t) = (1 * f)(t) = \int_0^t 1 \cdot f(r)\, dr \neq f(t).$$

For convolution, 1 is not the multiplicative identity. Rather, convolution of f with 1 corresponds to integration of f. For example, if $f(t) = t^n$, then

$$(t^n * 1) = \int_0^t r^n\, dr = \frac{t^{n+1}}{n+1} \neq t^n.$$

The delta function turns out to be the multiplicative identity for convolution since

$$(f * \delta)(t) = \int_0^t f(t-r)\delta(r)\, dr = f(t).$$

Convolution can be used to compute the inverse Laplace transform of many functions.

EXAMPLE 6.2   Use convolution to compute $L^{-1}\{H\}$ when

$$H(s) = \frac{1}{s^2(s-3)}.$$

First Solution: Since $L\{t\} = s^{-2}$ and $L\{e^{3t}\} = (s-3)^{-1}$, then

$$L^{-1}\{H\} = L^{-1}\{(s-3)^{-1}\} * L^{-1}\{s^{-2}\} = e^{3t} * t$$

$$= \int_0^t e^{3(t-r)}r\,dr = e^{3t}\int_0^t e^{-3r}r\,dr$$

$$= e^{3t}\left[\frac{re^{-3r}}{-3} - \frac{e^{-3r}}{9}\right]_0^t$$

$$= -\frac{t}{3} - \frac{1}{9} + \frac{e^{3t}}{9}.$$

Second Solution: Since $L^{-1}\{1/s\} = 1$ and $L^{-1}\{(s-3)^{-1}\} = e^{3t}$, then

$$L^{-1}\{H\} = 1 * (1 * e^{3t}) = 1 * \frac{e^{3t} - 1}{3}$$

$$= \frac{e^{3t}}{9} - \frac{t}{3} - \frac{1}{9}.$$

In these solutions we have used the fact that convolution is associative and commutative so that we can do the convolutions in any order we please. Recall also that convolution with 1 corresponds to integration. ∎

EXAMPLE 6.3   Write h in the form $f * g$ when

$$H(s) = \frac{1}{(s^2 + 4)^2}.$$

There are many possible solutions. For example, since

$$H(s) = \left(\frac{1}{s^2+4}\right)\left(\frac{1}{s^2+4}\right) \quad \text{and} \quad L^{-1}\left\{\frac{1}{s^2+4}\right\} = \frac{1}{2}\sin 2t,$$

then $h(t) = (\frac{1}{2}\sin 2t) * (\frac{1}{2}\sin 2t)$. On the other hand,

$$H(s) = \left(\frac{-1}{4s}\right)\frac{-4s}{(s^2+4)^2} = \left(\frac{-1}{4s}\right)\left(\frac{d}{ds}\left\{\frac{2}{s^2+4}\right\}\right),$$

so that

$$h(t) = L^{-1}\left\{\frac{-1}{4s}\right\} * L^{-1}\left\{\frac{-4s}{(s^2+4)^2}\right\} = \left(\frac{-1}{4}\right) * (-t\sin 2t).$$

One could also write

$$h(t) = [\tfrac{1}{2} * (\sin 2t)] * (\cos 2t)$$
$$= \tfrac{1}{4}(1 - \cos 2t) * (\cos 2t).$$

Our second solution is probably the best solution since it yields the easiest integral. Indeed, using integration by parts, we compute

$$h(t) = \left(-\frac{1}{4}\right) * (-t \sin 2t) = \frac{1}{4} \int_0^t r \sin 2r \, dr$$

$$= \frac{1}{4}\left[r \frac{\cos 2r}{-2} \Big|_0^t + \frac{1}{2} \int_0^t \cos 2r \, dr \right]$$

$$= \frac{1}{4}\left[-\frac{r \cos 2r}{2} + \frac{1}{4} \sin 2r \right]_0^t$$

$$= -t \frac{\cos 2t}{8} + \frac{1}{16} \sin 2t. \quad \blacksquare$$

EXAMPLE 6.4   Compute $h(t) = (t^{-1/4}) * t^{5/4}$.

Recall that $L\{t^v\} = \Gamma(v+1)/s^{v+1}$ for any $v > -1$. Here Γ is the gamma function. Hence

$$L\{h\} = L\{t^{-1/4} * t^{5/4}\} = L\{t^{-1/4}\}L\{t^{5/4}\}$$

$$= \frac{\Gamma(\frac{3}{4})\Gamma(\frac{9}{4})}{s^{3/4}s^{9/4}} = \left[\frac{\Gamma(\frac{3}{4})\Gamma(\frac{9}{4})}{2}\right]\frac{2}{s^3}.$$

Hence

$$h(t) = \left[\frac{\Gamma(\frac{3}{4})\Gamma(\frac{9}{4})}{2}\right]t^2. \quad \blacksquare$$

PROBLEMS

1. Show that for any continuous functions f, g, and k

   (a) $f * (g + k) = f * g + f * k$.   (b) $f * (g * k) = (f * g) * k$.

2. Find the Laplace transform of each function.

   (a) $\int_0^t (t - r)^3 \sin 4r \, dr$.   (b) $\int_0^t (t - r)^2 e^{-3r} \, dr$.

   (c) $\int_0^t \sin (t - r)(-r \cos 2r) \, dr$.   (d) $\int_0^t \cos 2(t - r) \sin \pi r \, dr$.

   (e) $\int_0^t (t - r)(-r) \cos r \, dr$.   (f) $\int_0^t (t - r)^7 r^2 \, dr$.

3. Use the convolution theorem to find the inverse Laplace transform. Evaluate the resulting integrals when possible.

   (a) $\dfrac{1}{(s^2 + 1)(s^2 + 4)}$.   (b) $\dfrac{1}{s^2(s + 1)^2}$.

   (c) $\dfrac{s}{(s + 2)(s^2 + 9)}$.   (d) $\dfrac{1}{s^{3/2}(s^2 + 4)}$.

4. Given any function f of class Λ, show that

   (a) $\int_0^t \int_0^{r_1} f(r_2) \, dr_2 \, dr_1 = \int_0^t (t - r)f(r) \, dr$.

(b) $\int_0^t \int_0^{r_1} \int_0^{r_2} f(r_3)\, dr_3\, dr_2\, dr_1 = \int_0^t \frac{(t-r)^2}{2} f(r)\, dr.$

(c) $(1 * 1 * \overbrace{\ldots * 1}^{n \text{ times}}) * f = \left[\dfrac{t^{n-1}}{(n-1)!} \right] * f.$

5. Evaluate each integral.

   (a) $\int_0^t (t-r)^{10} r^3\, dr.$

   (b) $t^a * t^b * t^c$, where a, b and $c > 0$.

6. Given a continuous function f defined on $0 \le t < \infty$, the **one-half integral** of f is defined as

$$I_{1/2}(f) = \frac{1}{\Gamma(1/2)} (t^{-1/2} * f).$$

[Note that $\Gamma(\tfrac{1}{2}) = \sqrt{\pi}$.]

   (a) Show that $I_{1/2}(I_{1/2}(f))(t) = \int_0^t f(r)\, dr.$

   (b) Show that

$$I_{1/2}\left(\int_0^t f(r)\, dr \right) = \int_0^t I_{1/2}(f)(r)\, dr = I_{1/2}(I_{1/2}(I_{1/2}(f)))(t).$$

   (c) Compute $I_{1/2}(p)$ when $p(t) = \sum_{j=0}^n a_j t^j$ is a polynomial.

7. For any $v > 0$ the vth-**fractional integral** of a function f is defined by the relation

$$I_v(f) = \frac{1}{\Gamma(v)} (t^{v-1} * f).$$

   (a) Show that if v is a positive integer, then $I_v(f)$ is the v-fold integral of f. *Hint:* See Problem 4.

   (b) Show that for any $v > 0$ and $\mu > 0$

$$I_v(I_\mu(f)) = I_\mu(I_v(f)) = I_{\mu+v}(f).$$

   (c) Given a polynomial $p(t) = \sum_{j=0}^n a_j t^j$ and given $v > 0$, compute $I_v(p).$

   (d) Recall that $e^z = \sum_{n=0}^\infty z^n/n!$. Let a be any real number. Compute $I_v(e^{at})$ as a series.

   (e) For any positive number b compute $I_v(\sin bt).$

   (f) For any positive number b compute $I_v(\cos bt).$

8. Let $I_{1/2}$ be the half-integral defined in Problem 6. We shall define a $\tfrac{1}{2}$-**fractional derivative** by the formula

$$D^{1/2} f = \frac{d}{dt} (I_{1/2}(f)).$$

As with whole derivatives, $D^{1/2}$ may exist or may not exist. It depends on what function f is chosen.

   (a) Given a polynomial $p(t) = \sum_{j=0}^n a_j t^j$, show that $(D^{1/2} p)(t)$ need not exist when $t = 0$. Compute $D^{1/2} p$ for $t > 0$.

(b) For any real number b compute $D^{1/2}(e^{bt})$, $t > 0$.

(c) Compute $D^{1/2}(D^{1/2}p)$ when $p(t) = \sum_{j=0}^{n} a_j t^j$ and $t > 0$.

9. The **point kinetics model** for a single-core nuclear reactor was discussed in Chapter 1. These equations have the form

$$p' = (\rho(t) - \beta)p + \sum_{i=1}^{m} \lambda_i c_i + S(t), \qquad p(0) = p_0$$

$$c_i' = \beta_i p - \lambda_i c_i, \qquad c_i(0) = c_{i0}, \qquad 1 \le i \le m$$

where β_i and λ_i are positive constants, $\beta = \sum_{i=1}^{m} \beta_i$, and $S(t)$ is a known function. The unknowns are p and the c_i.

(a) Show that $p(t)$ satisfies an equation of the form

$$p'(t) = (\rho(t) - \beta)p(t) + \int_0^t g(t - r)p(r)\,dr + f(t).$$

Compute $g(t)$ and $f(t)$.

(b) Compute $P = L\{p\}$ when $\rho(t) \equiv S(t) \equiv 0$.

10. Given the initial value problem

$$y^{(N)} + \sum_{j=0}^{N-1} b_j y^{(j)} = cu(t), \qquad y(0) = y'(0) = \ldots = y^{(N-1)}(0) = 0,$$

where the b_j and c are real numbers. Define $p(s) = s^N + \sum_{j=0}^{N-1} b_j s^j$.

(a) Show that $Y = L\{y\}$ can be written in the form $Y(s) = H(s)L\{u\}$. Compute $H(s)$.

(b) Show that if $H(iw) \ne 0$ and if $u(t) = \cos(wt)$, then

$$Y(s) = |H(iw)|L\{\cos(wt + \alpha)\} + Y_c(s),$$

where $\tan \alpha = \text{Im}\,[H(iw)]/\text{Re}\,[H(iw)]$ and $L^{-1}\{Y_c\}$ solves the corresponding homogeneous equation.

6.7   SOME CONTROL THEORY

Consider a nonhomogeneous second-order linear differential equation with constant coefficients

(7.1) $\qquad a_2 \dfrac{d^2 x}{dt^2} + a_1 \dfrac{dx}{dt} + a_0 x = u(t), \qquad x(0) = x_0, \dfrac{dx}{dt}(0) = x_0'.$

We shall think of (7.1) as a mathematical description of some physical device. This device will be viewed as a black box. The quantities $x(t)$ and $x'(t)$ determine the *state* of the device at time t. According to (7.1), the device is in the state (x_0, x_0') at time zero. At time zero a signal $u(t)$ is input to the device and an output signal $x(t)$ is obtained (see Figure 6.9).

The output $x(t)$ can be written as the sum of the complementary solution, that is, the solution of

(7.2) $\qquad a_2 x_c'' + a_1 x_c' + a_0 x_c = 0, \qquad x_c(0) = x_0, \qquad x_c'(0) = x_0'$

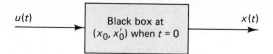

Figure 6.9. An input–output system.

and the solution of the nonhomogeneous problem

(7.3) $$a_2 x_p'' + a_1 x_p' + a_0 x_p = u(t), \qquad x_p(0) = x_p'(0) = 0.$$

The solution of (7.2) has Laplace transform

(7.4) $$X_c(s) = \frac{(s a_2 + a_1) x_0 + a_2 x_0'}{a_2 s^2 + a_1 s + a_0}.$$

The solution of (7.3) has Laplace transform

(7.5) $$X_p(s) = \frac{1}{a_2 s^2 + a_1 s + a_0} U(s).$$

The term $H(s) = (a_2 s^2 + a_1 s + a_0)^{-1}$ is the **transfer function** for the differential equation. The inverse Laplace transform $h = L^{-1}\{H\}$ solves (7.3) with $u(t) = \delta(t)$; that is, it is the output (or response) to the impulse input $\delta(t)$. Hence h is often called the **impulse response** function. From (7.5) we see that $x_p = h * u$, where $*$ denotes convolution. This part of the solution shows how the device processes an input $u(t)$. The solution $x_c(t)$ of (7.2) depends on x_0 and x_0' but is independent of $u(t)$. In most control situations $x_c(t)$ tends to zero as $t \to \infty$ (see Problem 5). Thus $x_c(t)$, and hence x_0 and x_0', soon become unimportant relative to the term $x_p(t)$. It is an accurate and useful description of the situation to separate the effects of $u(t)$ from those of x_0 and x_0'. This is done in Figure 6.10. The black box is initially at the zero state. The transfer function $H(s)$ characterizes the black box.

Figure 6.10 represents a typical **open-loop control device.** The output of the device is $x_p = h * u$. This output is determined (or controlled) by the input $u(t)$. Also common in control theory is the use of **feedback.** By this we mean that the input $u(t)$ depends on the output $x(t)$. For example, the output $x(t)$ might be scaled and then compared to a reference signal $r(t)$, that is $u(t) = r(t) - K x(t)$, as in Figure 6.11.

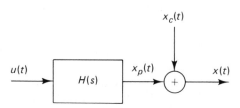

Figure 6.10. Open-loop control system.

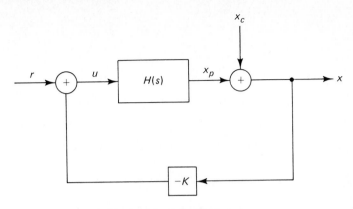

Figure 6.11. A feedback system.

The addition of feedback will change the control device into a new and different device. It will alter the differential equation. If in (7.1) $u = r(t) - Kx(t)$, then $x(t)$ will solve

$$a_2 x'' + a_1 x' + a_0 x = r(t) - Kx$$

or

$$a_2 x'' + a_1 x' + (a_0 + K)x = r(t), \qquad x(0) = x_0, \qquad x'(0) = x'_0.$$

The transfer function of this new device is

$$H_K(s) = \frac{1}{a_2 s^2 + a_1 s + a_0 + K}.$$

EXAMPLE 7.1.   For the open-loop system

(7.6) $$x'' + 2x' = u(t)$$

find the transfer function $H(s)$ and the impulse response function. Solve the equation when $u(t) = 1$, $x(0) = 0$, and $x'(0) = 0$. Find the transfer function for the feedback system

(7.7) $$w'' + 2w' = r(t) - Kw(t)$$

when $0 < K < 1$. Determine the solution of (7.7) when $r(t) = 1$, $w(0) = 0$, and $w'(0) = 0$.

The transfer function for (7.6) is

$$H(s) = \frac{1}{s(s + 2)} = \frac{1}{2s} - \frac{1}{2(s + 2)}.$$

Hence

$$h(t) = L^{-1}\{H\} = \tfrac{1}{2} - \tfrac{1}{2}e^{-2t}.$$

If $u(t) = 1$, $x(0) = 0$, and $x'(0) = 0$, then

$$X(s) = H(s)L\{u\} = \frac{1}{s^2(s + 2)}$$

$$= \frac{1}{2s^2} - \frac{1}{4s} + \frac{1}{4(s + 2)}.$$

Hence

$$x(t) = \tfrac{1}{2}t - \tfrac{1}{4} + \tfrac{1}{4}e^{-2t}.$$

Notice that this solution becomes unbounded as $t \to \infty$. Indeed,

$$\lim_{t \to \infty} \left[x(t) - \frac{2t - 1}{4} \right] = 0,$$

so that $x(t) \cong (2t - 1)/4$ when t is large.

The transfer function for the feedback system (7.7) is

$$H_K(s) = \frac{1}{s^2 + 2s + K} = \frac{1}{(s + 1)^2 - (1 - K)}$$

$$= \frac{1}{(s + 1) - \sqrt{1 - K}} \frac{1}{(s + 1) + \sqrt{1 - K}}.$$

Hence one can easily compute

$$H_K(s) = \frac{1}{2\sqrt{1 - K}} \left[\frac{1}{s + 1 - \sqrt{1 - K}} - \frac{1}{s + 1 + \sqrt{1 - K}} \right].$$

It follows that $h_K = L^{-1}\{H_K\}$ is

$$h_K(t) = \frac{1}{2\sqrt{1 - K}} \left[e^{-(1 - \sqrt{1 - K})t} - e^{-(1 + \sqrt{1 - K})t} \right].$$

If $r(t) = 1$, then $w = h_K * 1$, that is,

$$w(t) = \int_0^t \frac{1}{2\sqrt{1 - K}} \left[e^{-(1 - \sqrt{1 - K})r} - e^{-(1 + \sqrt{1 - K})r} \right] dr$$

or

$$(7.8) \qquad w(t) = \frac{1}{K} + \frac{1}{2\sqrt{1 - K}} \left[\frac{e^{-(1 + \sqrt{1 - K})t}}{1 + \sqrt{1 - K}} - \frac{e^{-(1 - \sqrt{1 - K})t}}{1 - \sqrt{1 - K}} \right].$$

The two exponentials in (7.8) tend to zero as $t \to \infty$. Hence $w(t) \cong K^{-1}$ for t large. The addition of feedback has radically altered the nature of the solution. The response to a unit function changes from $x(t) \cong (2t - 1)/4$ to $x(t) \cong K^{-1}$ for large t. ∎

The ideas explained here can be generalized considerably. For example, if feedback is added to (7.1), this feedback may depend on both of the state variables $x(t)$ and $x'(t)$. A typical situation is

$$u(t) = r(t) - c_1 x(t) - c_2 x'(t)$$

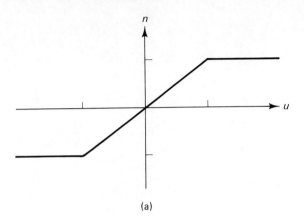

(a)

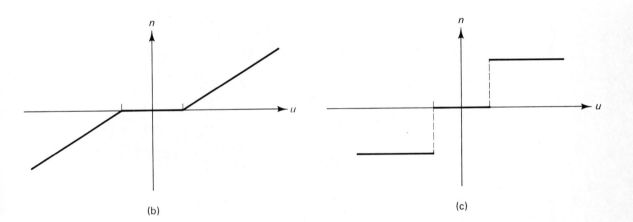

(b)   (c)

Figure 6.12 (a) Saturation nonlinearity. (b) Nonlinearity with dead zone. (c) Relay with dead zone.

for some constants c_1 and c_2. Often, the feedback is nonlinear, that is,

$$u(t) = n(r(t) - c_1 x(t) - c_2 x'(t)),$$

where $n(u)$ is an odd, continuous function such that $n(u) \geq 0$ for $u > 0$. Some typical functions $n(u)$ are graphed in Figure 6.12. Notice that these functions are all *nonlinear*. Also, the order of the differential equation can be larger than 2, or systems of differential equations can be used. One of the more challenging control problems is the control of robots (see Photo 16). In robotics the governing equations are highly nonlinear systems of equations.

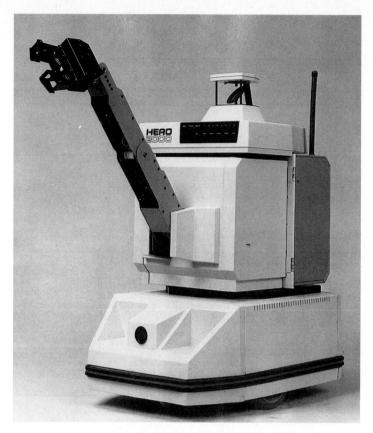

Photo 16. A mobile robot. (Courtesy of Heath Company.)

PROBLEMS

In Problems 1–4, find the transfer function for the given open-loop control system and compute the impulse response function. Then set $u = r - Kx$ and determine the transfer function of the resulting feedback system.

1. $x'' + 4x' + 4x = u(t)$.

2. $2x'' + 8x = u(t)$.

3. $x''' + 2x'' + x' = u(t)$.

4. $x''' + x'' + 4x' + 4x = u(t)$.

5. Show that if a_0, a_1, and a_2 are all positive, then all solutions of (7.2) tend to zero as $t \to \infty$. Consider the cases $a_1^2 > 4a_2a_0$, $a_1^2 = 4a_2a_0$, and $a_1^2 < 4a_2a_0$ separately.

6. Determine the impulse response function for (7.7) when $K = 1$ and when $K = 2$.

7. (a) Solve (7.7) when $r(t) = 1$, $w(0) = w'(0) = 0$, and $K = 1$. Determine the limit as $t \to \infty$ of the solution.

   (b) Repeat part (a) with $K = 2$.

8. In (7.3) let $u = r(t) - c_1x(t) - c_2x'(t)$.

   (a) Find the transfer function for this feedback system.

   (b) Assume that $a_1 + c_2 > 0$, $a_0 + c_1 > 0$, and $r(t) = r_0$ is constant. Compute the limit as $t \to \infty$ of the solution of (7.3).

9. (a) Solve $z'' + 4z = \sin 2t$, $z(0) = z'(0) = 0$.

(b) Solve $w'' + 4w = (\sin 2t - w')$, $w(0) = w'(0) = 0$.

(c) How does the feedback change the nature of the solution?

10. The cylindrical tank in Figure 6.13 has cross-sectional area A. Liquid is input at the rate of $u(t)$ liters per second. Flow resistance at the outflow orifice is R. If $h(t)$ is the height of the liquid in the tank at time t, then

$$Ah' = \text{net tank rate of flow} = \text{inflow rate} - \text{outflow rate} = u(t) - \frac{h}{R}$$

or

(7.9) $$h' = -\frac{1}{AR} h + \frac{1}{A} u(t).$$

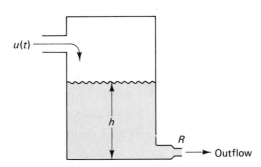

Figure 6.13. Tank flow problem.

(a) Compute the transfer function for the open-loop system (7.9).

(b) If $u = r(t) - Kh$, compute the transfer function of the resulting feedback system.

(c) Let $u = r(t) - Kh$ and let $r(t) = h_0$, where $h_0 > 0$ is a fixed constant. Solve the resulting differential equation for $h(t)$. Show that $h(t)$ has a limit $h(\infty)$ as $t \to \infty$. What is the feedback control causing the system to do? (Assume that $K > 0$.)

11. Two cylindrical tanks having cross-sectional areas A_1 and A_2 are connected as shown in Figure 6.14. Liquid is input to tank 1 at the rate $u(t)$ liters per second. The outflow orifices of the two tanks have flow resistances R_1 and R_2.

(a) Determine expressions for $A_1 h_1'$ and $A_2 h_2'$.

(b) Find a differential equation of the form

$$b_2 h_2'' + b_1 h_2' + b_0 h_2 = b_3 u(t)$$

which describes this system. Determine the transfer function for this open-loop control system.

(c) If $u(t) = u_0$ is constant, show that $h_1(t)$ and $h_2(t)$ have limits as $t \to \infty$. Compute these limits.

(d) If in part (b) we use feedback of the form $u = K(H_1 - h_2)$, how can H_1 and $K > 0$ be chosen so that $h_2(t)$ tends to the limit $h_0 > 0$ as $t \to \infty$?

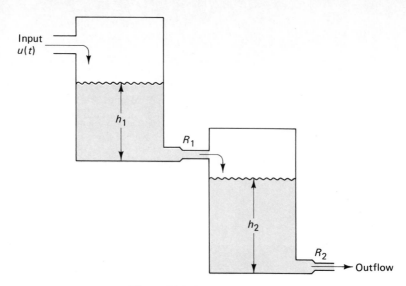

Figure 6.14. Two tank system.

12. Given the mechanical system in Figure 6.4, suppose that $u = f(t)$ is the input.

    (a) Compute the transfer function for the open-loop system.

    (b) If $u = f(t) = r(t) - kx(t)$, compute the transfer function for the resulting feedback system.

    (c) In part (b) if $r(t) = kx_0$, show that any solution of the resulting differential equations has a limit as $t \to \infty$. (Assume that $k > 0$.)

13. Let $p_1(s) = s^N + \sum_{j=0}^{N-1} b_j s^j$ and $p_2(s) = \sum_{j=0}^{M} c_j s^j$, where the terms b_j and c_j are real numbers and $N > M \geq 0$. Consider the control system

$$y^{(N)} + \sum_{j=0}^{N-1} b_j y^{(j)} = \sum_{j=0}^{M} c_j u^{(j)}.$$

    (a) Show that if $y(t)$ is a solution of this equation and if $Y = L\{y\}$, $U = L\{u\}$, then

$$Y(s) = H(s)U(s) + Y_H(s),$$

    where $Y_H = L\{y_H\}$ and y_H is a solution of the corresponding homogeneous equation. The function $H(s)$ is the **transfer function** for this open-loop system. Compute $H(s)$.

    (b) Show that $y = y_H + g * u$ for some functions g. How is g related to $H(s)$?

14. The rotational mechanical system in Figure 6.15 consists of a mass with moment of inertia $J > 0$, a spring of stiffness $K > 0$, and a viscous damping term with $B \geq 0$. A torque $u(t)$ is applied to the mass.

    (a) If feedback of the form $u = r(t) - L\theta'(t)$ is used, find the transfer function of the feedback system.

    (b) If $L > 0$ and if $u = w_0 - L\theta'(t)$, show that each solution of the system tends to a constant as $t \to \infty$. Compute the value of this constant.

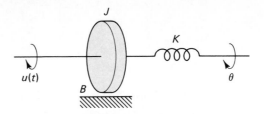

Figure 6.15. A rotational control system.

15. In Figure 6.15 assume that $J > 0$, $B > 0$, and $K = 0$. Let $w = \theta'$.

   (a) Show that $Jw' + Bw = u$.

   (b) Show if $u = w_0 - L\theta' = w_0 - Lw$ and if $\theta(t)$ is any solution of the rotational system, there are constants A and C such that

$$\lim_{t \to \infty} \{\theta(t) - [At + C]\} = 0.$$

   Compute A.

16. A simple home water heater was studied in Chapter 2. This system was depicted in Figure 2.11. The water tank is insulated to reduce heat loss to the room. A heater can be turned on and off to control the water temperature $T(t)$ (in degrees Fahrenheit) of the tank water. The temperature T satisfies an equation of the form

$$CT' + f(t)S[T - T_i(t)] + \frac{T - T_a}{R} = h(t),$$

   when C, S, and R are positive constants, $f(t)$ is the rate at which hot water is used, T_i is the temperature at which water is input to the tank, T_a is the temperature of the air that surrounds the tank, and $h(t)$ is the rate of heat flow from the water heater. Assume that $f(t) = f_0$, $T_i(t) = T_I$, and $T_a(t) = T_A$ are constant.

   (a) If $h(t) = T_c - KT(t)$, where $K > 0$, what value of T_c must be used in order that all solutions of $T(t)$ tend to 150°F as $t \to \infty$? Home water heaters are not built with such feedback controls. Why do you think that this is the case?

   (b) A control which is more realistic than that in part (a) is

$$h(T) = \begin{cases} h_0 & \text{if } T \le 150, \\ 0 & \text{if } T > 150 \end{cases}$$

   where h_0 is a fixed positive constant. Show that with this feedback, the differential equation for $T(t)$ is nonlinear.

6.8 INTEGRAL EQUATIONS

Certain types of integral equations can be studied using Laplace transforms. The equations must be linear Volterra equations of convolution type, that is, equations of the form

(8.1) $$\int_0^t k(t - r)y(r)\, dr = f(t)$$

or

(8.2) $$y(t) + \int_0^t k(t - r)y(r) \, dr = f(t).$$

In both of these cases $k(t)$ and $f(t)$ are given known functions while $y(t)$ is the unknown.

In equation (8.1) we note that if $y(t)$ is a solution and if $y(t)$ is continuous on $0 \leq t < \infty$, then on taking $t = 0$ in (8.1) we see that $f(0)$ must be zero. Hence we shall assume for now that $f(0) = 0$. (The case $f(0) \neq 0$ will be taken up later.) We solve (8.1) by taking Laplace transforms. This gives $K(s)Y(s) = F(s)$ or

(8.3) $$Y(s) = \frac{F(s)}{K(s)}.$$

If we can determine the inverse Laplace transform of $F(s)/K(s)$, then (8.1) is solved.

EXAMPLE 8.1   Solve the **Abel equation**

$$\int_0^t \frac{1}{\sqrt{t - r}} \, y(r) \, dr = f(t)$$

when $f(0) = 0$ and f' is of class Λ. In particular, solve for $y(t)$ when $f(t) = t$.
Recall that $L\{t^{-1/2}\} = \Gamma(\tfrac{1}{2})/\sqrt{s}$, where Γ denotes the gamma function. It can be shown that $\Gamma(\tfrac{1}{2}) = \sqrt{\pi}$. Hence

$$\frac{\sqrt{\pi}}{\sqrt{s}} \, Y(s) = F(s)$$

or

$$Y(s) = \frac{\sqrt{s}}{\sqrt{\pi}} \, F(s) = \frac{1}{\pi} \frac{\sqrt{\pi}}{\sqrt{s}} \{sF(s)\}.$$

Since $f(0) = 0$, then $L\{f'\} = sF(s) - f(0) = sF(s)$. Thus,

$$Y(s) = \frac{1}{\pi} L\{t^{-1/2}\}L\{f'\}$$

and

$$y(t) = \frac{1}{\pi} (t^{-1/2} * f') = \frac{1}{\pi} \int_0^t \frac{1}{\sqrt{t - r}} f'(r) \, dr.$$

If $f(t) = t$, then $f'(t) = 1$ and

$$y(t) = \frac{1}{\pi} \int_0^t \frac{1}{\sqrt{t - r}} \cdot 1 \, dr = \frac{1}{\pi} \int_0^t \frac{dr}{\sqrt{r}} = \frac{2}{\pi} \sqrt{t}. \quad \blacksquare$$

EXAMPLE 8.2   Solve for $y(t)$ when

$$\int_0^t e^{-(t-r)} y(r)\, dr = f(t).$$

In particular, find the solution when $f(t) = t^{1/2}$.

Inasmuch as

$$\frac{1}{s+1}\, Y(s) = F(s),$$

then

$$Y(s) = (s+1)F(s) = sF(s) + F(s)$$
$$= \{L\{f'\} + f(0)\} + F(s).$$

Taking inverse transforms gives

$$y(t) = f'(t) + f(0)\delta(t) + f(t),$$

where $\delta(t)$ is the delta function. If $f(0) \neq 0$, then $y(t)$ cannot be a function in the usual sense. Rather, it is a generalized function (since it includes a δ function).

If $f(t) = t^{1/2}$, then $y = t^{1/2} + \frac{1}{2}t^{-1/2} = (2t+1)/2\sqrt{t}$ for $0 < t < \infty$. In this case $f'(t)$ is not defined when $t = 0$. The solution $y(t)$ is also not defined at $t = 0$. ∎

To solve (8.2), take Laplace transforms and rearrange to obtain

$$Y(s) + K(s)Y(s) = F(s)$$

or

$$Y(s) = \frac{F(s)}{1 + K(s)}.$$

If the inverse transform can be computed, then $y(t)$ is found.

EXAMPLE 8.3   Solve

$$y(t) + 2\int_0^t \cos(t-r)y(r)\, dr = 1.$$

Laplace transforming the equation yields

$$Y(s) + \frac{2s}{s^2+1}\, Y(s) = \frac{1}{s}$$

or

$$Y(s) = \frac{s^2+1}{s(s^2+2s+1)} = \frac{s^2+1}{(s+1)^2 s} = \frac{1}{s} - \frac{2}{(s+1)^2}.$$

Hence

$$y(t) = 1 - 2te^{-t}. \quad \blacksquare$$

EXAMPLE 8.4   Solve for $w(t)$ in

$$w(t) = 1 - \int_0^t \frac{1}{\sqrt{t-r}} w(r) \, dr, \qquad 0 \le t < \infty.$$

In this case, since $\Gamma(\frac{1}{2}) = \sqrt{\pi}$,

$$W(s) = \frac{1}{s} - \frac{\sqrt{\pi}}{\sqrt{s}} W(s).$$

A little algebra shows that

$$W(s) = \left(1 + \frac{\sqrt{\pi}}{\sqrt{s}}\right)^{-1} \frac{1}{s} = \frac{\sqrt{s}}{(\sqrt{s} + \sqrt{\pi})s} = \frac{1}{\sqrt{s}(\sqrt{s} + \sqrt{\pi})}$$

$$= \frac{\sqrt{s} - \sqrt{\pi}}{\sqrt{s}(s - \pi)} = \frac{1}{s - \pi}\left(1 - \frac{\sqrt{\pi}}{\sqrt{s}}\right).$$

The inverse Laplace transform of $W(s)$ is

$$(8.4) \qquad\qquad w(t) = e^{\pi t} - e^{\pi t} * \frac{1}{\sqrt{t}}$$

$$= e^{\pi t} - \int_0^t e^{\pi(t-r)} r^{-1/2} \, dr.$$

Under the change of variables $\pi r = u^2$ the last integral (8.4) can be written as

$$e^{\pi t} \int_0^t e^{-\pi r} r^{-1/2} \, dr = e^{\pi t} \int_0^{\sqrt{\pi t}} e^{-u^2} \frac{2}{\sqrt{\pi}} \, du.$$

Hence

$$w(t) = e^{\pi t}\left(1 - \frac{2}{\sqrt{\pi}} \int_0^{\sqrt{\pi t}} e^{-u^2} \, du\right)$$

or

$$w(t) = e^{\pi t}(1 - \text{erf}(\sqrt{\pi t})) = e^{\pi t} \, \text{erfc}(\sqrt{\pi t})$$

where erf is the error function and erfc is the complementary error function. $\blacksquare$

Integral equations of the form (8.2) occur in a variety of situations involving renewal. As an example we shall consider a simple economics model involving renewal of an investment and a depreciation policy. Such models have recently been of interest to the U.S. Agency for International Development and to some underdeveloped countries. Many simplifying assumptions are used. All goods, be they consumer goods or services, natural resources, investment or capital goods, or the service of labor, are lumped together and are viewed as consisting of a single homogeneous physical unit. Consumers are assumed to have a fixed propensity to save; that is, they save a fixed portion $S(0 < S < 1)$ of their disposable income. Business savings are assumed to occur in the form of a depreciation policy.

A *project* is a nonnegative function $a(t)$ where $a(t - r)$ is the rate of return at time t of a unit investment at time r. It is assumed that a fixed project has been chosen and that all savings are immediately reinvested in the same project (i.e., the project is *continually renewed*). The depreciation policy is specified by nonnegative function $d(t)$, where $d(t - r)$ is the rate of business reinvestment at time t from a project started at time r.

The gross national product $x(t)$ at time t is the sum of all returns from investments $v(r)$ made between time zero and time t in accordance with the project $a(t)$ plus a term $b(t)$ that will account for external sources of income (e.g., returns on investment that were made before time zero). Thus

$$(8.5) \qquad x(t) = \int_0^t a(t - r)v(r)\, dr + b(t).$$

Similarly, the total business savings up to time t is

$$(8.6) \qquad u(t) = \int_0^t d(t - r)v(r)\, dr + c(t),$$

where $c(t)$ is a term that accounts for all external sources of savings. The net natural product (or disposable income) is gross national product minus savings, that is,

$$(8.7) \qquad y(t) = x(t) - u(t).$$

Consumer savings is $Sy(t)$. Hence total investment at time t is

$$(8.8) \qquad v(t) = u(t) + Sy(t).$$

Equations (8.5)–(8.8) are four equations for the four unknown functions $x(t)$, $y(t)$, $u(t)$, and $v(t)$. The quantity of most interest is $y(t)$. The four equations can be reduced to one equation of type (8.2) for $y(t)$ as follows. From (8.7) we see that

$$y - d * y = (x - u) - d * (x - u).$$

Now use (8.5) and (8.6) to compute

$$y - d * y = (a * v + b) - (d * v + c) - d * (a * v + b - d * v - c)$$

or

$$(8.9) \quad y - d * y = (a - d) * (v - d * v) + b - c - d * (b - c).$$

From (8.6) and (8.8) we see that

$$v - d * v = v - (u - c) = (v - u) + c = Sy + c.$$

This and (8.9) give

$$y - d * y = (a - d) * (Sy + c) + b - c - d * b + d * c,$$

which is easily rearranged to see that

$$y = (Sa + (1 - S)d) * y + (b - c + a * c - b * d).$$

Hence

(8.10)

$$y(t) = \int_0^t [Sa(t - r) + (1 - S) d(t - r)]y(r) \, dr + f(t),$$

$$f(t) = b(t) - c(t) + \int_0^t [a(t - r)c(r) - b(t - r) d(r)] \, dr.$$

Since the income stream $y(t)$ solves (8.10), clearly it depends on the project $a(t)$ and the depreciation policy $d(t)$. In a given situation S and $f(t)$ are apparently fixed, while $a(t)$ and $d(t)$ can be chosen to maximize the value of the income stream. A common method of assigning a value to the income stream $y(t)$ is to use the **present** or **discounted value** (see Problems 14–16 of Section 6.1). Given an agreed-upon interest rate I, the **present value** of $y(t)$ is

(8.11)
$$Y(I) = \int_0^\infty e^{-It}y(t) \, dt.$$

This value takes into account the time value of the commodity. Income that will be received in the future is given a lower value than the same amount of goods to be received immediately.

Since the present value of $y(t)$ given in (8.10) is just the Laplace transform of $y(t)$ at the value $s = I$, this value can be computed from (8.10) *without first solving* (8.10) *for* $y(t)$. Indeed, from (8.10),

$$Y(I) = [SA(I) + (1 - S)D(I)]Y(I) + F(I)$$

or

(8.12)
$$Y(I) = [1 - SA(I) - (1 - S)D(I)]^{-1}F(I).$$

Different policies $a(t)$ and $d(t)$ can be compared by computing the corresponding $Y(I)$ using (8.12). Those policies are better that produce larger values of $Y(I)$.

PROBLEMS

In Problems 1–13, solve using Laplace transforms. In some problems the solution may be a generalized function.

1. $\int_0^t e^{2(t-r)}y(r) \, dr = t.$

2. $\int_0^t \frac{1}{\sqrt{t-r}} y(r) \, dr = t^2.$

3. $\int_0^t \sin 2(t - r)y(r) \, dr = t - \sin t.$

4. $\int_0^t \sin 2(t - r)y(r) \, dr = \sin t.$

5. $\int_0^t (t - r)^{1/3} y(r) \, dr = t^{3/2}.$

6. $\int_0^t (t - r)^{3/2} y(r) \, dr = t^{3/2}.$

7. $\int_0^t (t - r)^{3/2} y(r) \, dr = t^{1/2}.$ Hint: $L\{\delta'\} = s.$

8. $\int_0^t (t - r)^{5/2} y(r) \, dr = t^{1/2}.$

9. $\int_0^t \sin \pi(t - r)y(r) \, dr = 1.$

10. $\int_0^t e^{t-r} \sin 2(t - r)y(r) \, dr = t^3.$

11. $\int_0^t e^{-2(t-r)}(t - r)^{-1/2} y(r) \, dr = 1.$

12. $\int_0^t (t - r)^{-1/2} y(r) \, dr = \cos t.$ **13.** $\int_0^t \sin (t - r) y(r) \, dr = t J_0(t).$

In Problems 14–20, solve using Laplace transforms.

14. $y(t) + 2 \int_0^t \cos (t - r) y(r) \, dr = t.$ **15.** $y(t) + \int_0^t 2 \cos (t - r) y(r) \, dr = \sin 2t.$

16. $y(t) + \int_0^t 7 \sin [3(t - r)] y(r) \, dr = 1.$ **17.** $y(t) - \int_0^t \sin (t - r) y(r) \, dr = \sin t.$

18. $y(t) - 2 \int_0^t \cos (t - r) y(r) \, dr = 1.$ **19.** $y(t) - 2 \int_0^t \cos (t - r) y(r) \, dr = t e^t.$

20. $y(t) + 4 \int_0^t \dfrac{1}{\sqrt{t - r}} \, y(r) \, dr = 1.$

21. Show that if $g(t, r)$ and $\partial g(t, r)/\partial t$ are continuous, then

$$\frac{d}{dt} \left(\int_0^t g(t, r) \, dr \right) = g(t, t) + \int_0^t \frac{\partial g}{\partial t} (t, s) \, ds.$$

22. (a) Show that if $y(t)$ is the solution of Problem 14, then

$$y'(t) + 2y(t) - 2 \int_0^t \sin (t - r) y(r) \, dr = 1.$$

   Use Problem 21.

   (b) Show that $y'' + 2y' + y = t$, $y(0) = 0$, and $y'(0) = 1$.

   (c) Is the solution of this initial value problem the same as the solution of the integral equation?

23. Suppose that $k(t)$ and $f(t)$ are continuously differentiable and $f(0) = 0$.

   (a) If $y(t)$ is a continuous solution of

$$\int_0^t k(t - r) y(r) \, dr = f(t),$$

   use Problem 21 to show that

$$k(0) y(t) + \int_0^t k'(t - r) y(r) \, dr = f'(t).$$

   (b) Show that if a continuous function $f(t)$ satisfies $f(0) = 0$ and $y(t)$ solves the second integral equation, then it must solve the first one.

24. For the delta function we define $\delta * \delta = \delta$.

   (a) Show that for any continuous functions f_1 and f_2 and any constants c_1 and c_2,

$$(c_1 \delta + f_1) * (c_2 \delta + f_2) = c_1 c_2 + c_1 f_2 + c_2 f_1 + f_1 * f_2.$$

   (b) Show that if $s(t)$ solves the equation

$$s(t) + \int_0^t k(t - r) s(r) \, dr = -k(t),$$

   then $(\delta + s) * (\delta + k) = (\delta + k) * (\delta + s) = \delta$.

   (c) Show that if $y(t)$ is a continuous solution of

$$y(t) + \int_0^t k(t - r) y(r) \, dr = f(t),$$

   and if $s(t)$ is given as in part (b), then $y = (\delta + s) * f$ is the solution.

25. Suppose that in (8.10) one has $f(t) = e^{-a_1 t}$, $d(t) = a_2 e^{-a_2 t}$, and $a(t) = e^{-a_3 t}$, where $a_1 > 0$, $a_2 > 0$, and $0 < a_3 < 1$.

(a) Compute the present value $Y(I)$.

(b) Is $Y(I)$ an increasing function of a_2?

(c) Is $Y(I)$ an increasing function of a_3?

26. Use Laplace transforms to solve for $y(t)$ in

$$y'(t) = y(t) + 4 \int_0^t e^{-2(t-r)} y(r)\, dr, \qquad y(0) = 1.$$

27. Compute the present value of $y(t)$ at interest rate I.

(a) $y(t) = \int_0^t [0.05(t - r)^{-1/2} + 0.95 e^{-(t-r)}] y(r)\, dr + 2e^{-2t}$.

(b) $y'(t) - 3y(t) = \int_0^t \log(t - r) y(r)\, dr,\ y(0) = 1$.

(c) $y''(t) = \int_0^t J_0(2(t - r)) y(s)\, ds,\ y(0) = 0,\ y'(0) = 1$.

TABLE OF LAPLACE TRANSFORMS

Function	Transform	Section
1	$\dfrac{1}{s}$	6.1
e^{at}	$\dfrac{1}{s - a}$	6.1
$u_c(t)$	$\dfrac{e^{-cs}}{s}$	6.1
t^n	$\dfrac{n!}{s^{n+1}}$	6.1
$\dfrac{\sin at}{t}$	$\arctan\left(\dfrac{a}{s}\right)$	6.1
$t^{-1/2}$	$\dfrac{\sqrt{\pi}}{\sqrt{s}}\quad (\sqrt{\pi} = 1.7724538509\ldots)$	6.1
$t^v\ (v > -1)$	$\dfrac{\Gamma(v + 1)}{s^{v+1}}$	6.1
$\sinh at$	$\dfrac{a}{s^2 - a^2}$	6.1
$\cosh at$	$\dfrac{s}{s^2 - a^2}$	6.1

TABLE OF LAPLACE TRANSFORMS *(continued)*

Function	Transform	Section
$t^n e^{at}$	$\dfrac{n!}{(s-a)^{n+1}}$	6.1
$\log t$	$\dfrac{-\gamma - \log s}{s}$ $(\gamma = 0.5772156\ldots)$	6.1
$t^v \log t \ (v > -1)$	$\dfrac{\Gamma'(v+1) - \log s\,\Gamma(v+1)}{s^{v+1}}$	6.1
$\sin bt$	$\dfrac{b}{s^2 + b^2}$	6.2
$\cos bt$	$\dfrac{s}{s^2 + b^2}$	6.2
$e^{at} \sin bt$	$\dfrac{b}{(s-a)^2 + b^2}$	6.2
$e^{at} \cos bt$	$\dfrac{s-a}{(s-a)^2 + b^2}$	6.2
$Si(t) = \displaystyle\int_0^t \dfrac{\sin r}{r}\,dr$	$\dfrac{1}{s} \arctan\left(\dfrac{1}{s}\right)$	6.2
$J_0(at)$	$\dfrac{1}{\sqrt{s^2 + a^2}}$	6.2 and 6.3
$\text{erf}\,(t)$	$\dfrac{1}{s} e^{s^2/4} \text{erf}\left(\dfrac{s}{2}\right)$	6.2
$\text{erf}\,(\sqrt{t})$	$\dfrac{1}{s\sqrt{s+1}}$	6.2
$\delta(t - c)$	e^{-cs}	6.4
$c_1 f_1(t) + c_2 f_2(t)$	$c_1 F_1(s) + c_2 F_2(s)$	6.1
$(-t)^n f(t)$	$\dfrac{d^n}{ds^n} F(s)$	6.1
$\dfrac{f(t)}{t}$	$\displaystyle\int_s^\infty F(r)\,dr$	6.1
$e^{at} f(t)$	$F(s-a)$	6.2
$f''(t)$	$s^2 F(s) - sf(0) - f'(0)$	6.2
$f^{(n)}(t)$	$s^n F(s) - s^{n-1} f(0) - \ldots - f^{(n-1)}(0)$	6.2
$\displaystyle\int_0^t f(r)\,dr$	$\dfrac{1}{s} F(s)$	6.2

TABLE OF LAPLACE TRANSFORMS *(concluded)*

Function	Transform	Section
$f(t) = f(t + p)$	$\dfrac{\int_0^p e^{-st}f(t)\,dt}{1 - e^{-sp}}$	6.2
$f(t) = \sum\limits_{n=0}^{\infty} a_n t^n$	$F(s) = \sum\limits_{n=0}^{\infty} \dfrac{a_n n!}{s^{n+1}}$	6.2
f real valued	$\overline{F(s)} = F(\bar{s})$	6.3
$u_c(t)f(t - c)$	$e^{-cs}F(s)$	6.4
$u_c(t)e^{b(t-c)}f(t - c)$	$e^{-cs}F(s - b)$	6.4
$f(at)$	$\dfrac{1}{a}F\left(\dfrac{s}{a}\right)$	6.4
$\dfrac{1}{a}e^{-bt/a}f\left(\dfrac{t}{a}\right)$	$F(as + b)$	6.4
$\int_0^t f(t - r)g(r)\,dr$	$F(s)G(s)$	6.6

CHAPTER REVIEW

The **Laplace transform** of a piecewise continuous function $f(t)$ is defined as the integral

$$L\{f\} = F(s) = \int_0^\infty e^{-st} f(t)\,dt.$$

If $|f(t)| \le M\,e^{at}$ for all large t (where $M > 0$ and a is any real number), then $F(s)$ will exist for all $s > a$. A table of Laplace transforms appears on page 340.
Given a linear differential equation with constant coefficients,

$$ay'' + by' + cy = g(t), \quad y(0) = a_0,\ y'(0) = a_1,$$

then $L\{y\} = Y(s)$ satisfies

$$a(s^2 Y(s) - sa_0 - a_1) + b(sY(s) - a_0) + cY(s) = G(s).$$

One can solve for $Y(s)$ in the last equation and then evaluate $y(t) = L^{-1}\{Y(s)\}$. Integral equations of convolution type can be solved by a similar procedure.

CHAPTER REVIEW PROBLEMS

Solve for $y(t)$ in Problems 1–5.

1. $y'' + y = \delta(t - 2), \quad y(0) = y'(0) = 0.$

2. $y'' + 2y = 2u_1(t), \quad y(0) = y'(0) = 0.$

3. $y'' + y' - 12y = e^t, \quad y(0) = 1, \quad y'(0) = -1.$

4. $y'' + 2y' + 10y = \delta(t), \quad y(0) = 0, \quad y'(0) = 1.$

5. $y'' - 4y' + 4y = e^{2t}$, $\quad y(0) = y'(0) = 0$.

6. Compute the Laplace transform of $y(t)$ when

$$ty'' + 2y' + ty = 0, \qquad y(0) = 1, \qquad y'(0) = 1.$$

Compute $L\{y\}$ in Problems 7–9.

7. $y(t) = \begin{cases} 1 & \text{if } 0 \le t < 1 \\ -1 & \text{if } 1 \le t < \infty. \end{cases}$

8. $y(t) = \begin{cases} 0 & \text{if } 0 \le t < 2 \\ t & \text{if } 2 \le t < \infty. \end{cases}$

9. $y(t) + \int_0^t (t - s)^3 y(s)\, ds = \sin 2t$.

CHAPTER SEVEN

Systems of Linear Equations

Chapter 7 contains a study of systems of differential equations and their applications. The chapter starts with a general introduction. Then basic matrix theory and the theory of determinates are reviewed in detail. Eigenvalues and eigenvectors of a matrix are introduced and discussed. The matrix notation is needed to discuss systems problems and to talk about the structure of their solutions. The eigenvalue–eigenvector results are used to solve linear first-order systems of differential equations with constant coefficients. The cases of simple real, simple complex, and multiple (real or complex) eigenvalues are considered separately. Solutions methods for nonhomogeneous (or forced) systems are studied in two ways, first using the variation of constants formula and then using Laplace transforms.

7.1   *INTRODUCTION*

In this chapter we study systems of linear differential equations and their solutions. Such systems consist of two or more simultaneous differential equations in two or more unknowns. An example of such a system is

(1.1)
$$x' = 5x - 2y + 5t + 3$$
$$y' = 4x - y + 4t + 2.$$

These two equations must be solved simultaneously for the unknown functions $x(t)$ and $y(t)$ since each equation contains both of the unknowns.

By a system of n **first-order linear differential equations** we mean a set of n simultaneous equations of the form

$$x_1' = a_{11}(t)x_1 + a_{12}(t)x_2 + \ldots + a_{1n}(t)x_n + g_1(t)$$

$$x_2' = a_{21}(t)x_1 + a_{22}(t)x_2 + \ldots + a_{2n}(t)x_n + g_2(t)$$

(E)

$$\vdots$$

$$x_n' = a_{n1}(t)x_1 + a_{n2}(t)x_2 + \ldots + a_{nn}(t)x_n + g_n(t).$$

The functions $a_{ij}(t)$ and $g_k(t)$ are known functions while $x_1(t), x_2(t), \ldots, x_n(t)$ are the unknowns. The functions $a_{ij}(t)$ are called the **coefficients** of the linear system (E). We say that system (E) has **constant coefficients** when each $a_{ij}(t)$ is a constant function. The terms $g_k(t)$ are called **forcing terms**. (E) is called **homogeneous** when $g_k(t)$ is zero for all $k = 1, 2, \ldots, n$. (E) is called **nonhomogeneous** (or forced) if at least one $g_k(t)$ is not zero.

System (1.1) can be put in the form (E) as follows. Set $x_1 = x$ and $x_2 = y$ in (1.1) so that

(1.2)

$$x_1' = 5x_1 - 2x_2 + (5t + 3)$$

$$x_2' = 4x_1 - x_2 + (4t + 2).$$

This is a system of two equations in two unknowns. This system is nonhomogeneous and has constant coefficients. The system

(1.3)

$$x_1' = (3t)x_1 - x_2$$

$$x_2' = -4x_1 + (\log t)x_2,$$

with $t > 0$, is homogeneous and has variable coefficients.

Initial conditions for (E) have the form

(IC) $x_1(t_0) = b_1, \quad x_2(t_0) = b_2, \quad \ldots, \quad x_n(t_0) = b_n$

where $t_0, b_1, b_2, \ldots, b_n$ are given real numbers. The basic existence and uniqueness theorem for (E) can be stated as follows.

THEOREM 1.1: EXISTENCE AND UNIQUENESS

Suppose that $a_{ij}(t)$ and $g_k(t)$ are given real-valued, continuous functions on an open interval $J = (a, b)$. Then for any t_0 in J and for any real numbers $b_1, b_2, \ldots, b_n$ there is one and only one set of functions $\{x_1(t), x_2(t), \ldots, x_n(t)\}$ that solves (E) and also satisfies (IC). The functions $x_1(t), \ldots, x_n(t)$ are defined for all t in J and solve (E) over the entire interval J.

If no initial conditions are given, we shall usually seek a general solution of system (E). A general solution contains n arbitrary constants. Given any initial condition (IC), these constants can be specified in such a way that (IC) is true.

For example, in (1.2) the coefficients and the forcing terms are all defined and continuous over any interval J. We shall use $J = (-\infty, \infty)$ since this is the largest possible interval. Hence for any given initial conditions

$$(1.4) \qquad x_1(t_0) = b_1, \qquad x_2(t_0) = b_2,$$

there is exactly one solution of (1.2) that also satisfies the initial conditions (1.4). This solution is defined for all t on the real line. The pair of functions

$$(1.5) \qquad \begin{aligned} x_1(t) &= c_1 e^{3t} + c_2 e^t - t \\ x_2(t) &= c_1 e^{3t} + 2c_2 e^t + 2 \end{aligned}$$

is a solution of (1.2). To check the first equation, compute

$$x_1' = 3c_1 e^{3t} + c_2 e^t - 1$$

and

$$5x_1 - 2x_2 + 5t + 3 = 5(c_1 e^{3t} + c_2 e^t - t) - 2(c_1 e^{3t} + 2c_2 e^t + 2) + 5t + 3$$
$$= 3c_1 e^{3t} + c_2 e^t - 1 = x_1'.$$

A similar computation verifies that the second equation in (1.2) is also true. Hence (1.5) is a solution of (1.2) that contains two arbitrary constants c_1 and c_2. As we shall later see, it is a general solution. The constants c_1 and c_2 can be specified by giving an initial condition. For example, if we require that $x_1(0) = 1$ and $x_2(0) = -2$, these conditions can be used in (1.5) to see that

$$c_1 e^0 + c_2 e^0 - 0 = c_1 + c_2 = 1$$

and

$$c_1 e^0 + 2c_2 e^0 + 2 = c_1 + 2c_2 + 2 = -2.$$

Solving for c_1 and c_2 gives $c_1 = 6$, $c_2 = -5$.

In (1.3) the coefficient $a_{22}(t) = \log t$. This function is defined and continuous for $t > 0$ but is not defined for $t \le 0$. Hence, in order to apply Theorem 1.1 the interval J must be contained in $(0, \infty)$. We choose J to be the largest such interval, $J = (0, \infty)$. We can be sure that any solution of (1.3) will be defined over $0 < t < \infty$. Initial conditions for (1.3) have the form

$$x_1(t_0) = b_1, \qquad x_2(t_0) = b_2.$$

Here b_1 and b_2 can be any real numbers, while t_0 is any *positive* real number.

Systems of differential equations arise in a variety of situations. One of the first settings where they were applied were mechanics problems (Photo 17). Many such problems are nonlinear but can sometimes be approximated by linear ones. Other mechanics problems are linear. An example of a linear system is illustrated in Figure 7.1. This system contains two masses and three linear springs arranged as shown. Let y_i denote the displacement of the mass m_i from its equilibrium position with positive displacements measured to the right. The masses are subject to viscous frictional forces with coefficients B_1 and B_2 and are subject to external forces $f_1(t)$ and $f_2(t)$.

Photo 17. Full moon–half earth. (Courtesy of the National Aeronautics and Space Administration.)

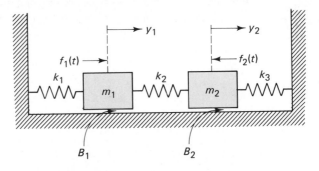

Figure 7.1. Two mass translational system.

By Newton's second law of motion it follows that $m_i y_i''$ equals the sum of the forces acting on the mass m_i. Hence

$$(1.6) \quad \begin{aligned} m_1 y_1'' &= -k_1 y_1 - k_2(y_1 - y_2) - B_1 y_1' + f_1(t) \\ m_2 y_2'' &= -k_2(y_2 - y_1) - k_3 y_2 - B_2 y_2' - f_2(t). \end{aligned}$$

The motion is completely specified if the initial displacements and initial velocities of the masses are known, that is, if

(1.7) $y_1(0) = y_{10},$ $y_1'(0) = v_{10},$ $y_2(0) = y_{20},$ $y_2'(0) = v_{20}$

are specified.

System (1.6) can be reduced to a system of first-order equations as follows. Let $v_1 = y_1'$ and $v_2 = y_2'$ be the velocities of the two masses. Hence

$$m_1 y_1'' = m_1 v_1' = -k_1 y_1 - k_2(y_1 - y_2) - B_1 v_1 + f_1(t)$$

and

$$m_2 y_2'' = m_1 v_2' = -k_2(y_2 - y_1) - k_3 y_2 - B_2 v_2 - f_2(t).$$

Hence four first-order equations that are equivalent to (1.6) are

(1.8)
$$y_1' = v_1,$$
$$v_1' = -\frac{1}{m_1}(k_1 + k_2)y_1 - \frac{B_1}{m_1}v_1 + \frac{k_2}{m_1}y_2 + \frac{1}{m_1}f_1(t),$$
$$y_2' = v_2,$$
$$v_2' = \frac{k_2}{m_2}y_1 - \frac{1}{m_2}(k_2 + k_3)y_2 - \frac{1}{m_2}B_2 v_2 - \frac{1}{m_2}f_2(t).$$

The two equations $y_1' = v_1$ and $y_2' = v_2$ are rather trivial. They are no more than definitions of the velocities v_1 and v_2. However, these two equations are necessary in order to replace (1.6) by four first-order linear equations.

System (1.8) has the form of (E) with $x_1 = y_1$, $x_2 = v_1$, $x_3 = y_2$, and $x_4 = v_2$. The initial conditions (1.7) have the form (IC) with $t_0 = 0$. System (1.8) has constant coefficients and is nonhomogeneous.

Linear equations of order $n > 1$ can always be reduced to systems of first-order equations by the simple device of giving derivatives new names. For example, given

(1.9) $y''' + 3y'' - 2ty' + y = \sin t,$

define $x_1 = y$, $x_2 = y'$, and $x_3 = y''$. Then

$$\frac{dx_1}{dt} = \frac{dy}{dt} = x_2,$$

$$\frac{dx_2}{dt} = \frac{d}{dt}(y') = y'' = x_3,$$

and

$$\frac{dx_3}{dt} = \frac{d}{dt}(y'') = y'''$$

$$= -3y'' + 2ty' - y + \sin t$$
$$= -3x_3 + 2tx_2 - x_1 + \sin t.$$

Hence an equivalent system is

$$x_1' = x_2$$

(1.10) $$x_2' = x_3$$

$$x_3' = -x_1 + 2tx_2 - 3x_3 + \sin t.$$

Initial conditions for (1.9) have the form

$$y(t_0) = b_1, \qquad y'(t_0) = b_2, \qquad y''(t_0) = b_3.$$

In the new notation these initial conditions become

(1.11) $$\qquad x_1(t_0) = b_1, \qquad x_2(t_0) = b_2, \qquad x_3(t_0) = b_3.$$

The pair (1.10) and (1.11) have the form of (E) and of (IC) with $n = 3$.

The technique used to reduce (1.9) to system (1.10) will work for any nth-order equation of the form $y^{(n)} = f(t, y, y', y'', \ldots, y^{(n-1)})$. Define $x_1 = y, x_2 = y', \ldots, x_n = y^{(n-1)}$. The resulting system of equations is

$$x_1' = x_2,$$

$$x_2' = x_3$$

$$\vdots$$

$$x_{n-1}' = x_n$$

$$x_n' = f(t, x_1, x_2, \ldots, x_n).$$

The technique of reducing an nth-order equation to a system of first-order equations is simple but rather important. All of the standard techniques for numerically solving a differential equation using a digital computer depend on first writing the equation as an equivalent system. Hence before numerically solving (1.9), it would first be necessary to rewrite it in the form (1.10). Similarly, equations (1.6) must be reduced to a system of first-order equations such as (1.8) before a numerical solution can be attempted. Students who will need to use computers to solve differential equations should be sure to master this technique.

Compartmentalized systems occur in a variety of applications. Scientists (and especially engineers) have studied such systems a great deal in recent years. Compartmental systems are systems that can be viewed as a set of compartments each of which contains material. This material can be transferred between the compartments, but no material is lost or consumed. We shall restrict attention to linear compartmental systems.

Figure 7.2 is a sketch of a compartmental system that contains four compartments. Material is transferred between compartments as indicated by the arrows. The rates of transfer are indicated by the constants λ_j. For example, compartment 1 loses material to compartments 2 and 3. It receives material from no compartment. Let $x_1(t)$ be the amount of material in compartment 1 at time t. Then according to Figure 7.2,

$$x_1' = -\lambda_1 x_1 - \lambda_2 x_1.$$

Compartment 2 receives material from compartment 1 at the rate $\lambda_1 x_1$. Compartment 2 loses material to compartment 4 at the rate $\lambda_3 x_2$. Hence

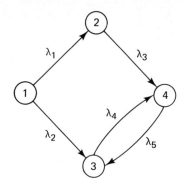

Figure 7.2. Four compartmental system.

$$x_2' = \lambda_1 x_1 - \lambda_3 x_2.$$

Similarly, $x_3' = \lambda_2 x_1 - \lambda_4 x_3 + \lambda_5 x_4$ and $x_4' = \lambda_3 x_2 + \lambda_4 x_3 - \lambda_5 x_4$. The complete system of equations is

(1.12)

$$x_1' = -\lambda_1 x_1 - \lambda_2 x_1$$

$$x_2' = \lambda_1 x_1 - \lambda_3 x_2$$

$$x_3' = \lambda_2 x_1 - \lambda_4 x_3 + \lambda_5 x_4$$

$$x_4' = \lambda_3 x_2 + \lambda_4 x_3 - \lambda_5 x_4.$$

Initial conditions are $x_i(0) = b_i$ for $i = 1, 2, 3, 4$. Normally, the constants b_i are nonnegative for physical reasons. It can then be shown that the solution terms $x_i(t)$ will also be nonnegative.

A particularly interesting and important example of a compartmental system arises in the study of carcinogenesis (i.e., the development of cancer). Authorities believe that carcinogenesis involves the processes of *transformation* and *growth*. Cells are divided into two groups (or compartments): normal cells and transformed cells. Transformation occurs when a normal cell is changed in such a way that it can generate a tumor. Through cell division this transformed cell becomes a colony or *clone*. When a clone becomes sufficiently large it is a detectable tumor.

Carcinogenesis can be initiated, for example, by exposure of normal cells to certain chemicals or to radiation such as x-rays, ultraviolet light, or radiation produced by radioactive materials. Realistic mathematical theories of carcinogenesis would be very useful in the determination of acceptable environmental concentrations of carcinogens and the estimation of the consequences of exceeding these acceptable concentrations. Direct tests on human beings are considered unethical or even immoral. Moreover, there are many scientific problems associated with human testing. For example, at low environmental doses of possible carcinogens large numbers of people would be needed in order to obtain meaningful results. These huge numbers of people would have to be followed for very long periods of time, often 20 to 40 years. In addition, these large numbers of people would have to be carefully environmentally controlled with nearly impossible precision. (Consider, for example, the problem of how many thousands of people could avoid unknown exposure to asbestos insulation in their work environments!)

Because of the many problems involved in human testing, scientists normally use controlled laboratory tests on small animals such as mice or rats. Such laboratory testing also has certain associated problems. For one thing, such testing is expensive. Hence in a given test, at most a few hundred lab animals are used. If a carcinogen at low environmental levels will cause, say, between 50 and 100 cancers per 100,000 population, then clearly no reliable results can be obtained with a few hundred lab animals unless large doses of the carcinogen are used. Moreover, there are occasional interspecific differences in chemistry. For example, arsenic compounds cause cancer in lab animals but do not seem to cause human cancer. There may occasionally be chemicals that cause human cancer but do not affect lab animals. Even for known carcinogens downsizing from large doses for laboratory mice to low-level doses for human beings is largely a matter of guesswork rather than science. A better theoretical understanding of carcinogenesis should give scientists a better understanding of the mechanisms of carcinogenesis and prove helpful in estimating the consequences to various species of low-level doses.

N. Arley and S. Ivensen were pioneers in the mathematical theory of carcinogenesis. Their theory can be described as follows. Let $p_n(t)$ be the probability that a cell is normal at time t, let $p_T(t)$ be the probability that a cell transforms at time t, and let λ be the probability rate of transition. Then

$$(1.13) \qquad \begin{aligned} p'_n &= -\lambda p_n, & p_n(0) &= 1 \\ p'_T &= \lambda p_n, & p_T(0) &= 0. \end{aligned}$$

It is assumed that $\lambda = \lambda_s + kc$, where $\lambda_s \geq 0$ is the spontaneous transition probability, $k > 0$ is a constant, and c is the concentration of the carcinogen in the cell's environment. (In general, c may depend on time. We shall deal here only with the case where c is constant.) System (1.13) is easily solved to obtain

$$p_n(t) = e^{-\lambda t}, \qquad p_T(t) = 1 - e^{-\lambda t}.$$

The Ivensen–Arley model seems to be too simple to be of much use in explaining human carcinogenesis. Other researchers have proposed more complicated systems, with two or more transitions necessary to change a normal cell into a clone progenitor. They also assume that normal and transformed cells may die. Such a two-stage model is sketched in Figure 7.3. There are four compartments. The first is normal cells. The second contains cells that have suffered one transition. The third contains cells that have suffered two transitions and are cancer progenitors. The fourth compartment contains the dead cells. The corresponding system of differential equations is

$$(1.14) \qquad \begin{aligned} p'_1 &= -\lambda_1 p_1 - \mu_1 p_1, & p_1(0) &= 1, \\ p'_2 &= \lambda_1 p_1 - \lambda_2 p_2 - \mu_2 p_2, & p_2(0) &= 0, \\ p'_3 &= \lambda_2 p_2 - \mu_3 p_3, & p_3(0) &= 0, \\ p'_4 &= \mu_1 p_1 + \mu_2 p_2 + \mu_3 p_3, & p_4(0) &= 0. \end{aligned}$$

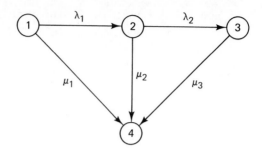

Figure 7.3. Two-stage carcinogenesis model.

In a similar manner one can develop three-stage, four-stage, or n-stage models. All of these models provide examples of interesting and potentially useful systems of linear differential equations.

PROBLEMS

In Problems 1–5, reduce the given initial value problem to an equivalent initial value problem for a first-order system.

1. $y'' + 3y' - y = t$, $y(0) = 1$, $y'(0) = -2$.

2. $z''' - 3z'' + 2z' - z = \sin t$, $z(0) = 1$, $z'(0) = 0$, $z''(0) = 3$.

3. $z^{(4)} = z$, $z(0) = 1$, $z'(0) = 0$, $z''(0) = -2$, $z'''(0) = \pi$.

4. $z'' = z + y$, $z(0) = 1$, $z'(0) = 0$.
    $y'' = 2z - y'$, $y(0) = -1$, $y'(0) = 3$.

5. $z' = 4z + 5x - x'$, $z(0) = 1$.
    $x''' + 4x' - x + z = x'' + \cos t$, $x(0) = x'(0) = 0$, $x''(0) = 2$.

6. Find the solution of (1.2) that satisfies the following initial conditions. Use the solution (1.5).

(a) $x_1(0) = -1$, $x_2(0) = -2$.

(b) $x_1(0) = 1$, $x_2(0) = -1$.

(c) $x_1(2) = 1$, $x_2(2) = -1$.

7. Find a general solution of $x_1' = x_2$, $x_2' = -4x_1 + t$. *Hint:* $x_1'' = x_2' = -4x_1 + t$.

8. Find a general solution of $x_1' = 2x_2$, $x_2' = -2x_1 + 3$. *Hint:* Compute x_1''.

9. In (1.6) the momentum of the ith mass is $p_i = m_i y_i'$ for $i = 1, 2$. Reduce (1.6) to an equivalent first-order system of equations in the four unknowns y_1, p_1, y_2, and p_2.

10. In (1.9) let $z_1 = y$, $z_2 = 3y'$, and $z_3 = 9y''$. Reduce (1.9) to an equivalent system of three first-order equations in the unknowns z_1, z_2, and z_3. (This transformation has the effect of scaling the derivatives of y. This trick is sometimes useful when solving differential equations numerically on a computer.)

11. For the equation $y^{(n)} = f(t, y, y', \ldots, y^{(n-1)})$, let $S > 0$ be a fixed real number and let $x_j = S^{j-1} y^{(j-1)}$ for $j = 1, 2, \ldots, n$. Reduce the given differential equation to a first-order system of equations in the unknowns x_j, $1 \leq j \leq n$.

12. Consider the differential equation

$$\sum_{i=0}^{n} a_i y^{(i)} = \sum_{i=0}^{n} b_i u^{(i)},$$

where $a_n > 0$, the a_i and b_i are real numbers, and $u(t)$ is a known function. Define

$$x_1 = a_n y - b_n u$$

$$x_2 = a_{n-1} y - b_{n-1} u + x_1'$$

$$x_3 = a_{n-2} y - b_{n-2} u + x_2'$$

$$\vdots$$

$$x_n = a_1 y - b_1 u + x_{n-1}'.$$

(a) Compute x_1' from the given expression and substitute in the expression for x_2. Next compute x_2' and substitute into the expression for x_3. Continue this process to show that

$$x_n' = \sum_{i=1}^{n} [a_i y^{(i)} - b_i u^{(i)}].$$

(b) Show that $x_n' = b_0 u - a_0 y$.

(c) Write the differential equation as an equivalent first-order system in the unknowns $x_1, x_2, \ldots, x_n$.

(d) Determine constants α_i such that $y = \sum_{i=1}^{n} \alpha_i x_i + \alpha_{n+1} u$.

13. (a) Given the mechanical system depicted Figure 7.4, write a system of three second-order equations in the unknowns y_1, y_2, and y_3 which describe the motion of the masses.

(b) Write an equivalent first-order system in terms of the positions and velocities of the masses.

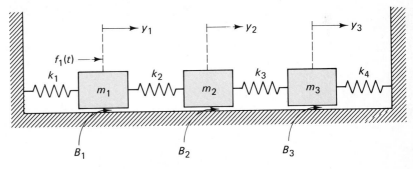

Figure 7.4. Three-mass translational system.

14. The law of mass action and its use in chemical kinetics was discussed in Chapter 2. Reread this material from Chapter 2 and then write differential equations for each reaction.

(a) $X \underset{k_{-1}}{\overset{k_1}{\rightleftharpoons}} Y \overset{k_2}{\longrightarrow} Z.$

(b) $X \underset{k_{-1}}{\overset{k_1}{\rightleftharpoons}} Y \underset{k_{-2}}{\overset{k_2}{\rightleftharpoons}} Z.$

(c) $X \underset{k_{-1}}{\overset{k_1}{\rightleftharpoons}} Y \overset{k_2}{\longrightarrow} Z \overset{k_3}{\longrightarrow} X.$

(d) $X \underset{k_{-1}}{\overset{k_1}{\rightleftharpoons}} Y \underset{k_{-2}}{\overset{k_2}{\rightleftharpoons}} Z \underset{k_{-3}}{\overset{k_3}{\rightleftharpoons}} X.$

In all cases the system is assumed to be closed and well stirred. All important parameters such as temperature or pressure are assumed to be held constant.

15. In Problem 14, the system of equations that describes the chemical kinetics will satisfy a conservation law. For example, in part (a) the sum of the concentrations of X, Y, and Z is constant (i.e., $x + y + z = c$). Determine the appropriate conservation law for the reactions in Problem 14, parts (b)–(d).

16. In (1.12) suppose that $x_i(0) = x_{i0} \geq 0$ for $i = 1, 2, 3, 4$. Let $c = x_1(0) + x_2(0) + x_3(0) + x_4(0)$. Show that for these initial conditions the solution satisfies

$$x_1(t) + x_2(t) + x_3(t) + x_4(t) = c$$

for all real numbers t.

17. Consider the linear compartmental system sketched in Figure 7.5. Write a system of differential equations that describe the time behavior of this system. Show that the conservation law $x_1(t) + x_2(t) + x_3(t) + x_4(t) = c$ is true for any solution of this first-order system of differential equations.

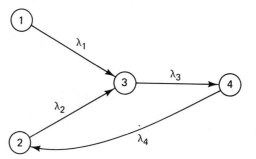

Figure 7.5. Compartmentalized system.

18. Given the linear compartmentalized system sketched in Figure 7.6, write a system of first-order differential equations that describe the time behavior of this system. Find a suitable conservation law for this system.

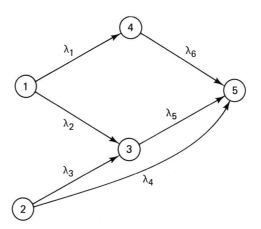

Figure 7.6. Compartmentalized system.

19. In system (1.13) show that $p_n(t) + p_T(t) = 1$ for all real numbers t.

20. Solve (1.13) when

$$c(t) = \begin{cases} c_0 & \text{for } 0 \leq t \leq t_1 \\ 0 & \text{for } t \geq t_1. \end{cases}$$

21. Solve (1.13) when $c(t) = c_0 e^{-\mu t}$ and $\mu > 0$.

22. Show that any solution of (1.14) satisfies the conservation law $p_1(t) + p_2(t) + p_3(t) + p_4(t) = 1$ for all real numbers t.

23. Consider the three-stage carcinogenesis model depicted in Figure 7.7. Here compartment 1 is normal cells and compartment 5 is dead cells. Write out the system of first-order linear differential equations that describe this three-stage model.

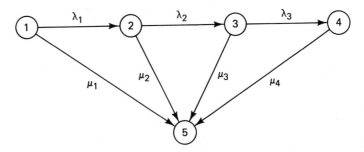

Figure 7.7. Three-stage carcinogenesis model.

24. A two-car train ascending a grade of angle $\theta > 0$ is sketched in Figure 7.8. The locomotive with mass m_l produces a force u in the forward direction. The cars each have mass m_c. The couplings between cars are modeled as a linear spring of stiffness k plus a viscous damper with damping coefficient B. Air resistance is assumed to produce viscous friction with damping coefficient B_c for each car and B_l for the locomotive.

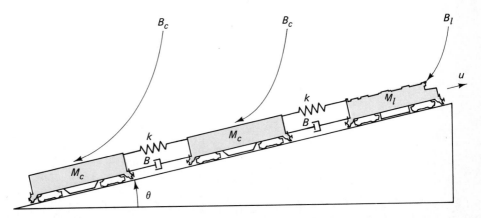

Figure 7.8. Two-car train uphill.

(a) Use Newton's second law in order to write three second-order differential equations that describe the behavior of the two cars and the locomotive.

(b) Write these three equations as an equivalent system of six first-order equations whose unknowns are the positions and velocities of the three masses.

(c) Suppose that another identical car is added to the train. Find a system of eight first-order differential equations that describe the motion.

7.2   ELIMINATION

In Section 7.1 it was shown that any nth-order linear equation can be written as an equivalent system of n first-order linear equations. Conversely, most systems of n first-order linear equations with smooth coefficients can be reduced to an equivalent nth-order equation. This fact can be used to find solutions of some systems.

For simplicity, only systems of two equations with constant coefficients will be considered, that is, systems of the form

$$x_1' = a_{11}x_1 + a_{12}x_2 + g_1(t)$$
$$x_2' = a_{21}x_1 + a_{22}x_2 + g_2(t). \tag{2.1}$$

Differentiating the first equation in (2.1) gives

$$x_1'' = a_{11}x_1' + a_{12}x_2' + g_1'(t).$$

This and the second equation in (2.1) give

$$\tag{2.2} x_1'' = a_{11}x_1' + a_{12}[a_{21}x_1 + a_{22}x_2 + g_2(t)] + g_1'(t).$$

From the first equation in (2.1) it follows that

$$a_{12}x_2 = [x_1' - a_{11}x_1 - g_1(t)].$$

This can be used in (2.2) to see that

$$x_1'' = a_{11}x_1' + a_{12}a_{21}x_1 + a_{22}[x_1' - a_{11}x_1 - g_1(t)] + a_{12}g_2(t) + g_1'(t)$$

or

$$\tag{2.3} x_1'' = (a_{11} + a_{22})x_1' + (a_{12}a_{21} - a_{11}a_{22})x_1 + [a_{12}g_2(t) - a_{22}g_1(t) + g_1'(t)]$$

Since (2.3) is linear with constant coefficients, it can be solved by the methods of Chapter 3 or Chapter 6.

EXAMPLE 2.1   Solve

$$x_1' = 5x_1 - 2x_2$$
$$x_2' = 4x_1 - x_2.$$

From the first equation we find

$$x_1'' = 5x_1' - 2x_2'.$$

Now use the second equation to substitute for x_2', that is,

$$x_1'' = 5x_1' - 2[4x_1 - x_2]$$
$$= 5x_1' - 8x_1 + 2x_2.$$

From the first equation it follows that $2x_2 = 5x_1 - x_1'$. Hence

$$x_1'' = 5x_1' - 8x_1 + [5x_1 - x_1']$$

or

$$x_1'' - 4x_1' + 3x_1 = 0.$$

This equation has the solution

(2.4) $$x_1 = c_1 e^{3t} + c_2 e^t.$$

Since

$$x_1' = 3c_1 e^{3t} + c_2 e^t$$

and since $x_2 = (5x_1 - x_1')/2$, then

$$x_2 = \tfrac{5}{2}[c_1 e^{3t} + c_2 e^t] - \tfrac{1}{2}[3c_1 e^{3t} + c_2 e^t]$$

or

(2.5) $$x_2 = c_1 e^{3t} + 2c_2 e^t.$$

Since c_1 and c_2 are arbitrary, (2.4) and (2.5) constitute a general solution of the first-order system. ■

EXAMPLE 2.2   Solve

$$x_1' = x_1 + 2x_2 + 1$$
$$x_2' = 3x_1 + 2x_2 + t.$$

As in Example 2.1, we differentiate and then substitute. This yields

$$x_1'' = x_1' + 2x_2'$$
$$= x_1' + 2(3x_1 + 2x_2 + t)$$
$$= x_1' + 6x_1 + 4x_2 + 2t$$
$$= x_1' + 6x_1 + 2(x_1' - x_1 - 1) + 2t$$
$$= 3x_1' + 4x_1 + 2t - 2.$$

Hence

(2.6a) $$x_1 = c_1 e^{4t} + c_2 e^{-t} - \tfrac{1}{2}t + \tfrac{7}{8}.$$

Since $2x_2 = x_1' - x_1 - 1$, then

$$x_2 = \frac{1}{2}\left(4c_1 e^{4t} - c_2 e^{-t} - \frac{1}{2}\right) - \frac{1}{2}\left(c_1 e^{4t} + c_2 e^{-t} - \frac{t}{2} + \frac{7}{8}\right) - \frac{1}{2}$$

or

(2.6b) $x_2 = \dfrac{3}{2} c_1 e^{4t} - c_2 e^{-t} - \dfrac{19}{16} + \dfrac{t}{4}.$

Of course, one can reverse the roles of x_1 and x_2. The calculation goes as follows:

$$x_2'' = 3x_1' + 2x_2' + 1$$
$$= 3(x_1 + 2x_2 + 1) + 2x_2' + 1$$
$$= 3x_1 + 6x_2 + 2x_2' + 4$$
$$= (x_2' - 2x_2 - t) + 6x_2 + 2x_2' + 4$$

or

$$x_2'' = 3x_2' + 4x_2 - t + 4.$$

Hence

(2.7a) $x_2 = d_1 e^{4t} + d_2 e^{-t} + \dfrac{t}{4} - \dfrac{19}{16}$

and $x_1 = (x_2' - 2x_2 - t)/3$, that is,

$$x_1 = \frac{1}{3}\left(4d_1 e^{4t} - d_2 e^{-t} + \frac{1}{4} \right) - \frac{2}{3}\left(d_1 e^{4t} + d_2 e^{-t} + \frac{t}{4} - \frac{19}{16} \right) - \frac{t}{3},$$

so

(2.7b) $x_1 = \dfrac{2}{3} d_1 e^{4t} - d_2 e^{-t} - \dfrac{t}{2} + \dfrac{7}{8}.$

The two solutions (2.6) and (2.7) are different but equivalent. This equivalence can be seen by taking $d_1 = 3c_1/2$ and $d_2 = -c_2$. ■

ELIMINATION AND CONTROL THEORY

In control theory it is useful to have, for a given open-loop control system, both a state-space representation and an input–output representation. For second-order systems the state-space representation has the form

$$x_1' = a_{11}x_1 + a_{12}x_2 + b_1 u(t)$$
$$x_2' = a_{21}x_1 + a_{22}x_2 + b_2 u(t)$$
$$y(t) = c_1 x_1(t) + c_2 x_2(t) + du(t).$$

The function $u(t)$ is the (known) system input and $y(t)$ is the (unknown) output. The input–output representation is obtained by finding a second-order differential equation satisfied by $y(t)$. The representation is found by a technique similar to elimination.

EXAMPLE 2.3   Find the input–output representation for

$$x_1' = -x_1 + x_2 - u(t)$$
$$x_2' = -2x_1 - 3u(t)$$
$$y = x_1 + u(t).$$

We obtain y' and y'' as follows:

$$y' = x_1' + u' = (-x_1 + x_2 - u) + u'$$

$$y'' = -x_1' + x_2' - u' + u''$$
$$= (x_1 - x_2 + u) + (-2x_1 - 3u) - u' + u''$$
$$= -x_1 - x_2 - 2u - u' + u''.$$

We now use the equations for y, y', and y'' to eliminate x_1 and x_2. First $x_1 = y - u$. Hence $y' = -(y - u) + x_2 - u + u'$ or

$$x_2 = y' + y - u'.$$

Now we substitute in the equation for y'', that is,

$$y'' = -(y - u) - (y' + y - u') - u' + u''$$

or

$$y'' + y' + 2y = u'' + u. \quad \blacksquare$$

PROBLEMS   In Problems 1–8, find a general solution of the system.

1. $x_1' = x_1 + x_2$
   $x_2' = x_2.$

2. $x_1' = x_1 + 2x_2 + 1$
   $x_2' = 3x_1 + 2x_2.$

3. $x_1' = -2x_1 + x_2 + e^t$
   $x_2' = -x_1 - 4x_2.$

4. $x_1' = -12x_1 + 17x_2$
   $x_2' = -4x_1 + 4x_2.$

5. $y_1' = 8y_1 - y_2$
   $y_2' = 4y_1 + 12y_2.$

6. $z_1' = 2z_1 + z_2$
   $z_2' = -4z_1 + 2z_2 + t.$

7. $x' = 8x - 8y$
   $y' = x + 4y.$

8. $w_1' = w_1 + 2w_2 + 1$
   $w_2' = 3w_1 + 2w_2.$

In Problems 9–14, solve the initial value problem.

9. $x_1' = -x_1 + 5x_2,$ $x_1(0) = 0$
   $x_2' = -2x_1 + 5x_2,$ $x_2(0) = -1.$

10. $x_1' = -2x_1 - x_2,$ $x_1(0) = 1$
   $x_2' = 4x_1 - 2x_2 + e^{2t},$ $x_2(0) = 0.$

11. $x_1' = 5x_1 - 2x_2,$ $x_1(0) = 0$
   $x_2' = 4x_1 - x_2 + e^{-t},$ $x_2(0) = 0.$

12. $w_1' = -w_1 + 5w_2 + t,$ $w_1(0) = 2$
   $w_2' = -2w_1 + 5w_2,$ $w_2(0) = -1.$

13. $z_1' = -2z_1 + 3z_2 + \sin t,$ $z_1(0) = 2$
   $z_2' = -z_1 + 4z_2,$ $z_2(0) = 0.$

14. $y_1' = -y_1 - y_2 - e^{-t},$ $y_1(0) = 0$
   $y_2' = -4y_1 - y_2 + 2e^{-t},$ $y_2(0) = 0.$

15. Use elimination to find a general solution of the following system of three equations.

$$x_1' = x_1 + 2x_2 + 2x_3$$

$$x_2' = x_2$$

$$x_3' = 2x_1 + 3x_2 + x_3.$$

Hint: Use $x_2 = c_2 e^t$ and then eliminate in the first and third equations.

16. Use elimination in

$$x_1' = x_1 + tx_2, \qquad x_2' = 2x_1 + x_2$$

to find a second-order differential equation solved by x_1.

17. For each of control system find a second-order equation that is solved by the output function $y(t)$.

(a) $x_1' = -2x_1 + x_2 + u(t)$
    $x_2' = -x_1 - u(t)$
    $y = x_1.$

(b) $x_1' = -3x_1 + \frac{3}{2}u(t)$
    $x_2' = x_1 - x_2$
    $y = x_1 + x_2.$

18. (a) Show that the following two control systems have the same input–output equation.

$$x_1' = -x_1 + u(t) \qquad w_1' = w_2$$

$$x_2' = -3x_2 + u(t) \qquad w_2' = -3w_1 + 4w_2 + u(t)$$

$$y = \tfrac{3}{4}(x_1 + x_2) \qquad y = 3w_1 + \tfrac{3}{2}w_2.$$

(b) Compare your input–output equation with the corresponding equation for Problem 17, part (b). Can you guess how many different state-space representatives can have the same input–output equations?

19. Consider the system in Figure 7.9 consisting of two cylindrical tanks with cross-sectional areas A_1 and A_2. Fluid is input to tank one at the rate $u(t)$. The output orifice to tank i is assumed to have hydraulic resistance R_i. If h_i is the height of the liquid in tank i at time t, then

$$A_i h_i' = \text{net tank rate of flow}$$

$$= \text{tank input rate–tank output rate.}$$

Hence

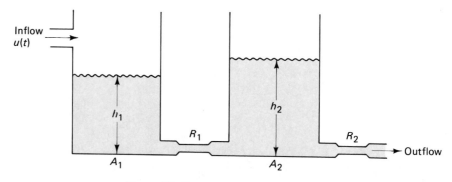

Figure 7.9. Two tanks on the same level.

$$A_1 h_1' = u(t) - \frac{h_1 - h_2}{R_1}$$

$$A_2 h_2' = \frac{h_1 - h_2}{R_1} - \frac{h_2}{R_2}.$$

(a) If we consider the output of this tank system to be the rate of outflow from the second tank through its second orifice, then

$$y = \frac{1}{R_2} h_2.$$

Find a second-order equation that is solved by y.

(b) If we consider the output of this system to be the liquid level in the first tank, then $y = h_1$. Find a second-order equation that is solved by y.

7.3   MATRICES

The method of elimination discussed in Section 7.2 is a satisfactory method of solution only when the number of unknowns is small. To develop an understanding of the properties of systems of first-order linear differential equations and to develop efficient methods of solution for such systems, it is desirable to use matrix–vector notation and to use certain powerful ideas and results from matrix theory. This section contains an introduction to matrix theory.

A **matrix** is a rectangular array of real or complex numbers. Examples are

$$(3.1) \qquad \begin{pmatrix} 2 & 1 & 0 \\ 3 & -1 & 7 \end{pmatrix}, \quad \begin{pmatrix} -1 & 1 \\ 3 & 4 \end{pmatrix}, \quad \begin{pmatrix} 1 \\ -2i \\ 3 \end{pmatrix}, \quad \begin{pmatrix} 1 & 2 \\ -1 & 0 \\ 3 & 7 \end{pmatrix}, \quad (2, 4+i).$$

The **size** of a matrix is determined by the number of rows and columns in the matrix. The first example of (3.1) has two rows and three columns and hence has size 2 by 3 (written 2×3). The remaining examples have sizes 2×2, 3×1, 3×2, and 1×2. A general $n \times m$ matrix $\mathbf{A}$ has the form

$$(3.2) \qquad \mathbf{A} = \begin{pmatrix} a_{11} & a_{12} & \cdots & a_{1m} \\ a_{21} & a_{22} & \cdots & a_{2m} \\ \vdots & & & \\ a_{n1} & a_{n2} & \cdots & a_{nm} \end{pmatrix}.$$

The entries a_{ij} are assigned subscripts according to their position in the array. Thus a_{ij} is the number in the ith row and jth column. For example, if

$$\mathbf{A} = \begin{pmatrix} 2 & 1 & 0 \\ 3 & -1 & 7 \end{pmatrix},$$

then $a_{11} = 2$, $a_{12} = 1$, $a_{13} = 0$, $a_{21} = 3$, and so on. The matrix $\mathbf{A}$ in (3.2) is often denoted by the symbols

$$\mathbf{A} = (a_{ij})_{n \times m}.$$

A is a **real matrix** if all entries a_{ij} are real numbers. Otherwise, **A** is called a **complex matrix.** In (3.1) the first, second, and fourth examples are real matrices and the third and fifth are complex.

A matrix contains the idea of *position* and *order* for a given set of numbers. Thus the four matrices

$$(1, 2), \quad \begin{pmatrix} 1 \\ 2 \end{pmatrix}, \quad (2, 1), \quad \begin{pmatrix} 2 \\ 1 \end{pmatrix}$$

are all different matrices. In general, two matrices **A** and **B** are called **equal** when they are the same size and the corresponding entries of **A** and **B** are all equal. Thus if

$$\mathbf{A} = (a_{ij})_{n \times m}, \qquad \mathbf{B} = (b_{ij})_{k \times r},$$

then **A** = **B** if and only if $n = k$, $m = r$, and $a_{ij} = b_{ij}$ for all i and j ($1 \le i \le n$, $1 \le j \le m$). For example,

$$\begin{pmatrix} a & b \\ 0 & 1 \end{pmatrix} = \begin{pmatrix} 1 & \pi \\ c & 1 \end{pmatrix}$$

if and only if $a = 1$, $b = \pi$, and $c = 0$.

A matrix $\mathbf{A} = (a_{ij})_{n \times m}$ is called **square** if $n = m$. Among the examples in (3.1) only the second matrix is square. A square matrix **A** is **diagonal** if $a_{ij} = 0$ whenever $i \ne j$, that is,

$$\mathbf{A} = \begin{pmatrix} a_{11} & 0 & 0 & \dots & 0 \\ 0 & a_{22} & 0 & \dots & 0 \\ \vdots & & & & \\ 0 & 0 & 0 & \dots & a_{nn} \end{pmatrix} = \operatorname{diag}(a_{11}, a_{22}, \dots, a_{nn}).$$

For example,

$$\operatorname{diag}(2, -1) = \begin{pmatrix} 2 & 0 \\ 0 & -1 \end{pmatrix},$$

$$\operatorname{diag}(1, 1, -2, 4, \pi) = \begin{pmatrix} 1 & 0 & 0 & 0 & 0 \\ 0 & 1 & 0 & 0 & 0 \\ 0 & 0 & -2 & 0 & 0 \\ 0 & 0 & 0 & 4 & 0 \\ 0 & 0 & 0 & 0 & \pi \end{pmatrix}.$$

Column vectors of dimension n are matrices of size $n \times 1$. For example,

$$\begin{pmatrix} 1 \\ 2 \end{pmatrix}, \quad \begin{pmatrix} a \\ b \\ c \end{pmatrix}, \quad \begin{pmatrix} x_1 \\ x_2 \\ x_3 \\ x_4 \end{pmatrix}$$

are, respectively, column vectors of dimension 2, 3, and 4. **Row vectors of dimension** n are matrices of size $1 \times n$. For example,

$$(2, -1), \quad (x_1, x_2, x_3), \quad (1, 4, 5, a)$$

are, respectively, row vectors of dimension 2, 3, and 4.

The **transpose** of **A**, denoted by $\mathbf{A}^T$, is the matrix obtained from **A** by interchanging the rows and columns of **A**. Thus if $\mathbf{A} = (a_{ij})_{n \times m}$, then $\mathbf{A}^T = (a_{ji})_{m \times n}$. For example, the transposes of the matrices in (3.1) are

$$\begin{pmatrix} 2 & 3 \\ 1 & -1 \\ 0 & 7 \end{pmatrix}, \quad \begin{pmatrix} -1 & 3 \\ 1 & 4 \end{pmatrix}, \quad (1, -2i, 3), \quad \begin{pmatrix} 1 & -1 & 3 \\ 2 & 0 & 7 \end{pmatrix}, \quad \begin{pmatrix} 2 \\ 4+i \end{pmatrix}.$$

The transpose provides a handy way to write column vectors without using large amounts of space. For example,

$$(2, 1)^T, \quad (y_1, y_2, y_3)^T, \quad (1, 2, 0, -\pi)^T$$

are column vectors of dimension 2, 3, and 4.

Given two matrices $\mathbf{A} = (a_{ij})_{n \times m}$ and $\mathbf{B} = (b_{ij})_{r \times k}$, the **product AB** can be defined if and only if the number of columns of **A** equals the number of rows of **B** (i.e., $m = r$). When $m = r$, the product $\mathbf{C} = \mathbf{AB}$ has size $n \times k$, that is,

$$\mathbf{C} = (c_{ij})_{n \times k} = (a_{ij})_{n \times m}(b_{ij})_{m \times k} = \mathbf{AB}.$$

The (i, j)th entry of **C** is defined to be

$$c_{ij} = \sum_{s=1}^{m} a_{is}b_{sj}.$$

For example, $(1, 2)$ is 1×2, $(3, -1)^T$ is 2×1, so that

$$(1, 2)\begin{pmatrix} 3 \\ -1 \end{pmatrix} = [1 \cdot 3 + 2(-1)] = (1)_{1 \times 1}.$$

Similarly,

$$\begin{pmatrix} 3 & 4 \\ 1 & -1 \end{pmatrix}_{2 \times 2} \begin{pmatrix} 2 \\ -1 \end{pmatrix}_{2 \times 1} = \begin{pmatrix} 3 \cdot 2 + 4(-1) \\ 1 \cdot 2 + (-1)(-1) \end{pmatrix}_{2 \times 1} = \begin{pmatrix} 2 \\ 3 \end{pmatrix},$$

$$(2, 1)_{1 \times 2}\begin{pmatrix} 1 & 2 & -2 \\ -1 & 0 & 3 \end{pmatrix}_{2 \times 3} = (1, 4, -1)_{1 \times 3},$$

and

$$\begin{pmatrix} 2 & 1 \\ 1 & 0 \end{pmatrix}\begin{pmatrix} 1 & -1 \\ 1 & 1 \end{pmatrix} = \begin{pmatrix} 3 & -1 \\ 1 & -1 \end{pmatrix}, \quad \begin{pmatrix} 3 \\ -1 \end{pmatrix}(1, 2) = \begin{pmatrix} 3 & 6 \\ -1 & -2 \end{pmatrix}.$$

Matrix multiplication can be used to compactly write systems of linear algebraic equations. For example, consider

$$2x + 3y + z = 4$$

(3.3) $$x - y + 2z = 0$$

$$x + y + 3z = -1.$$

The **coefficient matrix** for this system is

$$A = \begin{pmatrix} 2 & 3 & 1 \\ 1 & -1 & 2 \\ 1 & 1 & 3 \end{pmatrix},$$

$\mathbf{x} = (x, y, z)^T$ is the vector unknown, and the terms on the right are grouped in the vector $\mathbf{b} = (4, 0, -1)^T$. With this notation the system can be written as

(3.4) $$\mathbf{Ax} = \mathbf{b}.$$

The reader should check to see that under the rules of matrix multiplication (3.3) really is the same as (3.4).

When writing a linear system in the matrix–vector form (3.4) it is important to use a consistent order for the variables and to use the zero coefficient to indicate the absence of an unknown. Thus the system

$$x + 3y = 1$$
$$z - 3y = 2$$

should be rewritten in the form

$$x + 3y + 0 \cdot z = 1$$
$$0 \cdot x - 3y + z = 2,$$

to make it clear what the coefficients are. The coefficient matrix, vector unknown, and the right-hand side then are

$$\begin{pmatrix} 1 & 3 & 0 \\ 0 & -3 & 1 \end{pmatrix}, \quad (x, y, z)^T, \quad (1, 2)^T,$$

and the matrix–vector form of the system is

$$\begin{pmatrix} 1 & 3 & 0 \\ 0 & -3 & 1 \end{pmatrix} \begin{pmatrix} x \\ y \\ z \end{pmatrix} = \begin{pmatrix} 1 \\ 2 \end{pmatrix}.$$

Two matrices $\mathbf{A}$ and $\mathbf{B}$ can be **added** if and only if they are the same size. Given $\mathbf{A} = (a_{ij})_{n \times m}$ and $\mathbf{B} = (b_{ij})_{n \times m}$ of the same size, the sum is

$$\mathbf{A} + \mathbf{B} = (a_{ij} + b_{ij})_{n \times m}.$$

For example,

$$\begin{pmatrix} 2 & -1 & 3 \\ 0 & 4 & 2 \end{pmatrix} + \begin{pmatrix} 0 & 1 & 4 \\ 2 & 0 & 2 \end{pmatrix} = \begin{pmatrix} 2 & 0 & 7 \\ 2 & 4 & 4 \end{pmatrix},$$

$$(1, 2, 3) + (-1, 0, 5) = (0, 2, 8),$$

$$\begin{pmatrix} 1 \\ 2 \\ 3 \end{pmatrix} + \begin{pmatrix} -2 \\ -3 \\ 0 \end{pmatrix} = \begin{pmatrix} -1 \\ -1 \\ 3 \end{pmatrix}, \qquad \begin{pmatrix} 2 & 2 \\ -1 & 1 \end{pmatrix} + \begin{pmatrix} x & 4 \\ 7 & a \end{pmatrix} = \begin{pmatrix} x+2 & 6 \\ 6 & a+1 \end{pmatrix}.$$

Matrix addition and multiplication can be combined to compactly write linear systems of first-order differential equations. For example, in

(3.5)
$$x_1' = 3x_1 - 2x_2 + \sin t$$
$$x_2' = x_1 + x_2 + 1,$$

the vector unknown, coefficient matrix, and forcing function are

$$\mathbf{x} = \begin{pmatrix} x_1 \\ x_2 \end{pmatrix}, \qquad \mathbf{A} = \begin{pmatrix} 3 & -2 \\ 1 & 1 \end{pmatrix}, \qquad \mathbf{g}(t) = \begin{pmatrix} \sin t \\ 1 \end{pmatrix}.$$

We will use the convention that

$$\mathbf{x}' = \begin{pmatrix} x_1 \\ x_2 \end{pmatrix}' = \begin{pmatrix} x_1' \\ x_2' \end{pmatrix}.$$

Hence (3.5) is equivalent to the first-order (vector) system

$$\mathbf{x}' = \mathbf{A}\mathbf{x} + \mathbf{g}(t).$$

Initial conditions for (3.5) have the form $x_1(t_0) = d_1$, $x_2(t_0) = d_2$. These initial conditions can also be expressed in vector form as

$$\mathbf{x}(t_0) = \mathbf{d},$$

where $\mathbf{d} = (d_1, d_2)^T$.

When expressing systems of first-order linear differential equations in vector–matrix notation it is important to use a consistent order for the variables and to use the zero coefficient to indicate the absence of a term. Thus the system

(3.6)
$$x_1' = x_1 + 3x_2 + t, \qquad x_1(0) = 2$$
$$x_2' = x_3 - 3x_2, \qquad x_2(0) = 0$$
$$x_3' = x_1 + x_2 + \sin t, \qquad x_3(0) = -1,$$

should be rewritten in the form

$$x_1' = x_1 + 3x_2 + 0\cdot x_3 + t, \qquad x_1(0) = 2$$
$$x_2' = 0\cdot x_1 - 3x_2 + x_3 + 0, \qquad x_2(0) = 0$$
$$x_3' = x_1 + x_2 + 0\cdot x_3 + \sin t, \qquad x_3(0) = -1.$$

It is now clear that with

$$\mathbf{x} = \begin{pmatrix} x_1 \\ x_2 \\ x_3 \end{pmatrix}, \quad A = \begin{pmatrix} 1 & 3 & 0 \\ 0 & -3 & 1 \\ 1 & 1 & 0 \end{pmatrix}, \quad \mathbf{g}(t) \equiv \begin{pmatrix} t \\ 0 \\ \sin t \end{pmatrix}, \quad \mathbf{d} = \begin{pmatrix} 2 \\ 0 \\ -1 \end{pmatrix},$$

the system (3.6) is equivalent to

$$\mathbf{x}' = A\mathbf{x} + \mathbf{g}(t), \qquad \mathbf{x}(0) = \mathbf{d}.$$

A **scalar** c means a real or a complex number c. **Multiplication** of a matrix $A = (a_{ij})_{n \times m}$ **by a scalar** c is defined by

$$cA = (ca_{ij})_{n \times m}.$$

For example,

$$-2 \begin{pmatrix} 2 & -1 \\ 3 & 0 \end{pmatrix} = \begin{pmatrix} -4 & 2 \\ -6 & 0 \end{pmatrix}, \qquad 2(3, 4, -2, 2) = (6, 8, -4, 4)$$

and

$$2 \begin{pmatrix} 2 & -2 & 3 \\ 1 & 1 & 0 \end{pmatrix} + (-1) \begin{pmatrix} 0 & 4 & 0 \\ -1 & 0 & 1 \end{pmatrix} = \begin{pmatrix} 4 & -4 & 6 \\ 2 & 2 & 0 \end{pmatrix} + \begin{pmatrix} 0 & -4 & 0 \\ 1 & 0 & -1 \end{pmatrix}$$

$$= \begin{pmatrix} 4 & -8 & 6 \\ 3 & 2 & -1 \end{pmatrix}.$$

Matrix addition, matrix multiplication, and scalar multiplication can often be used to express the same result in different ways. For example,

$$\begin{pmatrix} 2 & 3 & -1 \\ 0 & 2 & -1 \\ 1 & 0 & 3 \end{pmatrix} \begin{pmatrix} c_1 \\ c_2 \\ c_3 \end{pmatrix} = c_1 \begin{pmatrix} 2 \\ 0 \\ 1 \end{pmatrix} + c_2 \begin{pmatrix} 3 \\ 2 \\ 0 \end{pmatrix} + c_3 \begin{pmatrix} -1 \\ -1 \\ 3 \end{pmatrix}.$$

Engineers normally express the state-space representation of control systems using vector–matrix notation. For example, the control system of Example 2.3 can be written as

$$\begin{aligned} x_1' &= -x_1 + x_2 - u(t) \\ (3.7) \qquad x_2' &= -2x_1 + 0 \cdot x_2 - 3u(t) \\ y &= x_1 + u(t). \end{aligned}$$

Define

$$\mathbf{x} = \begin{pmatrix} x_1 \\ x_2 \end{pmatrix}, \quad A = \begin{pmatrix} -1 & 1 \\ -2 & 0 \end{pmatrix}, \quad \mathbf{b} = \begin{pmatrix} -1 \\ -3 \end{pmatrix}, \quad \mathbf{c} = \begin{pmatrix} 1 \\ 0 \end{pmatrix}.$$

Then the control system (3.7) can be written as

$$\mathbf{x}' = A\mathbf{x} + \mathbf{b}u(t), \qquad y = \mathbf{c}^T\mathbf{x} + u(t).$$

The control $u(t)$ is a scalar that multiplies the vector **b**.

Multiple input–multiple output control systems can also be conveniently written using vector matrix notation. For example, the system

$$x_1' = x_1 - x_2 + u_1(t)$$

$$x_2' = x_2 + x_3 + u_2(t)$$

$$x_3' = x_1 - x_2 - x_3 + 2u_1(t) - u_2(t)$$

$$y_1 = x_1 + x_2 + u_1(t)$$

$$y_2 = x_1 - x_3 - u_2(t)$$

can be written as

$$\begin{pmatrix} x_1 \\ x_2 \\ x_3 \end{pmatrix}' = \begin{pmatrix} 1 & -1 & 0 \\ 0 & 1 & 1 \\ 1 & -1 & -1 \end{pmatrix} \begin{pmatrix} x_1 \\ x_2 \\ x_3 \end{pmatrix} + \begin{pmatrix} 1 & 0 \\ 0 & 1 \\ 2 & -1 \end{pmatrix} \begin{pmatrix} u_1(t) \\ u_2(t) \end{pmatrix}$$

$$\begin{pmatrix} y_1 \\ y_2 \end{pmatrix} = \begin{pmatrix} 1 & 1 & 0 \\ 1 & 0 & -1 \end{pmatrix} \begin{pmatrix} x_1 \\ x_2 \\ x_3 \end{pmatrix} + \begin{pmatrix} 1 & 0 \\ 0 & -1 \end{pmatrix} \begin{pmatrix} u_1(t) \\ u_2(t) \end{pmatrix}.$$

This control system has the form

$$\mathbf{x}' = \mathbf{A}\mathbf{x} + \mathbf{b}u(t), \qquad \mathbf{y} = \mathbf{C}\mathbf{x} + \mathbf{D}u(t),$$

where $\mathbf{u}(t)$ is the (vector) input to the control system and $\mathbf{y} = (y_1, y_2)^T$ is the (vector) output.

PROBLEMS

1. Suppose that

$$\mathbf{A} = \begin{pmatrix} 2 & 1 \\ -1 & 4 \end{pmatrix}, \qquad \mathbf{B} = \begin{pmatrix} 1 & -1 \\ 2 & 4 \end{pmatrix}, \qquad \mathbf{x} = \begin{pmatrix} 1 \\ -2 \end{pmatrix}, \qquad \mathbf{y} = \begin{pmatrix} 0 \\ 3 \end{pmatrix}.$$

Compute the following.

(a) $3\mathbf{A} + 2\mathbf{B}$.

(b) $2\mathbf{A}\mathbf{x} + 5\mathbf{y}$.

(c) $\mathbf{A}\mathbf{B} + 3\mathbf{A}^T$.

(d) $\mathbf{B}\mathbf{A}\mathbf{x} - 2\mathbf{y} + 3\mathbf{x}$.

(e) $\mathbf{A}\mathbf{B} - \mathbf{B}\mathbf{A}$.

(f) $\mathbf{A} + \mathbf{y}\mathbf{x}^T$.

(g) $(2 + i)\mathbf{x} + i\mathbf{y}$.

2. Suppose that

$$\mathbf{A} = \begin{pmatrix} 1 & 2 & 1 \\ -1 & 0 & 2 \\ 3 & 1 & 1 \end{pmatrix}, \qquad \mathbf{B} = \begin{pmatrix} 1 & 1 & 0 \\ 0 & 2 & 0 \\ 0 & 1 & 3 \end{pmatrix}, \qquad \mathbf{x} = \begin{pmatrix} 1 \\ 0 \\ -1 \end{pmatrix}, \qquad \mathbf{y} = \begin{pmatrix} 2 \\ 1 \\ 0 \end{pmatrix}.$$

Compute the following.

(a) $2(\mathbf{A} + \mathbf{A}^T) - \mathbf{B}$.

(b) $\mathbf{A}^T\mathbf{B} + 2\mathbf{A}$.

(c) $\mathbf{x}^T\mathbf{A} + 3(\mathbf{x} + \mathbf{y})^T$.

(d) $\mathbf{x}^T\mathbf{A}\mathbf{y}$.

(e) $AB - BA$. 　　　　　　　　　　　(f) $2(yx^T)y + x$.

(g) $iAx + (2 + i)y$.

3. Write each system of linear equations in the vector–matrix form $Ax = b$.

(a) $3x_1 - x_2 = 0,\ 2x_1 + 3x_2 = 1$.

(b) $x_2 - x_1 = 4,\ x_2 + x_1 = -1$.

(c) $2x_1 - x_3 = 4,\ x_1 + x_2 + x_3 = 0,\ x_2 + x_3 = 1$.

(d) $x_1 + x_2 = 1,\ x_2 + x_3 = 2,\ x_3 + x_4 = -1,\ x_4 + x_1 = 1$.

(e) $2x_1 + ix_2 = 3,\ ix_1 + x_2 = 3 + i$.

4. Write each system of differential equations in the vector–matrix form $x' = Ax + g(t)$, $x(\tau) = d$.

(a) $\begin{aligned} x_1' &= 3x_1 - x_2 + 6, & x_1(0) &= 0 \\ x_2' &= x_1 + 2x_2 + t, & x_2(0) &= 0. \end{aligned}$ 　　　(b) $\begin{aligned} x_1' &= x_2 + 3, & x_1(1) &= 6 \\ x_2' &= -x_1 + \sin t, & x_2(1) &= -1. \end{aligned}$

(c) $\begin{aligned} x_1' &= x_2 - x_1, & x_1(0) &= 0 \\ x_2' &= x_1 + x_3 + t, & x_2(0) &= 4 \\ x_3' &= x_2 - x_1, & x_3(0) &= -1. \end{aligned}$ 　　　(d) $\begin{aligned} S_1' &= 3(S_1 - S_2 - t), & S_1(0) &= 0 \\ S_2' &= -3(S_1 - S_2 + 1), & S_2(0) &= 1. \end{aligned}$

5. Use the transformation $x_1 = y$, $x_2 = y'$, etc., to reduce the given equation to a first-order system. Write this system in vector–matrix notation.

(a) $y'' - y' + y = 0,\ y(0) = 1,\ y'(0) = -1$.

(b) $y'' + 2y' - 3y = \sin t,\ y(-1) = y'(-1) = 0$.

(c) $y''' + 2y'' + 3y' + 4y = t^2,\ y(1) = 1,\ y'(1) = -1,\ y''(1) = 2$.

(d) $y^{(4)} + y = 0,\ y(0) = y''(0) = 1,\ y'(0) = y'''(0) = -1$.

6. Write each control system in the vector–matrix form $x' = Ax + bu$, $y = cx + du$. The input $u(t)$ and the output y will be scalar valued in some cases and vector valued in others.

(a) $\begin{aligned} x_1' &= -2x_1 + x_2 + u(t) \\ x_2' &= -x_1 - u(t) \\ y &= x_1 + 2u(t). \end{aligned}$ 　　　(b) $\begin{aligned} x_1' &= -3x_1 + \tfrac{3}{2}u(t) \\ x_2' &= x_1 - x_2 \\ y &= x_1 + x_2. \end{aligned}$

(c) $\begin{aligned} w_1' &= w_2 \\ w_2' &= -3w_1 + 4w_2 + u(t) \\ y &= 3w_1 + \tfrac{3}{2}w_2. \end{aligned}$ 　　　(d) $\begin{aligned} x_1' &= -2x_1 + x_2 + u_1(t) \\ x_2' &= 2(x_2 - x_1) + u_2(t) \\ y &= x_1 + 2x_2 + u_2(t). \end{aligned}$

(e) $\begin{aligned} x_1' &= x_2 + u_2(t) \\ x_2' &= -3x_1 + 4x_2 + u_1(t) - u_2(t) \\ y_1 &= 3x_1 + \tfrac{3}{2}x_2 \\ y_2 &= x_1 - x_2 + u_1(t) - u_2(t). \end{aligned}$ 　　(f) $\begin{aligned} R_1' &= 3R_1 - R_2 + u(t) \\ R_2' &= 2(u(t) - R_1) \\ y_1 &= R_1 - u(t) \\ y_2 &= R_1 - R_2. \end{aligned}$

The following definition is needed in Problems 7–11. If $A(t) = (a_{ij}(t))_{n \times m}$ is a matrix, then the derivative of $A(t)$ with respect to t is defined by

$$A'(t) = (a_{ij}'(t))_{n \times m}.$$

7. Let $g(t) = (e^t + e^{-t},\ 2t + 1)^T$. Compute the following.

(a) $g'(t)$. 　　　　　　　　　　　　(b) $g''(t)$.

(c) $\dfrac{d}{dt}\left[\begin{pmatrix} 2 & 1 \\ 3 & 2 \end{pmatrix}\mathbf{g}(t)\right].$

(d) $\dfrac{d}{dt}\left[\mathbf{g}(t)^T\mathbf{g}(t)\right].$

8. Given that

$$\mathbf{X}(t) = \begin{pmatrix} e^{3t} & e^t \\ e^{3t} & 2e^t \end{pmatrix}, \qquad \mathbf{A} = \begin{pmatrix} 5 & -2 \\ 4 & -1 \end{pmatrix}, \qquad \mathbf{d} = \begin{pmatrix} 2 \\ 1 \end{pmatrix},$$

compute the following.

(a) $\mathbf{X}'(t) - \mathbf{A}\mathbf{X}(t)$.

(b) $\mathbf{y}'(t) - \mathbf{A}\mathbf{y}(t)$, where $\mathbf{y} = \mathbf{X}\mathbf{d}$.

(c) $\mathbf{Y}'(t) - \mathbf{Y}(t)\mathbf{A}^T$, where $\mathbf{Y} = \mathbf{X}^T$.

9. For what value of a does $\mathbf{x}(t) = (4e^{2t}, ae^{2t})^T$ solve

$$\mathbf{x}' = \begin{pmatrix} 3 & -2 \\ 2 & -2 \end{pmatrix}\mathbf{x}?$$

10. For what value of λ does $\mathbf{x}(t) = (1, 3)^T e^{\lambda t}$ solve

$$\mathbf{x}' = \begin{pmatrix} 2 & -1 \\ 3 & -2 \end{pmatrix}\mathbf{x}?$$

11. For what value of $\mathbf{g}(t)$ does $\mathbf{x}(t) = (t, 1)^T$ solve

$$\mathbf{x}' = \begin{pmatrix} 2 & -1 \\ 3 & -2 \end{pmatrix}\mathbf{x} + \mathbf{g}(t)?$$

12. For what value of b does

$$\mathbf{x} = \begin{pmatrix} \cos bt & \sin bt \\ -\sin bt & \cos bt \end{pmatrix}\begin{pmatrix} 1 \\ i \end{pmatrix}.$$

solve

$$\mathbf{x}' = \begin{pmatrix} 0 & 2 \\ -2 & 0 \end{pmatrix}\mathbf{x}?$$

7.4   MATRIX ALGEBRA

Any two matrices $\mathbf{A}$ and $\mathbf{B}$ of the same size can be added, that is,

$$(a_{ij})_{n \times m} + (b_{ij})_{n \times m} = (a_{ij} + b_{ij})_{n \times m}.$$

Since $a_{ij} + b_{ij} = b_{ij} + a_{ij}$ for all i and j, then

$$\mathbf{A} + \mathbf{B} = \mathbf{B} + \mathbf{A}.$$

Thus matrix addition is **commutative.** It is also **associative,** that is,

$$(\mathbf{A} + \mathbf{B}) + \mathbf{C} = \mathbf{A} + (\mathbf{B} + \mathbf{C}),$$

for all matrices $\mathbf{A}$, $\mathbf{B}$, and $\mathbf{C}$ of a given size.

The $n \times m$ **zero matrix 0** is the matrix of that size such that all entries are zero. Thus

$$\begin{pmatrix} 0 & 0 \\ 0 & 0 \end{pmatrix}, \quad (0, 0, 0), \quad \begin{pmatrix} 0 & 0 \\ 0 & 0 \\ 0 & 0 \end{pmatrix}, \quad \begin{pmatrix} 0 \\ 0 \end{pmatrix}$$

are the zero matrices of sizes 2×2, 1×3, 3×2, and 2×1. The $n \times m$ zero matrix has the property that

$$\mathbf{A} + \mathbf{0} = \mathbf{0} + \mathbf{A} = \mathbf{A}$$

for all matrices $\mathbf{A}$ of size $n \times m$.

Scalar multiplication of $\mathbf{A}$ by c is defined by $c\mathbf{A} = (ca_{ij})$. This multiplication satisfies the following **distributive laws:**

$$c(\mathbf{A} + \mathbf{B}) = c\mathbf{A} + c\mathbf{B}, \qquad (c_1 + c_2)\mathbf{A} = c_1\mathbf{A} + c_2\mathbf{A}$$

for all $n \times m$ matrices $\mathbf{A}$ and $\mathbf{B}$. Note that

$$\mathbf{A} + (-1)\mathbf{A} = \mathbf{0}.$$

The term $(-1)\mathbf{A}$ is often written as $-\mathbf{A}$.

Matrix multiplication is associative and distributive with respect to matrix addition. Hence, for all $\mathbf{A}$, $\mathbf{B}$, $\mathbf{C}$, etc., of the proper sizes

$$\mathbf{A}(\mathbf{BC}) = (\mathbf{AB})\mathbf{C}, \qquad \mathbf{A}(\mathbf{B} + \mathbf{D}) = \mathbf{AB} + \mathbf{AD}$$

and

$$(\mathbf{E} + \mathbf{F})\mathbf{A} = \mathbf{EA} + \mathbf{FA}.$$

All of the algebraic rules mentioned so far are straightforward extensions of the rules of arithmetic for real and complex numbers. Students usually have no trouble remembering and applying these rules. There are two ways in which matrix multiplication is different from ordinary multiplication of numbers. These are *commutativity* and *existence of inverses*.

Matrix multiplication is *not commutative*. Given two matrices $\mathbf{A} = (a_{ij})_{n \times m}$ and $\mathbf{B} = (b_{ij})_{m \times k}$, the product $\mathbf{AB}$ is not necessarily equal to $\mathbf{BA}$. Indeed, the product $\mathbf{BA}$ is not even defined unless $n = k$. If $\mathbf{AB}$ and $\mathbf{BA}$ are both defined, they do not have to be equal. For example,

$$\begin{pmatrix} 2 & 1 \\ 3 & 0 \end{pmatrix}\begin{pmatrix} 1 & 4 \\ 0 & 1 \end{pmatrix} = \begin{pmatrix} 2 & 9 \\ 3 & 12 \end{pmatrix}$$

and

$$\begin{pmatrix} 1 & 4 \\ 0 & 1 \end{pmatrix}\begin{pmatrix} 2 & 1 \\ 3 & 0 \end{pmatrix} = \begin{pmatrix} 14 & 1 \\ 3 & 0 \end{pmatrix} \neq \begin{pmatrix} 2 & 9 \\ 3 & 12 \end{pmatrix}.$$

These two matrices do not commute. Noncommuting examples of size $n \times n$ can be found for any integer $n \geq 2$.

The $n \times n$ **identity matrix,** denoted by **I,** is the diagonal matrix of size $n \times n$ all of whose diagonal entries are 1, that is,

$$\mathbf{I} = \text{diag}(1, 1, \ldots, 1) = \begin{pmatrix} 1 & 0 & 0 & \ldots & 0 \\ 0 & 1 & 0 & \ldots & 0 \\ 0 & 0 & 1 & \ldots & 0 \\ & \vdots & & & \\ 0 & 0 & 0 & \ldots & 1 \end{pmatrix}.$$

Thus

$$\begin{pmatrix} 1 & 0 \\ 0 & 1 \end{pmatrix}, \quad \begin{pmatrix} 1 & 0 & 0 \\ 0 & 1 & 0 \\ 0 & 0 & 1 \end{pmatrix}, \quad \begin{pmatrix} 1 & 0 & 0 & 0 \\ 0 & 1 & 0 & 0 \\ 0 & 0 & 1 & 0 \\ 0 & 0 & 0 & 1 \end{pmatrix}$$

are the identity matrices of sizes 2×2, 3×3, and 4×4. From the definition of matrix multiplication it follows that if **I** is of size $n \times n$, then

$$\mathbf{AI} = \mathbf{A}, \qquad \mathbf{IB} = \mathbf{B}$$

for all $m \times n$ matrices **A** and all $n \times m$ matrices **B**. For example,

$$\begin{pmatrix} 2 & 1 \\ 3 & 0 \end{pmatrix}\begin{pmatrix} 1 & 0 \\ 0 & 1 \end{pmatrix} = \begin{pmatrix} 1 & 0 \\ 0 & 1 \end{pmatrix}\begin{pmatrix} 2 & 1 \\ 3 & 0 \end{pmatrix} = \begin{pmatrix} 2 & 1 \\ 3 & 0 \end{pmatrix},$$

and

$$\begin{pmatrix} 1 & 0 & -1 \\ 2 & 1 & 0 \end{pmatrix}\begin{pmatrix} 1 & 0 & 0 \\ 0 & 1 & 0 \\ 0 & 0 & 1 \end{pmatrix} = \begin{pmatrix} 1 & 0 & -1 \\ 2 & 1 & 0 \end{pmatrix},$$

$$\begin{pmatrix} 1 & 0 \\ 0 & 1 \end{pmatrix}\begin{pmatrix} 1 & 0 & -1 \\ 2 & 1 & 0 \end{pmatrix} = \begin{pmatrix} 1 & 0 & -1 \\ 2 & 1 & 0 \end{pmatrix}.$$

Given an $n \times n$ matrix **A,** the **inverse** of **A** (if it exists) is that matrix **B** such that $\mathbf{AB} = \mathbf{I}$. The inverse of **A** is usually written as $\mathbf{A}^{-1}$. Notice that we only talk about inverses of *square* matrices and that even for square matrices, the inverse need not always exist. For example, the matrix

$$\mathbf{A} = \begin{pmatrix} 1 & 1 \\ -1 & -1 \end{pmatrix}$$

has no inverse. This can be seen as follows. Suppose that we try to find **B** such that $\mathbf{AB} = \mathbf{I}$, that is,

(4.1) $$\begin{pmatrix} 1 & 1 \\ -1 & -1 \end{pmatrix}\begin{pmatrix} b_{11} & b_{12} \\ b_{21} & b_{22} \end{pmatrix} = \begin{pmatrix} 1 & 0 \\ 0 & 1 \end{pmatrix}.$$

This left side is

(4.2)
$$\begin{pmatrix} b_{11} + b_{21} & b_{12} + b_{22} \\ -b_{11} - b_{21} & -b_{12} - b_{22} \end{pmatrix}.$$

If b_{11} and b_{21} are chosen so that $b_{11} + b_{21} = 1$, then $-b_{11} - b_{21}$ must be -1. Similarly, if $b_{12} + b_{22} = 0$, then $-b_{12} - b_{22} = 0$. Hence (4.2) will be

$$\begin{pmatrix} 1 & 0 \\ -1 & 0 \end{pmatrix} \neq \begin{pmatrix} 1 & 0 \\ 0 & 1 \end{pmatrix}.$$

On many occasions it would be handy for $\mathbf{A}^{-1}$ to always exist. A lamentable fact of life is that $\mathbf{A}^{-1}$ need not exist.

If $\mathbf{A}^{-1}$ exists, then $\mathbf{A}\mathbf{A}^{-1} = \mathbf{A}^{-1}\mathbf{A} = \mathbf{I}$, that is, $\mathbf{A}$ and $\mathbf{A}^{-1}$ commute. Moreover, there is only one inverse since

$$\mathbf{AB} = \mathbf{I}, \qquad \mathbf{AC} = \mathbf{I}$$

imply that $\mathbf{AB} = \mathbf{AC}$. Hence

(4.3)
$$\mathbf{B(AB)} = \mathbf{B(AC)}.$$

The left side of (4.3) equals $\mathbf{(BA)B} = \mathbf{IB} = \mathbf{B}$ and the right side is $\mathbf{(BA)C} = \mathbf{IC} = \mathbf{C}$. Thus $\mathbf{B} = \mathbf{C}$.

If the inverse of $\mathbf{A}$ is known or is easily found, the system

(4.4)
$$\mathbf{Ac} = \mathbf{b}$$

of n simultaneous linear equations in the unknown $\mathbf{c}$ is easily solved. Multiply on the left by $\mathbf{A}^{-1}$. Then $\mathbf{A}^{-1}(\mathbf{Ac}) = (\mathbf{A}^{-1}\mathbf{A})\mathbf{c} = \mathbf{Ic} = \mathbf{c}$. Hence

$$\mathbf{c} = \mathbf{A}^{-1}\mathbf{b}.$$

Methods for computing $\mathbf{A}^{-1}$ will be discussed in Section 7.5.

In the system (4.4), **elimination** is often the best way to obtain the solution. The first step is to find the **augmented matrix.** For example, in the system

$$c_1 - 3c_2 = -1$$
$$3c_1 - 2c_2 = 2,$$

the coefficient matrix and right-hand side are

$$\mathbf{A} = \begin{pmatrix} 1 & -3 \\ 3 & -2 \end{pmatrix}, \qquad \mathbf{b} = \begin{pmatrix} -1 \\ 2 \end{pmatrix}.$$

The augmented matrix M is

(4.5)
$$\mathbf{M} = \begin{pmatrix} 1 & -3 & -1 \\ 3 & -2 & 2 \end{pmatrix}.$$

It is made up of the columns of $\mathbf{A}$ followed by one more column made up of the elements of $\mathbf{b}$. The augmented matrix will now be reduced to an equivalent problem in which all of the entries below the diagonal are zero. This reduction is accomplished by using the following **elementary row operations.**

ELEMENTARY ROW OPERATIONS

---

1. Replace a row of **M** by a constant multiple k of that row where $k \neq 0$.
2. Replace a row of **M** by the sum of that row and a multiple of some other row.
3. Interchange two rows of **M**.

We can reduce **M**, given in (4.5) by adding to the last row (-3) times the first row, that is,

$$\mathbf{M}_R = \begin{pmatrix} 1 & -3 & -1 \\ 0 & 7 & 5 \end{pmatrix}.$$

The reduced matrix $\mathbf{M}_R$ is equivalent to the problem

(4.6)
$$\begin{aligned} c_1 - 3c_2 &= -1 \\ 7c_2 &= 5. \end{aligned}$$

Back substitution can be applied to solve (4.6). By back substitution we mean to start with the last equation, solve for c_2, and work upward. This gives

$$c_2 = \tfrac{5}{7}$$

and then

$$c_1 - 3(\tfrac{5}{7}) = -1, \qquad c_1 = \tfrac{15}{7} - 1 = \tfrac{8}{7}.$$

Elementary row operations allow one to replace the original system of equations by a new system which is equivalent to the old one in the sense that it has exactly the same solutions. For example, multiplying the first row of M by a constant $k \neq 0$ corresponds to multiplying the first equation in the system by k. The new system has the very same solutions as the old one. Similarly, interchanging the first and the third rows of M corresponds to interchanging the first and third equations. The new system is clearly equivalent to the old one. What we wish to do is to use elimination to reduce the original system of equations to a *triangular* one. The triangular system can be solved quite simply by back substitution. The following examples illustrate this procedure.

EXAMPLE 4.1   Use elimination to solve for c_1, c_2, and c_3 in

$$\begin{aligned} c_1 - c_2 &= 2 \\ 2c_1 - 3c_2 + c_3 &= 0 \\ -c_1 - c_2 + 4c_3 &= 1. \end{aligned}$$

The augmented matrix is

$$\begin{pmatrix} 1 & -1 & 0 & 2 \\ 2 & -3 & 1 & 0 \\ -1 & -1 & 4 & 1 \end{pmatrix}.$$

First we eliminate the entries 2 and -1 in the first column. Add (-2) times row 1 to row 2 and then add the first row to the third row. This gives

$$\begin{pmatrix} 1 & -1 & 0 & 2 \\ 0 & -1 & 1 & -4 \\ 0 & -2 & 4 & 3 \end{pmatrix}.$$

To eliminate the entry -2 in the second column (and at the same time keep the zero entries in the first column), we add (-2) times the second row to the third, that is,

$$\begin{pmatrix} 1 & -1 & 0 & 2 \\ 0 & -1 & 1 & -4 \\ 0 & 0 & 2 & 11 \end{pmatrix}.$$

This matrix is reduced. It is equivalent to the system

$$c_1 - c_2 = 2$$
$$-c_2 + c_3 = -4$$
$$2c_3 = 11.$$

Back substitution gives $c_3 = \frac{11}{2}$,

$$-c_2 + \tfrac{11}{2} = -4, \qquad c_2 = \tfrac{11}{2} + 4 = \tfrac{19}{2},$$

and

$$c_1 - \tfrac{19}{2} = 2, \qquad c_1 = \tfrac{19}{2} + 2 = \tfrac{23}{2}. \quad \blacksquare$$

EXAMPLE 4.2   Use elimination to solve

$$c_1 - c_2 + c_3 = 0$$
$$c_1 - c_2 + 2c_3 = 4$$
$$c_2 + c_3 = 1.$$

The augmented matrix is

$$\begin{pmatrix} 1 & -1 & 1 & 0 \\ 1 & -1 & 2 & 4 \\ 0 & 1 & 1 & 1 \end{pmatrix}.$$

Add (-1) times the first row to the second:

$$\begin{pmatrix} 1 & -1 & 1 & 0 \\ 0 & 0 & 1 & 4 \\ 0 & 1 & 1 & 1 \end{pmatrix}.$$

Now interchange the second and third rows to obtain the reduced matrix

$$\begin{pmatrix} 1 & -1 & 1 & 0 \\ 0 & 1 & 1 & 1 \\ 0 & 0 & 1 & 4 \end{pmatrix}.$$

Back substitution yields $c_3 = 4$, $c_2 = -3$, and $c_1 = -7$. ■

If A^{-1} does not exist, then (4.4) will have no solution or will have infinitely many solutions. If there are infinitely many solutions, elimination can be used to find these solutions.

EXAMPLE 4.3   Solve the system

$$\begin{aligned} c_1 - c_2 - c_3 &= 1 \\ c_1 + 2c_2 + 2c_3 &= 0 \\ 2c_1 + c_2 + c_3 &= 1. \end{aligned}$$

The augmented matrix is

$$\begin{pmatrix} 1 & -1 & -1 & 1 \\ 1 & 2 & 2 & 0 \\ 2 & 1 & 1 & 1 \end{pmatrix}.$$

Adding (-1) times the first row to the second and (-2) times the first row to the third gives

$$\begin{pmatrix} 1 & -1 & -1 & 1 \\ 0 & 3 & 3 & -1 \\ 0 & 3 & 3 & -1 \end{pmatrix}.$$

Subtracting the second row from the third gives

$$\begin{pmatrix} 1 & -1 & -1 & 1 \\ 0 & 3 & 3 & -1 \\ 0 & 0 & 0 & 0 \end{pmatrix}.$$

This matrix is reduced since all subdiagonal entries are zero. This reduced matrix is equivalent to the three equations

$$\begin{aligned} c_1 - c_2 - c_3 &= 1 \\ 3c_2 + 3c_3 &= -1 \\ 0 &= 0. \end{aligned}$$

Whenever there are infinitely many solutions, elimination will always produce one or more equations of the form $0 = 0$. The last equation gives no information. In the second equation we can solve for c_2 in terms of c_3 (or c_3 in terms of c_2), that is,

$$c_2 = -\tfrac{1}{3} - c_3.$$

This is used in the first equation to obtain

$$c_1 - (-\tfrac{1}{3} - c_3) - c_3 = 1, \qquad c_1 = \tfrac{2}{3}.$$

A solution is

$$\mathbf{c} = \begin{pmatrix} c_1 \\ c_2 \\ c_3 \end{pmatrix} = \begin{pmatrix} \tfrac{2}{3} \\ -\tfrac{1}{3} - c_3 \\ c_3 \end{pmatrix},$$

where c_3 is an arbitrary constant. ■

When there is no solution, elimination will produce a contradictory equation of the form $0 = 1$ or $0 = -2$, etc.

EXAMPLE 4.4   Solve for c_1, c_2, and c_3 in

$$
\begin{aligned}
c_1 - c_2 - c_3 &= 1 \\
c_1 + 2c_2 + 2c_3 &= 0 \\
2c_1 + c_2 + c_3 &= -3.
\end{aligned}
$$

In this case the augmented matrix will reduce to

$$\begin{pmatrix} 1 & -1 & -1 & 1 \\ 0 & 3 & 3 & -1 \\ 0 & 0 & 0 & -4 \end{pmatrix}.$$

The corresponding set of algebraic equations is

$$
\begin{aligned}
c_1 - c_2 - c_3 &= 1 \\
3c_2 + 3c_2 &= -1 \\
0 &= -4.
\end{aligned}
$$

Since $0 = -4$ is not possible, there is no solution. ■

PROBLEMS   **1.** Find *all* solutions $\mathbf{c} = (c_1, c_2)^T$.

(a) $\begin{pmatrix} 2 & 1 \\ 1 & 1 \end{pmatrix} \mathbf{c} = \begin{pmatrix} 1 \\ 2 \end{pmatrix}$.

(b) $\begin{pmatrix} 1 & -1 \\ -1 & 1 \end{pmatrix} \mathbf{c} = \begin{pmatrix} 0 \\ 0 \end{pmatrix}$.

(c) $\begin{pmatrix} 1 & -1 \\ -2 & 2 \end{pmatrix} \mathbf{c} = \begin{pmatrix} -1 \\ 3 \end{pmatrix}$.

(d) $\begin{pmatrix} 2 & 3 \\ 2 & 1 \end{pmatrix} \mathbf{c} = 4\mathbf{c}$.

(e) $\begin{pmatrix} 2i & 1 \\ -1 & 1 \end{pmatrix} \mathbf{c} = \begin{pmatrix} 0 \\ 0 \end{pmatrix}.$

2. Find *all* solutions $\mathbf{c} = (c_1, c_2, c_3)^T$.

(a) $\begin{array}{rcl} c_1 - c_2 & = & 1 \\ c_1 + c_2 - 5c_3 & = & 2 \\ 2c_1 - 3c_2 + c_3 & = & 0. \end{array}$

(b) $\begin{array}{rcl} c_1 + 2c_2 & = & 1 \\ -3c_1 + c_2 + c_3 & = & 0 \\ 2c_2 + c_3 & = & 0. \end{array}$

(c) $\begin{pmatrix} 1 & -3 & 0 \\ 5 & 1 & -1 \\ 6 & -6 & -2 \end{pmatrix} \mathbf{c} = 2\mathbf{c}.$

(d) $\begin{pmatrix} 4 & 2 & 2 \\ 1 & 5 & 1 \\ -2 & -4 & 0 \end{pmatrix} \mathbf{c} = \mathbf{0}.$

(e) $\begin{array}{rcl} 2c_1 + 5c_2 + 4c_3 & = & 8 \\ c_1 - 3c_2 + 2c_3 & = & -10 \\ 3c_1 + 12c_2 + 9c_3 & = & 6. \end{array}$

(f) $\begin{array}{rcl} c_1 - c_2 + 4c_3 & = & c_1 \\ 3c_1 + 2c_2 - c_3 & = & -4c_2 \\ 2c_1 + c_2 - c_3 & = & -c_3. \end{array}$

(g) $\begin{pmatrix} 1 & 0 & 0 \\ -4 & 1 & 0 \\ 3 & 6 & 2 \end{pmatrix} \mathbf{c} = \mathbf{0}.$

(h) $\begin{pmatrix} 1 & 0 & 0 \\ -4 & 1 & 0 \\ 3 & 6 & 2 \end{pmatrix} \mathbf{c} = \mathbf{c}.$

3. Show that

$$\mathbf{A} = \begin{pmatrix} 2 & 0 & 1 \\ -1 & 2 & 1 \\ 1 & 2 & 2 \end{pmatrix}$$

has no inverse. *Hint:* See Problem 4.

4. Show that if $\mathbf{Ax} = \mathbf{0}$ for some vector $\mathbf{x} \neq \mathbf{0}$, then $\mathbf{A}$ has no inverse.

5. Show that if $\mathbf{AB} = \mathbf{BA}$, then for any positive integers m and k, $\mathbf{A}^m \mathbf{B}^k = \mathbf{B}^k \mathbf{A}^m$.

6. Show that if $\mathbf{A}^{-1}$ and $\mathbf{B}^{-1}$ exist, then $(\mathbf{AB})^{-1}$ exists and $(\mathbf{AB})^{-1} = \mathbf{B}^{-1}\mathbf{A}^{-1}$.

7. Show that if $\mathbf{A}$ is an invertible 2×2 matrix, then $\mathbf{AB} = \mathbf{I}$ if and only if the first column of $\mathbf{B}$ is the solution of $\mathbf{Ac}_1 = (1, 0)^T$ and the second column of $\mathbf{B}$ is the solution of $\mathbf{Ac}_2 = (0, 1)^T$.

8. Compute $\mathbf{A}^{-1}$ for each matrix. *Hint:* See Problem 7.

(a) $A = \begin{pmatrix} 1 & 1 \\ -3 & 2 \end{pmatrix}.$

(b) $A = \begin{pmatrix} 3 & -1 \\ -2 & 1 \end{pmatrix}.$

(c) $A = \begin{pmatrix} 2 & 1 \\ 0 & 2 \end{pmatrix}.$

(d) $A = \begin{pmatrix} 2+i & 1 \\ 1 & 1 \end{pmatrix}.$

9. Suppose that $\mathbf{A} = \text{diag}(3, -1, 4)$. Compute $\mathbf{A}^{-1}$. *Hint:* $\mathbf{A}^{-1}$ will be a diagonal matrix.

10. Show that a diagonal matrix is invertible if all diagonal entries are nonzero.

11. Show that if $\mathbf{A}^{-1}$ exists, then $(\mathbf{A}^T)^{-1}$ exists and equals $(\mathbf{A}^{-1})^T$.

7.5 DETERMINANTS AND THEIR USES

We now study the determinant, a scalar-valued function defined for all square matrices. It is defined as follows. The determinant of a 1×1 matrix (a_{11}) is

$$\det (a_{11}) = a_{11}.$$

The determinant of a 2×2 matrix is

(5.1) $\qquad \det \begin{pmatrix} a_{11} & a_{12} \\ a_{21} & a_{22} \end{pmatrix} = \begin{vmatrix} a_{11} & a_{12} \\ a_{21} & a_{22} \end{vmatrix} = a_{11}a_{22} - a_{12}a_{21}.$

Thus the determinant of a 2×2 matrix is the product of the entries on the diagonal minus the product of the two off-diagonal entries. These 2×2 determinants can be quickly computed. For example,

$$\begin{vmatrix} 2 & -1 \\ 3 & 1 \end{vmatrix} = 2 \cdot 1 - (-1)3 = 5, \qquad \begin{vmatrix} 4 & 5 \\ -2 & -1 \end{vmatrix} = 4(-1) - 5(-2) = 6.$$

The determinant of a 3×3 matrix is defined in terms of determinants of three 2×2 submatrices:

(5.2) $\qquad \det \begin{pmatrix} a_{11} & a_{12} & a_{13} \\ a_{21} & a_{22} & a_{23} \\ a_{31} & a_{32} & a_{33} \end{pmatrix} = \begin{vmatrix} a_{11} & a_{12} & a_{13} \\ a_{21} & a_{22} & a_{23} \\ a_{31} & a_{32} & a_{33} \end{vmatrix}$

$$= a_{11} \begin{vmatrix} a_{22} & a_{23} \\ a_{32} & a_{33} \end{vmatrix} - a_{12} \begin{vmatrix} a_{21} & a_{23} \\ a_{31} & a_{33} \end{vmatrix} + a_{13} \begin{vmatrix} a_{21} & a_{22} \\ a_{31} & a_{32} \end{vmatrix}.$$

For example,

$$\begin{vmatrix} 2 & 3 & -1 \\ 0 & 1 & 4 \\ 1 & -2 & 3 \end{vmatrix} = 2 \begin{vmatrix} 1 & 4 \\ -2 & 3 \end{vmatrix} - 3 \begin{vmatrix} 0 & 4 \\ 1 & 3 \end{vmatrix} + (-1) \begin{vmatrix} 0 & 1 \\ 1 & -2 \end{vmatrix}$$

$$= 2[11] - 3[-4] - [-1] = 35.$$

Now consider an $n \times n$ matrix $\mathbf{A} = (a_{ij})$. The determinant of $\mathbf{A}$ will be defined in terms of $(n - 1) \times (n - 1)$ determinants in the manner of (5.2). The matrix obtained from $\mathbf{A}$ by deleting the ith row and the jth column is called the ijth **minor** of $\mathbf{A}$ and is denoted by $\mathbf{A}_{ij}$. The minor $\mathbf{A}_{ij}$ corresponds in a natural way to the ijth entry a_{ij} since it is obtained from $\mathbf{A}$ by deleting the row and the column that contain a_{ij}. The ijth **cofactor** is $(-1)^{i+j} \det \mathbf{A}_{ij}$. The determinant of $\mathbf{A}$ is defined in terms of cofactors as

(5.3) $\qquad \det \mathbf{A} = |\mathbf{A}| = \sum_{j=1}^{n} a_{1j}(-1)^{1+j} \det \mathbf{A}_{1j}$

$$= a_{11} \det \mathbf{A}_{11} - a_{12} \det \mathbf{A}_{12} + a_{13} \det \mathbf{A}_{13} + \dots$$
$$+ (-1)^n a_{1n} \det \mathbf{A}_{1n}.$$

When $n = 3$ this reduces to (5.2).

The definition (5.3) of det $\mathbf{A}$ is a *definition by induction*. This means that the determinant of an $n \times n$ matrix $\mathbf{A}$ is computed in terms of determinants of certain $(n-1) \times (n-1)$ matrices.

EXAMPLE 5.1   Compute det $\mathbf{A}$, where

$$\mathbf{A} = \begin{pmatrix} 1 & 0 & -1 & 0 \\ 4 & 7 & 0 & 2 \\ 1 & 1 & -1 & 1 \\ 2 & 0 & 2 & 1 \end{pmatrix}.$$

By (5.3)

$$\det \mathbf{A} = (1) \begin{vmatrix} 7 & 0 & 2 \\ 1 & -1 & 1 \\ 0 & 2 & 1 \end{vmatrix} - (0) \begin{vmatrix} 4 & 0 & 2 \\ 1 & -1 & 1 \\ 2 & 2 & 1 \end{vmatrix} + (-1) \begin{vmatrix} 4 & 7 & 2 \\ 1 & 1 & 1 \\ 2 & 0 & 1 \end{vmatrix}$$

$$- (0) \begin{vmatrix} 4 & 7 & 0 \\ 1 & 1 & -1 \\ 2 & 0 & 2 \end{vmatrix}$$

$$= \begin{vmatrix} 7 & 0 & 2 \\ 1 & -1 & 1 \\ 0 & 2 & 1 \end{vmatrix} - \begin{vmatrix} 4 & 7 & 2 \\ 1 & 1 & 1 \\ 2 & 0 & 1 \end{vmatrix} = (-17) - (7) = -24. \quad \blacksquare$$

Clearly, determinants of $n \times n$ matrices when $n \geq 4$ are complicated objects. In order to minimize complications and to compute determinants efficiently it will be necessary to borrow some ideas and rules (really theorems) from linear algebra. These rules will be stated and explained in the remainder of this section.

Rule (Mi) If two rows (or two columns) of $\mathbf{A}$ are interchanged, the determinant of the resulting matrix is $-\det \mathbf{A}$.

For example,

$$\begin{vmatrix} 2 & 1 \\ -1 & 4 \end{vmatrix} = 9 = - \begin{vmatrix} -1 & 4 \\ 2 & 1 \end{vmatrix} = - \begin{vmatrix} 1 & 2 \\ 4 & -1 \end{vmatrix}.$$

Rule (Mii) The determinant of $\mathbf{A}$ can be computed by expanding across any row

$$\det \mathbf{A} = a_{i1}(-1)^{i+1} \det \mathbf{A}_{i1} + a_{i2}(-1)^{i+2} \det \mathbf{A}_{i2} + \ldots + a_{in}(-1)^{i+n} \det \mathbf{A}_{in}$$

or down any column

$$\det \mathbf{A} = a_{1j}(-1)^{1+j} \det \mathbf{A}_{1j} + a_{2j}(-1)^{2+j} \det \mathbf{A}_{2j} + \ldots + a_{nj}(-1)^{n+j} \det \mathbf{A}_{nj}.$$

EXAMPLE 5.2   In Example 5.1 the determinant can be evaluated by expanding down the second column. We find that

$$\det \mathbf{A} = -(0)\begin{vmatrix} 4 & 0 & 2 \\ 1 & -1 & 1 \\ 2 & 2 & 1 \end{vmatrix} + (7)\begin{vmatrix} 1 & -1 & 0 \\ 1 & -1 & 1 \\ 2 & 2 & 1 \end{vmatrix} - (1)\begin{vmatrix} 1 & -1 & 0 \\ 4 & 0 & 2 \\ 2 & 2 & 1 \end{vmatrix}$$

$$+ (0)\begin{vmatrix} 1 & -1 & 0 \\ 4 & 0 & 2 \\ 1 & -1 & 1 \end{vmatrix}$$

$$= 7\begin{vmatrix} 1 & -1 & 0 \\ 1 & -1 & 1 \\ 2 & 2 & 1 \end{vmatrix} - \begin{vmatrix} 1 & -1 & 0 \\ 4 & 0 & 2 \\ 2 & 2 & 1 \end{vmatrix} = 7[-4] - [-4] = -24.$$

On the other hand, expanding across the last row gives

$$\det \mathbf{A} = (-2)\begin{vmatrix} 0 & -1 & 0 \\ 7 & 0 & 2 \\ 1 & -1 & 1 \end{vmatrix} + 0\begin{vmatrix} 1 & -1 & 0 \\ 4 & 0 & 2 \\ 1 & -1 & 1 \end{vmatrix} - (2)\begin{vmatrix} 1 & 0 & 0 \\ 4 & 7 & 2 \\ 1 & 1 & 1 \end{vmatrix}$$

$$+ (1)\begin{vmatrix} 1 & 0 & -1 \\ 4 & 7 & 0 \\ 1 & 1 & -1 \end{vmatrix}$$

$$= -2[5] + 0 - 2[5] + [-4] = -24. \quad\blacksquare$$

It will usually be advantageous to expand across a row or down a column that has several zero entries. Since it is not necessary to compute the cofactor $(-1)^{i+j} \det \mathbf{A}_{ij}$ when $a_{ij} = 0$, this strategy minimizes work.

Rule (Miii) For any constant c, if c times any row (or any column) is added to a second row (or second column), the determinant is unchanged.

This rule can often be exploited in order to replace a given matrix $\mathbf{A}$ by another matrix $\mathbf{A}_0$ having many zero entries and such that $\det \mathbf{A} = \det \mathbf{A}_0$. For example, if

$$\mathbf{A} = \begin{pmatrix} 1 & 2 & 1 \\ 1 & 2 & -1 \\ 2 & 1 & 3 \end{pmatrix}, \qquad \mathbf{A}_0 = \begin{pmatrix} 0 & 0 & 2 \\ 1 & 2 & -1 \\ 2 & 1 & 3 \end{pmatrix},$$

then $\mathbf{A}_0$ is obtained from $\mathbf{A}$ by subtracting the second row from the first. Hence

$$\det \mathbf{A} = \det \mathbf{A}_0 = 2\begin{vmatrix} 1 & 2 \\ 2 & 1 \end{vmatrix} = -6.$$

Rule (Miv) If a row or column of **A** is multiplied by a constant k, then the determinant of the resulting matrix is $k \det \mathbf{A}$.

For example,

$$\begin{vmatrix} 2 & 2 \\ 6 & 1 \end{vmatrix} = 2 \begin{vmatrix} 1 & 2 \\ 3 & 1 \end{vmatrix}, \qquad \begin{vmatrix} 50 & 100 & 25 \\ 1 & 0 & 3 \\ 0 & 1 & 1 \end{vmatrix} = 25 \begin{vmatrix} 2 & 4 & 1 \\ 1 & 0 & 3 \\ 0 & 1 & 1 \end{vmatrix},$$

and

$$\begin{vmatrix} 2e^t & -e^{2t} & 3e^{-t} \\ 2e^t & e^{2t} & 0 \\ e^t & 0 & e^{-t} \end{vmatrix} = e^t \begin{vmatrix} 2 & -e^{2t} & 3e^{-t} \\ 2 & e^{2t} & 0 \\ 1 & 0 & e^{-t} \end{vmatrix}$$

$$= e^t e^{2t} \begin{vmatrix} 2 & -1 & 3e^{-t} \\ 2 & 1 & 0 \\ 1 & 0 & e^{-t} \end{vmatrix}$$

$$= e^t e^{2t} e^{-t} \begin{vmatrix} 2 & -1 & 3 \\ 2 & 1 & 0 \\ 1 & 0 & 1 \end{vmatrix}.$$

$$= e^{2t}[1] = e^{2t}.$$

An **upper triangular matrix** $\mathbf{A} = (a_{ij})_{n \times n}$ is a square matrix for which $a_{ij} = 0$ when $i > j$. For example,

$$\begin{pmatrix} 2 & 1 \\ 0 & -1 \end{pmatrix}, \quad \begin{pmatrix} 0 & 1 \\ 0 & 2 \end{pmatrix}, \quad \begin{pmatrix} -1 & 2 & 0 \\ 0 & 3 & 4 \\ 0 & 0 & 1 \end{pmatrix}, \quad \begin{pmatrix} 1 & -2 & -3 \\ 0 & 0 & 2 \\ 0 & 0 & -1 \end{pmatrix}$$

are all upper triangular matrices. A matrix **A** is called **lower triangular** when its transpose $\mathbf{A}^T$ is upper triangular. Examples of lower triangular matrices are

$$\begin{pmatrix} 1 & 0 \\ 3 & 2 \end{pmatrix}, \quad \begin{pmatrix} 1 & 0 \\ 0 & 2 \end{pmatrix}, \quad \begin{pmatrix} -1 & 0 & 0 \\ 3 & 2 & 0 \\ 1 & 1 & 3 \end{pmatrix}, \quad \begin{pmatrix} 3 & 0 & 0 \\ 0 & -\pi & 0 \\ 0 & 1 & \pi \end{pmatrix}.$$

According to the results in Section 7.4, any matrix **A** can be reduced to an upper (or lower) triangular matrix $\mathbf{A}_0$ by a sequence of elementary row operations. The three types of elementary row operators are to multiply a row by a nonzero constant k, to interchange two rows, and to replace a row by the sum of that row and a constant multiple of a second row. The matrix obtained from **A** by one of these three elementary row operation will have determinant $k \det$ **A**, $-\det \mathbf{A}$, or $\det \mathbf{A}$, respectively. Hence when a matrix **A** is reduced to an upper triangular matrix $\mathbf{A}_0$, there is a known constant K such that

$$\det \mathbf{A} = K \det \mathbf{A}_0.$$

The determinant of an upper triangular matrix is easily computed. Indeed, if we expand down the first column, then since all but one entry in the first column is zero, it follows that

$$\det \mathbf{A}_0 = \begin{vmatrix} a_{11} & a_{12} & a_{13} & \cdots & a_{1n} \\ 0 & a_{22} & a_{23} & \cdots & a_{2n} \\ \vdots & \vdots & \vdots & & \vdots \\ 0 & 0 & 0 & \cdots & a_{nn} \end{vmatrix} = a_{11} \begin{vmatrix} a_{22} & a_{23} & \cdots & a_{2n} \\ 0 & a_{33} & \cdots & a_{3n} \\ \vdots & \vdots & & \vdots \\ 0 & 0 & \cdots & a_{nn} \end{vmatrix}.$$

Continue to expand down the first column of the remaining determinants to compute

$$\det \mathbf{A}_0 = a_{11}a_{22} \begin{vmatrix} a_{33} & a_{34} & \cdots & a_{3n} \\ 0 & a_{44} & \cdots & a_{4n} \\ \vdots & \vdots & & \vdots \\ 0 & 0 & \cdots & a_{nn} \end{vmatrix} = \cdots = a_{11}a_{22} \ldots a_{nn}.$$

A similar argument works for lower triangular matrices. Thus the following result is true.

THEOREM 5.3

The determinant of a triangular matrix is the product of its diagonal entries.

For example,

$$\begin{vmatrix} 2 & 1 \\ 0 & -1 \end{vmatrix} = -2, \quad \begin{vmatrix} 0 & 1 \\ 0 & 2 \end{vmatrix} = 0, \quad \begin{vmatrix} -1 & 2 & 0 \\ 0 & 3 & 4 \\ 0 & 0 & -1 \end{vmatrix} = 3, \quad \begin{vmatrix} 2 & 0 & 0 \\ 0 & 3 & 0 \\ 0 & 0 & 4 \end{vmatrix} = 24$$

and if $\mathbf{I}$ is the $n \times n$ identity matrix, $\det \mathbf{I} = 1$ and $\det(-\mathbf{I}) = (-1)^n$.

EXAMPLE 5.4   Compute

$$\begin{vmatrix} 0 & 1 & 2 & 0 \\ 4 & 1 & 2 & -1 \\ 0 & 0 & 1 & 4 \\ 0 & 0 & 20 & 160 \end{vmatrix}.$$

Using elementary row operations

$$\begin{vmatrix} 0 & 1 & 2 & 0 \\ 4 & 1 & 2 & -1 \\ 0 & 0 & 1 & 4 \\ 0 & 0 & 20 & 160 \end{vmatrix} = -\begin{vmatrix} 4 & 1 & 2 & -1 \\ 0 & 1 & 2 & 0 \\ 0 & 0 & 1 & 4 \\ 0 & 0 & 20 & 160 \end{vmatrix} = -20\begin{vmatrix} 4 & 1 & 2 & -1 \\ 0 & 1 & 2 & 0 \\ 0 & 0 & 1 & 4 \\ 0 & 0 & 1 & 8 \end{vmatrix}$$

$$= -20\begin{vmatrix} 4 & 1 & 2 & -1 \\ 0 & 1 & 2 & 0 \\ 0 & 0 & 1 & 4 \\ 0 & 0 & 0 & 4 \end{vmatrix}$$

$$= (-20)[4 \cdot 1 \cdot 1 \cdot 4] = -320.$$

It would also make sense to do the computation by expanding down the first column. There is usually more than one reasonable way to compute a determinant. ∎

Rule (Mv) For any matrix $\mathbf{A}$, $\det \mathbf{A} = \det (\mathbf{A}^T)$.

For example,

$$\begin{vmatrix} a & b \\ c & d \end{vmatrix} = \begin{vmatrix} a & c \\ b & d \end{vmatrix}, \qquad \begin{vmatrix} 2 & 3 & 1 \\ -1 & 0 & 1 \\ 3 & 4 & 1 \end{vmatrix} = \begin{vmatrix} 2 & -1 & 3 \\ 3 & 0 & 4 \\ 1 & 1 & 1 \end{vmatrix}.$$

Rule (Mvi) Given two $n \times n$ matrices $\mathbf{A}$ and $\mathbf{B}$, $\det (\mathbf{AB}) = \det \mathbf{A} \det \mathbf{B}$.

For example,

$$\begin{pmatrix} 2 & 1 \\ -1 & 3 \end{pmatrix}\begin{pmatrix} 1 & 4 \\ 0 & 2 \end{pmatrix} = \begin{pmatrix} 2 & 10 \\ -1 & 2 \end{pmatrix},$$

and

$$\begin{vmatrix} 2 & 1 \\ -1 & 3 \end{vmatrix} = 7, \qquad \begin{vmatrix} 1 & 4 \\ 0 & 2 \end{vmatrix} = 2, \qquad \begin{vmatrix} 2 & 10 \\ -1 & 2 \end{vmatrix} = 14 = 7 \cdot 2.$$

Rule (Mvii) An $n \times n$ matrix $\mathbf{A}$ has an inverse if and only if $\det \mathbf{A} \neq 0$.

Hence the matrices

$$\begin{pmatrix} 2 & 1 \\ 4 & 2 \end{pmatrix}, \quad \begin{pmatrix} 2 & 3 & -1 \\ 1 & 0 & 1 \\ 0 & 3 & -3 \end{pmatrix}, \quad \begin{pmatrix} 1 & 2 & 1 \\ 2 & 4 & 2 \\ -1 & 1 & 1 \end{pmatrix}$$

have no inverse, while the matrices

$$\begin{pmatrix} 1 & 3 \\ -1 & \pi \end{pmatrix}, \quad \begin{pmatrix} 1 & 2 & 1 \\ 1 & 2 & 2 \\ -1 & 0 & 1 \end{pmatrix}, \quad \begin{pmatrix} 2 & 1 & 0 \\ 0 & 2 & 1 \\ 0 & 0 & 2 \end{pmatrix}$$

do. Moreover, when det $\mathbf{A} = D \neq 0$, the inverse can be expressed in terms of cofactors by the formula

$$\mathbf{A}^{-1} = \frac{1}{D}((-1)^{i+j}\det \mathbf{A}_{ij})^T = \frac{1}{D}((-1)^{i+j}\det \mathbf{A}_{ji}).$$

This formula provides a practical method of computing $\mathbf{A}^{-1}$ only when n is small. For $n = 2$ suppose that

$$\mathbf{A} = \begin{pmatrix} a_{11} & a_{12} \\ a_{21} & a_{22} \end{pmatrix}, \qquad D = a_{11}a_{22} - a_{12}a_{21} \neq 0.$$

Then

$$\mathbf{A}^{-1} = \frac{1}{D}\begin{pmatrix} a_{22} & -a_{21} \\ -a_{12} & a_{11} \end{pmatrix}^T = \frac{1}{D}\begin{pmatrix} a_{22} & -a_{12} \\ -a_{21} & a_{11} \end{pmatrix}.$$

For example,

$$\begin{pmatrix} 1 & 3 \\ -2 & -2 \end{pmatrix}^{-1} = \frac{1}{4}\begin{pmatrix} -2 & -3 \\ 2 & 1 \end{pmatrix} = \begin{pmatrix} -\frac{1}{2} & -\frac{3}{4} \\ \frac{1}{2} & \frac{1}{4} \end{pmatrix}$$

and

$$\begin{pmatrix} e^t & e^{-2t} \\ e^t & 2e^{-2t} \end{pmatrix}^{-1} = \frac{1}{e^{-t}}\begin{pmatrix} 2e^{-2t} & -e^{-2t} \\ -e^t & e^t \end{pmatrix} = \begin{pmatrix} 2e^{-t} & -e^{-t} \\ -e^{2t} & e^{2t} \end{pmatrix}.$$

Rule (Mviii) There is a nonzero vector $\mathbf{c}$ such that $\mathbf{Ac} = \mathbf{0}$ if and only if det $\mathbf{A} = 0$.

For example, if

$$\mathbf{A} = \begin{pmatrix} 2 & 3 & -1 \\ 1 & 0 & 1 \\ 0 & 3 & -3 \end{pmatrix},$$

then det $\mathbf{A} = 0$. Hence there is at least one $\mathbf{c} \neq \mathbf{0}$ such that $\mathbf{Ac} = \mathbf{0}$. In fact, there must be infinitely many such $\mathbf{c}$. The method of elimination can be used to reduce $\mathbf{A}$, that is,

$$\begin{pmatrix} 2 & 3 & -1 \\ 1 & 0 & 1 \\ 0 & 3 & -3 \end{pmatrix} \rightarrow \begin{pmatrix} 2 & 3 & -1 \\ 0 & -\frac{3}{2} & \frac{3}{2} \\ 0 & 3 & -3 \end{pmatrix} \rightarrow \begin{pmatrix} 2 & 3 & -1 \\ 0 & -\frac{3}{2} & \frac{3}{2} \\ 0 & 0 & 0 \end{pmatrix}.$$

Hence the solution $\mathbf{c} = (c_1, c_2, c_3)^T$ has components that satisfy

$$2c_1 + 3c_2 - c_3 = 0$$
$$-\tfrac{3}{2}c_2 + \tfrac{3}{2}c_3 = 0,$$

so that $c_2 = c_3$ and $c_1 = (c_3 - 3c_2)/2 = (c_3 - 3c_3)/2 = -c_3$. Hence $c = (-c_3, c_3, c_3)^T$ is a nonzero solution for any $c_3 \neq 0$.

A set $S = \{\mathbf{u}_1, \mathbf{u}_2, \ldots, \mathbf{u}_m\}$ of n-dimensional column vectors is called **linearly dependent** if there are constants $k_1, k_2, \ldots, k_m$, not all zero, such that

(5.4) $$k_1\mathbf{u}_1 + k_2\mathbf{u}_2 + \ldots + k_m\mathbf{u}_m = 0.$$

If (5.4) is true only when $k_1 = k_2 = \ldots = k_m = 0$, then the set S is called **linearly independent.** For example,

(5.5) $$\mathbf{u}_1 = \begin{pmatrix} 1 \\ 0 \\ -1 \end{pmatrix}, \qquad \mathbf{u}_2 = \begin{pmatrix} 1 \\ 1 \\ 0 \end{pmatrix}, \qquad \mathbf{u}_3 = \begin{pmatrix} 1 \\ -2 \\ -3 \end{pmatrix}$$

is linearly dependent since $3\mathbf{u}_1 - 2\mathbf{u}_2 - \mathbf{u}_3 = 0$. Any set that includes the zero vector is linearly dependent. For example, if

$$\mathbf{u}_1 = \begin{pmatrix} 1 \\ 2 \end{pmatrix}, \qquad \mathbf{u}_2 = \begin{pmatrix} 0 \\ 0 \end{pmatrix},$$

then $0 \cdot \mathbf{u}_1 + 1 \cdot \mathbf{u}_2 = 0$.

The case where m equals the dimension n is particularly interesting. Suppose that $\mathbf{u}_i = (u_{1i}, u_{2i}, \ldots, u_{ni})^T$ for $i = 1, 2, \ldots, n$ and suppose that $U = (u_{ij})_{n \times n}$. Hence U is the matrix whose columns are the vectors $\mathbf{u}_1, \mathbf{u}_2, \ldots, \mathbf{u}_n$, written in that order. Thus (5.4) can be written as

$$k_1 \begin{pmatrix} u_{11} \\ u_{21} \\ \vdots \\ u_{n1} \end{pmatrix} + k_2 \begin{pmatrix} u_{12} \\ u_{22} \\ \vdots \\ u_{n2} \end{pmatrix} + \ldots + k_n \begin{pmatrix} u_{1n} \\ u_{2n} \\ \vdots \\ u_{nn} \end{pmatrix} = U\mathbf{k} = 0,$$

where $\mathbf{k} = (k_1, k_2, \ldots, k_n)^T$. This system of algebraic equations will have a nonzero solution $\mathbf{k}$ if and only if $\det U = 0$. Hence S is linearly independent if $\det U \neq 0$ and is linearly dependent if $\det U = 0$. For example, the set

$$\mathbf{u}_1 = \begin{pmatrix} 1 \\ 2 \end{pmatrix}, \qquad \mathbf{u}_2 = \begin{pmatrix} 1 \\ -1 \end{pmatrix}$$

is linearly independent since

$$U = \begin{pmatrix} 1 & 1 \\ 2 & -1 \end{pmatrix} \quad \text{and} \quad \det U = -3 \neq 0.$$

The set (5.5) is linearly dependent since

$$U = \begin{pmatrix} 1 & 1 & 1 \\ 0 & 1 & -2 \\ -1 & 0 & -3 \end{pmatrix} \quad \text{and} \quad \det U = 0.$$

PROBLEMS

In Problems 1–11, compute the determinant of the matrix.

1. $\begin{pmatrix} 2 & 1 \\ -1 & 4 \end{pmatrix}.$

2. $\begin{pmatrix} 0 & 1 \\ -1 & 2 \end{pmatrix}.$

3. $\begin{pmatrix} i & 1 \\ 2 & -i \end{pmatrix}.$

4. $\begin{pmatrix} 1 & 0 & 1 \\ 0 & 1 & 2 \\ 1 & 1 & 3 \end{pmatrix}.$

5. $\begin{pmatrix} 2 & 1 & 0 \\ 0 & 3 & 2 \\ 1 & -1 & -1 \end{pmatrix}.$

6. $\begin{pmatrix} 0 & 1 & 2 & -1 \\ 2 & 0 & 0 & 0 \\ 1 & 4 & -1 & 2 \\ 1 & 1 & 1 & 1 \end{pmatrix}.$

7. $\begin{pmatrix} 1 & 1 & 2 & -1 \\ 0 & 2 & 0 & 3 \\ 0 & 0 & 4 & -1 \\ 0 & 0 & 0 & \pi \end{pmatrix}.$

8. $\begin{pmatrix} 1 & 4 & -1 & 2 \\ 1 & 1 & 1 & 1 \\ 2 & 0 & 0 & 3 \\ 0 & 2 & 2 & -1 \end{pmatrix}.$

9. $\begin{pmatrix} 1 & 2+i & 0 & 4 \\ 0 & 6 & \pi & 3i \\ 0 & 0 & \pi & 7 \\ 0 & 0 & 0 & \sqrt{2}i \end{pmatrix}.$

10. $\begin{pmatrix} 3-u & 2 \\ -1 & 1-u \end{pmatrix}.$

11. $\begin{pmatrix} -1-s & 3 & -1 \\ -3 & -1-s & 0 \\ 0 & 0 & 2-s \end{pmatrix}.$

12. Given **A**, find K and an upper triangular matrix $\mathbf{A}_0$ such that det $\mathbf{A} = K$ det $\mathbf{A}_0$.

(a) $\mathbf{A} = \begin{pmatrix} 1 & 0 & 2 \\ 1 & 1 & 3 \\ 0 & 1 & -1 \end{pmatrix}.$

(b) $\mathbf{A} = \begin{pmatrix} 1 & 0 & -1 \\ 2 & 1 & 4 \\ 3 & 2 & 3 \end{pmatrix}.$

(c) $\mathbf{A} = \begin{pmatrix} 0 & 0 & 2 \\ 1 & 3 & 3 \\ 0 & 1 & 4 \end{pmatrix}.$

13. Find the inverse of each matrix.

(a) $\begin{pmatrix} 1 & 1 \\ -1 & 3 \end{pmatrix}.$

(b) $\begin{pmatrix} 1 & 1 \\ 1 & -1 \end{pmatrix}.$

(c) $\begin{pmatrix} 0 & 2 \\ 1 & 4 \end{pmatrix}.$

(d) $\begin{pmatrix} 2 & 0 & 0 \\ 0 & 3 & 1 \\ 0 & 1 & 2 \end{pmatrix}.$

(e) $\begin{pmatrix} 2 & 1 & 0 \\ 0 & 2 & 0 \\ 0 & 0 & -1 \end{pmatrix}.$

(f) $\begin{pmatrix} e^{2t} & -e^{-2t} \\ e^{2t} & 2e^{-2t} \end{pmatrix}.$

(g) $\begin{pmatrix} e^t & 3e^{-t} \\ -e^t & e^{-t} \end{pmatrix}.$

14. Find all values of s such that the matrix had determinant zero.

(a) $\begin{pmatrix} 2-s & 0 \\ -1 & 2-s \end{pmatrix}.$

(b) $\begin{pmatrix} -s & -3 \\ 1 & 4-s \end{pmatrix}.$

(c) $\begin{pmatrix} 1-s & 4 \\ -1 & 3-s \end{pmatrix}.$

15. Find all solutions of each set of algebraic equations.

(a) $\begin{pmatrix} 2 & 1 \\ -1 & 2 \end{pmatrix} \begin{pmatrix} c_1 \\ c_2 \end{pmatrix} = \mathbf{0}.$

(b) $\begin{pmatrix} 1 & 1 \\ -3 & 3 \end{pmatrix} \begin{pmatrix} c_1 \\ c_2 \end{pmatrix} = \mathbf{0}.$

(c) $\begin{pmatrix} i & 1 \\ -1 & i \end{pmatrix} \begin{pmatrix} c_1 \\ c_2 \end{pmatrix} = \mathbf{0}.$

(d) $\begin{pmatrix} 2 & 1 & 0 \\ 0 & 2 & 0 \\ 0 & 0 & -1 \end{pmatrix} \begin{pmatrix} c_1 \\ c_2 \\ c_3 \end{pmatrix} = 2 \begin{pmatrix} c_1 \\ c_2 \\ c_3 \end{pmatrix}.$

(e) $\begin{pmatrix} 2 & 1 & 0 \\ 0 & 2 & 1 \\ 0 & 0 & -1 \end{pmatrix} \begin{pmatrix} c_1 \\ c_2 \\ c_3 \end{pmatrix} = 2 \begin{pmatrix} c_1 \\ c_2 \\ c_3 \end{pmatrix} + \begin{pmatrix} 1 \\ 0 \\ 0 \end{pmatrix}.$

16. Determine whether or not each set of vectors is linearly independent.

(a) $(1, 2)^T, (1, -1)^T.$

(b) $(1, i)^T, (2, 1)^T.$

(c) $(1, 1, 1)^T, (2, 0, -1)^T, (7, 1, -2)^T.$

(d) $(2, 1, 4)^T, (0, 1, 3)^T, (1, 0, 1)^T.$

(e) $(1, 2, 1)^T, (3, 0, 1)^T, (0, 2, 1)^T.$

(f) $(1, 0, 2, 4)^T, (0, 0, 2, 1)^T, (0, 0, 0, \sqrt{2})^T, (0, 4, 0, 0)^T.$

(g) $(1, 1)^T, (1, -1)^T, (2, 1)^T.$

(h) $(1, 0, 1)^T, (1, 1, 0)^T.$

17. Given Rule (Mii), show that $\det \mathbf{A} = \det \mathbf{A}^T.$

18. Show that if two rows (or two columns) of a matrix $\mathbf{A}$ are proportional, then $\det \mathbf{A} = 0.$

19. Given $\mathbf{A} = (a_{ij})_{n \times n}$, let $\mathbf{A}_{ij}$ be the ijth minor. Show that for any r and any s between 1 and n,

$$\sum_{j=1}^{n} (-1)^{s+j} \det \mathbf{A}_{js} a_{jr} = \begin{cases} 0 & \text{if } r \neq s \\ \det \mathbf{A} & \text{if } r = s. \end{cases}$$

Hint: The expression is the expansion down the sth column of some matrix $\mathbf{B}$. Find $\mathbf{B}$.

20. If $\det \mathbf{A} \neq 0$, prove that

$$\mathbf{A}^{-1} = \frac{1}{\det \mathbf{A}} ((-1)^{i+j} \mathbf{A}_{ji}).$$

Hint: Use Problem 19.

21. Show that if $\{\mathbf{u}_1, \mathbf{u}_2, \ldots, \mathbf{u}_n\}$ is a linearly independent set of column vectors of dimension n and if $\mathbf{v}$ is any n-dimensional column vector, there is one and only one set of numbers $c_1, c_2, \ldots, c_n$ such that $c_1 \mathbf{u}_1 + c_2 \mathbf{u}_2 + \ldots + c_n \mathbf{u}_n = \mathbf{v}.$

7.6   HOMOGENEOUS LINEAR SYSTEMS

Given an $n \times n$ matrix-valued function $\mathbf{A}(t) = (a_{ij}(t))_{n \times n}$ which is defined and continuous on an interval $J = (a, b)$, consider the homogeneous first-order linear system

(H) $$\mathbf{x}' = \mathbf{A}(t)\mathbf{x}.$$

Every solution of (H) will be defined over the entire interval J. A general solution of (H) will contain n arbitrary constants. The values of these constants can be specified in such a way that any initial condition

(IC) $$\mathbf{x}(t_0) = \mathbf{x}_0$$

is true, where t_0 is any point in the interval J and $\mathbf{x}_0$ is any n-dimensional column vector. Moreover, for (H) the following **principle of superposition** is true.

THEOREM 6.1: LINEAR COMBINATIONS

If $\mathbf{x}_1(t)$ and $\mathbf{x}_2(t)$ are two solutions of (H) and if c_1 and c_2 are any two constants, then $c_1\mathbf{x}_1(t) + c_2\mathbf{x}_2(t)$ is also a solution of (H).

To see that the theorem is true, let $\mathbf{x} = c_1\mathbf{x}_1 + c_2\mathbf{x}_2$. Then

$$\mathbf{x}' = c_1\mathbf{x}'_1 + c_2\mathbf{x}'_2 = c_1\big[\mathbf{A}(t)\mathbf{x}_1\big] + c_2\big[\mathbf{A}(t)\mathbf{x}_2\big]$$
$$= \mathbf{A}(t)\big[c_1\mathbf{x}_1 + c_2\mathbf{x}_2\big] = \mathbf{A}(t)\mathbf{x}.$$

Hence $\mathbf{x}$ is also a solution of (H).

By repeated application of Theorem 6.1, we see that if $\mathbf{x}_1, \mathbf{x}_2, \ldots, \mathbf{x}_k$ are all solutions of (H) and if $c_1, c_2, \ldots, c_k$ are given constants, then

$$c_1\mathbf{x}_1 + c_2\mathbf{x}_2 + \ldots + c_k\mathbf{x}_k$$

is a solution of (H). A particularly interesting case is $k = n$. Then

(6.1) $$\mathbf{x} = c_1\mathbf{x}_1 + c_2\mathbf{x}_2 + \ldots + c_n\mathbf{x}_n$$

is a solution of (H) that contains n arbitrary constants c_i.

A set $\{\mathbf{x}_1, \mathbf{x}_2, \ldots, \mathbf{x}_k\}$ of k solutions of (H) is called **linearly independent on** J whenever $c_1, c_2, \ldots, c_k$ are constants such that

(6.2) $$c_1\mathbf{x}_1(t) + c_2\mathbf{x}_2(t) + \ldots + c_k\mathbf{x}_k(t) = 0 \qquad \text{for all } t \in J,$$

then $c_1 = c_2 = \ldots = c_k = 0$. A set of n solutions $S = \{x_1, x_2, \ldots, x_n\}$ of (H) is called a **fundamental set of solutions** of (H) if S is a linearly independent set of solutions on J. Whenever S is a fundamental set of solutions, then (6.1) is a general solution of (H).

Given a set $S = \{\mathbf{x}_1, \mathbf{x}_2, \ldots, \mathbf{x}_n\}$ of solutions of (H), let $\mathbf{X}$ be the $n \times n$ matrix whose first column is made up of the entries of the solution $\mathbf{x}_1$, whose second column is made up of the entries of $\mathbf{x}_2$, and so on. Symbolically, we write

$$\mathbf{X}(t) = \big[\mathbf{x}_1(t), \mathbf{x}_2(t), \ldots, \mathbf{x}_n(t)\big].$$

The matrix $\mathbf{X}$ is called a **fundamental matrix** for (H) if S is a fundamental set of solutions. Given a vector $\mathbf{c} = (c_1, c_2, \ldots, c_n)^T \neq 0$, then

$$c_1\mathbf{x}_1(t) + c_2\mathbf{x}_2(t) + \ldots + c_n\mathbf{x}_n(t) = \mathbf{X}(t)\mathbf{c} = 0$$

implies that det $\mathbf{X}(t) = 0$ for all t in J. Conversely, if for some t_0 in J, we have det $\mathbf{X}(t_0) = 0$; then there is a $\mathbf{c} \neq \mathbf{0}$ such that $\mathbf{X}(t_0)\mathbf{c} = \mathbf{0}$. Hence $\mathbf{x}(t) = \mathbf{X}(t)\mathbf{c}$ satisfies (H) plus the initial condition $\mathbf{x}(t_0) = \mathbf{0}$, so $\mathbf{x}(t) = \mathbf{X}(t)\mathbf{c} \equiv \mathbf{0}$ on J. This proves the following result.

THEOREM 6.2: CHARACTERIZATION OF FUNDAMENTAL SETS

If $S = \{\mathbf{x}_1, \mathbf{x}_2, \ldots, \mathbf{x}_n\}$ is a set of n solutions of the system (H) and if $\mathbf{X} = [\mathbf{x}_1, \mathbf{x}_2, \ldots, \mathbf{x}_n]$, then the following statements are equivalent.

(a) S is a fundamental set of solutions of (H).
(b) $\mathbf{X}(t)$ is a fundamental matrix for (H).
(c) det $\mathbf{X}(t) \neq 0$ for all t in J.
(d) det $\mathbf{X}(t) \neq 0$ for at least one t in J.

If S is a fundamental set of solutions of (H), then

$$\mathbf{x}(t) = c_1\mathbf{x}_1 + c_2\mathbf{x}_2 + \ldots + c_n\mathbf{x}_n = \mathbf{X}(t)\mathbf{c},$$

with $\mathbf{c} = (c_1, c_2, \ldots, c_n)^T$, is a general solution of (H).

EXAMPLE 6.3   Solve the initial value problem

$$\mathbf{x}' = \begin{pmatrix} -1 & 6 \\ 1 & -2 \end{pmatrix}\mathbf{x}, \qquad \mathbf{x}(0) = \begin{pmatrix} 1 \\ 0 \end{pmatrix},$$

given the two solutions

$$\mathbf{x}_1(t) = \begin{pmatrix} 3 \\ 1 \end{pmatrix}e^t, \qquad \mathbf{x}_2(t) = \begin{pmatrix} -2 \\ 1 \end{pmatrix}e^{-4t}.$$

To check that the given functions are solutions, we compute

$$\begin{pmatrix} -1 & 6 \\ 1 & -2 \end{pmatrix}\begin{pmatrix} 3 \\ 1 \end{pmatrix}e^t = \begin{pmatrix} -3+6 \\ 3-2 \end{pmatrix}e^t = \begin{pmatrix} 3 \\ 1 \end{pmatrix}e^t = \left[\begin{pmatrix} 3 \\ 1 \end{pmatrix}e^t\right]'$$

and

$$\begin{pmatrix} -1 & 6 \\ 1 & -2 \end{pmatrix}\begin{pmatrix} -2 \\ 1 \end{pmatrix}e^{-4t} = \begin{pmatrix} 8 \\ -4 \end{pmatrix}e^{-4t} = \begin{pmatrix} -2 \\ 1 \end{pmatrix}(-4e^{-4t}) = \left[\begin{pmatrix} -2 \\ 1 \end{pmatrix}e^{-4t}\right]'.$$

Given $\mathbf{x}_1$ and $\mathbf{x}_2$, the matrix $\mathbf{X} = [\mathbf{x}_1, \mathbf{x}_2]$ is

$$\mathbf{X}(t) = \begin{pmatrix} 3e^t & -2e^{-4t} \\ e^t & e^{-4t} \end{pmatrix}.$$

Since $\det \mathbf{X}(t) = 5e^{-3t} \neq 0$, then $\{\mathbf{x}_1, \mathbf{x}_2\}$ is a fundamental set of solutions and $\mathbf{X}(t)$ is a fundamental matrix. A general solution is

$$\mathbf{x}(t) = c_1 \begin{pmatrix} 3 \\ 1 \end{pmatrix} e^t + c_2 \begin{pmatrix} -2 \\ 1 \end{pmatrix} e^{-4t} = \begin{pmatrix} 3e^t & -2e^{-4t} \\ e^t & e^{-4t} \end{pmatrix} \begin{pmatrix} c_1 \\ c_2 \end{pmatrix} = \mathbf{X}(t)\mathbf{c}.$$

We need to pick $\mathbf{c}$ so that

$$\mathbf{x}(0) = \begin{pmatrix} 1 \\ 0 \end{pmatrix} = \mathbf{X}(0)\mathbf{c} = \begin{pmatrix} 3 & -2 \\ 1 & 1 \end{pmatrix} \begin{pmatrix} c_1 \\ c_2 \end{pmatrix}.$$

Hence

$$\begin{pmatrix} c_1 \\ c_2 \end{pmatrix} = \begin{pmatrix} 3 & -2 \\ 1 & 1 \end{pmatrix}^{-1} \begin{pmatrix} 1 \\ 0 \end{pmatrix} = \begin{pmatrix} \frac{1}{5} & \frac{2}{5} \\ -\frac{1}{5} & \frac{3}{5} \end{pmatrix} \begin{pmatrix} 1 \\ 0 \end{pmatrix} = \begin{pmatrix} \frac{1}{5} \\ -\frac{1}{5} \end{pmatrix}. \quad \blacksquare$$

THEOREM 6.4: SOLUTION FORMULA

If $\mathbf{X}(t)$ is a fundamental matrix for (H), then for any t_0 in J and any vector $\mathbf{x}_0$ the solution of the initial value problem

$$\mathbf{x}' = \mathbf{A}\mathbf{x}, \qquad \mathbf{x}(t_0) = \mathbf{x}_0$$

is $\mathbf{x}(t) = \mathbf{X}(t)\mathbf{X}^{-1}(t_0)\mathbf{x}_0$.

To prove this result, note that if $\mathbf{c}$ is an arbitrary vector, then $\mathbf{x}(t) = \mathbf{X}(t)\mathbf{c}$ is a general solution. The vector $\mathbf{c}$ is determined from the initial condition, that is,

$$\mathbf{x}(t_0) = \mathbf{x}_0 = \mathbf{X}(t_0)\mathbf{c} \quad \text{or} \quad \mathbf{c} = \mathbf{X}(t_0)^{-1}\mathbf{x}_0.$$

Hence $\mathbf{x}(t) = \mathbf{X}(t)\mathbf{c} = \mathbf{X}(t)\mathbf{X}(t_0)^{-1}\mathbf{x}_0$, as required.

EXAMPLE 6.5   The reader can easily check that

(6.3)
$$\mathbf{x}' = \begin{pmatrix} 1 & 5 \\ -1 & 7 \end{pmatrix} \mathbf{x}$$

has a fundamental set of solutions

$$\mathbf{x}_1 = \begin{pmatrix} 1 \\ 1 \end{pmatrix} e^{6t}, \qquad \mathbf{x}_2 = \begin{pmatrix} 5 \\ 1 \end{pmatrix} e^{2t}.$$

Hence

$$\mathbf{X}(t) = \begin{pmatrix} e^{6t} & 5e^{2t} \\ e^{6t} & e^{2t} \end{pmatrix}$$

is a fundamental matrix. Since $\det \mathbf{X}(t) = -4e^{8t}$, then

$$\mathbf{X}(t)^{-1} = \frac{1}{-4e^{8t}} \begin{pmatrix} e^{2t} & -5e^{2t} \\ -e^{6t} & e^{6t} \end{pmatrix} = \begin{pmatrix} -\dfrac{e^{-6t}}{4} & \dfrac{5}{4}e^{-6t} \\ \dfrac{1}{4}e^{-2t} & -\dfrac{1}{4}e^{-2t} \end{pmatrix}.$$

Hence a general solution is

$$\mathbf{x}(t) = \begin{pmatrix} e^{6t} & 5e^{2t} \\ e^{6t} & e^{2t} \end{pmatrix} \begin{pmatrix} -\frac{1}{4}e^{-6t_0} & \frac{5}{4}e^{-6t_0} \\ \frac{1}{4}e^{-2t_0} & -\frac{1}{4}e^{-2t_0} \end{pmatrix} \mathbf{x}_0$$

$$= \begin{pmatrix} -\frac{1}{4}e^{6(t-t_0)} + \frac{5}{4}e^{2(t-t_0)} & \frac{5}{4}e^{6(t-t_0)} - \frac{5}{4}e^{2(t-t_0)} \\ -\frac{1}{4}e^{6(t-t_0)} + \frac{1}{4}e^{2(t-t_0)} & \frac{5}{4}e^{6(t-t_0)} - \frac{1}{4}e^{2(t-t_0)} \end{pmatrix} \mathbf{x}_0. \quad \blacksquare$$

Given the homogeneous linear equation (H), there is a corresponding **matrix differential equation,**

(M) $$\mathbf{X}' = \mathbf{A}(t)\mathbf{X}.$$

In (M) the unknown is the $n \times n$ matrix $\mathbf{X}(t)$. A matrix $\mathbf{X}(t)$ will solve (M) if and only if each column of $\mathbf{X}(t)$ is a solution of (H). Hence the matrix $\mathbf{X}(t)$ is simply a handy notation that allows one to keep track of n solutions $\{\mathbf{x}_1, \mathbf{x}_2, \ldots, \mathbf{x}_n\}$ of (H) with the one symbol $\mathbf{X} = [\mathbf{x}_1, \mathbf{x}_2, \ldots, \mathbf{x}_n]$. A unique solution of (M) can be specified by giving one matrix initial condition

(6.4) $$\mathbf{X}(t_0) = \mathbf{X}_0.$$

For example, the computations in Example 6.5 show that the unique solution of

$$\mathbf{X}_e' = \begin{pmatrix} 1 & 5 \\ -1 & 7 \end{pmatrix} \mathbf{X}_e, \qquad \mathbf{X}_e(0) = \mathbf{I}$$

is

$$\mathbf{X}_e(t) = \begin{pmatrix} -\frac{1}{4}e^{6t} + \frac{5}{4}e^{2t} & \frac{5}{4}e^{6t} - \frac{5}{4}e^{2t} \\ -\frac{1}{4}e^{6t} + \frac{1}{4}e^{2t} & \frac{5}{4}e^{6t} - \frac{1}{4}e^{2t} \end{pmatrix}.$$

The next result provides a way of replacing one fundamental matrix by a second one.

THEOREM 6.6: FUNDAMENTAL MATRICES

If $\mathbf{X}(t)$ is a fundamental matrix for (H) and if $\mathbf{C}$ is any $n \times n$ constant matrix, then $\mathbf{X}_1 = \mathbf{XC}$ is a solution of (M). If $\det \mathbf{C} \neq 0$, then $\mathbf{X}_1$ is also a fundamental matrix.

To see that the result is true, compute

$$\mathbf{X}'_1 = \mathbf{X}'\mathbf{C} = [\mathbf{A}(t)\mathbf{X}]\mathbf{C} = \mathbf{A}(t)[\mathbf{X}\mathbf{C}] = \mathbf{A}(t)\mathbf{X}_1.$$

Hence $\mathbf{X}_1$ solves (M). Moreover, $\det \mathbf{X}_1(t) = \det(\mathbf{X}(t)\mathbf{C}) = \det \mathbf{X}(t) \det \mathbf{C}$. Since $\det \mathbf{X}(t) \neq 0$, then $\det \mathbf{X}_1(t) \neq 0$ if and only if $\det \mathbf{C} \neq 0$.

EXAMPLE 6.7   Solve the matrix initial value problem

$$\mathbf{Y}' = \begin{pmatrix} -1 & 6 \\ 1 & -2 \end{pmatrix}\mathbf{Y}, \qquad \mathbf{Y}(t_0) = \mathbf{I}.$$

From Example 6.3 we see that

$$\mathbf{X}(t) = \begin{pmatrix} 3e^t & -2e^{-4t} \\ e^t & e^{-4t} \end{pmatrix}$$

solves the matrix differential equation. We can check that this matrix is a fundamental matrix by computing $\det \mathbf{X}(t_0) = 5e^{-3t_0} \neq 0$. Since

$$\mathbf{X}^{-1}(t_0) = \frac{1}{5e^{-3t_0}}\begin{pmatrix} e^{-4t_0} & 2e^{-4t_0} \\ -e^{t_0} & 3e^{t_0} \end{pmatrix} = \frac{1}{5}\begin{pmatrix} e^{-t_0} & 2e^{-t_0} \\ -e^{4t_0} & 3e^{4t_0} \end{pmatrix}.$$

then $\mathbf{Y}(t) = \mathbf{X}(t)\mathbf{X}^{-1}(t_0)$ is the required matrix solution, that is,

$$\mathbf{Y}(t) = \frac{1}{5}\begin{pmatrix} 3e^{t-t_0} + 2e^{-4(t-t_0)} & 6e^{t-t_0} - 6e^{-4(t-t_0)} \\ e^{t-t_0} - e^{-4(t-t_0)} & 2e^{t-t_0} + 3e^{-4(t-t_0)} \end{pmatrix}. \quad \blacksquare$$

PROBLEMS

1. For each system of equations, verify that the given functions are solutions. Decide whether or not the given set of solutions is a fundamental set of solutions.

(a) $\mathbf{x}' = \begin{pmatrix} 2 & -1 \\ 1 & 2 \end{pmatrix}\mathbf{x}, \quad \mathbf{x}_1 = e^{2t}\begin{pmatrix} \cos t \\ \sin t \end{pmatrix}, \quad \mathbf{x}_2 = e^{2t}\begin{pmatrix} -\sin t \\ \cos t \end{pmatrix}.$

(b) $\mathbf{x}' = \begin{pmatrix} 1 & 4 \\ 1 & 1 \end{pmatrix}\mathbf{x}, \quad \mathbf{x}_1 = \begin{pmatrix} 2 \\ 1 \end{pmatrix}e^{3t}, \quad \mathbf{x}_2 = \begin{pmatrix} 2 \\ -1 \end{pmatrix}e^{-t}.$

(c) $\mathbf{x}' = \begin{pmatrix} -1 & 1 & 0 \\ 0 & -1 & 0 \\ 0 & 0 & -1 \end{pmatrix}\mathbf{x}, \quad \mathbf{x}_1 = \begin{pmatrix} 0 \\ 0 \\ e^{-t} \end{pmatrix}, \quad \mathbf{x}_2 = \begin{pmatrix} e^{-t} \\ 0 \\ 0 \end{pmatrix}, \quad \mathbf{x}_3 = \begin{pmatrix} te^{-t} \\ e^{-t} \\ -e^{-t} \end{pmatrix}.$

(d) $\mathbf{x}' = \begin{pmatrix} -1 & 1 & 0 \\ 0 & -1 & 0 \\ 0 & 0 & 3 \end{pmatrix}\mathbf{x}, \quad \mathbf{x}_1 = \begin{pmatrix} 0 \\ 0 \\ e^{3t} \end{pmatrix}, \quad \mathbf{x}_2 = \begin{pmatrix} 0 \\ 0 \\ 0 \end{pmatrix}, \quad \mathbf{x}_3 = \begin{pmatrix} e^{-t} \\ 0 \\ 0 \end{pmatrix}.$

2. (a) Verify that $\mathbf{x}_1 = (1, 1)^T e^{-2t}$, $\mathbf{x}_2 = (3, -1)^T e^{2t}$ is a fundamental set of solutions of

$$\mathbf{x}' = \begin{pmatrix} 1 & -3 \\ -1 & -1 \end{pmatrix}\mathbf{x}.$$

(b) Find the fundamental matrix solution $\mathbf{X}_e(t)$ such that $\mathbf{X}_e(0) = \mathbf{I}$.

(c) Find the solution that satisfies $\mathbf{x}(0) = (0, -1)^T$.

3. (a) Verify

$$x_1 = \begin{pmatrix} 0 \\ 0 \\ e^{3t} \end{pmatrix}, \qquad x_2 = \begin{pmatrix} -e^{-t} \\ 0 \\ 0 \end{pmatrix}, \qquad x_3 = \begin{pmatrix} te^{-t} \\ e^{-t} \\ 0 \end{pmatrix}$$

is a fundamental set of solutions of

$$x' = \begin{pmatrix} -1 & 1 & 0 \\ 0 & -1 & 0 \\ 0 & 0 & 3 \end{pmatrix} x.$$

(b) Find the fundamental matrix that satisfies $X(0) = I$.

(c) Find the solution that satisfies $x(0) = (2, 1, 0)^T$.

4. Let $X = (x_{ij})_{2 \times 2}$ be a solution of (M) when $n = 2$ and let $D(t) = \det X(t)$.

(a) Show that

$$\frac{dD}{dt} = \begin{vmatrix} x'_{11} & x_{12} \\ x'_{21} & x_{22} \end{vmatrix} + \begin{vmatrix} x_{11} & x'_{12} \\ x_{21} & x'_{22} \end{vmatrix}.$$

(b) Show that

$$\frac{dD}{dt} = [a_{11}(t) + a_{22}(t)]D.$$

(c) Given part (b), show that either $D(t)$ is everywhere zero on J or else $D(t)$ is never zero on J.

(d) Suppose that $\det X(t) \neq 0$ on I. If X_1 is a second solution of (M), show there is a constant c such that $\det X_1(t) = c \det X(t)$.

5. Let Y and Z be solutions of (M) with $\det Y(t) \neq 0$ on I. Show that there is a constant matrix K such that $Z(t) = Y(t)K$ for all t in I. *Hint:* Let $Z = [z_1, z_2, \ldots, z_n]$ and $K = [k_1, \ldots, k_n]$. Show that there is a k_j such that $z_j(t) = Y(t)k_j$.

6. Recall that $y'' + 4y = 0$ is equivalent to

$$x' = \begin{pmatrix} 0 & 1 \\ -4 & 0 \end{pmatrix} x.$$

(a) Find a fundamental set of solutions of this system.

(b) Find the fundamental matrix $Y(t)$ such that $Y(t_0) = I$.

7. Given $y'' + 9y = 0$, let $x_1 = y$ and $x_2 = y'/3$.

(a) Reduce this second-order equation to an equivalent system for $x = (x_1, x_2)^T$.

(b) For the system found in part (a), find a set of fundamental solutions.

(c) Find the fundamental matrix for the system.

(d) Find the fundamental matrix $Y(t)$ such that $Y(t_0) = I$.

8. Show that the matrix initial value problem

$$Y' = A(t)Y, \qquad Y(t_0) = C$$

has a unique solution on J. *Hint:* Use the existence and uniqueness theorem for (H).

9. Given Problem 8, show that if $A(t)$ is continuous over J, then (M) has at least one fundamental matrix defined on J.

10. Suppose that $A(t) = A$ is independent of t. Let X be the solution of $X' = AX$ such that $X(0) = I$.

   (a) Show that for any real number t_0, $X_1(t) = X(t - t_0)$ is also a fundamental matrix.

   (b) By Problem 5 there is a constant matrix K such that $X(t - t_0) = X(t)K$. Show that $K = X(-t_0)$.

   (c) Given (b) show that $K = X(t_0)^{-1}$.

   (d) Show that $X(t - t_0) = X(t)X(t_0)^{-1}$.

   (e) Show that $X(t - t_0) = X(t)X(-t_0)$, that is, show $X(-t_0) = X(t_0)^{-1}$.

   (f) Show that $X(t + s) = X(t)X(s)$.

11. Let $A(t)$ be independent of time and let X solve

$$X' = AX, \qquad X(0) = I.$$

Show that $x_1 = X(t - t_0)x_0$ and $x_2 = X(t)X(t_0)^{-1}x_0$ both solve

$$x' = Ax, \qquad x(t_0) = x_0.$$

12. (a) Recall that the solution of the initial value problem (M) and (6.4) is unique. Using this, show that for any two fundamental matrices X_1 and X_2,

$$X_1(t)X_1^{-1}(t_0) = X_2(t)X_2^{-1}(t_0)$$

   for all t and t_0 in J.

   (b) Show that the solution of (M) and (6.4) is $X_i(t)X_i^{-1}(t_0)X_0$ for $i = 1$ and for $i = 2$.

7.7 *THE EIGENVALUE–EIGENVECTOR METHOD OF SOLUTION*

We will now develop a method of solution for the first-order system of differential equations

$$(7.1) \qquad\qquad\qquad x' = Ax$$

when A is independent of time. Since A is the coefficient matrix for the system, we say that (7.1) has **constant coefficients.** Our method of solution is a natural extension of the methods of solution developed in Chapters 3 and 4. We take as a trial solution

$$(7.2) \qquad\qquad\qquad x = e^{\lambda t}v,$$

where the constant λ and the vector v must be determined. On substituting (7.2) into (7.1) it follows that

$$\lambda e^{\lambda t}v = A(e^{\lambda t}v) = e^{\lambda t}Av$$

or

$$(7.3) \qquad\qquad\qquad (A - \lambda I)v = 0.$$

The zero vector $\mathbf{v} = \mathbf{0}$ provides a solution but not a very interesting one. In order that (7.3) have a *nonzero solution* $\mathbf{v}$, it is necessary that $\mathbf{A} - \lambda\mathbf{I}$ have determinant zero, that is,

$$(7.4) \qquad p(\lambda) = \det(\mathbf{A} - \lambda\mathbf{I}) = 0.$$

If $p(\lambda)$ is zero, then (7.3) will have infinitely many solutions.

EXAMPLE 7.1　　Find a general solution of

$$(7.5) \qquad \mathbf{x}' = \begin{pmatrix} 3 & -2 \\ -1 & 2 \end{pmatrix}\mathbf{x}.$$

In this case

$$p(\lambda) = \begin{vmatrix} 3 - \lambda & -2 \\ -1 & 2 - \lambda \end{vmatrix} = (3 - \lambda)(2 - \lambda) - 2$$

$$= \lambda^2 - 5\lambda + 4 = (\lambda - 1)(\lambda - 4).$$

Hence $\lambda_1 = 1$ or $\lambda_2 = 4$ will do.

For $\lambda_1 = 1$, (7.3) is

$$\begin{pmatrix} 2 & -2 \\ -1 & 1 \end{pmatrix}\begin{pmatrix} v_1 \\ v_2 \end{pmatrix} = \begin{pmatrix} 2v_1 - 2v_2 \\ -v_1 + v_2 \end{pmatrix} = \begin{pmatrix} 0 \\ 0 \end{pmatrix}.$$

The solution is $v_1 = v_2$, where v_2 is any constant. Hence

$$\mathbf{v} = \begin{pmatrix} v_2 \\ v_2 \end{pmatrix} = v_2 \begin{pmatrix} 1 \\ 1 \end{pmatrix}.$$

Since the solution will be multiplied by an arbitrary constant later, we shall take $v_2 = 1$ and obtain the solution

$$\mathbf{x}_1 = \begin{pmatrix} 1 \\ 1 \end{pmatrix} e^t.$$

For $\lambda_2 = 4$ (7.3) is

$$\begin{pmatrix} -1 & -2 \\ -1 & -2 \end{pmatrix}\begin{pmatrix} v_1 \\ v_2 \end{pmatrix} = \begin{pmatrix} -v_1 - 2v_2 \\ -v_1 - 2v_2 \end{pmatrix} = \begin{pmatrix} 0 \\ 0 \end{pmatrix}.$$

Hence $v_1 = -2v_2$ or $v = (-2v_2, v_2)^T = v_2(-2, 1)^T$. Since we can take v_2 to be any convenient nonzero value, we choose $v_2 = -1$ and obtain

$$\mathbf{x}_2 = \begin{pmatrix} 2 \\ -1 \end{pmatrix} e^{4t}.$$

A general solution is

$$\mathbf{x}(t) = c_1 \begin{pmatrix} 1 \\ 1 \end{pmatrix} e^t + c_2 \begin{pmatrix} 2 \\ -1 \end{pmatrix} e^{4t} = \begin{pmatrix} e^t & 2e^{4t} \\ e^t & -e^{4t} \end{pmatrix}\begin{pmatrix} c_1 \\ c_2 \end{pmatrix},$$

where c_1 and c_2 are arbitrary constants. A fundamental matrix is

(7.6)
$$X(t) = \begin{pmatrix} e^t & 2e^{4t} \\ e^t & -e^{4t} \end{pmatrix}. \quad \blacksquare$$

The function $p(\lambda)$ defined in (7.4) is a polynomial in λ of degree n. This polynomial is called the **characteristic polynomial** for $x' = Ax$. The **characteristic equation** is $p(\lambda) = 0$. The solutions $\lambda_1, \lambda_2, \ldots, \lambda_n$ of the characteristic equation are called the **eigenvalues** of A. Given an eigenvalue λ_i of A, a corresponding **eigenvector** v_i is a *nonzero* solution of $(A - \lambda_i I)v_i = 0$. For example, in Example 7.1 $\lambda_1 = 1$ and $\lambda_2 = 4$ are the eigenvalues of

$$A = \begin{pmatrix} 3 & -2 \\ -1 & 2 \end{pmatrix}.$$

Given the eigenvalue $\lambda_1 = 1$ an eigenvector has the form $v_1 = (v_1, v_1)^T$. For $\lambda_2 = 4$ we saw that the eigenvector is $v_2 = (-2v_2, v_2)^T$ for any nonzero constant v_2.

It can be shown that eigenvectors corresponding to different eigenvalues are linearly independent. Hence the following result is true.

THEOREM 7.2: EIGENVALUE–EIGENVECTOR METHOD

Suppose that A has n distinct eigenvalues $\lambda_1, \lambda_2, \ldots, \lambda_n$. Let v_i be an eigenvector corresponding to λ_i for $i = 1, 2, \ldots, n$. Then a general solution of (7.1) is

$$x(t) = c_1 e^{\lambda_1 t} v_1 + c_2 e^{\lambda_2 t} v_2 + \ldots + c_n e^{\lambda_n t} v_n.$$

The matrix

$$X(t) = [e^{\lambda_1 t} v_1, e^{\lambda_2 t} v_2, \ldots, e^{\lambda_n t} v_n]$$

is a fundamental matrix for $x' = Ax$.

The eigenvalue–eigenvector method of solution is reasonably straightforward but does require a bit of practice. The main problem for most students is to make sure to find a *nonzero solution* v of (7.3).

EXAMPLE 7.3   Find a general solution of

(7.7)
$$x' = \begin{pmatrix} 0 & 1 & 0 \\ 0 & 0 & 1 \\ -2 & 1 & 2 \end{pmatrix} x.$$

The characteristic equation is

$$\begin{vmatrix} -\lambda & 1 & 0 \\ 0 & -\lambda & 1 \\ -2 & 1 & 2-\lambda \end{vmatrix} = \lambda^2(2-\lambda) - 2 + \lambda = (2-\lambda)(\lambda^2 - 1).$$

Hence $\lambda_1 = -1$, $\lambda_2 = 1$, and $\lambda_3 = 2$ are eigenvalues. For $\lambda_1 = -1$ the eigenvector equation is $(\mathbf{A} - (-1)I)\mathbf{v} = \mathbf{0}$, that is,

$$\begin{pmatrix} 1 & 1 & 0 \\ 0 & 1 & 1 \\ -2 & 1 & 3 \end{pmatrix} \begin{pmatrix} v_1 \\ v_2 \\ v_3 \end{pmatrix} = \begin{pmatrix} v_1 + v_2 \\ v_2 + v_3 \\ -2v_1 + v_2 + 3v_3 \end{pmatrix} = \begin{pmatrix} 0 \\ 0 \\ 0 \end{pmatrix}.$$

Since $v_1 + v_2 = 0$, then $v_1 = -v_2$ and $v_2 + v_3 = 0$ gives $v_3 = -v_2$. The third equation is redundant. However, as a check against algebra errors we verify that the third equation is true, that is,

$$-2v_1 + v_2 + 3v_3 = -2(-v_2) + v_2 + 3(-v_2) = 0.$$

Hence $\mathbf{v}_1 = (-v_2, v_2, -v_2)^T$, where v_2 is any arbitrary *nonzero* constant. For example, we can choose $v_2 = -1$ so that

$$\mathbf{x}_1 = \begin{pmatrix} 1 \\ -1 \\ 1 \end{pmatrix} e^{-t}.$$

For $\lambda_2 = 1$ the eigenvector equation is

$$\begin{pmatrix} -1 & 1 & 0 \\ 0 & -1 & 1 \\ -2 & 1 & 1 \end{pmatrix} \begin{pmatrix} v_1 \\ v_2 \\ v_3 \end{pmatrix} = \begin{pmatrix} -v_1 + v_2 \\ -v_2 + v_3 \\ -2v_1 + v_2 + v_3 \end{pmatrix} = \begin{pmatrix} 0 \\ 0 \\ 0 \end{pmatrix}.$$

Now $-v_1 + v_2 = 0$ gives $v_1 = v_2$ and $-v_2 + v_3 = 0$ gives $v_3 = v_2$ or $\mathbf{v} = (v_2, v_2, v_2)^T$. The last equation is redundant but we check it, that is, $-2v_1 + v_2 + v_3 = -2v_2 + v_2 + v_2 = 0$. Since any *nonzero* v_2 will do, we use the convenient value $v_2 = 1$. This gives

$$\mathbf{x}_2 = \begin{pmatrix} 1 \\ 1 \\ 1 \end{pmatrix} e^t.$$

For $\lambda_3 = 2$ the eigenvector equation is

$$\begin{pmatrix} -2 & 1 & 0 \\ 0 & -2 & 1 \\ -2 & 1 & 0 \end{pmatrix} \begin{pmatrix} v_1 \\ v_2 \\ v_3 \end{pmatrix} = \begin{pmatrix} -2v_1 + v_2 \\ -2v_2 + v_3 \\ -2v_1 + v_2 \end{pmatrix} = \begin{pmatrix} 0 \\ 0 \\ 0 \end{pmatrix}.$$

Hence $v_2 = 2v_1$ and $v_3 = 2v_2 = 2(2v_1) = 4v_1$ or $v = (v_1, 2v_1, 4v_1)^T$, where v_1 is an *nonzero* constant. We take $v_1 = 1$ so that

$$\mathbf{x}_3 = \begin{pmatrix} 1 \\ 2 \\ 4 \end{pmatrix} e^{2t}.$$

A general solution is

(7.8)
$$\mathbf{x}(t) = c_1 \begin{pmatrix} 1 \\ -1 \\ 1 \end{pmatrix} e^{-t} + c_2 \begin{pmatrix} 1 \\ 1 \\ 1 \end{pmatrix} e^{t} + c_3 \begin{pmatrix} 1 \\ 2 \\ 4 \end{pmatrix} e^{2t}$$

$$= \begin{pmatrix} e^{-t} & e^{t} & e^{2t} \\ -e^{-t} & e^{t} & 2e^{2t} \\ e^{-t} & e^{t} & 4e^{2t} \end{pmatrix} \begin{pmatrix} c_1 \\ c_2 \\ c_3 \end{pmatrix}.$$

There are infinitely many sets of fundamental solutions and hence infinitely many fundamental matrices and infinitely many general solutions. For example, another set of fundamental solutions is

$$\begin{pmatrix} -1 \\ 1 \\ -1 \end{pmatrix} e^{-t}, \quad \begin{pmatrix} \frac{1}{2} \\ 1 \\ 2 \end{pmatrix} e^{2t}, \quad \begin{pmatrix} 2 \\ 2 \\ 2 \end{pmatrix} e^{t}.$$

Hence a general solution is

$$\mathbf{x}(t) = d_1 \begin{pmatrix} -1 \\ 1 \\ -1 \end{pmatrix} e^{-t} + d_2 \begin{pmatrix} \frac{1}{2} \\ 1 \\ 2 \end{pmatrix} e^{2t} + d_3 \begin{pmatrix} 2 \\ 2 \\ 2 \end{pmatrix} e^{t}.$$

This solution is equivalent to (7.8). It reduces to (7.8) when $d_1 = -c_1$, $d_2 = 2c_3$, and $d_3 = c_2/2$. ■

Let $\mathbf{X}_e(t)$ be the fundamental matrix for (7.1) that satisfies $\mathbf{X}_e(0) = \mathbf{I}$. Thus $\mathbf{X}_e$ solves

(7.9)
$$\mathbf{X}' = \mathbf{A}\mathbf{X}, \qquad \mathbf{X}(0) = \mathbf{I}.$$

When $n = 1$, this reduces to $x' = ax$, $x(0) = 1$. The solution is $x(t) = e^{at}$. By analogy we call the solution of (7.9) $e^{\mathbf{A}t}$. This **matrix exponential function** has many of the same properties as the usual exponential function.

THEOREM 7.4: MATRIX EXPONENTIAL

$\mathbf{X}_e(t) = e^{\mathbf{A}t}$ satisfies

(i) $e^{\mathbf{A} \cdot 0} = \mathbf{I}$,

(ii) $e^{\mathbf{A}(-t)} = (e^{\mathbf{A}t})^{-1}$ for all real numbers t, and

(iii) $e^{\mathbf{A}(t+s)} = e^{\mathbf{A}t} e^{\mathbf{A}s}$ for all real numbers t and s.

Property (i) is automatic in view of the initial condition in (7.9). The other two properties follow once we prove that $\mathbf{X}_e(t - r) = \mathbf{X}_e(t)\mathbf{X}_e(r)^{-1}$. To see this we note that $\mathbf{x}_1 = \mathbf{X}_e(t - r)\mathbf{d}$ and $\mathbf{x}_2 = \mathbf{X}_e(t)\mathbf{X}_e(r)^{-1}\mathbf{d}$ are both solutions of

$$\mathbf{x}' = \mathbf{Ax}, \qquad \mathbf{x}(r) = \mathbf{d}.$$

Since solutions of initial value problems are unique, then $\mathbf{X}_e(t - r)\mathbf{d} = \mathbf{X}_e(t)\mathbf{X}_e(r)^{-1}\mathbf{d}$ for all vectors $\mathbf{d}$. This means that

(7.10) $$\mathbf{X}_e(t - r) = \mathbf{X}_e(t)\mathbf{X}_e(r)^{-1}.$$

In (7.10) put $t = 0$ so that $\mathbf{X}_e(-r) = \mathbf{I}\mathbf{X}_e(r)^{-1} = \mathbf{X}_e(r)^{-1}$. This proves property (ii). To prove property (iii), put $r = -s$ in (7.10) so that

$$\mathbf{X}_e(t + s) = \mathbf{X}_e(t)\mathbf{X}_e(-s)^{-1} = \mathbf{X}_e(t)(\mathbf{X}_e(s)^{-1})^{-1} = \mathbf{X}_e(r)\mathbf{X}_e(s).$$

This proves property (iii).

In terms of the matrix exponential function,

$$\mathbf{x}' = \mathbf{Ax}, \qquad \mathbf{x}(t_0) = \mathbf{x}_0$$

has solution

$$\mathbf{x}(t) = e^{\mathbf{A}(t - t_0)}\mathbf{x}_0 = e^{\mathbf{A}t}e^{-\mathbf{A}t_0}\mathbf{x}_0.$$

EXAMPLE 7.5   Compute $e^{\mathbf{A}t}$ when

(7.11) $$\mathbf{A} = \begin{pmatrix} 3 & -2 \\ -1 & 2 \end{pmatrix}.$$

Note that $e^{\mathbf{A}t} = \mathbf{X}(t)\mathbf{X}(0)^{-1}$, where $\mathbf{X}(t)$ is any fundamental matrix for (7.1). For this $\mathbf{A}$, it was shown in (7.6) that a fundamental matrix is

$$\mathbf{X}(t) = \begin{pmatrix} e^t & 2e^{4t} \\ e^t & -e^{4t} \end{pmatrix}.$$

Hence the solution of (7.9) is $\mathbf{X}(t)\mathbf{X}(0)^{-1}$. Since

$$\mathbf{X}(0)^{-1} = \begin{pmatrix} 1 & 2 \\ 1 & -1 \end{pmatrix}^{-1} = \frac{1}{-3}\begin{pmatrix} -1 & -2 \\ -1 & 1 \end{pmatrix} = \begin{pmatrix} \dfrac{1}{3} & \dfrac{2}{3} \\ \dfrac{1}{3} & -\dfrac{1}{3} \end{pmatrix},$$

then

$$e^{\mathbf{A}t} = \begin{pmatrix} e^t & 2e^{4t} \\ e^t & -e^{4t} \end{pmatrix}\begin{pmatrix} \dfrac{1}{3} & \dfrac{2}{3} \\ \dfrac{1}{3} & -\dfrac{1}{3} \end{pmatrix}$$

or

(7.12) $$e^{\mathbf{A}t} = \begin{pmatrix} \dfrac{e^t}{3} + \dfrac{2}{3}e^{4t} & \dfrac{2}{3}e^t - \dfrac{2}{3}e^{4t} \\ \dfrac{e^t}{3} - \dfrac{e^{4t}}{3} & \dfrac{2}{3}e^t + \dfrac{e^{4t}}{3} \end{pmatrix}. \qquad \blacksquare$$

Comparing (7.11) and (7.12) it is clear that the matrix exponential function is a complicated function of **A**. There is usually no simple way to compute $e^{\mathbf{A}t}$ given **A**. Usually, the best way to compute $e^{\mathbf{A}t}$ is to solve the initial value problem (7.9).

EXAMPLE 7.6   For (7.7) compute $e^{\mathbf{A}t}$.

From (7.8) we see that a fundamental matrix is

$$\mathbf{X}(t) = \begin{pmatrix} e^{-t} & e^t & e^{2t} \\ -e^{-t} & e^t & 2e^{2t} \\ e^{-t} & e^t & 4e^{2t} \end{pmatrix}.$$

Hence $e^{\mathbf{A}t} = \mathbf{X}(t)\mathbf{X}(0)^{-1}$. A convenient way to compute

$$(7.13) \qquad \mathbf{X}(0)^{-1} = \begin{pmatrix} 1 & 1 & 1 \\ -1 & 1 & 2 \\ 1 & 1 & 4 \end{pmatrix}^{-1}$$

is **Gauss–Jordan elimination.** This elimination technique is done as follows.

1. Write the augmented matrix $[\mathbf{X}(0), \mathbf{I}]$, where **I** is the identity matrix of the same size as $\mathbf{X}(0)$.
2. Use the three elementary row operations to reduce $[\mathbf{X}(0), \mathbf{I}]$ to $[\mathbf{I}, \mathbf{B}]$.
3. The matrix **B** computed in step 2 is $\mathbf{X}(0)^{-1}$.

For the problem (7.13) the initial augmented matrix is

$$\begin{pmatrix} 1 & 1 & 1 & 1 & 0 & 0 \\ -1 & 1 & 2 & 0 & 1 & 0 \\ 1 & 1 & 4 & 0 & 0 & 1 \end{pmatrix}.$$

First zero out the terms -1 and 1 in the first column. To do this, add the first row to the second and add (-1) times the first row to the third. The result is

$$\begin{pmatrix} 1 & 1 & 1 & 1 & 0 & 0 \\ 0 & 2 & 3 & 1 & 1 & 0 \\ 0 & 0 & 3 & -1 & 0 & 1 \end{pmatrix}.$$

Multiply the second row by $\frac{1}{2}$ and the third row by $\frac{1}{3}$ to obtain

$$\begin{pmatrix} 1 & 1 & 1 & 1 & 0 & 0 \\ 0 & 1 & \frac{3}{2} & \frac{1}{2} & \frac{1}{2} & 0 \\ 0 & 0 & 1 & -\frac{1}{3} & 0 & \frac{1}{3} \end{pmatrix}.$$

To zero out the term in the first row, second column, add (-1) times the second row to the first:

$$\begin{pmatrix} 1 & 0 & -\frac{1}{2} & \frac{1}{2} & -\frac{1}{2} & 0 \\ 0 & 1 & \frac{3}{2} & \frac{1}{2} & \frac{1}{2} & 0 \\ 0 & 0 & 1 & -\frac{1}{3} & 0 & \frac{1}{3} \end{pmatrix}.$$

Now eliminate the entries $-\frac{1}{2}$ and $\frac{3}{2}$ in the third column. This gives

$$\begin{pmatrix} 1 & 0 & 0 & \frac{1}{3} & -\frac{1}{2} & \frac{1}{6} \\ 0 & 1 & 0 & 1 & \frac{1}{2} & -\frac{1}{2} \\ 0 & 0 & 1 & -\frac{1}{3} & 0 & \frac{1}{3} \end{pmatrix}.$$

The identity is now on the left. Hence

$$\mathbf{X}(0)^{-1} = \begin{pmatrix} \frac{1}{3} & -\frac{1}{2} & \frac{1}{6} \\ 1 & \frac{1}{2} & -\frac{1}{2} \\ -\frac{1}{3} & 0 & \frac{1}{3} \end{pmatrix}$$

and

$$e^{\mathbf{A}t} = \mathbf{X}(t)\mathbf{X}(0)^{-1}$$

$$= \begin{pmatrix} \dfrac{e^{-t}}{3} + e^t - \dfrac{e^{2t}}{3} & -\dfrac{e^{-t}}{2} + \dfrac{e^t}{2} & \dfrac{e^{-t}}{6} - \dfrac{e^t}{2} + \dfrac{e^{2t}}{3} \\[2mm] -\dfrac{e^{-t}}{3} + e^t - \dfrac{2}{3}e^{2t} & \dfrac{e^{-t}}{2} + \dfrac{e^t}{2} & -\dfrac{e^{-t}}{6} - \dfrac{e^t}{2} + \dfrac{2}{3}e^{2t} \\[2mm] \dfrac{e^{-t}}{3} + e^t - \dfrac{4}{3}e^{2t} & -\dfrac{e^{-t}}{2} + \dfrac{e^t}{2} & \dfrac{e^{-t}}{6} - \dfrac{e^t}{2} + \dfrac{4}{3}e^{2t} \end{pmatrix}. \quad \blacksquare$$

PROBLEMS

In Problems 1–8, find a general solution of the system and compute a fundamental matrix.

1. $\mathbf{x}' = \begin{pmatrix} 1 & 1 \\ 9 & 1 \end{pmatrix}\mathbf{x}.$

2. $\mathbf{x}' = \begin{pmatrix} 3 & -12 \\ -1 & 2 \end{pmatrix}\mathbf{x}.$

3. $\mathbf{x}' = \begin{pmatrix} 2 & 1 \\ 4 & -1 \end{pmatrix}\mathbf{x}.$

4. $\mathbf{x}' = \begin{pmatrix} 1 & 3 \\ -1 & 5 \end{pmatrix}\mathbf{x}.$

5. $\mathbf{x}' = \begin{pmatrix} -4 & 5 \\ -1 & 2 \end{pmatrix}\mathbf{x}.$

6. $\mathbf{x}' = \begin{pmatrix} -1 & 3 \\ 1 & 1 \end{pmatrix}\mathbf{x}.$

7. $\mathbf{x}' = \begin{pmatrix} 1 & 2 & -1 \\ 0 & -1 & 1 \\ -1 & -1 & -2 \end{pmatrix}\mathbf{x}.$

8. $\mathbf{x}' = \begin{pmatrix} 1 & -2 & -1 \\ -4 & -1 & 1 \\ 1 & -3 & -2 \end{pmatrix}\mathbf{x}.$

In Problems 9–16, solve the initial value problem.

9. $\mathbf{x}' = \begin{pmatrix} 1 & 1 \\ 9 & 1 \end{pmatrix}\mathbf{x}, \qquad \mathbf{x}(0) = \begin{pmatrix} 1 \\ 2 \end{pmatrix}$ (see Problem 1).

10. $\mathbf{x}' = \begin{pmatrix} 2 & 1 \\ 10 & -1 \end{pmatrix}\mathbf{x}, \qquad \mathbf{x}(0) = \begin{pmatrix} -2 \\ 1 \end{pmatrix}.$

11. $\mathbf{x}' = \begin{pmatrix} -2 & 1 \\ 2 & -3 \end{pmatrix}\mathbf{x}, \qquad \mathbf{x}(0) = \begin{pmatrix} 0 \\ \sqrt{2} \end{pmatrix}$

12. $\mathbf{x}' = \begin{pmatrix} -2 & 1 \\ 2 & -3 \end{pmatrix}\mathbf{x}, \qquad \mathbf{x}(3) = \begin{pmatrix} 0 \\ \sqrt{2} \end{pmatrix}$ (see Problem 11).

13. $\mathbf{x}' = \begin{pmatrix} -2 & 1 \\ 2 & -3 \end{pmatrix} \mathbf{x}, \qquad \mathbf{x}(-1) = \begin{pmatrix} 0 \\ \sqrt{2} \end{pmatrix}$ (see Problem 11).

14. $\mathbf{x}' = \begin{pmatrix} 1 & -1 & -2 \\ 1 & -2 & -3 \\ -4 & 1 & -1 \end{pmatrix} \mathbf{x}, \qquad \mathbf{x}(0) = \begin{pmatrix} 1 \\ -1 \\ 2 \end{pmatrix}$

15. $\mathbf{x}' = \begin{pmatrix} 1 & -1 & -2 \\ 1 & -2 & -3 \\ -4 & 1 & -1 \end{pmatrix} \mathbf{x}, \qquad \mathbf{x}(0) = \begin{pmatrix} 1 \\ 0 \\ 0 \end{pmatrix}$ (see Problem 14).

16. $\mathbf{x}' = \begin{pmatrix} 1 & -1 & -2 \\ 1 & -2 & -3 \\ -4 & 1 & -1 \end{pmatrix} \mathbf{x}, \qquad \mathbf{x}(\pi) = \begin{pmatrix} 1 \\ 0 \\ 0 \end{pmatrix}$ (see Problem 15).

In Problems 17–21, compute $e^{\mathbf{A}t}$ for the given $\mathbf{A}$. *Hint:* Given any fundamental matrix $\mathbf{X}(t)$, $e^{\mathbf{A}t} = \mathbf{X}(t)\mathbf{X}(0)^{-1}$.

17. $\begin{pmatrix} -1 & 3 \\ 1 & 1 \end{pmatrix}$ (see Problem 6).

18. $\begin{pmatrix} 1 & -6 \\ -1 & 2 \end{pmatrix}$.

19. $\begin{pmatrix} -1 & -3 \\ 1 & -5 \end{pmatrix}$.

20. $\begin{pmatrix} -1 & 1 & 0 \\ 0 & 2 & 1 \\ 0 & 0 & 1 \end{pmatrix}$.

21. $\begin{pmatrix} -1 & 1 & 2 \\ -1 & 2 & 3 \\ 4 & -1 & 1 \end{pmatrix}$ (see Problem 15).

22. Suppose that $\mathbf{A} = \text{diag}\,(a_1, a_2, \ldots, a_n)$, where $a_i \neq a_j$ when $i \neq j$.

(a) Compute all eigenvalues and corresponding eigenvectors for $\mathbf{A}$.

(b) Compute $e^{\mathbf{A}t}$.

23. Suppose that $\mathbf{A}$ can be partitioned into submatrices so that

$$\mathbf{A} = \begin{pmatrix} \mathbf{B} & \mathbf{0} \\ \mathbf{0} & \mathbf{C} \end{pmatrix}.$$

(a) Show that

$$e^{\mathbf{A}t} = \begin{pmatrix} e^{\mathbf{B}t} & \mathbf{0} \\ \mathbf{0} & e^{\mathbf{C}t} \end{pmatrix}.$$

(b) Given the results of Problems 17 and 18 compute $e^{\mathbf{A}t}$ when

$$\mathbf{A} = \begin{pmatrix} -1 & 3 & 0 & 0 \\ 1 & 1 & 0 & 0 \\ 0 & 0 & 1 & -6 \\ 0 & 0 & -1 & 2 \end{pmatrix}$$

24. (a) In Theorem 7.2 suppose that all eigenvalues λ_i are real and negative. Show that all solutions of $\mathbf{x}' = \mathbf{A}\mathbf{x}$ tend to zero as $t \to \infty$.

(b) Given the tank system depicted in Figure 7.9 on page 364, suppose that $u(t) = 0$. Show that all solutions tend to zero as $t \to \infty$.

25. The governing equation for the compartmental system in Figure 7.10 is

$$\mathbf{x}' = \begin{pmatrix} -\lambda_1 & 0 & 0 \\ \lambda_1 & -\lambda_2 & 0 \\ 0 & \lambda_2 & 0 \end{pmatrix} \mathbf{x}.$$

Assume that $\lambda_1 > 0$, $\lambda_2 > 0$, and $\lambda_1 \neq \lambda_2$.

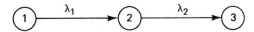

Figure 7.10. Linear compartmental system.

(a) Find a fundamental set of solutions of this system.

(b) Show that each solution has a limit as $t \to \infty$.

26. Two different concentrations C_1 and C_2 of a solution are separated by a membrane through which the solute can diffuse. The rate of diffusion is assumed proportional to the difference $C_1 - C_2$. The direction of diffusion is such that it will tend to equalize the concentrations. The governing equations are

$$\frac{dC_1}{dt} = -\frac{k}{V_1}(C_1 - C_2), \qquad \frac{dC_2}{dt} = \frac{k}{V_2}(C_1 - C_2),$$

where k is a positive constant and V_i is the volume of solution on the side with concentration C_i.

(a) Find a fundamental set of solutions of this system.

(b) Show that any $(C_1(t), C_2(t))^T$ has a limit $(C_1(\infty), C_2(\infty))^T$ as $t \to \infty$ and that $C_1(\infty) = C_2(\infty)$.

(c) Find the fundamental matrix for this system that satisfies $\mathbf{X}_e(0) = \mathbf{I}$.

27. (a) Solve $y'' - 3y' + 2y = 0$ for $y(t)$ using the techniques of Chapter 3.

(b) Write $y'' - 3y' + 2y = 0$ as an equivalent system of the form (7.1).

(c) Solve the system obtained in (b) and compare the answer with that obtained in (a).

7.8 COMPLEX EIGENVALUES

Given the first-order linear differential equation

(8.1) $$\mathbf{x}' = \mathbf{Ax},$$

when $\mathbf{A}$ is a real $n \times n$ matrix, the characteristic polynomial

$$p(\lambda) = \det(\mathbf{A} - \lambda\mathbf{I})$$

has real coefficients. Hence, if $\lambda = \alpha + i\beta$ is a complex eigenvalue, then the conjugate $\bar{\lambda} = \alpha - i\beta$ is also an eigenvalue. Suppose that $\mathbf{v}$ is an eigenvector corresponding to the eigenvalue λ, so that

(8.2) $$(\mathbf{A} - \lambda\mathbf{I})\mathbf{v} = \mathbf{0}.$$

Hence

(8.3)
$$\mathbf{x}_1 = e^{\lambda t}\mathbf{v}$$

is a solution of (8.1). Taking conjugates in (8.2), we see that

$$(\bar{\mathbf{A}} - \bar{\lambda}\mathbf{I})\bar{\mathbf{v}} = (\mathbf{A} - \bar{\lambda}\mathbf{I})\bar{\mathbf{v}} = \mathbf{0}.$$

Hence $\bar{\mathbf{v}}$ is an eigenvector corresponding to $\bar{\lambda}$ and $\mathbf{x}_2 = e^{\bar{\lambda}t}\bar{\mathbf{v}} = \bar{\mathbf{x}}_1$ is a solution. These solutions are complex valued. To obtain two equivalent real-valued solutions, we take the real and the imaginary parts of $\mathbf{x}_1(t)$. Thus

$$\mathbf{y}_1(t) = \text{Re}\,[\mathbf{x}_1(t)] = \tfrac{1}{2}[\mathbf{x}_1(t) + \mathbf{x}_2(t)]$$

and

$$\mathbf{y}_2(t) = \text{Im}\,[\mathbf{x}_1(t)] = \frac{1}{2i}\,[\mathbf{x}_1(t) - \mathbf{x}_2(t)]$$

are the sought-after pair of real-valued solutions.

THEOREM 8.1: COMPLEX EIGENVALUES

If $\mathbf{A}$ is a real matrix and if $\lambda = \alpha + i\beta$ is a complex eigenvalue of $\mathbf{A}$ with corresponding eigenvector $\mathbf{v}$, then

$$\mathbf{y}_1(t) = \text{Re}\,[e^{\lambda t}\mathbf{v}] \quad \text{and} \quad \mathbf{y}_2(t) = \text{Im}\,[e^{\lambda t}\mathbf{v}]$$

are two linearly independent real-valued solutions of (8.1).

EXAMPLE 8.2   Find a real-valued set of fundamental solutions of

(8.4)
$$\mathbf{x}' = \begin{pmatrix} 2 & 3 \\ -3 & 2 \end{pmatrix}\mathbf{x}.$$

The characteristic equation is $\lambda^2 - 4\lambda + 13 = 0$. The characteristic roots are $\lambda_1 = 2 + 3i$ and $\lambda_2 = 2 - 3i$. For $\lambda_1 = 2 + 3i$ the eigenvector equation is

$$\begin{pmatrix} -3i & 3 \\ -3 & -3i \end{pmatrix}\begin{pmatrix} v_1 \\ v_2 \end{pmatrix} = \begin{pmatrix} -3iv_1 + 3v_2 \\ -3v_1 - 3iv_2 \end{pmatrix} = \begin{pmatrix} 0 \\ 0 \end{pmatrix}.$$

The solution is $v_2 = iv_1$, where v_1 is any nonzero constant. We take $v_1 = 1$ so that $\mathbf{v} = (1, i)^T$ is an eigenvector. A complex-valued solution is

$$\mathbf{x}_1(t) = e^{(2+3i)t}\begin{pmatrix} 1 \\ i \end{pmatrix}$$

$$= e^{2t}(\cos 3t + i \sin 3t)\left[\begin{pmatrix} 1 \\ 0 \end{pmatrix} + i\begin{pmatrix} 0 \\ 1 \end{pmatrix}\right]$$

$$= e^{2t}\left[\cos 3t\begin{pmatrix} 1 \\ 0 \end{pmatrix} + i\cos 3t\begin{pmatrix} 0 \\ 1 \end{pmatrix} + i\sin 3t\begin{pmatrix} 1 \\ 0 \end{pmatrix} - \sin 3t\begin{pmatrix} 0 \\ 1 \end{pmatrix}\right]$$

$$= e^{2t}\left[\begin{pmatrix} \cos 3t \\ -\sin 3t \end{pmatrix} + i\begin{pmatrix} \sin 3t \\ \cos 3t \end{pmatrix}\right].$$

Two linearly independent real-valued solutions are

$$e^{2t}\begin{pmatrix} \cos 3t \\ -\sin 3t \end{pmatrix} \quad \text{and} \quad e^{2t}\begin{pmatrix} \sin 3t \\ \cos 3t \end{pmatrix}.$$

A general solution is

$$\mathbf{x}(t) = c_1 e^{2t}\begin{pmatrix} \cos 3t \\ -\sin 3t \end{pmatrix} + c_2 e^{2t}\begin{pmatrix} \sin 3t \\ \cos 3t \end{pmatrix}$$

or

$$\mathbf{x}(t) = \begin{pmatrix} e^{2t}\cos 3t & e^{2t}\sin 3t \\ -e^{2t}\sin 3t & e^{2t}\cos 3t \end{pmatrix}\begin{pmatrix} c_1 \\ c_2 \end{pmatrix} = \mathbf{X}(t)\begin{pmatrix} c_1 \\ c_2 \end{pmatrix}.$$

The fundamental matrix $\mathbf{X}(t)$ satisfies $\mathbf{X}(0) = \mathbf{I}$. Hence

$$\mathbf{X}(t) = e^{\mathbf{A}t} = \begin{pmatrix} e^{2t}\cos 3t & e^{2t}\sin 3t \\ -e^{2t}\sin 3t & e^{2t}\cos 3t \end{pmatrix}. \quad \blacksquare$$

Theorem 8.1 can be applied to any system (8.1) of dimension $n \geq 2$.

EXAMPLE 8.3   Find a real-valued fundamental set of solutions of

$$\mathbf{x}' = \begin{pmatrix} 1 & 2 & 0 \\ -1 & -1 & 0 \\ 1 & 0 & -1 \end{pmatrix}\mathbf{x}.$$

The characteristic equation is

$$\begin{vmatrix} 1-\lambda & 2 & 0 \\ -1 & -1-\lambda & 0 \\ 1 & 0 & -1-\lambda \end{vmatrix} = (1-\lambda)(1+\lambda)^2 - 2(\lambda+1)$$

$$= (\lambda+1)(-1-\lambda^2) = -(\lambda+1)(\lambda^2+1) = 0.$$

Hence the eigenvalues are $\lambda_1 = i$, $\lambda_2 = -i$, and $\lambda_3 = -1$. For $\lambda_1 = i$ the eigenvector equation is

$$\begin{pmatrix} 1-i & 2 & 0 \\ -1 & -(1+i) & 0 \\ 1 & 0 & -(1+i) \end{pmatrix}\begin{pmatrix} v_1 \\ v_2 \\ v_3 \end{pmatrix} = \begin{pmatrix} (1-i)v_1 + 2v_2 \\ -v_1 - (1+i)v_2 \\ v_1 - (1+i)v_3 \end{pmatrix} = \begin{pmatrix} 0 \\ 0 \\ 0 \end{pmatrix}.$$

The solution is $v_1 = -(1+i)v_2$ and $v_3 = (1+i)^{-1}v_1 = -v_2$. We choose $v_2 = -1$. Thus $\mathbf{v}_1 = (1+i, -1, 1)^T$ is an eigenvector. Without further computation we can take $\mathbf{v}_2 = \bar{\mathbf{v}}_1 = (1-i, -1, 1)^T$ for $\lambda_2 = -i$. For $\lambda_3 = -1$, the eigenvector equation is

$$\begin{pmatrix} 2 & 2 & 0 \\ -1 & 0 & 0 \\ 1 & 0 & 0 \end{pmatrix}\begin{pmatrix} v_1 \\ v_2 \\ v_3 \end{pmatrix} = \begin{pmatrix} 2v_1 + 2v_2 \\ -v_1 \\ v_1 \end{pmatrix} = \begin{pmatrix} 0 \\ 0 \\ 0 \end{pmatrix}.$$

Hence $v_1 = 0$, $v_2 = 0$, and v_3 is arbitrary. We take $v_3 = 1$ so that $v_3 = (0, 0, 1)^T$. Since

$$\begin{pmatrix} 1+i \\ -1 \\ 1 \end{pmatrix} e^{it} = \left[\begin{pmatrix} 1 \\ -1 \\ 1 \end{pmatrix} + i \begin{pmatrix} 1 \\ 0 \\ 0 \end{pmatrix} \right] (\cos t + i \sin t)$$

$$= \left[\begin{pmatrix} 1 \\ -1 \\ 1 \end{pmatrix} \cos t - \begin{pmatrix} 1 \\ 0 \\ 0 \end{pmatrix} \sin t \right] + i \left[\begin{pmatrix} 1 \\ -1 \\ 1 \end{pmatrix} \sin t + \begin{pmatrix} 1 \\ 0 \\ 0 \end{pmatrix} \cos t \right]$$

$$= \begin{pmatrix} \cos t - \sin t \\ -\cos t \\ \cos t \end{pmatrix} + i \begin{pmatrix} \sin t + \cos t \\ -\sin t \\ \sin t \end{pmatrix},$$

then a fundamental set of solutions is

$$\mathbf{x}_1(t) = \begin{pmatrix} \cos t - \sin t \\ -\cos t \\ \cos t \end{pmatrix}, \qquad \mathbf{x}_2(t) = \begin{pmatrix} \sin t + \cos t \\ -\sin t \\ \sin t \end{pmatrix}, \qquad \mathbf{x}_3(t) = \begin{pmatrix} 0 \\ 0 \\ e^{-t} \end{pmatrix}. \quad \blacksquare$$

If **A** has more than one complex eigenvalue, the same technique can be applied separately to each eigenvalue.

EXAMPLE 8.4   Find a real-valued set of fundamental solutions of

$$(8.5) \qquad \mathbf{x}' = \begin{pmatrix} 0 & 1 & 1 & -3 \\ 0 & 3 & 0 & 1 \\ -1 & 3 & 0 & 1 \\ 0 & -1 & 0 & 3 \end{pmatrix} \mathbf{x}.$$

The characteristic equation is

$$\begin{vmatrix} -\lambda & 1 & 1 & -3 \\ 0 & 3-\lambda & 0 & 1 \\ -1 & 3 & -\lambda & 1 \\ 0 & -1 & 0 & 3-\lambda \end{vmatrix} = -\lambda \begin{vmatrix} 3-\lambda & 0 & 1 \\ 3 & -\lambda & 1 \\ -1 & 0 & 3-\lambda \end{vmatrix}$$

$$+ (-1) \begin{vmatrix} 1 & 1 & -3 \\ 3-\lambda & 0 & 1 \\ -1 & 0 & 3-\lambda \end{vmatrix}$$

$$= (-\lambda)[(3-\lambda)^2(-\lambda) - \lambda] - [-1 - (3-\lambda)^2]$$

$$= (\lambda^2 + 1)[(3-\lambda)^2 + 1] = (\lambda^2 + 1)(\lambda^2 - 6\lambda + 10).$$

The eigenvalues are $\pm i$ and $3 \pm i$. For $\lambda = i$ the eigenvector equation is

$$\begin{pmatrix} -i & 1 & 1 & -3 \\ 0 & 3-i & 0 & 1 \\ -1 & 3 & -i & 1 \\ 0 & -1 & 0 & 3-i \end{pmatrix} \begin{pmatrix} v_1 \\ v_2 \\ v_3 \\ v_4 \end{pmatrix} = \begin{pmatrix} -iv_1 + v_2 + v_3 - 3v_4 \\ (3-i)v_2 + v_4 \\ -v_1 + 3v_2 - iv_3 + v_4 \\ -v_2 + (3-i)v_4 \end{pmatrix} = \begin{pmatrix} 0 \\ 0 \\ 0 \\ 0 \end{pmatrix}.$$

A solution is $v_2 = v_4 = 0$, $v_3 = iv_1$. Hence $v = (1, 0, i, 0)^T$ will do. A solution of (8.5) is

$$
(8.6) \quad e^{it} \begin{pmatrix} 1 \\ 0 \\ i \\ 0 \end{pmatrix} = (\cos t + i \sin t) \left[\begin{pmatrix} 1 \\ 0 \\ 0 \\ 0 \end{pmatrix} + i \begin{pmatrix} 0 \\ 0 \\ 1 \\ 0 \end{pmatrix} \right] = \begin{pmatrix} \cos t \\ 0 \\ -\sin t \\ 0 \end{pmatrix} + i \begin{pmatrix} \sin t \\ 0 \\ \cos t \\ 0 \end{pmatrix}.
$$

For $\lambda = 3 + i$ the eigenvector equation is

$$
\begin{pmatrix} -3 - i & 1 & 1 & -3 \\ 0 & -i & 0 & 1 \\ -1 & 3 & -3 - i & 1 \\ 0 & -1 & 0 & -i \end{pmatrix} \begin{pmatrix} v_1 \\ v_2 \\ v_3 \\ v_4 \end{pmatrix} = \begin{pmatrix} -(3 + i)v_1 + v_2 + v_3 - 3v_4 \\ -iv_2 + v_4 \\ -v_1 + 3v_2 - (3 + i)v_3 + v_4 \\ -v_2 - iv_4 \end{pmatrix} = \begin{pmatrix} 0 \\ 0 \\ 0 \\ 0 \end{pmatrix}.
$$

The solution is $v_4 = iv_2$, $v_1 = (9 - 7i)v_2/(9 + 6i)$, $v_3 = (7 + 9i)v_2/(9 + 6i)$. An eigenvector is $v = (9 - 7i, 9 + 6i, 7 + 9i, -6 + 9i)^T$ and a solution of (8.5) is

$$
(8.7) \quad e^{3t}(\cos t + i \sin t) \left[\begin{pmatrix} 9 \\ 9 \\ 7 \\ -6 \end{pmatrix} + i \begin{pmatrix} -7 \\ 6 \\ 9 \\ 9 \end{pmatrix} \right]
$$

$$
= e^{3t} \begin{pmatrix} 9 \cos t + 7 \sin t \\ 9 \cos t - 6 \sin t \\ 7 \cos t - 9 \sin t \\ -6 \cos t - 9 \sin t \end{pmatrix} + ie^{3t} \begin{pmatrix} 9 \sin t - 7 \cos t \\ 9 \sin t + 6 \cos t \\ 7 \sin t + 9 \cos t \\ -6 \sin t + 9 \cos t \end{pmatrix}.
$$

Given (8.6) and (8.7), we see that a real-valued fundamental set of solutions is

$$
\begin{pmatrix} \cos t \\ 0 \\ -\sin t \\ 0 \end{pmatrix}, \begin{pmatrix} \sin t \\ 0 \\ \cos t \\ 0 \end{pmatrix}, e^{3t} \begin{pmatrix} 9 \cos t + 7 \sin t \\ 9 \cos t - 6 \sin t \\ 7 \cos t - 9 \sin t \\ -6 \cos t - 9 \sin t \end{pmatrix}, e^{3t} \begin{pmatrix} 9 \sin t - 7 \cos t \\ 9 \sin t + 6 \cos t \\ 7 \sin t + 9 \cos t \\ -6 \sin t + 9 \cos t \end{pmatrix}. \quad \blacksquare
$$

PROBLEMS

In Problems 1–8, find a real-valued set of fundamental solutions and compute a real fundamental matrix.

1. $x' = \begin{pmatrix} -2 & \pi \\ -\pi & -2 \end{pmatrix} x.$

2. $x' = \begin{pmatrix} -2 & -2 \\ 6 & 2 \end{pmatrix} x.$

3. $x' = \begin{pmatrix} 4 & -5 \\ 4 & -4 \end{pmatrix} x.$

4. $x' = \begin{pmatrix} 2 & 5 \\ -2 & 4 \end{pmatrix} x.$

5. $\mathbf{x}' = \begin{pmatrix} -3 & \sqrt{2} \\ -\sqrt{2} & -3 \end{pmatrix} \mathbf{x}.$

6. $\mathbf{x}' = \begin{pmatrix} 1 & -5 \\ 2 & -1 \end{pmatrix} \mathbf{x}.$

7. $\mathbf{x}' = \begin{pmatrix} 3 & -2 & 2 \\ 4 & -1 & 1 \\ 0 & 0 & 3 \end{pmatrix} \mathbf{x}.$

8. $\mathbf{x}' = \begin{pmatrix} -1 & 3 & 0 \\ -5 & -1 & 1 \\ -6 & 6 & 2 \end{pmatrix} \mathbf{x}.$

In Problems 9–16, solve the initial value problem.

9. $\mathbf{x}' = \begin{pmatrix} -1 & -1 \\ 3 & 1 \end{pmatrix} \mathbf{x}, \quad \mathbf{x}(0) = \begin{pmatrix} 0 \\ -2 \end{pmatrix}.$

10. $\mathbf{x}' = \begin{pmatrix} -1 & -1 \\ 3 & 1 \end{pmatrix} \mathbf{x}, \quad \mathbf{x}(0) = \begin{pmatrix} 1 \\ 0 \end{pmatrix}$ (see Problem 9).

11. $\mathbf{x}' = \begin{pmatrix} -1 & 2 \\ -2 & -1 \end{pmatrix} \mathbf{x}, \quad \mathbf{x}(0) = \begin{pmatrix} 2 \\ 1 \end{pmatrix}.$

12. $\mathbf{x}' = \begin{pmatrix} -1 & 2 \\ -2 & -1 \end{pmatrix} \mathbf{x}, \quad \mathbf{x}(0) = \begin{pmatrix} 1 \\ 1 \end{pmatrix}$ (see Problem 11).

13. $\mathbf{x}' = \begin{pmatrix} 4 & 1 \\ -2 & 2 \end{pmatrix} \mathbf{x}, \quad \mathbf{x}(0) = \begin{pmatrix} 2 \\ -1 \end{pmatrix}.$

14. $\mathbf{x}' = \begin{pmatrix} 4 & 1 \\ -2 & 2 \end{pmatrix} \mathbf{x}, \quad \mathbf{x}(0) = \begin{pmatrix} 0 \\ 2 \end{pmatrix}$ (see Problem 13).

15. $\mathbf{x}' = \begin{pmatrix} 1 & 2 & 0 \\ -3 & 1 & 1 \\ 0 & 2 & 1 \end{pmatrix} \mathbf{x}, \quad \mathbf{x}(0) = \begin{pmatrix} -1 \\ 1 \\ 0 \end{pmatrix}.$

16. $\mathbf{x}' = \begin{pmatrix} 1 & 2 & 0 \\ -3 & 1 & 1 \\ 0 & 2 & 1 \end{pmatrix} \mathbf{x}, \quad \mathbf{x}(0) = \begin{pmatrix} 0 \\ 0 \\ 1 \end{pmatrix}$ (see Problem 15).

17. Show that if $\mathbf{x}(t)$ solves $\mathbf{x}' = \mathbf{A}\mathbf{x}$, $\mathbf{x}(0) = \mathbf{d}$, then $\mathbf{x}(t - t_0)$ solves $\mathbf{x}' = \mathbf{A}\mathbf{x}$, $\mathbf{x}(t_0) = \mathbf{d}$.

Given the results of Problems 9–17, solve the initial value Problems 18–24.

18. $\mathbf{x}' = \begin{pmatrix} -1 & -1 \\ 3 & 1 \end{pmatrix} \mathbf{x}, \quad \mathbf{x}(3) = \begin{pmatrix} 0 \\ -2 \end{pmatrix}.$

19. $\mathbf{x}' = \begin{pmatrix} -1 & -1 \\ 3 & 1 \end{pmatrix} \mathbf{x}, \quad \mathbf{x}(-\pi) = \begin{pmatrix} 0 \\ -2 \end{pmatrix}.$

20. $\mathbf{x}' = \begin{pmatrix} -1 & -1 \\ 3 & 1 \end{pmatrix} \mathbf{x}, \quad \mathbf{x}(1) = \begin{pmatrix} 2 \\ 0 \end{pmatrix} = 2\begin{pmatrix} 1 \\ 0 \end{pmatrix}.$

21. $\mathbf{x}' = \begin{pmatrix} 4 & 1 \\ -2 & 2 \end{pmatrix} \mathbf{x}, \quad \mathbf{x}(-5) = \begin{pmatrix} 2 \\ -1 \end{pmatrix}.$

22. $\mathbf{x}' = \begin{pmatrix} 4 & 1 \\ -2 & 2 \end{pmatrix} \mathbf{x}, \quad \mathbf{x}(2\pi) = \begin{pmatrix} 2 \\ -1 \end{pmatrix} + \begin{pmatrix} 0 \\ 2 \end{pmatrix} = \begin{pmatrix} 2 \\ 1 \end{pmatrix}.$

23. $\mathbf{x}' = \begin{pmatrix} 1 & 2 & 0 \\ -3 & 1 & 1 \\ 0 & 2 & 1 \end{pmatrix} \mathbf{x}, \quad \mathbf{x}(10) = \begin{pmatrix} 0 \\ 0 \\ 1 \end{pmatrix}.$

24. $\mathbf{x}' = \begin{pmatrix} 1 & 2 & 0 \\ -3 & 1 & 1 \\ 0 & 2 & 1 \end{pmatrix}\mathbf{x}, \qquad \mathbf{x}(5) = \begin{pmatrix} -1 \\ 1 \\ 0 \end{pmatrix} + 2\begin{pmatrix} 0 \\ 0 \\ 1 \end{pmatrix} = \begin{pmatrix} -1 \\ 1 \\ 2 \end{pmatrix}.$

25. Recall that $\mathbf{X}_e(t) = e^{\mathbf{A}t}$ is the solution of $\mathbf{X}' = \mathbf{A}\mathbf{X}$, $\mathbf{X}(0) = \mathbf{I}$. Find $e^{\mathbf{A}t}$ for each matrix.

(a) $\begin{pmatrix} -1 & -1 \\ 3 & 1 \end{pmatrix}$ (see Problem 9).   (b) $\begin{pmatrix} -1 & 2 \\ -2 & -1 \end{pmatrix}$ (see Problem 11).

(c) $\begin{pmatrix} 4 & 1 \\ -2 & 2 \end{pmatrix}$ (see Problem 13).   (d) $\begin{pmatrix} 1 & 2 & 0 \\ -3 & 1 & 1 \\ 0 & 2 & 1 \end{pmatrix}$ (see Problem 15).

26. Find a real-valued set of fundamental solutions for

$$\mathbf{x}' = \begin{pmatrix} 1 & 2 & 1 & 0 & 0 \\ -2 & 1 & 0 & 0 & 0 \\ 0 & 0 & 3 & 0 & 1 \\ 0 & 0 & 0 & 0 & 2 \\ 0 & 0 & 0 & -2 & 0 \end{pmatrix}\mathbf{x}.$$

27. Show that for any real numbers a and b one has

$$e^{\begin{pmatrix} a & b \\ -b & a \end{pmatrix}t} = e^{at}\begin{pmatrix} \cos bt & \sin bt \\ -\sin bt & \cos bt \end{pmatrix}.$$

28. Consider the mechanical rotational system $\mathbf{x}' = \mathbf{w} \times \mathbf{x}$, where $\times$ denotes the vector cross product. Here $\mathbf{w} = (w_1, w_2, w_3)^T$ is a real 3-vector.

(a) Write this system in the form $\mathbf{x}' = \mathbf{A}\mathbf{x}$, where $\mathbf{A}$ is a 3×3 real matrix.

(b) Find a real-valued fundamental set of solutions.

(c) Show that all solutions of $\mathbf{x}' = \mathbf{w} \times \mathbf{x}$ are periodic. Compute the common period.

(d) Find all constant solutions.

29. Suppose that $\mathbf{x}' = \mathbf{A}\mathbf{x}$ and $\mathbf{x} = \mathbf{B}\mathbf{y}$, where $\det \mathbf{B} \neq 0$. Show that $\mathbf{y}' = (\mathbf{B}^{-1}\mathbf{A}\mathbf{B})\mathbf{y}$.

30. Suppose that $\mathbf{A}$ has n distinct eigenvalues λ_i with corresponding eigenvectors $\mathbf{v}_i$ for $i = 1, 2, 3, \ldots, n$. Let $\mathbf{V} = [\mathbf{v}_1, \ldots, \mathbf{v}_n]$ be the $n \times n$ matrix whose jth column is $\mathbf{v}_j$. Thus $\det \mathbf{V} \neq 0$. Let $\mathbf{D} = \text{diag}(\lambda_1, \ldots, \lambda_n)$.

(a) Show that $\mathbf{A}\mathbf{V} = \mathbf{V}\mathbf{D}$.

(b) Show that if $\mathbf{x}' = \mathbf{A}\mathbf{x}$ and $\mathbf{x} = \mathbf{V}\mathbf{y}$, then $\mathbf{y}' = \mathbf{D}\mathbf{y}$.

(c) Show that $\mathbf{x} = \mathbf{V} \text{diag}(e^{\lambda_1 t}, \ldots, e^{\lambda_n t})\mathbf{V}^{-1}\mathbf{x}(0)$.

31. (a) Solve $y'' + 4y = 0$ by the methods of Chapter 3.

(b) Write $y'' + 4y = 0$ as an equivalent system of the form (8.1).

(c) Solve the system obtained in (b) and compare with the solution obtained in (a).

7.9 MULTIPLE EIGENVALUES

In case $\mathbf{A}$ has distinct (real or complex) eigenvalues, the eigenvalue–eigenvector method discussed in Sections 7.7 and 7.8 can readily be applied to solve the system

(9.1) $\mathbf{x}' = \mathbf{A}\mathbf{x}.$

When $\mathbf{A}$ has eigenvalues of multiplicity greater than 1, it is much harder to obtain solutions since the eigenvector structure of $\mathbf{A}$ can be extremely complicated. Two examples will illustrate the variety of possibilities.

EXAMPLE 9.1

$$\mathbf{A} = \begin{pmatrix} 1 & 1 \\ -1 & 3 \end{pmatrix}.$$

The characteristic equation is $\lambda^2 - 4\lambda + 4 = (\lambda - 2)^2 = 0$. Hence $\lambda = 2$ is an eigenvalue of multiplicity 2. The eigenvector equation is

$$(\mathbf{A} - 2\mathbf{I})\mathbf{v} = \begin{pmatrix} -1 & 1 \\ -1 & 1 \end{pmatrix}\begin{pmatrix} v_1 \\ v_2 \end{pmatrix} = \begin{pmatrix} -v_1 + v_2 \\ -v_1 + v_2 \end{pmatrix} = \begin{pmatrix} 0 \\ 0 \end{pmatrix}.$$

Hence $v_2 = v_1$ and $\mathbf{v} = (v_1, v_1)^T$. A second, linearly independent eigenvector does not exist. Hence our method gives only the solution

$$\mathbf{x}_1 = v_1 \begin{pmatrix} 1 \\ 1 \end{pmatrix} e^{2t}.$$

of $\mathbf{x}' = \mathbf{A}\mathbf{x}$. To find a second solution we reason by analogy from the results in Chapter 3. Suppose that we try to find a solution of the form

(9.2) $\mathbf{x} = (\mathbf{v}_1 t + \mathbf{v}_2)e^{2t}.$

Then $\mathbf{x}' = [2(\mathbf{v}_1 t + \mathbf{v}_2) + \mathbf{v}_1]e^{2t}$, so that

$$[2\mathbf{v}_1 t + (2\mathbf{v}_2 + \mathbf{v}_1)]e^{2t} = \mathbf{A}[\mathbf{v}_1 t + \mathbf{v}_2]e^{2t}$$

or

$$(2\mathbf{v}_1)t + (2\mathbf{v}_2 + \mathbf{v}_1) = (\mathbf{A}\mathbf{v}_1)t + \mathbf{A}\mathbf{v}_2.$$

Hence it is necessary that

$$\mathbf{A}\mathbf{v}_1 = 2\mathbf{v}_1 \quad \text{and} \quad \mathbf{A}\mathbf{v}_2 = 2\mathbf{v}_2 + \mathbf{v}_1,$$

that is,

(9.3) $(\mathbf{A} - 2\mathbf{I})\mathbf{v}_1 = \mathbf{0}, \qquad (\mathbf{A} - 2\mathbf{I})\mathbf{v}_2 = \mathbf{v}_1.$

We see from (9.3) that (9.2) is a solution when $\mathbf{v}_1$ is an eigenvector for $\lambda = 2$ and $(\mathbf{A} - 2\mathbf{I})\mathbf{v}_2 = \mathbf{v}_1$. Hence if we choose $\mathbf{v}_1 = (1, 1)^T$, we must find $\mathbf{v}_2$ so that

$$(\mathbf{A} - 2\mathbf{I})\mathbf{v}_2 = \begin{pmatrix} -1 & 1 \\ -1 & 1 \end{pmatrix}\begin{pmatrix} v_1 \\ v_2 \end{pmatrix} = \mathbf{v}_1 = \begin{pmatrix} 1 \\ 1 \end{pmatrix}.$$

Hence $-v_1 + v_2 = 1$ or $v_2 = 1 + v_1$, where v_1 is arbitrary. We can choose v_1 to be any convenient value. We take $v_1 = 0$ so that (9.2) becomes

$$\mathbf{x}_2 = \left[\begin{pmatrix} 1 \\ 1 \end{pmatrix} t + \begin{pmatrix} 0 \\ 1 \end{pmatrix}\right] e^{2t} = \begin{pmatrix} t \\ t+1 \end{pmatrix} e^{2t}.$$

A general solution is

$$\mathbf{x} = c_1 \begin{pmatrix} 1 \\ 1 \end{pmatrix} e^{2t} + c_2 \begin{pmatrix} t \\ t+1 \end{pmatrix} e^{2t} = e^{2t} \begin{pmatrix} 1 & t \\ 1 & t+1 \end{pmatrix} \begin{pmatrix} c_1 \\ c_2 \end{pmatrix}. \quad \blacksquare$$

As the next example shows, multiple eigenvalues do not necessarily lead to factors of t in the solution.

EXAMPLE 9.2   Solve (9.1) when

$$\mathbf{A} = \begin{pmatrix} 2 & 0 & -1 \\ 0 & 2 & -1 \\ 0 & 0 & 1 \end{pmatrix}.$$

The characteristic equation is

$$\begin{vmatrix} 2-\lambda & 0 & -1 \\ 0 & 2-\lambda & -1 \\ 0 & 0 & 1-\lambda \end{vmatrix} = (2-\lambda)^2(1-\lambda) = 0.$$

Hence $\lambda_1 = 1$, $\lambda_2 = 2$, and $\lambda_3 = 2$. For $\lambda_1 = 1$ the eigenvector equation is

$$\begin{pmatrix} 1 & 0 & -1 \\ 0 & 1 & -1 \\ 0 & 0 & 0 \end{pmatrix} \begin{pmatrix} v_1 \\ v_2 \\ v_3 \end{pmatrix} = \begin{pmatrix} v_1 - v_3 \\ v_2 - v_3 \\ 0 \end{pmatrix} = \begin{pmatrix} 0 \\ 0 \\ 0 \end{pmatrix}.$$

This gives $v_1 = v_2 = v_3$, so that $\mathbf{v}_1 = (1, 1, 1)^T$ will do. For the double eigenvalue $\lambda_2 = \lambda_3 = 2$ the eigenvector equation is

$$(9.4) \qquad \begin{pmatrix} 0 & 0 & -1 \\ 0 & 0 & -1 \\ 0 & 0 & -1 \end{pmatrix} \begin{pmatrix} v_1 \\ v_2 \\ v_3 \end{pmatrix} = \begin{pmatrix} -v_3 \\ -v_3 \\ -v_3 \end{pmatrix} = \begin{pmatrix} 0 \\ 0 \\ 0 \end{pmatrix}.$$

Hence $v_3 = 0$ and v_1 and v_2 are any arbitrary real numbers. The eigenvectors are

$$(9.5) \qquad \begin{pmatrix} v_1 \\ v_2 \\ 0 \end{pmatrix} = v_1 \begin{pmatrix} 1 \\ 0 \\ 0 \end{pmatrix} + v_2 \begin{pmatrix} 0 \\ 1 \\ 0 \end{pmatrix}.$$

For $\lambda = 2$ we can choose *two linearly independent eigenvectors*, for example, $v_1 = (1, 0, 0)^T$ and $v_2 = (0, 1, 0)^T$. A general solution is

$$(9.6) \qquad \mathbf{x} = c_1 \begin{pmatrix} 1 \\ 1 \\ 1 \end{pmatrix} e^t + c_2 \begin{pmatrix} 1 \\ 0 \\ 0 \end{pmatrix} e^{2t} + c_3 \begin{pmatrix} 0 \\ 1 \\ 0 \end{pmatrix} e^{2t} = \begin{pmatrix} e^t & e^{2t} & 0 \\ e^t & 0 & e^{2t} \\ e^t & 0 & 0 \end{pmatrix} \begin{pmatrix} c_1 \\ c_2 \\ c_3 \end{pmatrix}.$$

No powers of t occur in the solution (9.6) because we found *two* linearly independent eigenvectors for the *double* eigenvalue $\lambda = 2$. $\blacksquare$

The general method of solution of (9.1) in case **A** has eigenvalues of multiplicity larger than 1 depends on the following concept:

GENERALIZED EIGENVECTORS AND CHAINS

We say that **v** is a **generalized eigenvector of A of rank** k associated with the eigenvalue λ if

$$(\mathbf{A} - \lambda\mathbf{I})^k\mathbf{v} = \mathbf{0} \quad \text{and} \quad (\mathbf{A} - \lambda\mathbf{I})^{k-1}\mathbf{v} \neq \mathbf{0}.$$

For such an eigenvector **v** we define a **chain of generalized eigenvectors of length** k as follows. Define $\mathbf{v}_k = \mathbf{v}$,

$$\mathbf{v}_{k-1} = (\mathbf{A} - \lambda\mathbf{I})\mathbf{v}_k = (\mathbf{A} - \lambda\mathbf{I})\mathbf{v},$$

$$\mathbf{v}_{k-2} = (\mathbf{A} - \lambda\mathbf{I})\mathbf{v}_{k-1} = (\mathbf{A} - \lambda\mathbf{I})^2\mathbf{v},$$

$$\vdots$$

$$\mathbf{v}_1 = (\mathbf{A} - \lambda\mathbf{I})\mathbf{v}_2 = (\mathbf{A} - \lambda\mathbf{I})^{k-1}\mathbf{v}.$$

For example, if **A** is given as in Example 9.1, then from (9.3) we see that $\mathbf{v}_2 = (0, 1)^T$ and $\mathbf{v}_1 = (1, 1)^T$ is a chain of generalized eigenvectors of length 2 associated with the eigenvalue $\lambda = 2$. In Example 9.2 each chain of generalized eigenvectors associated with the eigenvalue $\lambda = 2$ has *length 1*, that is, the generalized eigenvectors are just normal eigenvectors.

The chain structure of generalized eigenvectors can be quite complicated. The following results are true.

1. If $\{\mathbf{v}_1, \mathbf{v}_2, \ldots, \mathbf{v}_k\}$ is a chain of generalized eigenvectors of length k associated with an eigenvalue λ, then this chain is a linearly independent set.
2. Generalized eigenvectors of **A** associated with different eigenvalues are linearly independent.
3. If $S_1 = \{\mathbf{v}_1, \mathbf{v}_2, \ldots, \mathbf{v}_k\}$ and $S_2 = \{\mathbf{u}_1, \mathbf{u}_2, \ldots, \mathbf{u}_m\}$ are chains of generalized eigenvectors of length k and m associated with the same eigenvalue and if $\mathbf{v}_k$ and $\mathbf{u}_m$ are linearly independent, then S_1 union S_2 is a linearly independent set.
4. The sum of the length of all linearly independent chains associated with a given eigenvalue is equal to the multiplicity of the eigenvalue.

These facts can be used to compute a fundamental set of solutions of (9.1). First the eigenvalues are computed. Then the chains are computed in such a way that n linearly independent generalized eigenvectors are obtained. Suppose that $\{\mathbf{v}_1, \mathbf{v}_2, \ldots, \mathbf{v}_k\}$ is a chain of length k associated with an eigenvalue λ. Then $\mathbf{v}_1$ is an ordinary eigenvalue, that is, $(\mathbf{A} - \lambda\mathbf{I})\mathbf{v}_1 = \mathbf{0}$, so that

$$\mathbf{x}_1 = \mathbf{v}_1 e^{\lambda t}$$

is a solution. Next define

$$x_2 = (v_1 t + v_2)e^{\lambda t}.$$

Since $(A - \lambda I)v_2 = v_1$ and $(A - \lambda I)v_1 = 0$, then

$$x'_2 = [\lambda(v_1 t + v_2) + v_1]e^{\lambda t} = [(\lambda v_1)t + \lambda v_2 + v_1]e^{\lambda t}$$
$$= A[v_1 t + v_2]e^{\lambda t} = Ax_2.$$

Hence x_2 is a solution of (9.1) with $x_2(0) = v_2$. Next define

$$x_3 = \left[v_1 \left(\frac{t^2}{2} \right) + v_2 t + v_3 \right] e^{\lambda t}.$$

As in the previous case we see that x_3 solves (9.1). Since $x_3(0) = v_3$ is linearly independent of $x_2(0) = v_2$ and $x_1(0) = v_1$, then x_1, x_2, and x_3 are linearly independent solutions. This process is continued to

$$x_k = \left[v_1 \left(\frac{t^{k-1}}{(k-1)!} \right) + v_2 \left(\frac{t^{k-2}}{(k-2)!} \right) + \ldots + v_{k-1} t + v_k \right] e^{\lambda t}.$$

This determines a set of k linearly independent solutions of (9.1). The same construction is applied to each of the chains of A. In this way one obtains n linearly independent solutions of (9.1).

EXAMPLE 9.3   Find a fundamental set of solutions of (9.1) when

$$A = \begin{pmatrix} -2 & 0 & 0 & 0 & 0 & 0 \\ 0 & -1 & 1 & 0 & 0 & 0 \\ 0 & 0 & -1 & 0 & 0 & 0 \\ 0 & 0 & 0 & 3 & 0 & 0 \\ 0 & 0 & 0 & 0 & 3 & 1 \\ 0 & 0 & 0 & 0 & 0 & 3 \end{pmatrix}.$$

Since A is an upper triangular matrix, we can immediately say that the eigenvalues of A are $\lambda = -2$ with multiplicity 1, $\lambda = -1$ with multiplicity 2, and $\lambda = 3$ with multiplicity 3.

For $\lambda_1 = -2$ it is easy to see that $(A + 2I)v = 0$ reduces to

$$(0, v_2 + v_3, v_3, 5v_4, 5v_5 + v_6, 5v_6)^T = 0.$$

Hence $v_2 = v_3 = v_4 = v_5 = v_6 = 0$ and v_1 is arbitrary. We take $v_1 = 1$ so that

$$v_1 = (1, 0, 0, 0, 0, 0)^T, \qquad \lambda_1 = -2.$$

For $\lambda_2 = -1$ the eigenvector equation is $(A + I)v = 0$ or

$$(-v_1, v_3, 0, 4v_4, 4v_5 + v_6, 4v_6)^T = 0.$$

All components of v are zero except v_2, which is arbitrary. We take $v_2 = 1$ so that

$$v_2 = (0, 1, 0, 0, 0, 0)^T, \qquad \lambda_2 = \lambda_3 = -1.$$

Since only one eigenvalue was found while $\lambda = -1$ is a double root, there must be a generalized eigenvector. It must satisfy the equation

$$(\mathbf{A} + \mathbf{I})\mathbf{v} = \mathbf{v}_2$$

or

$$(-v_1, v_3, 0, 4v_4, 4v_5 + v_6, 4v_6)^T = (0, 1, 0, 0, 0, 0)^T.$$

The solution is $v_3 = 1$ and $v_2 = c$ arbitrary, while $v_1 = v_4 = v_5 = v_6 = 0$, that is,

$$\mathbf{v} = (0, 0, 1, 0, 0, 0)^T + c\mathbf{v}_2.$$

A convenient choice is $c = 0$, so that

$$\mathbf{v}_3 = (0, 0, 1, 0, 0, 0)^T.$$

For $\lambda = 3$ the eigenvector equation is $(\mathbf{A} - 3\mathbf{I})\mathbf{v} = \mathbf{0}$, that is,

$$(-5v_1, -4v_2 + v_3, -4v_3, 0, v_6, 0)^T = 0.$$

Hence $v_1 = v_2 = v_3 = v_6 = 0$ and v_4 and v_5 are arbitrary. This gives two linearly independent eigenvectors. Since $\lambda = 3$ is an eigenvalue of multiplicity 3, there must be one generalized eigenvector $\mathbf{u}$. It satisfies the equation $(\mathbf{A} - 3\mathbf{I})\mathbf{u} = (0, 0, 0, v_4, v_5, 0)^T$ for some choices of v_4 and v_5, that is,

$$(-5u_1, -4u_2 + u_3, -4u_3, 0, u_6, 0)^T = (0, 0, 0, v_4, v_5, 0)^T.$$

Clearly, $u_1 = u_2 = u_3 = 0$, $u_6 = v_5$ and $v_4 = 0$. This means that $\mathbf{u} = (0, 0, 0, u_4, u_5, v_5)^T$ and

$$(\mathbf{A} - 3\mathbf{I})\mathbf{u} = (0, 0, 0, 0, v_5, 0)^T.$$

Since u_4, u_5, and v_5 are arbitrary (except that $v_5 \neq 0$), we use the simple choices $u_4 = u_5 = 0$, $v_5 = 1$. This gives

$$\mathbf{u} = \mathbf{v}_6 = (0, 0, 0, 0, 0, 1)^T, \qquad \mathbf{v}_5 = (0, 0, 0, 0, 1, 0)^T$$

with $(\mathbf{A} - 3\mathbf{I})\mathbf{v}_6 = \mathbf{v}_5$. We now choose an eigenvector $\mathbf{v}_4$ for $\lambda = 3$ such that $\mathbf{v}_4$ and $\mathbf{v}_5$ are linearly independent. For example,

$$\mathbf{v}_4 = (0, 0, 0, 1, 0, 0)^T$$

will do. Notice that all eigenvectors and generalized eigenvectors are *nonzero*. The solution corresponding to the eigenvalue $\lambda_1 = -2$ is

$$\mathbf{x}_1 = \mathbf{v}_1 e^{-2t} = \begin{pmatrix} 1 \\ 0 \\ 0 \\ 0 \\ 0 \\ 0 \end{pmatrix} e^{-2t}.$$

The solutions obtained from the chain $\{\mathbf{v}_2, \mathbf{v}_3\}$ for $\lambda_2 = \lambda_3 = -1$ are

$$\mathbf{x}_2 = v_2 e^{-t} = \begin{pmatrix} 0 \\ 1 \\ 0 \\ 0 \\ 0 \\ 0 \end{pmatrix} e^{-t} \quad \text{and} \quad \mathbf{x}_3 = (\mathbf{v}_2 t + \mathbf{v}_3) e^{-t} = \begin{pmatrix} 0 \\ t \\ 1 \\ 0 \\ 0 \\ 0 \end{pmatrix} e^{-t}.$$

The solutions obtained from the eigenvector $\mathbf{v}_4$ and from the chain $\{\mathbf{v}_5, \mathbf{v}_6\}$ are

$$\mathbf{x}_4 = \mathbf{v}_4 e^{3t} = \begin{pmatrix} 0 \\ 0 \\ 0 \\ 1 \\ 0 \\ 0 \end{pmatrix} e^{3t}, \qquad \mathbf{x}_5 = \mathbf{v}_5 e^{3t} = \begin{pmatrix} 0 \\ 0 \\ 0 \\ 0 \\ 1 \\ 0 \end{pmatrix} e^{3t},$$

and

$$\mathbf{x}_6 = (\mathbf{v}_5 t + \mathbf{v}_6) e^{3t} = \begin{pmatrix} 0 \\ 0 \\ 0 \\ 0 \\ t \\ 1 \end{pmatrix} e^{3t}.$$

These six solutions constitute a fundamental set of solutions. A fundamental matrix is

$$\mathbf{X}(t) = \begin{pmatrix} e^{-2t} & 0 & 0 & 0 & 0 & 0 \\ 0 & e^{-t} & te^{-t} & 0 & 0 & 0 \\ 0 & 0 & e^{-t} & 0 & 0 & 0 \\ 0 & 0 & 0 & e^{3t} & 0 & 0 \\ 0 & 0 & 0 & 0 & e^{3t} & te^{3t} \\ 0 & 0 & 0 & 0 & 0 & e^{3t} \end{pmatrix}.$$

Since $\mathbf{X}(0) = \mathbf{I}$, then $\mathbf{X}(t) = e^{\mathbf{A}t}$. ∎

As Example 9.3 shows, the computation of all chains of generalized eigenvectors of a matrix may be a very complicated undertaking. If the eigenvalue λ is complex, the computation is the same in theory but is even more complicated in practice because of the need to do complex arithmetic. Complex conjugate pairs of solutions can be replaced by real-valued solutions, that is, the real and the imaginary parts of the complex solutions.

PROBLEMS

In Problems 1–12, find a general solution and a fundamental matrix for the system.

1. $\mathbf{x}' = \begin{pmatrix} 4 & 1 \\ -1 & 2 \end{pmatrix} \mathbf{x}.$

2. $\mathbf{x}' = \begin{pmatrix} 2 & 1 \\ -1 & 0 \end{pmatrix} \mathbf{x}.$

3. $\mathbf{x}' = \begin{pmatrix} 7 & -4 \\ 4 & -1 \end{pmatrix} \mathbf{x}.$

4. $\mathbf{x}' = \begin{pmatrix} 3 & -2 \\ 2 & -1 \end{pmatrix} \mathbf{x}.$

5. $\mathbf{x}' = \begin{pmatrix} -3 & 4 \\ -1 & 1 \end{pmatrix} \mathbf{x}.$

6. $\mathbf{x}' = \begin{pmatrix} 3 & 1 \\ -1 & 1 \end{pmatrix} \mathbf{x}.$

7. $\mathbf{x}' = \begin{pmatrix} 2 & 0 & 0 \\ 1 & 2 & 0 \\ -1 & 0 & 2 \end{pmatrix} \mathbf{x}.$

8. $\mathbf{x}' = \begin{pmatrix} -3 & 1 & 2 \\ 0 & -3 & 1 \\ 0 & 0 & -3 \end{pmatrix} \mathbf{x}.$

9. $\mathbf{x}' = \begin{pmatrix} 0 & 1 & 0 \\ 0 & 0 & 1 \\ 8 & -12 & 6 \end{pmatrix} \mathbf{x}.$

10. $\mathbf{x}' = \begin{pmatrix} 0 & 1 & 0 & 0 \\ 0 & 0 & 1 & 0 \\ 0 & 0 & 0 & 1 \\ -16 & 0 & 8 & 0 \end{pmatrix} \mathbf{x}.$

11. $\mathbf{x}' = \begin{pmatrix} 0 & 1 & 0 & 0 \\ 0 & 0 & 1 & 0 \\ 0 & 0 & 0 & 1 \\ -16 & 0 & -8 & 0 \end{pmatrix} \mathbf{x}.$

12. $\mathbf{x}' = \begin{pmatrix} 0 & 1 & 0 \\ 0 & 0 & 1 \\ 2 & -5 & 4 \end{pmatrix} \mathbf{x}.$

Given the solutions of Problems 1–12, solve Problems 13–18.

13. $\mathbf{x}' = \begin{pmatrix} 4 & 1 \\ -1 & 2 \end{pmatrix} \mathbf{x},$ $\qquad \mathbf{x}(0) = \begin{pmatrix} 1 \\ 1 \end{pmatrix}.$

14. $\mathbf{x}' = \begin{pmatrix} 2 & 1 \\ -1 & 0 \end{pmatrix} \mathbf{x},$ $\qquad \mathbf{x}(0) = \begin{pmatrix} 2 \\ 0 \end{pmatrix}.$

15. $\mathbf{x}' = \begin{pmatrix} 7 & -4 \\ 4 & -1 \end{pmatrix} \mathbf{x},$ $\qquad \mathbf{x}(0) = \begin{pmatrix} 0 \\ -1 \end{pmatrix}.$

16. $\mathbf{x}' = \begin{pmatrix} 3 & 1 \\ -1 & 1 \end{pmatrix} \mathbf{x},$ $\qquad \mathbf{x}(1) = \begin{pmatrix} 1 \\ 0 \end{pmatrix}.$

17. $\mathbf{x}' = \begin{pmatrix} 2 & 0 & 0 \\ 1 & 2 & 0 \\ -1 & 0 & 2 \end{pmatrix} \mathbf{x},$ $\qquad \mathbf{x}(0) = \begin{pmatrix} 0 \\ 1 \\ 0 \end{pmatrix}.$

18. $\mathbf{x}' = \begin{pmatrix} -3 & 1 & 2 \\ 0 & -3 & 1 \\ 0 & 0 & -3 \end{pmatrix} \mathbf{x},$ $\qquad \mathbf{x}(0) = \begin{pmatrix} 1 \\ 0 \\ 0 \end{pmatrix}.$

In Problems 19–23, compute e^{At} for the given **A**. *Hint:* Given any fundamental matrix $\mathbf{X}(t)$, $e^{At} = \mathbf{X}(t)\mathbf{X}(0)^{-1}$.

19. $\begin{pmatrix} 3 & -1 \\ 4 & -1 \end{pmatrix}.$

20. $\begin{pmatrix} 0 & 1 & 0 \\ 0 & 0 & 1 \\ -2 & 3 & 0 \end{pmatrix}.$

21. $\begin{pmatrix} 3 & 1 \\ -1 & 1 \end{pmatrix}$ (see Problem 6).

22. $\begin{pmatrix} 1 & 2 & 0 \\ 0 & 1 & 0 \\ 0 & 0 & -1 \end{pmatrix}$.

23. $\begin{pmatrix} 2 & 1 & 0 \\ 0 & 2 & 1 \\ 0 & 0 & 2 \end{pmatrix}$.

24. It is know that a real $n \times n$ matrix $\mathbf{A}$ that is symmetric (i.e., $\mathbf{A} = \mathbf{A}^T$) must have n mutually perpendicular eigenvectors. Suppose that $\mathbf{A}$ is such a matrix and that $S = \{\mathbf{v}_1, \mathbf{v}_2, \ldots, \mathbf{v}_n\}$ is a set of n mutually perpendicular eigenvectors.

(a) Show that S is a linearly independent set of vectors.

(b) Let $\mathbf{u}_k = \mathbf{v}_k/|\mathbf{v}_k|$ when $|\mathbf{v}_k| = $ length of $\mathbf{v}_k$. Show that $\mathbf{U} = [\mathbf{u}_1, \mathbf{u}_2, \ldots, \mathbf{u}_n]$ is a matrix with the property that $\mathbf{U}\mathbf{U}^T = \mathbf{U}^T\mathbf{U} = \mathbf{I}$.

(c) Show that $\mathbf{A}\mathbf{U} = \mathbf{U}\mathbf{D}$ for some diagonal matrix $\mathbf{D}$.

(d) If $\mathbf{x}' = \mathbf{A}\mathbf{x}$ and if $\mathbf{y} = \mathbf{U}^T\mathbf{x}$, then show that $\mathbf{y}' = \mathbf{D}\mathbf{y}$.

(e) Show that $e^{\mathbf{A}t} = \mathbf{U}e^{\mathbf{D}t}\mathbf{U}^T$.

25. Compute a fundamental matrix for

$$\mathbf{x}' = \begin{pmatrix} -2 & 1 & -2 \\ 1 & -2 & -2 \\ -2 & -2 & 1 \end{pmatrix}\mathbf{x}.$$

26. (a) Show that if

$$\mathbf{A} = \begin{pmatrix} a & b & 1 & 0 \\ -b & a & 0 & 1 \\ 0 & 0 & a & b \\ 0 & 0 & -b & a \end{pmatrix}$$

then $\lambda = a + ib$ is a double eigenvalue of $\mathbf{A}$.

(b) Find complex-valued vectors $\{\mathbf{v}_1, \mathbf{v}_2\}$ such that

$$(\mathbf{A} - (a + ib)\mathbf{I})\mathbf{v}_2 = \mathbf{v}_1, \qquad [\mathbf{A} - (a + ib)\mathbf{I}]\mathbf{v}_1 = \mathbf{0}, \qquad \mathbf{v}_1 \neq \mathbf{0}.$$

(c) Show that

$$\mathbf{y}_1 = \mathbf{v}_1 e^{(a+ib)t}, \qquad \mathbf{y}_2 = (\mathbf{v}_1 t + \mathbf{v}_2)e^{(a+ib)t}$$

are solutions of $\mathbf{x}' = \mathbf{A}\mathbf{x}$. Show that $\bar{\mathbf{y}}_1$ and $\bar{\mathbf{y}}_2$ are also solutions.

(d) Show that $\mathbf{x}_1 = \text{Re } \mathbf{y}_1$, $\mathbf{x}_2 = \text{Im } \mathbf{y}_1$, $\mathbf{x}_3 = \text{Re } \mathbf{y}_2$, and $\mathbf{x}_4 = \text{Im } \mathbf{y}_2$ comprise a real-valued fundamental set of solutions.

27. Show that

(a) $e^{\begin{pmatrix} \lambda & 1 \\ 0 & \lambda \end{pmatrix}t} = e^{\lambda t}\begin{pmatrix} 1 & t \\ 0 & 1 \end{pmatrix}$.

(b) $e^{\begin{pmatrix} \lambda & 1 & 0 \\ 0 & \lambda & 1 \\ 0 & 0 & \lambda \end{pmatrix}t} = e^{\lambda t}\begin{pmatrix} 1 & t & t^2/2 \\ 0 & 1 & t \\ 0 & 0 & 1 \end{pmatrix}$.

28. Let $p(s) = s^n + a_{n-1}s^{n-1} + \ldots + a_2 s^2 + a_1 s + a_0$,

$$A = \begin{pmatrix} 0 & 1 & 0 & \cdots & 0 \\ 0 & 0 & 1 & \cdots & 0 \\ \vdots & & & & \\ -a_0 & -a_1 & -a_2 & \cdots & -a_{n-1} \end{pmatrix}, \qquad b(s) = \begin{pmatrix} 1 \\ s \\ s^2 \\ \vdots \\ s^{n-1} \end{pmatrix}$$

so that

$$b'(s) = \begin{pmatrix} 0 \\ 1 \\ 2s \\ \vdots \\ (n-1)s^{n-2} \end{pmatrix}, \qquad b^{(2)}(s) = \begin{pmatrix} 0 \\ 0 \\ 2 \\ \vdots \\ (n-1)(n-2)s^{n-3} \end{pmatrix}, \qquad \text{etc.}$$

(a) Show that if $p(\lambda) = 0$, then $b(\lambda)$ is an eigenvector of A corresponding to the eigenvalue λ.

(b) Show that if $p(\lambda) = p'(\lambda) = 0$, then

$$(A - \lambda I)b'(\lambda) = b(\lambda), \qquad (A - \lambda I)b(\lambda) = 0.$$

(c) Show that if λ is a zero of $p(s)$ of multiplicity $k > 1$, then

$$\left\{ \frac{1}{(k-1)!} b^{(k-1)}(\lambda), \ldots, b^{(1)}(\lambda), b(\lambda) \right\}$$

is a chain of generalized eigenvector of A corresponding to the eigenvalue λ.

29. Write $y'' - 4y' + 4y = 0$ as a system of two equations. Compute all eigenvectors and generalized eigenvectors of the corresponding matrix A.

30. (a) Using the method of power series, show that $X' = AX$ has a solution of the form

$$X(t) = B_0 + B_1 t + B_2 t^2 + \ldots = \sum_{n=0}^{\infty} B_n t^n,$$

where B_0 is an arbitrary constant $n \times n$ matrix and $B_j = (A^j/j!)B_0$ for $j = 1, 2, 3, \ldots$.

(b) Compute e^{At} as a power series.

31. (a) Given

$$A = \begin{pmatrix} 0 & w \\ -w & 0 \end{pmatrix},$$

compute A^2, A^3, and A^4.

(b) Show that

$$A^{2k} = \begin{pmatrix} (-1)^k w^{2k} & 0 \\ 0 & (-1)^k w^{2k} \end{pmatrix},$$

for $k = 0, 1, 2, \ldots$.

(c) Show that

$$\mathbf{A}^{2k+1} = \begin{pmatrix} 0 & (-1)^k w^{2k+1} \\ (-1)^{k+1} w^{2k+1} & 0 \end{pmatrix},$$

for $k = 0, 1, 2, \ldots$.

(d) Compute the power series representation for $e^{\mathbf{A}t}$.

32. (a) For the compartmental system depicted in Figure 7.2, write the coefficient matrix $\mathbf{A}$ for the governing equations.

(b) Show that the eigenvalues of $\mathbf{A}$ are 0, $-\lambda_3$, $-(\lambda_1 + \lambda_2)$, and $-(\lambda_4 + \lambda_5)$.

(c) Find a fundamental set of solutions when $\lambda_i = 1$ for $1 \le i \le 5$.

(d) Find a fundamental set of solutions when $\lambda_1 = \lambda_2 = \lambda_4 = \lambda_5 = 2$ and $\lambda_3 = 4$.

33. (a) Solve $y'' - 2y' + y = 0$ using the methods of Chapter 3.

(b) Write this equation as an equivalent system of the form (9.1).

(c) Solve the system obtained in (b) and compare with the solution obtained in (a).

7.10 *NONHOMOGENEOUS SYSTEMS*

Given a continuous $n \times n$ matrix $\mathbf{A}(t)$ and a continuous n-vector-valued function $\mathbf{g}(t)$ defined on an open interval J, consider the nonhomogeneous (or forced) linear system

(10.1) $$\mathbf{x}' = \mathbf{A}(t)\mathbf{x} + \mathbf{g}(t).$$

We assume that a fundamental matrix $\mathbf{X}(t)$ can be found for the corresponding homogeneous system

(10.2) $$\mathbf{x}' = \mathbf{A}(t)\mathbf{x}.$$

Working by analogy from the known results for nth-order equations, we assume a trial solution of the form

(10.3) $$\mathbf{x} = \mathbf{X}(t)\mathbf{y},$$

where $\mathbf{y}$ is an unknown vector function. On substituting (10.3) into (10.1), we find that

(10.4) $$\mathbf{x}' = \mathbf{X}'\mathbf{y} + \mathbf{X}\mathbf{y}' = \mathbf{A}(\mathbf{X}\mathbf{y}) + \mathbf{g}.$$

Since $\mathbf{X}' = \mathbf{A}\mathbf{X}$, then (10.4) becomes

$$\mathbf{A}\mathbf{X}\mathbf{y} + \mathbf{X}\mathbf{y}' = \mathbf{A}\mathbf{X}\mathbf{y} + \mathbf{g}$$

or $\mathbf{X}\mathbf{y}' = \mathbf{g}$, that is,

$$\mathbf{y}'(t) = \mathbf{X}(t)^{-1}\mathbf{g}(t) \qquad \text{for all } t \text{ in } J.$$

Hence for any fixed τ in J we have

$$\mathbf{y}(t) = \mathbf{c} + \int_{\tau}^{t} \mathbf{X}(s)^{-1}\mathbf{g}(s) \, ds$$

and

(10.5)
$$x(t) = X(t)c + \int_\tau^t X(t)X(s)^{-1}g(s)\,ds.$$

Since c is an arbitrary constant vector, then (10.5) is a general solution of (10.1). The term $X(t)c$ is a general solution of the corresponding homogeneous system (10.2), while the integral term in (10.5) is a particular solution of (10.1).

THEOREM 10.1: VARIATION OF CONSTANTS

If $X(t)$ is any fundamental matrix for (10.2) and τ is any point in the interval J, then (10.5) is a general solution of (10.1). Moreover, the solution of the initial value problem

$$x' = A(t)x + g(t), \qquad x(t_0) = x_0$$

is

(10.6)
$$x(t) = X(t)X(t_0)^{-1}x_0 + \int_{t_0}^t X(t)X(s)^{-1}g(s)\,ds.$$

Only (10.6) needs further proof. In (10.5) we choose $\tau = t_0$ so that

$$x(t) = X(t)c + \int_{t_0}^t X(t)X(s)^{-1}g(s)\,ds.$$

When $t = t_0$ we require that

$$x(t_0) = X(t_0)c + 0 = x_0$$

or $c = X(t_0)^{-1}x_0$. This proves (10.6).

When $A(t) = A$ is a constant matrix, then given any fundamental matrix $X(t)$ of $x' = Ax$, we know that $e^{At} = X(t)X(0)^{-1}$ or $X(t) = e^{At}X(0)$. Thus $X(s)^{-1} = X(0)^{-1}(e^{As})^{-1} = X(0)^{-1}e^{-As}$,

$$X(t)X(t_0)^{-1} = [e^{At}X(0)][X(0)^{-1}e^{-At_0}] = e^{A(t-t_0)},$$

and

$$X(t)X(s)^{-1} = [e^{At}X(0)][X(0)^{-1}e^{-As}] = e^{A(t-s)}.$$

Thus (10.6) reduces to

$$x(t) = e^{A(t-t_0)}x_0 + \int_{t_0}^t e^{A(t-s)}g(s)\,ds.$$

EXAMPLE 10.2   Find a general solution of

$$x' = \begin{pmatrix} 1 & -1 \\ 2 & -1 \end{pmatrix} x + \begin{pmatrix} \cot t \\ 0 \end{pmatrix}.$$

The corresponding homogeneous system has eigenvalues $\pm i$. A complex-valued solution is

$$\begin{pmatrix} 1 \\ 1-i \end{pmatrix} e^{it} = \left[\begin{pmatrix} 1 \\ 1 \end{pmatrix} + i \begin{pmatrix} 0 \\ -1 \end{pmatrix} \right] [\cos t + i \sin t]$$

$$= \begin{pmatrix} \cos t \\ \cos t + \sin t \end{pmatrix} + i \begin{pmatrix} \sin t \\ \sin t - \cos t \end{pmatrix}.$$

A real-valued fundamental matrix is

$$\mathbf{X}(t) = \begin{pmatrix} \cos t & \sin t \\ \cos t + \sin t & \sin t - \cos t \end{pmatrix}.$$

Hence

$$e^{\mathbf{A}t} = \mathbf{X}(t)\mathbf{X}(0)^{-1} = \mathbf{X}(t) \begin{pmatrix} 1 & 0 \\ 1 & -1 \end{pmatrix}^{-1}$$

$$= \begin{pmatrix} \cos t + \sin t & -\sin t \\ 2 \sin t & \cos t - \sin t \end{pmatrix}.$$

The trial solution $\mathbf{x} = e^{\mathbf{A}t}\mathbf{y}$ leads to

$$\mathbf{y}'(t) = e^{-\mathbf{A}t}\mathbf{g}(t) = \begin{pmatrix} \cos t - \sin t & \sin t \\ -2 \sin t & \cos t + \sin t \end{pmatrix} \begin{pmatrix} \cot t \\ 0 \end{pmatrix}$$

$$= \begin{pmatrix} \cos t \cot t - \cos t \\ -2 \cos t \end{pmatrix} = \begin{pmatrix} \csc t - \sin t - \cos t \\ -2 \cos t \end{pmatrix}.$$

Integration gives

$$\mathbf{y}(t) = \begin{pmatrix} -\log |\csc t + \cot t| + \cos t - \sin t \\ -2 \sin t \end{pmatrix} + \mathbf{c}.$$

A general solution is $\mathbf{x} = e^{\mathbf{A}t}\mathbf{y}$, that is,

$$\mathbf{x}(t) = e^{\mathbf{A}t} \begin{pmatrix} c_1 \\ c_2 \end{pmatrix} + e^{\mathbf{A}t} \begin{pmatrix} -\log |\csc t + \cot t| + \cos t - \sin t \\ -2 \sin t \end{pmatrix}. \quad \blacksquare$$

PROBLEMS   In Problems 1–6, find a particular solution.

1. $\mathbf{x}' = \begin{pmatrix} 1 & -1 \\ 2 & -1 \end{pmatrix} \mathbf{x} + \begin{pmatrix} 1 \\ \sec t \end{pmatrix}$ (see Example 10.2).

2. $\mathbf{x}' = \begin{pmatrix} 3 & 1 \\ 5 & -1 \end{pmatrix} \mathbf{x} + \begin{pmatrix} 1 \\ e^t \end{pmatrix}.$

3. $\mathbf{x}' = \begin{pmatrix} 3 & 1 \\ 5 & -1 \end{pmatrix} \mathbf{x} + \begin{pmatrix} e^{4t} \\ 1 \end{pmatrix}$ (see Problem 2).

4. $\mathbf{x}' = \begin{pmatrix} 3 & -4 \\ 2 & -3 \end{pmatrix} \mathbf{x} + \begin{pmatrix} e^t \\ 1 \end{pmatrix}.$

5. $\mathbf{x}' = \begin{pmatrix} 3 & -4 \\ 2 & -3 \end{pmatrix} \mathbf{x} + \begin{pmatrix} e^t \\ e^t \end{pmatrix}$ (see Problem 4).

6. $\mathbf{x}' = \begin{pmatrix} 1 & 1 \\ 2 & 2 \end{pmatrix} \mathbf{x} + \begin{pmatrix} 0 \\ t \end{pmatrix}$.

7. Show that if α is not an eigenvalue of $\mathbf{A}$, then

(a) $\mathbf{x}' = \mathbf{A}\mathbf{x} + \mathbf{b}e^{\alpha t}$ has a particular solution of the form $\mathbf{x}_p(t) = \mathbf{q}e^{\alpha t}$ for some constant vector $\mathbf{q}$.

(b) $\mathbf{x}' = \mathbf{A}\mathbf{x} + (\mathbf{b}_0 + \mathbf{b}_1 t)e^{\alpha t}$ has a particular solution of the form $\mathbf{x}_p(t) = (\mathbf{q}_0 + \mathbf{q}_1 t)e^{\alpha t}$.

(c) $\mathbf{x}' = \mathbf{A}\mathbf{x} + (\sum_{j=0}^{N} \mathbf{b}_j t^j)e^{\alpha t}$ has a particular solution of the form $\mathbf{x}_p(t) = (\sum_{j=0}^{N} \mathbf{q}_j t^j)e^{\alpha t}$.

In Problems 8–10, solve using Problem 7.

8. $\mathbf{x}' = \begin{pmatrix} 0 & -2 \\ 2 & 0 \end{pmatrix} \mathbf{x} + \begin{pmatrix} t \\ 1 \end{pmatrix} e^t$, $\mathbf{x}(0) = \begin{pmatrix} 1 \\ 0 \end{pmatrix}$.

9. $\mathbf{x}' = \begin{pmatrix} 1 & 1 \\ 2 & 2 \end{pmatrix} \mathbf{x} + \begin{pmatrix} e^{2t} \\ e^{-t} \end{pmatrix}$, $\mathbf{x}(0) = \begin{pmatrix} 2 \\ -1 \end{pmatrix}$.

10. $\mathbf{x}' = \begin{pmatrix} 2 & -3 \\ 1 & -2 \end{pmatrix} \mathbf{x} + \begin{pmatrix} te^{2t} \\ 0 \end{pmatrix}$, $\mathbf{x}(0) = \begin{pmatrix} 0 \\ 0 \end{pmatrix}$.

11. Open-loop input–output control systems can be written in the form

$$\mathbf{x}' = \mathbf{A}\mathbf{x} + \mathbf{b}u(t), \qquad y = \mathbf{c}^T\mathbf{x} + du(t),$$

where $u(t)$ is the known input and y is the unknown output. Show that if $\mathbf{x}(0) = \mathbf{x}_0$ is known, then

(a) $\mathbf{x}(t) = e^{\mathbf{A}t}\mathbf{x}_0 + \int_0^t e^{\mathbf{A}(t-s)}\mathbf{b}u(s)\,ds$, and

(b) $y(t) = \mathbf{c}^T e^{\mathbf{A}t}\mathbf{x}_0 + du(t) + \int_0^t (\mathbf{c}^T e^{\mathbf{A}(t-s)}\mathbf{b})u(s)\,ds$.

The function $h(t) = \mathbf{c}^T e^{\mathbf{A}t}\mathbf{b}$ is called the **impulse response function** for the given control system.

In Problems 12–15, solve using Problem 11.

12. Consider the control system

$$\mathbf{x}' = \begin{pmatrix} 3 & 1 \\ 5 & -1 \end{pmatrix} \mathbf{x} + \begin{pmatrix} 0 \\ 1 \end{pmatrix} u(t), \qquad y = (1, 0)\mathbf{x} + u.$$

(a) Compute the impulse response function $h(t)$.

(b) Find the output y when $\mathbf{x}(0) = (0, 0)^T$ and $u(t) = 0$.

(c) Find the output y when $\mathbf{x}(0) = (1, -1)^T$ and $u(t) = 0$.

(d) Find the output y when $\mathbf{x}(0) = (1, -1)^T$ and $u(t) = 1$.

13. Find $y(t)$ when

$$\mathbf{x}' = \begin{pmatrix} 0 & 1 \\ -1 & 0 \end{pmatrix} \mathbf{x} + \begin{pmatrix} 1 \\ 1 \end{pmatrix} u, \qquad y = (1, 0)\mathbf{x}$$

and $\mathbf{x}_0 = (0, 0)^T$, $u(t) = \sin \pi t$.

14. Find $y(t)$ when

$$x' = \begin{pmatrix} 0 & w \\ -w & 0 \end{pmatrix} x + \begin{pmatrix} 1 \\ 0 \end{pmatrix} u, \qquad y = (1, 0)x$$

and $x_0 = (0, 1)^T$, $u(t) = \sin wt$.

15. Show that if $u(t) = 1$, then for any x_0 the output from

$$x' = \begin{pmatrix} 0 & 1 \\ -1 & -2 \end{pmatrix} x + \begin{pmatrix} 0 \\ 2 \end{pmatrix} u, \qquad y = (1, -1)x - u$$

has a finite limit as $t \to \infty$. Compute this limit, that is, compute

$$\lim_{t \to \infty} y(t).$$

7.11   LAPLACE TRANSFORMS

The Laplace transform was discussed in Chapter 6. It can be used to obtain the solution of initial value problems of the form

(11.1) $$\qquad\qquad x' = Ax + f(t), \qquad x(0) = x_0.$$

EXAMPLE 11.1   Solve

$$x_1' = 5x_1 - 2x_2 + 1, \qquad x_2' = 4x_1 - x_2$$

subject to the initial conditions $x_1(0) = 0$, $x_2(0) = 1$. Let $X_1(s)$ and $X_2(s)$ be the Laplace transforms of $x_1(t)$ and $x_2(t)$. Then

$$sX_1 = 5X_1 - 2X_2 + \frac{1}{s} \quad \text{and} \quad sX_2 - 1 = 4X_1 - X_2$$

or

$$(s - 5)X_1 + 2X_2 = \frac{1}{s},$$

$$-4X_1 + (s + 1)X_2 = 1.$$

This set of equations can be solved for X_1 and X_2 to obtain

$$X_1(s) = \frac{1 - s}{s(s - 1)(s - 3)} = \frac{1}{3s} - \frac{1}{3(s - 3)}$$

and

$$X_2(s) = \frac{s^2 - 5s + 4}{s(s - 1)(s - 3)} = \frac{4}{3s} - \frac{1}{3(s - 3)}.$$

Taking inverse Laplace transforms gives

$$x_1 = \frac{1 - e^{3t}}{3} \quad \text{and} \quad x_2 = \frac{4 - e^{3t}}{3}. \qquad \blacksquare$$

Laplace transforms can be applied to a system of order 3 or more in the same way. However, the algebra will be much more complicated. Laplace transforms can also be used to compute e^{At} given the matrix $\mathbf{A}$. Let $\mathbf{X}(t) = e^{At}$ so that

(11.2) $$\mathbf{X}' = \mathbf{AX}, \qquad \mathbf{X}(0) = \mathbf{I}.$$

Let $\mathbf{X}^*(s)$ be the Laplace transform of $\mathbf{X}(t)$. Then from (11.2) we see that

$$s\mathbf{X}^* - \mathbf{I} = \mathbf{AX}^*.$$

Hence $(s\mathbf{I} - \mathbf{A})\mathbf{X}^* = \mathbf{I}$ or

(11.3) $$\mathbf{X}^*(s) = L\{e^{At}\} = (s\mathbf{I} - \mathbf{A})^{-1}.$$

EXAMPLE 11.2   Compute e^{At} given that

$$\mathbf{A} = \begin{pmatrix} 1 & 1 \\ 3 & 3 \end{pmatrix}.$$

By (11.3) we have

$$\mathbf{X}^*(s) = \begin{pmatrix} s-1 & -1 \\ -3 & s-3 \end{pmatrix}^{-1} = \frac{1}{s(s-4)} \begin{pmatrix} s-3 & 1 \\ 3 & s-1 \end{pmatrix}$$

$$= \frac{1}{4} \begin{pmatrix} \dfrac{3}{s} + \dfrac{1}{s-4} & \dfrac{-1}{s} + \dfrac{1}{s-4} \\ \dfrac{-3}{s} + \dfrac{3}{s-4} & \dfrac{1}{s} + \dfrac{3}{s-4} \end{pmatrix}.$$

Thus

$$e^{At} = \frac{1}{4} \begin{pmatrix} 3 + e^{4t} & -1 + e^{4t} \\ -3 + 3e^{4t} & 1 + 3e^{4t} \end{pmatrix}. \qquad \blacksquare$$

A general formula for the solution of (11.1) can be obtained using Laplace transforms. Let $\mathbf{X}(s)$ be the Laplace transform of $\mathbf{x}$ and let $\mathbf{F}(s)$ be the Laplace transform of $\mathbf{f}$. Then

$$s\mathbf{X} - \mathbf{x}_0 = \mathbf{AX} + \mathbf{F}(s)$$

or $(s\mathbf{I} - \mathbf{A})\mathbf{X} = \mathbf{x}_0 + \mathbf{F}(s)$. Hence

(11.4) $$\mathbf{X} = (s\mathbf{I} - \mathbf{A})^{-1}\mathbf{x}_0 + (s\mathbf{I} - \mathbf{A})^{-1}\mathbf{F}(s).$$

By (11.3) we see that $(s\mathbf{I} - \mathbf{A})^{-1}\mathbf{x}_0 = L\{e^{At}\mathbf{x}_0\}$. The product $(s\mathbf{I} - \mathbf{A})^{-1}\mathbf{F}(s)$ is the convolution of e^{At} with $\mathbf{f}$. Hence taking the inverse Laplace transform of (11.4) gives

(11.5) $$\mathbf{x}(t) = e^{At}\mathbf{x}_0 + \int_0^t e^{A(t-r)}\mathbf{f}(r)\,dr.$$

The expression on the right in (11.5) is the variation of constants formula for the solution of (11.1).

PROBLEMS   In Problems 1–7, solve using Laplace transforms.

1. $\mathbf{x}' = \begin{pmatrix} -3 & 2 \\ 1 & -2 \end{pmatrix}\mathbf{x}, \qquad \mathbf{x}(0) = (1, 0)^T.$

2. $\mathbf{x}' = \begin{pmatrix} 2 & 1 \\ 4 & -1 \end{pmatrix}\mathbf{x}, \qquad \mathbf{x}(0) = (1, 1)^T.$

3. $\mathbf{x}' = \begin{pmatrix} \pi & 7 \\ -7 & 1 \end{pmatrix}\mathbf{x}, \qquad \mathbf{x}(0) = (0, 0)^T.$

4. $\mathbf{x}' = \begin{pmatrix} 2 & 5 \\ -2 & 4 \end{pmatrix}\mathbf{x} + \begin{pmatrix} 0 \\ 1 \end{pmatrix}, \quad \mathbf{x}(0) = (0, 0)^T.$

5. $\mathbf{x}' = \begin{pmatrix} -1 & 1 & 0 \\ 0 & 2 & 1 \\ 0 & 0 & 1 \end{pmatrix}\mathbf{x}, \qquad \mathbf{x}(0) = (1, 0, 1)^T.$

6. $2\dfrac{dw}{dx} + 4\dfrac{dz}{dx} + w - z = 3e^x, \; w(0) = 1.$

   $\dfrac{dw}{dx} + 2w = e^x - \dfrac{dz}{dx} - z, \; z(0) = 0.$

7. $\quad y_1' + y_2' + y_2 = 2y_1, \; y_1(0) = y_1'(0) = 0.$
   $\quad y_1'' - 3y_1' + y_2' - y_2 + 2y_1 = 0, \; y_2(0) = 1.$

In Problems 8–11, use the Laplace transform to compute e^{At}.

8. $A = \begin{pmatrix} -1 & 2 \\ -2 & -1 \end{pmatrix}.$

9. $A = \begin{pmatrix} -1 & 1 & 2 \\ -1 & 2 & 3 \\ 4 & -1 & 1 \end{pmatrix}.$

10. $A = \begin{pmatrix} -2 & -1 \\ 1 & 0 \end{pmatrix}.$

11. $A = \begin{pmatrix} 3 & 1 \\ -1 & 1 \end{pmatrix}.$

12. Consider the open-loop control system

$$\mathbf{x}' = A\mathbf{x} + \mathbf{b}u(t), \qquad y = \mathbf{c}^T\mathbf{x}, \qquad \mathbf{x}(0) = \mathbf{x}_0.$$

Use Laplace transforms to show that

(a) $\mathbf{x}(t) = e^{At}\mathbf{x}_0 + \displaystyle\int_0^t e^{A(t-s)}\mathbf{b}u(s)\, ds,$ and

(b) $y(t) = \mathbf{c}^T e^{At}\mathbf{x}_0 + \displaystyle\int_0^t \mathbf{c}^T e^{At}\mathbf{b}u(s)\, ds.$

The function $H(s) = \mathbf{c}^T(sI - A)^{-1}\mathbf{b}$ is called the **transfer function** associated with this control system.

In Problems 13 and 14, solve using Problem 12.

13. Consider the control system

$$\mathbf{x}' = \begin{pmatrix} 0 & 1 \\ -1 & 0 \end{pmatrix}\mathbf{x} + \begin{pmatrix} 1 \\ 1 \end{pmatrix}u(t), \qquad y = (1, 0)\mathbf{x}$$

(a) Compute the transfer function $H(s)$.

(b) Compute $h(t) = L^{-1}\{H(s)\}$.

(c) Find $y(t)$ when $\mathbf{x}(0) = (0, 0)^T$ and $u(t) = \sin\sqrt{2}t$.

14. Consider the control system,

$$\mathbf{x}' = \begin{pmatrix} 0 & 3 \\ -3 & 0 \end{pmatrix}\mathbf{x} + \begin{pmatrix} 1 \\ 0 \end{pmatrix}u, \qquad y = (1, 0)\mathbf{x}.$$

(a) Compute the transfer function $H(s)$.

(b) Compute $h(t) = L^{-1}\{H(s)\}$.

(c) Find $y(t)$ when $\mathbf{x}_0 = (0, 1)^T$ and $u(t) = \sin 3t$.

CHAPTER REVIEW

Systems of linear differential equations are normally reduced to first-order systems and then written in matrix–vector form $\mathbf{x}' = \mathbf{A}(t)\mathbf{x} + \mathbf{f}(t)$. If $\mathbf{f}(t) \equiv 0$, the system is **homogeneous** and, otherwise, **nonhomogeneous**. If $\mathbf{A}(t)$ is constant, then we say that the system has **constant coefficients**. The principle of superposition is true. Thus, if $\{\mathbf{x}_1, \dots, \mathbf{x}_n\}$ is a **fundamental set** of solutions of the homogeneous equation, then $\mathbf{x}_c = \sum c_i\mathbf{x}_i$ is a **general solution** of that equation. A **fundamental matrix** solution $\mathbf{X}$ is a matrix whose columns form a fundamental set.

Given a homogeneous system $\mathbf{x}' = \mathbf{Ax}$ with constant coefficients, the **eigenvalue–eigenvector** method can be used to determine a solution. Given *any* fundamental matrix $\mathbf{X}(t)$, then $e^{\mathbf{A}t} = \mathbf{X}(t)\mathbf{X}(0)^{-1}$. The **variation of parameters** formula (10.5) or (11.5) or Laplace transforms can be used to solve the corresponding nonhomogeneous equation.

CHAPTER REVIEW PROBLEMS

In Problems 1–2 find a general solution. Also compute $e^{\mathbf{A}t}$ for the given $\mathbf{A}$.

1. $\mathbf{x}' = \begin{pmatrix} 2 & -5 \\ 2 & -4 \end{pmatrix}\mathbf{x}.$

2. $\mathbf{x}' = \begin{pmatrix} 3 & -4 \\ 4 & -7 \end{pmatrix}\mathbf{x}.$

3. Write the following as a first-order system in vector matrix form.

(a) $x''' = x' + 3x + t,\ x(0) = 1,\ x'(0) = -1,\ x''(0) = 0.$

(b) $x'' = x + y,\ y'' = x' + y',\ x(0) = x'(0) = 0,\ y(0) = y'(0) = 1.$

4. Using variation of parameters find a particular solution.

$$\mathbf{x}' = \begin{pmatrix} 0 & 1 \\ -1 & 0 \end{pmatrix}\mathbf{x} + \begin{pmatrix} \cot x \\ 0 \end{pmatrix}.$$

5. Solve using Laplace transforms:

$$\mathbf{x}' = \begin{pmatrix} -3 & -1 \\ 1 & -1 \end{pmatrix}\mathbf{x} + \begin{pmatrix} 1 \\ 0 \end{pmatrix}e^{-t}, \qquad \mathbf{x}(0) = \begin{pmatrix} 0 \\ 0 \end{pmatrix}.$$

CHAPTER EIGHT

*Numerical Methods*_____

In this chapter we introduce methods for numerically approximating solutions of initial value problems of the form

$$(0.1) \qquad y' = f(x, y), \qquad y(a) = y_0, \qquad a \le x \le b.$$

In some interesting cases (0.1) can be solved exactly using methods discussed in Chapters 2 to 6. However, in most cases, either no exact solution is possible or the solution found may not be in a form where numerical values are easily obtained. For such equations the methods developed in this chapter can be used to approximate the desired solution.

Suppose that (0.1) has a solution $y = \varphi(x)$ on $a \le x \le b$. By a numerical approximation to $\varphi(x)$ we mean the following. The interval $[a, b]$ is partitioned by selecting points $x_0, x_1, x_2, \ldots, x_N$ with $a = x_0 < x_1 < x_2 < \ldots < x_N = b$. At each point x_j a numerical value y_j is given which is approximately equal to the value of solution at x_j, that is, $y_j \cong \varphi(x_j)$ (see Figure 8.1). The value of $\varphi(x)$ is not computed at other points $x = x_n$. These values must be estimated given the values at the points x_n. For $j = 0$ the initial condition in (0.1) gives the exact value $\varphi(a) = \varphi(x_0) = y_0$. The remaining approximations $y_1, y_2, \ldots, y_N$ are usually computed one at a time starting at the left and working to the right. In simple problems the approximations y_j can sometimes be computed using a hand-held calculator. However, the computations are usually done on a digital computer. A small computer such as the one pictured in Photo 18 will suffice for most problems of interest to students.

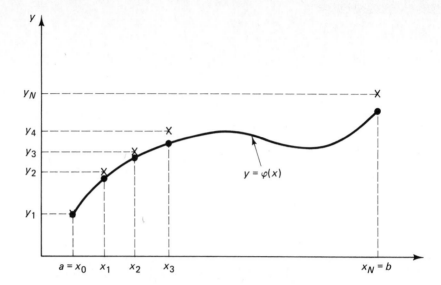

Figure 8.1. Numerical approximation.

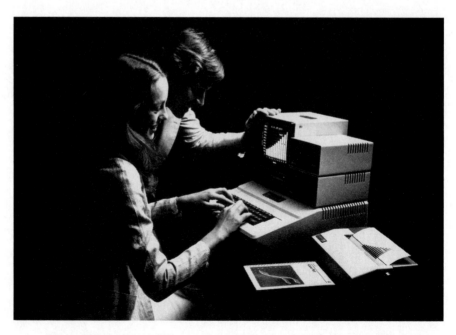

Photo 18. MacIntosh SE computers. (Courtesy of Apple Computer Inc.)

Before starting the material on the numerical solution of differential equations you may wish to become better acquainted with your computer. The following exercises are suggested. You may wish to do them in both single and double precision arithmetic.

1. (a) Compute $Z = \text{SQRT}(2.)$ (z is the square root of 2) and compare with

$$\sqrt{2} = 1.4142\ 13562\ 37309\ \ldots.$$

   (b) Then compute $W = Z{**}2$ (w is the square of z) and compare with 2. Just how accurate does your machine seem to be?

2. (a) Compute $Z = 4.{*}\text{ATAN}(1.)$ (z is 4 times the arctangent of 1) and compare with

$$\pi = 3.14159\ 26535\ 89793\ 23\ \ldots.$$

   (b) Compute $W = \text{SIN}(Z/2.)$ (w is the sine of z halves) and compare with $\sin(\pi/2) = 1$.

   (c) Compute $X = \text{COS}(Z)$ (x is the cosine of z) and compare with $\cos \pi = 1$.

   (d) Compute $Y = \text{SQRT}(Z)$ (y is the square root of z) and compare with

$$\sqrt{\pi} = 1.77245\ 38509\ 65516\ 027\ \ldots.$$

3. Verify that $\cos(x - y) - \cos x \cos y + \sin x \sin y = 0$. Compute this expression for some values of x and y; for example, let x and y run through the values $-10 \leq x, y \leq 10$ by steps of 0.2. Do you get something near zero?

4. Compute $Z = \text{EXP}(1.)$ (z is e raised to the first power) and compare with

$$e = 2.71828\ 18284\ 59045\ 23\ \ldots.$$

Your answers will depend on your machine and the software you use. If you want to find out why your answers are not completely accurate, pick up a book on numerical analysis and read about machine representation of floating point numbers, floating point arithmetic, and round off errors.

8.1   EULER'S METHOD

The Euler method is a simple method that we will use to illustrate the main features of the numerical solution of (0.1). More efficient, but also more complicated, methods will be introduced in later sections of this chapter. We consider the initial value problem

(1.1) $y' = f(x, y), \qquad y(a) = y_0.$

Assume that f and $\partial f / \partial y$ exist and are continuous in a region $D = \{(x, y) : a \leq x \leq b, A \leq y \leq B\}$. We assume that the true solution $y = \varphi(x)$ of (1.1) exists over $a \leq x \leq b$ and that $A < \varphi(x) < B$ there.

Given a point x in $[a, b)$, for small values of h, we can expand $\varphi(x + h)$ in the Taylor series

$$\varphi(x + h) = \varphi(x) + h\varphi'(x) + \frac{h^2}{2}\varphi''(x + \bar{h}),$$

where $\bar{h}$ is between zero and h. Since $\varphi'(x) = f(x, \varphi(x))$, then

(1.2) $$\varphi(x + h) = \varphi(x) + hf(x, \varphi(x)) + \frac{h^2}{2}\varphi''(x + \bar{h}).$$

When h is small, then approximately

(1.3) $$\varphi(x + h) \cong \varphi(x) + hf(x, \varphi(x)).$$

The approximation (1.3) will be used in (1.1) as follows. We divide the interval $[a, b]$ into N subintervals of size h so that $h = (b - a)/N$. We define

$$x_n = a + nh, \qquad 0 \le n \le N.$$

With $x = x_n$ and $x + h = x_{n+1}$ in (1.3) we see that

$$\varphi(x_{n+1}) \cong \varphi(x_n) + hf(x_n, \varphi(x_n)).$$

Hence it is natural to define the following approximations:

EULER'S METHOD

Define approximations y_n by

(1.4) $$y_{n+1} = y_n + hf(x_n, y_n), \qquad 0 \le n \le N - 1.$$

When h is small, we expect (1.4) to determine a good approximate solution at the grid points x_n. The approximations y_n are computed one at a time starting at the left. Since y_0 is given, then (1.4) can be used to compute y_1. Given y_1, (1.4) is used to compute y_2, and so on.

EXAMPLE 1.1   Consider $y' = 2y$, $y(0) = 3$, $0 \le x \le 1$.

The true solution is $\varphi(x) = 3e^{2x}$. Let us see how well Euler's method approximates this solution. For $N = 2$ we have $h = 0.5$. Since $y_0 = 3$, then by (1.4),

$$y_1 = y_0 + h(2y_0) = 3 + 0.5(2 \cdot 3) = 6,$$

$$y_2 = y_1 + h(2y_1) = 6 + 0.5(2 \cdot 6) = 12.$$

The errors in these two approximations are

$$e_1 = \varphi(0.5) - y_1 = 3e - 6 \cong 2.15485,$$

$$e_2 = \varphi(1) - y_2 = 3e^2 - 12 \cong 10.16717.$$

The step size $h = \frac{1}{2}$ is too large to achieve much accuracy. Let us repeat the calculation with $h = \frac{1}{4}$:

$$y_1 = y_0 + 0.25(2y_0) = 3 + \tfrac{3}{2} = 4.5$$

$$y_2 = 4.5 + 0.25(2)(4.5) = 6.75$$

$$y_3 = 6.75 + 0.25(2)(6.75) = 10.125$$

and

$$y_4 = 10.125 + 0.25(2)(10.125) = 15.1875.$$

The error at $x_4 = 1$ is

$$e_4 = \varphi(1) - y_4 = 3e^2 - 15.1875 = 6.97967.$$

The step size $h = \tfrac{1}{4}$ gives a more accurate approximation than $h = \tfrac{1}{2}$. Table 8.1 gives results for still smaller values of h. As h becomes smaller, the error in the Euler approximation decreases. For example, at $x_n = 0.5$, the error when $h =$

TABLE 8.1   Euler's Method

h	x_n	y_n	$\varphi(x_n)$	Error e_n
0.1	0.5	7.46496	8.15485	0.68985
	1.0	18.57521	22.16717	3.59196
0.05	0.5	7.78123	8.15485	0.37362
	1.0	20.18250	22.16717	1.98467
0.025	0.5	7.95989	8.15485	0.19495
	1.0	21.11200	22.16717	1.04720

0.1 is 0.68985. When h is halved to 0.05, the error goes down by approximately one-half to 0.37362. When h is halved again to 0.025, the error in the approximation is nearly halved again. The same situation occurs at $x_n = 1.0$ and, if checked, will also occur at $x_n = 0.1, 0.2$, or at any other grid point we choose. ■

EXAMPLE 1.2   Solve $y' = y^2$, $y(0) = \tfrac{1}{2}$, $0 \le x \le 1$ using Euler's method with $h = 0.2$.

Since $y_0 = 0.5$ is given, then

$$y_1 = y_0 + hy_0^2 = 0.5 + 0.2(0.5)^2 = 0.55$$

$$y_2 = 0.55 + 0.2(0.55)^2 = 0.6105$$

$$y_3 = 0.6105 + 0.2(0.6105)^2 \cong 0.68504$$

$$y_4 = 0.68504 + 0.2(0.68504)^2 \cong 0.77890$$

and

$$y_5 = 0.77890 + 0.2(0.77890)^2 \cong 0.90024.$$

By separation of variables the true solution is $\varphi(x) = (2 - x)^{-1}$. Hence the error at $x = 1.0$ is

$$e_5 = \varphi(1) - y_5 = 0.09976.$$

When h is halved to 0.1, then $y_{10} \cong 0.94221$ and the error at $x = 1.0$ is

$$e_{10} = \varphi(1) - y_{10} = 0.05780.$$

This is about one-half of the error when $h = 0.2$. When h is halved again to 0.05, then $y_{20} = 0.96852$ and the error is approximately halved to

$$e_{20} = \varphi(1) - y_{20} = 0.03148.$$

This tendency of the error to decrease in proportion to the decrease in step size will be explained theoretically in Section 8.5. ■

   If the function $f(x, y)$ in (1.1) is complicated, if the step h is very small, or if the interval $[a, b]$ is long, then Euler's method yields an extremely long and tedious computation. For example, imagine computing an approximation to

(1.5) $$y' = \sqrt{|\sin(x + 2 + y)|} + y^2 e^{-y} + \pi, \qquad y(0) = \sqrt{2}$$

over $0 \le x \le 50$ with $h = 0.01$! However, Euler's method is easy to program in Basic, Fortran, or Pascal. Once the programming has been done, even a small computer can calculate the Euler approximation to (1.5) in a few moments.

PROBLEMS

In Problems 1–6, use Euler's method to approximate the indicated value of the solution. Use $h = 0.1$ and then $h = 0.05$. Find the true solution of the problem and compute your errors.

1. $y' = -2y$, $y(0) = 1$. Find $y(1)$.

2. $y' = 1 + y^2$, $y(0) = 0$. Find $y(\frac{1}{2})$.

3. $y' = -y + 1$, $y(1) = 0$. Find $y(3)$.

4. $y' = y + 1 + x^2$, $y(0) = -1$. Find $y(1)$.

5. $y' = -2y + 6$, $y(0) = 3$. Find $y(1)$.

6. $y' = -2y + 6$, $y(-2) = 0$. Find $y(-1)$.

7. Euler's method is to be applied to the problem

$$y' = y, \qquad y(0) = y_0, \qquad 0 \le x \le b.$$

(a) Show that $y_n = (1 + h)^n y_0$ for $0 \le n \le N$, $h = b/N$.

(b) Show that $y_N = (1 + b/N)^N y_0$ and that

$$\lim_{N \to \infty} y_N = e^b y_0.$$

Hint: You will need a result from calculus concerning e.

8. Euler's method is to be applied to the problem

$$y' = Ay, \qquad y(0) = y_0, \qquad 0 \le x \le b.$$

(a) Show that $y_n = (1 + Ah)^n y_0$ for $0 \le n \le N$, $h = b/N$.

(b) Show that when $A > 0$

$$\lim_{N \to \infty} y_N = e^{Ab} y_0.$$

(c) For $A < 0$ compute the limit of y_N as $N \to \infty$.

9. The exact solution of

$$y' = 3y - 2x, \qquad y(0) = 1$$

is $\varphi(x) = \frac{7}{9}e^{3x} + \frac{2}{9} + \frac{2}{3}x$, $-\infty < x < \infty$.

(a) For $h = 0.1$ compute the Euler approximation to $\varphi(x)$ when $x = 0.2, 0.4$, and 0.6. Compute the errors in the approximations.

(b) Repeat part (a) with $h = 0.025$. Are the errors approximately $\frac{1}{4}$ of those in part (a)?

(c) Estimate how small h must be in order that Euler's method will approximate $\varphi(0.6)$ to three significant figures.

10. (a) In (1.1) show that the change of variable $t = -x$ results in the problem

$$\frac{dy}{dt} = -f(-t, y), \qquad y(-a) = y_0.$$

(b) How can Euler's method be used to solve

$$y' = f(x, y), \qquad y(a) = y_0$$

for $y(c)$ when $c < a$?

(c) Use Euler's method and a step size of $h = 0.02$ to approximate $y(-1)$ given that

$$y' = (\sin y)y + 1, \qquad y(0) = 0.$$

8.2   RUNGE–KUTTA METHODS

In this section we derive more efficient numerical methods by refining the Taylor series argument used in Section 8.1 to derive the Euler method. Taylor series will be used both directly and indirectly.

Given the problem

(2.1) $$y' = f(x, y), \qquad y(a) = y_0, \qquad a \le x \le b,$$

let N be a fixed integer, $h = (b - a)/N$, and $x_n = a + nh$ for $0 \le n \le N$. Since $x_{n+1} = x_n + h$, then using Taylor's theorem we see that

(2.2) $$\varphi(x_{n+1}) = \varphi(x_n) + h\varphi'(x_n) + \frac{h^2}{2}\varphi''(x_n) + \frac{h^3}{6}\varphi'''(\bar{x}_n),$$

where $\bar{x}_n$ is some point between x_n and x_{n+1}. From (2.1)

$$\varphi'(x_n) = f(x_n, \varphi(x_n))$$

and

$$\varphi''(x_n) = \left[\frac{d}{dx} f(x, \varphi(x))\right]_{x_n} = [f_x(x, \varphi(x)) + f_y(x, \varphi(x))\varphi'(x)]_{x_n}$$

$$= f_x(x_n, \varphi(x_n)) + f_y(x_n, \varphi(x_n))f(x_n, \varphi(x_n)).$$

If these formulas are used in (2.2) and if the last term on the right in (2.2) is dropped, we find that

$$\varphi(x_{n+1}) \cong \varphi(x_n) + hf(x_n, \varphi(x_n)) + \frac{h^2}{2}[f_x(x_n, \varphi(x_n)) + f_y(x_n, \varphi(x_n))f(x_n, \varphi(x_n))].$$

This formula is more accurate for small values of h than (1.3) since the term omitted is of the order of h^3. The corresponding numerical method, the **second-order Taylor series method**, is

$$(2.3) \qquad y_{n+1} = y_n + hf(x_n, y_n) + \frac{h^2}{2}[f_x(x_n, y_n) + f_y(x_n, y_n)f(x_n, y_n)].$$

EXAMPLE 2.1   The initial value problem

$$y' = y^2 + 1, \qquad y(0) = 0, \qquad 0 \le x \le 1$$

has solution $\varphi(x) = \tan x$. Since $f(x, y) = y^2 + 1$, then $f_x \equiv 0$ and $f_y(x, y) = 2y$. Hence (2.3) reduces to

$$(2.4) \qquad y_{n+1} = y_n + h(y_n^2 + 1) + h^2 y_n(y_n^2 + 1), \qquad y_0 = 0.$$

Table 8.2 contains some sample results for various values of h. This method is superior to Euler's method, since much more accuracy is obtained for a given amount of work. Notice that halving the step size h will reduce the error by approximately one-fourth. This is roughly the case between $h = 0.2$ and $h = 0.1$ and is more nearly the case between $h = 0.1$ and $h = 0.05$ ■

Taylor series methods give good results but can be complicated to use since it is necessary to compute the two partial derivatives f_x and f_y. Moreover, one must evaluate $f_x(x_n, y_n)$, $f_y(x_n, y_n)$, and $f(x_n, y_n)$ at each step. To avoid these difficulties we shall develop **indirect Taylor series methods,** that is, methods that allow the indirect computation of the Taylor series. These methods are called **Runge–Kutta methods.**

The general second-order Runge–Kutta method has the form

$$(2.5) \qquad y_{n+1} = y_n + h[\alpha_1 f(x_n, y_n) + \alpha_2 f(x_n + \beta h, y_n + \gamma hf(x_n, y_n))].$$

TABLE 8.2   *Power Series Method*

x_n	$h = 0.2$		$h = 0.1$		$h = 0.05$	
	y_n	e_n	y_n	e_n	y_n	e_n
0.2	0.20000	0.00271	0.20201	0.00070	0.20253	0.00018
0.4	0.41632	0.00647	0.42107	0.00173	0.42235	0.00045
0.6	0.67052	0.01361	0.68037	0.00377	0.68314	0.00099
0.8	0.99932	0.03031	1.02082	0.00882	1.02726	0.00238
1.0	1.47895	0.07846	1.53289	0.02452	1.55055	0.00686

The constants α_1, α_2, β, and γ must be determined by expanding the right-hand side of (2.5) in powers of h and then picking these constants so as to match as many terms as possible in the Taylor series for $\varphi(x_n + h)$. Define

$$\Phi(x, y, h) = \alpha_1 f(x, y) + \alpha_2 f(x + \beta h, y + \gamma h f(x, y)).$$

Using Taylor series for a function of two variables, we see that

(2.6) $\qquad \Phi(x, y, h) = \alpha_1 f(x, y) + \alpha_2 [f(x, y) + \beta h f_x + \gamma h f_y f$
$$+ h^2(\tfrac{1}{2}\beta^2 f_{xx} + \beta\gamma f_{xy} f + \tfrac{1}{2}\gamma^2 f_{yy} f^2)] + \mathcal{O}(h^3)$$

where $\mathcal{O}(h^3)$ denotes terms with a factor h^3. On collecting terms we see that $y_{n+1} = y_n + h\Phi(x_n, y_n, h)$, where

(2.7) $\qquad \Phi = (\alpha_1 + \alpha_2) f + (\alpha_2 \beta f_x + \alpha_2 \gamma f_y f) h$
$$+ \left(\frac{\alpha_2 \beta^2}{2} f_{xx} + \alpha_2 \beta\gamma f_{xy} f + \frac{\alpha_2 \gamma^2}{2} f_{yy} f^2 \right) h^2 + \mathcal{O}(h^3).$$

If $f(x, y)$ is smooth (i.e., f has continuous derivatives through order 3), then

$$\varphi(x_n + h) = \varphi(x_n) + h\left[\varphi'(x_n) + \frac{h}{2} \varphi''(x_n) + \frac{h^2}{6} \varphi'''(x_n) + \frac{h^3}{24} \varphi^{(4)}(\bar{x}_n) \right]$$

or

(2.8) $\quad \varphi(x_n + h) = \varphi(x_n) + h\left[f + \frac{h}{2} (f_x + f_y f) + \frac{h^2}{6} (f_{xx} + 2f_{xy}f \right.$

$$\left. + f_{yy}f^2 + f_x f_y + f_y^2 f) + \mathcal{O}(h^3) \right].$$

To match terms in (2.7) and (2.8), we need

(2.9) $\qquad\qquad \alpha_1 + \alpha_2 = 1, \qquad \alpha_2 \beta = \tfrac{1}{2}, \qquad \alpha_2 \gamma = \tfrac{1}{2}.$

Terms of order h^2 in (2.7) cannot be matched with the corresponding terms in (2.8).

SECOND-ORDER RUNGE–KUTTA FORMULAS

The algebraic system (2.9) has many solutions. It is easy to check that one such solution is $\alpha_1 = 0$, $\alpha_2 = 1$, and $\beta = \gamma = \tfrac{1}{2}$. The resulting Runge–Kutta method is

(2.10) $\qquad y_{n+1} = y_n + hf\left(x_n + \frac{h}{2}, y_n + \frac{h}{2} f(x_n, y_n) \right).$

The most popular choice is $\alpha_1 = \alpha_2 = \tfrac{1}{2}$ and $\beta = \gamma = 1$. This gives the **standard second-order Runge–Kutta** formula

(2.11) $\qquad y_{n+1} = y_n + \frac{h}{2} [f(x_n, y_n) + f(x_n + h, y_n + hf(x_n, y_n))].$

EXAMPLE 2.2   Use (2.11) to solve the initial value problem

$$y' = y^2, \qquad y(0) = 0.5, \qquad 0 \le x \le 1.$$

The exact solution is $\varphi(x) = (2 - x)^{-1}$. For convenience of computation, we write (2.11) in the form

$$k_{1n} = hf(x_n, y_n)$$

$$k_{2n} = hf(x_n + h, y_n + k_{1n})$$

$$y_{n+1} = y_n + \tfrac{1}{2}(k_{1n} + k_{2n}).$$

We choose $h = 0.2$. Since $y_0 = 0.5$, then

$$k_{10} = 0.2(0.5)^2 = 0.05$$

$$k_{20} = 0.2(0.5 + 0.05)^2 = 0.0605$$

and

$$y_1 = 0.5 + \tfrac{1}{2}(0.05 + 0.0605) = 0.55525.$$

Next compute

$$k_{11} = 0.2(0.55525)^2 \cong 0.06166$$

$$k_{21} = 0.2(0.55525 + 0.06166)^2 \cong 0.07612$$

and

$$y_2 = 0.55525 + \tfrac{1}{2}(0.07612 + 0.06166) \cong 0.62414.$$

The terms y_3, y_4, and y_5 are computed similarly. Results for several values of h are given in Table 8.3. Notice that when the step size is halved from $h = 0.2$ to $h = 0.1$, the error decreases by roughly one-fourth. This type of behavior can be predicted from the asymptotic error analysis given in Section 8.5. ∎

     More accurate Runge–Kutta formulas can be created. For example, fourth-order Runge–Kutta methods are of the form

$$k_{1n} = hf(x_n, y_n)$$

$$k_{2n} = hf(x_n + \beta_2 h, y_n + \gamma_{21} k_{1n})$$

$$k_{3n} = hf(x_n + \beta_3 h, y_n + \gamma_{31} k_{1n} + \gamma_{32} k_{2n})$$

$$k_{4n} = hf(x_n + \beta_4 h, y_n + \gamma_{41} k_{1n} + \gamma_{42} k_{2n} + \gamma_{43} k_{3n})$$

TABLE 8.3   Runge–Kutta Method

		$h = 0.2$			$h = 0.1$	$h = 0.05$
x_n	k_{1n}	k_{2n}	y_n	e_n	e_n	e_n
0.2	0.05000	0.06050	0.55525	0.00031	0.00008	0.00002
0.4	0.06166	0.07612	0.62414	0.00086	0.00023	0.00006
0.6	0.07791	0.09857	0.71238	0.00191	0.00051	0.00013
0.8	0.10150	0.13248	0.82937	0.00397	0.00108	0.00028
1.0	0.13757	0.18699	0.99165	0.00835	0.00230	0.00060

and

$$y_{n+1} = y_n + (\alpha_1 k_{1n} + \alpha_2 k_{2n} + \alpha_3 k_{3n} + \alpha_4 k_{4n}).$$

The constants β_j, α_j, and γ_{jk} must be chosen in order to match the terms in the Taylor series for $\varphi(x_n + h)$ up through terms of order h^5. An extremely popular and successful choice of the constants results in the following method:

CLASSICAL FOURTH-ORDER RUNGE–KUTTA

$$k_{1n} = hf(x_n, y_n)$$

$$k_{2n} = hf\left(x_n + \frac{h}{2}, y_n + \frac{1}{2}k_{1n}\right)$$

(2.12)

$$k_{3n} = hf\left(x_n + \frac{h}{2}, y_n + \frac{1}{2}k_{2n}\right)$$

$$k_{4n} = hf(x_n + h, y_n + k_{3n})$$

and

$$y_{n+1} = y_n + \frac{1}{6}(k_{1n} + 2k_{2n} + 2k_{3n} + k_{4n}).$$

The method is reasonably easy to program. Since it does not require a great deal of storage and since it gives rather accurate answers when h is only moderately small, it is a popular method for use on small computers.

EXAMPLE 2.3   Use the fourth-order Runge–Kutta method to solve the initial value problem of Example 2.2.
   We have $y' = y^2$, $y(0) = 0.5$, $0 \le x \le 1$. The exact solution is $\varphi(x) = (2 - x)^{-1}$. For $h = 0.2$, we have

$$k_{11} = hy_0^2 = 0.2(0.5)^2 = 0.05$$

$$k_{21} = h(y_0 + \tfrac{1}{2}k_{11})^2 = 0.2[0.5 + 0.5(0.05)]^2 \cong 0.05513$$

$$k_{31} = h(y_0 + \tfrac{1}{2}k_{21})^2 = 0.2[0.5 + 0.5(0.05513)]^2 \cong 0.05566$$

$$k_{41} = h(y_0 + k_{31})^2 = 0.2[0.5 + 0.05566]^2 \cong 0.06175$$

and

$$y_1 = y_0 + \tfrac{1}{6}(k_{11} + 2k_{21} + 2k_{31} + k_{41}) \cong 0.55556.$$

If this computation is carried out using a machine with 10-decimal-place accuracy, it is found that $y_1 = 0.555555245$ and the error $\varphi(0.2) - y_1 \cong 3.11 \times 10^{-7}$. It is interesting to compare this error with the corresponding error 3.10×10^{-4} made in using the second-order Runge–Kutta method. To achieve the same accuracy at $x = 0.2$ using the second-order Runge–Kutta method it would be necessary to use a step size of approximately 0.005. Hence one would need to take about 40 equally spaced steps in going from $x = 0$ to $x = 0.2$. ∎

Programming the fourth-order Runge–Kutta method is a bit more complicated than the programming of the other methods introduced thus far. Programming will be easier if the method is first broken down into a series of simpler steps. We suggest the following steps.

1. Obtain a, b, h, and $y(a)$. Set $n = 0$, $x_n = a$, $y_n = y(a)$.
2. Given x_n, y_n, and h, set $t = x_n$, $z = y_n$, and then evaluate $w = hf(t, z)$.
3. Set $k_{1n} = w$.
4. Set $t = x_n + h/2$, $z = y_n + k_{1n}/2$, and then evaluate $w = hf(t, z)$.
5. Set $k_{2n} = w$.
6. Set $t = x_n + h/2$, $z = y_n + k_{2n}/2$, and then evaluate $w = hf(t, z)$.
7. Set $k_{3n} = w$.
8. Set $t = x_n + h$, $z = y_n + k_{3n}$, and then evaluate $w = hf(t, z)$.
9. Set $k_{4n} = w$.
10. Set $y_{n+1} = y_n + (k_{1n} + 2k_{2n} + 2k_{3n} + k_{4n})/6$ and set $x_{n+1} = x_n + h$. Read out or otherwise save x_{n+1} and y_{n+1}.
11. If $x_{n+1} \geq b$, then stop. Otherwise, replace n by $n + 1$ and go to step 2.

The procedure requires a subroutine that will evalute $w = hf(t, z)$ given h, t, and z.

PROBLEMS

1. Solve each problem using the Taylor series method (2.3). Use $h = 0.1$ and then $h = 0.05$.

   (a) $y' = -2y$, $y(0) = 1$. Compute $y(1)$.

   (b) $y' = 1 + y^2$, $y(0) = 0$. Compute $y(1)$.

   (c) $y' = -y + 2 \cos x$, $y(0) = 1$. Compute $y(3)$.

   The true solutions of these problems are $\varphi(x) = e^{-2x}$, $\varphi(x) = \tan x$, and $\varphi(x) = \sin x + \cos x$. Using these solutions, compute the errors in your approximations.

2. Repeat Problem 1 for the standard second-order Runge–Kutta method given by (2.11).

3. Repeat Problem 1 for the classical fourth-order Runge–Kutta method. Compare your results with those obtained in Problem 1.

4. (a) The problem $y' = 1 + y^2$, $y(0) = 0$ has solution $\varphi(x) = \tan x$. Graph this solution over $0 \leq x < \pi/2$.

   (b) Use the second-order Runge–Kutta method (2.11) to solve this initial value problem over $0 \leq x \leq \pi/2$. Use $h = \pi/N$, $N = 20, 40, 80$, and 160. Does the method give an answer at $x = \pi/2$?

   (c) Graph the results obtained for $h = \pi/20$ and for $\pi/40$. Do your numerical results give any indication of a problem at $x = \pi/2$?

5. (a) Use the classical fourth-order Runge–Kutta method to solve the initial value problem $y' = -2y + 3$, $y(0) = 2$ for $y(1)$ and $y(2)$. Use $h = 0.2, 0.1, 0.05$, and 0.025.

   (b) Find the true solution of this problem. Then compute the errors in your approximations.

   (c) Calculate the ratio by which the errors decrease when h is halved.

6. Given that $y' = (\sin y)y + 1$, $y(0) = 0$, use the method given by (2.10) to compute $y(-1)$. Use $h = 0.1$ (see Problem 1 of Section 8.1).

7. Show that the Runge–Kutta scheme

$$k_{j+1, n} = hf\left(x_n + \frac{j}{3}h, y_n + \frac{j}{3}k_{jn}\right), \qquad j = 0, 1, 2$$

$$y_{n+1} = y_n + \frac{k_{1n} + 3k_{3n}}{4}$$

matches the Taylor series approximation for $\varphi(x_n + h)$ up through terms of order h^4.

8. Use a Runge–Kutta method to solve the epidemic model

$$\frac{dI}{dt} = kI(1 - I), \qquad I(0) = I_0$$

discussed in Section 2.2. Use several successively smaller values of h so that you are convinced that the results are accurate to two significant figures.
   Solve over $0 \le t \le 3$ for $k = 1$ and for $I_0 = \frac{1}{4}, \frac{1}{2}, 1$, and 2. Repeat these runs with $k = 2$. Do solutions seem to have the shapes indicated by Figure 2.6?

9. Use a Runge–Kutta method to solve the Michaelis–Menton problem

$$\frac{dp}{dt} = \frac{V(s_0 - p)}{s_0 - p + K_m}, \qquad p(0) = 0$$

accurately enough to graph the solutions. Try several different positive values of the constants V, s_0, and K_m and see what the solutions look like. Have fun!

10. Find the true solution of $y' = (x + y)^{-1}$, $y(0) = 1$. Can this solution be easily used to compute $y(2)$? Use a Runge–Kutta method to approximate $y(x)$ over $0 \le x \le 2$.

8.3   MULTISTEP METHODS

Given the initial value problem

(3.1) $y' = f(x, y), \qquad y(a) = y_0, \qquad a \le x \le b,$

let $\varphi(x)$ be the true solution, let $h = (b - a)/N$, and let $x_n = a + nh$ as before. Integration of $\varphi'(x) = f(x, \varphi(x))$ from x_n to x_{n+1} gives

(3.2) $\varphi(x_{n+1}) = \varphi(x_n) + \int_{x_n}^{x_{n+1}} f(s, \varphi(s))\, ds.$

If h is small, the integral can be approximated by replacing $f(s, \varphi(s))$ with $f(x_n, \varphi(x_n))$. The area under the curve $z = f(x, \varphi(x))$ in Figure 8.2 is replaced

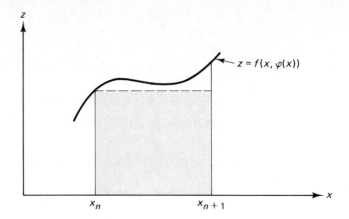

Figure 8.2. Rectangular approximation.

by the shaded area. In this case (3.2) is replaced by

$$\varphi(x_{n+1}) \cong \varphi(x_n) + \int_{x_n}^{x_{n+1}} f(x_n, \varphi(x_n))\, ds$$

$$\cong \varphi(x_n) + hf(x_n, \varphi(x_n)).$$

This approximation leads to the Euler method.

A more accurate approximation would be to replace $f(s, \varphi(s))$ by its average value at the two end points. This means that we are replacing the area under the curve $z = f(x, \varphi(x))$ in Figure 8.3 by the shaded trapezoidal area. This approximation in (3.2) gives

$$\varphi(x_{n+1}) \cong \varphi(x_n) + \frac{h}{2} \left[f(x_n, \varphi(x_n)) + f(x_{n+1}, \varphi(x_{n+1})) \right].$$

The corresponding numerical approximation is

(3.3) $$y_{n+1} = y_n + \frac{h}{2} \left[f(x_n, y_n) + f(x_{n+1}, y_{n+1}) \right].$$

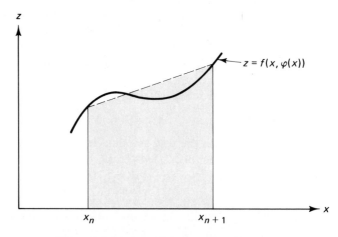

Figure 8.3. Trapezoidal approximation.

The difficulty in (3.3) is that the unknown value y_{n+1} appears on the right-hand side. This difficulty can be avoided by using the Euler method to predict a preliminary value y_{n+1}^*. This value is used on the right in (3.3) to obtain a corrected or final value of y_{n+1}. The method is as follows.

IMPROVED EULER METHOD

Given x_n, y_n and h,

$$y_{n+1}^* = y_n + hf(x_n, y_n),$$

$$y_{n+1} = y_n + \frac{h}{2}[f(x_n, y_n) + f(x_{n+1}, y_{n+1}^*)].$$

This predictor–corrector method is called the **improved Euler method** or **Heun method**.

EXAMPLE 3.1   Consider the problem $y' = 2y$, $y(0) = 3$, $0 \le x \le 1$.

This problem was solved by the Euler method in Example 1.1. The true solution is $\varphi(x) = 3e^{2x}$. For $N = 2$ we have $h = 0.5$. Since $y_0 = 3$, then

$$y_1^* = 3 + 0.5(2 \cdot 3) = 6,$$

$$y_1 = 3 + \frac{0.5}{2}[2 \cdot 3 + 2 \cdot 6] = 7.5$$

and

$$y_2^* = 7.5 + 0.5[2 \cdot (7.5)] = 15,$$

$$y_2 = 7.5 + \frac{0.5}{2}[2 \cdot (7.5) + 2(15)] = 18.75.$$

The errors in these two approximations are

$$e_1 = \varphi(0.5) - y_1 = 3e - 7.5 \cong 0.65485$$

$$e_2 = \varphi(1) - y_2 = 3e^2 - 18.75 \cong 3.41717.$$

The step size $h = \frac{1}{2}$ is too large to achieve much accuracy. Let us repeat the calculations with $h = \frac{1}{4}$:

$$y_1^* = 3 + \tfrac{1}{4}[2 \cdot 3] = 4.5,$$

$$y_1 = 3 + \tfrac{1}{8}[2 \cdot 3 + 2(4.5)] = 4.875,$$

$$y_2^* = 4.875 + \tfrac{1}{4}[2(4.875)] = 7.3125,$$

$$y_2 = 4.875 + \tfrac{1}{8}[2(4.875) + 2(7.3125)] = 7.921875,$$

$$y_3^* = 7.921875 + \tfrac{1}{4}[2(7.921875)] = 11.8828125,$$

$$y_3 = 7.921875 + \tfrac{1}{8}[2(7.921875) + 2(11.882125)] \cong 12.87304,$$

$$y_4^* = 12.87304 + \tfrac{1}{4}[2(12.87304)] \cong 19.30957,$$

and

$$y_4 = 12.87304 + \tfrac{1}{8}[2(12.87304) + 2(19.30957)] \cong 20.91870.$$

The error at $x_4 = 1$ is

$$e_4 = \varphi(1) - y_4 = 3e^2 - 20.91870 \cong 1.24847.$$

As expected, the step size $h = \tfrac{1}{4}$ gives a more accurate approximation than $h = \tfrac{1}{2}$. We also see that the improved Euler method is more accurate than the Euler method used in Example 1.1.

Table 8.4 gives results for still smaller values of h. As h grows smaller, the errors in the approximation decrease. Moreover, when h is halved, the error goes down approximately by a factor of 4. ■

TABLE 8.4   *Improved Euler's Method*

h	x_n			Error e_n
0.1	0.5	8.10812	8.15485	0.04672
	1.0	21.91389	22.16717	0.25327
0.05	0.5	8.14224	8.15485	0.01260
	1.0	22.09870	22.16717	0.06846
0.025	0.5	8.15157	8.15485	0.00327
	1.0	22.14938	22.16717	0.01779

More general methods based on approximation of an integral are available. One such method is the fourth-order **Adams–Bashforth** method,

$$(3.4) \qquad y_{n+1} = y_n + \frac{h}{24}[55f(x_n, y_n) - 59f(x_{n-1}, y_{n-1})$$

$$+ 37f(x_{n-2}, y_{n-2}) - 9f(x_{n-3}, y_{n-3})].$$

This method is a **multistep method**; that is, the values y_{n-j} are needed for $j = 0, 1, 2, 3$, in order to compute y_{n+1}. Hence starting values y_0, y_1, y_2, and y_3 are needed. Then (3.4) can be used to successively compute y_4, y_5, etc. Since problem (3.1) only provides y_0, some other method, such as the fourth-order Runge–Kutta, is needed to compute the remaining starting values y_1, y_2, and y_3.

The fourth-order **Adams–Moulton** method is

$$(3.5) \qquad y_{n+1} = y_n + \frac{h}{24}[9f(x_{n+1}, y_{n+1}) + 19f(x_n, y_n)$$

$$- 5f(x_{n-1}, y_{n-1}) + f(x_{n-2}, y_{n-2})].$$

This method, like (3.3), suffers the difficulty that y_{n+1} occurs on the right-hand side of (3.5). This difficulty is avoided by using the Adams–Bashforth formula (3.4) to predict a preliminary value y_{n+1}^*. This value is used in (3.5) to obtain a corrected or final value y_{n+1}. The computation goes as follows. Given x_n, h, y_n, y_{n-1}, y_{n-2}, and y_{n-3},

$$y^*_{n+1} = y_n + \frac{h}{24}\left[55f(x_n, y_n) - 59f(x_{n-1}, y_{n-1})\right.$$

$$\left. + 37f(x_{n-2}, y_{n-2}) - 9f(x_{n-3}, y_{n-3})\right],$$

$$y_{n+1} = y_n + \frac{h}{24}\left[9f(x_{n+1}, y^*_{n+1}) + 19f(x_n, y_n)\right.$$

$$\left. - 5f(x_{n-1}, y_{n-1}) + f(x_{n-2}, y_{n-2})\right].$$

This is the very popular and accurate **Adams predictor–corrector** method. This method is the basis for much of the work currently done on numerical solution of differential equations. Large computers, such as the one shown in Photo 19, come with software for solving systems of differential equations. This software normally uses Adams methods to approximate the desired solutions.

Photo 19. Cray Y–MP8 supercomputer. (Courtesy of Cray Research, Inc. and photographer Paul Shambroom.)

PROBLEMS

1. Solve each problem using the improved Euler method. Use $h = 0.1$ and then $h = 0.05$.

   (a) $y' = -2y$, $y(0) = 1$. Compute $y(1)$.

   (b) $y' = 1 + y^2$, $y(0) = 0$. Compute $y(1)$.

   (c) $y' = -y + 2\cos x$, $y(0) = 1$. Compute $y(3)$.

   The true solutions are $\varphi(x) = e^{-2x}$, $\varphi(x) = \tan x$, and $\varphi(x) = \sin x + \cos x$. Using these solutions, compute the errors in your approximations.

2. Solve Problem 1 using the following third-order Adams predictor–corrector scheme:

$$y_{n+1}^* = y_n + \frac{h}{12}[23f(x_n, y_n) - 16f(x_{n-1}, y_{n-1}) + 5f(x_{n-2}, y_{n-2})]$$

$$y_{n+1} = y_n + \frac{h}{12}[5f(x_{n+1}, y_{n+1}^*) + 8f(x_n, y_n) - f(x_{n-1}, y_{n-1})].$$

Use the known exact solutions to obtain the necessary starting values.

3. (a) Show that if the improved Euler method is applied to $y' = ky$, $y(0) = y_0$, then

$$y_{n+1} = \left[1 + hk + \frac{(hk)^2}{2}\right]y_n.$$

(b) Show that the true solution $\varphi(x)$ satisfies

$$\varphi(x_{n+1}) = \left[1 + hk + \frac{(hk)^2}{2} + \mathcal{O}(h)^3\right]\varphi(x_n).$$

4. (a) Show that the Adams–Bashforth method (3.4) will integrate the problem $y' = x^k$, $y(0) = 0$ exactly when $k = 0, 1, 2$.

(b) For what values of k will the Adams–Moulton method (3.5) integrate $y' = x^k$, $y(0) = 0$ exactly?

5. When using (3.3) one can correct more than once. If Euler's method is used as a predictor and (3.3) is corrected twice, the resulting method is

$$y_{n+1}^* = y_n + hf(x_n, y_n)$$

$$y_{n+1}^{**} = y_n + \frac{h}{2}[f(x_{n+1}, y_{n+1}^*) + f(x_n, y_n)]$$

$$y_{n+1} = y_n + \frac{h}{2}[f(x_{n+1}, y_{n+1}^{**}) + f(x_n, y_n)].$$

Use this method with $h = 0.1$ to solve

$$y' = 1 + y^2, \qquad y(0) = 0, \qquad 0 \le x \le 1.$$

Compare the results of this computation with the results obtained in Problem 1, part (b). Does the extra correction make a noticeable difference? Repeat for $y' = -2y$, $y(0) = 1$, $0 \le x \le 1$.

6. The problem $y' = -1000(y - \pi \cos x) - \pi \sin x$, $y(0) = \pi$ has true solution $\varphi(x) = \pi \cos x$. Use the predictor–corrector scheme in Problem 1 to solve $0 \le x \le 3$ when $h = 0.1$. Is your solution accurate? Repeat with $h = 0.05$ and $h = 0.01$. The general solution of this equation is

$$y = ce^{-1000x} + \pi \cos x.$$

The part of the solution e^{-1000x} changes much more rapidly than the part $\pi \cos x$. Equations that exhibit two or more radically different time behaviors are called **stiff**. Special numerical methods are usually needed for the solution of stiff problems.

7. Find the true solution of $y' = (1 + y^2)^{-1}$, $y(0) = 1$. Is it easy to use this solution to compute $y(2)$? Use the improved Euler method to solve for $y(x)$ over $0 \le x \le 2$. Use $h = 0.1$ and then $h = 0.05$.

8. Repeat Problem 7 for $y' = (x + y)^{-1}$, $y(0) = 1$.

8.4   SYSTEMS OF DIFFERENTIAL EQUATIONS

Systems of differential equations occur often in applications. Examples of systems and the initial value problem for systems were discussed in detail in Section 7.1. We study the system of m first-order differential equations

$$
\begin{aligned}
y_1' &= f_1(x, y_1, y_2, \ldots, y_m) \\
y_2' &= f_2(x, y_1, y_2, \ldots, y_m) \\
&\vdots \\
y_m' &= f_m(x, y_1, y_2, \ldots, y_m),
\end{aligned}
$$

(E)

on an interval $a \le x \le b$. Initial values for this system take the form

(I) $y_1(a) = A_1$, $y_2(a) = A_2$, $\ldots$, $y_m(a) = A_m$.

This general form is very clumsy and time consuming to write. To simplify the presentation we shall express this initial value problem in *vector notation*. Define

$$
\mathbf{y} = \begin{pmatrix} y_1 \\ y_2 \\ \vdots \\ y_m \end{pmatrix}, \qquad
\mathbf{f}(x, \mathbf{y}) = \begin{pmatrix} f_1(x, y_1, y_2, \ldots, y_m) \\ \vdots \\ f_m(x, y_1, y_2, \ldots, y_m) \end{pmatrix}
$$

$$
\mathbf{y}' = \begin{pmatrix} y_1' \\ y_2' \\ \vdots \\ y_m' \end{pmatrix}, \qquad
\mathbf{A} = \begin{pmatrix} A_1 \\ A_2 \\ \vdots \\ A_m \end{pmatrix}.
$$

Then (E) and (I) can be written as

(4.1) $\mathbf{y}' = \mathbf{f}(x, \mathbf{y})$, $\mathbf{y}(a) = \mathbf{A}$, $a \le x \le b$.

This looks like a single first-order equation but is really a compact notation for several equations.

EXAMPLE 4.1   The Volterra–Lotka predator–prey model (discussed in Section 2.7) has the form

(4.2) $\dfrac{dy_1}{dx} = y_1(a - by_2)$, $\dfrac{dy_2}{dx} = y_2(-c + fy_1)$,

where a, b, c, and f are fixed positive constants. Initial values take the form

$$
y_1(a) = A_1 > 0, \qquad y_2(a) = A_2 > 0.
$$

This problem has the form of (E) and (I) with $m = 2$, $f_1(x, y_1, y_2) = y_1(a - by_2)$, and $f_2(x, y_1, y_2) = y_2(-c + fy_1)$. Hence we take

$$\mathbf{y} = \begin{pmatrix} y_1 \\ y_2 \end{pmatrix}, \qquad \mathbf{A} = \begin{pmatrix} A_1 \\ A_2 \end{pmatrix}, \qquad \mathbf{f}(x, \mathbf{y}) = \begin{pmatrix} f_1(x, y_1, y_2) \\ f_2(x, y_1, y_2) \end{pmatrix}. \quad \blacksquare$$

Higher-order equations can also be reduced to systems.

EXAMPLE 4.2   Consider the pendulum problem (see Section 3.14)

(4.3) $$\frac{d^2\theta}{dx^2} + \frac{g}{l}\sin\theta = 0, \qquad \theta(0) = A_1, \qquad \theta'(0) = A_2,$$

where $\theta(x)$ is the unknown pendulum angle, g is the gravitation constant (in correct units), and l is the length of the pendulum rod.

We set $y_1 = \theta$ and $y_2 = \theta'$. Then $y_1' = \theta' = y_2$ and $y_2' = \theta'' = -(g/l)\sin\theta = -(g/l)\sin y_1$. Hence

$$y_1' = f_1(x, y_1, y_2) = y_2, \qquad\qquad y_1(a) = A_1$$

$$y_2' = f_2(x, y_1, y_2) = -\frac{g}{l}\sin y_1, \qquad y_2(a) = A_2. \quad \blacksquare$$

REDUCTION OF *m*th-ORDER EQUATIONS TO SYSTEMS

The general mth-order differential equation

$$y^{(m)} = f(x, y, y', y'', \dots, y^{(m-1)})$$

with initial conditions

$$y(a) = A_1, \quad y'(a) = A_2, \quad \dots, \quad y^{(m-1)}(a) = A_m$$

can be written as a system as follows. Define

$$y_1 = y, \quad y_2 = y', \quad y_3 = y'', \quad \dots, \quad y_m = y^{(m-1)}.$$

Then the equivalent first-order system problem is

$$y_1' = y_2, \qquad\qquad\qquad y_1(a) = A_1$$
$$y_2' = y_3, \qquad\qquad\qquad y_2(a) = A_2$$
$$\vdots \qquad\qquad\qquad\qquad\qquad \vdots$$
$$y_{m-1}' = y_m, \qquad\qquad\qquad y_{m-1}(a) = A_{m-1}$$
$$y_m' = f(x, y_1, y_2, \dots, y_m), \qquad y_m(a) = A_m.$$

If the initial value problem (E) for a system of differential equations is written in the vector notation (4.1), then the numerical methods discussed earlier in this chapter can be applied without any change. For example, Euler's method for (4.1) has the following form.

EULER'S METHOD FOR SYSTEMS

Given x_n, h and the vector $\mathbf{y}_n$, then

$$\mathbf{y}_{n+1} = \mathbf{y}_n + h\mathbf{f}(x_n, \mathbf{y}_n).$$

Here $\mathbf{y}_n$ is a vector approximation to the true solution $\boldsymbol{\varphi}(x_n)$. During computation this approximate solution $\mathbf{y}_n$ will normally be stored in a computer as an m-dimensional array, that is, $\mathbf{y}_n = (y_n(1), y_n(2), \ldots, y_n(m))^T$. Hence we define $y_n(k)$ to be the approximate value of the kth component $\varphi_k(x_n)$ of the true solution, that is,

$$\mathbf{y}_n = \begin{pmatrix} y_n(1) \\ y_n(2) \\ \vdots \\ y_n(m) \end{pmatrix} \cong \begin{pmatrix} \varphi_1(x_n) \\ \varphi_2(x_n) \\ \vdots \\ \varphi_m(x_n) \end{pmatrix} = \boldsymbol{\varphi}(x_n).$$

EXAMPLE 4.3   Apply Euler's method to the Volterra–Lotka predator–prey problem

(4.4) $$y_1' = y_1(3 - y_2), \qquad y_2' = y_2(-2 + y_1)$$

when $y_1(0) = 1$, $y_2(0) = 2$.

We shall approximate the solution at $x = 1$ using $h = \frac{1}{4}$. Let $f_1(x, y_1, y_2) = y_1(3 - y_2)$ and $f_2(x, y_1, y_2) = y_2(-2 + y_1)$. Then Euler's method is

$$y_{n+1}(1) = y_n(1) + hf_1(x_n, y_n(1), y_n(2))$$

$$y_{n+1}(2) = y_n(2) + hf_2(x_n, y_n(1), y_n(2)).$$

Since $y_0(1) = 1$ and $y_0(2) = 2$, then

$$\begin{aligned} y_1(1) &= 1 + \tfrac{1}{4}[1(3 - 2)] = 1.25 \\ y_1(2) &= 2 + \tfrac{1}{4}[2(-2 + 1)] = 1.5 \end{aligned} \quad \text{or} \quad \mathbf{y}_1 = \begin{pmatrix} 1.25 \\ 1.5 \end{pmatrix}.$$

Continuing this way gives

$$y_2(1) = 1.25 + \tfrac{1}{4}[1.25(3 - 1.5)] = 1.71875$$

$$y_2(2) = 1.5 + \tfrac{1}{4}[1.5(-2 + 1.25)] = 1.21875$$

and

$$y_3(1) = 1.71875 + \tfrac{1}{4}[1.71875(3 - 1.21875)] \cong 2.48413$$

$$y_3(2) = 1.21875 + \tfrac{1}{4}[1.21875(-2 + 1.71875)] \cong 1.13306$$

and then

$$y_4(1) = 2.48413 + \tfrac{1}{4}[2.48413(3 - 1.13306)] \cong 3.64356$$

$$y_4(2) = 1.13306 + \tfrac{1}{4}[1.13306(-2 + 2.48143)] \cong 1.27019.$$

Our approximation to the solution $\varphi(x)$ at $x = 1$ is

$$\mathbf{y}_4 = \begin{pmatrix} 3.64356 \\ 1.27019 \end{pmatrix} \cong \varphi(x). \quad \blacksquare$$

SECOND-ORDER RUNGE–KUTTA METHOD FOR SYSTEMS

The second-order Runge–Kutta method (2.11), written for the system (4.1), is as follows. Given x_n, h, and $\mathbf{y}_n$,

(4.5)
$$\mathbf{k}_{1n} = h\mathbf{f}(x_n, \mathbf{y}_n)$$
$$\mathbf{k}_{2n} = h\mathbf{f}(x_n + h, \mathbf{y}_n + \mathbf{k}_{1n})$$
$$\mathbf{y}_{n+1} = \mathbf{y}_n + \tfrac{1}{2}(\mathbf{k}_{1n} + \mathbf{k}_{2n}).$$

EXAMPLE 4.4　　Apply the second-order Runge–Kutta method to problem (4.4). Let $h = \tfrac{1}{4}$. Then

$$k_{10}(1) = hf_1(x_0, y_0(1), y_0(2))$$
$$= \tfrac{1}{4}[1(3 - 2)] = 0.25$$

$$k_{10}(2) = hf_2(x_0, y_0(1), y_0(2)) \qquad \text{and} \quad \mathbf{k}_{10} = \begin{pmatrix} 0.25 \\ -0.5 \end{pmatrix}.$$
$$= \tfrac{1}{4}[2(-2 + 1)] = -0.5$$

Next,

$$k_{20}(1) = hf_1(x_0 + h, y_0(1) + k_{10}(1), y_0(2) + k_{10}(2))$$
$$= \tfrac{1}{4}[(1 + 0.25)(3 - [2 - 0.5])] = 0.46875$$

$$k_{20}(2) = hf_2(x_0 + h, y_0(1) + k_{10}(1), y_0(2) + k_{10}(2))$$
$$= \tfrac{1}{4}[(2 - 0.5)(-2 + [1 + 0.25])] = -0.28125,$$

so that

$$\mathbf{k}_{20} = \begin{pmatrix} 0.46875 \\ -0.28125 \end{pmatrix}.$$

Finally,

$$y_1(1) = y_0(1) + \tfrac{1}{2}[k_{10}(1) + k_{20}(1)] = 1 + \tfrac{1}{2}[0.25 + 0.46875] \cong 1.35938$$

$$y_1(2) = y_0(2) + \tfrac{1}{2}[k_{10}(2) + k_{20}(2)] = 2 + \tfrac{1}{2}[-0.5 - 0.28125] \cong 1.60938.$$

Hence our approximate solution is

$$\mathbf{y}_1 = \begin{pmatrix} 1.35938 \\ 1.60938 \end{pmatrix}.$$

The reader should compute $\mathbf{y}_2$ given $\mathbf{y}_1$ above and $h = \frac{1}{4}$. The results should be

$$\mathbf{k}_{11} = \begin{pmatrix} 0.47260 \\ -0.25775 \end{pmatrix}, \qquad \mathbf{k}_{2|1} = \begin{pmatrix} 0.75495 \\ -0.05678 \end{pmatrix}, \qquad \mathbf{y}_2 = \begin{pmatrix} 1.97320 \\ 1.45212 \end{pmatrix}. \quad \blacksquare$$

A good general-purpose and reasonably efficient method for numerical solution of systems of the form (4.1) for use on a small computer is the fourth-order Runge–Kutta method. It is as follows.

FOURTH-ORDER RUNGE–KUTTA METHOD FOR SYSTEMS

Given x_n, h and $\mathbf{y}_n$, compute

$$\mathbf{k}_{1n} = h\mathbf{f}(x_n, \mathbf{y}_n)$$

$$\mathbf{k}_{2n} = h\mathbf{f}\left(x_n + \frac{h}{2}, \mathbf{y}_n + \frac{1}{2}\mathbf{k}_{1n} \right)$$

(4.6)

$$\mathbf{k}_{3n} = h\mathbf{f}\left(x_n + \frac{h}{2}, \mathbf{y}_n + \frac{1}{2}\mathbf{k}_{2n} \right)$$

$$\mathbf{k}_{4n} = h\mathbf{f}(x_n + h, \mathbf{y}_n + \mathbf{k}_{3n})$$

$$\mathbf{y}_{n+1} = \mathbf{y}_n + \tfrac{1}{6}(\mathbf{k}_{1n} + 2\mathbf{k}_{2n} + 2\mathbf{k}_{3n} + \mathbf{k}_{4n}).$$

We suggest that the program be broken down into the following steps.

1. Obtain a, b, h, and the initial conditions $A(i)$ for $i = 1, 2, \ldots, m$. Then set $n = 0$, $x_n = a$, and $y_n(i) = A(i)$ for $i = 1, 2, \ldots, m$.
2. Given x_n, $y_n(i)$ for $i = 1, 2, \ldots, m$ and h, set $t = x_n$, $z(i) = y_n(i)$ for $i = 1, 2, \ldots, m$. Then evaluate $w(i) = hf_i(t, \mathbf{z})$ for $i = 1, 2, \ldots, m$.
3. Set $k_{1n}(i) = w(i)$ for $i = 1, 2, \ldots, m$.
4. Set $t = x_n + h/2$, $z(i) = y_n(i) + k_{1n}(i)/2$ for $i = 1, 2, \ldots, m$. Then evaluate $w(i) = hf_i(t, \mathbf{z})$ for $i = 1, 2, \ldots, m$.
5. Set $k_{2n}(i) = w(i)$ for $i = 1, 2, \ldots, m$.
6. Set $t = x_n + h/2$, $z(i) = y_n(i) + k_{2n}(i)/2$ for $i = 1, 2, \ldots, m$. Then evaluate $w(i) = hf_i(t, \mathbf{z})$ for $i = 1, 2, \ldots, m$.
7. Set $k_{3n}(i) = w(i)$ for $i = 1, 2, \ldots, m$.

8. Set $t = x_n + h$, $z(i) = y_n(i) + k_{3n}(i)$ for $i = 1, 2, \ldots, m$. Then evaluate $w(i) = hf_i(t, \mathbf{z})$ for $i = 1, 2, \ldots, m$.

9. Set $k_{4n}(i) = w(i)$ for $i = 1, 2, \ldots, m$.

10. Set $y_{n+1}(i) = y_n(i) + (k_{1n}(i) + 2k_{2n}(i) + 2k_{3n}(i) + k_{4n}(i))/6$ for $i = 1, 2, \ldots, m$ and set $x_{n+1} = x_n + h$. Then read out or otherwise save x_{n+1} and $y_{n+1}(i)$ for $i = 1, 2, \ldots, m$.

11. If $x_{n+1} \geq b$, then stop. Otherwise, replace n by $n + 1$ and go to step 2.

The procedure requires a subroutine that will evaluate $f_i(t, \mathbf{z})$ given t and the vector $\mathbf{z}$.

PROBLEMS

1. The initial value problem

$$y_1' = y_1 + 2y_2 + 1, \qquad y_1(0) = \tfrac{7}{8}$$

$$y_2' = 3y_1 + 2y_2 + x, \qquad y_2(0) = -\tfrac{19}{16}$$

has true solution $\varphi_1(x) = -x/2 + \tfrac{7}{8}$ and $\varphi_2(x) = x/4 - \tfrac{19}{16}$. Numerically solve this system over $0 \leq x \leq 1$ for $h = 0.1$ and $h = 0.05$. Compute the errors made in your approximate solutions at $x = 1$.

   (a) Use the Euler method.

   (b) Use the second-order Runge–Kutta method (4.5).

2. Repeat Problem 1 for

$$y'' + 4y = 0, \qquad y(0) = 3, \qquad y'(0) = 0.$$

The true solution is $\varphi(x) = 3 \cos 2x$, $\varphi'(x) = -6 \sin 2x$. Use $h = 0.02$ and then $h = 0.01$.

3. Repeat Problem 1 for $y''' + 2y'' - y' - 2y = -x$, $y(0) = 1$, $y'(0) = -2$, $y''(0) = 5$. The true solution is $\varphi(x) = 5e^{-2x}/4 + x/2 - \tfrac{1}{4}$. Use $h = 0.02$ and then $h = 0.01$.

Program the fourth-order Runge–Kutta method and use it to solve Problems 4–7.

4. Solve the pendulum problem

$$\frac{d^2\theta}{dx^2} + \frac{g}{l} \sin \theta = 0$$

when $g = 9.80665$ meters/second^2 and $l = 0.5$ meter. Solve accurately enough to graph $\theta(x)$ and $\theta'(x)$ over $0 \leq x \leq 3$ for the following initial conditions:

   (a) $\theta(0) = \theta'(0) = 0.1$. (What is happening physically?)

   (b) $\theta(0) = 0.1 + 2\pi$, $\theta'(0) = 0.1$. [Compare with part (a)!]

   (c) $\theta(0) = 0$, $\theta'(0) = 25$. (What is happening physically?)

5. Solve the swing equation problem

$$M_1 y_1'' + D_1 y_1' = P_1 + c_{11} \sin (y_1 - y_2) - c_{12} \cos (y_1 - y_2)$$

$$M_2 y_2'' + D_2 y_2' = P_2 + c_{21} \sin (y_2 - y_1) - c_{22} \cos (y_2 - y_1)$$

when $M_1 = 1.2$, $M_2 = 1.4$, $D_1 = D_2 = 0.1$, $c_{11} = c_{12} = 3.3$, $c_{21} = c_{22} = 5.8$, $P_1 = 1.7$, and $P_2 = 0.5$. The initial conditions are $y_1(0) = y_1'(0) = y_2(0) = y_2'(0) = 0$. Graph $y_1(t)$ and $y_2(t)$ over $0 \le t \le 2$. Pick h small enough so that you can graph accurately.

6. For the Volterra–Lotka model

$$\frac{dy_1}{dx} = y_1(1 - y_2), \qquad \frac{dy_2}{dx} = y_2(-1 + y_1)$$

verify that solutions have the form shown in Figure 2.8 by solving the equation for several representative initial conditions. Graph your results in (y_1, y_2) space. Do solutions seem to be periodic? Is the period always the same? Have fun!

8.5 ERRORS AND ESTIMATES

For the initial value problem (1.1) the Euler method (1.4) can be written in the form

(5.1) $$y_{n+1} = y_n + h\Phi(x_n, y_n),$$

where $\Phi(x, y) = f(x, y)$. From (1.2) we see that the true solution $\varphi(x)$ satisfies the equation

(5.2) $$\varphi(x_{n+1}) = \varphi(x_n) + h\Phi(x_n, \varphi(x_n)) + E(x_n, h)h^2,$$

where

$$E(x, h) = \tfrac{1}{2}\varphi''(x + \bar{h}).$$

Moreover, $E(x, h)$ is continuous and bounded on $a \le x \le b, 0 < h \le 1$ since by (1.2) we have

$$E(x, h) = \frac{1}{h^2}\left[\varphi(x + h) - \varphi(x) - hf(x, \varphi(x))\right].$$

The term $E(x, h)h^2$ in (5.2) is called the **local truncation error** for the Euler method. The Euler method is called a **first-order** method because of the form of the truncation error.

The second-order Runge–Kutta method (2.5) can be written in the form (5.1), where $\Phi(x, y)$ is given in (2.5). The parameters α_1, α_2, β, and γ were chosen in such a way that the true solution $\varphi(x)$ satisfies

(5.3) $$\varphi(x_{n+1}) = \varphi(x_n) + h\Phi(x_n, \varphi(x_n)) + E(x_n, h)h^{p+1}.$$

Here $p = 2$ and $E(x, h)$ is a very complicated but also continuous and bounded function of x and h. The fourth-order Runge–Kutta method can also be written in the form (5.1). Moreover, (5.3) is true with $p = 4$.

For any numerical method of the form (5.1) such that (5.3) is true for some positive integer p and some continuous and bounded function $E(x, h)$, the term $E(x, h)h^{p+1}$ is called the **local truncation error**. The integer p is the **order** of the method. When h is small we see that the error is small at each step when using (5.1). These small errors may possibly accumulate as we go from step to step. However, this accumulated error cannot get too large. Indeed, the following result is true.

THEOREM 5.1: CONVERGENCE

Suppose that f, $\partial f/\partial y$, and φ satisfy the assumptions listed under (1.1). Suppose that there is a constant $L > 0$ such that

$$|\Phi(x, y_1) - \Phi(x, y_2)| \le L|y_1 - y_2|$$

for $a \le x \le b$, $A \le y_1, y_2 \le B$. Suppose that (5.3) is true for some positive integer p and some continuous function $E(x, h)$ with $|E(x, h)| \le E_0$ on $a \le x \le b$, $0 < h \le 1$. Let $y(x_n, h)$ be the approximate solution obtained by using (5.1) for some $h \in (0, 1)$. Then the maximum error in this approximation satisfies the estimate

$$(5.4) \qquad \max_{a \le x_n \le b} |\varphi(x_n) - y(x_n, h)| \le \frac{e^{L(b-a)} - 1}{L} E_0 h^p.$$

The estimate (5.4) shows that $y(x, h)$ becomes a better and better approximation to the solution $\varphi(x)$ as h gets smaller and smaller. It also shows that methods become more accurate when p is larger.

To prove the theorem, we let $e_n = \varphi(x_n) - y(x_n, h)$ be the error at x_n. Subtracting (5.1) from (5.3) gives

$$(5.5) \qquad e_{n+1} = e_n + h[\Phi(x_n, \varphi(x_n)) - \Phi(x_n, y(x_n, h))] + E(x_n, h)h^{p+1}.$$

Thus

$$|e_{n+1}| \le |e_n| + hL|\varphi(x_n) - y(x_n, h)| + |E(x_n, h)|h^{p+1}$$
$$\le |e_n| + hL|e_n| + E_0 h^{p+1}.$$

Since $|e_0| = 0$, then for $n = 0, 1, 2, \ldots$

$$(5.6) \qquad |e_{n+1}| \le (1 + hL)|e_n| + E_0 h^{p+1}.$$

From (5.6) we see that

$$|e_1| \le E_0 h^{p+1}$$
$$|e_2| \le (1 + hL)|e_1| + E_0 h^{p+1}$$
$$\le [(1 + hL) + 1]E_0 h^{p+1}$$
$$|e_3| \le (1 + hL)[(1 + hL) + 1]E_0 h^{p+1} + E_0 h^{p+1}$$
$$\le [1 + (1 + hL) + (1 + hL)^2]E_0 h^{p+1}$$

and in general

(5.7) $|e_n| \leq [1 + (1 + hL) + (1 + hL)^2 + \ldots + (1 + hL)^{n-1}]E_0 h^{p+1}.$

Any geometric series satisfies $1 + r + r^2 + \ldots + r^{n-1} = (1 - r^n)/(1 - r)$. We use this result in (5.7) with $r = 1 + hL$ to see that

$$|e_n| \leq \frac{1 - (1 + hL)^n}{1 - (1 + hL)} E_0 h^{p+1} = \frac{(1 + hL)^n - 1}{L} E_0 h^p.$$

Since $1 + hL \leq e^{hL}$, then $(1 + hL)^n \leq e^{nhL}$. Hence

$$|e_n| \leq \frac{e^{(nh)L} - 1}{L} E_0 h^p \leq \frac{e^{(b-a)L} - 1}{L} E_0 h^p,$$

since $nh \leq b - a$. This proves the theorem.

The conclusion of Theorem 5.1 can be stated in terms of order notation. In this notation $\mathcal{O}(h^p)$ means a term whose absolute value is at most a fixed constant K times h^p when $-1 \leq h \leq 1$. For example, $-3h^3 = \mathcal{O}(h^3)$ since $|-3h^3| \leq 3h^3$. Similarly, $-2h^2 + h = \mathcal{O}(h)$ since $|-2h^2 + h| \leq h(2 + |h|) \leq 3h$ when $-1 \leq h \leq 1$. In this order notation we see from Theorem 5.1 that $e_n = \mathcal{O}(h^p)$.

Theorem 5.1 is called a *convergence theorem*. It can be extended to systems of differential equations. Convergence theorems for multistep methods are more complicated and harder to prove. Note that (5.4) only gives an *upper bound* for the error. In most problems the actual errors are much smaller than (5.4) would indicate. Good estimates of the actual error can be obtained using **asymptotic error analysis.** This is done by first expanding the local truncation error. For example, consider the Euler method. When $f(x, y)$ has continuous second partial derivatives, then the true solution of (1.1) has Taylor series expansion

$$\varphi(x + h) = \varphi(x) + h\varphi'(x) + \frac{h^2}{2}\varphi''(x) + \frac{h^3}{6}\varphi'''(x + \bar{h})$$

$$= \varphi(x) + hf(x, \varphi(x)) + h^2\left[\frac{\varphi''(x)}{2} + \frac{h}{6}\varphi'''(x + \bar{h})\right]$$

This means that

$$E(x, h) = \frac{\varphi''(x)}{2} + \frac{h}{6}\varphi'''(x + \bar{h}) = E_1(x) + E_2(x, h)h.$$

Similarly, the local truncation error for a Runge–Kutta method can be written in the form

$$h^{p+1}E(x, h) = h^{p+1}[E_1(x) + E_2(x, h)h],$$

where $E_1(x)$ is a continuous function and $E_2(x, h)$ is a continuous and bounded function. Whenever this is true, (5.5) can be written in the form

$$e_{n+1} = e_n + h[\Phi_y(x_n, \varphi(x_n))e_n + \mathcal{O}(e_n^2)] + h^{p+1}[E_1(x_n) + hE_2(x_n, h)].$$

Define $\bar{e}_n = e_n/h^p$. Theorem 5.1 implies that $|e_n| = \mathcal{O}(h^p)$. Thus

(5.8) $$\bar{e}_{n+1} = \bar{e}_n + h[\Phi_y(x_n, \varphi(x_n))\bar{e}_n + E_1(x_n)] + \mathcal{O}(h^2).$$

Since (5.8) looks like the Euler method applied to

(5.9) $$z' = \Phi_y(x, \varphi(x))z + E_1(x), \qquad z(a) = 0,$$

then a proof similar to that of Theorem 5.1 will show that

$$\frac{e_n}{h^p} - z(x_n) = \bar{e}_n - z(x_n) = \mathcal{O}(h).$$

Thus the error e_n made in the approximation (5.3) satisfies

(5.10) $$e_n = z(x_n)h^p + \mathcal{O}(h^{p+1}),$$

where $z(x)$ is the solution of (5.9). This formula is called the **asymptotic error estimate.**

EXAMPLE 5.2   Consider the problem $y' = 3y + 6$, $y(0) = 0$, $0 \leq x \leq 0.5$. If Euler's method is used, then $f(x, y) = \Phi(x, y) = 3y + 6$. Thus $L = 3$ will do. The true solution is $\varphi(x) = 2e^{3x} - 2$. Hence $\varphi'(x) = 6e^{3x}$ and $\varphi''(x) = 18e^{3x}$. From (5.2) we see that

$$E(x, h) = \tfrac{1}{2}\varphi''(x + \bar{h}) = 9e^{3(x+\bar{h})}.$$

Thus

$$|E(x, h)| \leq 9e^{3(0.5)} = 9e^{1.5} = E_0.$$

Hence the error estimate (5.4) becomes

$$\max_{0 \leq x_n \leq 0.5} |\varphi(x_n) - y(x_n, h)| \leq \frac{e^{3(0.5-0)} - 1}{3} 9e^{1.5}h$$

$$\leq (e^{1.5} - 1)3e^{1.5}h \cong 46.81154h.$$

This formula overestimates the actual errors.

As pointed out above, $E_1(x) = \varphi''(x)/2$ for Euler's method. Hence $E_1(x) = 9e^{3x}$ in the present case. Since $\Phi_y(x, y) = 3$, then (5.9) is

$$z' = 3z + 9e^{3x}, \qquad z(0) = 0.$$

The solution of this problem is $z(x) = 9xe^{3x}$. Hence the asymptotic estimate of the error is

$$\varphi(x_n) - y(x_n, h) \cong 9x_n e^{3x_n}h.$$

For small values of h this is a much more accurate error estimate. ∎

For the Euler method $p = 1$. Thus (5.10) reduces to $\varphi(x_n) - y(x_n, h) = z(x_n)h + \mathcal{O}(h^2)$. When h is small the term $z(x_n)h$ contains most of the error. If we halve the step size, then

$$\varphi(x_n) - y\left(x_n, \frac{h}{2}\right) = z(x_n)\frac{h}{2} + \text{(very small)}.$$

Hence the error will be reduced by approximately $\frac{1}{2}$. This behavior was pointed out in Section 8.1. Similarly, for the second-order Runge–Kutta methods

$$\varphi(x_n) - y(x_n, h) = z(x_n)h^2 + \text{(very small)}$$

and

$$\varphi(x_n) - y\left(x_n, \frac{h}{2}\right) = z(x_n)\frac{h^2}{4} + \text{(very small)}.$$

Hence halving the step size h reduces the error by approximately a factor of $\frac{1}{4}$. Such behavior was observed in Section 8.2.

Round-off is also a source of errors. Since computing equipment represents numbers by a finite number of digits, it is not possible to represent most numbers exactly in the machine. This finite precision also means that addition, multiplication, and so on, are not done precisely in the machine. Errors caused by this finite precision are called *round-off errors*. In the method (5.1) suppose that at step n there is a round-off error r_n. The value actually computed by (5.1) will be a rounded approximation $\tilde{y}_n$. These values $\tilde{y}_n$ will satisfy the equation

(5.11) $\tilde{y}_{n+1} = \tilde{y}_n + h\Phi(x_n, \tilde{y}_n) + r_n.$

When the h is taken small enough, the local truncation errors may become smaller than the round-off errors r_n. At that point, taking a smaller h will not increase accuracy. Indeed, since a small h means more steps, it may decrease accuracy by allowing round-off errors to accumulate as the machine steps along. Many people, to their sorrow, have verified this prediction with their computations. The exact point h at which round-off errors can become a problem varies with the differential equation, the numerical method used, and the construction of the computer. Experience is needed in order to know where to stop. Be warned that round-off can be a problem and proceed with care!

PROBLEMS

If Problems 1–4 were solved using Euler's method, find the maximum possible error as predicted by Theorem 5.1. Find the asymptotic error $z(x_n)h$. Solve the problem using Euler's method and compare these predictions with the actual errors.

1. $y' = 2y - x$, $y(0) = 1$, $0 \le x \le 1$, $h = 0.05$.

2. $y' = 2y - x$, $y(0) = 1$, $0 \le x \le 1$, $h = 0.0125$.

3. $y' = -2y + x$, $y(0) = 1$, $0 \le x \le 1$, $h = 0.05$.

4. $y' = -4y + \sin x$, $y(0) = -\frac{1}{17}$, $0 \le x \le 1$, $h = 0.05$.

5. Write a program using Euler's method to solve

$$y' = 10^4(\sqrt{10} - \sqrt{9.9999})y, \quad y(0) = 1, \qquad 0 \le x \le 3.$$

Find the true solution of this problem. Compute the errors made at $x = 1$, $x = 2$, and $x = 3$ when you use $h = 0.05, 0.025, 0.0125$, etc. Repeat with the fourth-order Runge–Kutta method. Is there a point on your machine where decreasing h increases the error?

6. Show that

$$\left| e - \left(1 + \frac{1}{N} \right)^N \right| \le \frac{2.3354}{N}.$$

Hint: Apply Euler's method to $y' = y$, $y(0) = 1$, $0 \le x \le 1$.

7. Extend (5.4) to the case where y_0 is approximately $\varphi(a)$ but is not equal to $\varphi(a)$. Prove that

$$\max_{a \le x_n \le b} |\varphi(x_n) - w_n| \le |\varphi(a) - w_0| e^{L(b-a)} + \frac{e^{(b-a)} - 1}{L} \left(E_0 h^p + k_0 h^p + \frac{r_0}{h} \right).$$

8. Show that if w_n satisfies

$$w_{n+1} = w_n + h\Phi(x_n, w_n) + k_n h^{p+1} + r_n$$

with $|k_n| \le k_0$ and $|r_n| \le r_0$ and if $\varphi(x)$ satisfies (5.3), then

$$\max_{a \le x_n \le b} |\varphi(x_n) - w_n| \le |\varphi(a) - w_0| e^{L(b-a)} + \frac{e^{(b-a)} - 1}{L} \left(E_0 h^p + k_0 h^p + \frac{r_0}{h} \right).$$

9. Apply Problem 8 to (5.8) and (5.9) using $p = 1$ and $r_n = 0$. Show that (5.10) is true.

10. (a) Suppose that $\tilde{y}_n$ satisfies (5.11) with $\tilde{y}_0 = \varphi(a)$ and that (5.3) is true. If $|r_n| \le r_0$, use Problem 8 to show that

$$\max_{a \le x_n \le b} |\varphi(x_n) - \tilde{y}_n| \le \frac{e^{(b-a)L} - 1}{L} \left(E_0 h^p + \frac{r_0}{h} \right).$$

(b) Compute the minimum value of $E_0 h^p + r_0 h^{-1}$ for $h > 0$. Graph this function of h. At what value h_m does the minimum occur?

(c) If $r_0 / E_0 < 1$, how does h_m change with p?

(d) Does this result support the assertion that because of round-off error, h can be taken too small?

11. (*Richardson extrapolation*) Suppose that method (5.1) satisfies (5.3). According to the asymptotic error estimates,

(5.12) $\varphi(x_n) \cong y(x_n, h) + z(x_n)h^p$

or $z(x_n) \cong [\varphi(x_n) - y(x_n, h)]h^{-p}$. If we halve the step size h and repeat the computation, then

(5.13) $\varphi(x_n) \cong y\left(x_n, \frac{h}{2} \right) + \frac{z(x_n)h^p}{2^p}.$

$$\cong y\left(x_n, \frac{h}{2} \right) + \frac{\varphi(x_n) - y(x_n, h)}{2^p}.$$

Solving for $\varphi(x_n)$ gives the **extrapolated estimate**

(5.14) $$\varphi(x_n) \cong (2^p - 1)^{-1}\left[2^p y\left(x_n, \frac{h}{2}\right) - y(x_n, h)\right].$$

This is a more accurate estimate for $\varphi(x_n)$. Note that (5.12) and (5.13) can be solved for the error $z(x_n)h^p$, that is,

(5.15) $$z(x_n)h^p = \frac{y(x_n, h/2) - y(x_n, h)}{1 - 2^{-p}}.$$

This formula can be used to get an estimate of the error in (5.12) and to decide whether h is small enough.

(a) Apply Euler's method to Problem 1 with $h = 0.04$ and then with $h = 0.02$. Compute the errors in $y(x_n, h)$ for $h = 0.04$ at $x_n = 0.4$ and 1 by comparing with the true solution.

(b) Use the Richardson extrapolation (5.14) to obtain a better estimate of the solution.

(c) Estimate the errors $y(x_n) - y(x_n, h)$ for $h = 0.04$ by using (5.15). Compare with the actual errors obtained in part (a).

CHAPTER REVIEW

We wish to solve the problem $y' = f(x, y)$, $y(a) = y_0$ over the interval $a \le x \le b$. Let $h = (b - a)/N$ be the **step size** (for some fixed positive integer N). Let $x_n = a + nh$. **Euler's method** is

$$y_{n+1} = y_n + hf(x_n, y_n), \qquad \text{for } n = 0, 1, \ldots, N-1.$$

The value of y_0 is given. The computed values y_n are approximations to the solution y at $x = x_n$. Euler's method is **first order,** that is, the local truncation error is order h^2. **Runge–Kutta** methods are indirect Taylor series methods. The fourth-order Runge–Kutta method (2.12) is an effective solution method for small computers. It is relatively easy to program. **Multistep** methods are very effective but require more careful and extensive programming. Adams type methods (c.f. (3.4) and (3.5)) are commonly used on large computers. **Systems** of equations are solved by the same methods as single equations. ***n*th-order** equations are first turned into equivalent systems of n first-order equations and then solved.

CHAPTER REVIEW PROBLEMS

1. (a) Show that if Euler's method is applied to the problem
$$y' = 2y + 1, \qquad y(0) = 0,$$
one gets $y_n = [(1 + 2h)^n - 1]/2$.

(b) What is the exact solution of this initial value problem?

(c) If this problem is written as a system (4.1), then what is m?

2. Write the following problems as first-order systems of the form (4.1):
   (a) $y''' - 9y = 0$, $y(0) = 0$, $y'(0) = 1$, $y''(0) = 2$.
   (b) $w'' + xw' + x^2w = 0$, $w(0) = 0$, $w'(0) = 3$.

CHAPTER NINE

*Qualitative Analysis*_____

In this chapter we study differential equations of the form

(E) $$\frac{dy}{dt} = f(t, y),$$

where $f(t, y)$ is defined and continuous and has continuous partial derivatives on a set $D = \{(t, y): A_1 < t < B_1 \text{ and } A_2 < y < B_2\}$. Many interesting differential equations (E) cannot be solved or else the solution, when found, is not in a convenient form. Our purpose here is to see what information can be gained concerning the solutions of (E) without actually solving it. The student has already encountered some results of this type. For example, the basic existence and uniqueness theorem states that for any point (τ, a) in D there is exactly one solution of (E) that satisfies the initial condition

$$y(\tau) = a.$$

This information is independent of our ability to actually find the required solution. Much more detailed, useful, and interesting information about solutions will be presented in this chapter.

When $f(t, y)$ is independent of t, equation (E) is called **autonomous** (or sometimes **time invariant**). Such an equation has the form

(A) $$y' = f(y).$$

We shall be concerned here with autonomous equations (A) or autonomous systems. Autonomous systems of two equations are of the form

$$(A_2) \qquad\qquad y_1' = f_1(y_1, y_2), \qquad y_2' = f_2(y_1, y_2).$$

Many of the results for systems that are presented in this chapter could be generalized from two autonomous equations to n autonomous equations. For simplicity we shall usually stick with $n = 2$.

In Sections 9.1 and 9.2 we assume that the student is familiar with the first part of Chapter 2. In particular, separation of variables and solution of first-order linear equations will be needed. The method of solution of second-order linear equations with constant coefficients is also needed in Section 9.2. In order to understand Sections 9.3 and 9.4 the student must be familiar with the eigenvalue–eigenvector method of solution which is discussed in Chapter 7.

9.1 *ANALYSIS OF SCALAR EQUATIONS*

The differential equation

$$(1.1) \qquad\qquad \frac{dy}{dt} = \cos y$$

is separable. By separation of variables we see that

$$dt = \frac{dy}{\cos y} = \sec y\, dy,$$

so

$$(1.2) \qquad\qquad t + c = \log\left|\sec y + \tan y\right|.$$

Expression (1.2) determines solutions implicitly. This expression cannot easily be solved for y nor does the expression give much information about solutions. We shall now develop some theory that will yield detailed information about how solutions of (1.1) evolve with time.

Consider the problem

$$(1.3) \qquad\qquad y' = f(y), \qquad y(\tau) = a$$

where f is defined, continuous, and continuously differentiable on an interval $I = (A, B)$. Given any τ and any a in I there is a unique solution $y = \varphi(t, \tau, a)$ of (1.3). Since f is independent of t, the solutions $\varphi(t, \tau, a)$ satisfy the following interesting property.

THEOREM 1.1

For any real numbers t and τ and any $a \in I$, as long as the solution φ is defined it is true that

$$\varphi(t, \tau, a) = \varphi(t - \tau, 0, a).$$

To prove this, we note that $y = \varphi(t, 0, a)$ is the solution of $y' = f(y)$, $y(0) = a$. Hence $y_1(t) = \varphi(t - \tau, 0, a)$ solves

$$y_1' = \varphi'(t - \tau, 0, a) = f(\varphi(t - \tau, 0, a)) = f(y_1),$$

$$y_1(\tau) = \varphi(\tau - \tau, 0, a) = \varphi(0, 0, a) = a.$$

Hence y_1 solves (1.3). **By uniqueness of solutions, it is the same solution as** $\varphi(t, \tau, a)$.

The conclusion of Theorem 1.1 implies that for autonomous equations the initial time τ is not important. If we know what solutions are doing when $\tau = 0$, we can determine what solutions are doing for any other τ. Because of this we shall always take $\tau = 0$.

An **equilibrium point** (or **critical point**) of the equation

(A) $$y' = f(y)$$

is a point $\bar{a}$ in I such that $f(\bar{a}) = 0$. Note that $\bar{a}$ is an equilibrium point if and only if the constant function $y(t) \equiv \bar{a}$ is a solution of (A). This is true since

$$y'(t) \equiv 0 \equiv f(\bar{a}) = f(y(t)).$$

For example, to find equilibrium points of (1.1) we set $\cos y = 0$. The solutions are $\bar{a} = \pi/2 + n\pi$ for any integer n. Hence (1.1) has an infinite number of equilibrium points.

SIGN ANALYSIS

Given the differential equation (A), at each point b on the interval I the function $f(b)$ must be positive, negative, or zero. If $f(b)$ is zero, then b is an equilibrium point. If $f(b) > 0$, then a solution $y(t)$ that passes through b at time τ must be increasing since $y'(\tau) = f(y(\tau)) = f(b) > 0$. Similarly, if $f(b) < 0$, a solution passing through b must be decreasing. Let $[a_1, a_2]$ be an interval in I such that $f(a_1) = f(a_2) = 0$, while $f(y) > 0$ when $a_1 < y < a_2$. Then a_1 and a_2 are equilibrium points of (A), while solutions between a_1 and a_2 must be increasing toward a_2 as t increases and decreasing toward a_1 as t decreases. If $y(t)$ is a solution satisfying $y(0) = b$ with $a_1 < b < a_2$, it can be shown that

$$\lim_{t \to \infty} y(t) = a_2 \quad \text{and} \quad \lim_{t \to \infty} y(t) = a_1.$$

Similarly, if $f(a_1) = f(a_2) = 0$ while $f(y) < 0$ for $a_1 < y < a_2$, then solutions $y(t)$ starting between a_1 and a_2 must decrease as t increases and must satisfy

$$\lim_{t \to \infty} y(t) = a_1 \quad \text{and} \quad \lim_{t \to -\infty} y(t) = a_2.$$

EXAMPLE 1.2   For $y' = \cos y$, Figure 9.1 displays the regions where $f(y) = \cos y$ is positive or negative. For example, on $-\pi/2 < y < \pi/2$ the cosine is positive. Solutions in this region increase and approach the equilibrium point $\pi/2$ as $t \to \infty$. In the interval $\pi/2 < y < 3\pi/2$ the cosine is negative. Solutions in this region are decreasing and tend to $\pi/2$ as $t \to \infty$. Clearly, this sign analysis gives much more information about solutions than formula (1.2). ∎

The usefulness of sign analysis is even more apparent when the differential equation is not known precisely. In such situations it is not possible to find an analytic solution of (A) nor can one use a computer to approximate solutions. However, one can often obtain reasonably detailed and useful information about the behavior of solutions and thus about the physical situation that the equation describes. We shall now present an example of such an analysis. Since the example is from economics, it will be necessary to present a certain amount of economic theory in the process of developing the relevant differential equation.

Harrod–Domar Model. We wish to describe the famous Harrod–Domar model for economic growth. This model describes a closed, self-sufficient economic community. All output is lumped together and considered to be a single homogeneous commodity. The net output of this commodity is called Y. A fraction s (with $0 < s < 1$) of the output is saved and the rest is consumed. Let $K(t)$ be the capital at time t. By capital we mean the sum of all of the means of production, such as machines, buildings, roads, and so on. All savings are invested in capital, so that

(1.4)
$$\frac{dK}{dt} = sY.$$

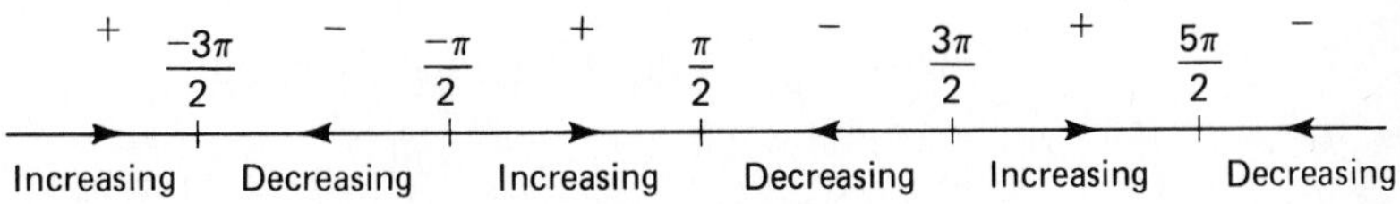

Figure 9.1. Sign analysis of $y' = \cos y$.

We assume that the factors necessary for production are labor L and capital K. Hence output Y is assumed to have the form

(1.5)
$$Y = P(K, L).$$

The **production function** P is assumed to be independent of time (e.g., there are no seasonal variations and no technological changes). We also assume that the production function $P(K, L)$ shows *constant returns to scale*. This means that if L and K are doubled (or tripled, etc.), then Y will double (or triple, etc.). Mathematically, the assumption is that for all $\lambda > 0$

(1.6)
$$P(\lambda K, \lambda L) = \lambda P(K, L).$$

(Thus P is homogeneous of degree 1; see Section 2.3.) Combining (1.4) and (1.5) gives

(1.7)
$$\frac{dK}{dt} = sP(K, L).$$

We also assume that the labor force is growing according to the simple growth law

(1.8)
$$\frac{dL}{dt} = gL.$$

The two equations (1.7) and (1.8) determine an autonomous system of equations for the unknowns $K(t)$ and $L(t)$. This system is analyzed as follows. First solve (1.8) for L, that is,

$$L(t) = L(0)e^{gt}.$$

Next introduce the variable $r = K/L$, the ratio of capital to labor. Hence $K = rL = rL(0)e^{gt}$ and

$$\frac{dK}{dt} = L(0)e^{gt}\frac{dr}{dt} + grL(0)e^{gt} = \left(\frac{dr}{dt} + gr\right)L.$$

This expression is used in (1.7) to see that

$$\left(\frac{dr}{dt} + gr\right)L = sP(K, L).$$

Now use (1.6) with $\lambda = L$ to obtain

$$\left(\frac{dr}{dt} + gr\right)L = sLP\left(\frac{K}{L}, 1\right) = sLP(r, 1).$$

Hence r satisfies the differential equation

(1.9)
$$\frac{dr}{dt} = sP(r, 1) - gr.$$

The behavior of solutions of (1.9) depends on the production function P, the savings rate s; and the growth rate g. A typical situation is graphed in

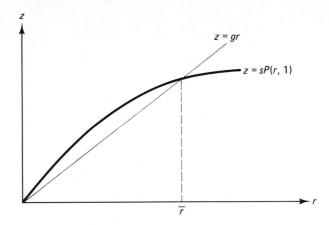

Figure 9.2. Harrod–Domar model.

Figure 9.2. We are making the economically reasonable assumption that the graph of $P(r, 1)$ passes through the origin. Moreover, we assume that $P(r, 1)$ is an increasing and convex function of r (i.e., $\partial P/\partial r > 0$ and $\partial^2 P/\partial r^2 \leq 0$). The curves $sP(r, 1)$ and gr intersect at one point $\bar{r} > 0$. Hence $\bar{r}$ is an equilibrium point of (1.9); $sP(r, 1) - gr$ is positive when $0 < r < \bar{r}$ and is negative when $r > \bar{r}$. Our sign analysis argument shows that all positive solutions of (1.9) must tend to $\bar{r}$ as $t \to \infty$. Thus the capital–labor ratio must tend to $\bar{r}$ as time goes on. Since $r(t) = K(t)/L(t)$, then for large times $K(t) \cong \bar{r}L(t)$ and

$$Y(t) = P(K(t), L(t)) \cong P(\bar{r}L(t), L(t)) = L(t)P(\bar{r}, 1).$$

Hence as time goes on, output will grow at about the same rate as labor and output per worker will become nearly constant. These conclusions are independent of whether $0 < r(0) < \bar{r}$ or $r(0) > \bar{r}$. The system self-adjusts toward the equilibrium $\bar{r}$. Notice that $r = 0$ is also an equilibrium point but not a very interesting one. If we start with $r = 0$ (i.e., no capital), there is no production.

   The savings rate s and the growth rate g of the labor force might be measured with reasonable precision. However, the production function $P(K, L)$ cannot, by the nature of things, be known precisely. If P is not known, then (1.9) can never be solved. The best that can be done from a mathematical point of view is to obtain general information about solutions. This we have done. From the economic point of view the work has just begun. On the surface the assumption that $P(r, 1)$ has the shape given in Figure 9.2 is reasonable. But is it the only possibility? Is assumption (1.8) about labor growth reasonable? Is it reasonable to lump all output into one commodity? What are the economic implications of our assumptions and of our conclusions? The interested reader can pursue these subjects further by going to the economics literature.

PROBLEMS

In Problems 1–4, determine all equilibrium points. Use sign analysis to describe the behavior of all nonequilibrium solutions.

1. $y' = y(y + 1)(y - 2)$.   **2.** $y' = y \sin y$.

3. $y' = y^3 + y$.   **4.** $y' = 1 - \dfrac{6}{y^2 + 4}$.

5. Suppose that the situation for (1.9) is as depicted by Figure 9.3. Find all equilibrium solutions. Discuss the behavior (as t increases) of all nonequilibrium solutions. Show that the state of the economy (after a long time) depends very much on the choice of $r(0)$.

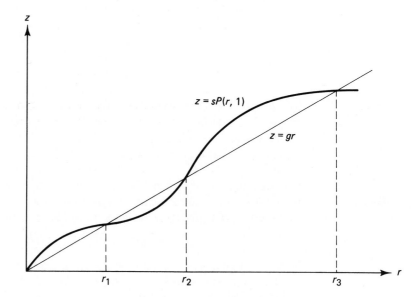

Figure 9.3. Alternative model.

6. Let $sP(r, 1)$ be as graphed in Figure 9.3. Show that the number of equilibrium points of (1.9) will vary depending on the choice of g.

7. For (A) suppose that $[b_1, b_2]$ is a subinterval of I on which $f(y)$ is never zero. Show that any solution $y(t)$ of (A) with $b_1 \le y(0) \le b_2$ must leave this subinterval after a finite amount of time.

8. Using Problem 7, show that if $f(a_1) = 0$, $f(a_2) = 0$, and $f(a) \ne 0$ when $a_1 < a < a_2$, then all solutions $y(t)$ such that $a_1 < y(0) < a_2$ must tend to a_1 or to a_2 as $t \to \infty$.

9.2 STABILITY

Suppose that $f(y)$ is continuously differentiable on an interval I and the point $\bar{a}$ in I is an equilibrium point of

(A) $y' = f(y)$.

We call $\bar{a}$ **stable** if all solutions that start near $\bar{a}$ remain near $\bar{a}$ for all future time. We say that $\bar{a}$ is **unstable** if this is not true. The formal definitions of stability go as follows.

DEFINITION 2.1: STABILITY

Let $\bar{a}$ be a critical point of (A).

(i) $\bar{a}$ is called **stable** if for any $\varepsilon > 0$ there is a $\delta > 0$ such that if $y(t)$ is any solution of (A) with $|y(0) - \bar{a}| < \delta$, then $|y(t) - \bar{a}| < \varepsilon$ for all $t \geq 0$.

(ii) $\bar{a}$ is called **unstable** if it is not stable; that is, there is an $\varepsilon > 0$ such that for any $\delta > 0$ there is at least one solution $y(t)$ of (A) with $0 < |y(0) - \bar{a}| < \delta$ and $|y(t_1) - \bar{a}| > \varepsilon$ for some $t_1 > 0$.

(iii) $\bar{a}$ is called **asymptotically stable** if it is stable and in addition there is an $R > 0$ such that when $y(t)$ is a solution of (A) with $|y(0) - \bar{a}| < R$, then $y(t) \to \bar{a}$ as $t \to \infty$ (i.e., $\lim_{t \to \infty} y(t) = \bar{a}$).

EXAMPLE 2.2 $y' = cy, \bar{a} = 0$.

The equation can be solved or stability can be checked by sign analysis (see Figure 9.4). If $c < 0$, then solutions starting near zero remain near zero and tend to zero as $t \to \infty$. Hence, if $c < 0$, then zero is asymptotically stable. If

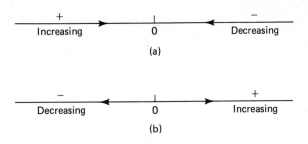

Figure 9.4. (a) $y' = cy, c < 0$. (b) $y' = cy, c > 0$.

$c > 0$, then any nonzero solution, no matter how close it starts to zero, will go away from zero. Hence the equilibrium is unstable. If $c = 0$, all solutions are constants. Solutions starting near zero will automatically stay near zero but do not tend toward zero. For $c = 0$, the equilibrium at zero is stable but not asymptotically stable. ∎

EXAMPLE 2.3   The differential equation $y' = y^2(y + 1)(y - 1)(y - 2)$ has equilibria at $0, -1, 1$, and 2. A sign analysis of the equation is given in Figure 9.5. The equilibrium

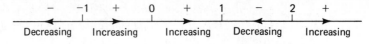

Figure 9.5. $y' = y^2(y + 1)(y - 1)(y - 2)$.

-1 is unstable since all nearby solutions go away. The equilibrium 0 is unstable. Nearby negative solutions are fine, but nearby positive solutions go away from 0. The equilibrium at 1 is stable, indeed asymptotically stable. Clearly, 2 is unstable. ∎

Our definitions of equilibria and of stability carry over to systems of equations. Given the system

(2.1) $$y_1' = f_1(y_1, y_2), \qquad y_2' = f_2(y_1, y_2)$$

a point $P = (a_1, a_2)$ is called an **equilibrium point** (or **critical point**) of (2.1) if

$$f_1(a_1, a_2) = 0, \qquad f_2(a_1, a_2) = 0.$$

DEFINITION 2.4: STABILITY–PLANAR SYSTEMS

Let $P = (a_1, a_2)$ be an equilibrium point of (2.1).

(i) P is **stable** if for any $\varepsilon > 0$ there is a $\delta > 0$ such that if $(y_1(t), y_2(t))$ is a solution of (2.1) with

$$|y_1(0) - a_1| < \delta \quad \text{and} \quad |y_2(0) - a_2| < \delta,$$

then $|y_1(t) - a_1| < \varepsilon$ and $|y_2(t) - a_2| < \varepsilon$ for all $t \geq 0$.
(ii) P is called **unstable** if it is not stable.
(iii) P is called **asymptotically stable** if it is stable and in addition there is an $R > 0$ such that if $(y_1(t), y_2(t))$ is any solution of (2.1) with

$$|y_1(0) - a_1| < R \quad \text{and} \quad |y_2(0) - a_2| < R,$$

then $y_1(t) \to a_1$ and $y_2(t) \to a_2$ as $t \to \infty$.

The various types of stability can sometimes be checked by **graphing** the solutions of (2.1) in the (y_1, y_2) plane. The (y_1, y_2) plane is called the **phase plane**. Given a solution of (2.1) the parametric solution curve $(y_1(t), y_2(t))$ in the phase plane is called an **orbit** or **trajectory** or **path** of (2.1). Notice that this orbit is a curve in *2-space*, while the graph of the actual solution is the curve $(t, y_1(t), y_2(t))$ in *3-space*.

EXAMPLE 2.5   Consider the linear mechanical system depicted in Figure 9.6 where $K > 0$, $M > 0$, and $B \geq 0$. If y is the displacement of the mass M from its equilibrium position, then by Newton's law

(2.2) $$My'' = -Ky - By'.$$

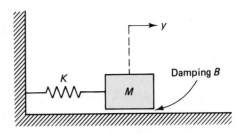

Figure 9.6. A mass-spring system.

To write (2.2) as a system of two equations, we introduce the variables $y_1 = y$ and $y_2 = y'$. Hence

(2.3) $$y_1' = y_2, \qquad y_2' = -\frac{K}{M}y_1 - \frac{B}{M}y_2.$$

System (2.3) is a **phase-space representation** of (2.2). The only equilibrium for (2.3) is $P = (0, 0)$, that is, $y_1 = y_2 = 0$.

Consider first the case $B = 0$. Here (2.2) reduces to

(2.4) $$My'' = -Ky$$

and has general solution $y = A \cos (wt + \theta)$, where $A \geq 0$ and θ are arbitrary constants and $w = \sqrt{K/M}$. In phase space the solution is

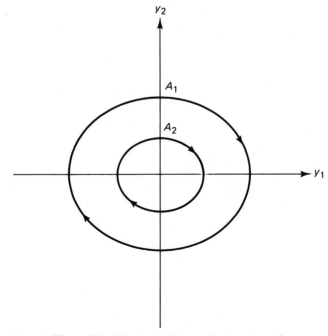

Figure 9.7. Solutions with $B = 0$, $A_2 > A_1 > 0$.

$$y_1 = A \cos(wt + \theta)$$

$$y_2 = -Aw \sin(wt + \theta).$$

Some typical solutions are graphed in Figure 9.7. Since

$$y_1^2 + \left(\frac{y_2}{w}\right)^2 = A^2,$$

it is clear that each solution lies on an ellipse centered at the origin. Each trajectory traverses an ellipse in the clockwise direction as t increases. If the initial
conditions of a solution are close to the origin, that solution stays on an ellipse
which is close to the origin. From this, we see that the origin is a stable
equilibrium.

Suppose that $B > 0$. The roots of the characteristic equation for (2.2) are

$$\lambda_1 = -\frac{B - \sqrt{B^2 - 4MK}}{2} \quad \text{and} \quad \lambda_2 = -\frac{B + \sqrt{B^2 - 4MK}}{2}.$$

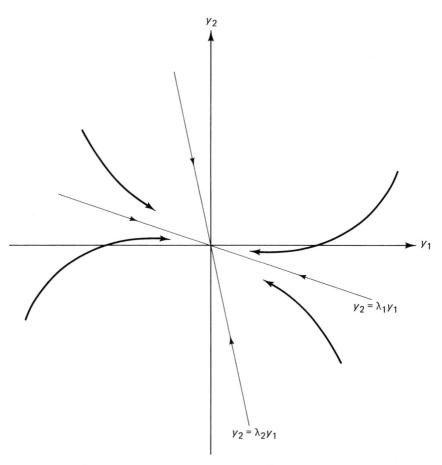

Figure 9.8. Solutions when $B^2 > 4MK$.

If $B^2 - 4MK > 0$, then λ_1 and λ_2 are both real and negative. Solutions have the form

(2.5)
$$y_1 = c_1 e^{\lambda_1 t} + c_2 e^{\lambda_2 t}$$
$$y_2 = \lambda_1 c_1 e^{\lambda_1 t} + \lambda_2 c_2 e^{\lambda_2 t}.$$

In (2.5) if $c_2 = 0$, the solution is on the line $y_2 = \lambda_1 y_1$. Since $\lambda_1 < 0$ and $y_1 = c_1 e^{\lambda_1 t}$, both y_1 and y_2 tend to zero as $t \to \infty$. This line of solutions is graphed in Figure 9.8. Similarly, if $c_1 = 0$, the solution (1.5) lies on the line $y_2 = \lambda_2 y_1$. Since $\lambda_2 < 0$, these solutions tend to the origin as $t \to \infty$. When c_1 and c_2 are both nonzero, solutions still tend to the origin as $t \to \infty$. Several such solutions are graphed in Figure 9.8. When $B^2 > 4MK$ the origin is asymptotically stable.

If $B^2 = 4MK$, then $\lambda = -B/2 < 0$ is a double root. The solutions

$$y_1 = (c_1 + c_2 t)e^{\lambda t}$$
$$y_2 = \lambda(c_1 + c_2 t)e^{\lambda t} + c_2 e^{\lambda t}$$

are graphed in Figure 9.9. The origin is asymptotically stable.

The most interesting case is $0 < B^2 < 4MK$. The eigenvalues

$$\lambda = -\frac{B \pm i\sqrt{4MK - B^2}}{2}$$

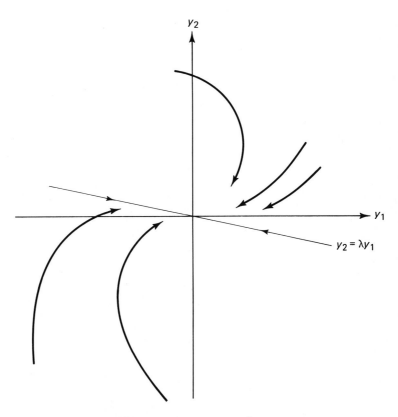

Figure 9.9. Solutions when $B^2 = 4MK$.

are complex. A general solution is

$$y_1 = Ae^{(-B/2)t} \cos(wt + \theta)$$

$$y_2 = -\frac{B}{2} Ae^{-(B/2)t} \cos(wt + \theta) - wAe^{-(B/2)t} \sin(wt + \theta)$$

where $w = 4MK - B^2$ and $A \geq 0$ and θ are arbitrary constants. Let A_1 and θ_1 satisfy $A_1 \sin \theta_1 = BA/2$ and $A_1 \cos \theta_1 = wA$. Then

$$y_2 = -(A_1 \sin \theta_1 \cos(wt + \theta) + A_1 \cos \theta_1 \sin(wt + \theta))e^{-(B/2)t}$$

or

$$y_2 = -A_1 e^{-(B/2)t} \sin(wt + \theta + \theta_1).$$

Hence both y_1 and y_2 oscillate about zero. Because of the term $e^{-(B/2)t}$ in each function, both y_1 and y_2 tend to zero as $t \to \infty$. The trajectories turn out to be spirals of the type shown in Figure 9.10. The equilibrium at the origin is asymptotically stable.   ■

Our analysis of (2.2) is typical of the analysis of many physical systems. The physical system is represented mathematically as a system of first-order differential equations—a phase-space representation. By solving or by other analysis we graph the orbits of the differential equations. The mathematical results represented by the graphs must be interpreted in order to see what is going on

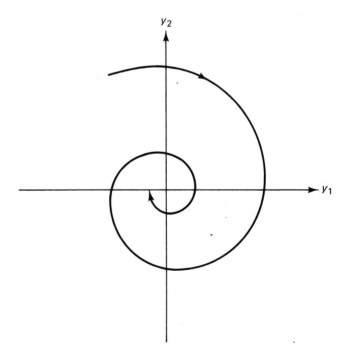

Figure 9.10. Solutions when $0 < B^2 < 4MK$.

in the physical system. Here (2.3) is our phase-space representation of the mechanical system. We interpret y_1 as the deviation of the center of mass from its equilibrium value and y_2 as the velocity of the mass. When the damping B is zero (or is so near zero that it can safely be ignored), we say that (2.2) is undamped. We see from Figure 9.7 that the mass oscillates back and forth between a maximum value $\bar{y}_1$ and a minimum value $-\bar{y}_1$. The velocity y_2 is zero when y_1 attains its maximum or its minimum. The speed of the mass is maximized when y_1 is passing through the value zero. There is only one equilibrium, $y_1 = y_2 = 0$. This is the type of motion seen in the pendulum of a grandfather clock. If the clock is working correctly, the damping will be so small that it can be ignored over time periods of a few hours. The pendulum seems to oscillate in the manner described.

The physical system is called overdamped when $B^2 > 4MK$. From Figure 9.8 we see that neither the position nor the velocity have significant oscillations. The orbits rush head-long for the origin. This type of motion can be observed in the suspension system of a car. Above each wheel of a car there is a large stiff spring and a damper (the shock absorber). When the suspension system is working correctly, it will level the car with little or no "bounce."

The system is underdamped when $0 < B^2 < 4MK$. Here damping is present but is light. This situation is typical of our experiences with everyday springs. The situation graphed in Figure 9.10 is also consistent with our everyday experiences. The shape of the orbits indicates that both position and velocity oscillate back and forth. However, the damping causes these oscillations to grow smaller and smaller. The system approaches equilibrium as t grows large.

In all situations the origin is a stable or an asymptotically stable equilibrium for (2.3). The mechanical system (2.2) can never be unstable.

Stability considerations are **important** in a variety of mechanical systems. You may remember seeing jerky motion picture footage of pre-Wright brothers'

Photo 20. Interceptor 400 aircraft. (Courtesy of Prop–Jets, Inc.)

airplanes. They usually crashed immediately. Stability and control were among *the* major problems for the inventors of the first airplanes. It was the Wright brothers' genius to find some of the first solutions to these problems. Thanks to the work of generations of engineers/designers, sophisticated techniques have been developed to solve problems of control and stability in modern aircraft (see Photo 20).

PROBLEMS

In Problems 1–4, find all equilibrium points and determine their stability type.

1. $y' = y(y^2 - 1)(y^2 - 4)$.

2. $y' = y^2(y^2 - 1)(y^2 - 4)$.

3. $y' = \sin y$.

4. $y' = y \sin y$.

5. Suppose that the economic model (1.9) has P, s, and g of the form shown in Figure 9.2. Determine the stability properties of the equilibrium $\bar{r}$.

6. Suppose that the economic model (1.9) has P, s, and g of the form shown in Figure 9.3. Determine the stability properties of r_1, r_2, and r_3.

7. For system (2.1), suppose that f_1 and f_2 are defined, continuous, and have continuous partial derivatives with respect to y_1 and y_2 in a region $D = \{(y_1, y_2) : A_i < y_i < B_i$ for $i = 1, 2\}$. Let $\varphi_1(t, \tau, a_1, a_2)$ and $\varphi_2(t, \tau, a_1, a_2)$ be the solution of (2.1) that satisfies the initial conditions

$$\varphi_1(\tau, \tau, a_1, a_2) = a_1, \qquad \varphi_2(\tau, \tau, a_1, a_2) = a_2.$$

Show that for $i = 1, 2$

$$\varphi_i(t, \tau, a_1\, a_2) = \varphi_i(t - \tau, 0, a_1, a_2).$$

Hint: Generalize the proof of Theorem 1.1.

In Problems 8–12, write the equation as an equivalent system. Solve the equation and use this solution to find a solution of the equivalent system. From the solution determine the stability properties of the equilibrium at the origin.

8. $y'' + 4y = 0$.

9. $y'' - 4y = 0$.

10. $y'' + y' - 2y = 0$.

11. $y'' + 3y' + 2y = 0$.

12. $y'' - 3y' + 2y = 0$.

13. The problem $y'' + y + y^3 = 0$ was studied in Example 1.5 of Section 3.1. A phase-plane plot of some typical solutions is shown in Figure 3.1. Using this information, show that the equilibrium at the origin is stable but not asymptotically stable.

14. Show that the trajectories of

$$w_1' = -f_1(w_1, w_2), \qquad w_2' = -f_2(w_1, w_2)$$

are the same as those of (2.1) except that the direction of travel of the solution is reversed.

15. Graph in phase space the trajectories of

$$w_1' = -w_2, \qquad w_2' = \frac{K}{M} w_1 + \frac{B}{M} w_2$$

when $B = 0$, when $B^2 > 4MK$, and when $0 < B^2 < 4MK$. *Hint:* Use Problem 14 and Example 2.5.

16. (a) In (2.2) let $z_1 = y$ be the displacement of the mass and $z_2 = My'$ be the momentum of the mass. Find a phase-space representation (i.e., an equivalent system of first-order equations) for (2.2) in terms of z_1 and z_2.

    (b) Let A be any 2×2 invertible matrix, that is,

$$A = \begin{pmatrix} a_{11} & a_{12} \\ a_{21} & a_{22} \end{pmatrix}, \qquad \det A \neq 0$$

and let

$$\begin{pmatrix} y \\ y' \end{pmatrix} = A \begin{pmatrix} w_1 \\ w_2 \end{pmatrix}.$$

Find a phase-space representation for (2.2) in terms of w_1 and w_2.

    (c) How many phase-space representations can you find for (2.2)?

17. In Section 3.14 it was shown that a frictionless pendulum consisting of a mass M suspended by a weightless, inflexible rod of length l is described mathematically by the equation

$$\frac{d^2\theta}{dt^2} + \frac{g}{l}\sin\theta = 0,$$

where g is the gravitational constant (in correct units) and θ is the angular deviation of the mass from the rest position $\theta = 0$.

    (a) Find a phase-space representation using $y_1 = \theta$, $y_2 = \theta'$.

    (b) Find all equilibrium points for the system obtained in part (a).

    (c) Show that total energy $E(y_1, y_2) = My_2^2/2 + Mg(1 - \cos y_1)/l$ is constant along any solution.

    (d) Near the equilibrium point $(0, 0)$ graph the curves $E(y_1, y_2) = c$ when c is a small positive constant. Argue that this equilibrium is stable.

    (e) Show that the equilibrium $(\pi, 0)$ is a saddle point for the surface $Z = E(y_1, y_2)$. Graph the curves $E(y_1, y_2) = c$ that lie near $(\pi, 0)$. Is $(\pi, 0)$ stable or unstable? Does your answer make sense physically?

9.3 LINEAR SYSTEMS

The system

(3.1)
$$\mathbf{y}' = \begin{pmatrix} -1 & 6 \\ 1 & -2 \end{pmatrix}\mathbf{y}$$

can be solved using the eigenvalue–eigenvector method discussed in Chapter 7. By this method we see that two linearly independent solutions are

$$\mathbf{y}_1 = \begin{pmatrix} 3 \\ 1 \end{pmatrix}e^t \quad \text{and} \quad \mathbf{y}_2 = \begin{pmatrix} -2 \\ 1 \end{pmatrix}e^{-4t}.$$

A general solution is $\mathbf{y} = c_1\mathbf{y}_1 + c_2\mathbf{y}_2$. In particular,

$$\mathbf{y} = c_1 \binom{3}{1} e^t$$

is a solution for any real number c_1. It satisfies the initial condition $\mathbf{y}(0) = (3c_1, c_1)^T$. If $|c_1|$ is small, then $\mathbf{y}(0)$ is near the equilibrium at the origin. As t increases the solution moves away from the origin along the line $y_1 = 3y_2$. If $c_1 = 0$, then $\mathbf{y} = c_2(-2, 1)^T e^{-4t}$. These solutions move along the line $y_1 = -2y_2$ toward the origin. These trajectories, as well as some trajectories with c_1 and c_2 both nonzero, are graphed in Figure 9.11. Clearly, the equilibrium at $(0, 0)$ is unstable.

The system

(3.2)
$$\mathbf{y}' = \begin{pmatrix} 2 & 3 \\ -3 & 2 \end{pmatrix} \mathbf{y}$$

can be solved by the eigenvalue–eigenvector method. The eigenvalues $\lambda = 2 \pm 3i$ are complex. A complex solution is

$$e^{(2+3i)t} \binom{1}{i}.$$

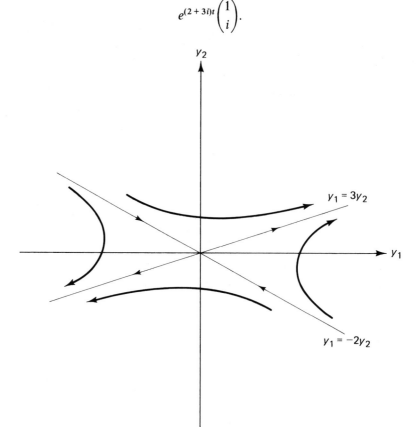

Figure 9.11. An unstable linear system.

Hence two real-valued solutions are

$$y_1 = e^{2t} \begin{pmatrix} \cos 3t \\ -\sin 3t \end{pmatrix} \quad \text{and} \quad y_2 = e^{2t} \begin{pmatrix} \sin 3t \\ \cos 3t \end{pmatrix}.$$

The general solution is $\mathbf{y} = c_1\mathbf{y}_1 + c_2\mathbf{y}_2$. The following argument shows that the origin is unstable. For any c_1,

$$\mathbf{y}(t) = c_1 e^{2t} \begin{pmatrix} \cos 3t \\ -\sin 3t \end{pmatrix}$$

is a solution with initial value $\mathbf{y}(0) = (c_1, 0)^T$. When c_1 is small, this initial value is near $(0, 0)^T$. But $\mathbf{y}(n\pi/3) = c_1 e^{2n\pi/3} (1, 0)^T$ when $n = 2, 4, 6, \ldots$. Hence $\mathbf{y}(n\pi/3)$ is far from the origin when n is large.

The orbits of (3.2) are spirals. This can be seen by going to polar coordinates (r, θ). Since $r^2 = y_1^2 + y_2^2$, then

$$\begin{aligned} (r^2)' = 2rr' &= 2y_1 y_1' + 2y_2 y_2' \\ &= 2y_1(2y_1 + 3y_2) + 2y_2(-3y_1 + 2y_2) \\ &= 4y_1^2 + 4y_2^2 = 4r^2 \end{aligned}$$

or $r' = 2r$. Similarly, since $\theta = \arctan(y_2/y_1)$, then

$$\theta' = \frac{1}{1 + (y_2/y_1)^2} \frac{y_1 y_2' - y_2 y_1'}{y_1^2} = \frac{-3y_1^2 - 3y_2^2}{y_1^2 + y_2^2} = -3.$$

Hence a system equivalent to (3.2) is

$$r' = 2r, \qquad \theta' = -3.$$

The solution of this system is

$$r = r(0)e^{2t}, \qquad \theta = -3t + \theta(0).$$

Such curves represent orbits that spiral away from the origin.

The analysis of these two examples can easily be generalized. The following theorem is true.

THEOREM 3.1: UNSTABLE CASE

Let **A** be a real, $n \times n$ matrix. If there is an eigenvalue λ such that either $\lambda > 0$ or $\operatorname{Re} \lambda > 0$, then the origin is an unstable equilibrium for the system

$$(3.3) \qquad\qquad \mathbf{y}' = \mathbf{A}\mathbf{y}.$$

If the matrix **A** has a real eigenvalue λ that is positive, then clearly, $\operatorname{Re} \lambda > 0$. Hence in Theorem 3.1 we usually just say that **A** has an eigenvalue λ "with positive real part." Such a matrix **A** is called an **unstable matrix**. A matrix **A** is called **stable** if all eigenvalues have negative real parts.

THEOREM 3.2: STABLE CASE

If $\mathbf{A}$ is a real $n \times n$ matrix that is stable, then the origin is an asymptotically stable equilibrium for system (3.3).

We can see why Theorem 3.2 should be true by considering some examples. First consider the system

$$(3.4) \qquad \mathbf{y}' = \begin{pmatrix} -1 & -5 \\ 1 & -7 \end{pmatrix} \mathbf{y}.$$

The eigenvalues of this matrix are $-6 < 0$ and $-2 < 0$. By the eigenvalue–eigenvector method we see that a general solution is

$$\mathbf{y} = c_1 \begin{pmatrix} 1 \\ 1 \end{pmatrix} e^{-6t} + c_2 \begin{pmatrix} 5 \\ 1 \end{pmatrix} e^{-2t}$$

$$= \begin{pmatrix} e^{-6t} & 5e^{-2t} \\ e^{-6t} & e^{-2t} \end{pmatrix} \begin{pmatrix} c_1 \\ c_2 \end{pmatrix} = \mathbf{Y}(t) \begin{pmatrix} c_1 \\ c_2 \end{pmatrix}.$$

From the fundamental matrix $\mathbf{Y}(t)$ we can compute

$$e^{\mathbf{A}t} = \mathbf{Y}(t)\mathbf{Y}(0)^{-1}$$

$$= \begin{pmatrix} -\frac{1}{4}e^{-6t} + \frac{5}{4}e^{-2t} & \frac{5}{4}e^{-6t} - \frac{5}{4}e^{-2t} \\ -\frac{1}{4}e^{-6t} + \frac{1}{4}e^{-2t} & \frac{5}{4}e^{-6t} - \frac{1}{4}e^{-2t} \end{pmatrix}.$$

The solution of (3.4) that satisfies the initial condition

$$(3.5) \qquad \mathbf{y}(0) = \mathbf{a} = \begin{pmatrix} a_1 \\ a_2 \end{pmatrix}$$

is

$$\mathbf{y}(t) = \mathbf{Y}(t)\mathbf{Y}(0)^{-1}\mathbf{a} = e^{\mathbf{A}t}\mathbf{a}.$$

Each term in $e^{\mathbf{A}t}$ contains one of the factors e^{-6t} or e^{-2t}. Hence the solution $\mathbf{y}(t)$ must tend to zero as $t \to \infty$.

The matrix $\mathbf{A}$ in the system

$$(3.6) \qquad \mathbf{y}' = \begin{pmatrix} -1 & -1 \\ 1 & -3 \end{pmatrix} \mathbf{y}$$

has the double eigenvalue $\lambda = -2$. A general solution is

$$\mathbf{y} = c_1 \begin{pmatrix} 1 \\ 1 \end{pmatrix} e^{-2t} + c_2 \begin{pmatrix} t \\ t - 1 \end{pmatrix} e^{-2t}$$

$$= e^{-2t} \begin{pmatrix} 1 & t \\ 1 & t - 1 \end{pmatrix} \begin{pmatrix} c_1 \\ c_2 \end{pmatrix} = \mathbf{Y}(t) \begin{pmatrix} c_1 \\ c_2 \end{pmatrix}.$$

By L'Hospital's rule

$$\lim_{t \to \infty} te^{-2t} = \lim_{t \to \infty} \frac{t}{e^{2t}} = 0.$$

Hence each term in the fundamental solution $\mathbf{Y}(t)$ tends to zero as $t \to \infty$. As before, the solution of (3.6) that satisfies the initial conditions (3.5) is

$$\mathbf{y}(t) = \mathbf{Y}(t)\mathbf{Y}(0)^{-1}\mathbf{a} = e^{\mathbf{A}t}\mathbf{a}.$$

This solution tends to zero as $t \to \infty$.

A matrix $\mathbf{A}$ such that all eigenvalues λ of $\mathbf{A}$ satisfy $\operatorname{Re} \lambda \le 0$ and at least one eigenvalue of $\mathbf{A}$ has zero real part is called a **critical matrix**. Critical matrices are not covered by either Theorem 3.1 or Theorem 3.2. If $\mathbf{A}$ is a critical matrix, then determining the stability properties of the zero solution of (3.3) is extremely complex and will not be treated here.

PROBLEMS

In Problems 1–5 determine whether the given matrix is stable, unstable, or critical.

1. $\begin{pmatrix} 3 & -2 \\ -1 & 2 \end{pmatrix}$.

2. $\begin{pmatrix} -1 & -2 \\ -1 & -2 \end{pmatrix}$.

3. $\begin{pmatrix} -1 & -3 \\ -3 & -1 \end{pmatrix}$.

4. $\begin{pmatrix} -1 & -3 \\ 1 & -5 \end{pmatrix}$.

5. $\begin{pmatrix} -3 & 1 & 0 \\ 0 & -3 & 1 \\ -2 & 1 & -1 \end{pmatrix}$.   *Hint:* One eigenvalue is $\lambda = -1$.

6. Show that if $\mathbf{A}$ is a stable matrix, then $-\mathbf{A}$ is unstable.

7. The matrix

$$\mathbf{A} = \begin{pmatrix} -1 & 1 \\ -1 & 1 \end{pmatrix}$$

is critical. Show that for this $\mathbf{A}$ the zero solution of (3.3) is unstable. *Hint:* Solve the system.

8. The matrix

$$\mathbf{A} = \begin{pmatrix} 0 & 2 & 1 \\ -2 & 0 & 0 \\ 0 & 0 & -1 \end{pmatrix}$$

is critical. Show that for this $\mathbf{A}$ the zero solution of (3.3) is stable.

9. (a) For problem (3.4) and (3.5) show that there are constants K_1 and K_2 such that the solution satisfies

$$|y_i(t)| \le (K_1 e^{-6t} + K_2 e^{-2t})(|a_1| + |a_2|)$$

for $i = 1, 2$. (The constants K_1 and K_2 do not depend on a_1 and a_2.)

(b) Using part (a), prove rigorously that the zero solution of (3.4) is asymptotically stable.

10. Precisely prove Theorem 3.1 for an $n \times n$ matrix $\mathbf{A}$ that has a real and positive eigenvalue.

11. (a) Show that if $y'' + ay' + by = 0$ is written as an equivalent two-dimensional system $\mathbf{y}' = \mathbf{Ay}$, then the characteristic equation for $\mathbf{A}$ is $\lambda^2 + a\lambda + b = 0$.

(b) Show that if $a > 0$ and $b > 0$, then $\mathbf{A}$ is a stable matrix.

9.4 ALMOST LINEAR SYSTEMS

Physical devices are almost never as simple as our mathematical idealizations of them. For example, consider the mechanical system depicted in Figure 9.6. We have assumed that when the spring is compressed (or stretched) by an amount y, the spring tries to expand (or contract) and produces a reactive force $f_k = -Ky$. The term K is called the stiffness of the spring. Actual metal springs only approximate this ideal. They will always produce a reactive force $f_k = -F(y)$, where F satisfies the conditions

(4.1) $F(0) = 0$ and $F'(y) > 0.$

Moreover, $F(y)$ will be approximately equal to Ky when y is small enough. The range of values y where $F(y) \cong Ky$ is a satisfactory approximation is called the **linear range** of the spring.

Mathematically, the governing equation for the system is

(4.2) $My'' = -F(y) - By'.$

This equation is usually replaced by the approximation

(4.3) $My'' = -Ky - By',$

where $K = F'(0)$. Going from (4.2) to (4.3) is called **linearization** [i.e., we linearize $F(y)$ about $y = 0$]. Linearization is very common in engineering and science. A natural question is whether or not the solutions of the linear approximation behave in a similar manner to the solutions of the nonlinear equation. Clearly, some restrictions are necessary. For example, in (4.2) a large velocity y' will eventually produce a large displacement y. Hence, if the linearization is to be valid for any length of time, then not only $|y|$ but also $|y'|$ must remain reasonably small.

We consider the problem of determining stability of the zero solution of **almost linear systems.** These systems have the form

(4.4)
$$y_1' = a_{11}y_1 + a_{12}y_2 + G_1(y_1, y_2)$$
$$y_2' = a_{21}y_1 + a_{22}y_2 + G_2(y_1, y_2).$$

We assume that G_1 and G_2 are small when y_1 and y_2 are small in the sense that

(4.5) $G_i(0, 0) = 0$ and $\dfrac{\partial G_i}{\partial y_j}(0, 0) = 0$ for $i, j = 1, 2.$

Since G_1 and G_2 are small, the **linear approximation** (or **linearized system**) is

$$w_1' = a_{11}w_1 + a_{12}w_2, \qquad w_2' = a_{21}w_1 + a_{22}w_2.$$

EXAMPLE 4.1   Consider the system

$$y_1' = y_1 + 2y_2 + y_1 y_2$$
$$y_2' = y_1 + y_1^2 + y_2^2 + y_1^3.$$

Here $G_1(y_1, y_2) = y_1 y_2$ and $G_2(y_1, y_2) = y_1^2 + y_2^2 + y_1^3$. It is easy to check that these functions satisfy (4.5). The linear approximation is

$$w_1' = w_1 + 2w_2, \qquad w_2' = w_1. \quad \blacksquare$$

THEOREM 4.2: LINEARIZATION

Consider system (4.4), where G_1 and G_2 are defined and continuous on a set $D = \{(y_1, y_2): |y_i| < A_i \text{ for } i = 1, 2\}$, G_1 and G_2 have continuous partial derivatives in D, and (4.5) is true. Let $\mathbf{A}$ be the matrix

$$\mathbf{A} = \begin{pmatrix} a_{11} & a_{12} \\ a_{21} & a_{22} \end{pmatrix}.$$

   (i) If $\mathbf{A}$ is stable, that is, all eigenvalues of $\mathbf{A}$ have negative real parts, then the origin is an asymptotically stable equilibrium point for system (4.4).
   (ii) If $\mathbf{A}$ is unstable, that is, $\mathbf{A}$ has at least one eigenvalue with positive real part, then the origin is unstable.
   (iii) Otherwise, $\mathbf{A}$ is critical and linearization provides no stability information.

EXAMPLE 4.3   The system given in Example 4.1 satisfies the conditions of Theorem 4.2. The linear approximation has the coefficient matrix

$$\mathbf{A} = \begin{pmatrix} 1 & 2 \\ 1 & 0 \end{pmatrix}.$$

The characteristic equation for this matrix is $\lambda^2 - \lambda - 2 = (\lambda - 2)(\lambda + 1)$. The eigenvalues are $\lambda_1 = -1$ and $\lambda_2 = 2$. Since $\lambda_2 = 2$ is real and positive, it has a positive real part. Hence the origin is an unstable equilibrium for the nonlinear system. $\quad \blacksquare$

EXAMPLE 4.4   Consider the equation $y'' + y' + e^y - 1 = 0$. Introduce new variables $y_1 = y$ and $y_2 = y'$. Then

$$(4.6) \qquad\qquad y_1' = y_2, \qquad y_2' = -y_2 - e^{y_1} + 1.$$

Since $e^{y_1} - 1 = y_1 + y_1^2/2 + y_1^3/3! + \ldots$, the linearized system is

(4.7) $w_1' = w_2, \qquad w_2' = -w_2 - w_1.$

System (4.6) has the form (4.4) with $G_1 \equiv 0$ and $G_2(y_1) = 1 - e^{y_1} + y_1$. Clearly, $G_2(0) = 0$. Since $G_2'(y_1) = -e^{y_1} + 1$, then $G_2'(0) = -1 + 1 = 0$. Hence Theorem 4.2 can be applied. The characteristic equation for (4.7) is $\lambda^2 + \lambda + 1 = 0$. The eigenvalues are $-\frac{1}{2} \pm i\sqrt{3}/2$. Since both eigenvalues have negative real parts, the origin is asymptotically stable.   ■

EXAMPLE 4.5   Consider the mechanical system (4.2) when $M > 0$, $B \geq 0$ and $K = F'(0) > 0$. Let $y_1 = y$ and $y_2 = y'$ so that

(4.8)
$$y_1' = y_2$$
$$y_2' = -F(y_1) - By_2 = -Ky_1 - By_2 + (Ky_1 - F(y_1)).$$

This system has the form of (4.4) with $G_1 \equiv 0$ and $G_2(y_1) = Ky_1 - F(y_1) = F'(0)y_1 - F(y_1)$. Clearly, $G_2(0) = G_2'(0) = 0$, so that Theorem 4.2 can be applied.

The linear equation (4.3) was analyzed in detail in Example 2.5. From that analysis we see that if $B = 0$, the linear system has complex eigenvalues $\pm i\sqrt{K/M}$. This is a critical case, so that no stability information is obtained. If $B > 0$, all eigenvalues have negative real parts. Hence if $B > 0$, the origin is an asymptotically stable equilibrium point for the nonlinear system (4.8).   ■

In our discussion of linearization we have always assumed that the equilibrium point of interest is the origin $(0, 0)$. In practical problems an equilibrium point (a_1, a_2) under study need not be at the origin. When this happens the transformation $w_1 = y_1 - a_1$ and $w_2 = y_2 - a_2$ will reduce the given system of differential equations to a new system of differential equations to which Theorem 4.2 may be applied. This transformation technique is discussed in detail in the problem section.

PROBLEMS   In Problems 1–13, write the given equation or system in the form (4.4). Decide what Theorem 4.2 says about the stability of the equilibrium at the origin.

1. $y_1' = -y_1 + 3y_2 + y_1y_2$
   $y_2' = y_1 + y_2 + y_1^4.$

2. $y_1' = y_2 + y_1 \sin y_2 + y_2^2$
   $y_2' = -2y_1 - 3y_2 - y_1y_2^2.$

3. $z' = -z + 2u + u(\cos u - 1)$
   $u' = -2z - u + u^2.$

4. $x_1' = -x_1 + x_2$
   $x_2' = x_1^2 + x_1 + x_2^2.$

5. $y_1' = -2y_1 - 2y_2$
   $y_2' = 4y_1 + 2y_2 + y_1y_2^2.$

6. $x' = x - 5y$
   $y' = -y + 2 \sin x.$

7. $3z'' + 2z' = -2z - z^3.$

8. $x'' + x' = \sin x.$

9. $y'' + 6y = 2y' + yy'.$

10. $y'' + y' = 1 - \cos y - (y')^3.$

11. $z'' + z = z' \sin z.$

12. $z'' + (z')^3 + z = 0.$

13. $y'' + 3y' + y^3 = -y.$

14. For what values of B is the origin an asymptotically stable equilibrium point for

$$y_1' = y_1 + \frac{y_2}{1 + y_1}$$

$$y_2' = -2y_1 - By_2.$$

For what values of B is the origin unstable? Are there values of B where you cannot tell?

15. Suppose that $P = (a_1, a_2)$ is an equilibrium point for

(4.8) $y_1' = f_1(y_1, y_2), \qquad y_2' = f_2(y_1, y_2).$

Let $w_1 = y_1 - a_1$ and $w_2 = y_2 - a_2$, so that

(4.9) $w_1' = f_1(w_1 + a_1, w_2 + a_2), \qquad w_2' = f_2(w_1 + a_1, w_2 + a_2).$

(a) Show that the origin is an equilibrium for (4.9).

(b) Show that if the origin in (4.9) is unstable, then P is an unstable equilibrium for (4.8).

(c) Show that if the origin in (4.9) is asymptotically stable, then P is an asymptotically stable equilibrium for (4.8).

In Problems 16–20, use Problem 15 and Theorem 4.2 to analyze the stability properties of the indicated equilibrium points.

16. $y_1' = y_1(2 - y_2), y_2' = -y_2(1 - y_1), P = (1, 2)$.

17. $y'' + 3y' + (y^2 - 1)y = 0, y = \pm 1, 0$ and $y' = 0$.

18. $x'' + x' + \sin x = 0, x = n\pi$ and $x' = 0$.

19. $y'' + \sin y = 0, y = n\pi$ and $y' = 0$.

20. $y'' + y' + (y - 1)^3 = 0, y = 1, y' = 0$.

What's ahead? Is there chaos in your future?

Classical qualitative analysis emphasizes equilibrium points and periodic solutions together with their stability. An exciting new topic in qualitative analysis is the theory of "chaos" and "strange attractors." Here is a world where little is what it seems and intuition is often of no help. It is also a world of regularity within irregularity and endless interesting pictures. Figures 9.12 and 9.13 are examples of the butterfly pattern obtained from the Lorenz equations

$$x' = \sigma(y - x), \qquad y' = \rho x - y - xz, \qquad z' = xy - \beta z,$$

where $\sigma = 10$, $\beta = 2.666\ldots$, and ρ is 26.5 in Figure 9.12 and 29 in Figure 9.13. In 1963 E. N. Lorenz proposed this system as a model for two-dimensional convection. The butterflies are the points where a three-dimensional orbit of this system hits the x–z plane. These figures were generated using the program "DYNAMICS" written by James Yorke of the University of Maryland. This program is a public domain program which allows one to watch chaos as it evolves, and to make pictures of the results.

Figure 9.12. Lorenz butterfly, rho $= 26.5$.

For a fascinating glimpse into the world of chaos recommended reading is the book *Chaos* by James Gleick (Viking Press, 1987). Chaos is not just a mathematical abstraction. One can build circuits that are chaotic or tend to strange attractors. P. Bartissol and L. Chua of the University of California at Berkeley have recently studied a "double hook" strange attractor in an article which appeared in the Institute for Electrical and Electronic Engineer's *Transactions on Circuits and Systems*. One can build a rather simple circuit (or set up a rather simple third-order differential equation) and watch the double hook behavior evolve. In order for a system of differential equations to exhibit chaotic behavior, it must be *nonlinear* and of at least *third order*. The double hook equations are nonlinear and third order. The next interesting question—find a profitable way to use chaos!

CHAPTER REVIEW

A system $\mathbf{y}' = \mathbf{f}(t, \mathbf{y})$ is called **autonomous** when $\mathbf{f}$ does not depend on the time t. An **equilibrium point** of this system is a point $\mathbf{a}$ for which $\mathbf{f}(t, \mathbf{a}) = 0$ for all t. Equilibrium points can be **unstable, stable** or **asymptotically stable** (see Definition 2.4). The stability type of equilibrium points of scalar autonomous equations can be checked by **sign analysis**. A **linear** system of the form $\mathbf{y}' = \mathbf{A}\mathbf{y}$ is asymptotically stable if all eigenvalues λ of $\mathbf{A}$ have negative real parts and is unstable if at least one eigenvalue λ has positive real parts. These stability tests also apply to almost linear systems $\mathbf{y}' = \mathbf{A}\mathbf{y} + \mathbf{G}(\mathbf{y})$ when $\mathbf{G}(\mathbf{y})$ is small in the sense of (4.5).

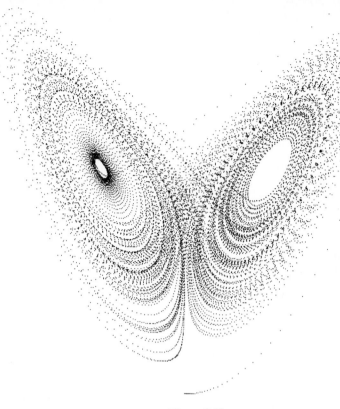

Figure 9.13.

CHAPTER REVIEW PROBLEMS

In Problems 1–3 determine all equilibrium points and decide whether each is unstable, asymptotically stable, or neither.

1. $y' = y^3 - 3y^2 + 2y$.

2. $y'' + 2y' + y = 0$. *Hint:* First rewrite as a system.

3. $y_1' = 4y_1 + y_2$, $y_2' = 2y_1 + y_2$.

In Problems 4 and 5 determine whether the origin is asymptotically stable or unstable.

4. $y_1' = y_2$, $y_2' = -y_1 - e^{y_2} + 1$.

5. $y_1' = 4y_1 + y_1y_2 - y_2^3 + y_2$, $y_2' = 2y_1 + y_1\sin y_2 + y_2$.

CHAPTER TEN

*Fourier Series*_____

Given a function $f(x)$ we wish to study the question of when $f(x)$ can be written as a trigonometric series of the form

$$(0.1) \qquad f(x) = \frac{a_0}{2} + \sum_{n=1}^{\infty} (a_n \cos nx + b_n \sin nx).$$

Such series are required when studying periodic solutions of linear differential equations with periodic forcing and when studying periodic solutions of non-linear differential equations. They are also used in the study of many physical problems that are modeled by partial differential equations. We shall first develop the basic properties of these series and then study their convergence properties. We show when (0.1) can be integrated or differentiated. A complex form of the series (0.1) will be developed. In the last section our results are used to study periodic solutions of some ordinary differential equations.

10.1 *EULER–FOURIER FORMULAS*

Consider a trigonometric series of the form

$$(1.1) \qquad f(x) = \frac{a_0}{2} + \sum_{n=1}^{\infty} (a_n \cos nx + b_n \sin nx).$$

We assume that $f(x)$ is a function that is defined over $-\pi \le x \le \pi$. We ask whether constants a_n and b_n can be found so that (1.1) is true.

First recall that $e^{inx} = \cos nx + i \sin nx$. Hence

$$\cos nx = \frac{1}{2}(e^{inx} + e^{-inx})$$

and

$$\sin nx = \frac{1}{2i}(e^{inx} - e^{-inx}).$$

From these relations it is clear that when n and m are integers, then

(1.2) $\int_{-\pi}^{\pi} \cos nx \cos mx \, dx$

$$= \frac{1}{4} \int_{-\pi}^{\pi} (e^{inx} + e^{-inx})(e^{imx} + e^{-imx}) \, dx$$

$$= \frac{1}{4} \int_{-\pi}^{\pi} (e^{i(n+m)x} + e^{i(n-m)x} + e^{i(m-n)x} + e^{-i(n+m)x}) \, dx.$$

If $n \neq m$, then

$$\int_{-\pi}^{\pi} e^{i(n+m)x} \, dx = \int_{-\pi}^{\pi} \left[\cos(n+m)x + i \sin(n+m)x\right] dx = 0.$$

Similarly, the other three integrals in (1.2) are also zero. If $n = m$, then the right side of (1.2) equals

$$\frac{1}{4} \int_{-\pi}^{\pi} (e^{2nix} + 1 + 1 + e^{-2nix}) \, dx = \frac{1}{4}(0 + 2\pi + 2\pi + 0) = \pi.$$

Hence for $n, m = 1, 2, 3, \ldots$

(1.3) $\int_{-\pi}^{\pi} \cos nx \cos mx \, dx = \begin{cases} \pi & \text{if } n = m \\ 0 & \text{if } n \neq m. \end{cases}$

By similar arguments

(1.4) $\int_{-\pi}^{\pi} \sin nx \sin mx \, dx = \begin{cases} \pi & \text{if } n = m \\ 0 & \text{if } n \neq m, \end{cases}$

(1.5) $\int_{-\pi}^{\pi} \sin nx \cos mx \, dx = 0,$

and

(1.6) $\int_{-\pi}^{\pi} \sin nx \, dx = \int_{-\pi}^{\pi} \cos mx \, dx = 0,$

for $n, m = 1, 2, 3, \ldots$.

To determine a_0 we integrate (1.1) from $-\pi$ to π and use (1.6). This gives

(1.7) $\int_{-\pi}^{\pi} f(x) \, dx = \int_{-\pi}^{\pi} \left(\frac{a_0}{2} + \sum_{n=1}^{\infty} (a_n \cos nx + b_n \sin nx)\right) dx$

$$= \int_{-\pi}^{\pi} \frac{a_0}{2} \, dx + \sum_{n=1}^{\infty} \left(a_n \int_{-\pi}^{\pi} \cos nx \, dx + b_n \int_{-\pi}^{\pi} \sin nx \, dx\right)$$

$$= \pi a_0.$$

To find a_m for $m \geq 1$, multiply (1.1) by cos mx, integrate from $-\pi$ to π, and use (1.3), (1.5), and (1.6). The result is

$$(1.8) \quad \int_{-\pi}^{\pi} f(x) \cos mx \, dx = \int_{-\pi}^{\pi} \left[\frac{a_0}{2} + \sum_{n=1}^{\infty} (a_n \cos nx + b_n \sin nx) \right] \cos mx \, dx$$

$$= a_m \int_{-\pi}^{\pi} \cos^2 mx \, dx = a_m \pi.$$

From (1.7) and (1.8) we see that

$$(1.9) \qquad\qquad a_n = \frac{1}{\pi} \int_{-\pi}^{\pi} f(x) \cos nx \, dx, \qquad n = 0, 1, 2, \ldots.$$

Similarly, multiplying (1.1) by sin nx and integrating gives

$$(1.10) \qquad\qquad b_n = \frac{1}{\pi} \int_{-\pi}^{\pi} f(x) \sin nx \, dx, \qquad n = 1, 2, 3, \ldots.$$

The coefficients a_n and b_n are called the **Fourier coefficients** of $f(x)$. Formulas (1.9) and (1.10) are the **Euler–Fourier formulas** for these coefficients. The resulting trigonometric series is called the **Fourier series** for $f(x)$. We write

$$(1.11) \qquad\qquad f(x) \sim \frac{a_0}{2} + \sum_{n=1}^{\infty} (a_n \cos nx + b_n \sin nx)$$

to denote the fact that $f(x)$ has the given Fourier series expansion. Notice that each term in the series on the right in (1.11) is 2π-periodic [i.e., cos $n(x + 2\pi) = $ cos nx and sin $n(x + 2\pi) = $ sin nx]. Hence the series must be 2π-periodic. If the series is to represent the function f, then f must also be 2π-periodic, that is, $f(x + 2\pi) = f(x)$. Henceforth, given a function $f(x)$ defined on $-\pi < x \leq \pi$, we shall *require* that $f(x)$ is defined outside of this basic interval in such a way that $f(x + 2\pi) = f(x)$ for all real numbers x.

EXAMPLE 1.1   Find the Fourier series for the function $f(x) = x$, $-\pi < x \leq \pi$.
     The Euler–Fourier formulas yield

$$a_0 = \frac{1}{\pi} \int_{-\pi}^{\pi} x \, dx = 0.$$

For $n \geq 1$ we integrate by parts to compute

$$a_n = \frac{1}{\pi} \int_{-\pi}^{\pi} x \cos nx \, dx$$

$$= \frac{1}{\pi} \left[x \frac{\sin nx}{n} \bigg|_{-\pi}^{\pi} - \frac{1}{n} \int_{-\pi}^{\pi} \sin nx \, dx \right] = 0$$

and

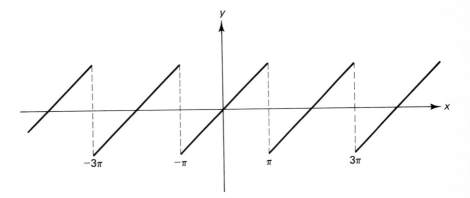

Figure 10.1. Periodic extension of $f(x) = x$.

$$b_n = \frac{1}{\pi} \int_{-\pi}^{\pi} x \sin nx\, dx$$

$$= \frac{1}{\pi} \left[-x \frac{\cos nx}{n} \Big|_{-\pi}^{\pi} + \frac{1}{n} \int_{-\pi}^{\pi} \cos nx\, dx \right]$$

$$= -\frac{2}{n} \cos n\pi = \left(-\frac{2}{n} \right) (-1)^n = \frac{2}{n} (-1)^{n+1}.$$

Hence, on $-\pi < x \le \pi$,

(1.12) $x \sim 2(\sin x - \tfrac{1}{2} \sin 2x + \tfrac{1}{3} \sin 3x - \tfrac{1}{4} \sin 4x + \ldots).$

The series (1.12) is the Fourier series of the function x in the interval $-\pi < x \le \pi$. At points outside $(-\pi, \pi)$ it is the Fourier series of the function obtained by extending x periodically with period 2π. This function is graphed in Figure 10.1 ∎

It can be shown that the series (1.12) will converge to $f(x) = x$ at all points x in the interval $-\pi < x < \pi$. It does not converge to $f(x)$ at $x = \pi$. Indeed, $\sin n\pi = 0$ for all integers n. Thus the series converges to zero there. Hence it would seem more natural to define $f(\pi) = 0$. Changing the definition of any function f at $x = \pi$ (or at any other single point) will not affect the integrals (1.9) and (1.10). The resulting function will have the same Fourier series. If the function $f(x)$ represents a signal, the value of $f(x)$ at any single point x_0 (or any finite set of points) is not usually physically significant. If the value of $f(x)$ were changed at a finite set of points on $(-\pi, \pi)$, then from an engineering point of view the new function would still represent the same signal. Similarly, if $f(x)$ is used as the forcing function for a differential equation (as in Section 10.8), then changing the value of $f(x)$ at a finite set of points will be seen not to cause any change in the solution of the differential equation. Hence in this chapter we shall feel free to change $f(x)$ at a point or leave $f(x)$ undefined at a point (or at a finite set of points) on $(-\pi, \pi)$ whenever this is convenient. Such changes will not change the Fourier series of f and are usually physically unimportant.

Let $f(x)$ be defined on $-\infty < x < \infty$. We say that f is **piecewise continuous** if on any finite interval $A \le x \le B$ f is continuous except possibly at a finite set of points x_j. At these points x_j we require that the one-sided limits

$$f(x_j^-) = \lim_{x \to x_j^-} f(x), \qquad f(x_j^+) = \lim_{x \to x_j^+} f(x)$$

exist and are finite. We do not require that the limits $f(x_j^-)$ and $f(x_j^+)$ be equal. When they are not equal we say that f has a **jump discontinuity** at x_j. For example, the function graphed in Figure 10.1 is piecewise continuous. It has jump discontinuities at the points $n\pi$ with n odd. Any continuous function f is automatically piecewise continuous. For example, $f(x) = \cos \alpha x$ and $g(x) = \sin \alpha x$ are piecewise continuous.

A function $f(x)$ defined on $-\infty < x < \infty$ is said to be **of class** D if it is piecewise continuous and if between consecutive jump discontinuities x_j and x_{j+1} the function $f'(x)$ exists and is continuous while

$$\lim_{u \to 0^+} \frac{f(x_j + u) - f(x_j^+)}{u} \quad \text{and} \quad \lim_{u \to 0^-} \frac{f(x_{j+1} + u) - f(x_{j+1}^-)}{u}$$

both exist and are finite.

EXAMPLE 1.2   Define $f(x) = x$ over $0 \le x \le \pi$ and $f(x) = -\pi$ over $-\pi < x < 0$. Extend f 2π-periodically. The resulting function is graphed in Figure 10.2. We shall show that this function is of class D.

The function f is clearly piecewise continuous with jump discontinuities at $x = n\pi$ for $n = 0, \pm 1, \pm 2, \ldots$. In the interval $(x_j, x_{j+1}) = (0, \pi)$, $f'(x) = 1$ is continuous and

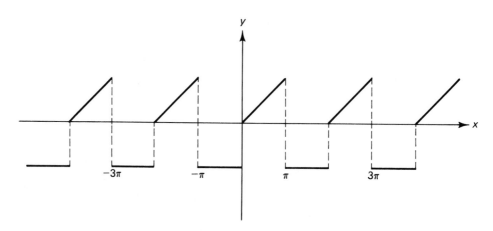

Figure 10.2. A function of class D.

$$\lim_{u \to 0^+} \frac{f(x_j + u) - f(x_j^+)}{u} = \lim_{u \to 0^+} \frac{f(u) - f(0^+)}{u}$$

$$= \lim_{u \to 0^+} \frac{u - 0}{u} = 1.$$

Similarly,

$$\lim_{u \to 0^-} \frac{f(x_{j+1} + u) - f(x_{j+1}^-)}{u} = \lim_{u \to 0^-} \frac{f(\pi + u) - f(\pi^-)}{u}$$

$$= \lim_{u \to 0^-} \frac{(u + \pi) - \pi}{u} = 1.$$

The same or a similar argument works on any interval $(n\pi, (n + 1)\pi)$. Hence f is of class D. ∎

The following result is proved in Section 10.5.

THEOREM 1.3: A RESULT OF DIRICHLET

If f is a 2π-periodic function of class D, then for any real number x the Fourier series for f converges to $\frac{1}{2}[f(x^+) + f(x^-)]$ at jump discontinuities and to $f(x)$ at points x where f is continuous.

EXAMPLE 1.4 Let $f(x) = x$ on $-\pi < x \le \pi$ and $f(x + 2\pi) = f(x)$ (see Figure 10.1). This function f is of class D. According to Theorem 1.3, the Fourier series (1.12) converges to zero when $x = n\pi$ for any odd integer n and to $f(x)$ when $x \ne n\pi$.

For $-\pi < x < \pi$ define

$$s_1(x) = 2 \sin x,$$

$$s_2(x) = 2 \sin x - \sin 2x,$$

$$s_3(x) = 2 \sin x - \sin 2x + \tfrac{2}{3} \sin 3x,$$

and in general

$$s_N(x) = 2 \sum_{n=1}^{N} \frac{(-1)^{n+1}}{n} \sin nx.$$

Then $s_N(x)$ should approximate x in the interval $(-\pi, \pi)$ when N is large. ∎

Figure 10.3 shows how $s_N(x)$ approximates $f(x)$ when $N = 4$ and $N = 10$. Notice that $s_{10}(x)$ is a better approximation than $s_4(x)$ over most of the interval, but neither function approximates very well near the points of discontinuity. Near the discontinuity $s_N(x)$ will sharply peak above $f(x)$ and then go down

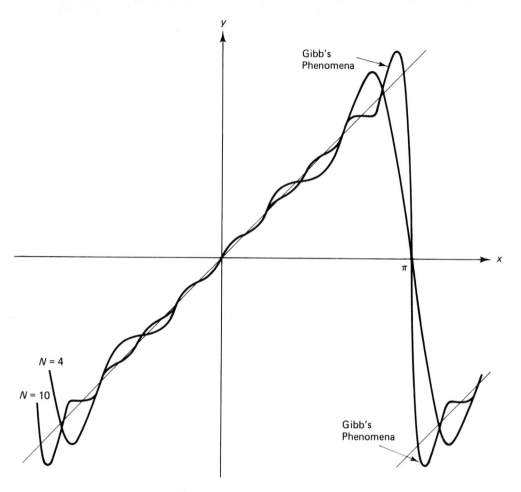

Figure 10.3. $s_4(x)$ and $s_{10}(x)$ approximations.

too far to a negative peak below $f(x)$. Such undesirable peaking near a discontinuity is typical of Fourier series approximations. The term **Gibb's phenomenon** is used to describe this peaking.

EXAMPLE 1.5   Let $f(x) = x$ on $0 \leq x \leq \pi$, $f(x) = -\pi$ on $-\pi < x < 0$, and $f(x + 2\pi) = f(x)$. It was shown in Example 1.2 that this f is of class D. The Fourier coefficients for f are computed as follows. For $n = 0$

$$a_0 = \frac{1}{\pi} \int_{-\pi}^{\pi} f(x)\, dx = \frac{1}{\pi} \int_{-\pi}^{0} f(x)\, dx + \frac{1}{\pi} \int_{0}^{\pi} f(x)\, dx$$

$$= \frac{1}{\pi} \int_{-\pi}^{0} (-\pi)\, dx + \frac{1}{\pi} \int_{0}^{\pi} x\, dx = -\frac{\pi}{2},$$

and for $n \geq 1$

$$a_n = \frac{1}{\pi} \int_{-\pi}^{\pi} f(x) \cos nx \, dx$$

$$= \frac{1}{\pi} \int_{-\pi}^{0} (-\pi) \cos nx \, dx + \frac{1}{\pi} \int_{0}^{\pi} x \cos nx \, dx.$$

The first integral is zero. Using integration by parts on the second integral, we see that

$$a_n = 0 + \frac{1}{\pi} \int_{0}^{\pi} x \cos nx \, dx$$

$$= \frac{1}{\pi} \left[x \frac{\sin nx}{n} \Big|_{0}^{\pi} - \int_{0}^{\pi} \frac{\sin nx}{n} \, dx \right]$$

$$= \frac{1}{\pi} \frac{\cos n\pi - 1}{n^2} = \frac{1}{n^2 \pi} ((-1)^n - 1).$$

Similarly,

$$b_n = \frac{1}{\pi} \int_{-\pi}^{\pi} f(x) \sin nx \, dx$$

$$= \frac{1}{\pi} \int_{-\pi}^{0} (-\pi) \sin nx \, dx + \frac{1}{\pi} \int_{0}^{\pi} x \sin nx \, dx$$

$$= \frac{1 - \cos n\pi}{n} - \frac{\cos n\pi}{n} = \frac{1}{n} (1 - 2(-1)^n).$$

Thus

$$(1.13) \qquad f(x) \sim -\frac{\pi}{4} + \sum_{n=1}^{\infty} \left[\frac{(-1)^n - 1}{n^2 \pi} \cos nx + \frac{1 - 2(-1)^n}{n} \sin nx \right]$$

$$= -\frac{\pi}{4} + \left(-\frac{2}{\pi} \cos x + 3 \sin x \right) - \frac{1}{2} \sin 2x$$

$$+ \left(-\frac{2}{9\pi} \cos 3x + \sin 3x \right) - \frac{1}{4} \sin 4x + \dots .$$

The series converges to $f(x)$ when $x \neq n\pi$. If $x = 0$, the series converges to

$$\frac{f(x^+) + f(x^-)}{2} = \frac{0 + (-\pi)}{2} = -\frac{\pi}{2}.$$

Hence

$$-\frac{\pi}{2} = -\frac{\pi}{4} + \sum_{n=1}^{\infty} \frac{1}{n^2 \pi} ((-1)^n - 1)$$

$$= -\frac{\pi}{4} - \frac{2}{\pi} \left(1 + \frac{1}{9} + \frac{1}{25} + \dots \right).$$

By rearranging we obtain the interesting result that

$$\frac{\pi^2}{8} = 1 + \frac{1}{9} + \frac{1}{25} + \ldots = \sum_{k=1}^{\infty} \frac{1}{(2k-1)^2}. \quad \blacksquare$$

Fourier series are used in electronics to represent periodic signals $f(x)$. The *n*th harmonic component of the signal $f(x)$ in (1.11) is

(1.14) $a_n \cos nx + b_n \sin nx.$

The *power* in the *n*th component is $\sqrt{2\pi}(a_n^2 + b_n^2)$. The power in such a component can easily be determined using an oscilloscope such as that in Photo 21. Undergraduate students who take electronics labs will probably do this and related oscilloscope experiments.

Engineers often build devices that will process signals $f(x)$. Typically, this processing attempts to preserve or to amplify certain desirable components of $f(x)$ while eliminating (or at least minimizing) certain undesirable components. It is necessary to understand the theory of Fourier series in order to understand how such devices are designed.

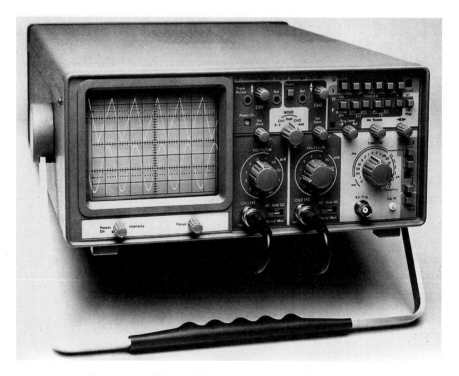

Photo 21. A digital oscilloscope. (Courtesy of Gould, Inc.)

PROBLEMS   In Problems 1–9, compute the Fourier series of the given function f. Verify that each function is of class D and determine at which points x the Fourier series converges of $f(x)$.

1. $f(x) = \begin{cases} 1 & \text{on } -\pi < x \le 0 \\ -1 & \text{on } 0 < x \le \pi. \end{cases}$ **2.** $f(x) = \begin{cases} 0 & \text{on } -\pi < x \le 0 \\ \pi & \text{on } 0 < x \le \pi. \end{cases}$

3. $f(x) = \begin{cases} 0 & \text{on } -\pi < x < 0 \\ x & \text{on } 0 \le x \le \pi. \end{cases}$ **4.** $f(x) = \begin{cases} x & \text{on } -\pi < x \le 0 \\ 1 & \text{on } 0 < x \le \pi. \end{cases}$

5. $f(x) = \begin{cases} 0 & \text{on } -\pi < x \le 0 \\ \sin x & \text{on } 0 < x \le \pi. \end{cases}$

6. $f(x) = 1 + 2 \sin 2x - \cos x$. *Hint:* Most of the Fourier coefficients are zero!

7. $f(x) = \pi + \sum\limits_{n=1}^{10} \dfrac{1}{n} \sin nx$.

8. $f(x) = \sin^2 x$. *Hint:* First use a trig identity.

9. $f(x) = \begin{cases} -1 & \text{on } -\pi < x < 0 \\ 1 & \text{on } 0 < x < \pi \\ 0 & \text{at } x = 0 \text{ and } x = \pi. \end{cases}$

   Hint: See Problem 1.

10. (a) Show that the series

$$\sum_{n=1}^{\infty} \left(\frac{1}{n^2} \cos nx + \frac{(-1)^n}{n^3} \sin nx \right)$$

   converges at each $x \in (-\pi, \pi]$. Let $g(x)$ be the function to which the series converges.

   (b) Compute the Fourier series of $g(x)$.

11. Compute the Fourier series for $f(x) = x^2$, $-\pi < x \le \pi$. Use this Fourier series and Theorem 1.3 to compute the numerical value of the sum

$$1 - \frac{1}{4} + \frac{1}{9} - \frac{1}{16} + \ldots = \sum_{n=1}^{\infty} \frac{(-1)^{n+1}}{n^2}.$$

12. Use the Fourier series for $f(x) = x$, $-\pi < x \le \pi$ and Theorem 1.3 to compute the numerical value of the sum

$$1 - \frac{1}{3} + \frac{1}{5} - \frac{1}{9} + \ldots = \sum_{n=1}^{\infty} \frac{(-1)^{n+1}}{(2n-1)}.$$

13. Let $f(x)$ be a 2π-periodic and piecewise continuous function with Fourier series (1.11).

   (a) Show that for any real number A

$$\int_A^{A+2\pi} f(x)\, dx = \int_{-\pi}^{\pi} f(x)\, dx.$$

   (b) Show that for any real number A

$$a_n = \frac{1}{\pi} \int_A^{A+2\pi} f(x) \cos nx\, dx$$

and

$$b_n = \frac{1}{\pi} \int_A^{A+2\pi} f(x) \sin nx \, dx.$$

14. Let $f(x) = x$ on $0 \le x < 2\pi$ and $f(x + 2\pi) = f(x)$.

(a) Graph $f(x)$ over $-4\pi \le x \le 6\pi$.

(b) Compute the Fourier series for f (use Problem 13 with $A = 0$).

15. Let $f(x) = x^2$ on $0 \le x < 2\pi$ and $f(x + 2\pi) = f(x)$.

(a) Graph $f(x)$ over $-4\pi \le x \le 6\pi$.

(b) Compute the Fourier series for f (use Problem 13).

10.2 *SINE AND COSINE SERIES*

For certain special classes of functions it is possible to show that many of the Fourier coefficients are always zero. This is useful information since the Fourier coefficients that are known to be zero need not be computed. The purpose of this section is to investigate two important classes of such functions.

Let $f(x)$ be a real-valued function defined over an interval $-\infty < x < \infty$. We say that $f(x)$ is **odd** if

$$f(-x) = -f(x)$$

and that $f(x)$ is **even** if

$$f(-x) = f(x)$$

for all x on $0 \le x < \infty$. For example, x, x^3, and $\sin \alpha x$ are odd, while 1, x^2, and $\cos \alpha x$ are even. The graph of an odd function is symmetric with respect to the origin. The graph of an even function is symmetric with respect to the y-axis.

If $f(x)$ is odd, then for any $A > 0$

$$\int_{-A}^{A} f(x) \, dx = \int_0^A f(x) \, dx + \int_{-A}^0 f(x) \, dx.$$

Let $s = -x$ in the second integral. Since f is odd, then

$$\int_{-A}^0 f(x) \, dx = \int_A^0 f(-s)(-ds) = \int_0^A f(-s) \, ds$$

$$= -\int_0^A f(s) \, ds = -\int_0^A f(x) \, dx.$$

Hence if f is odd, then for any $A > 0$

(2.1)
$$\int_{-A}^{A} f(x) \, dx = \int_0^A f(x) \, dx - \int_0^A f(x) \, dx = 0.$$

When $f(x)$ is even, then by a similar calculation

$$\int_{-A}^{A} f(x)\,dx = \int_{0}^{A} f(x)\,dx + \int_{-A}^{0} f(x)\,dx$$

$$= \int_{0}^{A} f(x)\,dx + \int_{0}^{A} f(-s)\,ds$$

$$= \int_{0}^{A} f(x)\,dx + \int_{0}^{A} f(s)\,ds$$

Hence if f is even, then for any $A > 0$

(2.2)
$$\int_{-A}^{A} f(x)\,dx = 2 \int_{0}^{A} f(x)\,dx.$$

If $f(x)$ and $g(x)$ are both odd, then

$$f(-x)g(-x) = (-f(x))(-g(x)) = (-1)^2 f(x)g(x) = f(x)g(x).$$

Thus we see that the product of two odd functions is an even function. By similar calculations one can prove that odd times even is odd and even times even is even. These facts will be useful in proving the next theorem.

THEOREM 2.1: FOURIER SINE AND COSINE SERIES

Let $f(x)$ be a 2π-periodic piecewise continuous function. If f is odd, then its Fourier series has only sine terms. The Fourier coefficients are given by

(2.3)
$$a_n = 0, \qquad b_m = \frac{2}{\pi} \int_{0}^{\pi} f(x) \sin mx\,dx$$

for $n = 0, 1, 2, \ldots$ and $m = 1, 2, 3, \ldots$.

If $f(x)$ is even, its Fourier series has only cosine terms. The Fourier coefficients are given by the formulas

(2.4)
$$a_n = \frac{2}{\pi} \int_{0}^{\pi} f(x) \cos nx\,dx, \qquad b_m = 0$$

for $n = 0, 1, 2, \ldots$ and $m = 1, 2, 3, \ldots$.

To see that the theorem is true suppose that f is odd. Since $\cos nx$ is even, the product $f(x) \cos nx$ is odd and by (2.1)

$$a_n = \frac{1}{\pi} \int_{-\pi}^{\pi} f(x) \cos nx\,dx = 0.$$

Similarly, $f(x) \sin mx$ is even. By (2.2)

$$b_m = \frac{1}{\pi} \int_{-\pi}^{\pi} f(x) \sin mx\,dx = \frac{2}{\pi} \int_{0}^{\pi} f(x) \sin mx\,dx.$$

A similar proof works when $f(x)$ is even.

EXAMPLE 2.2   Let $f(x) = x$ on $-\pi < x < \pi$ and $f(\pi) = 0$. Then f (extended to be 2π-periodic) is odd. Its Fourier coefficients satisfy $a_n = 0$ and

$$b_n = \frac{2}{\pi} \int_0^\pi x \sin nx \, dx = \frac{2}{n}(-1)^{n+1}.$$

This series agrees with the one computed in Section 10.1.   ∎

EXAMPLE 2.3   Define $f(x) = 0$ on $-\pi/2 < x < \pi/2$ and $f(x) = 1$ on $-\pi < x < -\pi/2$ or $\pi/2 < x < \pi$. Let $f(\pm\pi/2) = 1/2$ and $f(x + 2\pi) = f(x)$. The resulting function, graphed in Figure 10.4, is clearly even. Hence $b_n = 0$ for all $n \geq 1$,

$$a_0 = \frac{2}{\pi} \int_0^\pi f(x) \, dx = \frac{2}{\pi} \int_{\pi/2}^\pi dx = 1$$

and

$$a_n = \frac{2}{\pi} \int_0^\pi f(x) \cos nx \, dx = \frac{2}{\pi} \int_{\pi/2}^\pi \cos nx \, dx$$

$$= \frac{2}{n\pi}\left(-\sin\frac{n\pi}{2}\right).$$

The resulting Fourier series is

$$f(x) \sim \frac{1}{2} + \frac{2}{\pi}\left(-\cos x + \frac{\cos 3x}{3} - \frac{\cos 5x}{5} + \cdots\right)$$

$$= \frac{1}{2} + \frac{2}{\pi}\sum_{k=1}^\infty \frac{(-1)^k}{2k - 1}\cos(2k - 1)x.   ∎$$

When $a_n = 0$ for all n, the resulting Fourier series is called a **Fourier sine series**. If $b_n = 0$ for n, the series is called a **Fourier cosine series**. A series that contains both sine and cosine terms is sometimes called a **full Fourier series**, to distinguish it from a sine or cosine series.

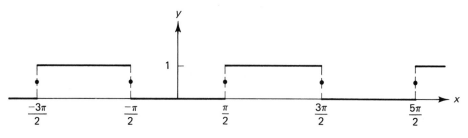

Figure 10.4. A square wave.

In many situations a function $f(x)$ is initially given only over an interval $0 < x < \pi$. This function can be extended in various ways to $-\pi < x < 0$. For example, if $f(x)$ is extended as an even function [i.e., $f(x) = f(-x)$ on $-\pi < x < 0$], then f will have a Fourier cosine series. On the other hand, an odd extension of f would yield a Fourier sine series. Either Fourier series would represent the original function over the original interval $(0, \pi)$.

EXAMPLE 2.4   Find a Fourier cosine series representation for the function $f(x) = x$, $0 < x < \pi$.

The function must be extended evenly over $-\pi < x < 0$. Hence $f(x) = -x = |x|$ on $-\pi \le x \le 0$. The resulting function is now extended periodically. This function is the sawtooth function depicted in Figure 10.5. The Fourier coefficients for this function satisfy $b_n = 0$,

$$a_0 = \frac{2}{\pi} \int_0^\pi x \, dx = \pi$$

and

$$a_n = \frac{2}{\pi} \int_0^\pi x \cos nx \, dx = \frac{2}{n^2 \pi} (\cos n\pi - 1)$$

$$= \frac{2}{n^2 \pi} ((-1)^n - 1).$$

Hence

$$f(x) \sim \frac{\pi}{2} - \frac{4}{\pi} \left(\cos x + \frac{1}{9} \cos 3x + \frac{1}{25} \cos 5x + \ldots \right). \quad \blacksquare$$

On the other hand, to obtain a sine series representation for the function $f(x) = x$, $0 < x < \pi$, we must extend f as an odd function, that is, $f(x) = x$ on $-\pi < x < 0$ and then $f(x + 2\pi) = f(x)$. (We will take $f(0) = f(\pi) = 0$.) The resulting function is graphed in Figure 10.1. Its Fourier series is (1.12). The functions depicted in Figures 10.1 and 10.5 are equal over $0 < x < \pi$ but are quite different overall.

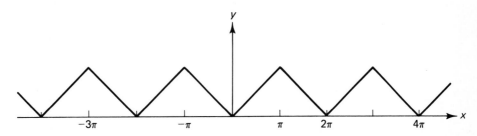

Figure 10.5. A sawtooth wave.

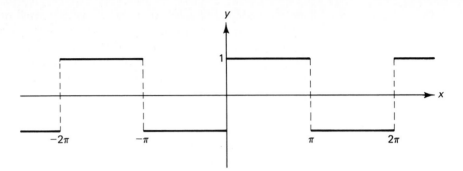

Figure 10.6. A square wave.

EXAMPLE 2.5   Find a Fourier sine series representation for the function $f(x) = 1$ on $0 < x < \pi$.
We extend f as an odd function, that is, $f(x) = -1$ on $-\pi < x < 0$, then
$f(0) = f(\pi) = 0$ and then $f(x + 2\pi) = f(x)$. The resulting function is the square
wave graphed in Figure 10.6. Since f is odd, then $a_n = 0$ for $n \geq 0$ while

$$b_n = \frac{2}{\pi} \int_0^\pi \sin nx \, dx = \frac{2}{n\pi}[-\cos n\pi + 1]$$

$$= \frac{2}{n\pi}[1 - (-1)^n].$$

Hence

$$f(x) \sim \frac{4}{\pi}\left(\sin x + \frac{1}{3}\sin 3x + \frac{1}{5}\sin 5x + \ldots\right)$$

$$= \frac{4}{\pi}\sum_{k=1}^{\infty}\frac{1}{2k-1}\sin(2k-1)x. \quad \blacksquare$$

PROBLEMS

1. Let $f(x) = 1$ on $0 < x < \pi$. Extend f as an even function over $(-\pi, 0)$ and then
2π-periodically. Graph the resulting function and compare this graph with Figure
10.6. What is the Fourier series for this function? What is a good way to define
$f(0)$ and $f(\pi)$?

2. Let $f(x) = x^2$ on $0 < x < \pi$.

   (a) Find a Fourier cosine-series representation for this function. Graph over $-3\pi <$
   $x < 5\pi$ the 2π-periodic function represented by this cosine series.

   (b) Find a Fourier sine series representation for this function. Graph over $-3\pi <$
   $x < 5\pi$ the 2π-periodic function represented by this sine series.

   (c) Using the Fourier series from part (a), compute the sum $\sum_{n=1}^{\infty}(-1)^{n+1}/n^2$.

3. Find a Fourier sine series for the function $f(x) = \cos x$, $0 < x < \pi$. Graph over $-3\pi < x < 5\pi$ the 2π-periodic function represented by this series. What is the natural way to define f at $x = 0$ and π?

4. Let $f(x) = \sin x$ on $0 < x < \pi$. Find the Fourier cosine series representation for f. Show that this series represents the 2π-periodic function $F(x) = |\sin x|$.

5. Let $f(x)$ be a 2π-periodic function such that

$$f(x) = \begin{cases} 1 & \text{on } 0 < x < \dfrac{\pi}{2} \\[2mm] 0 & \text{on } \dfrac{\pi}{2} < x < \dfrac{3\pi}{2}, \\[2mm] -1 & \text{on } \dfrac{3\pi}{2} < x < 2\pi. \end{cases} \quad f(0) = 0, \quad f\left(\dfrac{\pi}{2}\right) = \dfrac{1}{2}, \quad f\left(\dfrac{3\pi}{2}\right) = -\dfrac{1}{2}$$

(a) Show that $f(x)$ is odd.

(b) Find the Fourier series for f.

6. Let f be the 2π-periodic function such that

$$f(x) = \begin{cases} 0 & \text{on } 0 < x < \dfrac{\pi}{2} \\[2mm] 1 & \text{on } \dfrac{\pi}{2} < x < \dfrac{3\pi}{2} \\[2mm] 0 & \text{on } \dfrac{3\pi}{2} < x < 2\pi. \end{cases}$$

(a) Show that $f(x)$ is even. (How should one define f at 0, $\pi/2$, and $3\pi/2$?)

(b) Find the Fourier series for f.

7. Suppose that $f(x)$ is 2π-periodic and also satisfies

$$f(x + \pi) = -f(x).$$

(a) Show that the Fourier coefficients a_n and b_n are zero whenever n is even.

(b) Show that whenever n is odd, then

$$a_n = \frac{2}{\pi} \int_0^\pi f(x) \cos nx \, dx, \qquad b_n = \frac{2}{\pi} \int_0^\pi f(x) \sin nx \, dx.$$

(c) Show that the square wave depicted in Figure 10.6 satisfies the property $f(x + \pi) = -f(x)$.

8. Suppose that f is a function of class D such that

$$f(x) \sim b_1 \sin x + b_3 \sin 3x + b_5 \sin 5x + \ldots.$$

(a) Show that $f(x)$ is odd.

(b) Show that $f(x + \pi) = -f(x)$. *Hint:* Use Theorem 1.3.

9. Let $g(x) = x^2$ on $0 \le x < \pi$, $g(x) = -(x - \pi)^2$ on $\pi \le x < 2\pi$ and $g(x + 2\pi) = g(x)$. Compute the Fourier series for g. Graph $g(x)$ over $-3\pi < x < 5\pi$.

10. Let $n(y)$ be a continuous and odd function.

   (a) Show that $f(x) = n(\sin x)$ is odd.

   (b) Show that $f(x + \pi) = -f(x)$.

   (c) What form will the Fourier series for f take?

11. In Problem 10, let $n(y) = 0$ on $0 \le y \le \frac{1}{2}$ and $n(y) = 2y - 1$ if $y > \frac{1}{2}$.

   (a) Graph $f(x) = n(\sin x)$ over $-3\pi < x < 5\pi$.

   (b) Compute the Fourier series for f.

10.3 ARBITRARY PERIODS

We wish to extend the notion of Fourier series from 2π-periodic functions to periodic functions with arbitrary periods. Recall that a function f defined over $-\infty < x < \infty$ is T-**periodic** when $f(x + T) = f(x)$ for all x. We shall set $T = 2c$ and work with $f(x)$ on the interval $-c < x < c$. To obtain a Fourier series for f we change variables to $t = \pi x/c$ and let $F(t) = f(ct/\pi)$. The function F is 2π-periodic in t. Hence F has Fourier series

$$F(t) = f\left(\frac{ct}{\pi}\right) \sim \frac{a_0}{2} + \sum_{n=1}^{\infty} (a_n \cos nt + b_n \sin nt).$$

Since $ct/\pi = x$, this means that

(3.1) $$f(x) \sim \frac{a_0}{2} + \sum_{n=1}^{\infty} a_n \cos\left(\frac{n\pi x}{c}\right) + b_n \sin\left(\frac{n\pi x}{c}\right).$$

Moreover, by the change of variables $x = ct/\pi$ we see that

(3.2) $$a_n = \frac{1}{\pi} \int_{-\pi}^{\pi} f\left(\frac{ct}{\pi}\right) \cos nt \, dt = \frac{1}{c} \int_{-c}^{c} f(x) \cos\left(\frac{n\pi x}{c}\right) dx.$$

Similarly,

(3.3) $$b_n = \frac{1}{c} \int_{-c}^{c} f(x) \sin\left(\frac{n\pi x}{c}\right) dx.$$

EXAMPLE 3.1   Find the Fourier series for $f(x)$ when

$$f(x) = \begin{cases} 0 & \text{on } -2 \le x < 0 \\ x & \text{on } \ \ 0 \le x < 2. \end{cases}$$

In this case $c = 2$ (and $T = 4$) while

$$a_0 = \frac{1}{2} \int_{-2}^{2} f(x)\, dx = \frac{1}{2} \int_0^2 x\, dx = 1,$$

$$a_n = \frac{1}{2} \int_{-2}^{2} f(x) \cos\left(\frac{n\pi x}{2}\right) dx = \frac{1}{2} \int_0^2 x \cos\left(\frac{n\pi x}{2}\right) dx$$

$$= \frac{1}{2}\left[\frac{2x}{n\pi} \sin\left(\frac{n\pi x}{2}\right)\Big|_0^2 - \int_0^2 \frac{2}{n\pi} \sin\left(\frac{n\pi x}{2}\right) dx \right]$$

$$= \frac{1}{2}\left(\frac{2}{n\pi}\right)^2 (\cos n\pi - 1) = \frac{2}{n^2\pi^2}((-1)^n - 1),$$

and

$$b_n = \frac{1}{2} \int_{-2}^{2} f(x) \sin\left(\frac{n\pi x}{2}\right) dx = \frac{1}{2} \int_0^2 x \sin\left(\frac{n\pi x}{2}\right) dx$$

$$= -\frac{2 \cos n\pi}{n\pi} = \frac{2}{n\pi}(-1)^{n+1}.$$

Hence

$$f(x) \sim \frac{1}{2} + \sum_{n=1}^{\infty} \left(\frac{2}{n^2\pi^2}((-1)^n - 1) \cos\left(\frac{n\pi x}{2}\right) + \frac{2}{n\pi}(-1)^{n+1} \sin\left(\frac{n\pi x}{2}\right) \right). \quad \blacksquare$$

If $f(x)$ is $2c$-periodic and even, its Fourier series is a cosine series. Then $b_n = 0$ for $n \geq 1$ and

$$a_n = \frac{2}{c} \int_0^c f(x) \cos\left(\frac{n\pi x}{c}\right) dx, \qquad n \geq 0.$$

Similarly, if $f(x)$ is odd, its Fourier coefficients satisfy $a_n = 0$ for $n \geq 0$ and

$$b_n = \frac{2}{c} \int_0^c f(x) \sin\left(\frac{n\pi x}{c}\right) dx, \qquad n \geq 1.$$

EXAMPLE 3.2   Find the Fourier sine series for the function $f(x) = \pi$ on $0 < x < 1$.
We extend $f(x)$ odd to $-1 < x < 0$ and then periodically of period 2. Thus $a_n = 0$ for all n and

$$b_n = \frac{2}{1} \int_0^1 \pi \sin n\pi x\, dx = -\frac{2}{n}(\cos n\pi - 1)$$

$$= \frac{2}{n}(1 - (-1)^n).$$

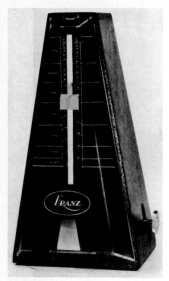

The required Fourier series is

$$f(x) \sim 4\left(\sin \pi x + \frac{1}{3}\sin 3\pi x + \frac{1}{5}\sin 5\pi x + \ldots\right)$$

$$= 4\sum_{k=1}^{\infty}\frac{1}{2k-1}\sin(2k-1)\pi x. \quad \blacksquare$$

Some Facts and Comments

A metronome (see Photo 22) is a mechanical device which can be used to generate an acoustical signal of any desired period, or equivalently desired frequency, within a wide range. The mass on the hinged front arm is adjusted up or down to select the desired frequency (measured in beats per minute). The device is powered by a keywound spring. Much more sophisticated electronic devices are now available for generating periodic signals of a given frequency. Such devices are used by engineers (and indeed by metronome manufacturers) in clocks, buzzers, metronomes, music and voice synthesizers, and so on.

Photo 22. A keywound metronome. (Courtesy of Franz Manufacturing Company, Inc.)

PROBLEMS

1. Find the Fourier series for each T-periodic function where $T = 2c$.

   (a) $f(x) = x$ over $-3 < x < 3$, $c = 3$.

   (b) $f(x) = |x|$ over $-\sqrt{2} < x < \sqrt{2}$, $c = \sqrt{2}$.

   (c) $f(x) = \begin{cases} 0 & \text{on } -1 < x < 0 \\ 1 & \text{on } \quad 0 < x < 1 \end{cases}$, $c = 1$.

   (d) $f(x) = \left|\sin \dfrac{\pi x}{2}\right|$ over $-2 < x < 2$, $c = 2$.

   (e) $f(x) = \cos x$ over $-\dfrac{\pi}{2} < x < \dfrac{\pi}{2}$, $c = \dfrac{\pi}{2}$.

   (f) $f(x) = 1 + 3\sin \pi x + \cos 2\pi x - \sin 3\pi x$, $-1 < x < 1$, $c = 1$.

   (g) $f(x) = \sin^2\left(\dfrac{\pi x}{\sqrt{3}}\right)$ over $-\sqrt{3} < x < \sqrt{3}$, $c = \sqrt{3}$.

2. Let f be the function defined by

$$f(x) = \begin{cases} 0 & \text{on } 0 < x < 1 \\ 1 & \text{on } 1 \leq x < 2. \end{cases}$$

   (a) Compute the Fourier sine series for f with $c = 2$.

   (b) Compute the Fourier cosine series for f with $c = 2$.

3. Let f be a T-periodic function of class D and let $T = 2c$.

(a) Using Theorem 1.3 show that the Fourier series for f converges to $[f(x^+) + f(x^-)]/2$ for each real number x.

(b) Show that each function in Problem 1 is of class D.

4. Suppose that f is a T-periodic function with $T = 2c$. Assume that $f(x + c) = -f(x)$ for all x.

(a) Show that the Fourier coefficients a_n and b_n are zero if n is even.

(b) Show that if n is odd, then

$$a_n = \frac{2}{c} \int_0^c f(x) \cos\left(\frac{n\pi x}{c}\right) dx, \quad \text{and} \quad b_n = \frac{2}{c} \int_0^c f(x) \sin\left(\frac{n\pi x}{c}\right) dx.$$

5. Let f be the function defined by

$$f(x) = \min\left\{1, 2\sin\frac{\pi x}{c}\right\}, \qquad 0 \le x < c$$

and $f(-x) = -f(x)$ on $-c < x < 0$.

(a) Show that f is odd.

(b) Show that $f(x + c) = -f(x)$ for all x.

(c) Compute the Fourier series for f.

6. If f is a T-periodic function with $T = 2c$, then f is said to have **frequency** $w = 2\pi/T = \pi/c$.

(a) Show that such a function has Fourier series

$$f(x) \sim \frac{a_0}{2} + \sum_{n=1}^{\infty} (a_n \cos nwx + b_n \sin nwx).$$

(b) Show that for $n \ge 1$.

$$a_n = \frac{w}{\pi} \int_{-\pi/w}^{\pi/w} f(x) \cos(nwx)\, dx.$$

(c) Find similar formulas for a_0 and for b_n.

7. Let $f(x)$ be T-periodic, where $T = 2c$.

(a) Show that for any real number A

$$\int_A^{A+T} f(x)\, dx = \int_0^T f(x)\, dx = \int_{-c}^c f(x)\, dx.$$

(b) Show that the Fourier coefficients for f satisfy

$$a_n = \frac{2}{T} \int_A^{T+A} f(x) \cos\left(\frac{2n\pi x}{T}\right) dx, \qquad n \ge 0$$

and

$$b_n = \frac{2}{T} \int_A^{T+A} f(x) \sin\left(\frac{2n\pi x}{T}\right) dx, \qquad n \ge 1.$$

8. Using Problem 7, compute the Fourier series for the T-periodic function that satisfies the condition given.

(a) $f(x) = x^2$ on $0 \leq x < 1$, $T = 1$.

(b) $f(x) = e^x$ on $0 \leq x < 2$, $T = 2$.

(c) $f(x) = x$ on $-1 \leq x < 3$, $T = 4$.

9. Suppose that $f(x)$ is a given T-periodic function.

(a) Show that f is (mT)-periodic for any positive integer m.

(b) Show that the Fourier expansions of f as a T-periodic function and as a $2T$-periodic function yield the same infinite series.

10.4   BESSEL'S INEQUALITY

Let $f(x)$ be a 2π-periodic, square-integrable function with

$$f(x) \sim \frac{a_0}{2} + \sum_{n=1}^{\infty} (a_n \cos nx + b_n \sin nx).$$

Define the partial sums $s_N(x)$ of the Fourier series by

$$s_N(x) = \frac{a_0}{2} + \sum_{n=1}^{N} (a_n \cos nx + b_n \sin nx).$$

Consider the nonnegative integral

$$(4.1) \qquad \int_{-\pi}^{\pi} [f(x) - s_N(x)]^2 \, dx = \int_{-\pi}^{\pi} f(x)^2 \, dx - 2 \int_{-\pi}^{\pi} f(x) s_N(x) \, dx$$

$$+ \int_{-\pi}^{\pi} s_N(x)^2 \, dx.$$

Using the relations (1.3)–(1.6), we see that

$$\int_{-\pi}^{\pi} s_N(x)^2 \, dx = \int_{-\pi}^{\pi} \left[\frac{a_0}{2} + \sum_{n=1}^{N} (a_n \cos nx + b_n \sin nx) \right]^2 dx$$

$$= \int_{-\pi}^{\pi} \left(\frac{a_0}{2} \right)^2 dx + \sum_{n=1}^{N} \left(a_n^2 \int_{-\pi}^{\pi} \cos^2 nx \, dx + b_n^2 \int_{-\pi}^{\pi} \sin^2 nx \, dx \right)$$

$$= \pi \left[\frac{a_0^2}{2} + \sum_{n=1}^{N} (a_n^2 + b_n^2) \right].$$

Moreover,

$$\int_{-\pi}^{\pi} f(x)s_N(x)\,dx = \int_{-\pi}^{\pi} f(x)\left[\frac{a_0}{2} + \sum_{n=1}^{N} a_n \cos nx + b_n \sin nx\right] dx$$

$$= \frac{a_0}{2} \int_{-\pi}^{\pi} f(x)\,dx$$

$$+ \sum_{n=1}^{N} \left(a_n \int_{-\pi}^{\pi} f(x) \cos nx\,dx + b_n \int_{-\pi}^{\pi} f(x) \sin nx\,dx\right)$$

$$= \pi\left[\frac{a_0^2}{2} + \sum_{n=1}^{N} (a_n^2 + b_n^2)\right].$$

Hence (4.1) reduces to

$$(4.2) \quad \int_{-\pi}^{\pi} [f(x) - s_n(x)]^2\,dx = \int_{-\pi}^{\pi} f(x)^2\,dx - 2\pi\left[\frac{a_0^2}{2} + \sum_{n=1}^{N} (a_n^2 + b_n^2)\right]$$

$$+ \pi\left[\frac{a_0^2}{2} + \sum_{n=1}^{N} (a_n^2 + b_n^2)\right]$$

$$= \int_{-\pi}^{\pi} f(x)^2\,dx - \pi\left[\frac{a_0^2}{2} + \sum_{n=1}^{N} (a_n^2 + b_n^2)\right].$$

Since the left side of (4.2) is nonnegative, then

$$(4.3) \qquad \pi\left[\frac{a_0^2}{2} + \sum_{n=1}^{N} (a_n^2 + b_n^2)\right] \le \int_{-\pi}^{\pi} f(x)^2\,dx.$$

Since (4.3) is true for any integer $N \ge 1$, it is also true in the limit as $N \to \infty$. This proves the following result.

THEOREM 4.1: BESSEL'S INEQUALITY

Let $f(x)$ be defined on $[-\pi, \pi]$ with $f(x)^2$ integrable there. If a_n and b_n are the Fourier coefficients for f, then

$$(4.4) \qquad \frac{a_0^2}{2} + \sum_{n=1}^{\infty} (a_n^2 + b_n^2) \le \frac{1}{\pi} \int_{-\pi}^{\pi} f(x)^2\,dx < \infty.$$

We notice that since the series in (4.4) is convergent, its nth term must go to zero, that is, $a_n^2 + b_n^2 \to 0$ as $n \to \infty$. Hence a_n and b_n must also tend to zero as $n \to \infty$. This proves the next result.

COROLLARY 4.2

Under the assumptions of Theorem 4.1

$$\lim_{n \to \infty} \int_{-\pi}^{\pi} f(x) \cos nx \, dx = \lim_{n \to \infty} \int_{-\pi}^{\pi} f(x) \sin nx \, dx = 0.$$

We say that $s_N(x)$ **converges to** $f(x)$ **in the mean** if

$$\lim_{N \to \infty} \int_{-\pi}^{\pi} [f(x) - s_N(x)]^2 \, dx = 0.$$

From (4.2) we see that $s_N(x)$ converges to $f(x)$ in the mean if and only if

(4.5)
$$\frac{1}{\pi} \int_{-\pi}^{\pi} f(x)^2 \, dx = \frac{a_0^2}{2} + \sum_{n=1}^{\infty} (a_n^2 + b_n^2).$$

The relation (4.5) is called **Parseval's equation.** It can be shown that Parseval's equation is true for any function $f(x)$ such that $f(x)^2$ is integrable over $[-\pi, \pi]$.

PROBLEMS

1. Let $f(x)$ be a function defined on $-c \leq x < c$ and square integrable there. Let a_n and b_n be the Fourier coefficients of f.

   (a) Show that

   $$\frac{a_0^2}{2} + \sum_{n=1}^{\infty} (a_n^2 + b_n^2) \leq \frac{1}{c} \int_{-c}^{c} f(x)^2 \, dx.$$

   (b) Show that

   $$\lim_{n \to \infty} \int_{-c}^{c} f(x) \cos \left(\frac{n\pi x}{c} \right) dx = \lim_{n \to \infty} \int_{-c}^{c} f(x) \sin \left(\frac{n\pi x}{c} \right) dx = 0.$$

   (c) Write out the Parseval equation for such a function f. What form does the Parseval equation take if f is odd? If f is even?

2. Use the Parseval equation and the series

   $$x \sim \sum_{n=1}^{\infty} \frac{2(-1)^{n+1}}{n} \sin nx, \qquad -\pi < x < \pi$$

   to evaluate the series $\sum_{n=1}^{\infty} 1/n^2$.

3. Use the Parseval relation and the series

   $$x^2 \sim \frac{\pi^2}{3} + 4 \sum_{n=1}^{\infty} \frac{(-1)^n}{n^2} \cos nx, \qquad -\pi < x < \pi$$

   to evaluate the series $\sum_{n=1}^{\infty} 1/n^4$.

4. Let $f(x) = \cos \alpha x$ on $-\pi < x < \pi$, where α is a fixed positive number.

(a) Show that

$$\cos \alpha x \sim \frac{\alpha \sin \pi \alpha}{\pi} \left(\frac{1}{\alpha^2} + \sum_{n=1}^{\infty} (-1)^n \frac{2}{\alpha^2 - n^2} \cos nx \right).$$

(b) Evaluate the series $\sum_{n=1}^{\infty} 1/(\alpha^2 - n^2)$. *Hint:* Set $x = \pi$ in the series in part (a).

(c) Evaluate the series $\sum_{n=1}^{\infty} (\alpha^2 - n^2)^{-2}$ by using the Parseval equation.

5. Verify directly that Corollary 4.2 is true when f is a continuous, 2π-periodic function whose derivative f' is also continuous. *Hint:* Integrate by parts.

10.5   CONVERGENCE OF FOURIER SERIES

Suppose that $f(x)$ is a 2π-periodic function of class D with

$$f(x) \sim \frac{a_0}{2} + \sum_{n=1}^{\infty} (a_n \cos nx + b_n \sin nx).$$

Let

$$s_N(x) = \frac{a_0}{2} + \sum_{n=1}^{N} (a_n \cos nx + b_n \sin nx)$$

be the Nth partial sum of the Fourier series for f. We wish to prove Theorem 1.3, that is, we wish to show that $s_N(x)$ converges to $[f(x^+) + f(x^-)]/2$ as $N \to \infty$. By the definition of the Fourier coefficients a_n and b_n we see that

$$s_N(x) = \frac{1}{2\pi} \int_{-\pi}^{\pi} f(t) \, dt + \sum_{n=1}^{N} \left[\frac{1}{\pi} \left(\int_{-\pi}^{\pi} f(t) \cos nt \, dt \right) \cos nx \right.$$

$$\left. + \frac{1}{\pi} \left(\int_{-\pi}^{\pi} f(t) \sin nt \, dt \right) \sin nx \right]$$

$$= \frac{1}{\pi} \int_{-\pi}^{\pi} f(t) \left[\frac{1}{2} + \sum_{n=1}^{N} \cos nt \cos nx + \sin nt \sin nx \right] dt$$

$$= \frac{1}{\pi} \int_{-\pi}^{\pi} f(t) \left[\frac{1}{2} + \sum_{n=1}^{N} \cos n(t - x) \right] dt$$

$$= \frac{1}{\pi} \int_{-\pi}^{\pi} f(t) K_N(t - x) \, dt,$$

where $K_N(t)$ is the **Dirichlet kernel** defined by the relation

$$K_N(t) = \frac{1}{2} + \sum_{n=1}^{N} \cos nt.$$

LEMMA 5.1

$$K_N(t) = \frac{\sin\left[(N + \frac{1}{2})t\right]}{2\sin(t/2)}.$$

The lemma is proved by considering the exponential sum

(5.1)
$$S = e^{it} + e^{2it} + \ldots + e^{Nit}$$
$$= e^{it} + (e^{it})^2 + \ldots + (e^{it})^N$$
$$= e^{it}\frac{e^{iNt} - 1}{e^{it} - 1} = \frac{e^{i(N + 1/2)t} - e^{it/2}}{e^{it/2} - e^{-it/2}}$$

or

(5.2)
$$S = \frac{\cos(N + 1/2)t + i\sin(N + 1/2)t - \cos(t/2) - i\sin(t/2)}{2i\sin(t/2)}.$$

From (5.1) we see that the real part of S is $K_N(t) - \frac{1}{2}$. Hence, by (5.2),

$$K_N(t) = \frac{1}{2} + \text{Re } S$$

$$= \frac{1}{2} + \frac{\sin(N + 1/2)t - \sin(t/2)}{2\sin(t/2)}$$

$$= \frac{\sin(N + 1/2)t}{2\sin(t/2)},$$

as required.

Since K_N and f are 2π-periodic, then

$$s_N(x) = \frac{1}{\pi}\int_{-\pi}^{\pi} f(t)K_N(t - x)\,dt = \frac{1}{\pi}\int_{-\pi-x}^{\pi-x} f(x + u)K_N(u)\,du$$

or

(5.3)
$$s_N(x) = \frac{1}{\pi}\int_{-\pi}^{\pi} f(x + u)K_N(u)\,du.$$

Since K_N is even, we can replace u by $-u$ in the integral (5.3) to obtain

(5.4)
$$s_N(x) = \frac{1}{\pi}\int_{-\pi}^{\pi} f(x - u)K_N(u)\,du.$$

Averaging (5.3) and (5.4) gives

$$s_N(x) = \frac{1}{\pi}\int_{-\pi}^{\pi} \frac{f(x + u) + f(x - u)}{2}K_N(u)\,du.$$

The integrand is even, so that

(5.5)
$$s_N(x) = \frac{2}{\pi} \int_0^\pi \frac{f(x + u) + f(x - u)}{2} K_N(u)\, du.$$

Notice that

$$\frac{2}{\pi} \int_0^\pi K_N(t)\, dt = \frac{2}{\pi} \int_0^\pi \left[\frac{1}{2} + \sum_{n=1}^N \cos nt \right] dt = 1.$$

Hence for any x

(5.6)
$$\frac{f(x^+) + f(x^-)}{2} = \frac{2}{\pi} \int_0^\pi \frac{f(x^+) + f(x^-)}{2} K_N(u)\, du.$$

Subtracting (5.5) from (5.6) gives

(5.7)
$$\frac{f(x^+) + f(x^-)}{2} - s_N(x) = \frac{1}{\pi} \int_0^\pi [f(x^+) - f(x + u)] K_N(u)\, du$$

$$+ \frac{1}{\pi} \int_0^\pi [f(x^-) - f(x - u)] K_N(u)\, du.$$

Recall that f is of class D. Hence the limit

$$\lim_{u \to 0^+} \frac{f(x^+) - f(x + u)}{2 \sin (u/2)} = \lim_{u \to 0^+} \frac{f(x^+) - f(x + u)}{u} \left[\frac{u}{2 \sin (u/2)} \right]$$

exists and is finite. Hence the two functions

$$\varphi_1(u) = \frac{f(x^+) - f(x + u)}{2 \sin (u/2)} \sin \left(\frac{u}{2} \right)$$

and

$$\varphi_2(u) = \frac{f(x^+) - f(x + u)}{2 \sin (u/2)} \cos \left(\frac{u}{2} \right)$$

are bounded, square-integrable functions. The first integral on the right in (5.7) equals

$$\frac{1}{\pi} \int_0^\pi \frac{f(x^+) - f(x + u)}{2 \sin (u/2)} \sin \left(N + \frac{1}{2} \right) u\, du$$

$$= \frac{1}{\pi} \int_0^\pi \varphi_1(u) \cos Nu\, du + \frac{1}{\pi} \int_0^\pi \varphi_2(u) \sin Nu\, du.$$

By Corollary 4.2 each of these integrals tends to zero as $N \to \infty$. Since the second integral in (5.7) can be treated in the same way, we see that (5.7) tends to zero as $N \to \infty$. Finally, we note that if x is a point of continuity of f, then $f(x^+) = f(x)$, and $f(x^-) = f(x)$. Thus

$$\frac{f(x^+) + f(x^-)}{2} = f(x).$$

Hence, by (5.7), we see that $s_N(x) \to f(x)$ as $N \to \infty$. This completes the proof of Theorem 1.3.

If $f(x)$ is a T-periodic function of class D with $T = 2c$, we can change variables to $x = ct/\pi$ and use the previous proof in order to see that the following result is true.

THEOREM 5.2: DIRICHLET'S CONVERGENCE RESULT

Let $f(x)$ be a T-periodic function of class D. Let $w = 2\pi/T$ and let

$$(5.8) \qquad s_N(x) = \frac{a_0}{2} + \sum_{n=1}^{N} (a_n \cos nwx + b_n \sin nwx).$$

Then $s_N(x)$ converges to $[f(x^+) + f(x^-)]/2$ as $N \to \infty$ for any real number x.

The theorem asserts, under rather mild conditions on f, that the Fourier series for f converges to f at all points of continuity. The convergence is often not rapid and, as pointed out in Section 10.1, the Gibbs phenomenon occurs near points of discontinuity. Convergence can be hastened and Gibbs' oscillations can be reduced by using the **method of σ-factors**. This method goes as follows.

Given $N \geq 1$, replace the partial sum (5.8) by the sum

$$(5.9) \qquad S_N(x) = \frac{a_0}{2} + \sum_{n=1}^{N} (a_n \sigma_n) \cos nwx + (b_n \sigma_n) \sin nwx$$

where

$$\sigma_n = \frac{\sin (n\pi/N)}{n\pi/N}, \qquad n = 1, 2, \ldots, N.$$

The sum $S_N(x)$ is the required approximation.

EXAMPLE 5.3   Figure 10.7 illustrates the effect of the σ-process. The square wave

$$(5.10) \qquad f(x) = \begin{cases} 1 & \text{on} \quad 0 < x < \pi \\ -1 & \text{on} \quad -\pi < x < \pi \end{cases}$$

with $f(x + 2\pi) = f(x)$ is depicted in Figure 10.7. Some typical curves $s_N(x)$ and $S_N(x)$ are also depicted. The square wave has Fourier series

$$f(x) \sim \frac{4}{\pi}\left(\sin x + \frac{1}{3} \sin 3x + \frac{1}{5} \sin 5x + \ldots \right).$$

For N even

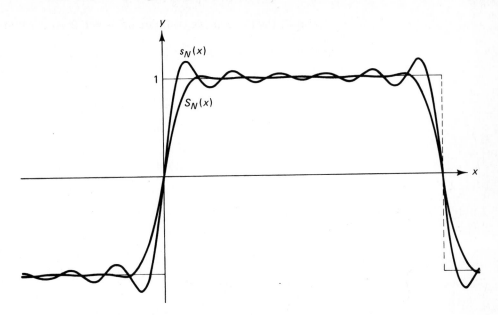

Figure 10.7. A square wave and the sigma-process.

$$s_N(x) = \frac{4}{\pi}\left[\sin x + \frac{1}{3}\sin 3x + \ldots + \frac{1}{N-1}\sin(N-1)x\right],$$

while

$$S_N(x) = \frac{4N}{\pi^2}\left[\sin x \sin\left(\frac{\pi}{N}\right) + \frac{1}{9}\sin 3x \sin\left(\frac{3\pi}{N}\right) + \ldots \right.$$

$$\left. + \frac{1}{(N-1)^2}\sin(N-1)x \sin\left(\frac{(N-1)\pi}{N}\right)\right].$$

Unwanted oscillations are drastically reduced and convergence is accelerated through the use of $S_N(x)$. ∎

The reason that the σ-process eliminates most of the unwanted oscillations in the approximation $s_N(x)$ is not hard to find. The σ-process integrates $s_N(x)$ to smooth out unwanted wiggles. The following result is true.

THEOREM 5.4: σ-FACTORS AND SMOOTHING

Let $s_N(x)$ and $S_N(x)$ be given by (5.8) and (5.9). Let $w = 1$ (for simplicity). Then

$$S_N(x) = \frac{N}{2\pi}\int_{-\pi/N}^{\pi/N} s_N(x+t)\,dt.$$

To prove the theorem we compute for $n = 1, 2, \ldots, N$ that

$$\frac{N}{2\pi} \int_{-\pi/N}^{\pi/N} \cos n(x + t)\, dt = \frac{N}{2\pi} \int_{-\pi/N}^{\pi/N} (\cos nx \cos nt - \sin nx \sin nt)\, dt$$

$$= \frac{N}{2\pi} \left[\cos nx \, \frac{2 \sin (n\pi/N)}{n} \right] = (\cos nx)\sigma_n.$$

Similarly,

$$\frac{N}{2\pi} \int_{-\pi/N}^{\pi/N} \sin n(x + t)\, dt = (\sin nx)\sigma_n.$$

Hence

$$\frac{N}{2\pi} \int_{-\pi/N}^{\pi/N} s_N(x + t)\, dt$$

$$= \frac{N}{2\pi} \int_{-\pi/N}^{\pi/N} \left[\frac{a_0}{2} + \sum_{n=1}^{N} (a_n \cos n(x + t) + b_n \sin n(x + t)) \right] dt$$

$$= \frac{a_0}{2} + \sum_{n=1}^{N} a_n(\cos nx)\sigma_n + b_n(\sin nx)\sigma_n = S_N(x).$$

Whenever it is necessary to sum a Fourier series, the σ-process is highly recommended. It will speed convergence and will greatly reduce problems caused by the Gibbs phenomenon.

PROBLEMS

1. Suppose that $f(x)$ is a continuously differentiable function on $0 \leq x \leq c$.

   (a) To what will the Fourier cosine series for f converge when $0 \leq x \leq c$? Prove your answer.

   (b) To what will the Fourier sine series for f converge when $0 \leq x \leq c$? Prove your answer.

2. Let $f(x)$ be the T-periodic function that satisfies the conditions given below. Verify that f is of class D. To what will the Fourier series for the function converge at each $x \in [0, T]$?

   (a) $f(x) = 1$ on $-\pi \leq x < 0$, $f(x) = 2$ on $0 \leq x < \pi$, and $T = 2\pi$.

   (b) $f(x) = x^2$ on $0 \leq x < \sqrt{3}$ and $T = \sqrt{3}$.

   (c) $f(x) = x^2$ on $-1 \leq x < 3$ and $T = 4$.

   (d) $f(x) = \sin x$ on $0 \leq x < \pi$ and $T = \pi$.

   (e) $f(x) = \sin x$ on $0 < x \leq 2$ and $T = 2$.

3. Show that if f is a 2π-periodic function defined by

$$f(x) = 1 + \sum_{n=1}^{\infty} \left(\frac{1}{n^2} \cos nx + (-1)^n e^{-n} \sin nx \right),$$

then the Fourier series for f converges to f for all real numbers x.

Hint: $\left| \dfrac{1}{n^2} \cos nx \right| \leq \dfrac{1}{n^2}$ and $\sum_{n=1}^{\infty} \dfrac{1}{n^2}$ converges.

4. Let $f(x)$ be a square wave given by (5.10).

(a) For $N = 10$ compute $s_N(x)$ and $S_N(x)$. Graph the errors $e_N(x) = f(x) - s_N(x)$ and $E_N(x) = f(x) - S_N(x)$, $0 \le x \le \pi$.

(b) The **arithmetic mean approximation** is defined as

$$\mathscr{S}_N(x) = \frac{1}{N}[s_0(x) + s_1(x) + \ldots + s_{N-1}(x)].$$

Compute $\mathscr{S}_N(x)$ when $N = 10$. Graph $\mathscr{S}_N(x)$ and graph the error $\mathscr{E}_N(x) = f(x) - \mathscr{S}_N(x)$, $0 \le x \le \pi$. Does $S_N(x)$ or $\mathscr{S}_N(x)$ give a more realistic approximation? *Hint:* Use a computer or a calculator to compute the errors.

5. Let $f(x) = x(\pi - x)$ for $-\pi \le x \le \pi$. For $N = 6$ compute $s_N(x)$ and $S_N(x)$ as well as the errors

$$e_N(x) = f(x) - s_N(x), \quad E_N(x) = f(x) - S_N(x).$$

Graph these errors over $-\pi \le x \le \pi$. Repeat the problem for $N = 8$ and $N = 10$. Does the σ-process seem to give a better approximation? *Hint:* Use a computer or a calculator to compute the errors.

6. Explain why the following function is not of class D.

$$f(x) = \begin{cases} \sqrt{x} & \text{on} & 0 \le x \le \pi, \\ -1 & \text{on} & -\pi \le x < 0. \end{cases}$$

10.6 OPERATIONS ON FOURIER SERIES

Let $f(x)$ be a piecewise continuous, T-periodic function with $T = 2c$. Then the function F defined by

$$(6.1) \qquad\qquad F(x) = \int_{-c}^{x} f(t)\, dt$$

is continuous in x. F will be T-periodic if it satisfies the condition $F(-c) = F(c)$. Since $F(-c) = 0$, this reduces to

$$(6.2) \qquad\qquad \int_{-c}^{c} f(t)\, dt = ca_0 = 0.$$

Hence the following theorem is true.

THEOREM 6.1: PERIODIC INTEGRALS OF PERIODIC FUNCTIONS

Let f be a T-periodic, piecewise-continuous function with $T = 2c$. Then the integral (6.1) determines a T-periodic function if and only if (6.2) is true. Moreover, if (6.2) is true, then F is of class D.

If F is periodic, it has a convergent Fourier series expansion

$$F(x) = \frac{A_0}{2} + \sum_{n=1}^{\infty}\left(A_n \cos\left(\frac{n\pi x}{c}\right) + B_n \sin\left(\frac{n\pi x}{c}\right)\right).$$

For $n \geq 1$ integration by parts gives

$$A_n = \frac{1}{c}\int_{-c}^{c} F(x)\cos\left(\frac{n\pi x}{c}\right) dx$$

$$= \left[\frac{1}{n\pi} F(x)\sin\left(\frac{n\pi x}{c}\right)\Big|_{-c}^{c} - \frac{1}{n\pi}\int_{-c}^{c} F'(x)\sin\left(\frac{n\pi x}{c}\right) dx\right]$$

$$= \frac{-c}{n\pi}\left(\frac{1}{c}\int_{-c}^{c} f(x)\sin\frac{n\pi x}{c} dx\right).$$

Hence $A_n = -(c/n\pi)b_n$, where b_n is the corresponding Fourier sine coefficient for $f(x)$. Similarly, $B_n = ca_n/n\pi$ and

(6.3) $$A_0 = -\frac{1}{c}\int_{-c}^{c} xf(x)\, dx.$$

Hence the following result is true.

THEOREM 6.2: INTEGRATION OF FOURIER SERIES

If f is a T-periodic function with $T = 2c$ and if $a_0 = 0$, so that

(6.4) $$f(x) \sim \sum_{n=1}^{\infty}\left[a_n \cos\left(\frac{n\pi x}{c}\right) + b_n \sin\left(\frac{n\pi x}{c}\right)\right],$$

then each side of (6.4) can be integrated to obtain

(6.5) $$\int_{-c}^{x} f(s)\, ds \sim \frac{A_0}{2} + \sum_{n=1}^{\infty}\left(\frac{c}{n\pi} a_n \sin\frac{n\pi x}{c} - \frac{c}{n\pi} b_n \cos\frac{n\pi x}{c}\right)$$

where A_0 is given by (6.3). The series in (6.5) converges for each x on the real line.

EXAMPLE 6.3   Let $f(x) = 1$ on $0 < x < 1$ and $f(x) = -1$ on $-1 < x < 0$. Then

$$f(x) \sim \frac{4}{\pi}\left(\sin \pi x + \frac{1}{3}\sin 3\pi x + \frac{1}{5}\sin 5\pi x + \ldots\right)$$

$$= \frac{4}{\pi}\sum_{k=1}^{\infty} \frac{1}{2k-1}\sin (2k-1)\pi x.$$

For x in the interval $-1 < x < 1$,

$$\int_{-1}^{x} f(x)\, dx = |x| - 1.$$

Hence in $-1 < x < 1$

$$|x| - 1 \sim \frac{A_0}{2} + \frac{4}{\pi}\left(-\frac{\cos \pi x}{\pi} - \frac{1}{9\pi}\cos 3\pi x - \frac{1}{25\pi}\cos 5\pi x - \cdots\right)$$

$$= \frac{A_0}{2} - \frac{4}{\pi^2}\left(\cos \pi x + \frac{1}{9}\cos 3\pi x + \frac{1}{25}\cos 5\pi x + \cdots\right)$$

$$= \frac{A_0}{2} - \frac{4}{\pi^2}\sum_{k=1}^{\infty}\frac{1}{(2k-1)^2}\cos(2k-1)\pi x$$

or

(6.6) $$|x| \sim \left(1 + \frac{A_0}{2}\right) - \frac{4}{\pi^2}\sum_{k=1}^{\infty}\frac{1}{(2k-1)^2}\cos(2k-1)\pi x.$$

The constant term $1 + A_0/2$ can be determined in either of two ways. If we use (6.3), then

$$1 + \frac{A_0}{2} = 1 - \frac{1}{2}\int_{-1}^{1} x f(x)\, dx = 1 - \frac{1}{2}\int_{-1}^{1}|x|\, dx = \frac{1}{2}.$$

Alternatively, $1 + A_0/2$ is one-half of the zero Fourier coefficient of $|x|$, that is,

$$1 + \frac{A_0}{2} = \frac{1}{2}\int_{-1}^{1}|x|\, dx = \frac{1}{2}.$$

By either calculation we see that the function g defined by $g(x) = |x|$ on $-1 < x < 1$ and $g(x + 2) = g(x)$ has Fourier series expansion

$$|x| \sim \frac{1}{2} - \frac{4}{\pi^2}\sum_{k=1}^{\infty}\frac{1}{(2k-1)^k}\cos(2k-1)\pi x. \quad \blacksquare$$

If $f(x)$ is a T-periodic, piecewise-continuous function with $T = 2c$ such that its mean value $a_0/2$ is not zero, then the function $h(x) = f(x) - a_0/2$ does have mean value zero. Thus $f(x) = a_0/2 + h(x)$ and Theorem 6.2 applies to $h(x)$. Since for any u and v

$$\int_{u}^{v} f(x)\, dx = \int_{-c}^{v} f(x)\, dx - \int_{-c}^{u} f(x)\, dx = \int_{-c}^{v} h(x)\, dx - \int_{-c}^{u} h(x)\, dx + \int_{u}^{v}\frac{a_0}{2}\, dx,$$

then

$$\int_{u}^{v} f(x)\, dx = \int_{u}^{v}\frac{a_0}{2}\, dx + \sum_{n=1}^{\infty}\int_{u}^{v}\left[a_n \cos\left(\frac{n\pi x}{c}\right) + b_n \sin\left(\frac{n\pi x}{c}\right)\right] dx.$$

This proves the following result.

THEOREM 6.4: DEFINITE INTEGRALS OF SERIES

If f is a T-periodic, piecewise-continuous function with $T = 2c$, then for any real numbers u and v the integral

$$\int_u^v f(x)\, dx$$

can be computed by integrating the Fourier series for f term by term.

EXAMPLE 6.5   From Example 6.3 we know that

$$|x| \sim \frac{1}{2} - \frac{4}{\pi^2} \sum_{k=1}^{\infty} \frac{1}{(2k-1)^2} \cos(2k-1)\pi x, \qquad -1 < x < 1.$$

Hence

$$\int_0^{1/2} |x|\, dx = \frac{1}{4} - \frac{4}{\pi^2} \sum_{k=1}^{\infty} \frac{1}{(2k-1)^2} \int_0^{1/2} \cos(2k-1)\pi x\, dx$$

or

$$\frac{1}{8} = \frac{1}{4} - \frac{4}{\pi^3} \sum_{k=1}^{\infty} \frac{(-1)^{k+1}}{(2k-1)^3}.$$

This expression can be rearranged to obtain the interesting result that

$$\frac{\pi^3}{32} = \sum_{k=0}^{\infty} \frac{(-1)^{k+1}}{(2k-1)^3} = 1 - \frac{1}{3^3} + \frac{1}{5^3} - \frac{1}{7^3} + \cdots. \quad \blacksquare$$

Fourier series can often be differentiated. However, differentiation is a more delicate operation than integration and must be done with care. The following result is true.

THEOREM 6.6: DIFFERENTIATION OF SERIES

Let f be a T-periodic, continuous function with $T = 2c$. Suppose that $f'(x)$ exists with at most finitely many exceptions over $-c \le x \le c$ and f' is of class D. Then the Fourier series for $f'(x)$ is obtained from the Fourier series for $f(x)$ by term-by-term differentiation.

To see that the result is true, we first recall that $f'(x)$ has a convergent Fourier series

$$f'(x) \sim \frac{a_0}{2} + \sum_{n=1}^{\infty} \left[a_n \cos\left(\frac{n\pi x}{c}\right) + b_n \sin\left(\frac{n\pi x}{c}\right) \right].$$

Since f is T-periodic with $T = 2c$, then

$$a_0 = \frac{1}{c} \int_{-c}^{c} f'(x) \, dx = \frac{1}{c} [f(c) - f(-c)] = 0.$$

Hence

(6.7) $$f'(x) \sim \sum_{n=1}^{\infty} \left[a_n \cos\left(\frac{n\pi x}{c}\right) + b_n \sin\left(\frac{n\pi x}{c}\right) \right].$$

Since

$$\int_{-c}^{x} f'(t) \, dx = f(x) - f(-c),$$

then (6.7) and Theorem 6.2 imply that

$$f(x) = [f(-c) + K] + \sum_{n=1}^{\infty} \left[\frac{c}{n\pi} a_n \sin\left(\frac{n\pi x}{c}\right) - \frac{c}{n\pi} b_n \cos\left(\frac{n\pi x}{c}\right) \right].$$

The derivative of this series is (6.7). Hence the theorem is true.

EXAMPLE 6.7   The function $f(x) = |x|$, $-1 \le x \le 1$ with $f(x + 2) = f(x)$ has series expansion (6.6). Now $f'(x)$ exists except when x is an integer and $f'(x)$ is the square wave

$$f'(x) = \begin{cases} 1 & \text{if} \quad 0 < x < 1 \\ -1 & \text{if} \ -1 < x < 0, \end{cases}$$

that is, f' is of class D. The derivative of the series (6.6) is the Fourier series for the square wave $f'(x)$, that is,

$$f'(x) \sim \frac{4}{\pi} \sum_{k=1}^{\infty} \frac{1}{2k - 1} \sin(2k - 1)\pi x. \quad \blacksquare$$

EXAMPLE 6.8   Let $f(x) = (x^2 - \pi^2)^2 = (x - \pi)^2(x + \pi)^2$ on $-\pi \le x \le \pi$ and $f(x + 2\pi) = f(x)$. It can be shown that

$$f(x) \sim \frac{48\pi^4}{90} + 48 \sum_{n=1}^{\infty} \frac{(-1)^{n+1}}{n^4} \cos nx.$$

Clearly, the derivative $f'(x)$ exists on $-\pi < x < \pi$. At $x = \pm\pi$ the derivative also exists. Indeed, it is zero! Hence $f'(x) = 2(x - \pi)(x + \pi)^2 + 2(x - \pi)^2(x + \pi) = 4x(x^2 - \pi^2)$ for all x on $-\pi \le x \le \pi$ and $f'(x)$ is of class D. Thus

$$f'(x) = 4x(x^2 - \pi^2) = 48 \sum_{n=1}^{\infty} \frac{(-1)^n}{n^3} \sin nx, \qquad -\pi \le x \le \pi.$$

Now $f''(x) = 12x^2 - 4\pi^2$ exists for $-\pi \le x \le \pi$ (including $x = \pi$ and $x = -\pi$) and f'' is of class D. Hence

$$f''(x) = 12x^2 - 4\pi^2 = 48 \sum_{n=1}^{\infty} \frac{(-1)^n}{n^2} \cos nx, \qquad -\pi \le x \le \pi.$$

The derivative $f'''(x) = 24x$ exists for $-\pi < x < \pi$, but no derivative exists at $x = \pm\pi$. Nevertheless, f''' is of class D and

(6.8) $$f'''(x) = 24x \sim 48 \sum_{n=1}^{\infty} \frac{(-1)^{n+1}}{n} \sin nx, \qquad -\pi < x < \pi.$$

This formula was computed in Section 10.1 [see (1.12)]. ∎

The Fourier series (6.8), or equivalently the Fourier series

(6.9) $$g(x) = x \sim 2 \sum_{n=1}^{\infty} \frac{(-1)^{n+1}}{n} \sin nx, \qquad -\pi < x < \pi$$

cannot be differentiated further by using Theorem 6.6. At first glance it would seem that this function satisfies the hypotheses of the theorem. However, $g(x)$ must be extended 2π-periodically outside the basic interval $-\pi < x < \pi$. Hence it is not continuous at $\pm\pi, \pm3\pi, \ldots$. Notice that the formal derivative of the series (6.9) is

(6.10) $$2 \sum_{n=1}^{\infty} (-1)^{n+1} \cos nx.$$

This series does not converge at any point x. However, it is possible to make some sense out of (6.10) by using the *unit impulse function*.

The unit impulse function $\delta(x)$ was introduced in Chapter 6. It is a generalized function which satisfies the condition that

$$\int_{-c}^{c} h(x)\delta(x - u) \, dx = h(u)$$

for any continuous function h and any $u \in (-c, c)$. This means that the 2π-periodic function which equals $\delta(x - \pi)$ over $-\pi < x \le \pi$ has Fourier coefficients

$$\frac{1}{\pi} \int_{-\pi}^{\pi} \delta(x - \pi) \cos nx \, dx = \frac{1}{\pi} \int_{0}^{2\pi} \delta(x - \pi) \cos nx \, dx = \frac{\cos n\pi}{\pi} = \frac{(-1)^n}{\pi}$$

and

$$\frac{1}{\pi} \int_{0}^{2\pi} \delta(x - \pi) \sin nx \, dx = \frac{\sin n\pi}{\pi} = 0.$$

Hence $\delta(x - \pi)$ would seem to have Fourier series

(6.11) $$\delta(x - \pi) \sim \frac{1}{\pi}\left(\frac{1}{2} + \sum_{n=1}^{\infty} (-1)^n \cos nx\right).$$

Comparing (6.9), (6.10), and (6.11) we see that formally

$$g'(x) = 1 - 2\pi \, \delta(x - \pi).$$

Even though (6.11) is not a valid Fourier series and $\delta(x - \pi)$ is not a genuine function; it is possible to make sense out of (6.11) by using the σ-process introduced in Section 10.5. Since the Nth partial sum from (6.11) is

$$s_N(x) = \frac{1}{\pi}\left(\frac{1}{2} + \sum_{n=1}^{N} (-1)^n \cos nx\right)$$

then the σ-process gives the approximation

$$S_n(x) = \frac{1}{\pi}\left(\frac{1}{2} + \sum_{n=1}^{N} \frac{(-1)^n}{(n\pi)/N} \sin nx\right).$$

The graph of a typical $S_N(x)$ is shown in Figure 10.8. As N grows larger, the spike of $S_N(x)$ at $x = \pi$ becomes higher and narrower and the ripples around $x = \pi$ become smaller and smaller. Thus the functions $S_N(x)$ do indeed approximate $\delta(x - \pi)$. The Fourier series (6.11) has meaning in the sense that it σ-sums to $\delta(x - \pi)$.

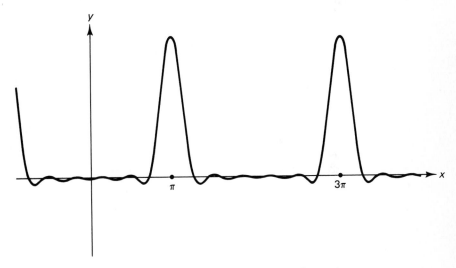

Figure 10.8. A σ-approximation to $\delta(x - \pi)$.

PROBLEMS

1. Let $f_1(x) = x$ on $-\pi < x < \pi$ and $f(x + 2\pi) = f(x)$ so that

$$f_1(x) \sim 2 \sum_{n=1}^{\infty} \frac{(-1)^{n+1}}{n} \sin nx.$$

Using this and Theorem 6.2, compute the Fourier series of each function.

(a) $f_2(x) = x^2$, $-\pi < x < \pi$.

(b) $f_3(x) = x^3$, $-\pi < x < \pi$.

(c) $f_4(x) = x^4$, $-\pi < x < \pi$.

2. Given that

$$|x| \sim \frac{\pi}{2} - \frac{4}{\pi} \sum_{k=1}^{\infty} \frac{1}{(2k-1)^2} \cos(2k-1)x, \qquad -\pi < x < \pi$$

compute the Fourier series for the function

$$f(x) = x^2 \operatorname{sgn} x = \begin{cases} x^2 & \text{if } 0 \le x < \pi \\ -x^2 & \text{if } -\pi < x < 0. \end{cases}$$

3. Let $f(x)$ be the 4-periodic function such that

$$f(x) = \begin{cases} -\dfrac{x}{2} & \text{if } -2 < x < 0 \\[2mm] \dfrac{x^2}{2} - \dfrac{x}{2} & \text{if } 0 \le x < 2 \end{cases}$$

so that

$$f(x) \sim \frac{4}{\pi^2} \sum_{n=1}^{\infty} \frac{(-1)^{n+2}}{n^2} \cos\left(\frac{n\pi x}{2}\right) + \frac{(-1)^n - 1}{\pi n^3} \sin\left(\frac{n\pi x}{2}\right) - \frac{1}{3}.$$

(a) Verify that the hypotheses of Theorem 6.6 are true.

(b) Compute the Fourier series for $f'(x)$.

(c) Verify that $f'(x)$ does not satisfy the hypotheses of Theorem 6.6.

4. Let f and g be $2c$-periodic functions with Fourier series

$$f(x) \sim \frac{a_0}{2} + \sum_{n=1}^{\infty} \left[a_n \cos\left(\frac{n\pi x}{c}\right) + b_n \sin\left(\frac{n\pi x}{c}\right) \right]$$

and

$$g(x) \sim \frac{A_0}{2} + \sum_{n=1}^{\infty} \left[A_n \cos\left(\frac{n\pi x}{c}\right) + B_n \sin\left(\frac{n\pi x}{c}\right) \right].$$

(a) Show that for any constants α and β, the function h defined by $h(x) = \alpha f(x) + \beta g(x)$ is $2c$-periodic.

(b) Show that

$$h(x) \sim \frac{\alpha a_0 + \beta A_0}{2} + \sum_{n=1}^{\infty} \left[(\alpha a_n + \beta A_n) \cos\left(\frac{n\pi x}{c}\right) + (\alpha b_n + \beta B_n) \sin\left(\frac{n\pi x}{c}\right) \right].$$

(c) Compute the Fourier series for $h(x) = x + |x|$, $-\pi < x < \pi$.

(d) Compute the Fourier series for $h(x) = 2x - |x|$, $-\pi < x < \pi$.

5. (a) Find the (formal) Fourier series for the 2π-periodic function such that $f(x) = \delta(x)$, $-\pi < x \le \pi$.

(b) Compute the σ-appproximation $S_N(x)$ when $N = 8$.

6. Solve the differential equation

$$y' = \sum_{n=1}^{\infty} \left[a_n \cos\left(\frac{n\pi x}{c}\right) + b_n \sin\left(\frac{n\pi x}{c}\right) \right], \qquad y(0) = 1.$$

7. Show that if

$$\sum_{n=1}^{\infty} (|a_n| + |b_n|) < \infty,$$

then the Fourier series

$$\frac{a_0}{2} + \sum_{n=1}^{\infty} \left[a_n \cos\left(\frac{n\pi x}{c}\right) + b_n \sin\left(\frac{n\pi x}{c}\right) \right]$$

converges *uniformly* on $-\infty < x < \infty$.

8. (a) Show that for any real numbers C and D,

$$|CD| \le \frac{C^2 + D^2}{2}.$$

(b) Show that

$$\sum_{n=1}^{N} |C_n D_n| \le \frac{1}{2} \sum_{n=1}^{N} (C_n^2 + D_n^2).$$

(c) Show that if

$$\sum_{n=1}^{\infty} C_n^2 < \infty \quad \text{and} \quad \sum_{n=1}^{\infty} D_n^2 < \infty,$$

then

$$\sum_{n=1}^{\infty} |C_n D_n| < \infty.$$

9. Suppose that $f(x)$ is a $2c$-periodic continuous function whose derivative $f'(x)$ is piecewise continuous with

$$f'(x) \sim \sum_{n=1}^{\infty} \left[a_n \cos\left(\frac{n\pi x}{c}\right) + b_n \sin\left(\frac{n\pi x}{c}\right) \right].$$

(a) Show that for some constant A_0

$$f(x) = \frac{A_0}{2} + \sum_{n=1}^{\infty} \left[\frac{c}{n\pi} a_n \sin\left(\frac{n\pi x}{c}\right) - \frac{c}{n\pi} b_n \cos\left(\frac{n\pi x}{c}\right) \right].$$

(b) Using Problems 7 and 8, show that the Fourier series for f converges to $f(x)$ uniformly on $-\infty < x < \infty$.

10. Let $f(x)$ be defined by the series

$$f(x) = 2 + \sum_{n=1}^{\infty} e^{-n} \cos nx + (-1)^n e^{-2n} \sin nx.$$

(a) Show that this series converges uniformly to $f(x)$.

(b) Compute the Fourier series for $f'(x)$ and $f''(x)$. Do these series converge uniformly?

Hint: Use Problem 7.

10.7 THE COMPLEX FORM OF A FOURIER SERIES

Any T-periodic function with $T = 2c$ that is square integrable over $(-c, c)$ has a Fourier series. Since

$$e^{i(n\pi x/c)} = \cos\left(\frac{n\pi x}{c}\right) + i \sin\left(\frac{n\pi x}{c}\right)$$

for any integer n, this Fourier series can be written in the form

(7.1) $$f(x) \sim \sum_{n=-\infty}^{\infty} d_n e^{i(n\pi x/c)}.$$

This expansion is called the **complex form** of the Fourier series for f. The numbers d_n called the **complex Fourier coefficients** of f. They are computed according to the following theorem.

THEOREM 7.1: COMPLEX FORM OF FOURIER SERIES

If $f(x)$ is a T-periodic function with $T = 2c$, then f has the complex Fourier series (7.1) where

$$d_n = \frac{1}{2c}\int_{-c}^{c} f(x)e^{-i(n\pi x/c)}\, dx.$$

To prove the theorem, first consider $n = 0$, where

$$d_0 = \frac{1}{2c}\int_{-c}^{c} f(x)\, dx = \frac{1}{2}a_0.$$

For $n \geq 1$,

$$d_n = \frac{1}{2c}\int_{-c}^{c} f(x)e^{-i(n\pi x/c)}\, dx$$

$$= \frac{1}{2c}\int_{-c}^{c} f(x)\left[\cos\left(\frac{n\pi x}{c}\right) - i\sin\left(\frac{n\pi x}{c}\right)\right]dx$$

$$= \frac{1}{2}\left[\frac{1}{c}\int_{-c}^{c} f(x)\cos\left(\frac{n\pi x}{c}\right)dx - \frac{i}{c}\int_{-c}^{c} f(x)\sin\left(\frac{n\pi x}{c}\right)dx\right]$$

$$= \frac{1}{2}[a_n - ib_n].$$

Similarly,

$$d_{-n} = \frac{1}{2c}\int_{-c}^{c} f(x)e^{i(n\pi x)/c}\, dx = \frac{1}{2}[a_n + ib_n],$$

so that

$$d_n e^{i(n\pi x/c)} + d_{-n} e^{-i(n\pi x/c)} = \frac{1}{2} [a_n - ib_n] \left[\cos\left(\frac{n\pi x}{c}\right) + i \sin\left(\frac{n\pi x}{c}\right) \right]$$

$$+ \frac{1}{2} [a_n + ib_n] \left[\cos\left(\frac{n\pi x}{c}\right) - i \sin\left(\frac{n\pi x}{c}\right) \right]$$

$$= a_n \cos\left(\frac{n\pi x}{c}\right) + b_n \sin\left(\frac{n\pi x}{c}\right).$$

Thus the series (7.1) can be written as

$$f(x) \sim d_0 + \sum_{n=1}^{\infty} \left(d_n e^{i(n\pi x/c)} + d_{-n} e^{-i(n\pi x/c)} \right)$$

$$= \frac{a_0}{2} + \sum_{n=1}^{\infty} \left[a_n \cos\left(\frac{n\pi x}{c}\right) + b_n \sin\left(\frac{n\pi x}{c}\right) \right],$$

as required.

EXAMPLE 7.2   Let $f(x) = x$ on $-1 < x < 1$ and $f(x + 2) = f(x)$. Then $d_0 = 0$ and

$$d_n = \frac{1}{2} \int_{-1}^{1} x e^{-in\pi x} \, dx = \frac{1}{2} \left[x \frac{e^{-in\pi x}}{-in\pi} \Big|_{-1}^{1} + \int_{-1}^{1} \frac{e^{-in\pi x}}{in\pi} \, dx \right]$$

$$= \frac{-1}{2} \left[\frac{e^{in\pi}}{in\pi} + \frac{e^{-in\pi}}{in\pi} - \frac{e^{in\pi}}{(in\pi)^2} + \frac{e^{-in\pi}}{(in\pi)^2} \right].$$

Since $e^{in\pi} = e^{-in\pi} = -1$, then $d_n = (-1)^{n+1}/(in\pi)$ and

$$f(x) \sim \sum_{n=1}^{\infty} \frac{(-1)^{n+1}}{in\pi} e^{in\pi x} + \sum_{n=-\infty}^{-1} \frac{(-1)^{n+1}}{in\pi} e^{in\pi x}$$

$$= \sum_{n=1}^{\infty} \frac{(-1)^{n+1}}{in\pi} \left[e^{in\pi x} - e^{-in\pi x} \right]. \quad \blacksquare$$

The convergence properties of complex Fourier series are the same as those of the ordinary Fourier series. Moreover, (7.1) can always be integrated term by term. It can be differentiated term by term when the function f is continuous and f' is piecewise continuous.

The idea of a Fourier series can be generalized further using the notion of orthogonal functions. A sequence of real- or complex-valued functions $\{\varphi_n(x)\}$ is said to be **orthogonal** on the interval $[a, b]$ if

(7.2) $$\int_a^b \varphi_n(x)\overline{\varphi_m(x)} \, dx \begin{cases} = 0 & \text{if } n \neq m \\ \neq 0 & \text{if } n = m. \end{cases}$$

For example, if $\varphi_n(x) = \sin nx$ for $n \geq 1$, then

$$\int_0^\pi \varphi_n(x)\overline{\varphi_m(x)} \, dx = \int_0^\pi \sin nx \sin mx \, dx = \begin{cases} 0 & \text{if } n \neq m \\ \dfrac{\pi}{2} & \text{if } n = m. \end{cases}$$

Hence $\{\sin nx : n = 1, 2, 3, \ldots\}$ is orthogonal on $[0, \pi]$. By (1.3)–(1.6) we see that the sequence

(7.3)
$$\{1, \sin x, \cos x, \sin 2x, \cos 2x, \ldots\}$$

is orthogonal on $[-\pi, \pi]$. Finally, the sequence

(7.4)
$$\{1, e^{ix}, e^{-ix}, e^{2ix}, e^{-2ix}, \ldots\}$$

is orthogonal on $[-\pi, \pi]$ since

$$\int_{-\pi}^{\pi} e^{inx}\overline{e^{imx}} \, dx = \int_{-\pi}^{\pi} e^{inx}e^{-imx} \, dx = \begin{cases} 0 & \text{if } n \neq m \\ 2\pi & \text{if } n = m. \end{cases}$$

Given an orthogonal sequence $\{\varphi_n(x) : n = 1, 2, 3, \ldots\}$ and a function $f(x)$, we wish to determine whether there are constants c_n such that

(7.5)
$$f(x) = \sum_{n=1}^{\infty} c_n \varphi_n(x).$$

To determine c_m we multiply (7.5) by $\overline{\varphi_m(x)}$ and then integrate from a to b. Since (7.2) is true, then

$$\int_a^b f(x)\overline{\varphi_m(x)} \, dx = \sum_{n=1}^{\infty} c_n \int_a^b \varphi_n(x)\overline{\varphi_m(x)} \, dx$$

$$= c_m \int_a^b |\varphi_m(x)|^2 \, dx.$$

Hence

(7.6)
$$c_m = \frac{\int_a^b f(x)\overline{\varphi_m(x)} \, dx}{\int_a^b |\varphi_m(x)|^2 \, dx}.$$

GENERALIZED FOURIER SERIES

The coefficients c_m determined by (7.6) are called the **generalized Fourier coefficients** of $f(x)$ [with respect to the orthogonal sequence $\{\varphi_n(x)\}$]. The corresponding **generalized Fourier series** is $\sum c_n \varphi_n(x)$. We write

(7.7)
$$f(x) \sim \sum_{n=1}^{\infty} c_n \varphi_n(x).$$

When $\{\varphi_n(x)\}$ is given by (7.3), the generalized Fourier series (7.7) will reduce to the ordinary Fourier series discussed in Section 10.1. If $\{\varphi_n(x) = \sin nx : n = 1, 2, 3, \ldots\}$, then (7.7) reduces to the sine series discussed in Section 10.2. If $\{\varphi_n(x)\}$ is given by (7.4), then (7.7) is the complex Fourier series (7.1). There are many other interesting choices of orthogonal sequences. Some examples are given in the problem section.

PROBLEMS   In Problems 1–5, find the complex form of the Fourier series of the T-periodic function.

1. $f(x) = 1$ on $0 < x < \pi$, $f(x) = -1$ on $-\pi < x < 0$, $T = 2\pi$.

2. $f(x) = \cos x$, $T = 2\pi$ (most coefficients will be zero).

3. $f(x) = \sin\left(\dfrac{n\pi x}{c}\right)$, $T = 2c$.

4. $f(x) = 0$ on $-1 < x < 0$, $f(x) = 1$ on $0 < x < 1$, $T = 2$.

5. $f(x) = e^x$, $-c < x < c$, $T = 2c$.

6. (a) Show that if f is a T-periodic function, then for any real number A its complex Fourier coefficients satisfy
$$d_n = \frac{1}{T}\int_A^{A+T} f(x)e^{-i(2n\pi x/T)}\,dx.$$

   (b) Compute the complex Fourier expansion of
$$f(x) = e^x, \qquad 0 \le x \le 2\pi, \qquad T = 2\pi.$$

   (c) Compute the complex Fourier series for
$$f(x) = x \text{ on } -1 \le x \le 5, \qquad T = 6.$$

7. Show that for any real-valued, T-periodic function $f(x)$, the complex Fourier coefficients d_n and d_{-n} are complex conjugates, that is $d_{-n} = \bar{d}_n$.

8. Let $f(x)$ be a T-periodic function with $T = 2c$ which satisfies the property that $f(x + c) = -f(x)$. Show that all even Fourier coefficients are zero, that is, $d_n = 0$ whenever n is an even integer.

9. (*Frequency form*) Let f be a T-periodic function. Then $w = 2\pi/T$ is the **frequency** of f. Show that
$$f(x) \sim \sum_{n=-\infty}^{\infty} d_n e^{inwx},$$
where
$$d_n = \frac{w}{2\pi}\int_0^{2\pi/w} f(x)e^{-inwx}\,dx.$$

10. Using the fact that $\sin nx = (e^{inx} - e^{-inx})/2i$, expand
$$f(x) \sim \sum_{n=1}^{\infty} a_n \sin nx$$
in a complex Fourier series.

11. Show that each sequence is orthogonal on the given interval.

    (a) $\{1, \cos x, \cos 2x, \cos 3x, \ldots\}$ on $[0, \pi]$.

    (b) The sequence (7.3) on $[0, 2\pi]$.

    (c) $\{\sin (n\pi x/a) : n \ge 1\}$ on $[0, a]$.

    (d) $\{\exp (in\pi x/a) : n = 0, \pm 1, \pm 2, \ldots\}$ on $[-a, a]$.

12. Show that if $\varphi_n(x)$ is orthogonal on $[0, a]$, then $\psi_n(x) = \varphi_n(xa/b)$ is orthogonal on $[0, b]$.

13. Let $P_n(x)$ be the Legendre polynomials, that is,

$$P_0 = 1, \quad P_1 = x, \quad P_2 = \frac{3x^2}{2} - \frac{1}{2}, \quad P_3 = \frac{5x^3}{2} - \frac{3x}{2},$$

$$P_4 = \frac{35x^4}{8} - \frac{15x^2}{4} + \frac{3}{8}, \quad \ldots.$$

Let $\varphi_n(x) = P_{n-1}(x)$ for $n = 1, 2, 3, \ldots$ and $[a, b] = [-1, 1]$.

(a) It is known that $\int_{-1}^{1} P_n(x)P_m(x) \, dx = 0$ if $n \neq m$. Prove this when n and m are between 0 and 3.

(b) Determine the generalized Fourier series for $f(x) = x(x - 1)$.

(c) Determine the first three generalized Fourier coefficients for $f(x) = |x|^{1/4}$.

14. Let $H_n(x)$ be the Hermite polynomials, that is,

$$H_0 = 1, \quad H_1 = 2x, \quad H_2 = 4x^2 - 2, \quad H_3 = 8x^3 - 12x,$$

$$H_4 = 16x^4 - 48x^2 + 12, \ldots.$$

It can be shown that $\varphi_n(x) = H_{n-1}(x) \exp(-x^2/2)$ is orthogonal on the interval $(-\infty, \infty)$.

(a) Determine the generalized Fourier series for $f(x) = (3x + 2)e^{-x^2/2}$.

(b) Find the generalized Fourier coefficients for the function $F(x) = f(x) \exp(-x^2/2)$ when f is given.

15. Let $\{\varphi_n(x)\}$ be a sequence of orthogonal functions on $[a, b]$ such that $\varphi_1(x) = 1$. Show that

$$\int_a^b \varphi_n(x) \, dx = 0 \qquad \text{for } n \geq 2.$$

16. Let $\{\varphi_n(x)\}$ be a sequence of orthogonal functions on $[a, b]$.

(a) Show that for any m and n

$$\int_a^b |\varphi_n(x) + \varphi_m(x)|^2 \, dx = \int_a^b |\varphi_n(x)|^2 \, dx + \int_a^b |\varphi_m(x)|^2 \, dx.$$

(b) For any constants g_n and any positive integer N show that

$$\int_a^b \left| \sum_{n=0}^{N} g_n \varphi_n(x) \right|^2 \, dx = \sum_{n=0}^{N} |g_n|^2 \int_a^b |\varphi_n(x)|^2 \, dx.$$

17. Let $\{\varphi_n(x)\}$ be an orthogonal sequence on $[a, b]$ such that

$$\int_a^b |\varphi_n(x)|^2 \, dx = 1 \qquad \text{for all } n.$$

Let f be a continuous function on $[a, b]$ and let c_n be the generalized Fourier coefficients of $f(x)$. Define $s_N(x) = \sum_{n=1}^{N} c_n \varphi_n(x)$ for any integer $N \geq 1$.

(a) Show that $\int_a^b |s_N(x)|^2 \, dx = \sum_{n=1}^{N} |c_n|^2$.

(b) Show that $\int_a^b |f(x)|^2 \, dx \geq \sum_{n=1}^{N} |c_n|^2$.

(c) Show that $c_n \to 0$ as $n \to \infty$.

Hint: Generalize the proof of Theorem 4.1.

10.8 PERIODICALLY FORCED DIFFERENTIAL EQUATIONS

We wish to find all periodic solutions of the differential equation

$$(8.1) \qquad\qquad y' + 2y = f(x)$$

when $f(x)$ is a fixed 2π-periodic function. It will be convenient to expand $f(x)$ in its complex Fourier series so that (8.1) takes the form

$$(8.2) \qquad\qquad y' + 2y = \sum_{n=-\infty}^{\infty} f_n e^{inx}.$$

Since we wish $y(x)$ to be 2π-periodic, we assume that it can be expanded in a Fourier series, that is,

$$(8.3) \qquad\qquad y(x) \sim \sum_{n=-\infty}^{\infty} y_n e^{inx}.$$

The coefficients y_n must be determined from the differential equation (8.2). Since

$$y'(x) \sim \sum_{n=-\infty}^{\infty} in y_n e^{inx},$$

then (8.2) becomes

$$\sum in y_n e^{inx} + 2 \sum y_n e^{inx} = \sum f_n e^{inx}.$$

Hence the coefficients y_n must satisfy $in y_n + 2 y_n = f_n$, that is,

$$y_n = \frac{1}{2 + in} f_n.$$

The 2π-periodic solution is

$$y(x) = \sum_{n=-\infty}^{\infty} \frac{1}{2 + in} f_n e^{inx}.$$

Now consider the general problem of determining a T-periodic solution of $Ly = f(x)$, where

$$(8.4) \qquad\qquad Ly = y^{(M)} + \alpha_{M-1} y^{(M-1)} + \ldots + \alpha_0 y,$$

where $\alpha_0, \ldots, \alpha_{M-1}$ are real constants and where

$$(8.5) \qquad\qquad f(x) \sim \sum_{n=-\infty}^{\infty} f_n e^{inwx}.$$

Here $w = 2\pi/T$ is the frequency and T is the period of the function $f(x)$. We assume a solution of the form

$$y(x) = \sum_{n=-\infty}^{\infty} y_n e^{inwx}.$$

Since

$$y'(x) = \sum_{n=-\infty}^{\infty} (inw)y_n e^{inwx},$$

$$\vdots$$

$$y^{(M)}(x) = \sum_{n=-\infty}^{\infty} (inw)^M y_n e^{inwx},$$

then

$$Ly = \sum_{n=-\infty}^{\infty} [(inw)^M + \alpha_{M-1}(inw)^{M-1} + \ldots + \alpha_1(inw) + \alpha_0]y_n e^{inwx}$$

$$= \sum_{n=-\infty}^{\infty} p(inw)y_n e^{inwx},$$

where $p(s) = s^M + \alpha_{M-1}s^{M-1} + \ldots + \alpha_1 s + \alpha_0$ is the characteristic polynomial for the operator L. The differential equation becomes

$$Ly = \sum p(inw)y_n e^{inwx} = \sum f_n e^{inwx} = f(x).$$

If $p(inw) \neq 0$ for all n, then $y_n = p(inw)^{-1}f_n$ and

(8.6)
$$y(x) = \sum_{n=-\infty}^{\infty} p(inw)^{-1}f_n e^{inwx}$$

is the desired solution. The following theorem is true.

THEOREM 8.1: PERIODIC FORCING–PERIODIC SOLUTIONS

Let f be a piecewise-continuous, T-periodic function with Fourier expansion (8.5). Suppose that the characteristic polynomial $p(s)$ for the differential operator (8.4) satisfies $p(inw) \neq 0$ for all integers n. Then $Ly = f(x)$ has a unique T-periodic solution $y(x)$ whose Fourier series is given by (8.6).

EXAMPLE 8.2   Find all 2π-periodic solutions of

$$y'' + 2y' + y = \sin x.$$

Here we have $f(x) = \sin x = (e^{ix} - e^{-ix})/2i$, so that $f_1 = 1/2i$, $f_{-1} = -1/2i$, and all other $f_n = 0$. Since $p(s) = s^2 + 2s + 1 = (s+1)^2$, then $p(in) = (in+1)^2 \neq 0$ when $-\infty < n < \infty$. Hence Theorem 8.1 applies. By that theorem the 2π-periodic solution is

$$y_p(x) = \frac{1}{p(i)}\left[\frac{1}{2i}\right]e^{ix} + \frac{1}{p(-i)}\left[-\frac{1}{2i}\right]e^{-ix}$$

$$= -\frac{1}{4}e^{ix} - \frac{1}{4}e^{-ix} = -\frac{1}{2}\cos x.$$

A general solution of the equation is

$$y(x) = (c_1 + c_2 x)e^{-x} + y_p(x). \quad \blacksquare$$

EXAMPLE 8.3   Find all 2-periodic solutions of

(8.7) $$y'' + 4y = f(x)$$

when $f(x)$ is the square-wave function

$$f(x) = \begin{cases} 1 & \text{on} \quad 0 < x < 1 \\ -1 & \text{on} \quad -1 < x < 0 \end{cases}, \quad f(x+2) = f(x).$$

The Fourier series for f is

$$f(x) \sim \frac{4}{\pi} \sum_{k=1}^{\infty} \frac{1}{2k-1} \sin(2k-1)\pi x$$

$$= \frac{4}{\pi} \sum_{k=1}^{\infty} \frac{1}{2k-1} \left[\frac{1}{2i} e^{i(2k-1)\pi x} - \frac{1}{2i} e^{-i(2k-1)\pi x} \right].$$

The characteristic polynomial $p(s) = s^2 + 4$ is zero only when $s = \pm 2i$. Hence the unique 2-periodic solution of (8.7) is

$$y_p(x) = \frac{4}{\pi} \sum_{k=1}^{\infty} \frac{1}{(2k-1)2i} \left[\frac{e^{i(2k-1)\pi x}}{p((2k-1)\pi i)} - \frac{e^{-i(2k-1)\pi x}}{p(-(2k-1)\pi i)} \right]$$

or

(8.8) $$y_p(x) = \frac{4}{\pi} \sum_{k=1}^{\infty} \frac{1}{(2k-1)[4-(2k-1)^2\pi^2]} \sin(2k-1)\pi x.$$

A general solution of (8.7) is

$$y(x) = c_1 \cos 2x + c_2 \sin 2x + y_p(x).$$

The first two terms of $y(x)$ are 2π-periodic and the last term is 2-periodic. Only when $c_1 = c_2 = 0$ is the solution periodic of period 2. $\quad \blacksquare$

The component of the function (8.5) with frequency nw is

$$f_n e^{inwx} + f_{-n} e^{-inwx}.$$

The solution (8.6) of $Ly = f(x)$ will alter such a frequency component but will never introduce components not already present in f. This is so because the nw-component of the solution (8.6) is

$$\frac{1}{p(inw)} f_n e^{inwx} + \frac{1}{p(-inw)} f_{-n} e^{-inwx}.$$

This component is zero whenever $f_n = f_{-n} = 0$. Also the solution (8.6) tends to attenuate the high-frequency components. This happens because

$$p(inw) = (inw)^M + \ldots + inw\alpha_1 + \alpha_0 \cong (inw)^M$$

when n is large. Hence the coefficient $f_n/p(inw) \cong f_n/(inw)^M$ is small when n is large. Similarly, $f_{-n}/p(-inw)$ is small. Engineers express this by saying that the differential equation **filters** the higher-frequency components. For example, consider the differential equation (8.7). The solution (8.8) is

$$y_p(x) = \frac{4}{\pi}\left(\frac{1}{4-\pi^2}\sin x + \frac{1}{3[4-9\pi^2]}\sin 3\pi x\right.$$

$$\left. + \frac{1}{5[4-25\pi^2]}\sin 5\pi x + \ldots\right)$$

$$\cong -\frac{4}{\pi}(0.17037\sin \pi x + 0.00393\sin 3\pi x$$

$$+ 0.00082\sin 5\pi x + 0.00005\sin 7\pi x + \ldots)$$

$$\cong -\frac{4}{\pi}(0.17037)\sin \pi x + \text{(small terms)}.$$

The differential equation has so filtered the square-wave input that the solution (or output) is essentially the sinusoidal term

$$-\frac{4}{\pi}(0.17037)\sin \pi x = -0.21692\sin \pi x.$$

It is typical that differential equations of order 2 or more very rapidly attenuate the higher-frequency components.

EXAMPLE 8.4   Solve $y'' + y' + 10y = f(x)$ when $f(x)$ is the square wave given in Example 8.3. The periodic solution is

$$y_p(x) = \frac{4}{\pi}\sum_{n \text{ odd}}\frac{1}{n}\frac{1}{2i}\left(\frac{e^{in\pi x}}{p(in\pi)} - \frac{e^{-in\pi x}}{p(-in\pi)}\right),$$

where $p(in\pi) = (in\pi)^2 + in\pi + 10 = (10 - n^2\pi^2) + in\pi$. Now

(8.9) $\quad \dfrac{1}{2i}\left(\dfrac{e^{in\pi x}}{p(in\pi)} - \dfrac{e^{-in\pi x}}{p(-in\pi)}\right) = \text{Im}\left(\dfrac{e^{in\pi x}}{p(in\pi)}\right)$

$$= \text{Im}\left(\frac{\cos n\pi x + i\sin n\pi x}{(10 - n^2\pi^2) + in\pi}\right)$$

$$= \frac{(10 - n^2\pi^2)\sin n\pi x - n\pi\cos n\pi x}{(10 - n^2\pi^2)^2 + (n\pi)^2}.$$

Let $R_n = [(10 - n^2\pi^2)^2 + (n\pi)^2]^{1/2}$ and let $\theta_n \in [0, 2\pi)$ be chosen so that $\cos\theta_n = (10 - n^2\pi^2)/R_n$ and $\sin\theta_n = -n\pi/R_n$. Then (8.9) has the form

$$\frac{1}{R_n}(\cos\theta_n \sin n\pi x + \sin\theta_n \cos n\pi x) = \frac{1}{R_n}\sin(n\pi x + \theta_n).$$

Hence the periodic solution can be written in the form

(8.10)
$$y_p(x) = \frac{4}{\pi} \sum_{n \text{ odd}} \frac{1}{nR_n} \sin(n\pi x + \theta_n).$$

If we think of the differential equation as a method of processing the input $f(x)$, we see from (8.10) that the nth harmonic $(4/n\pi) \sin n\pi x$ is changed to

$$\frac{4}{n\pi} \frac{1}{R_n} \sin(n\pi x + \theta_n),$$

that is, the amplitude has been multiplied by R_n^{-1} and the phase has been shifted by θ_n. The general solution of the equation is

(8.11)
$$y(x) = e^{-x/2}\left(c_1 \cos\sqrt{\frac{39}{4}}\, x + c_2 \sin\sqrt{\frac{39}{4}}\, x\right) + y_p(x).$$

As time x increases, the first term in this solution will go to zero, leaving only the periodic term $y_p(x)$. Notice also that

(8.12)
$$y_p(x) = \frac{4}{\pi}\left(\frac{1}{R_1}\sin(\pi x + \theta_1) + \frac{1}{3R_3}\sin(3\pi x + \theta_3)\right.$$

$$\left. + \frac{1}{5R_5}\sin(5\pi x + \theta_5) + \ldots\right)$$

$$\cong \frac{4}{\pi}(0.31804 \sin(\pi x - 1.52931) + 0.00420 \sin(3\pi x + 3.26059)$$

$$+ 0.00084 \sin(5\pi x + 3.20785) + \ldots).$$

Since 0.00420 is only about 1% of 0.31804, 0.00084 is only about 0.3%, and so on, we see from (8.11) and (8.12) that after waiting a short time, the solution is essentially

$$y(x) \cong \frac{4}{\pi} 0.31084 \sin(\pi x - 1.52931).$$

For all practical purposes, the differential equation $y'' + y' + 10y = f(x)$ has changed the square wave $f(x)$ into a sine wave. ∎

PROBLEMS

1. Let $f(x) = \cos x + 2 \sin 2x$ and $T = 2\pi$.
   (a) Find the complex Fourier series for f.
   (b) Find a general solution of $y'' - 9y = f(x)$.
   (c) Find a general solution of $y'' + y' + y = f(x)$.

2. Let $f(x) = 0$ on $-1 < x < 0$, $f(x) = 1$ on $0 \le x < 1$ and $T = 2$.
   (a) Find the complex Fourier series for f.
   (b) Find a general solution of $y'' + 4y = f(x)$.
   (c) Find a general solution of $y'' - 4y = f(x)$.

3. Find all periodic solutions of

$$y'' + y' + y = \sum_{n=1}^{\infty} \frac{1}{n^3} \cos nx.$$

4. Find a general solution of

$$y'' + y = \sum_{n=1}^{\infty} \frac{1}{n^2} \cos nx.$$

Hint: Solve $y'' + y = \cos x$ by the methods of Chapter 3 or 6. Then let $f(x) = \sum_{n=2}^{\infty} n^{-2} \cos nx$.

5. (a) Solve

$$y'' + y' + 5y = \cos x, \qquad y(0) = 1, \qquad y'(0) = 0.$$

(b) Write your solution in the form

$$y(x) = y_T(x) + A \sin (x + \theta).$$

(c) How large must x be before $|y_T(x)| < A/100$?

6. Let $Ly = y^{(M)} + \ldots + \alpha_1 y' + \alpha_0 y$ and $p(s) = s^M + \ldots + \alpha_1 s + \alpha_0$.

(a) Show that $Ly = 0$ has a T-periodic solution if and only if $p(2\pi n i / T) = 0$ for some integer n.

(b) Let $f(x)$ be a T-periodic, continuous function. How can the method of solution by Fourier series be modified to solve $Ly = f$ when $p(2n\pi i / T) = 0$ for the some integer $n \geq 1$?

7. Let $f(x) = \delta(x)$ be the unit impulse function on $-\pi < x \leq \pi$ and $f(x + 2\pi) = f(x)$.

(a) Compute the complex Fourier series for f. Does this series converge at any value of x?

(b) Find the unique 2π-periodic solution $y_p(x)$ of

$$y'' + 2y' + 3y = f(x).$$

(c) Show that the Fourier series for y_p converges at all real numbers x. *Hint:* See Problem 7 of Section 10.6.

8. Let $f(x)$ be a T-periodic square wave with $T = 2c$ such that

$$f(x) \sim \sum_{n \text{ odd}} \frac{1}{n} \sin \frac{n\pi x}{c}.$$

(a) Find the unique periodic solution $y_p(x)$ of

$$y'' + 0.1 y' + 10y = f(x).$$

(b) Show that y_p can be written in the form

$$y_p(x) = \sum_{n \text{ odd}} \frac{1}{nR_n} \sin \left(\frac{n\pi x}{c} + \theta_n \right).$$

(c) Compute $(nR_n)^{-1}$ and θ_n for $n = 1, 3, 5$, when $c = 1$. Put y_p in the form

$$y_p(x) = A_1 \sin (n\pi x + \theta_1) + A_3 \sin (3\pi x + \theta_2) + A_5 \sin (5\pi x + \theta_3) + \ldots.$$

Is this solution nearly sinusoidal?

9. Let f be T-periodic with $T = 2c$ and assume that $f(x + c) = -f(x)$ for all x. Show that the Fourier coefficients of f satisfy

(a) $f_m = 0$ if m is even.

(b) $f_m = \dfrac{2}{c} \int_0^c f(x) e^{-(im\pi x/c)} \, dx$ if m is odd.

CHAPTER REVIEW

If $f(x)$ is a periodic function with period $T = 2c$, the **Fourier series** for f has the form

$$f(x) \sim \frac{a_0}{2} + \sum_{n=1}^{\infty} \left[a_n \cos\left(\frac{n\pi x}{c}\right) + b_n \sin\left(\frac{n\pi x}{c}\right) \right].$$

The **Fourier coefficients** are given by the relations

$$a_n = \frac{1}{c} \int_{-c}^{c} f(x) \cos\left(\frac{n\pi x}{c}\right) dx \quad \text{and} \quad b_n = \frac{1}{c} \int_{-c}^{c} f(x) \sin\left(\frac{n\pi x}{c}\right) dx.$$

If $f(x)$ is **odd**, then

$$a_n = 0, \qquad b_n = \frac{2}{c} \int_0^c f(x) \sin\left(\frac{n\pi x}{c}\right) dx.$$

If $f(x)$ is **even**, then

$$a_n = \frac{2}{c} \int_0^c f(x) \cos\left(\frac{n\pi x}{c}\right) dx, \qquad b_n = 0.$$

The coefficients satisfy the **Parseval equation**

$$\frac{1}{c} \int_{-c}^{c} f(x)^2 \, dx = \frac{a_0^2}{2} + \sum_{n=1}^{\infty} (a_n^2 + b_n^2).$$

The **complex form** of a Fourier series is

$$f(x) \sim \sum_{n=-\infty}^{\infty} d_n \, e^{i(n\pi x/c)}, \qquad \text{where} \quad d_n = \frac{1}{2c} \int_{-c}^{c} f(x) \, e^{-i(n\pi x/c)} \, dx.$$

Fourier series can be integrated term by term. They can be differentiated term by term when the function f' is of class D (Theorem 6.6). These facts are useful when solving linear differential equations $Ly = p(x)$ for a periodic y.

CHAPTER REVIEW PROBLEMS

1. Let $f(x) = 2$ on $0 < x < c$, $f(x) = -1$ on $-c < x < 0$, and $f(x + 2c) \equiv f(x)$. Find the Fourier series for $f(x)$.

2. Let $g(x) = 3e^{2x}$ on $-\pi < x < \pi$ and $g(x + 2\pi) \equiv g(x)$. Compute the complex Fourier series for $g(x)$.

3. Find a general solution of $y'' + 2y' + 10y = \sum_{n=1}^{\infty} \dfrac{1}{n} \cos n\pi x$.

4. Let $f(x) = 1 - |x|$ over $0 < x < 2$.

   (a) If we extend $f(x)$ evenly to $-2 < x < 0$, what formula determines $f(x)$ over that interval?

   (b) If we extend $f(x)$ oddly to $-2 < x < 0$, what formula determines $f(x)$ over that interval?

CHAPTER ELEVEN

Separation of Variables

In this chapter we study partial differential equations and their solutions. Partial differential equations arise in many branches of science, for example in electromagnetic theory, elasticity, fluid mechanics, heat transfer, acoustics, and quantum mechanics. We shall study the *heat equation*, the *wave equation*, and the *Laplace equation*. These equations are important examples of the three major types of linear partial differential equations. We shall discuss what initial and/or boundary conditions are needed in order to specify one and only one solution and we shall show how many important problems can be solved by the method of separation of variables.

By a partial differential equation we mean an equation that contains an unknown function u and partial derivatives of u. For example,

$$(0.1) \qquad \frac{\partial u}{\partial x} + \frac{\partial u}{\partial y} u = x \quad \text{and} \quad \frac{\partial w}{\partial t} + 3 \frac{\partial w}{\partial x} = 0$$

are partial differential equations for the unknown functions $u(x, y)$ and $w(t, x)$, while

$$(0.2) \qquad \frac{\partial u}{\partial t} = k \frac{\partial^2 u}{\partial x^2}, \qquad \frac{\partial^2 v}{\partial x^2} + \frac{\partial^2 v}{\partial y^2} = 0, \qquad \frac{\partial^2 w}{\partial t^2} = c^2 \frac{\partial^2 w}{\partial x^2}$$

are partial differential equations for the unknown functions $u(t, x)$, $v(x, y)$, and $w(t, x)$.

The order of a partial differential equation is the order of the highest derivative that occurs in the equation. For example, both equations in (0.1) are first order, while all those in (0.2) are second order. We shall be concerned mainly with second-order problems of the types given in (0.2). These three equations are, respectively, the heat equation, the Laplace equation, and the wave equation. We shall often use the subscript notation for derivatives. In this notation (0.1) is written as

$$u_x + u_y u = x \quad \text{and} \quad w_t + 3w_x = 0,$$

while (0.2) is written as

$$u_t = k u_{xx}, \qquad v_{xx} + v_{yy} = 0, \qquad w_{tt} = c^2 w_{xx}.$$

Photo 23. Fatigue failure. (Sample courtesy of Prof. L. W. Zachary.)

Photo 24. Fatigue detail. (Sample courtesy of Prof. L. W. Zachary.)

Partial differential equations have many applications. Photos 23 and 24 provide a dramatic illustration of one use. These photos show a worm gear which was on the end of a steel shaft. The shaft had a diameter of slightly more than 10 cm. The stratified lines indicate fatigue cracking caused by vibration. When the cracking progressed far enough the sample necked and then broke. Metal structures are normally designed and analyzed by using partial differential equation models. Vibration analysis is a standard part of a structural engineer's tool kit since excessive vibration can have catastrophic results.

11.1   THE HEAT EQUATION IN ONE DIMENSION

In this section we derive the equation of heat flow in a uniform material and show what initial and boundary conditions are naturally associated with this equation. By a *uniform material* we mean a homogeneous material that is isotropic (i.e., there are no preferred directions for heat flow). Consider the thin bar of length b and with uniform cross section pictured in Figure 11.1. The sides are assumed to be insulated so that heat can enter or leave the bar only at the two ends $x = 0$ and $x = b$. Thus heat flow in the bar can be assumed to occur only in the x-direction.

$x = 0$ $x = b$

Figure 11.1. Heat flow in a bar.

Let $u(t, x)$ be the temperature of the bar at point x and time t and let $q(t, x)$ be the rate of heat flow there. We assume the **Fourier law of heat conduction,** that is,

$$(1.1) \qquad q(t, x) = -\kappa \frac{\partial u}{\partial x}.$$

Here κ is a positive constant called the **thermal conductivity.** This constant depends only on the material making up the bar. If this material has density ρ and specific heat c, the law of conservation of energy implies that

$$(1.2) \qquad \frac{\partial}{\partial t}(\rho c u) = -\frac{\partial}{\partial x} q(t, x).$$

Combining (1.1) and (1.2) we obtain the heat equation

$$(E) \qquad u_t = k^2 u_{xx}$$

where $k = \sqrt{\kappa/\rho c} > 0$. The constant k^2, called the **thermal diffusivity,** has been determined for most common materials.

The heat equation (E) describes all kinds of one-dimensional heat flow. For example, suppose that a pane of window glass, which is initially at temperature T, is placed in a window. If the surface area of the glass is large, it is reasonable to assume that we have an infinite slab of glass. If the outside air temperature is $T_1 = 20°F$ while the inside air temperature is $T_2 = 70°F$, heat will flow through the slab from inside to outside and (E) will be true (see Figure 11.2).

The heat equation (E) by itself will not determine the unknown temperature $u(t, x)$. For example, in our window glass example, the temperature $u(t, x)$ at

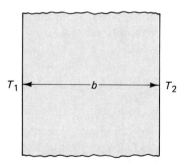

T_1 b T_2

Figure 11.2. Heat flow in a slab.

time t and positive x will be different when the window is initially at $100°F$ from when it is initially at $-40°F$. Clearly, $u(t, x)$ depends on the initial temperature of the glass. We shall assume that

(IC) $$u(0, x) = f(x), \qquad 0 < x < b$$

where $f(x)$ is the known initial temperature distribution. Condition (IC) is called an **initial condition.**

Even (E) and (IC) together do not determine $u(t, x)$. In our window glass example the heat flow will depend on the air temperature in the room and outside. The heat flow can be very different depending on whether the day is warm or cold. Clearly, it is important to know what is happening at the two boundaries $x = 0$ and $x = b$. We shall assume **boundary conditions** of the form

(BC) $$u(t, 0) = T_1 \quad \text{and} \quad u(t, b) = T_2 \qquad \text{for all } t > 0.$$

The three conditions (E), (IC), and (BC) do determine a unique solution $u(t, x)$. Heat flow problems will always be specified by giving the equation, an initial condition and boundary conditions. For example,

(P$_1$)
$$\begin{cases} u_t = 3u_{xx} & \text{for } 0 < x < 2, t > 0 \\ u(0, x) = 1 + x^2 & \text{for } 0 < x < 2 \\ u(t, 0) = 0, \quad u(t, 2) = 30 & \text{for } t > 0 \end{cases}$$

is such a heat problem. Here $k = \sqrt{3}, b = 2, f(x) = 1 + x^2, T_1 = 0,$ and $T_2 = 30$.

It will be convenient to have (E), (IC), and (BC) written in operator notation. Let L be the operator defined by

$$Lw = w_t - k^2 w_{xx}.$$

Here $w(t, x)$ is any function with continuous second partial derivatives. It is important to notice that L is **linear,** that is,

$$L(c_1 w_1 + c_2 w_2) = c_1 L w_1 + c_2 L w_2$$

for all constants c_1 and c_2 and all functions w_1 and w_2. In terms of L, (E) is written as

(E) $$Lu = u_t - k^2 u_{xx} = 0.$$

This equation is *homogeneous.* The corresponding nonhomogeneous equation would be $Lu = F$, where F is some known nonzero function.

Similarly, the initial condition (IC) can be written as

(IC) $$L_I u = f.$$

Here $L_I w(x) = w(0, x)$. The boundary conditions can be written as

(BC) $$L_1 u = T_1, \qquad L_2 u = T_2$$

where $(L_1 u)(t) = u(t, 0)$ and $(L_2 u)(t) = u(t, b)$. The initial condition is homogeneous if $f \equiv 0$. Otherwise, it is nonhomogeneous. Similarly, (BC) is homogeneous if $T_1 = T_2 = 0$ and is nonhomogeneous otherwise.

HOMOGENEOUS BOUNDARY CONDITIONS

In all of the subsequent discussions it will be important to keep track of which conditions on the unknown function u are homogeneous and which are not. If the condition has the form $Mu = f$ for some linear operator M, then clearly **homogeneous** means that f is zero. However, there will not always be an obvious linear operator M around. In such circumstances we shall consider a condition homogeneous if whenever u_1 and u_2 satisfy the condition, then so does every linear combination $c_1u_1 + c_2u_2$ for any constants c_1 and c_2. (Clearly combinations of the form $\sum_{i=1}^{N} c_i u_i$ will also satisfy the condition.) For example, we see that the condition "$u(t, x)$ remains bounded as $t \to \infty$ for all $x \in [0, b]$" is a homogeneous condition. A "homogeneous condition" requires a specified set of functions u. This set must satisfy the condition that whenever u_1 and u_2 are in the set and c_1 and c_2 are constants, then $c_1u_1 + c_2u_2$ is in the set.

PROBLEMS

1. (a) Prove that $Lw = w_t - k^2 w_{xx}$ is a linear operator.

   (b) Prove that the boundary operators $(L_1 w)(t) = w(t, 0)$ and $(L_2 w)(t) = w(t, b)$ are linear.

   (c) Show that if $u_1, u_2, \ldots, u_n$ solve (E) and $c_1, c_2, \ldots, c_n$ are constants, then $c_1u_1 + c_2u_2 + \ldots + c_nu_n$ solves (E).

   (d) Show that if $u_1, u_2, \ldots, u_n$ solve (E) and satisfy the homogeneous boundary conditions $L_1 u = L_2 u = 0$, then for any constants c_i, $u = c_1u_1 + c_2u_2 + \ldots + c_nu_n$ solves (E) and the two homogeneous boundary conditions.

2. Even in a uniform material the parameters ρ, c, and κ do not have to be constants. For example, the density ρ might be dependent in a significant way on the temperature if the temperature variation is large.

   (a) Assume that $\rho(u)$, $c(u)$, and $\kappa(u)$ depend on u. Use (1.1) and (1.2) to derive an equation of heat flow.

   (b) Show that if ρ and c are constant while $\kappa = du_x^\alpha$ for some positive constants d and α, then the equation of heat flow is

$$L^*u = u_t - \frac{d(\alpha + 1)}{\rho c} u_x^\alpha u_{xx} = 0.$$

   (c) Show that L^* obtained in part (b) is *not* a linear operator.

3. If the material described in (1.1) and (1.2) is not homogeneous, then ρ, c, and κ may depend on x.

   (a) Derive the equation of heat flow when ρ, c, and κ are functions of x.

   (b) Write your equation in the form $Lu = 0$.

   (c) Show that the L you obtain is linear.

4. Let D be a three-dimensional volume and let D_0 be any subvolume with boundary S_0. Let n be the outward unit normal on S_0. Suppose that $u(t, x, y, z)$ is the tem-

perature and $q(t, x, y, z)$ is the rate of heat flow. If no energy is generated or consumed inside of D, the law of conservation of energy implies that

$$\frac{d}{dt} \iiint_{D_0} \rho c u(t, x, y, z) \, dx \, dy \, dz = -\iint_{S_0} q(t, x, y, z) \cdot n \, dS.$$

(a) Use the divergence theorem to show that

$$\iiint_{D_0} \text{div } q \, dx \, dy \, dz = \iint_{S_0} q \cdot n \, dS.$$

(b) Show that

$$\iiint_{D_0} \left[\frac{\partial}{\partial t} (\rho c u) + \text{div } q \right] dx \, dy \, dz = 0.$$

(c) Show that if part (b) is true for all subvolumes D_0 of D and if ρ, c, u, and div q are continuous functions, then

$$\frac{\partial}{\partial t} (\rho c u) = -\text{div } q.$$

5. In Problem 4, suppose that the Fourier law $q = -\kappa \text{ grad } u$ holds.

(a) Show that

$$\frac{\partial}{\partial t} (\rho c u) = \frac{\partial}{\partial x} (\kappa u_x) + \frac{\partial}{\partial y} (\kappa u_y) + \frac{\partial}{\partial z} (\kappa u_z).$$

(b) Show that if ρ, c, and κ are constants, then

$$u_t = k^2 (u_{xx} + u_{yy} + u_{zz}), \qquad k = \sqrt{\frac{\kappa}{\rho c}}.$$

(c) Show that if heat flows only in the x-direction, then the result in part (b) reduces to the heat equation (E).

6. Verify that each of the following conditions is homogeneous.

(a) $u(t, 0) = 0$ for all $t > 0$.

(b) $u_x(0, x) = 0$ for all x, $0 < x < b$.

(c) $u(t, x) \to 0$ as $t \to \infty$ for all x, $0 < x < b$.

(d) $u(x, y)$ is bounded on $0 \le y < \infty$ for each x in $(0, a)$.

(e) $u_x(t, b) = 0$ for all $t > 0$.

(f) $\alpha u(t, 0) - \beta u_x(t, 0) = 0$ for all $t > 0$.

(g) $u(r, \theta + 2\pi) = u(r, \theta)$ for $0 \le r \le R$, $-\infty < \theta < \infty$.

(h) $u(r, \theta)$ is bounded as $r \to 0^+$ for each θ in the range $-\infty < \theta < \infty$.

11.2   SOLUTION OF THE HEAT PROBLEM

We shall now solve the one-dimensional heat problem in the special case where the boundary conditions are homogeneous. Hence we seek a solution $u(t, x)$ defined for $0 < x < b$, $t > 0$, of the problem

(P)
$$\begin{cases} u_t - k^2 u_{xx} = 0 \\ u(0, x) = f(x) \\ u(t, 0) = 0, \qquad u(t, b) = 0. \end{cases}$$

We shall solve (P) by the method of **separation of variables.** According to this method, we first attempt to solve only the homogeneous portions of (P). Hence we shall temporarily ignore the initial condition $u(0, x) = f(x)$. We concentrate on the equation and the boundary conditions. We seek a nonzero solution of these which has the form

(2.1) $u(t, x) = T(t)X(x).$

Substituting (2.1) into the equation $Lu \equiv u_t - k^2 u_{xx} = 0$ gives

$$T'X = k^2 TX'',$$

where prime denotes the derivative (i.e., $T' = dT/dt$ and $X'' = d^2X/dx^2$). This equation can be rewritten in the form

(2.2) $$\frac{T'}{k^2 T} = \frac{X''}{X}.$$

In (2.2), the t variable has been **separated** from the x variable, that is, the left side of (2.2) depends only on t and the right side only on x. Since (2.2) is true for all $t > 0$ and all x in $(0, b)$, we can fix x while varying t. From this we see that the left side of (2.2) must be constant. Similarly, if we fix t and vary x in (2.2), we see that the right side must equal the same constant, that is,

$$\frac{T'}{k^2 T} = \mu = \frac{X''}{X}.$$

This leads to the two ordinary differential equations

(2.3) $T'(t) = \mu k^2 T(t)$

and

(2.4) $X''(x) = \mu X(x).$

Any solution of $Lu = 0$ of the form (2.1) must satisfy (2.3) and (2.4) for some constant μ.

Now consider the boundary conditions. Since u has the form (2.1), $L_1 u = 0$ implies that

$$u(t, 0) = T(t)X(0) = 0 \qquad \text{for all } t > 0.$$

One solution is $T(t) \equiv 0$. However, this would mean that $u(t, x) = T(t)X(x) \equiv 0$. Since we require that $u \not\equiv 0$, we see that what is needed is

(2.5) $X(0) = 0.$

Similarly, the second boundary condition $L_2 u = 0$ gives

(2.6) $X(b) = 0.$

The three conditions (2.4), (2.5), and (2.6) are now combined to obtain

$$\text{(BVP)} \qquad X'' - \mu X = 0, \qquad X(0) = 0, \qquad X(b) = 0.$$

This problem is a **boundary value problem** for the unknown function X since the two side conditions $X(0) = X(b) = 0$ are given at the boundaries of the interval $0 < x < b$.

Our boundary value problem must be solved in different ways depending on whether μ is zero, positive, or negative. When $\mu = 0$, then (2.4) reduces to $X'' = 0$. Hence X must have the form

$$X(x) = c_1 x + c_2.$$

Now $X(0) = c_2 = 0$, so that $X(x) = c_1 x$. But $X(b) = c_1 b = 0$, so c_1 is also zero. Hence there is no nonzero solution of (BVP) when $\mu = 0$. When $\mu > 0$, then

$$X(x) = c_1 e^{\sqrt{\mu} x} + c_2 e^{-\sqrt{\mu} x}.$$

The requirement $X(0) = 0$ means that $c_2 = -c_1$. Thus

$$X(x) = c_1(e^{\sqrt{\mu} x} - e^{-\sqrt{\mu} x}).$$

Now

$$X(b) = c_1(e^{\sqrt{\mu} b} - e^{-\sqrt{\mu} b}) = 0$$

can happen only when $c_1 = 0$. Hence there are no nonzero solutions of (BVP) when $\mu > 0$.

The case $\mu < 0$ turns out to be more interesting. Since $\mu < 0$, it is convenient to write $\mu = -\lambda^2$ where $\lambda > 0$. Thus we consider the equation

$$X'' + \lambda^2 X = 0.$$

Solutions have the form

$$X(x) = c_1 \sin \lambda x + c_2 \cos \lambda x.$$

Since $X(0) = c_2 = 0$, we see that $X(x)$ must have the form

$$X(x) = c_1 \sin \lambda x.$$

The second boundary condition implies that

$$X(b) = c_1 \sin \lambda b = 0.$$

We cannot allow $c_1 = 0$ since that gives $X(x) \equiv 0$. Thus we require that $\sin \lambda b = 0$. This means that $\lambda b = n\pi$ or $\lambda = n\pi/b$ for some integer n. The nonzero solutions of (BVP) are

$$(2.7) \qquad X_n(x) = d_n \sin \frac{n\pi x}{b}, \qquad \mu_n = -\left(\frac{n\pi}{b}\right)^2,$$

where d_n is an arbitrary constant. If $n = 0$ in (2.7), then $X_0(x) = 0$. Hence we require $n \neq 0$. For negative integers we have

$$X_{-n}(x) = d_{-n} \sin \left(\frac{-n\pi x}{b}\right) = (-d_{-n}) \sin \left(\frac{n\pi x}{b}\right).$$

Since $-d_{-n}$ is just an arbitrary constant, this solution is the same as $X_n(x)$. Thus we take $n = 1, 2, 3, \ldots$ in (2.7).

Now put $\mu = \mu_n = -(n\pi/b)^2$ into (2.3) and solve for T. The result is

$$(2.8) \qquad\qquad T_n(t) = g_n e^{-(n\pi k/b)^2 t}$$

where g_n is an arbitrary constant. The corresponding solution (2.1) is

$$(2.9) \qquad\qquad u_n(t, x) = d_n g_n e^{-(n\pi k/b)^2 t} \sin\left(\frac{n\pi x}{b}\right),$$

where n is any positive integer.

We now use the fact that the equation and the boundary conditions are linear and homogeneous. This implies that if the solutions (2.9) are multiplied by constants c_n and summed, the resulting function will again satisfy the equation and the boundary conditions. Hence

$$(2.10) \qquad\qquad u(t, x) = \sum_{n=1}^{\infty} c_n u_n(t, x)$$

will solve the homogeneous portions of (P) provided that the series converges. Let $b_n = c_n d_n g_n$ be a new arbitrary constant and write (2.10) in the form

$$(2.11) \qquad\qquad u(t, x) = \sum_{n=1}^{\infty} b_n e^{-(n\pi k/b)^2 t} \sin\left(\frac{n\pi x}{b}\right).$$

We wish to pick the constants b_n in (2.11) in such a way that $u(t, x)$ will satisfy the initial condition in (P). Setting $t = 0$ in (2.11) and using $u(0, x) = f(x)$, we see that the b_n must be picked in such a way that

$$(2.12) \qquad\qquad f(x) = \sum_{n=1}^{\infty} b_n \sin\left(\frac{n\pi x}{b}\right), \qquad 0 < x < b.$$

Now (2.12) can be satisfied if the b_n are chosen to be the Fourier sine series coefficients of f, that is,

$$(2.13) \qquad\qquad b_n = \frac{2}{b} \int_0^b f(x) \sin\left(\frac{n\pi x}{b}\right) dx.$$

The solution of (P) is (2.11) and (2.13).

EXAMPLE 2.1   For $0 < x < 1$ and $t > 0$, solve

$$u_t - 4u_{xx} = 0$$

$$u(0, x) = 1$$

$$u(t, 0) = 0, \qquad u(t, 1) = 0.$$

In this case, separation of variables gives

$$u(t, x) = \sum_{n=1}^{\infty} b_n e^{-(2n\pi)^2 t} \sin n\pi x$$

and

$$b_n = 2 \int_0^1 1 \cdot \sin n\pi x \, dx = \frac{2}{n\pi} \left[(-1)^{n+1} + 1 \right].$$

Hence

(2.14) $$u(t, x) = \sum_{n \text{ odd}} \frac{4}{n\pi} e^{-(2n\pi)^2 t} \sin n\pi x$$

$$= \sum_{m=1}^{\infty} \frac{4}{(2m-1)\pi} e^{-[2(2m-1)\pi]^2 t} \sin (2m-1)\pi x. \quad \blacksquare$$

The method of separation of variables will be used over and over in this chapter for various equations and boundary conditions. The student should learn the method rather than attempting to memorize formulas. In going over the method, the student will see that arbitrary constants were supplied in three places. The arbitrary constants d_n and g_n in (2.7) and (2.8) were not needed. An arbitrary constant can be supplied when the solutions u_n are added to get (2.10). In the future, we shall not put in arbitrary constants as we go along. Rather, we will supply them in the infinite sum.

PROBLEMS   In Problems 1–5, solve the heat flow problem.

1. $u_t = u_{xx}$, $u(0, x) = 3 \sin x + 2 \sin 2x$, $u(t, 0) = u(t, \pi) = 0$.

2. $u_t = 2u_{xx}$, $u(0, x) = 1$, $u(t, 0) = u(t, \pi) = 0$.

3. $v_t - 9v_{xx} = 0$, $v(0, x) = x$, $v(t, 0) = v(t, 1) = 0$.

4. $\dfrac{\partial u}{\partial t} = \dfrac{\partial^2 u}{\partial x^2}$, $u(0, x) = \displaystyle\sum_{n=1}^{\infty} \frac{1}{n^2} \sin nx$, $u(t, 0) = u(t, \pi) = 0$.

5. $\dfrac{\partial w}{\partial t} = 5 \dfrac{\partial^2 w}{\partial x^2}$, $w(0, x) = 0$, $w(t, 0) = w(t, 2) = 0$.

6. (a) Show that if separation of variables is applied to the problem

$$u_t = k^2 u_{xx} + cu$$

$$u(0, x) = f(x)$$

$$u(t, 0) = u(t, b) = 0,$$

one obtains the associated equation

$$T' = k^2 \mu T$$

and the boundary value problem

$$X'' + \frac{c}{k^2} X = \mu X, \qquad X(0) = 0, \qquad X(b) = 0.$$

Solve each problem using separation of variables.

(b) $u_t = u_{xx} + u$, $u(0, x) = 1$, $u(t, 0) = u(t, \pi) = 0$.

(c) $u_t = u_{xx} - u$, $u(0, x) = 1$, $u(t, 0) = u(t, \pi) = 0$.

(d) $u_t = 4u_{xx} + 3u$, $u(0, x) = x$, $u(t, 0) = u(t, 1) = 0$.

7. In Problem (P), suppose that $f(x)$ is a piecewise continuous function such that $|f(x)| \leq M$ on $0 \leq x \leq b$. Show that the solution $u(t, x)$ of (P) satisfies

$$|u(t, x)| \leq 2Me^{-(\pi k/b)^2 t}(1 - e^{-(\pi k/b)^2 t})^{-1}$$

for all $t > 0$ and for $0 < x < b$. Then show that

$$\lim_{t \to \infty} u(t, x) = 0.$$

8. Let $\delta(x)$ denote the unit impulse function. Solve

$$u_t = u_{xx}, \qquad u(t, 0) = u(t, \pi) = 0, \qquad u(0, x) = \frac{\pi}{2}\delta\left(x + \frac{\pi}{2}\right).$$

The following information will be needed when doing the remainder of this problem set. Given the problem

(P$_1$) $u_t = k^2 u_{xx}$, $u(0, x) = f(x)$, $u(t, 0) = T_1$, $u(t, b) = T_2$

the corresponding **steady-state problem** is

(P$_s$) $0 = k^2 U_{xx}$, $U(0) = T_1$, $U(b) = T_2$.

This is a heat problem in which the solution $U(x)$ is independent of time. [Since there is no time, then (P$_s$) has no initial condition.] The steady-state problem (P$_s$) will be needed when doing Problems 9–17.

9. Show the solution of (P$_s$) is

$$U(x) = (T_2 - T_1)\left(\frac{x}{b}\right) + T_1.$$

10. (a) Let $w(t, x) = u(t, x) - U(x)$. Show that w solves the heat problem

$$w_t = k^2 w_{xx}, \qquad w(t, 0) = 0, \qquad w(t, b) = 0$$

$$w(0, x) = g(x) \equiv f(x) - (T_2 - T_1)\left(\frac{x}{b}\right) - T_1.$$

(b) Show that the solution of (P$_1$) is

$$u(t, x) = U(x) + \sum_{n=1}^{\infty} g_n e^{-(n\pi k/b)^2 t} \sin\left(\frac{n\pi x}{b}\right).$$

In Problems 11–14, solve using the results of Problems 9 and 10.

11. $u_t = u_{xx}$, $u(0, x) = 0$, $u(t, 0) = 1$, $u(t, 3) = 3$.

12. $u_t = 3u_{xx}$, $u(0, x) = x$, $u(t, 0) = 0$, $u(t, \pi) = 1$.

13. $u_t = 3u_{xx}$, $u(0, x) = 2x$, $u(t, 0) = 0$, $u(t, \pi) = \pi$.

14. $u_t = k^2 u_{xx}$, $u(0, x) = A + Bx$, $u(t, 0) = T_1$, $u(t, b) = T_2$, where A and B are constants.

15. Determine the corresponding steady-state problem. Then solve the equation.

(a) $u_t = u_{xx} + u$, $u(0, x) = f(x)$, $u(t, 0) = 1$, $u(t, 2) = 0$.

(b) $u_t = u_{xx} - 4u$, $u(0, x) = h(x)$, $u(t, 0) = 1$, $u(t, 1) = 0$.

16. Suppose that a large glass panel 1 inch thick is initially at 20°F. It is placed in a wall when the outside temperature is 0°F and the inside temperature is 70°F. Given that $k^2 = 0.023$ feet^2/second for this glass, compute the temperature $u(t, x)$.

17. (a) For aluminum $k^2 \cong 3.33$, for common steel $k^2 \cong 0.48$ and for pine $k^2 \cong 0.006$. Repeat Problem 16 for a panel of aluminum, steel, and pine.

    (b) Show that for any of these panels.

    $$\lim_{t \to \infty} u(t, x) = 840x.$$

    (c) For which panel does $u(t, x)$ approach $840x$ the fastest? the slowest?

11.3 HEAT PROBLEMS WITH INSULATED BOUNDARIES

The heat equation was solved in Section 11.2 subject to the condition that the ends of the insulated bar were held at temperature zero. If, instead, the ends of the bar are **insulated,** the boundary conditions will be

$$u_x(t, 0) = 0, \qquad u_x(t, b) = 0.$$

The corresponding heat problem is

(P$_1$)
$$\begin{cases} u_t - k^2 u_{xx} = 0 \\ u_x(t, 0) = u_x(t, b) = 0 \\ u(0, x) = f(x). \end{cases}$$

This problem can be solved by the method of separation of variables. We first find all nonzero solutions of the homogeneous portions of (P$_1$) of the form $u(t, x) = T(t)X(x)$. Putting this u in the heat equation gives

$$T'X = k^2 TX''$$

or

(3.1)
$$\frac{T'}{k^2 T} = \frac{X''}{X}.$$

Since the variables in (3.1) are separated, each side must equal a constant μ. Thus

(3.2)
$$T' = k^2 \mu T$$

and

(3.3)
$$X'' - \mu X = 0.$$

The boundary conditions imply that

$$u_x(t, 0) = T(t)X'(0) = 0, \qquad u_x(t, b) = T(t)X'(b) = 0,$$

and hence that $X'(0) = X'(b) = 0$. This and (3.3) lead to the boundary value problem

(BVP$_1$)
$$X'' - \mu X = 0, \qquad X'(0) = X'(b) = 0.$$

If $\mu > 0$, the solution of (3.3) has the form

$$X(x) = c_1 \cosh \sqrt{\mu}\, x + c_2 \sinh \sqrt{\mu}\, x.$$

Thus

$$X'(0) = \sqrt{\mu}\, c_1 \sinh 0 + \sqrt{\mu}\, c_2 \cosh 0 = \sqrt{\mu}\, c_2 = 0.$$

Thus $c_2 = 0$ and $X(x) = c_1 \cosh \sqrt{\mu}\, x$. This means that

$$X'(b) = \sqrt{\mu}\, c_1 \sinh \sqrt{\mu}\, b = 0.$$

This can happen only if $c_1 = 0$. Hence (BVP$_1$) has no nonzero solution when $\mu > 0$.

If $\mu = 0$, then $X(x) = c_1 x + c_2$ and $X'(x) = c_1$. If $c_1 = 0$, then $X'(0) = X'(b) = 0$. Thus, for $\mu = 0$, any nonzero constant is a solution. If $\mu < 0$, then let $\mu = -\lambda^2$. In terms of the new parameter λ the equation is

$$X'' + \lambda^2 X = 0.$$

It has solution

$$X(x) = c_1 \cos \lambda x + c_2 \sin \lambda x.$$

Since $X'(x) = -\lambda c_1 \sin \lambda x + \lambda c_2 \cos \lambda x$, then $X(0) = \lambda c_2 = 0$ implies that $c_2 = 0$. Thus $X(x) = c_1 \cos \lambda x$ and

$$X'(b) = -\lambda c_1 \sin \lambda b = 0.$$

To get a nonzero solution $X(x)$ it is necessary that $\sin \lambda b = 0$, that is, $\lambda = n\pi/b$ for $n = 1, 2, 3, \ldots$. Hence nonzero solutions of (BVP$_1$) are

$$X_n(x) = \begin{cases} 1/2 & \text{if } n = 0 \\ \cos\left(\dfrac{n\pi x}{b}\right) & \text{if } n = 1, 2, 3, \ldots. \end{cases}$$

Since $\mu_n = -(n\pi/b)^2$, then by (3.2) we have

$$T_n(t) = e^{-(n\pi k/b)^2 t}$$

and $u_n(t, x) = T_n(t) X_n(x)$. The functions $u_n(t, x)$ will satisfy the heat equation and the boundary conditions. Hence, for any constants a_n such that the series converges so will

(3.4)
$$u(t, x) = \sum_{n=0}^{\infty} a_n u_n(t, x).$$

The solution (3.4) can be rewritten as

(3.5)
$$u(t, x) = \frac{a_0}{2} + \sum_{n=1}^{\infty} a_n e^{-(n\pi k/b)^2 t} \cos\left(\frac{n\pi x}{b}\right).$$

We wish to choose the constants a_n so that $u(0, x) = f(x)$ is true, that is, so that

$$f(x) = \frac{a_0}{2} + \sum_{n=1}^{\infty} a_n \cos\left(\frac{n\pi x}{b}\right).$$

This is accomplished by letting the a_n be the Fourier cosine coefficients of f, that is

(3.6) $$a_0 = \frac{2}{b} \int_0^b f(x)\, dx \quad \text{and} \quad a_n = \frac{2}{b} \int_0^b f(x) \cos\left(\frac{n\pi x}{b}\right) dx.$$

Then (3.5) and (3.6) give the desired solution.

EXAMPLE 3.1   Solve the problem

$$u_t = 4u_{xx}, \qquad u_x(t, 0) = u_x(t, 1) = 0, \qquad u(0, x) = x.$$

The method of separation of variables gives

$$u(t, x) = \frac{a_0}{2} + \sum_{n=1}^{\infty} a_n e^{-4n^2\pi^2 t} \cos n\pi x,$$

where

$$a_0 = 2 \int_0^1 x\, dx = 1$$

and

$$a_n = 2 \int_0^1 x \cos n\pi x\, dx = \frac{2}{n^2\pi^2} ((-1)^n - 1).$$

Hence

$$u(t, x) = \frac{1}{2} - \frac{4}{\pi^2} \sum_{n \text{ odd}} \frac{1}{n^2} e^{-4n^2\pi^2 t} \cos n\pi x. \qquad \blacksquare$$

SOLVING BY SEPARATION OF VARIABLES

In the solution of (P_1) we first identified the homogeneous part of the problem and then found all solutions $u_n(t, x) = T_n(t)X_n(x)$ of this homogeneous part. Only at the end did we form the sum (3.4) and solve the nonhomogeneous part of (P_1). In separation of variables problems it will always be necessary to first identify the *homogeneous conditions* in the problem and to hold off trying to satisfy the nonhomogeneous conditions until all solutions of the homogeneous part of the problem are in hand.

PROBLEMS   In Problems 1–7, solve using separation of variables.

   1. $u_t = u_{xx}, \quad u_x(t, 0) = u_x(t, \pi) = 0, \quad u(0, x) = \pi - x.$

   2. $u_t = 3u_{xx}, \quad u_x(t, 0) = u_x(t, 2) = 0, \quad u(0, x) = x.$

3. $v_t = 2v_{xx}$, $v_x(t, 0) = v_x(t, \pi) = 0$, $v(0, x) = \sin x$.

4. $V_t = V_{xx}$, $V_x(t, 0) = V_x(t, 5) = 0$, $V(0, x) = 1$.

5. $R_t = 3R_{xx}$, $R_x(t, 0) = R_x(t, 3) = 0$, $R(0, x) = 0$.

6. $u_t = u_{xx} + 3u$, $u_x(t, 0) = u_x(t, \pi) = 0$, $u(0, x) = 1 + \cos x$.

7. $u_t = 2u_{xx} - \pi u$, $u_x(t, 0) = u_x(t, 1) = 0$, $u(0, x) = x$.

8. The **steady-state** problem corresponding to

$$(3.7) \quad u_t = k^2 u_{xx} + cu, \quad u_x(t, 0) = T_1, \quad u_x(t, b) = T_2, \quad u(0, x) = f(x)$$

is

$$(3.8) \qquad 0 = k^2 U_{xx} + cU, \quad U_x(0) = T_1, \quad U_x(b) = T_2.$$

(a) Solve (3.8) when $c < 0$.

(b) Show that (3.8) has a solution when $c = 0$ if and only if $T_1 = T_2$.

(c) For $c > 0$ when does (3.8) have a unique solution for all T_1 and T_2?

9. (a) Show that if u solves (3.7) and U solves (3.8), then $w(t, x) = u(t, x) - U(x)$ solves

$$w_t = k^2 w_{xx} + cw, \quad w_x(t, 0) = w_x(t, b) = 0, \quad w(0, x) = g(x)$$

where $g(x) = f(x) - U(x)$.

(b) Solve $u_t = u_{xx} - u$, $u_x(t, 0) = 1$, $u_x(t, 1) = 0$, $u(0, x) = f(x)$.

10. In (P_1) suppose that f is piecewise continuous with $|f(x)| \le M$ for $0 < x < b$.

(a) Show that the Fourier coefficients of f satisfy $|a_m| \le 2M$ for $m \ge 0$.

(b) Show that the solution of (P_1) satisfies

$$\lim_{t \to \infty} u(t, x) = \frac{1}{b} \int_0^b f(x)\, dx.$$

(c) Give a physical interpretation of part (b). Does part (b) agree with your intuition?

11.4   NEWTON COOLING

Newton's law of cooling states that a body radiates heat from its surface at a rate proportional to the difference between the skin temperature of the body and the temperature $\bar{u}$ of the surrounding medium. For example, in a slab of material of thickness b, if the surface at $x = 0$ cools by radiation, the boundary condition at $x = 0$ is

$$-\frac{\partial u}{\partial x}(t, 0) = -h_0(u(t, 0) - \bar{u}_0),$$

where h_0 is a positive constant. If the surface at $x = b$ cools by radiation, then the boundary condition at $x = b$ is

$$\frac{\partial u}{\partial x}(t, b) = -h_1(u(t, b) - \bar{u}_1),$$

where h_1 is a positive constant.

For example, let us solve the one-dimensional heat equation in a slab where the surface at $x = 0$ is held at temperature zero and the surface at $x = b$ radiates into a medium at temperature zero. The mathematical problem to solve is

(4.1)
$$\begin{cases} u_t = k^2 u_{xx}, & u(0, x) = f(x), \\ u(t, 0) = 0, & u_x(t, b) + hu(t, b) = 0. \end{cases}$$

Separation of variables will be used. We first find all nonzero solutions $u(t, x) = T(t)X(x)$ of the equation and the boundary conditions. By an easy calculation, we obtain the equation

(4.2)
$$T' = \mu k^2 T$$

and the boundary value problem

(4.3) $$X'' - \mu X = 0, \qquad X(0) = 0, \qquad X'(b) + hX(b) = 0.$$

The student can check that (4.3) has no nonzero solutions when $\mu > 0$ and when $\mu = 0$. When $\mu < 0$ we set $\mu = -\lambda^2$. Solutions of (4.3) then have the form

$$X(x) = c_1 \sin \lambda x + c_2 \cos \lambda x.$$

Since $X(0) = c_2 = 0$, then $X(x) = c_1 \sin \lambda x$. The second boundary condition implies that

(4.4) $$\lambda c_1 \cos \lambda b + hc_1 \sin \lambda b = 0.$$

Since $X(x) \not\equiv 0$, then $c_1 \neq 0$. Thus (4.4) implies that

(4.5)
$$-\frac{\lambda}{h} = \tan \lambda b.$$

Since (4.5) is a transcendental equation, solutions λ cannot be found exactly. Solutions can be obtained by numerical approximation procedures. (Tables can be found in the book of Abramowitz and Stegun.) We can also see that there are roots by graphing, that is, by finding the points of intersection of the two curves $y = \tan \lambda b$ and $y = -\lambda/h$. This is done in Figure 11.3. We see from that figure that there are infinitely many roots λ_n with $\pi/(2b) < \lambda_1 < 3\pi/(2b) < \lambda_2 < 5\pi/(2b) < \lambda_3 < \ldots$.

Nonzero solutions of (4.3) have the form

$$X_n(x) = \sin \lambda_n z.$$

Since $\mu_n = -\lambda_n^2$, then from (4.2) we see that

$$T_n(t) = e^{-\lambda_n^2 k^2 t}$$

and $u_n(t, x) = T_n(t)X_n(x)$. To satisfy the initial condition, we first form the sum

(4.6)
$$u(t, x) = \sum_{n=1}^{\infty} c_n e^{-\lambda_n^2 k^2 t} \sin \lambda_n x.$$

The constants c_n must be chosen so that

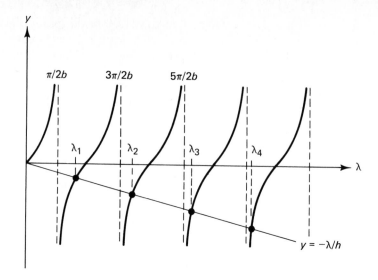

Figure 11.3. Graphical determination of roots of (4.5).

$$(4.7) \qquad f(x) = \sum_{n=1}^{\infty} c_n \sin \lambda_n x.$$

Since $\lambda_n \neq n\pi/b$, then (4.7) is not a Fourier series. However, the constants c_n can be determined using integrals. The following result is needed.

THEOREM 4.1: ORTHOGONALITY

Let $X_n(x) = \sin \lambda_n x$ be the nonzero solutions of (4.3). Then the following orthogonality relation is true:

$$\int_0^b X_n(x) X_m(x)\, dx = 0 \qquad \text{when } n \neq m.$$

To prove this result, note that $X_n'' = -\lambda_n^2 X_n$ and $X_m'' = -\lambda_m^2 X_m$. Thus

$$-\lambda_n^2 \int_0^b X_n X_m\, dx = \int_0^b X_n'' X_m\, dx$$

$$= X_n' X_m \Big|_0^b - \int_0^b X_n' X_m'\, dx$$

$$= [X_n' X_m - X_n X_m']_0^b + \int_0^b X_n X_m''\, dx$$

$$= [X_n' X_m - X_n X_m']_0^b - \lambda_m^2 \int_0^b X_n X_m\, dx.$$

In this calculation, integration by parts was used twice. Since X_n and X_m satisfy the boundary conditions in (4.1), then

$$[X'_n X_m - X_n X'_m]_0^b = X'_n(b) X_m(b) - X_n(b) X'_m(b)$$
$$= (-h X_n(b)) X_m(b) - X_n(b)(-h X_m(b)) = 0.$$

This means that

(4.8) $$-\lambda_n^2 \int_0^b X_n X_m \, dx = -\lambda_m^2 \int_0^b X_n X_m \, dx.$$

Since $n \neq m$, then $\lambda_n^2 \neq \lambda_m^2$. Thus the only way (4.8) can be true is for the integral to be zero. This proves the theorem.

We use Theorem 4.1 in (4.7) as follows (see Section 10.7). Multiply (4.7) by $X_k(x)$ and then integrate from zero to b. The result is

$$\int_0^b f(x) X_k(x) \, dx = c_k \int_0^b X_k(x)^2 \, dx$$

or

(4.9) $$c_k = \frac{\int_0^b f(x) X_k(x) \, dx}{\int_0^b X_k(x)^2 \, dx}, \qquad k = 1, 2, 3, \ldots.$$

Since

$$\int_0^b X_n(x)^2 \, dx = \int_0^b \sin^2 \lambda_n x \, dx = \frac{1}{2} \int_0^b (1 - \cos 2\lambda_n x) \, dx$$

$$= \frac{b}{2} - \frac{\sin 2\lambda_n b}{4\lambda_n} = \frac{b}{2} - \frac{\sin \lambda_n b \cos \lambda_n b}{2\lambda_n}$$

$$= \frac{b}{2} - \frac{\sin \lambda_n b \cos \lambda_n b}{2(-h \tan \lambda_n b)}$$

$$= \frac{b}{2} + \frac{\cos^2 \lambda_n b}{2h},$$

then we can write

$$c_n = \frac{\int_0^b f(x) X_n(x) \, dx}{b/2 + (\cos^2 \lambda_n b)/2h}.$$

EXAMPLE 4.2   Solve

$$u_t = 9 u_{xx}, \qquad u(t, 0) = 0, \qquad u_x(t, 1) + 2u(t, 1) = 0, \qquad u(0, x) = 1.$$

The solution is

$$u(t, x) = \sum_{n=1}^{\infty} c_n e^{-9\lambda_n^2 t} \sin \lambda_n x$$

where λ_n solves $-\lambda/2 = \tan \lambda$. The constants c_n are determined by the formula

$$c_n = \frac{\int_0^1 \sin \lambda_n x \, dx}{\frac{1}{2} + \cos^2 \lambda_n/4} = \frac{4}{\lambda_n}\left(\frac{1 - \cos \lambda_n}{2 + \cos^2 \lambda_n}\right). \quad \blacksquare$$

1. Solve by separation of variables.

(a) $u_t = u_{xx}$, $u(t, 0) = 0$, $u_x(t, \pi) + u(t, \pi) = 0$, $u(0, x) = \pi - x$.

(b) $u_t = 3u_{xx}$, $u(t, 0) = 0$, $u_x(t, 2) + u(t, 2) = 0$, $u(0, x) = x$.

2. Given the problem

(4.10) $u_t = k^2 u_{xx}$, $u(t, 0) = T_1$, $u_x(t, b) + h[u(t, b) - \bar{u}] = 0$, $u(0, x) = f(x)$,

the corresponding **steady-state problem** is

(4.11) $k^2 U_{xx} = 0$, $U(0) = T_1$, $U_x(b) + h[U(b) - \bar{u}] = 0$.

(a) Solve (4.11) for $U(x)$.

(b) Define $w(t, x) = u(t, x) - U(x)$. Show that $w(t, x)$ satisfies a heat problem with homogeneous boundary conditions.

(c) Find $u(t, x)$.

3. Consider the problem

$u_t = k^2 u_{xx}$, $-u_x(t, 0) + hu(t, 0) = 0$, $u(t, b) = 0$, $u(0, x) = f(x)$.

(a) Use separation of variables to find an associated differential equation for $T(t)$ and a boundary value problem for $X(x)$.

(b) Find all nonzero solutions $X_n(x)$ of the boundary value problem.

(c) Show that if $n \neq m$, then $\int_0^b X_n X_m \, dx = 0$.

(d) Solve for $u(t, x)$.

4. (a) Repeat Problem 3 for

$u_t = k^2 u_{xx}$, $u(t, 0) = u_x(t, b) = 0$, $u(0, x) = f(x)$.

(b) Let $F(x)$ be a $4b$-periodic function which is odd and which satisfies the conditions

$F(x) = f(x)$ on $0 \leq x \leq b$, $F(x + b) = F(-x + b)$ on $0 \leq x \leq b$.

Show that $F(x + 2b) = -F(x)$ and hence that all even terms in the Fourier series for F are zero (see Problem 7 of Section 10.2).

(c) Show that

$$F(x) \sim \sum_{n=1,\, n \text{ odd}}^{\infty} b_n \sin\left(\frac{n\pi x}{2b}\right)$$

where

$$b_n = \frac{1}{b}\int_0^{2b} F(x) \sin\left(\frac{n\pi x}{2b}\right) dx = \frac{2}{b}\int_0^b f(x) \sin\left(\frac{n\pi x}{2b}\right) dx.$$

5. Repeat Problem 3 for

$u_t = k^2 u_{xx}$, $u_x(t, 0) = u(t, b) = 0$, $u(0, x) = f(x)$.

6. For the problem

$$\rho(x)c(x)\frac{\partial u}{\partial t} = \frac{\partial}{\partial x}\left(\kappa(x)\frac{\partial u}{\partial x}\right) + d(x)u,   u(0, x) = f(x)$$

$$u(t, 0) = 0,   u_x(t, b) + hu(t, b) = 0$$

apply separation of variables. Determine the associated differential equation for $T(t)$ and boundary value problem for $X(x)$.

7. Write a computer program to evaluate the constants λ_n determined in Example 4.1. Evaluate λ_n, c_n, and $9\lambda_n^2$ for several values of n.

11.5 THE LAPLACE EQUATION ON A RECTANGLE

Heat flow in a two-dimensional medium is described by the partial differential equation $u_t = k^2(u_{xx} + u_{yy})$. The corresponding **time-independent** or **steady-state** equation is

(5.1) $$u_{xx} + u_{yy} = 0.$$

This equation is called the two-dimensional Laplace equation. This equation, and its three-dimensional analog,

$$u_{xx} + u_{yy} + u_{zz} = 0,$$

arise in the study of electrostatics, gravitation, elasticity, and numerous other areas.

Since there is no time variable in (5.1), there is no associated initial condition. However, boundary conditions must be specified in order to obtain a unique solution. On the rectangle

$$R = \{(x, y): 0 \le x \le a, 0 \le y \le b\}$$

a typical problem is

(R$_1$)
$$\begin{cases} u_{xx} + u_{yy} = 0 & \text{on } 0 < x < a, \quad 0 < y < b \\ u(x, 0) = f_1(x), \quad u(x, b) = f_2(x) & \text{for } 0 < x < a \\ u(0, y) = 0, \quad u(a, y) = 0, & \text{for } 0 < y < b. \end{cases}$$

These conditions are illustrated in Figure 11.4.

We shall solve (R$_1$) using separation of variables. The homogeneous portions of (R$_1$) are the first and third lines. We seek a nonzero solution of the first and third lines of (R$_1$) of the form $u(x, y) = X(x)Y(y)$. Since

$$X''Y + XY'' = 0,$$

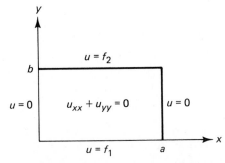

Figure 11.4. A Laplace problem.

then $-X''/X = Y''/Y$ separates the variables. We are led, by the usual calculations, to the associated differential equation

(5.2) $$Y'' - \mu Y = 0$$

and the boundary value problem

(5.3) $$X'' + \mu X = 0, \qquad X(0) = X(a) = 0.$$

Problem (5.3) was solved in Section 11.2. The only nonzero solutions of (5.3) are

$$X_n(x) = \sin\left(\frac{n\pi x}{a}\right), \qquad \mu_n = \left(\frac{n\pi}{a}\right)^2$$

for $n = 1, 2, 3, \ldots$. Using $\mu_n = (n\pi/a)^2$ in (5.2), we find that

$$Y_n(y) = a_n \cosh\left(\frac{n\pi y}{a}\right) + b_n \sinh\left(\frac{n\pi y}{a}\right),$$

where a_n and b_n are arbitrary constants. We now form the sum

(5.4) $$u(x, y) = \sum_{n=1}^{\infty} \left(a_n \cosh\left(\frac{n\pi y}{a}\right) + b_n \sinh\left(\frac{n\pi y}{a}\right)\right) \sin\left(\frac{n\pi x}{a}\right).$$

Using $y = 0$ in (5.4), we see that

$$f_1(x) = \sum_{n=1}^{\infty} a_n \sin\left(\frac{n\pi x}{a}\right).$$

This means that the a_n's must be the Fourier sine coefficients of f_1, that is,

(5.5) $$a_n = \frac{2}{a} \int_0^a f_1(x) \sin\left(\frac{n\pi x}{a}\right) dx.$$

The second boundary condition leads to the equation

$$f_2(x) = \sum_{n=1}^{\infty} \left(a_n \cosh\left(\frac{n\pi b}{a}\right) + b_n \sinh\left(\frac{n\pi b}{a}\right)\right) \sin\left(\frac{n\pi x}{a}\right).$$

This means that the constants

$$B_n = \left(a_n \cosh\left(\frac{n\pi b}{a}\right) + b_n \sinh\left(\frac{n\pi b}{a}\right)\right)$$

must be the Fourier sine coefficients of f_2. Thus

(5.6) $$B_n = \frac{2}{a} \int_0^a f_2(x) \sin\left(\frac{n\pi x}{a}\right) dx.$$

In terms of the Fourier coefficients, a_n and B_n, we have

$$b_n = \frac{B_n - a_n \cosh(n\pi b/a)}{\sinh(n\pi b/a)}.$$

Hence the solution of (R_1) is

$$u(x, y) = \sum_{n=1}^{\infty} \left\{ a_n \left[\cosh\left(\frac{n\pi y}{a}\right) - \coth\left(\frac{n\pi b}{a}\right) \sinh\left(\frac{n\pi y}{a}\right) \right] \right.$$

$$\left. + B_n \sinh\left(\frac{n\pi y}{a}\right) \operatorname{csch}\left(\frac{n\pi b}{a}\right) \right\} \sin\left(\frac{n\pi x}{a}\right),$$

where the a_n and B_n are given in (5.5) and (5.6).

EXAMPLE 5.1   Solve

$$u_{xx} + u_{yy} = 0, \qquad u(x, 0) = 0, \qquad u(x, \pi) = 1, \qquad u(0, y) = u(1, y) = 0.$$

In this example, $a = 1$, $b = \pi$, $f_1(x) \equiv 0$, and $f_2(x) \equiv 1$. This means that all $a_n = 0$, while

$$B_n = 2 \int_0^1 \sin n\pi x \, dx = \frac{2}{n\pi} [1 + (-1)^{n+1}].$$

The solution is

$$u(x, y) = \sum_{n=1}^{\infty} \frac{2}{n\pi} [1 + (-1)^{n+1}] \frac{\sinh n\pi y}{\sinh n\pi^2} \sin n\pi x. \quad \blacksquare$$

The problem

$$(\mathbf{R}_2) \qquad \begin{cases} u_{xx} + u_{yy} = 0 & \text{on } 0 < x < a, 0 < y < b \\ u(x, 0) = u(x, b) = 0 & \text{on } 0 < x < a \\ u(0, y) = g_1(y) & \text{on } 0 < y < b \\ u(a, y) = g_2(y) & \text{on } 0 < y < b \end{cases}$$

is solved in a similar manner. The student should compare the boundary values in $(\mathbf{R}_1)$ and $(\mathbf{R}_2)$ and note where u is zero and where it is not. It should be clear that if the solutions of $(\mathbf{R}_1)$ and $(\mathbf{R}_2)$ are added together, the result is a solution of the problem specified in Figure 11.5. This problem has general boundary values specified on all four sides of the rectangle R.

DIRICHLET PROBLEM IN A REGION G

Given a bounded region G with boundary B, the **Dirichlet problem** for G has the form

$$u_{xx} + u_{yy} = 0 \qquad \text{for } (x, y) \text{ in } G$$

with u equal to some given function f on the boundary of G, that is,

$$u(x, y) = f(x, y) \qquad \text{for } (x, y) \text{ in } B.$$

Problems (R_1) and (R_2) are Dirichlet problems with $G = R$ and with f zero over parts of B. Figure 11.5 specifies the general Dirichlet problem for a rectangle.

The Dirichlet boundary conditions given in Figure 11.5 are not the only physically interesting boundary conditions for the Laplace equation. Examples of other interesting boundary conditions are given in the problem section.

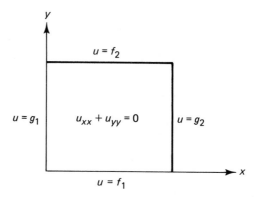

Figure 11.5. Dirichlet problem on a rectangle.

PROBLEMS

In Problems 1–6, solve the Dirichlet problem using separation of variables.

1. $u_{xx} + u_{yy} = 0$, $u(x, 0) = x$, $u(x, 1) = 0$, $u(0, y) = 0$, $u(\pi, y) = 0$.

2. $u_{xx} + u_{yy} = 0$, $u(x, 0) = x$, $u(x, 1) = 0$, $u(0, y) = 0$, $u(\pi, y) = 1$.

3. $2u_{xx} + u_{yy} = 0$, $u(x, 0) = 1$, $u(x, 3) = 1$, $u(0, y) = 0$, $u(\pi, y) = 0$.

4. $3u_{xx} + 4u_{yy} = 0$, $u(x, 0) = 0$, $u(x, \pi) = 0$, $u(0, y) = y$, $u(\pi, y) = y$.

5. $u_{xx} + 2u_{yy} + 3u_y = 0$, $u(x, 0) = 0$, $u(x, 1) = 1$, $u(0, y) = 0$, $u(1, y) = 0$.

6. $u_{xx} + u_{yy} = 0$ on $-1 < x, y < 1$, $u(x, -1) = x$, $u(x, 1) = 0, u(-1, y) = 0, u(1, y) = 0$. (Hard problem! Be careful!)

In Problems 7–10, solve by separation of variables. Notice that the boundary conditions are not necessarily Dirichlet boundary conditions. Proceed with care!

7. $u_{xx} + u_{yy} = 0$, $u(x, 0) = x$, $u(x, \pi) = 0$, $u_x(0, y) = u_x(\pi, y) = 0$.

8. $9u_{xx} + u_{yy} = 0$, $u(x, 0) = 0$, $u(x, 1) = 1 + x$, $u_x(0, y) = u_x(\pi, y) = 0$.

9. $u_{xx} + u_{yy} = 0$, $u_y(x, 0) = 0$, $u_y(x, 2) = 0$, $u(0, y) = y$, $u(\pi, y) = 1$.

10. $u_{xx} + 2u_{yy} + 3u_y = 0$, $u(x, 0) = 0$, $u(x, 1) = x, u_x(0, y) = 0$, $u_x(1, y) = 0$.

11. (a) Show that for any constant K, $u(x, y) \equiv K$ solves

$$u_{xx} + u_{yy} = 0, \qquad u_y(x, 0) = u_y(x, 1) = 0, \qquad u_x(0, y) = u_x(1, y) = 0.$$

(b) Show that

$$u_{xx} + u_{yy} = 0, \qquad u_x(0, y) = u_x(1, y) = 0$$

$$u_y(x, 0) = f_1(x), \qquad u_y(x, 1) = f_2(x)$$

does not have a unique solution.

12. (a) Show that separation of variables applied to

$$u_{xx} + u_{yy} = 0, \qquad u(0, y) = 0, \qquad u(1, y) + u_x(1, y) = 0$$

$$u(x, 0) = f(x), \qquad u(x, 1) = 0$$

leads to the boundary value problem

$$X'' - \mu X = 0, \qquad X(0) = 0, \qquad X(1) + X'(1) = 0.$$

(b) Find all nonzero solutions $X(x)$ of this boundary value problem (see Section 11.4).

(c) Solve for $u(x, y)$.

13. Consider the problem

$$\begin{array}{ll} u_{xx} + u_{yy} = 0 & \text{on } 0 < x < a, \quad 0 < y < \infty. \\[4pt] u(x, 0) = f(x) & \text{on } 0 < x < a. \\[4pt] u(0, y) = u(a, y) = 0 & \text{on } 0 < y < \infty. \end{array}$$

$u(x, y)$ remains bounded as $y \to \infty$.

(a) Show that separation of variables leads to the boundary value problem

$$X'' - \mu X = 0, \qquad X(0) = X(a) = 0$$

and to the equation

$$Y'' + \mu Y = 0$$

with the side condition that $Y(y)$ is bounded as $y \to \infty$.

(b) Find all nonzero solutions $X_n(x)$ and μ_n of the boundary value problem.

(c) Find all *bounded* solutions of $Y_n'' + \mu_n Y_n = 0$.

(d) Solve for $u(x, y)$.

11.6 THE LAPLACE EQUATION ON A DISK

In polar coordinates $x = r \cos \theta$, $y = r \sin \theta$ the Laplace equation

(6.1) $$u_{xx} + u_{yy} = 0$$

becomes

$$(rU_r)_r + \frac{1}{r} U_{\theta\theta} = 0,$$

where $U(r, \theta) = u(r \cos \theta, r \sin \theta)$. Hence the Dirichlet problem on a disk

$$D = \{(x, y): x^2 + y^2 \le A^2\}$$

can be written as

$$\begin{cases} (rU_r)_r + \dfrac{1}{r}U_{\theta\theta} = 0 & \text{in } 0 < r < A \\[2mm] U(A, \theta) = f(\theta) & \text{on } 0 \le \theta < 2\pi. \end{cases}$$

(6.2)

Here f is a given function. There are two "hidden boundary conditions" that must be attached to (6.2) to make the problem meaningful. First we must require that the solution of (6.2) be 2π-periodic in θ. Second, since (6.1) must be satisfied at $x = y = 0$, then $U(r, \theta)$ must surely be defined and bounded when $r = 0$. Hence the problem that we wish to solve is not (6.2). Rather it is

(D)

$$\begin{cases} (rU_r)_r + \dfrac{1}{r}U_{\theta\theta} = 0, & 0 < r < A, \quad 0 \le \theta < 2\pi \\[2mm] U(A, \theta) = f(\theta) \\[2mm] U(r, \theta + 2\pi) = U(r, \theta) \\[2mm] U(r, \theta) \text{ is bounded as } r \to 0^+. \end{cases}$$

We solve (D) by separation of variables. From $U = R(r)\Theta(\theta)$ we see that $(rR')'\Theta + R\Theta''/r = 0$ or

$$\frac{r(rR')'}{R} = -\frac{\Theta''}{\Theta} = \mu.$$

Hence $R(r)$ must satisfy

(6.3) $r^2R'' + rR' - \mu R = 0,$ $R(r)$ bounded as $r \to 0^+$

and Θ must be a 2π-periodic solution of

(6.4) $\Theta'' + \mu\Theta = 0.$

Since (6.4) is a second-order equation, the two periodic boundary conditions $\Theta(\pi) = \Theta(-\pi)$ and $\Theta'(\pi) = \Theta'(-\pi)$ are enough to ensure that Θ is 2π-periodic. Hence Θ must be a nonzero solution of the boundary value problem

(6.5) $\Theta'' + \mu\Theta = 0,$ $\Theta(\pi) = \Theta(-\pi),$ $\Theta'(\pi) = \Theta'(-\pi).$

There are no nonzero, 2π-periodic solutions of (6.5) when $\mu < 0$. This is easily checked. When $\mu = 0$, then $\Theta = c_1\theta + c_2$. The solution is periodic whenever $c_1 = 0$ (i.e., Θ is any constant). When $\mu > 0$ let $\lambda = \sqrt{\mu}$ so that

$$\Theta(\theta) = c_1 \cos \lambda\theta + c_2 \sin \lambda\theta$$

and

$$\Theta'(b) = -\lambda c_1 \sin \lambda\theta + \lambda c_2 \cos \lambda\theta.$$

To satisfy the boundary conditions, we require that

$$c_1 \cos \lambda\pi + c_2 \sin \lambda\pi = c_1 \cos(-\lambda\pi) + c_2 \sin(-\lambda\pi)$$

and

$$-\lambda c_1 \sin \lambda\pi + \lambda c_2 \cos \lambda\pi = -\lambda c_1 \sin(-\lambda\pi) + \lambda c_2 \cos(-\lambda\pi).$$

Since the cosine is an even function and the sine is an odd function, these conditions reduce to

(6.6) $$2 \sin \lambda \pi = 0.$$

Thus $\lambda = n$, $\mu = n^2$, and

$$\Theta_n(\theta) = a_n \cos n\theta + b_n \sin n\theta,$$

where a_n and b_n are arbitrary constants.

When $\mu = n^2$, (6.3) is the Euler equation

$$r^2 R_n'' + r R_n' - n^2 R_n = 0.$$

Solutions have the form $R_n = c_n r^n + d_n r^{-n}$. Since R_n must be bounded as $r \to 0^+$, then $d_n = 0$. Thus we take $R_n(r) = r^n$ and

$$U_n(r, \theta) = \begin{cases} a_0 & \text{if } n = 0 \\ r^n(a_n \cos n\theta + b_n \sin n\theta) & \text{if } n = 1, 2, 3, \ldots. \end{cases}$$

In order to satisfy the boundary condition $U(A, \theta) = f(\theta)$ we sum the solutions U_n to obtain

(6.7) $$U(r, \theta) = a_0 + \sum_{n=1}^{\infty} r^n(a_n \cos n\theta + b_n \sin n\theta).$$

It is required that

(6.8) $$U(A, \theta) = a_0 + \sum_{n=1}^{\infty} A^n(a_n \cos n\theta + b_n \sin n\theta) = f(\theta).$$

To satisfy (6.8), we let a_0, $A^n a_n$, and $A^n b_n$ be the Fourier coefficients of f. Thus

$$a_0 = \frac{1}{2\pi} \int_0^{2\pi} f(\theta) \, d\theta,$$

$$a_n = \frac{1}{A^n \pi} \int_0^{2\pi} f(\theta) \cos n\theta \, d\theta,$$

and

$$b_n = \frac{1}{A^n \pi} \int_0^{2\pi} f(\theta) \sin n\theta \, d\theta,$$

for $n = 1, 2, 3, \ldots.$

EXAMPLE 6.1   Solve the Laplace equation in the disk $x^2 + y^2 < 4$ subject to the boundary condition that $U(2, \theta) = \theta$ when $0 \leq \theta < 2\pi$.

In this case we have

$$a_0 = \frac{1}{2\pi} \int_0^{2\pi} \theta \, d\theta = \pi,$$

$$2^n a_n = \frac{1}{\pi} \int_0^{2\pi} \theta \cos n\theta \, d\theta = 0,$$

and

$$2^n b_n = \frac{1}{\pi} \int_0^{2\pi} \theta \sin n\theta \, d\theta = -\frac{2}{n}.$$

Thus

$$u(r, \theta) = \pi - 2 \sum_{n=1}^{\infty} \left(\frac{r}{2}\right)^n \frac{1}{n} \sin n\theta. \quad \blacksquare$$

Since the solution of problem (D) is unique, the following interesting result is true.

THEOREM 6.2: MEAN VALUE THEOREM

If $u(x, y)$ solves (D), then

$$u(0,0) = \frac{1}{2\pi} \int_0^{2\pi} f(\theta) \, d\theta.$$

The result is true because (6.7) implies that

$$u(0, 0) = U(0, \theta) = a_0 = \frac{1}{2\pi} \int_0^{2\pi} f(\theta) \, d\theta.$$

COROLLARY 6.3

The solution $u(x, y)$ of (D) cannot attain a strict maximum in the interior of the disk.

The result is proved by a contradiction argument. Suppose that there is a point $(\bar{x}, \bar{y})$ with $\bar{x}^2 + \bar{y}^2 = R_1^2 < R^2$ such that $u(\bar{x}, \bar{y}) > u(x, y)$ whenever $0 < (x - \bar{x})^2 + (y - \bar{y})^2 \leq \delta^2$ for some $\delta < R - R_1$. Define $u_1(x, y) = u(x + \bar{x}, y + \bar{y})$. Then $u_1(x, y)$ solves the Laplace equation in the disk $x^2 + y^2 < \delta^2$ and $u_1(0, 0) > u_1(x, y)$ for all (x, y) on the boundary $x^2 + y^2 = \delta^2$. This would mean that the mean value of $u_1(x, y)$ over the boundary $x^2 + y^2 = \delta^2$ is smaller than $u_1(0, 0)$. But Theorem 6.2 states that it equals $u_1(0, 0)$, a contradiction. The conclusion of Corollary 6.3 can be strengthened. For more details, see the problem section.

SOLUTION NOTE

The first, third and fourth conditions in (D) are *homogeneous* conditions. The second equation $U(A, \theta) = f(\theta)$ is nonhomogeneous (unless $f \equiv 0$). Notice that we followed the usual pattern of solution by separation of variables. First, all solutions $U_n(r, \theta)$ of the three homogeneous conditions in (D) were found. Only at the end did we form the sum (6.7) and attempt to solve the nonhomogeneous condition.

PROBLEMS

In Problems 1–6, solve the Dirichlet problem (D) for the boundary condition given.

1. $f(\theta) = 2\theta - 1$ on $0 \le \theta < 2\pi, A = 1.$ **2.** $f(\theta) = \theta$ on $-\pi \le \theta < \pi, A = 1.$

3. $f(\theta) = \begin{cases} 1 & \text{if } 0 \le \theta < \pi \\ 0 & \text{if } -\pi \le \theta < 0 \end{cases}, A = 2.$ **4.** $f(\theta) = |\theta|$ on $-\pi \le \theta < \pi, A = \sqrt{3}.$

5. $f(\theta) = 1 + \sum\limits_{n=1}^{\infty} e^{-n} \sin n\theta, A = 4.$ **6.** $f(\theta) = 0$ on $-\pi/4 \le \theta < 7\pi/4, A = 5.$

7. Solve the Laplace equation in the half-disk $D_0 = \{(x, y): x^2 + y^2 < A^2, y > 0\}$ subject to the boundary conditions

$$U(A, \theta) = g(\theta), \qquad 0 \le \theta \le \pi$$

$$U(r, 0) = U(r, \pi) = 0, \qquad 0 \le r < A.$$

8. Solve the Laplace equation in the half-disk $D_0 = \{(x, y): x^2 + y^2 < A^2, y > 0\}$ subject to the boundary conditions

$$U(A, \theta) = g(\theta), \qquad \text{on } 0 \le \theta \le \pi$$

$$U_\theta(r, 0) = U_\theta(r, \pi) = 0, \qquad \text{on } 0 \le r < A.$$

9. Solve the Laplace equation on the annulus $A = \{(x, y): 1 < x^2 + y^2 < 4\}$ subject to the boundary conditions

$$U(1, \theta) = g_1(\theta), \qquad U(2, \theta) = g_2(\theta) \qquad \text{for } 0 \le \theta < 2\pi.$$

10. Solve the Laplace equation in the unbounded region $x^2 + y^2 > A^2$ subject to the two conditions

$$U(A, \theta) = f(\theta) \qquad \text{on } 0 \le \theta < 2\pi,$$

$$U(r, \theta) \text{ is bounded as } r \to \infty.$$

11. (a) Show that $U(r, \theta) = \log (r/A)$ solves the Laplace equation when $r > A$ and the boundary condition $U(A, \theta) = 0.$

(b) Show that in Problem 10, if the requirement that $U(r, \theta)$ remains bounded as $r \to \infty$ is dropped, then the problem has more than one solution (in fact, infinitely many solutions).

12. (a) Show that the solution of (D) can be written in the form

$$U(r, \theta) = \frac{1}{\pi} \int_{-\pi}^{\pi} \left[\frac{1}{2} + \sum_{n=1}^{\infty} \left(\frac{r}{A} \right)^n \cos n(\theta - s) \right] f(s) \, ds.$$

(b) Show that

$$\sum_{n=0}^{\infty} \left(\frac{r}{A} \right)^n \cos n\theta = Re \left[\sum_{n=0}^{\infty} \left(\frac{r}{A} \right)^n e^{in\theta} \right]$$

$$= Re \left(1 - \frac{r}{A} e^{i\theta} \right)^{-1}$$

and then that

$$1 + 2 \sum_{n=1}^{\infty} \left(\frac{r}{A} \right)^n \cos n(\theta - s) = \frac{A^2 - r^2}{A^2 - 2rA \cos(\theta - s) + r^2}.$$

13. Let u solve $u_{xx} + u_{yy} = 0$ and let $U(r, \theta) = u(r \cos \theta, r \sin \theta)$ be its polar representation. Show that

$$U_r = u_x \cos \theta + u_y \sin \theta$$

$$U_\theta = u_x(-r \sin \theta) + u_y(r \cos \theta).$$

Continue this computation to show that

$$\frac{1}{r} (rU_r)_r + \frac{1}{r^2} U_{\theta\theta} = u_{xx} + u_{yy}.$$

14. Show that if $w_{xx} + w_{yy} > 0$ in $x^2 + y^2 < R^2$, then w cannot attain a maximum in the interior of the disk. *Hint:* At any such maximum one would have $w_{xx} \leq 0$.

15. (*Maximum Principle*) Show that if $u(x, y)$ solves (D) and if $f(\theta) \leq M$ on $0 \leq \theta \leq 2\pi$, then $u(x, y) \leq M$ when $x^2 + y^2 < R^2$. *Hint:* Apply Problem 14 to $w(x, y) = u(x, y) + \varepsilon(x^2 + y^2)$ to see that $u(x, y) \leq w(x, y) \leq M + \varepsilon R^2$. Then let $\varepsilon \to 0^+$.

16. (a) (*Maximum Principle*) Show that if $u_{xx} + u_{yy} = 0$ in the rectangle $R = \{(x, y) : A_1 < x < A_2, B_1 < y < B_2\}$ and if $u(x, y) \leq M$ on the boundary of R, then $u(x, y) \leq M$ in the interior of R. *Hint:* Modify the proof used in Problem 15.

(b) Can you generalize the result to regions other than rectangles?

17. (a) In Problem 15, show that if $f(\theta) \geq m$ on $0 \leq \theta \leq 2\pi$, then $u(x, y) \geq m$ when $x^2 + y^2 < R^2$. *Hint:* Apply Problem 15 to $-u$.

(b) Show that if $f(\theta) \equiv 0$, then $u \equiv 0$.

(c) Show that (D) has at most one solution.

18. Show that if $|f(\theta)| \leq M$ on $0 \leq \theta \leq 2\pi$ for some $M > 0$, then the series in (6.7) converges for all r with $0 \leq r < R$.

11.7 THE WAVE EQUATION

The wave equation

(7.1) $$u_{tt} = c^2 u_{xx}$$

can be used to described a variety of physical phenomena. For example, consider a perfectly flexible, homogeneous, and elastic string stretched between two supports on the x-axis as shown in Figure 11.6. (See also Photo 25 for an interesting practical application.) Let $u(t, x)$ be the vertical displacement of the string at time t and position x. If u is small, then u will satisfy (7.1). In this

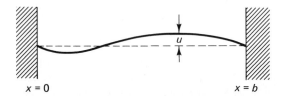

Figure 11.6. Elastic string problem.

Photo 25. Sunshine Skyway Bridge, Tampa Bay, Florida—Designed by Figg and Muller Engineers, Inc. (high level approaches and main span) (Photograph by Ray Stanyard).

string problem $c = \sqrt{T/\rho}$, where ρ is the density of the string and T is an elastic constant for the string.

Since (7.1) is second order in t, two initial conditions are needed. These are the **initial position**

$$(7.2) \qquad\qquad u(0, x) = f(x)$$

and the **initial velocity**

$$(7.3) \qquad\qquad u_t(0, x) = g(x),$$

where f and g are known functions. Since the string is fixed at the ends $x = 0$ and $x = b$, then u must also satisfy the two boundary conditions

$$(7.4) \qquad\qquad u(t, 0) = 0, \qquad u(t, b) = 0.$$

The four conditions (7.1)–(7.4) determine $u(t, x)$ completely. The *homogeneous* part of the problem is (7.1) and (7.4).

The wave equation occurs in many acoustical and elastic problems. For example, consider a cylindrical bar made up of a homogeneous elastic material and oriented along the x-axis as shown in Figure 11.7. If the bar is stretched or contracted in such a way that the planes $x =$ constant are displaced in the x-direction by an amount $u(t, x)$, then u will satisfy (7.1). Here $c = \sqrt{E/\rho}$, where ρ is the density of the material and E is its Young's modulus. Initial and boundary conditions such as (7.2)–(7.4) must also be given in order to specify u completely.

The wave problem (7.1)–(7.4) can be solved by the method of separation of variables. We first seek a nonzero solution $u(t, x) = T(t)X(x)$ of (7.1) and (7.4). Thus $T''X = c^2 TX''$ and

$$\frac{T''}{c^2 T} = \frac{X''}{X} = -\mu$$

for some constant μ. The boundary conditions (7.4) imply that $X(0) = X(b) = 0$. Hence we are led to the equation

$$(7.5) \qquad\qquad T'' + \mu c^2 T = 0$$

and the boundary value problem

$$(7.6) \qquad X'' + \mu X = 0, \qquad X(0) = X(b) = 0.$$

The boundary value problem (7.6) was solved in Section 11.2. The solution is

$$X_n(x) = \sin\left(\frac{n\pi x}{b}\right) \quad \text{and} \quad \mu_n = \left(\frac{n\pi}{b}\right)^2, \qquad n = 1, 2, 3, \ldots.$$

Figure 11.7. Elastic bar.

Given μ_n, the solution of (7.5) is

$$T_n(t) = a_n \cos\left(\frac{n\pi ct}{b}\right) + b_n \sin\left(\frac{n\pi ct}{b}\right)$$

where a_n and b_n are arbitrary constants. Thus

$$u_n(t, x) = \left[a_n \cos\left(\frac{n\pi ct}{b}\right) + b_n \sin\left(\frac{n\pi ct}{b}\right)\right] \sin\left(\frac{n\pi x}{b}\right)$$

satisfies (7.1) and (7.4).

We now sum the functions $u_n(t, x)$ to form

(7.7) $\qquad u(t, x) = \sum_{n=1}^{\infty} \left[a_n \cos\left(\frac{n\pi ct}{b}\right) + b_n \sin\left(\frac{n\pi ct}{b}\right)\right] \sin\left(\frac{n\pi x}{b}\right).$

Then initial condition (7.2) will be satisfied if

$$f(x) = \sum_{n=1}^{\infty} a_n \sin\left(\frac{n\pi x}{b}\right).$$

Hence the constants a_n must be the Fourier sine coefficients of f, that is,

(7.8) $\qquad\qquad\qquad a_n = \frac{2}{b} \int_0^b f(x) \sin\left(\frac{n\pi x}{b}\right) dx.$

From (7.7) we see that

$$u_t(t, x) = \sum_{n=1}^{\infty} \left(\frac{n\pi c}{b}\right) \left[-a_n \sin\left(\frac{n\pi ct}{b}\right) + b_n \cos\left(\frac{n\pi ct}{b}\right)\right] \sin\left(\frac{n\pi x}{b}\right).$$

Hence, (7.3) reduces to

$$g(x) = \sum_{n=1}^{\infty} \left(\frac{n\pi c}{b}\right) b_n \sin\left(\frac{n\pi x}{b}\right)$$

or

(7.9) $\qquad\qquad b_n\left(\frac{n\pi c}{b}\right) = \frac{2}{b} \int_0^b g(x) \sin\left(\frac{n\pi x}{b}\right) dx.$

The solution $u(t, x)$ is specified by (7.7)–(7.9).

EXAMPLE 7.1   Solve the wave problem

$$u_{tt} = 4u_{xx}$$

$$u(0, x) = x(x - \pi), \qquad u_t(0, x) = 0$$

$$u(t, 0) = u(t, \pi) = 0.$$

The solution has the form

$$u(t, x) = \sum_{n=1}^{\infty} \left[a_n \cos(2nt) + b_n \sin(2nt)\right] \sin nx.$$

The first initial condition implies that

$$x(x - \pi) \sim \sum_{n=1}^{\infty} a_n \sin nx,$$

while the second implies that

$$0 \sim \sum_{n=1}^{\infty} 2nb_n \sin nx.$$

Hence $b_n = 0$ for $n = 1, 2, 3, \ldots$, while

$$a_n = \frac{2}{\pi} \int_0^{\pi} x(x - \pi) \sin nx \, dx = \frac{4}{\pi n^3} (\cos n\pi - 1).$$

Thus

$$u(t, x) = \sum_{n=1}^{\infty} \frac{4}{n^3 \pi} [(-1)^n - 1] \cos (2nt) \sin nx. \quad \blacksquare$$

When $g(x) \equiv 0$ the solution (7.7) takes the form

$$u(t, x) = \sum_{n=1}^{\infty} a_n \cos \left(\frac{n\pi ct}{b} \right) \sin \left(\frac{n\pi x}{b} \right)$$

$$= \sum_{n=1}^{\infty} \frac{a_n}{2} \left[\sin \frac{n\pi(x - ct)}{b} + \sin \frac{n\pi(x + ct)}{b} \right]$$

or

(7.10) $\qquad u(t, x) = \frac{1}{2} \sum_{n=1}^{\infty} a_n \sin \frac{n\pi(x - ct)}{b} + \frac{1}{2} \sum_{n=1}^{\infty} a_n \sin \frac{n\pi(x + ct)}{b}.$

The series

$$\sum_{n=1}^{\infty} a_n \sin \frac{n\pi x}{b}$$

represents the odd-periodic extension of $f(x)$. If we call this extension $F(x)$, then (7.10) reduces to

(7.11) $\qquad u(t, x) = \frac{1}{2}[F(x - ct) + F(x + ct)].$

The result (7.11) is that the wave form $F(x)$ is seen to split into a wave $F(x - ct)/2$, which moves to the right with speed c and a wave $F(x + ct)/2$ which moves to the left with speed c. This splitting of the initial waveform is illustrated in Figure 11.8 for a triangular initial condition.

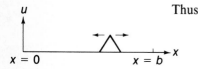

u

$x = 0 \qquad\qquad x = b$

etc.

Figure 11.8. Splitting of a solution as t grows.

PROBLEMS

In Problems 1–8, solve using separation of variables.

1. $u_{tt} = 2u_{xx}, \quad u(0, x) = x, \quad u_t(0, x) = 0, \quad u(t, 0) = u(t, \pi) = 0.$

2. $9u_{tt} = u_{xx}, \quad u(0, x) = 0, \quad u_t(0, x) = x(x - \pi), \quad u(t, 0) = u(t, \pi) = 0.$

3. $4u_{tt} = 9u_{xx}$, $u(0, x) = 1$, $u_t(0, x) = 0$, $u(t, 0) = u(t, 1) = 0$.

4. $u_{tt} = \pi^2 u_{xx}$, $u(0, x) = x$, $u_t(0, x) = 1$, $u(t, 0) = u(t, 1) = 0$.

5. $u_{tt} = u_{xx} + u$, $u(0, x) = 1$, $u_t(0, x) = 0$, $u(t, 0) = u(t, 1) = 0$.

6. $u_{tt} = u_{xx} - u$, $u(0, x) = 1$, $u_t(0, x) = 0$, $u(t, 0) = u(t, 1) = 0$.

7. $u_{tt} = u_{xx}$, $u(0, x) = x$, $u_t(0, x) = 0$, $u_x(t, 0) = u_x(t, 1) = 0$.

8. $u_{tt} = 4u_{xx}$, $u(0, x) = 0$, $u_t(0, x) = x - \frac{1}{2}$, $u_x(t, 0) = u_x(t, 1) = 0$.

A **damped wave equation** has the form

$$u_{tt} + bu_t = c^2 u_{xx},$$

where $b > 0$ is the damping constant. In Problems 9–12, solve the damped problem using separation of variables.

9. $u_{tt} + 2u_t = u_{xx}$, $u(0, x) = x$, $u_t(0, x) = 0$, $u(t, 0) = u(t, \pi) = 0$.

10. $v_{tt} + 2v_t = 4v_{xx}$, $v(0, x) = 0$, $v(t, 0) = v(t, \pi) = 0$,

$$v_t(0, x) = \begin{cases} 0 & \text{on } 0 < x < 1 \\ 1 & \text{on } 1 < x < \pi. \end{cases}$$

11. $u_{tt} + 2u_t = 2u_{xx}$, $u(0, x) = 0$, $u(t, 0) = u(t, \pi) = 0$, $u_t(0, x) = \sum_{n=1}^{\infty} 2^{-n} \sin nx$.

12. $w_{tt} + bw_t = c^2 w_{xx}$, $w(0, x) = f(x)$, $w_t(0, x) = 0$, $w(t, 0) = 0$, $w(t, a) = 0$,   where $b < (2c\pi)/a$.

13. In a long, thin pipe, air movement is essentially one-dimensional. If $P(t, x)$ is the pressure of the air in the pipe, then P satisfies the equation

$$P_{tt} = c^2 P_{xx}.$$

If the ends of the pipe are sealed, then

$$P_x(t, 0) = P_x(t, b) = 0.$$

Find P given that

$$P(0, x) = f(x), \qquad P_t(0, x) = 0.$$

14. Let $X(x)$ be a nonzero solution of the boundary value problem

$$X^{(4)} - \mu X = 0, \qquad X(0) = X''(0) = X(b) = X''(b) = 0.$$

(a) Use integration by parts twice to show that

$$\int_0^b X(x)X^{(4)}(x)\, dx = \int_0^b X''(x)^2\, dx.$$

(b) Show that if $X \not\equiv 0$, then $\mu \geq 0$.

15. Flexure of a uniform elastic beam of length b whose ends are simply supported is modeled by

$$\frac{\partial^2 u}{\partial t^2} = -c^2 \frac{\partial^4 u}{\partial x^4}$$

$$u(t, 0) = u_{xx}(t, 0) = u(t, b) = u_{xx}(t, b) = 0.$$

Photo 26. Long reach industrial robot. (Courtesy of Cincinnati Milacron Co.)

Here $c > 0$ and $u(t, x)$ is the deflection of the beam. Find $u(t, x)$ when

$$u(0, x) = f(x), \qquad u_t(0, x) = g(x).$$

Hint: Use separation of variables and Problem 14.

Other boundary conditions are also of interest. The beam in Photo 26 has one **cantilevered** end and one **free** end. The boundary conditions at the cantilevered end have the form $u(t, 0) = u_x(t, 0) = 0$ and at the free end have the form $u_{xx}(t, b) = u_{xxx}(t, b) = 0$.

16. Let $u(t, x)$ be given by (7.7) and suppose that F and G are the periodic functions such that

$$F(x) = \sum_{n=1}^{\infty} a_n \sin\left(\frac{n\pi x}{b}\right), \qquad G(x) = \sum_{n=1}^{\infty} b_n \cos\left(\frac{n\pi x}{b}\right).$$

(a) Show that

$$u(t, x) = \tfrac{1}{2}[F(x - ct) + F(x + ct)] + \tfrac{1}{2}[G(x - ct) - G(x + ct)].$$

(b) Show that $u(t, x)$ is periodic in t of period T_1. Compute T_1.

(c) Show that $u(t, x)$ is periodic in x of period T_2. Compute T_2.

(d) Is it possible that $u(t, x) \to 0$ as $t \to \infty$?

17. Sound will travel along a thin, uniform elastic rod according to the equation

$$u_{tt} = c^2 u_{xx},$$

where $u(t, x)$ is the deflection along the rod and c is the speed of sound in the material. (For example, if the rod is 1% carbon steel, then $c \cong 5080$ meters per second.) If

$$u(t, 0) = 0 \quad \text{and} \quad u_x(t, b) = 0,$$

then find $u(t, x)$ satisfying

$$u(0, x) = f(x), \qquad u_t(0, x) = 0.$$

Hint: See Problem 4 of Section 11.4.

11.8 *D'ALEMBERT'S SOLUTION TO THE WAVE EQUATION*

The solution (7.11) makes it clear that the two quantities $z = x + ct$ and $w = x - ct$ are significant variables when solving the wave equation. We wish to express the wave equation

$$u_{tt} - c^2 u_{xx} = 0$$

in terms of these two new variables. Let $U(z, w) = u(t, x)$ so that

$$u_x = U_z \frac{\partial z}{\partial x} + U_w \frac{\partial w}{\partial x} = U_z + U_w$$

and

$$u_{xx} = [U_z + U_w]_z \frac{\partial z}{\partial x} + [U_z + U_w]_w \frac{\partial w}{\partial x}$$

$$= U_{zz} + 2U_{zw} + U_{ww}.$$

Similarly,

$$u_{tt} = c^2[U_{zz} - 2U_{zw} + U_{ww}].$$

Thus

$$u_{tt} - c^2 u_{xx} = -4c^2 U_{zw} = 0,$$

so that U satisfies the partial differential equation

(8.1) $$U_{zw} = 0.$$

The new equation (8.1) is easily solved. Integrating (8.1) with respect to w gives

$$U_z = H(z),$$

where H is an arbitrary function of z. Integration with respect to z gives

$$U(z, w) = \int H(z)\, dz + k(w),$$

where k is an arbitrary function of w. Thus U is any function of the form

$$U(z, w) = h(z) + k(w),$$

where h and k are any twice continuously differentiable functions. Since $z = x + ct$ and $w = x - ct$, then

(8.2) $$u(t, x) = h(x + ct) + k(x - ct)$$

is a general solution of the wave equation.

Consider now the initial value problem

(8.3) $$\begin{cases} u_{tt} = c^2 u_{xx} & \text{for } -\infty < x < \infty, t > 0 \\ u(0, x) = f(x) \quad \text{and} \quad u_t(0, x) = g(x) & \text{for } -\infty < x < \infty, \end{cases}$$

where g has one and f two continuous derivatives. Notice that the solution must be defined over the entire real line $-\infty < x < \infty$. Hence no boundary conditions are needed. The solution of (8.3) must have the form (8.2). The problem is to pick the functions h and k in such a way that the initial conditions in (8.3) are true, that is, so that

(8.4) $$u(0, x) = h(x) + k(x) = f(x)$$

and

$$u_t(0, x) = ch'(x) - ck'(x) = g(x).$$

Integrating the last equation gives

(8.5) $$h(x) - k(x) = \frac{1}{c}\int_0^x g(s)\, ds + K$$

for some constant K. Averaging (8.4) and (8.5) yields

$$h(x) = \frac{1}{2}\left[f(x) + \frac{1}{c}\int_0^x g(s)\, ds + K \right]$$

while (8.4) minus (8.5) yields

$$k(x) = \frac{1}{2}\left[f(x) - \frac{1}{c}\int_0^x g(s)\, ds - K \right].$$

Hence

$$u(t, x) = \frac{1}{2}\left[f(x + ct) + \frac{1}{c}\int_0^{x+ct} g(s)\, ds + K \right]$$

$$+ \frac{1}{2}\left[f(x - ct) - \frac{1}{c}\int_0^{x-ct} g(s)\, ds - K \right].$$

The constants $K/2$ and $-K/2$ add to zero. The two integrals can be combined. The resulting solution formula is

---

D'ALEMBERT'S FORMULA

(8.6) $u(t, x) = \frac{1}{2}[f(x + ct) + f(x - ct)] + \frac{1}{2c}\int_{x-ct}^{x+ct} g(s)\, ds.$

EXAMPLE 8.1   On $-\infty < x < \infty$, $t > 0$ solve

$$u_{tt} = 9u_{xx}, \qquad u(0, x) = e^{-|x|}, \qquad u_t(0, x) = xe^{-x^2}.$$

The d'Alembert formula yields

$$u(t, x) = \frac{1}{2}\left[e^{-|x+3t|} + e^{-|x-3t|} \right] + \frac{1}{6}\int_{x-3t}^{x+3t} se^{-s^2}\, ds$$

$$= \frac{1}{2}\left[e^{-|x+3t|} + e^{-|x-3t|} \right] - \frac{1}{12}\left[e^{-(x+3t)^2} - e^{-(x-3t)^2} \right]. \quad \blacksquare$$

The lines

$$x - ct = \text{constant} \quad \text{and} \quad x + ct = \text{constant}$$

are called **characteristics** for the equation $u_{tt} = c^2 u_{xx}$. Given any point (t_0, x_0) in the (t, x) plane the two characteristics that pass through this point are

$$x - ct = (x_0 - ct_0) = d_1 \quad \text{and} \quad x + ct = (x_0 + ct_0) = d_2.$$

We see from (8.6) that $u(t_0, x_0)$ is determined by the two numbers $f(d_1)$ and $f(d_2)$ and the values $g(s)$ in the interval $d_1 \le s \le d_2$ (see Figure 11.9). The values of f and g over $[d_1, d_2]$ uniquely determine u at (t_0, x_0) as well as at all other points (t, x) in the shaded triangle. Conversely, the values of f and g on $d_1 \le x \le d_2$ can influence the solution $u(t, x)$ only at those points which can be connected to some point in $[d_1, d_2]$ by a characteristic. This region of influence is graphed in Figure 11.10. For points in the crosshatched region II $u(t, x)$ is completely

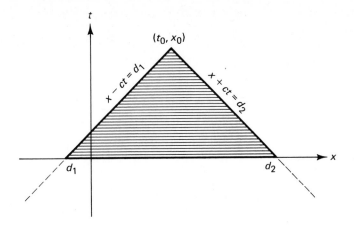

Figure 11.9. Region of dependence of $u(t_0, x_0)$.

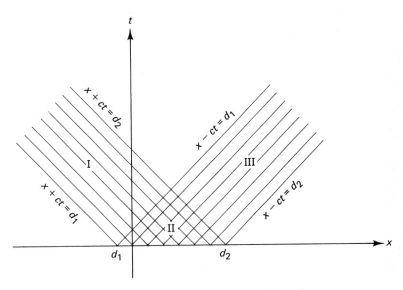

Figure 11.10. Region of influence of $[d_1, d_2]$.

determined. If (t, x) is in the hatched regions I or III, then $u(t, x)$ is influenced by these values of f and g but is not completely determined by them.

PROBLEMS   In Problems 1–4, solve (8.3) for the given f and g.

    1. $f(x) = \sin \pi x, \quad g(x) \equiv 0, \quad c = 2.$

    2. $f(x) \equiv 0, \quad g(x) = \cos 3x, \quad c = 2.$

    3. $f(x) = \operatorname{sech} x, \quad g(x) = x(x^2 + 1)^{-1}, \quad c = 3.$

    4. $f(x) = e^{-x^2}, \quad g(x) = -2xe^{-x^2}, \quad c = 1.$

5. In (8.3), what values of f and g will give

$$u(t, x) = \cos \pi(x + ct)?$$

6. In (8.3), what values of f and g will give

$$u(t, x) = \cos \pi(x - ct)?$$

7. Given $g(x) = x(1 + x^2)^{-1}$.

(a) For what $f(x)$ will the solution $u(t, x)$ of (8.3) be a wave traveling to the right, that is, u will have the form

$$u(t, x) = h(x - ct)?$$

(b) For what $f(x)$ will $u(t, x)$ be a wave traveling to the left?

8. (a) In (8.3), given f, what must g be in order that u be a wave traveling to the right [i.e., $u(t, x) = h(x - ct)$ for some h]?

(b) What must g be in order that u be a wave traveling to the left?

9. Given the half-line problem

$$u_{tt} = c^2 u_{xx} \qquad \text{for } t > 0, x > 0$$

(8.7) $$u(0, x) = f_1(x) \quad \text{and} \quad u_t(0, x) = g_1(x) \qquad \text{for } x > 0$$

$$u(t, 0) = 0 \qquad \text{for } t > 0.$$

let f and g be the odd extensions of f_1 and g_1 to $-\infty < x < \infty$ and let u solve (8.3) for this f and g. Show that $u(t, 0) = 0$ for all $t > 0$ and hence that $u(t, x)$ solves (8.7).

10. Solve the half-line problem

$$\begin{cases} u_{tt} = c^2 u_{xx} \qquad \text{for } t > 0 \text{ and } x > 0 \\ u(0, x) = f_2(x) \quad \text{and} \quad u_t(0, x) = g_2(x) \qquad \text{for } x > 0 \\ u_x(t, 0) = 0 \qquad \text{for } t > 0. \end{cases}$$

Hint: Extend f_2 and g_2 as even functions to $-\infty < x < \infty$ and proceed as in Problem 9.

11. Let $u(t, x)$ solve (8.3) and let d_1 and d_2 be real numbers with $d_1 < d_2$.

(a) Show that if $f(x) \equiv g(x) \equiv 0$ for $x \geq d_2$ and for $x \leq d_1$, then $u(t, x)$ must be zero except when

$$d_1 < x + ct < d_2 \quad \text{or} \quad d_1 < x - ct < d_2.$$

(b) Show that if $f(x) \equiv g(x) \equiv 0$ when $d_1 \leq x \leq d_2$, then $u(t, x)$ must be zero when

$$d_1 \leq x + ct \leq d_2 \quad \text{and} \quad d_1 \leq x - ct \leq d_2.$$

11.9 SEPARATION OF VARIABLES AND BESSEL FUNCTIONS

On a disk $x^2 + y^2 < R^2$ the heat equation

(9.1) $$u_t = k^2(u_{xx} + u_{yy})$$

is best changed to polar coordinates $x = r \cos \theta$, $y = r \sin \theta$. In polar coordinates (9.1) is written as

$$(9.2) \qquad u_t = \frac{k^2}{r} \left[(ru_r)_r + \frac{1}{r} u_{\theta\theta} \right].$$

Since the solution must be 2π-periodic in θ, we require the boundary condition

$$(9.3) \qquad u(t, r, \theta) = u(t, r, \theta + 2\pi).$$

Since (9.1) must be true at the origin $x = y = 0$, the u must be defined and bounded at $r = 0$. Hence u must solve the boundary condition

$$(9.4) \qquad u(t, r, \theta) \text{ is bounded as } r \to 0^+.$$

We wish to solve the heat equation subject to the initial and boundary conditions $u(0, r, \theta) = f(r)$ and $u(t, a, \theta) = 0$. Notice that these two conditions are independent of θ. Hence we expect that u will also be independent of θ. This means that our problem reduces to

$$(P_2) \qquad \begin{cases} u_t = \dfrac{k^2}{r} [ru_r]_r & \text{for } t > 0 \text{ and } 0 < r < a, \\[2mm] u(t, a) = 0 \quad \text{and} \quad u(t, r) \text{ is bounded } ar\ r \to 0^+, \\[2mm] u(0, r) = f(r) & \text{on } 0 < r < a \end{cases}$$

where f is a given function. This problem will be solved by separation of variables. The first two lines of (P_2) contain the *homogeneous* part of the problem. We first seek nonzero solutions $u(t, r) = T(t)R(r)$ of the first two lines of (P_2). Thus

$$T'R = \frac{k^2}{r} T(rR')'$$

or

$$\frac{T'}{k^2 T} = \frac{(rR')'}{rR} = -\lambda^2$$

for some constant λ. Hence, T must satisfy the equation

$$(9.5) \qquad T' + k^2\mu T = 0$$

and R the boundary value problem

$$(9.6) \qquad (rR')' + \lambda^2 rR = 0, \qquad R(a) = 0 \text{ and } R(r) \text{ bounded as } r \to 0^+.$$

To solve (9.6), first change variables to $x = \lambda r$ so that

$$\frac{dR}{dr} = \frac{dR}{dx}\frac{dx}{dr} = \frac{dR}{dx}\lambda \quad \text{and} \quad \frac{d^2R}{dr^2} = \frac{d^2R}{dx^2}\lambda^2.$$

Thus (9.6) becomes

$$x\frac{d^2R}{dx^2} + \frac{dR}{dx} + xR = 0.$$

This is a Bessel equation of order $v = 0$. This equation was studied in Sections 5.4 and 5.5. Solutions are tabulated in Table 5.3. For $v = 0$, two linearly independent solutions are $J_0(x)$ and $Y_0(x)$, while a general solution is

$$R(x) = c_1 J_0(x) + c_2 Y_0(x).$$

Since $Y_0(x)$ contains the term $(2/\pi) \log (x/2)$, it is not bounded as $r \to 0^+$. Hence c_2 must be zero and $R(x) = c_1 J_0(x)$. Bounded solutions of (9.6) have the form

$$R(r) = c_1 J_0(\lambda r).$$

The boundary condition $R(a) = c_1 J_0(\lambda a) = 0$ implies that λa must be a zero of J_0. The function $J_0(x)$ has infinitely many positive zeros x_n (see, e.g., Table 5.2). Thus

$$\lambda_n = \frac{x_n}{a},$$

where x_n is the nth zero of $J_0(x)$ and

$$R_n(r) = J_0(\lambda_n r) = J_0\left(\frac{x_n r}{a}\right).$$

From (9.5) it follows that

$$T_n(t) = e^{-(kx_n/a)^2 t}$$

and hence that $u_n(t, r) = \exp\left[-t(kx_n/a)^2\right]R_n(r)$.

Our solution of (P₂) must have the form

(9.7)
$$u(t, r) = \sum_{n=1}^{\infty} b_n e^{-(kx_n/a)^2 t} R_n(r),$$

where the constants b_n are chosen so that

(9.8)
$$f(r) = \sum_{n=1}^{\infty} b_n R_n(r).$$

In can be shown (see the problem section) that

$$\int_0^a R_n(r) R_m(r) r \, dr = 0 \qquad \text{if } n \neq m.$$

Hence the constants b_n can be found as follows. Multiply (9.8) by $r R_m(r)$ and integrate to obtain

$$\int_0^a f(r) R_m(r) r \, dr = \sum_{n=1}^{\infty} b_n \int_0^a R_n(r) R_m(r) r \, dr = b_m \int_0^a R_m^2(r) r \, dr.$$

Thus

(9.9)
$$b_m = \frac{\int_0^a f(r) R_m(r) r \, dr}{\int_0^a R_m^2(r) r \, dr}.$$

The coefficients (9.9) are called the **Fourier–Bessel coefficients** for f and (9.8) is called the **Fourier–Bessel expansion** of f. The series (9.7) with b_m given by (9.9) is the required solution of (P$_2$).

PROBLEMS

1. Solve (P$_2$) with the following data:

    (a) $f(r) = 2J_0(x_3 r) - J_0(x_5 r), \ k = a = 1.$

    (b) $f(r) = \sum_{n=1}^{100} n^{-2} J_0(\lambda_n r), \ k = a = 2.$

    (c) $f(r) = \sum_{n=1}^{N} A_n J_0(\lambda_n r)$, general k and a.

2. Let $R_n(x) = J_0(\lambda_n x)$ as above so that $(rR_n')' + \lambda_n^2 r R_n = 0$.

    (a) Multiply by rR_n' and show that

    $$[(rR_n')^2]' + (\lambda_n r)^2 (R_n^2)' = 0.$$

    (b) Integrate the expression above and show that $\int_0^a R_n(r)^2 r \, dr = \dfrac{a^2 R_n'(a)^2}{2\lambda_n^2}.$

    (c) It is known that $J_0'(x) = -J_1(x)$. Use this to show that $\int_0^a [R_n(r)]^2 r \, dr = \dfrac{a^2}{2} [J_1(x_n)]^2.$

3. (a) It is known that

    $$\frac{d}{dx}[xJ_1(x)] = xJ_0(x).$$

    Use this expression to compute the Fourier–Bessel expansion for the function $f(r) \equiv 1$.

    (b) Solve (P$_2$) when $f(r) \equiv 1$.

    (c) Assume that $a = k = 1$. Use the accompanying table to compute the first six Fourier coefficients of the solution series.

n	x_n	$J_1(x_n)$
1	2.404856	+0.5191475
2	5.520078	−0.3402648
3	8.653728	+0.2714523
4	11.791534	−0.2324598
5	14.930918	+0.2065464
6	18.071064	−0.1877288

4. On the disk $0 \le r < a, \ -\infty < \theta < \infty$, solve the wave equation

    $$u_{tt} = \frac{c^2}{r}\left[(ru_r) + \frac{1}{r}u_{\theta\theta}\right]$$

    subject to the boundary conditions

    $$u(t, a, \theta) = 0,$$

    $$u(t, r, \theta) = u(t, r, \theta + 2\pi),$$

    $$u(t, r, \theta) \text{ bounded as } r \to 0^+,$$

and each of the following the initial conditions.

(a) $u(0, r, \theta) = f(r)$, $u_t(0, r, \theta) = 0$.

(b) $u(0, r, \theta) = 0$, $u_t(0, r, \theta) = g(r)$.

Hint: u will be independent of θ in each case.

(c) $u(0, r, \theta) = 2J_0(x_2 r) + 4J_0(x_4 r)$,
$u_t(0, r, \theta) = J_0(x_1 r) - 3J_0(x_3 r)$, $a = c = 1$.

Hint: u will be independent of θ in each case.

5. On a right circular cylinder, given symmetry in θ, the Laplace equation $u_{xx} + u_{yy} + u_{zz} = 0$ becomes $(1/r)[ru_r]_r + u_{zz} = 0$, $0 < r < a$, $0 < z < b$. Here cylindrical coordinates are used. Solve this equation for $u(r, z)$ subject to the conditions that $u(r, z)$ is bounded as $r \to 0^+$, $u(r, 0) = f(r)$, $u(r, b) = g(r)$ and to one of the following boundary conditions:

(a) $u(a, z) = 0$, or

(b) $\dfrac{\partial u}{\partial r}(a, z) = 0$.

6. Let $\varphi(r)$ be a bounded, nonconstant solution on $0 < r \le a$ of

$$(r\varphi')' + \mu r\varphi = 0, \qquad \varphi(a) = 0.$$

(a) Integrate this equation to show that

$$r_2\varphi'(r_2) - r_1\varphi'(r_1) = -\mu \int_{r_1}^{r_2} s\varphi(s)\, ds.$$

(b) Show that $\lim r\varphi'(r) = L$ exists as $r \to 0^+$.

(c) Show that for $0 < r < a$,

$$r\varphi'(r) = L - \mu \int_0^r s\varphi(s)\, ds.$$

(d) Show that

$$\lim_{r \to 0+} r\varphi'(r) = L = 0.$$

Hint: Solve for $\varphi'(r)$ in part (c). Then integrate from r to a. Examine the resulting expression.

7. Let $\varphi(r)$ be as in Problem 6.

(a) Use integration by parts to show that

$$\int_r^a [s\varphi'(s)]'\varphi(s)\, ds = -r\varphi'(r)\varphi(r) - \int_r^a s\varphi'(s)^2\, ds.$$

(b) Use the differential equation to show that

$$\int_r^a [s\varphi'(s)]'\varphi(s)\, ds = -\mu \int_r^a s\varphi(s)^2\, ds.$$

(c) Show that

$$\mu = \frac{\displaystyle\int_0^a s\varphi'(s)^2\, ds}{\displaystyle\int_0^a s\varphi(s)^2\, ds}.$$

(d) Show that μ must be positive. *Hint:* First show that $\varphi'(a) \ne 0$.

8. For $i = 1, 2$ let R_i be a bounded, nonconstant, continuous solution on $0 < r \le a$ of

$$(rR_i')' + \mu_i r R_i = 0, \qquad R_i(a) = 0.$$

(a) Show that

$$\int_r^a (rR_1')'R_2 \, dr = [rR_1'(r)R_2(r) - rR_1(r)R_2'(r)]_r^a + \int_r^a (rR_2')'R_1 \, dr.$$

(b) Use part (a) and Problem 4 to show that

$$-\mu_1 \int_0^a rR_1R_2 \, dr = -\mu_2 \int_0^a rR_1R_2 \, dr.$$

(c) Show that if $\mu_1 \neq \mu_2$, then

$$\int_0^a rR_1R_2 \, dr = 0.$$

9. Using Problem 6, show that if $R_n(r)$ solves (9.6) with $\lambda_n = x_n/a$, then

$$\int_0^a R_k(r)R_m(r)r \, dr = 0.$$

for any integers k and m with $k \neq m$.

CHAPTER REVIEW

The heat equation, wave equation, and Laplace equation were studied in this chapter.

In order to solve the **heat equation**

$$u_t = ku_{xx}$$

in a region $0 < x < b$, $t > 0$, it is necessary to have a boundary condition at $x = 0$ and at $x = b$ plus one initial condition.

For the **wave equation**

$$u_{tt} = c^2 u_{xx},$$

it is necessary to have a boundary condition at $x = 0$ and at $x = b$ plus two initial conditions.

For the **Laplace equation**

$$w_{xx} + w_{yy} = 0,$$

it is necessary to have boundary conditions around the entire boundary of the region of interest. It is important to distinguish between **homogeneous** and **nonhomogeneous** boundary conditions.

Solutions of these three problems were obtained by using the method of **separation of variables.** It is assumed that the equation plus the homogeneous boundary conditions can be solved by a product of the form

$$u(t, x) = T(t)X(x)$$

(or $w(x, y) = X(x)Y(y)$). The unknown function $X(x)$ (or $Y(y)$) was seen to solve a **boundary value problem.** Once the two unknown functions were found, the superposition principle was used to form an infinite series of terms u_n. The nonhomogeneous conditions and Fourier series techniques were used to determine the unknown constants in the series.

CHAPTER REVIEW PROBLEMS

Solve Problems 1–4 using separation of variables.

1. $u_t = 2u_{xx}$, $u_x(t, 0) = u_x(t, 1) = 0$, $u(0, x) = x$.

2. $v_t = v_{xx}$, $v(t, 0) = v(t, \pi) = 0$, $v(0, x) = x^2$.

3. $u_{xx} + u_{yy} = 0$, $u_x(0, y) = u_x(1, y) = 0$, $u(x, 0) = 0$, $u(x, 1) = x^2$.

4. $w_{tt} = 4w_{xx}$, $w(t, 0) = w(t, \pi) = 0$, $w(0, x) = 1$ and

$$w_t(0, x) = \sum_{n=1}^{\infty} \frac{1}{n^2} \sin nx.$$

5. Solve the Laplace equation over the circle $x^2 + y^2 < 4$ subject to the boundary condition that

$$U(2, \theta) = \begin{cases} 0 & \text{on} \quad -\pi < \theta \le 0, \\ \theta & \text{on} \quad 0 < \theta \le \pi. \end{cases}$$

Hint: Use polar coordinates as in (6.2).

6. Find the steady state solution of the following problems:

(a) $u_{tt} = 3u_{xx} - 4x^3$, $u(t, 0) = u(t, 1) = 0$.

(b) $v_t = v_{xx}$, $v(t, 0) = A$, $v_x(t, 1) = B$.

References

Chapter 1   1. Z. Akcasu, G. S. Lellouche, and L. M. Shotkin, *Mathematical Methods in Nuclear Reactor Dynamics*, Academic Press, New York, 1971.

2. J. Endrenyi, *Reliability Modeling in Electrical Power Systems*, Wiley, New York, 1978.

3. G. F. Simmons, *Differential Equations*, McGraw-Hill, New York, 1972.

Chapter 2   4. J. J. D'Azzo and C. H. Houpis, *Linear Control Systems Analysis and Design*, McGraw-Hill, New York, 1975.

5. A. Cornish-Bowden, *Fundamentals of Enzyme Kinetics*, Butterworth, London, 1974.

6. H. I. Freedman, *Deterministic Mathematical Models in Population Ecology*, Marcel Dekker, New York, 1980.

7. A. Higdon and W. B. Stiles, *Engineering Mechanics*, Vol. II, Prentice-Hall, Englewood Cliffs, N.J., 1962.

8. L. Michaelis and M. E. Menton, *Biochem. Z.*, Vol 49 (1913), p. 333.

9. R. Peral, *The Biology of Population Growth*, Alfred A. Knopf, New York, 1930.

10. S. I. Rubinow, *Mathematical Problems in the Biological Sciences*, SIAM, Philadelphia, 1973.

11. R. M. Solow, A Contribution to the Theory of Economic Growth, *Q. J. Econ.*, Vol. 70 (1956), pp. 65–94.

12. F. F. Verhulst, Notice sur la loi que la population suit dans son acroissemont, *Corr. Math. Phys.*, Vol. 10 (1838), p. 113.

Chapters 3 and 4   13. F. Brauer and J. A. Nohel, *Ordinary Differential Equations*, W. A. Benjamin, New York, 1967.

14. E. D. Rainville and P. E. Bedient, *Elementary Differential Equations*, 6th ed., Macmillan, New York, 1981.

15. S. L. Ross, *Introduction to Ordinary Differential Equations*, 3rd ed., Wiley, New York, 1980.

16. M. R. Spiegel, *Applied Differential Equations*, 3rd ed., Prentice-Hall, Englewood Cliffs, N.J., 1981.

Chapter 5

17. M. Abramowitz and I. A. Stegun, Eds., *Handbook of Mathematical Functions with Formulas, Graphs and Mathematical Tables*, National Bureau of Standards, Applied Mathematics Series, 1970.

18. G. Birkhoff and G. C. Rota, *Ordinary Differential Equations*, 3rd ed., Wiley, New York, 1978.

19. G. Frobenius, Ueber die Integration der linearen Differentialgleichungen durch Reihen, *J. Math.*, Vol. 76 (1873), pp. 214–235.

20. L. Fuchs, Zur Theorie der linearen Differentialgleichungen mit veränderlichen Coeffizienten, *J. Math.*, Vol. 66 (1866), pp. 121–160; Vol. 68 (1868), pp. 345–385.

Chapter 6
(See also Ref. 4.)

21. R. V. Churchill, *Operational Mathematics*, McGraw-Hill, New York, 1958.

22. A. Erdelyi, Ed., *Tables of Integral Transforms*, McGraw-Hill, New York, 1954 (especially Vol. 1).

23. A. P. Sage, *Linear Systems Control*, Matrix Publishers, Beaverton, Oreg., 1978.

24. M. R. Spiegel, *Theory and Problems of Laplace Transforms*, Schaum Publishing Co., New York, 1965.

Chapter 7
(See also
Refs. 3 and 4.)

25. H. Campbell, *An Introduction to Matrices, Vectors and Linear Programming*, 2nd ed., Prentice-Hall, Englewood Cliffs, N.J., 1977.

26. C. C. MacDuffee, *Theory of Matrices*, Chelsea, New York, 1946.

27. A. J. Vandr, *Nutrition, Stress and Toxic Chemicals*, University of Michigan Press, Ann Arbor, Mich., 1981.

28. A. Whittemore and J. B. Keller, Quantitative Theories of Carcinogenesis, *SIAM Rev.*, Vol. 20 (1978), pp. 1–30.

Chapter 8

29. K. E. Atkinson, *An Introduction to Numerical Analysis*, Wiley, New York, 1978.

30. S. D. Conte, *Elementary Numerical Analysis*, McGraw-Hill, New York, 1965.

Chapter 9
(See also
Refs. 11 and 13.)

31. M. D. Intriligator, *Mathematical Optimization and Economic Theory*, Prentice-Hall, Englewood Cliffs, N.J., 1971.

32. J. P. LaSalle and S. Lefschetz, *Stability by Liapunov's Direct Method*, Academic Press, New York, 1961.

33. E. N. Lorenz, Deterministic Non-periodic Flows, *J. Atmos. Sci.*, Vol. 20 (1963), pp. 130–141.

34. P. Bartissol and L. O. Chua, The Double Hook, *IEEE Transactions on Circuits and Systems*, Vol. 35 (1988), pp. 1512–1522.

Chapters 10 and 11

35. M. Abramowitz and I. Stegun, Eds., *Handbook of Mathematical Functions*, Dover, New York, 1965.

36. P. V. Churchill, *Fourier Series and Boundary Value Problems*, McGraw-Hill, New York, 1963.

37. R. Haberman, *Elementary Applied Partial Differential Equations*, Prentice-Hall, Englewood Cliffs, N.J., 1983.

38. C. Lanczos, *Applied Analysis*, Prentice-Hall, Englewood Cliffs, N.J., 1956 (especially Chapter IV).

39. I. N. Sneddon, *Fourier Series*, Free Press, Glencoe, Ill., 1961.

40. M. J. Lighthill, *Fourier Analysis and Generalized Functions*, Cambridge University Press, London, 1964.

Answers to Selected Problems_____

Section 1.2 **1.** Ordinary, third order **3.** Ordinary, second order
5. Ordinary, third order **7.** Partial, second order
9. Just substitute the formula into the equation. (**11** and **13** are done the same way.)
15. $y = 2e^{-3x}$ **17.** $y = e^{3x} - e^{2x}$
19. Since $f(x, y) = y^{1/3}$, then $\partial f/\partial y = \frac{1}{3}y^{-2/3}$ does not exist at $y = 0$.
21. $I' = 2I(1 - I - R) - I, \ R' = -3R + I$

Section 2.1 **1.** $y = (\frac{3}{2}x^2 + c)^{1/3}$ **3.** $y = (1 + ce^{e^x})^{-1}$
5. $y = \tan(\log|\sqrt{1 + x^2} + x| + c)$ **7.** $u = c(1 + t) - 1$
9. $y = \sin(\frac{1}{2}\arcsin x + (x/2)\sqrt{1 - x^2} + c)$

11. $y = 2 - e^{-3x}$ **13.** $\dfrac{y - 2}{y - 1} = \dfrac{2}{3}e^{[x^2 - x + x^{-1} - (1/2) + \log x]}$

15. $y = (2 + \log x)^{-1}$

Section 2.2 **1.** $k = \log 3, \ \tau = \dfrac{\log 2}{\log 3} \cong 0.63$ hour

3. 8.72×10^{-5} gram; 1.146×10^{-6} gram
5. (a) At most 8.04 years, independent of age
    (b) At most 160.72 years, independent of age
8. (a) $y = 2(4 - 3e^{2x})^{-1/2}$ (c) $y = 0$ (e) $p = 5(1 + 4e^{-10x})^{-1}$
11. (a) 1521 years **13.** $0.25 \times 10^{-5}r$ micrograms
15. (b) $P(t) = KP_0[P_0 - (P_0 - K)e^{-kt}]^{-1}$ tends to K as $t \to \infty$
17. (a) $P = \pi + (1 - \pi)e^{-2t}$ (c) $P = 10 - 9e^{-3t}$

Section 2.3 **1.** (a) Two (b) Not homogeneous (c) Three
    (d) One (e) One (f) Two
    3. Yes **4.** No **5.** Yes

582

7. No   **9.** Yes   **11.** $z = ct^2 - t$

13. $y^3 + 3yx^2 = c$ **15.** $(y - 3x)^{1/5}(y + 2x)^{4/5} = 1$

17. $y = 2x \tan (2 \log |x| + \arctan (-0.5))$

19. $N^2 + 2Nt - t^2 = 4$ **25.** $(y + x)^3 = c(y - x)$

27. $\log |x| + c = 2\sqrt{y/x} - y/x$

29. (b) $\sec\left(\dfrac{y + 4x}{x}\right) + \tan\left(\dfrac{y + 4x}{x}\right) = cx$ and $y = \left(\dfrac{\pi}{2} + n\pi - 4\right)x$

31. $\tan (M - x) = x + c$ **33.** $\sec\left(\dfrac{w + s}{s}\right) + \tan\left(\dfrac{w + s}{s}\right) = sc$

Section 2.4   **1.** $e^x + x^2/2 + y^2/2 = c$ **3.** Not exact   **5.** $x^3y - xy^3 + y^2/2 = c$

              7. $t^2 + z^2 = c$ **9.** Not exact   **11.** Not exact

              13. $\sin (xy) - x^2 = \sin 2 - 1$ **15.** $y \sin t + t^2 e^y - 3y = \pi^2/4$

              19. $3y^2/2 + 4y = x - x^2 + c$ (separates)   **21.** $1/y + \log |y| = 1/x + c$ (separates)

              23. $y = -x \log (c_1 - \log |x|)$ (homogeneous)

              25. $e^y - 2x^2y - \log |x| = c$ (exact)

              27. $y = x \tan (\log |x| + c)$ (homogeneous)

Section 2.5   **1.** $(y/x^2) = c$ **3.** $\log |y/x| = c_1$

              5. $\log |y| + x^2/2 - 1/(2y^2) = c$ **7.** $\mu = e^{-y}$ and $xye^{-y} = c$

              9. $\mu = e^x$ and $y = x^2 + ce^{-x}$

              11. $\mu = (x - 1)^{-1}$ and $y^2/2 = \log |x - 1| + c$

              13. $\mu = y$ and $-xy^2 + (y^2 - 2y + 2)e^y = c$ **15.** $\mu = (xy)^{-1}$ and $e^{xy}x = cy$

              19. $y = x/(cx + 4)$ (separates)   **21.** $\mu = N$ and $N^2 + N \sin t = c$

Section 2.6   **1.** $y = ce^{\pi x} - 4/\pi$ **3.** $y = ce^{x^2/2} + 1$

              5. $y = (c + \log |x|)/(1 + x^2)$ **7.** $x = ce^{-\sin t} - 1 + 2 \sin t - \sin^2 t$

              9. $y = ce^{x - x \log x}$ **11.** $y = x - 2e^{-x}$

              13. $N = \frac{1}{10}e^{-3t} - \frac{1}{10} \cos t + \frac{3}{10} \sin t$ **15.** $x^3y = 1/(2e) - 1/(2e^{x^2})$

              17. $z = \frac{10}{13}e^{-3t} + \frac{3}{13} \cos 2t + \frac{2}{13} \sin 2t$ **19.** $(\cos x)s = -1 - \log |\cos x|$

              21. (a) $-\infty < x < \infty$ (c) $\pi/2 < x < 3\pi/2$

                     (e) $0 < x < 2$ (g) $-\infty < x < 0$

              25. $\eta = -1/2$ **29.** (a) $R = 0.22648$

              31. (a) $R = 70.82$ **37.** $z = ce^t + \frac{1}{2} \cos t - \frac{3}{2} \sin t$

              39. $y^2/x^2 = 1 + (\log |x| + c)^2$ **41.** $\mu = x^{-2}$ and $y + \sin (y/x) = c$

Section 2.7   **1.** $y = (ce^{2x} + x + \frac{1}{2})^{-1/2}$ **3.** $y = (1 + ce^{x^2})^{-1/2}$ **5.** $R = (ce^{-4t} - 1)^{-1/4}$

              7. $(x + 2)^2 - 2(x + 2)(y - 3) - (y - 3)^2 = c$

              9. $\dfrac{(x + 1)^2(y + 2)}{y + 2x + 4} = c$

              11. $\log |y + x + 2| + \dfrac{2x + 1}{x + y + 2} = \log 4 + \frac{1}{4}$

              13. $w = ax + by + c$ gives $dw/dx = a + bf(w)$

              15. $\sqrt{2}(x + c) = \arctan [\sqrt{2}(x + 2y + 1)]$

              17. (a) $P = \dfrac{30(2 + \cos t)}{((90/p_0) - 29)e^{-3t} + 20 + 9 \cos t + 3 \sin t}$

Section 2.8   **1.** 46.6 feet

              3. $h(t) = h_0 + v_0 t - gt^2/2$ where $h_0 = $ initial height and $v_0 = $ initial velocity. Maximal height occurs when $t = v_0/g$

5. $v(t) = (e^{-kt/m} - 1)mg(\sin \alpha)/k$

7. $\alpha = 45°$

9. 2423 feet

11. $k = gm/|v_T|$, v_T = terminal velocity

13. 19.96 seconds

15. $v(3) = -73.12$ feet/second, $a(3) = 4880$ feet

17. 170 feet

19. (a) $t^* = 43.88$ seconds and $v(t^*) = -125$ feet/second

(b) $t^* = 45.10$ seconds and $v(t^*) = -50$ meters/second

21. Period $= 2\pi\sqrt{M/K}$

23. (a) $y = \frac{1}{2}\sin(\sqrt{1545.6}\,t + \pi/2)$

(b) $-\frac{1}{2}\sin(\sqrt{1545.6}\,t + \pi/2)$

(c) $-3\sin(\sqrt{1545.6}\,t)/\sqrt{1545.6}$

25. (a) $\frac{1}{2}\sin(\sqrt{1030.4}\,t + \pi/2)$

(c) $-3\sin(\sqrt{1030.4}\,t)/\sqrt{1030.4}$

29. $My'' + (K_1 + K_2)y = 0$ and $y = A\sin(\sqrt{(K_1 + K_2)/M}\,t + B)$

31. (a) $3\sin[4(t - 2) + \pi/2]$ (c) $-\frac{3}{4}\sin 4(t - 5)$ (d) Zero

Section 2.9

1. (a) $dp/dt = ks_1$, $s_1 + p = c$

(c) $dx_1/dt = k_1s_1 - k_2x_1$, $dx_2/dt = k_2x_1 - k_3x_2$, $dp/dt = k_3x_2$, $s_1 + x_1 + x_2 + p = c$

(e) $dp/dt = ks_1^2$, $s_1 + 2p = c$ (f) $dp/dt = ks_1^2 - k_{-1}p$, $s_1 + 2p = c$

2. (a) $p = c$, $s_1 = 0$

(b) $s_1 = 0$, $p = \dfrac{k_2c}{k_2 + k_{-2}}$, $x = \dfrac{k_{-2}c}{k_2 + k_{-2}}$

(c) $s_1 = x_1 = x_2 = 0$, $p = c$

3. $p = 4 - 4e^{-3t}$ **5.** $p = (c + q) - ce^{-kt}$ **7.** $p = q$

9. $s_1 = 0$, $p = \dfrac{k_{-2}p_0 - k_2x_0}{k_2 + k_{-2}}e^{-(k_2 + k_{-2})t} + \dfrac{k_2(x_0 + p_0)}{k_2 + k_{-2}}$

11. $p = s_0/2 - s_0/(2 + 4ks_0t)$ **13.** $p = s_0/3 - (s_0/3)(6ks_0^2t + 1)^{-1/2}$

15. $p = (4e^t - 3)/(2e^t - 1)$

17. The answers can be computed from $p = \dfrac{ak_1}{k_1 + k_{-1}}(1 - e^{-t(k_1 + k_{-1})})$

19. $p = (a + b) - ae^{-[2t + (12/\pi)\sin(\pi t/12)]}$

Review Problems Chapter 2

1. $y = ce^{(\cos x/3)}$ (separates)

3. Substitute $z = x + y - 2$. Then $y = 2 - x + \tan(x - 1 + \pi/4)$

5. $xy - 3x^2/2 - 8x - 2y = c$ (exact)

7. $y^3x = y^5/5 + c$ (linear in x)

9. $y = c/(xe^x) + 1/x$ (linear in y)

11. $x^3 + xy - e^{-y} = c$ (exact)

13. $x^2 + e^{xy} + y^2/2 = c$ (exact)

15. $y = (3^{2/3} + [2x/3])^{3/2}$ (separates)

17. $t = (y + c)e^y$ (linear in t)

19. $(\sin x)(\sin y) = c$ (separates)

21. $\sqrt{1 + y^3}\,x = c$ (linear in x)

23. $e^{-y} + e^x = c$ (separates)

25. $y = -2 + ce^{(x^2/2 - x)}$ (separates)

27. $y^3 + 3yt^2 + 4t^3 = c$ (homogeneous)

29. $(s - 2)/s = (\pi - 2)e^{t^2/4}/\pi$ (separates)

30. Substitute $w = 6x + 3y + 5$

33. $3B^3 - 3xB^2 - 2x^3 = c$ (homogeneous)

35. $N^2 = c_2t - t^2$ (homogeneous)

36. Bernoulli equation, use $y = w^{1/2}$

37. $x = y^2(2\log|y| + c)$ (linear in x)

38. Bernoulli equation, use $y = w^{-1}$

39. $y = \sin(x + \pi/4)$ (separates)

45. (a) Substitute $w_1 = w + \frac{3}{2}$, $x_1 = x - \frac{1}{2}$

(b) Substitute $w = 2t + y + 1$

49. (a) $5\log 5/\log \frac{5}{2}$ seconds

(b) $50°$

(c) $T(t) = 50 - 30e^{-tk}$, $k = \frac{1}{5}\log\frac{5}{2}$

Section 3.1   **1.** $y = \log|x| + c_1/x + c_2$ **3.** $y = c_2 e^{c_1 x}$ **5.** $A = c_1 e^{-1/u} + c_2$
             7. $y = \sin x$ **9.** $y = \tan(x/2)$ **11.** $y = e^{2(x-1)}$
             13. $y = x^2/2 + \frac{3}{2}$

             15. $y = 2 + \log\left|\dfrac{x^2 - 3}{2}\right|$ (Use $z = p^{-1}$ to solve.)

Section 3.2   **1.** Homogeneous, constant coefficient, $J = (-\infty, \infty)$
             3. Nonhomogeneous, variable coefficient, $J = (-\infty, 0)$ or $(0, \infty)$
             5. Homogeneous, variable coefficients, $J = (-\infty, -1), (-1, 1)$ or $(1, \infty)$
             7. $J = (-2, 2)$
             9. (a) $y'' + 3y' - xy$ (b) $3y'' - 3y' - 3xy$
                  (c) $3y''' - 3xy' - 3y$ (d) $3y''' - 3xy'$
             11. (a) $6e^x$ (b) Zero
                  (c) $2x^2 + 6x + 2$ (d) $(r^2 + 3r + 2)e^{rx}$

Section 3.3   **1.** Independent   **3.** Independent
             5. Dependent   **7.** Independent
             9. (a) $y = e^{-2x}/3 + 2e^x/3$ (b) $y = -2e^{-2x}/3 - e^x/3$ (c) $y = 0$
                  (d) $y = -e^{-2(x-\log 2)}/3 + e^{x-\log 2}/3 = -4e^{-2x}/3 + e^x/6$
            12. $w(0) = 1,\ w(1) = e^{-1},\ w(2) = e^{-2}$
            13. $w(1) = 5e^3,\ w(-1) = 5e^{-3}$
            15. $y = c \sin x$ for any constant c
            17. $y = (2 \cos x)/(\cos 1)$
            19. $y = \frac{4}{7}(x - x^{-2})$

Section 3.4   **1.** $y = c_1 e^{3x} + c_2 e^{-x}$ **3.** $y = c_1 e^{2x} + c_2 e^{-2x}$
             5. $y = c_1 e^{(1+\sqrt{3})t} + c_2 e^{(1-\sqrt{3})t}$ **7.** $y = (c_1 + c_2 x)e^{-x/2}$
             9. $y = (e^x + e^{-x})/2$ **11.** $y = e^{2(x-1)} - 1$
            13. $y = xe^{4x}$ **15.** $y = (e^{-2x} - e^{3x})/5$
            17. (b) $y = \cosh \alpha x$ (c) $y = (\sinh \alpha x)/\alpha$
           21. (a) $y = e^x + (e^{-x} - e^{2x})/3$ **23.** (b) $y = \cosh 4(x - 2)$
                  (b) $y = (\frac{1}{4} + x/2)e^x - e^{-x}/4$ (c) $y = [\sinh 3(x + 1)]/3$
                  (c) $y = x^2 e^x$

Section 3.5   **1.** $y = c_1 \cos 3x + c_2 \sin 3x$
            3. $y = e^{-x/4}(c_1 \cos(\sqrt{7}x/4) + c_2 \sin(\sqrt{7}x/4))$
            5. $y = \cos\sqrt{2}x + \sqrt{2}\sin\sqrt{2}x$ **7.** $y = e^x(\cos 4x - \frac{1}{4}\sin 4x)$
            9. $y = \cosh 2t = (e^{2t} + e^{-2t})/2$ **11.** $P = e^{2t}(c_1 \cos t + c_2 \sin t)$
           13. $N = e^{2x}(c_1 \cos 3x + c_2 \sin 3x)$
           15. (a) $y = \cos\sqrt{3}x - (1/\sqrt{3})\sin\sqrt{3}x$
                  (b) $y = \cos\sqrt{3}(x - 3) - (1/\sqrt{3})\sin\sqrt{3}(x - 3)$
                  (e) $y = -\frac{1}{2}e^{-(x-1)}\sin 4(x - 1)$ (i) $y = \sin\sqrt{2}(x + \sqrt{\pi})$
           17. $y = (e^x + \cos x - \sin x)/2$
           21. $y = (\pi \sin 2x)/(2 \sin 2)$
           23. $y = -\sin 3x$
           25. $y = e^{x-2}\sin 4x/\sin 8$

Section 3.6   **1.** $y = c_1 e^{-x} + c_2 e^{-2x} + e^x/6$ **3.** $y = (c_1 + c_2 x)e^{2x} + \frac{3}{4}$
             5. $y = c_1 e^{-x} + c_2 e^{-2x} + 3$ **7.** $y = c_1 \cos\sqrt{3}x + c_2 \sin\sqrt{3}x + e^x/4$

9. $y = e^{-x/2}(c_1 \cos (\sqrt{3}x/2) + c_2 \sin (\sqrt{3}x/2)) + e^{2x}/7$

11. $y = \cos 2x + (5/6) \sin 2x + (\sin x)/3$ **13.** $y = -\frac{5}{20}e^{-x} + \frac{4}{20}e^{-2x} + e^{3x}/20$

15. $y = \frac{3}{4}e^{2x} + e^{-2x}/4 - e^x$ **17.** $y = c_1e^x + c_2e^{2x} + e^{-x}/2 + 2xe^x$

Section 3.7   **1.** $y = c_1 \cos x + c_2 \sin x + 1 + x$

3. $y = e^{-x/2}[c_1 \cos (\sqrt{11}x/2) + c_2 \sin (\sqrt{11}x/2)] + e^{2x}/9$

5. $y = c_1e^{2x} + c_2e^{3x} + e^{-x}/12$ **7.** $y = c_1 + c_2e^{-x} + 4x$

9. $y = c_1 \cos x + c_2 \sin x + (x - 1)e^x/2$ **11.** $y = c_1 + c_2e^{-2x} + x(x - 1)/4$

13. $N = c_1e^t + c_2e^{2t} + e^{-t}/6$ **15.** $y = (c_1 + c_2x)e^{2x} + x^2e^{2x}/2$

17. $y = -e^x/2 - 5e^{-x}/6 + e^{2x}/3$ **19.** $B = (-\frac{1}{4} + 5x/4)e^{2x} + (x + 1)/4$

21. $B = 3e^t/2 + e^{-t}/2 - t^2 - 2$ **23.** $y = -x^2e^{2x}/2$

25. $y_p = x(A_0 + A_1x + A_2x^2)e^x + (B_0 + B_1x + B_2x^2)e^{-x}$

27. $y_p = (A_0 + A_1x + A_2x^2 + A_3x^3) + Be^{2x}$

31. $y = 1 - \sin x/\cos 2$

33. No solution

Section 3.8   **1.** $y = c_1 \cos 2x + c_2 \sin 2x + e^x[(\cos x)/5 + (\sin x)/10]$

3. $y = (c_1 + c_2x)e^{-x} - (\cos x)/2$

5. $y = c_1e^x + c_2e^{-x} - e^x(\cos 2x + \sin 2x)/8$

7. $y = c_1e^{\sqrt{5}x} + c_2e^{-\sqrt{5}x} - (\cos x)/6$

9. $R = c_1 \cos x + c_2 \sin x - (x \cos x)/2$

11. $y = e^{-x}(c_1 \cos \sqrt{3}x + c_2 \sin \sqrt{3}x) + (\sin 2x)/4$

13. $y = e^x(c_1 \cos \sqrt{3}x + c_2 \sin \sqrt{3}x) + (e^x \sin x)/2$

15. $y_p = e^x[(Ax + B) \cos 2x + (Cx + D) \sin 2x]$

17. $y_p = x[(A_0 + A_1x + A_2x^2) \cos x + (B_0 + B_1x + B_2x^2) \sin x]$

19. $y_p = xe^{2x}[(A + Bx) \cos x + (C + Dx) \sin x]$

21. $y = 2 \cos 2t - \frac{2}{3} \sin 2t + \frac{1}{3} \sin t$

23. $B = \cos x + x \sin x$

25. $y = (\frac{46}{50} - (135x/50))e^{3x} + (x^2/2)e^{3x} + \frac{4}{50} \cos x - \frac{3}{50} \sin x$

27. $y = -2e^{-s} + \frac{5}{6}e^{-2s} + \frac{3}{2} - \frac{1}{3}e^s$

Section 3.9   **1.** $y_p = x \sin x + (\cos x) \log |\cos x|$

3. $Q_p = x(\log |x| - 1)e^{2x}$ or $y_p = x \log |x|e^{2x}$

5. $R_p = -e^{-3x} \log |x|$ **7.** $y_p = -\frac{1}{2} \tan^2 x \cos x + \tan x \sin x$

9. $y_p = \frac{4}{15}x^{5/2}e^x$ **11.** $y = \frac{4}{15}x^{5/2}e^x + 1$

13. $y = -6x + \frac{7}{2}x^2 + \frac{3}{2}$ **15.** $y = x^2 - x \log x - \frac{1}{2}x(\log x)^2$

Section 3.10   **1.** $y = c_1x^{-3} + c_2x^2$ **3.** $y = c_1xe^{-x} + c_2x$ **5.** $y_p = -\frac{1}{8} - \frac{2}{21}e^{3x}$

7. $y_p = -\frac{4}{27}x^{-1/2}$ **9.** $y_p = -\frac{1}{4}e^{2x}$ **11.** $y_p = \frac{3}{2}x^2e^{4x}$

13. $B = c_1x^2 + c_2x^{-1}$ **15.** $R = c_2e^r + c_1(r + 1)$

Section 3.11   **1.** $y = c_1x^2 + c_2x^3$ **3.** $y = c_1x^{-4} + c_2x^2$ **5.** $y = c_1x + c_2x^{1/2}$

7. $y = x^{1/2}\{c_1 \cos [\sqrt{3}(\log x)/2] + c_2 \sin [\sqrt{3}(\log x)/2]\}$

9. $y = c_1x^3 + c_2x^{-2} - \frac{1}{6}$ **11.** $y = (c_1 + c_2 \log x)x^{-1} + \frac{4}{9}x^{1/2}$

13. $y = c_1x + c_2x^{-5} + x^2/7$ **15.** $y = \frac{5}{3}x^2 - \frac{2}{3}x^5$

17. $y = \frac{4}{7}x^4 - \frac{3}{7}x^{-3}$ **19.** $y = \frac{13}{10}x^3 + \frac{13}{15}x^{-2} - x/6$

21. (a) $y = (1 - \log (x + 1))(x + 1)$

(b) $y = |x - 2|^{1/2}\left(3 \cos \left(\frac{\sqrt{3}}{2} \log |x - 2|\right) + (5/\sqrt{3}) \sin \left(\frac{\sqrt{3}}{2} \log |x - 2|\right)\right)$

(c) $y = [1 - 4 \log (1 - x)](1 - x)^3$ (d) $y = \frac{1}{2}(x + 1)^4 + (x + 1)^{-3} - \frac{1}{2}$

22. (a) $y = c_1 t^2 + c_2 t^{-3}$ (c) $N = [c_1 + c_2 \log s] s^{1/2}$

     (e) $V = [c_1 + c_2 \log (u - 1)](u - 1)^{-1}$

Section 3.12   **1.** Period $= \pi$

     (a) $y = \sin (2t + \pi/2)$ (b) $y = \sin 2t$

     (c) $y = \sqrt{2} \sin (2t + \pi/4)$

     (d) $y = (\sqrt{37}/2) \sin (2t + 4.5472 \ldots)$

3. $y = 0.05 \cos \sqrt{5}$ period $= 2\pi/\sqrt{5}$, amplitude $= 0.05$

5. $y = 0.1 \cos \sqrt{10}\, t$, period $= 2\pi/\sqrt{10}$, amplitude $= 0.1$

7. $y = \frac{5}{96} \cos \sqrt{618.24}\, t$

9. (a) $y = e^{-t/2}[\frac{1}{5} \cos (\sqrt{15}\, t/2) + \sin (\sqrt{15}\, t/2)/(5\sqrt{15})]$

     (b) $y = (\frac{1}{5} + t/10)e^{-t/2}$ (c) $y = \frac{4}{15}e^{-t} - \frac{1}{15}e^{-4t}$

     (g) $y = 0$ (i) $y = \frac{1}{2} \cos 2t - \frac{1}{4} \sin 2t$

11. $y = e^{-t/20}[\frac{1}{10} \cos (\sqrt{39.99}\, t/2) + (1/100\sqrt{39.99}) \sin (\sqrt{39.99}t/2)]$

13. $y = -\frac{1}{2} \cos (17.084437t)$

15. $y = e^{-0.444822t}[\frac{1}{10} \cos (3.130836t) + 0.0142078 \sin (3.130836t)]$

17. $2\pi \sqrt{\dfrac{1.99}{50.5(32.2)}} \le T \le 2\pi \sqrt{\dfrac{2.01}{49.5(32.2)}}$

19. (a) $u = g \sin \theta (M_c + M_l) + (B_c + B_l)v_0$

     (b) First let $y_l = v_0 t + a_0$ and $y_c = v_0 t + a_1$.

       Then $a_0 - a_1 = [gM_c \sin \theta + B_c v_0]/K$

21. $u = g \sin \theta (M_l + M_c) + (B_l + B_c)v_0$

Section 3.13   **1.** (a) $y = \cos \sqrt{2}\, t$ (b) $y = -\sqrt{2} \sin \sqrt{2}\, t$

     (c) $y = \frac{3}{2} + \frac{5}{2} \cos 2t$ on $0 \le t \le t_1 = \frac{1}{2} \cos^{-1} \frac{3}{5}$

       $y = 3 \cos \sqrt{2}(t - t_1) - (4/\sqrt{2}) \sin \sqrt{2}(t - t_1)$

       on $t_1 \le t \le t_2 = t_1 + \sqrt{2} \sin^{-1} (3/\sqrt{17})$

       $y = -\frac{3}{2} - \frac{5}{2} \cos 2(t - t_2)$ on $t_2 \le t \le t_3 = t_2 + \cos^{-1} \frac{3}{5}$

       $y = 3 \cos \sqrt{2}(t - t_3) - (4/\sqrt{2}) \sin \sqrt{2}(t - t_3)$ on $t_3 \le t \le t_4 = t_3 + \sqrt{2} \sin (3/\sqrt{17})$

       $y = \frac{3}{2} + \frac{5}{2} \cos 2(t - t_4)$ on $t_4 \le t \le t_5 = t_4 + \frac{1}{2} \cos^{-1} \frac{3}{5}$

     (d) $y = 0$

2. (a) $y = \cos \sqrt{2}(t - 1)$

3. (a) $y = \cos t$ (d) $y = 2 \cos (t - \pi)$

     (e) $y = -t^2 + 3$ on $-1 \le t \le 1$

       $y = -2\sqrt{2} \sin (t - 1 - \pi/4)$ on $1 \le t \le 1 + \pi/2$

       $y = (t - 1 - \pi/2)^2 - 3$ on $1 + \pi/2 \le t \le 3 + \pi/2$

       $y = 2\sqrt{2} \sin (t - 3 - \pi/2)$ on $3 + \pi/2 \le t \le 3 + \pi$

       $y = -(t - 3 - \pi)^2 + 3$ on $3 + \pi \le t \le 4 + \pi$

5. $y = p = 0$ **7.** Energy $= \dfrac{M}{2} a_1^2 + \dfrac{K}{2} a_0^2$

8. (a) $e - 3.5$ (b) $e^{-1} + \frac{1}{2}$

Section 3.14   **1.** (a) $\theta = 0.3 \sin (3t + \pi/2)$ (b) $\theta = 0.3 \sin (3t - 3 + \pi/2)$

     (c) $\theta = \frac{2}{3} \sin 3t$ (d) $\theta = \frac{2}{3} \sin (3t + 9)$

     (e) $\theta = 0$ (f) $\theta = (\sqrt{34}/15) \sin (3t + 0.5404195)$

3. (a) $\theta = e^{-t/2}(\cos(t/2) + \sin(t/2))$　　　　(b) $\theta = -2e^{-t/2}\sin(t/2)$

(c) $\theta = \frac{1}{2}\exp(-1 + \sqrt{2}/2)t + \frac{1}{2}\exp(-1 - \sqrt{2}/2)t$

(d) $\theta = [\pi + (1 + \pi/\sqrt{2})t]e^{-t/\sqrt{2}}$

(e) $\theta = [\pi + (1 + \pi/\sqrt{2})(t - 1)]e^{-(t-1)/\sqrt{2}}$

(f) $\theta = 0$

5. $J = 225/(4\pi^2)$　　　　　　　　　7. $\theta = (\sqrt{865}/4)\sin(t/\sqrt{6} + 0.0340076)$

9. $n\pi$ for any integer n

11. (b) $\theta = e^{-t/10}0.1047358\sin(5.7146t + 1.5532991)$

(c) $t > 6.93$ seconds

Section 3.15　1. (a) $y = \frac{2}{15}\cos 2x + \sin 2x - \frac{2}{15}\cos 3x$

(b) $y = \frac{17}{15}\cos 2x - \frac{1}{2}\sin 2x - \frac{2}{15}\cos 3x$

(c) $y = 2\cos 2x + (x/12)\sin 2x$　　　　(d) $y = (x/12)\sin 2x$

(e) $y = -\frac{8}{9}\cos 2x + \frac{1}{2}\sin 2x - \frac{1}{9}\cos x$　　(f) $y = \frac{1}{9}\cos 2x - \frac{1}{9}\cos x$

3. (a) $y = B_1\cos 4x + B_2\sin 4x + \frac{15}{16}x\sin 4x$

(b) $y = B_1\cos 4x + B_2\sin 4x + [15/(32 - 2c^2)]\cos(cx)$

5. $c = (m/n)\sqrt{7}$, where $m \neq n$ and m and n are relatively prime integers

7. $c_m = \sqrt{7}/2$

9. (a) $y = F(-Bc\cos ct + (K - c^2M)\sin ct)/(B^2c^2 + (K - c^2M)^2)$

11. (b) $Z_p = (27 + 11i)e^{(2+i)t}/68$

(c) $y = \text{Re }Z_p = e^{2t}(27\cos t - 11\sin t)/68$

Section 3.16　1. (a) $Q = e^{-5000t}(B_1\cos 5000\sqrt{3}\,t + B_2\sin 5000\sqrt{3}\,t$

(b) Let $B_1 = 1$, $B_2 = 1/\sqrt{3}$

3. (a) $Q \cong e^{-25t/3}(B_1\cos(25\sqrt{11{,}999}\,t/3) + B_2\sin(25\sqrt{11{,}999}\,t/3))$

$+ (0.0001)\cos t + 2 \times 10^{-9}\sin t$

(b) $Q \cong B_1\cos(1000\sqrt{5/6}\,t) + B_2\sin(1000\sqrt{5/6}\,t) + 0.0001\cos t$

5. $Q_p = F[(C^{-1} - c^2L)\cos(ct) + Rc\sin(ct)]/[(C^{-1} - c^2L)^2 + (cR)^2]$

7. (a) $v \equiv E$　　　　　　　　　(c) $v \equiv E, i \equiv f(E)$

Review Problems　1. (a) $y = [2/(2 - \sqrt{2}x)]^2$　　　　(b) $B = 2^{3/2}(x + 2)^{3/2}/3 - \frac{2}{3}$
Chapter 3　　(c) $y = \pm x^2/2 - 1$

3. (a) $R = c_1e^{-t} + c_2e^{7t}$　　　　　(b) $B = cr^{-1}$

(c) $y = (c_1 + c_2x)e^{3x}$　　　　　　(d) $y = c_1t^3 + c_2t^{-2}$

(e) $B = |s|^{1/2}\left[c_1\cos\left(\frac{\sqrt{7}}{2}\log|s|\right) + c_2\sin\left(\frac{\sqrt{7}}{2}\log|s|\right)\right]$

4. (b) $y = -\frac{2}{3}\sin 2t + \frac{1}{3}\sin t$　　　　(d) $B = \frac{3}{4} - \frac{1}{2}\log|s| + s^2/4$

(f) $y = (2x)^{-1} + (2x^3)^{-1}$

5. $B_p = s^3/2$　　　　　　　　　7. $B = c_1x^{(3+\sqrt{5})/2} + c_2x^{(3-\sqrt{5})/2}$

9. $y = e^{-x/6}(c_1\cos(\sqrt{11}x/6) + c_2\sin(\sqrt{11}x/6)) + 1$

11. $B = x^{1/2}[c_1\cos(\sqrt{5}/2)\log x + c_2\sin(\sqrt{5}/2)\log x]$

13. (a) All $x_0 \neq 0$　　　　　　　14. (a) $-1 < x < 1$

(b) All $x_0 \neq \pm\pi/2, \pm3\pi/2, \pm5\pi/2, \ldots$　　(d) $-\pi/2 < x < \pi/2$

17. (a) $c_0 = \sqrt{K/J}$

(b) $c = (m/n)\sqrt{K/J}$, where n and m are relatively prime integers and $n/m \neq 1$

Section 4.1　1. Constant coefficients　　　　3. Variable coefficients

5. Yes　　　　　　　　　　　　　7. No

9. Yes   **11.** Yes

12. $y = \frac{7}{4}e^x - \frac{5}{4}e^{-x} + \frac{1}{2}\cos x - 5\sin x + \sin 2x$

Section 4.2

1. $y = c_1 e^{3x} + e^{-3x/2}(c_2 \cos (3\sqrt{3}x/2) + c_3 \sin (3\sqrt{3}x/2))$

3. $y = (c_1 + c_2 x)e^{\sqrt{3}x} + (c_3 + c_4 x)e^{-\sqrt{3}x}$ **5.** $y = c_1 + c_2 e^x + c_3 e^{2x}$

7. $y = c_1 e^{7x} + c_2 e^{-x/2} + c_3 e^{-2x}$

9. $y = c_1 e^{-x} + c_2 e^{\sqrt{2}x} + c_3 e^{-\sqrt{2}x} + c_4 \cos \sqrt{2}x + c_5 \sin \sqrt{2}x$

11. $\{e^x, \cos 2x, \sin 2x\}$, $W(0) = 10$ **13.** $\{e^{-x}, e^{2x}, e^{-2x}\}$, $W(0) = 12$

15. $y = \frac{1}{2}e^x - \frac{1}{2}\cos x - \frac{1}{2}\sin x$ **17.** $y = e^x - 1 - x$

19. $B = e^s + e^{-s} + \cos s - \sin s$

22. (a) $y = \frac{1}{2}e^{x-1} - \frac{1}{2}\cos (x-1) - \frac{1}{2}\sin (x-1)$

   (c) $R = [1 - 3(x-\pi) + 4(x-\pi)^2]e^{2(x-\pi)}$

   (f) $y = e^{x+10} + e^{-(x+10)} + \cos (x+10) - \sin (x+10)$

23. $y = c_1 x + c_2 \cos (\sqrt{3} \log |x|) + c_3 \sin (\sqrt{3} \log |x|)$ will do on $-\infty < x < 0$ and on $0 < x < \infty$

Section 4.3

1. $y = c_1 e^{3x} + e^{-3x/2}[c_2 \cos (3\sqrt{3}x/2) + c_3 \sin (3\sqrt{3}x/2)] - e^x/26$

3. $y = c_1 e^{-x/2} + e^{x/4}[c_2 \cos (\sqrt{3}x/4) + c_3 \sin (\sqrt{3}x/4)] + [16 \cos x + 2 \sin x]/65$

5. $N = c_1 e^x + e^{-x/2}[c_2 \cos (\sqrt{3}x/2) + c_3 \sin (\sqrt{3}x/2)] + (x^2/6 - x/3)e^x$

7. $y = c_1 e^x + c_2 e^{-x} + c_3 \cos x + c_4 \sin x - (x \sin x)/4$

9. $y = -2 \sin x + (x^2/2) + 2x$ **11.** $y_p = Ax^2 e^x + (Bx^3 + Cx^2)e^{-x}$

14. $p(s) = s^5 + s^4 - 4s$ satisfies $p(0) = 0$ and $p(\sqrt{2}i) \neq 0$. Thus $y_p = A \cos \sqrt{2}t + B \sin \sqrt{2}t + Cx$

15. $N_p = (Ax + B)e^{2x} + (Cx + D)e^{-2x}$

17. $y_p = e^{-\pi x}(A \cos 3x + B \sin 3x) + (Cx + D)$

20. (a) $y_p = e^{x-1}/26$

   (c) $y_p = \frac{1}{65}[16 \cos (x + (\pi/2)) + 2 \sin (x + (\pi/2))] = (-16 \sin x + 2 \cos x)/65$

   (e) $N_p = e^{-1}[(x+1)^2/6 - (x+1)/3]e^{x+1}$

22. (a) $y_p = -1$ (do directly)

   (b) $y_p = (3x/4)e^x - (x/2) \sin x + 4$ [use Problems 7, 8, and part (a)]

Section 4.4

1. $y = c_1 + c_2 e^x + c_3 e^{-x} - 3x^2/2 - 3$

2. $N = c_1 + c_2 \cos x + c_3 \sin x + \log |\sec x + \tan x| - x \cos x + \sin x \log |\cos x|$

3. $y = c_1 x + c_2 x^3 + c_3 x^{-1} + x^5/48$. Note that $g(x) = x^2$ not x^5.

5. (a) $Y(x) = \frac{1}{2}e^x - \frac{1}{2}\cos x - \frac{1}{2}\sin x$

   (c) $Y(x) = \frac{1}{5} - e^{-x}(\frac{1}{5}\cos 2x + \frac{1}{10}\sin 2x)$

7. (b) $y = \frac{8}{105}x^{7/2}e^x + (c_1 x^2/2 + c_2 x + c_3)e^x$

Review Problems Chapter 4

1. $y = c_1 e^{2x} + c_2 e^{-2x} + c_3 e^{-x} - 2x - 1$

3. $y = c_1 e^x + c_2 \cos x + c_3 \sin x - 2 + \dfrac{x}{4}(\cos x - \sin x)$

5. $y = c_1 + c_2 \cos x + c_3 \sin x + \sec x + \cos x \log |\cos x| + (\tan x - x) \sin x$

Section 5.1

1. (a) 1   (c) $\frac{1}{2}$ (e) ∞

   (g) $\frac{1}{4}$ (i) ∞ (k) ∞

2. (a) Diverges at $x = 1$ and $x = -1$ (d) Converges at $x = 1$ and $x = -1$

3. (a) $\sum_{n=0}^{\infty} [(-1)^n(n+1) + 1]x^n$ (c) $-1 + \sum_{n=1}^{\infty} [(-1)^{n-1}n - 1]x^n$

   (e) $\sum_{n=2}^{\infty} (n-1)x^n$ (g) $\sum_{n=0}^{\infty} [1/(2n)! + 1]x^{2n}$

4. (b) $\displaystyle\sum_{k=1}^{\infty} \frac{(-1)^{k-1}}{(2k+1)!} x^{2k+1} = x - \sin x$

(d) $1 + \sum_{k=0}^{\infty} \dfrac{2}{(2k+1)!} x^{2k+1} = 1 + 2 \sinh x$

(g) $\sum_{k=1}^{\infty} x^{2k}/k!$

5. (a) $\sum_{n=0}^{\infty} (n+2)(n+1)x^n$ (c) $\sum_{n=0}^{\infty} \dfrac{x^n}{(n+3)^2}$

(e) $\sum_{n=0}^{\infty} \dfrac{(n+3)(n+2)(n+1)}{(n+3)!} x^n = \sum_{n=0}^{\infty} \dfrac{x^n}{n!}$

6. (b) $\sum_{n=0}^{\infty} \dfrac{3^n e^3}{n!} (x-1)^n$ (d) $\sum_{n=1}^{\infty} \dfrac{(-1)^{n-1}}{n} (x-1)^n$

(f) $5 + (-5)(x+1) + (x+1)^2$ (h) $\sum_{n=0}^{\infty} \dfrac{(-1)^n}{3^{n+1}} (x-2)^n$

(j) $\sum_{n=0}^{\infty} (-1)^n (x-1)^n$ (l) $-\sum_{n=0}^{\infty} \dfrac{x^{2n}}{2^{n+1}}$

7. (a) 1   (b) $\sum_{n=0}^{\infty} \dfrac{(-1)^n}{2n+1} u^{2n+1}$

10. $R = 1$ **11.** $R = 1$ **13.** $R = 1$ **15.** $R = 3$

17. $\sum_{k=0}^{\infty} \dfrac{(-1)^k}{(2k+1)!(2k+1)} x^{2k+1}$ **19.** $\sum_{k=0}^{\infty} \dfrac{1}{(2k+1)!(2k+1)} x^{2k+1}$

21. $1 - \dfrac{2}{\sqrt{\pi}} \sum_{n=0}^{\infty} \dfrac{(-1)^n}{(2n+1)n!} x^{2n+1}$ **23.** $\sum_{n=0}^{\infty} \dfrac{(-1)^n}{(2n+1)!(4n+3)} \left(\dfrac{\pi}{2}\right)^{2n+1} x^{4n+3}$

25. $f(x) = 0 + x - x^2/2 + \ldots$ **27.** $\tan x = 0 + x - 0 \cdot x^2 + \ldots$

29. (a) 2   (c) $\sqrt{2}$ (e) 1   (g) 3

Section 5.2   **1.** $y = a_0 \sum_{k=0}^{\infty} \dfrac{(2x)^{2k}}{(2k)!} + \dfrac{a_1}{2} \sum_{k=0}^{\infty} \dfrac{(2x)^{2k+1}}{(2k+1)!}$

3. $y = a_0(1 - x^2) + a_1 \left[x - \sum_{k=1}^{\infty} \dfrac{1 \cdot 3 \ldots (2k-3)}{(2k+1)!} x^{2k+1} \right]$

5. $y = a_0 \left[1 + \sum_{k=1}^{\infty} \dfrac{(-1)^k 1 \cdot 4 \ldots (3k-2)}{(3k)!} (x-1)^{3k} \right]$

$+ a_1 \left[x + \sum_{k=1}^{\infty} \dfrac{(-1)^k}{(3k+1)!} 2 \cdot 5 \ldots (3k-1)(x-1)^{3k+1} \right]$

7. $N = a_0 \sum_{k=0}^{\infty} \dfrac{(-1)^k}{k! 2^k} x^{2k}$

9. $y = a_0 \left[1 + \sum_{k=1}^{\infty} \dfrac{(-1)^k 1 \cdot 5 \ldots (4k-3)}{(4k)!} x^{4k} \right]$

$+ a_1 \left[x + \sum_{k=1}^{\infty} \dfrac{(-1)^k 2 \cdot 4 \ldots (4k-2)}{(4k+1)!} x^{4k+1} \right]$

$+ a_2 \left[x^2 + 2 \sum_{k=1}^{\infty} \dfrac{(-1)^k 1 \cdot 3 \cdot 7 \ldots (4k-1)}{(4k+2)!} x^{4k+2} \right]$

11. $R = 2 \sum_{k=1}^{\infty} \dfrac{(-1)^{k+1}(x-1)^{3k}}{2 \cdot 3 \cdot 5 \cdot 6 \ldots (3k-1)(3k)} + \sum_{k=1}^{\infty} \dfrac{(-1)^{k+1}(x-1)^{3k+1}}{3 \cdot 4 \cdot 6 \cdot 7 \ldots (3k)(3k+1)}$

$+ \sum_{k=0}^{\infty} \dfrac{(-1)^k(x-1)^{3k+2}}{1 \cdot 2 \cdot 4 \cdot 5 \ldots (3k+1)(3k+2)}$

13. $y = 2 + 4x^2$

15. $B = \pi t$

17. $y = x + \dfrac{ax^3}{3!} + \left(a^2 + \dfrac{3}{2}\right)\dfrac{x^5}{5!} + \left(a^3 + 13\dfrac{a}{2}\right)\dfrac{x^7}{7!} + \cdots$

19. $y = x + \dfrac{ax^3}{3!} + \left(a^2 - \dfrac{3}{2}\right)\dfrac{x^5}{5!} + \left(a^3 - 13\dfrac{a}{2}\right)\dfrac{x^7}{7!} + \cdots$

21. (a) $y = 1 - x - x^3/6 + x^4/12 + \cdots$
   (b) $y = x + x^3/6 - x^4/12 + x^5/30 + \cdots$

22. (a) $y_1 = 1 + x - x^2/2 - x^4/48 + \cdots$ **23.** $L = 2$ is predicted

25. (a) $y = c\left[1 + \displaystyle\sum_{n=1}^{\infty} \dfrac{a(a-1)(a-2)\ldots(a-n+1)}{n!}\, x^n\right]$

Section 5.3   **1.** (a) $y_1(x, b) = 1 + \displaystyle\sum_{k=1}^{\infty} \dfrac{-b(4-b)(16-b)\ldots((2k-2)^2 - b)}{(2k)!}\, x^{2k}$

$y_2(x, b) = x + \displaystyle\sum_{k=1}^{\infty} \dfrac{(1-b)(9-b)\ldots((2k-1)^2 - b)}{(2k+1)!}\, x^{2k+1}$

   (d) $1, x, 2x^2 - 1, 4x^3 - 3x, 8x^4 - 8x^2 + 1$

2. $b = n(n+2); \ 1, 2x, 4x^2 - 1, 8x^3 - 4x$

5. $P_6(x) = (231x^6 - 315x^4 + 105x^2 - 5)/16$

6. (a) $y_1(x, b) = 1 + \displaystyle\sum_{k=1}^{\infty} \dfrac{(-b)(4-b)(4k-4-b)}{(2k)!}\, x^{2k}$

7. (c) $1, 2x, 4x^2 - 2, 8x^3 - 12x$ **9.** $H_4(x) = 16x^4 - 48x^2 + 12$

Section 5.4   **4.** $R = \infty$

Section 5.5   **1.** (a) $-2\sqrt{\pi}$ (b) $4\sqrt{\pi}/3$
   (d) $\sqrt{\pi}/2$ (f) $945\sqrt{\pi}/32$

2. (b) -4.0184

3. (a) $h(n) = 1 \cdot 5 \ldots (4n - 3)$ (b) -4.8341

4. Both zero

7. (b) $J_{-1/2}(x) = (\cos x)/\sqrt{x}, \ J_{1/2}(x) = (\sin x)/\sqrt{x}$
   (c) $Y_{1/2}(x) = (-\cos x)/\sqrt{x} \ [\text{by } (5.6)]$

8. By (5.6), $Y_{3/2}(x) = J_{-3/2}(x), \ y = c_1 J_{3/2}(x) + c_2 J_{-3/2}(x)$

10. $R = \infty$

11. (b) $y = c_1 J_{\sqrt{2}}(\sqrt{3}e^x) + c_2 Y_{\sqrt{2}}(\sqrt{3}e^x)$ **12.** (b) $y = \sqrt{x}(c_1 J_{\sqrt{5}/2}(x) + c_2 Y_{\sqrt{5}/2}(x))$

Section 5.6   **1.** (a) $x_0 = 0$ is a regular singular point
   (c) $x_0 = 0, 1; \ x = 1$ is a regular singular point
   (e) $x_0 = 1, -1;$ both are regular singular points

2. (a) $y_1 = \displaystyle\sum_{n=0}^{\infty} \dfrac{(-1)^n}{n!(1 + 2\sqrt{2})\ldots(n + 2\sqrt{2})}\, x^{n+\sqrt{2}}$

$y_2 = \displaystyle\sum_{n=0}^{\infty} \dfrac{(-1)^n}{n!(1 - 2\sqrt{2})\ldots(n - 2\sqrt{2})}\, x^{n-\sqrt{2}}$

   (c) $y_1 = x^i\left[1 + \displaystyle\sum_{n=1}^{\infty} \dfrac{x^n}{n!(1 + 2i)(2 + 2i)\ldots(n + 2i)}\right]$

$y_2 =$ the conjugate of y_1 and $x^i = \cos(\log x) + i \sin(\log x)$

(d) $y_1 = 1 + \sum\limits_{n=1}^{\infty} \dfrac{2^n(x+2)^n}{n!5 \cdot 7 \ldots (2n+3)}$

$y_2 = (x+2)^{-3/2}\left[1 + \sum\limits_{n=1}^{\infty} \dfrac{2^n(x+2)^n}{n!(-1)\cdot 1 \cdot 3 \ldots (2n-3)}\right]$

5. (a) $y_1 = |x|^{\sqrt{2}} \sum\limits_{n=0}^{\infty} \dfrac{(-1)^n x^n}{n!(1 + 2\sqrt{2}) \ldots (n + 2\sqrt{2})}$

$y_2 = |x|^{-\sqrt{2}} \sum\limits_{n=0}^{\infty} \dfrac{(-1)^n x^n}{n!(1 - 2\sqrt{2}) \ldots (n - 2\sqrt{2})}$

7. $y_1 = \cos(\log x)[1 + x/5 - x^2/40 + \ldots]$
$\quad - \sin(\log x)[-2x/5 - 3x^2/40 - 7x^3/1566 - \ldots]$

$y_2 = \sin(\log x)[1 + x/5 - x^2/40 + \ldots]$
$\quad + \cos(\log x)[-2x/5 - 3x^2/40 - 7x^3/1566 - \ldots]$

Section 5.7   **1.** $y_1 = 1 - 2x + x^2/2$
$y_2 = (1 - 2x + x^2/2)\log x + [5x - 9x^2/4 + x^3/18 + \ldots]$

3. $y_1 = x^2 - \dfrac{x^3}{2} + \sum\limits_{n=2}^{\infty} \dfrac{(-1)^n 6}{n!(n+2)(n+3)} x^{n+2}$

$y_2 = x^{-1} - \tfrac{1}{2}$

5. (b) $k = n$ an integer
(c) $p_0(x) = 1,\ p_1(x) = 1 - x,\ p_2(x) = 1 - 2x + x^2/2$
(d) $y_1 = 1,\ y_2 = \log x + [x + x^2/2!2 + x^3/3!3 + x^4/4!4 + \ldots]$
(e) $y_1 = 1 - x,\ y_2 = (1 - x)\log x + [3x - x^2/4 - x^3/36 - x^4/288 - \ldots]$

7. (b) $k \neq -\tfrac{1}{4} + m^2/4$ with m an integer
$y_1 = x^{r_1} \sum\limits_{n=0}^{\infty} a_n x^n,\ y_2 = x^{r_2} \sum\limits_{n=0}^{\infty} b_n x^n$
(c) $k = -\tfrac{1}{4}$
$y_1 = x^{1/2} \sum\limits_{n=0}^{\infty} a_n x^n,\ y_2 = y_1 \log x + x^{1/2} \sum\limits_{n=1}^{\infty} b_n x^n$
(d) $k = -\tfrac{1}{4} + m^2/4,\ m \neq 0$
$y_1 = x^{(m+1)/2} \sum\limits_{n=0}^{\infty} a_n x^n,\ y_2 = a y_1 \log x + x^{(1-m)/2} \sum\limits_{n=0}^{\infty} b_n x^n$

9. (a) Irregular if $B \neq 0$ or $C \neq 0$ (b) Regular
(c) Irregular   (d) Irregular
(e) Regular

10. (c) $\tfrac{1}{4}$ and $\tfrac{3}{4}$

11. (c) $y_2 = (-\log x)y_1 + x^{-1} \sum\limits_{n=1}^{\infty} b_n x^{-n}$

Review Problems
Chapter 5   **1.** $y = c_0\left[1 + \sum\limits_{k=1}^{\infty} \dfrac{\alpha^{2k} x^{3k}}{2 \cdot 3 \cdot 5 \cdot 6 \ldots (3k-1)(3k)}\right] + c_1\left[x + \sum\limits_{k=1}^{\infty} \dfrac{\alpha^{2k} x^{3k+1}}{3 \cdot 4 \cdot 6 \cdot 7 \ldots (3k)(3k+1)}\right]$

3. $y = c_0\left[1 + \sum\limits_{k=1}^{\infty} \dfrac{(-1)^k x^k}{1 \cdot 4 \cdot 7 \ldots (3k-2)k!}\right] + c_1\left[1 + \sum\limits_{k=1}^{\infty} \dfrac{(-1)^k x^k}{k!5 \cdot 8 \ldots (3k+2)}\right]x^{2/3}$

Section 6.1   **1.** (a) Piecewise continuous   (b) Continuous
(c) Piecewise continuous   (d) Neither
(e) Piecewise continuous   (f) Piecewise continuous
(g) Piecewise continuous   (h) Continuous
(i) Neither

4. (a) $2!/s^3$ (c) $2/(s-4)$
(e) $3/(s^2 + 1) + 2s/(s^2 + 1)^2 = (3s^2 + 2s + 3)/(s^2 + 1)^2$

(g) $2/s^3 + 12/s^4$

(i) $\frac{1}{2}((s-a)^{-1} - (s+a)^{-1}) = a/(s^2 - a^2)$

5. (a) $a/(s^2 + a^2)$ $\qquad\qquad$ (c) $a/[(s-b)^2 + a^2]$

6. (a) $\pi/2 - \tan^{-1}(s/a) = \tan^{-1}(a/s)$ $\qquad$ (c) $\pi/2 - \tan^{-1}((s-b)/a)$

7. (b) $2s/(s^2 + 1)^2$ $\qquad\qquad$ (d) $3!/(s-2)^4$

9. (c) $L(t \log t) = \dfrac{\Gamma'(2) - \log s}{s^2} = \dfrac{1 + \Gamma'(1) - \log s}{s^2}$

$$L(t^2 \log t) = \frac{\Gamma'(3) - 2\log s}{s^3} = \frac{3 + 2\Gamma'(1) - 2\log s}{s^3}$$

10. (a) $(e^{-as} - e^{-bs})/s$

(b) $L[t\chi_{[a,b]}] = \dfrac{e^{-as} + ase^{-as}}{s^2} - \dfrac{e^{-bs} + bse^{-bs}}{s^2}$

11. (b) $F(s) = (1 - 2e^{-3s} + (3\pi + 1)e^{-\pi s} - 3\pi e^{-7s})/s$

12. $F(s) = (-e^{-2s} + 3e^{-5s})/s$ $\qquad\qquad$ **14.** (a) \$238.15

15. (b) *Hint:* Recall that $e = \lim_{n\to\infty}(1 + 1/n)^n$. Let $n = N/I$.

16. (b) \$1210.31 $\qquad\qquad$ (c) \$1099.01

Section 6.2 **1.** (a) $2/[(s-1)^2 + 4]$ $\qquad$ (b) $3/[(s+a)^2 + 9]$ $\qquad$ (d) $e^{-2(s-3)}/(s-3)$

(f) $\tan^{-1}\left(\dfrac{1}{s-4}\right) = \dfrac{\pi}{2} - \tan^{-1}(s-4)$ $\qquad$ (h) $\dfrac{1}{2}\left[\dfrac{s-b}{(s-b)^2 + 4} - \dfrac{s+b}{(s+b)^2 + 4}\right]$

(j) $-[\pi^2 - (s-2)^2]/[(s-2)^2 + \pi^2]^2$

2. (a) $(3 + s^2)/[s(s^2 + 4)]$ $\qquad\qquad$ (c) $(s^2 + 1)^{-1}(s^2 - 3s - 4)^{-1}$

(e) $(s^2 - s + 1)/[s(s^3 - 2s - 1)]$ $\qquad$ (g) $1/[s^2(s^2 + 1)]$

(i) $(cs^2 + cb^2 + s)/[(s^2 + b^2)(s + a)]$

4. (a) $(1 + e^{-\pi s})/[(1 - e^{-2\pi s})(s^2 + 1)]$ $\qquad$ (c) $(1 - e^{-s})^2/[s(1 - e^{-2s})]$

(e) $(1 + e^{-\pi s})/[(1 - e^{-\pi s})(s^2 + 1)]$ (the period is π)

6. (b) $(1 - 1/(2s^2) + 1\cdot 3/[1\cdot 2s^4] - \ldots)/s = (1 + s^2)^{-1/2}$

(c) $\dfrac{2}{\sqrt{\pi}}\displaystyle\sum_{k=0}^{\infty}\dfrac{(-1)^k}{k!}\dfrac{(2k)!}{s^{2k+2}}$ $\qquad$ (d) $1/[s(s+1)^{1/2}]$ $\qquad$ (e) $s^{-1}e^{-1/(4s)}$

8. (a) $F(3i) = -2/5 = \overline{F(-3i)}$

(c) $F(a + ib) = \dfrac{2}{(a + ib)^2 + 4} = \overline{F(a - ib)}$

11. (a) $(w\cos a + s\sin a)/(s^2 + w^2)$

(c) $(us^2 - uw^2 + u^3)((w + u)^2 + s^2)^{-1}((w - u)^2 + s^2)^{-1}$

12. (a) $(2s + 5)((s + 3)^2 + 1)^{-1}$ $\qquad\qquad$ **13.** $x(t) = \cos 2t,\ y(t) = \sin 2t$

14. $X(s) = 20(s^2 - s + 8)^{-1},\ Y(s) = 2(s + 1)(s^2 - s + 8)^{-1}$

Section 6.3 **1.** $y = \frac{2}{5}e^{2t} + \frac{3}{5}e^{-3t}$ $\qquad\qquad$ **3.** $R = 3\cosh 2t = \frac{3}{2}(e^{2t} + e^{-2t})$

5. $y = -\frac{2}{3}\sin 3t$ $\qquad\qquad$ **7.** $y = -e^{-2t}$

9. $y = -\frac{2}{21} + e^{7t}/35 + e^{-3t}/15$

11. $N = -\frac{1}{144} + t/12 + e^{-t/2}(\cos(\sqrt{47}t/2) - (23/\sqrt{47})\sin(\sqrt{47}t/2))/144$

13. $y = -t/7 + \frac{4}{147} + 3e^{7t}/490 - e^{-3t}/30$

15. $y = -e^{-2t}/9 + 4e^t/9 + \frac{2}{3}e^{-t/2}(\cos(\sqrt{3}t/2) - (1/\sqrt{3})\sin(\sqrt{3}t/2))$

17. $x = e^{-t/2}(\cos(\sqrt{15}t/2) - (1/\sqrt{15})\sin(\sqrt{15}t/2))$

19. $y = -e^t\cosh(\sqrt{2}t) + e^t\sinh(\sqrt{2}t)/\sqrt{2}$

21. $y = e^{2t}$ **23.** $y = (\sin t)/8 + \frac{7}{24} \sin 3t$

25. $y = \frac{19}{51}e^{4t} + \frac{11}{15}e^{-2t} - \frac{9}{85}\cos t - \frac{2}{85}\sin t$

27. Since $L[-t \cos t] = \dfrac{d}{ds} s/(s^2 + 1) = 2/(s^2 + 1)^2 - 1/(s^2 + 1)$, then

$(s^2 + 1)^{-2} = L[-(t/2)\cos t + \frac{1}{2}\sin t]$; thus $y = (-t/2)\cos t + \frac{1}{2}\sin t$

29. $y = -(e^{-t}/10)[2\cos t + \sin t] + \frac{6}{5}\cosh 2t - \frac{1}{20}\sinh 2t$

31. $R = (e^{-t}/5)(\cosh 2t + \frac{3}{2}\sinh 2t) + (3\sin t - \cos t)/5$

33. $y = \frac{43}{10}e^{-t} - \frac{29}{13}e^{-2t} - \frac{9}{130}\cos 3t - \frac{7}{130}\sin 3t$

35. $Y(s) = \displaystyle\int_s^\infty \exp(s^2/2 + s^3/3 - u^2/2 - u^3/3)2(u-1)\,du$

39. (a) $\frac{4}{3} - e^{-t}/8 - \frac{7}{4}e^t + \frac{13}{24}e^{3t}$ (b) $e^{-t}/4 - \frac{5}{4}e^{3t}$

    (c) $-\frac{2}{3} + \frac{3}{4}e^t - e^{-3t}/12$ (d) $3 - 3\cos t + 2\sin t$

40. (a) $x = a_0 e^{-Bt/2M}\cos(\sqrt{K/M - B^2/(4M^2)}\,t)$

$\qquad + \dfrac{2a_1 M + Ba_0}{\sqrt{4MK - B^2}} e^{-Bt/2M}\sin(\sqrt{K/M - B^2/(4M^2)}\,t)$

Section 6.4

1. $f(t) = u_1(t) + u_3(t)$, $F(s) = e^{-s}/s + e^{-3s}/s$

3. $f(t) = (t-1)u_1(t) + u_1(t) - t$, $F(s) = e^{-s}/s^2 + e^{-s}/s - s^{-2}$

5. $f(t) = e^6 u_2(t)e^{3(t-2)}$, $F(s) = e^{-2(s-3)}/(s-3)$

7. $F(s) = e^{-s}/s + e^{-2s}/s + e^{-3s}/s - e^{-\pi s}/s^2 - \pi e^{-\pi s}/s$

9. $\frac{1}{2}u_1(t)\sin 2(t-1)$

11. $(e^{-t}/\sqrt{5})\sin\sqrt{5}t - u_\pi(t)(e^{-(t-\pi)}/\sqrt{5})\sin\sqrt{5}(t-\pi)$

13. $u_{1/2}(t)(-e^{-5(t-1/2)} + e^{(t-1/2)})/6$

15. $u_2(t)/7 + \frac{3}{7} - \frac{1}{7}u_2(t)e^{-2(t-2)}[\cos\sqrt{3}(t-2) + (2/\sqrt{3})\sin\sqrt{3}(t-2)]$

$\qquad - \frac{3}{7}e^{-2t}[\cos\sqrt{3}t + (2/\sqrt{3})\sin\sqrt{3}t]$

17. $y = \frac{1}{4} + 5e^{4t}/12 - 2e^t/3 - u_5(t)[\frac{1}{4} + e^{4(t-5)}/12 - e^{t-5}/3]$

19. $u = xe^{-x} + u_5(x)[1 - e^{-(x-5)} - (x-5)e^{-(x-5)}]$

21. $w = \frac{1}{5} + (4e^{-t}/5)\cos 2t + (e^{-t}/10)\sin 2t + (u_\pi(t)/5)$

$\qquad (1 - e^{-(t-\pi)}[\cos 2(t-\pi) + (\sin 2(t-\pi))/2])$

23. $R = \frac{1}{2} - e^{-2x}/2 - u_1(x)[1 - e^{-2(x-1)}] + u_2(x)[1 - e^{-2(x-2)}]/2$

25. $y = \cos t + u_1(t)[1 + (t-1) - \cos(t-1) - \sin(t-1)]$

27. $N = 1 - e^{-t} - te^{-t} + t^3 e^{-t}/3 - u_2(t)[1 - e^{-(t-2)} - (t-2)e^{-(t-2)}$

$\qquad - (t-2)^2 e^{-(t-2)}/2 - (t-2)^3 e^{-(t-2)}/6]$

29. $(s^2 + b^2)^{-1/2}$

30. (a) $(te^{t/2})/4$ (b) $\frac{1}{4}(t/4)^3 e^{-3t/4}$

    (c) $\frac{1}{4}(t-1)e^{(t-1)/2}u_1(t)$ (h) $\displaystyle\int_0^t 2e^{-5u/2}[\sin(u/2)/u]\,du$

33. (b) $w = e^{-(x-2)^2}$

Section 6.5

1. $y = e^{-t} - e^{-2t} + u_\pi(t)(e^{-(t-\pi)} - e^{-2(t-\pi)})$

3. $y = 2u_1(t)e^{2(t-1)}(t-1) - u_2(t)e^{2(t-2)}(t-2)$

5. $N = \pi u_2(x)\sinh(x-2) - \pi u_4(x)\sinh(x-4)$

7. $w = 2\cos t - u_{3\pi/2}(t)\sin(t - 3\pi/2)$

9. $R = \pi u_\pi(x)\sin 3(x - \pi) = -\pi u_\pi(x)\sin 3x$

11. (a) se^{-cs} (b) $s^2 e^{-cs}$ (c) $s(e^{-cs} - e^{-ds})$

13. (b) $\delta(t - c)$

Section 6.6

2. (a) $24/[s^4(s^2 + 16)]$ (c) $(4 - s^2)/[(s^2 + 1)(s^2 + 4)^2]$

    (e) $(4 - s^2)/[s^2(s^2 + 4)]$

3. (a) $\sin t * (\sin 2t)/2 = -\frac{1}{6}\sin 2t + \frac{1}{3}\sin t$　　　　　　(c) $e^{-2t} * \cos 3t$

5. (a) $(10!3!/14!)t^{14}$

6. (c) $\sum_{j=0}^{n} (a_j j!/\Gamma(j + 3/2))t^{j + 1/2}$

7. (c) $\sum_{j=0}^{n} (a_j j!/\Gamma(j + v + 1))t^{j+v}$　　　　(d) $\sum_{n=0}^{\infty} (a^n/\Gamma(n + v + 1))t^{n+v}$

8. (a) $D^{1/2}p$ will not exist at $t = 0$ if $a_0 \neq 0$

$D^{1/2}p(t) = \sum_{j=0}^{n} (a_j j!/\Gamma(j + 1/2))t^{j - 1/2}$

(c) $\sum_{j=1}^{n} ja_j t^{j-1}$

9. (a) $g(t) = \sum_{i=1}^{m} \lambda_i e^{-\lambda_i t}\beta_i$

$f(t) = S(t) + \sum_{i=1}^{m} \lambda_i c_{i0} e^{-\lambda_i t}$

(b) $[p(0) + \sum_{i=1}^{m} \lambda_i c_{i0}/(s + \lambda_i)]/[s + \beta - \sum_{i=1}^{m} \lambda_i \beta_i/(s + \lambda_i)]$

Section 6.7　**1.** $H(s) = (s + 2)^{-2}; h(t) = te^{-2t}; H_K(s) = (s^2 + 4s + 4 + K)^{-1}$

3. $H(s) = s^{-1}(s + 1)^{-2}; h(t) = 1 - e^{-t}(1 + t); H_K(s) = [s(s + 1)^2 + K]^{-1}$

6. For $K = 1$, $H_1(s) = (s + 1)^{-2}$, and $h_1(t) = te^{-t}$

7. $w_1(t) = 1 - e^{-t} - te^{-t} \to 1$ as $t \to \infty$ $(K = 1)$

8. (b) $r_0/(a_0 + c_1)$

9. (a) $(\sin 2t - 2t\cos 2t)/8$

(b) $e^{-t/2}(\frac{1}{2}\cos\sqrt{15}t + (1/4\sqrt{15})\sin\sqrt{15}t) - \frac{1}{2}\cos 2t$

10. (c) $h(t) = \dfrac{h_0 R}{1 + KR}(1 + ce^{-(1 + KR)t/AR}); h(\infty) = h_0 R(1 + KR)^{-1}$

11. (b) $A_2 h_2' + (R_2^{-1} + A_2/(R_1 A_1))h_2' + h_2/(R_1 R_2 A_1) = u/(R_1 A_1)$

(c) $h_1(\infty) = R_1 u_0; h_2(\infty) = R_2 u_0$　　　　(d) Need $(R_2 H_1 K)/(1 + KR_2) = h_0$

12. (a) $H(s) = (Ms^2 + Bs + K)^{-1}$

13. (a) $H(s) = p_2(s)/p_1(s)$　　　　　　　　　(b) $g = L^{-1}(H)$

14. (b) $\theta(t) \to w_0/K$　　　　　　　　　　**15.** (b) $A = w_0/(B + L)$

Section 6.8　**1.** $y = 1 - 2t$　　　　　　　　　　　**3.** $y = 2t - \frac{3}{2}\sin t$

4. $y = \frac{1}{2}\delta(t) + \frac{3}{2}\sin t$　　　　　**5.** $y = (3\sqrt{\pi}\,t^{1/6})/(4\Gamma(\frac{4}{3})\Gamma(\frac{7}{6}))$

7. $y = \frac{2}{3}\delta'(t)$　　　　　　　　　　　**9.** $y = \pi^{-1}\delta'(t) + \pi$

11. $y = (t^{-1/2}/\pi)e^{-2t} + \sqrt{2/\pi}\,\text{erf}(\sqrt{2t})$　　**13.** $y = \delta(t) + J_0'(t)$

15. $y = -\frac{12}{25}e^{-t} + \frac{4}{5}te^{-t} + \frac{12}{25}\cos 2t + \frac{9}{25}\sin 2t$

17. $y = t$　　　　　　　　　　　　　　**19.** $y = t^3 e^t/3 + t^2 e^t + te^t$

22. (c) Yes

25. (a) $Y(I) = \dfrac{(I + a_3)(I + a_2)}{(I + a_1)((I + a_3)(I + a_2) - S(I + a_2) - a_2(1 - s)(I + a_3))}$

(b) Yes　　　　　　　　　　　　　(c) No, decreasing

26. $y = e^{-3t}/5 + \frac{4}{5}e^{2t}$

27. (b) $Y(I) = I(I^2 - 3I - \Gamma'(1) - \log(I))^{-1}$

(c) $Y(I) = \sqrt{I^2 + 4}/(I^2\sqrt{I^2 + 4} - 1)$

Review Problems　**1.** $y = u_2(t)\sin(t - 2)$　　　**3.** $y = \frac{1}{2}e^{3t} - \frac{1}{10}e^t + \frac{3}{5}e^{-4t}$

Chapter 6　　**5.** $y = \frac{1}{2}t^2 e^{2t}$

7. $y = 1 - 2u_1(t)$ so $Y(s) = \dfrac{1}{s} - \dfrac{2}{s}e^{-s}$

9. $Y(s) = 2s^4/[(s^2 + 4)(s^4 + 6)]$

Section 7.1　**1.** $x_1' = x_2, x_2' = t + x_1 - 3x_2, x_1(0) = 1, x_2(0) = -2$

3. $x_1' = x_2, x_2' = x_3, x_3' = x_4, x_4' = x_1$

$x_1(0) = 1, x_2(0) = 0, x_3(0) = -2, x_4(0) = \pi$

5. $x_1' = 4x_1 + 5x_2 - x_3$, $x_2' = x_3$, $x_3' = x_4$, $x_4' = -4x_3 + x_2 - x_1 + x_4 + \cos t$
$x_1(0) = 1$, $x_2(0) = x_3(0) = 0$, $x_4(0) = 2$

6. (a) $c_1 = 2, c_2 = -3$ (c) $c_1 = 9e^{-6}, c_2 = -6e^{-2}$

7. $x_1 = c_1 \sin 2t + c_2 \cos 2t + t/4$
$x_2 = 2c_1 \cos 2t - 2c_2 \sin 2t + \frac{1}{4}$

9. $y_1' = p_1/m_1$, $p_1' = -k_1 y_1 - k_2(y_1 - y_2) - (B_1/m_1)p_1 + f_1(t)$
$y_2' = p_2/m_2$, $p_2' = -k_2(y_2 - y_1) - k_3 y_2 - (B_2/m_2)p_2 - f_2(t)$
$y_i(0) = y_{i0}$, $p_i(0) = m_i v_{i0}$ for $i = 1, 2$

11. $x_1' = x_2/S$, $x_2' = x_3/S, \ldots, x_{n-1}' = x_n/S$
$x_n' = S^{n-1} f(t, x_1, x_2/S, \ldots, x_n/S^{n-1})$

12. (d) $\alpha_1 = a_n^{-1}$, $\alpha_{n+1} = b_n/a_n$, $\alpha_i = 0$ for $2 \le i \le n$

13. (a) $m_1 y_1'' = f_1(t) - y_1 k_1 - k_2(y_1 - y_2) - B_1 y_1'$
$m_2 y_2'' = -k_2(y_2 - y_1) + k_3(y_3 - y_2) - B_2 y_2'$
$m_3 y_3'' = -k_3(y_3 - y_2) - k_4 y_3 - B_3 y_3'$

14. (a) $x' = -k_1 x + k_{-1} y$, $y' = k_1 x - k_{-1} y - k_2 y$, $z' = k_2 y$

15. $x + y + z = $ constant in all cases

17. $x_1' = -\lambda_1 x_1$, $x_2' = -\lambda_2 x_2 + \lambda_4 x_4$
$x_3' = -\lambda_3 x_3 + \lambda_1 x_1 + \lambda_2 x_2$, $x_4' = -\lambda_4 x_4 + \lambda_3 x_3$

21. $P_n(t) = \exp\left(-\lambda_s t + (Kc_0/\mu)[1 - e^{-\mu t}]\right)$, $P_T(t) = 1 - P_n(t)$

24. (a) $M_1 y_1'' = u - M_1 g \sin\theta - B_1 y_1' - B(y_1' - y_2') - k(y_1 - y_2)$
$M_c y_2'' = -B_c y_2' - B(y_2' - y_1') - B(y_2' - y_3') - k(y_2 - y_1) - k(y_2 - y_3) - M_c g \sin\theta$
$M_c y_3'' = -B_c y_3' - B(y_3' - y_2') - k(y_3 - y_2) - M_c g \sin\theta$

Section 7.2

1. $x_1 = c_1 e^t + c_2 t e^t$, $x_2 = c_2 e^t$

3. $x_1 = (c_1 + c_2 t)e^{-3t} + 5e^t/16$, $x_2 = (c_2 - c_1 - c_2 t)e^{-3t} - e^t/16$

5. $y_1 = e^{10t}(c_1 + c_2 t)$, $y_2 = -e^{10t}(2c_1 + c_2 + c_2 t)$

7. $x = e^{6t}(c_1 \cos 2t + c_2 \sin 2t)$, $y = e^{6t}[(c_1 - c_2)\cos 2t + (c_2 + c_1)\sin 2t]/4$

9. $x_1 = -5e^{2t}\sin t$, $x_2 = -e^{2t}[3\sin t + \cos t]$

11. $x_1 = e^t/2 - e^{3t}/4 - e^{-t}/4$, $x_2 = e^t - e^{3t}/4 - 3e^{-t}/4$

13. $z_1 = c_1 e^{(1+\sqrt{6})t} + c_2 e^{(1-\sqrt{6})t} + [11\sin t - 7\cos t]/20$
$z_2 = c_1(1 + \sqrt{6}/3)e^{(1+\sqrt{6})t} + c_2(1 - \sqrt{6}/3)e^{(1-\sqrt{6})t} + [-\cos t + 3\sin t]/20$
$c_1 = (33 - 32\sqrt{6}/3)/40$, $c_2 = (33 + 32\sqrt{6}/3)/40$

15. $x_1 = c_1 e^{-t} - (3c_2/2)e^t + c_3 e^{3t}$, $x_2 = c_2 e^t$
$x_3 = -c_1 e^{-t} - c_2 e^t + c_3 e^{3t}$

17. (a) $y'' + 2y' + y = u' - u$ (b) $y'' + 4y' + 3y = \frac{3}{2}u' + 3u$

19. (a) $(R_1 R_2 A_1 A_2)y'' + (A_1 R_1 + A_1 R_2 + A_2 R_2)y' + y = u$

Section 7.3

1. (a) $\begin{pmatrix} 8 & 1 \\ 1 & 20 \end{pmatrix}$ (b) $\begin{pmatrix} 0 \\ -3 \end{pmatrix}$ (d) $\begin{pmatrix} 12 \\ -48 \end{pmatrix}$ (f) $\begin{pmatrix} 2 & 1 \\ 2 & -2 \end{pmatrix}$

2. (a) $\begin{pmatrix} 3 & 1 & 8 \\ 2 & -2 & 6 \\ 8 & 5 & 1 \end{pmatrix}$

3. (a) $\begin{pmatrix} 3 & -1 \\ 2 & 3 \end{pmatrix}\begin{pmatrix} x_1 \\ x_2 \end{pmatrix} = \begin{pmatrix} 0 \\ 1 \end{pmatrix}$ (c) $\begin{pmatrix} 2 & 0 & -1 \\ 1 & 1 & 1 \\ 0 & 1 & 1 \end{pmatrix}\begin{pmatrix} x_1 \\ x_2 \\ x_3 \end{pmatrix} = \begin{pmatrix} 4 \\ 0 \\ 1 \end{pmatrix}$

4. (a) $\mathbf{x}' = \begin{pmatrix} 3 & -1 \\ 1 & 2 \end{pmatrix}\mathbf{x} + \begin{pmatrix} 6 \\ t \end{pmatrix}$, $\mathbf{x}(0) = \begin{pmatrix} 0 \\ 0 \end{pmatrix}$

5. (a) $\mathbf{x}' = \begin{pmatrix} 0 & 1 \\ -1 & 1 \end{pmatrix} x, \ \mathbf{x}(0) = \begin{pmatrix} 1 \\ -1 \end{pmatrix}$

(c) $\mathbf{x}' = \begin{pmatrix} 0 & 1 & 0 \\ 0 & 0 & 1 \\ -4 & -3 & -2 \end{pmatrix} \mathbf{x} + \begin{pmatrix} 0 \\ 0 \\ t^2 \end{pmatrix}, \ \mathbf{x}(1) = \begin{pmatrix} 1 \\ -1 \\ 2 \end{pmatrix}$

6. (a) $\mathbf{x}' = \begin{pmatrix} -2 & 1 \\ -1 & 0 \end{pmatrix} \mathbf{x} + \begin{pmatrix} 1 \\ -1 \end{pmatrix} u(t), \ y = (1, 0)\mathbf{x} + 2u(t)$

(c) $\mathbf{w}' = \begin{pmatrix} 0 & 1 \\ -3 & 4 \end{pmatrix} \mathbf{w} + \begin{pmatrix} 0 \\ 1 \end{pmatrix} u(t), \ y = (3, \frac{3}{2})\mathbf{w}$

(e) $\mathbf{x}' = \begin{pmatrix} 0 & -1 \\ -3 & 4 \end{pmatrix} \mathbf{x} + \begin{pmatrix} 0 & 1 \\ 1 & -1 \end{pmatrix} \mathbf{u}, \ y = \begin{pmatrix} 3 & \frac{3}{2} \\ 1 & -1 \end{pmatrix} \mathbf{x} + \begin{pmatrix} 0 & 0 \\ 1 & -1 \end{pmatrix} \mathbf{u}$

7. (b) $\mathbf{g}''(t) = (e^t + e^{-t}, 0)^T$ (d) $2e^{2t} - 2e^{-2t} + 8t + 4$

8. (a) $\mathbf{0}$ **9.** $a = 2$

11. $\mathbf{g}(t) = (2 - 2t, 2 - 3t)^T$

Section 7.4

1. (a) $\begin{pmatrix} -1 \\ 3 \end{pmatrix}$ (c) No solution   (e) $\begin{pmatrix} 0 \\ 0 \end{pmatrix}$

2. (a) $(4, 3, 1)^T$ (c) $(0, 0, 0)^T$

(e) $(\frac{102}{11}, \frac{28}{11}, -\frac{64}{11})^T$ (g) $(0, 0, 0)^T$

8. (a) $\begin{pmatrix} \frac{2}{5} & -\frac{1}{5} \\ \frac{3}{5} & \frac{1}{5} \end{pmatrix}$ (c) $\begin{pmatrix} \frac{1}{2} & -\frac{1}{4} \\ 0 & \frac{1}{2} \end{pmatrix}$

9. Diagonal $(\frac{1}{3}, -1, \frac{1}{4})$

Section 7.5

1. 9   **3.** -1 **5.** 0   **7.** 8π

9. $6\pi\sqrt{2}i$ **11.** $(2 - s)(s^2 + 2s + 10)$

12. (a) $\mathbf{A}_0 = \begin{pmatrix} 1 & 0 & 2 \\ 0 & 1 & 1 \\ 0 & 0 & -2 \end{pmatrix}$, $K = 1$ will do

13. (a) $\begin{pmatrix} \frac{3}{4} & -\frac{1}{4} \\ \frac{1}{4} & \frac{1}{4} \end{pmatrix}$ (c) $\begin{pmatrix} -2 & 1 \\ \frac{1}{2} & 0 \end{pmatrix}$ (f) $\begin{pmatrix} \dfrac{2e^{-2t}}{3} & \dfrac{e^{-2t}}{3} \\ -\dfrac{e^{2t}}{3} & \dfrac{e^{2t}}{3} \end{pmatrix}$

14. (a) $s = 2$

15. (a) $(0, 0)^T$ (c) $(K, -iK)^T$ for any real number K

(e) $(K, 1, 0)^T$ for any number K

16. (a) Independent   (c) Dependent   (e) Independent

Section 7.6

1. (a) Yes   (c) Yes   (d) No

6. (a) $\begin{pmatrix} \cos 2t & \sin 2t \\ -2\sin 2t & 2\cos 2t \end{pmatrix}$ (b) $\begin{pmatrix} \cos 2(t - t_0) & \dfrac{\sin 2(t - t_0)}{2} \\ -2\sin 2(t - t_0) & \cos 2(t - t_0) \end{pmatrix}$

7. (a) $\mathbf{x}' = \begin{pmatrix} 0 & 3 \\ -3 & 0 \end{pmatrix} \mathbf{x}$ (c) $\begin{pmatrix} \cos 3t & \sin 3t \\ -\sin 3t & \cos 3t \end{pmatrix}$

Section 7.7   **1.** $\mathbf{x} = c_1 \begin{pmatrix} 1 \\ 3 \end{pmatrix} e^{4t} + c_2 \begin{pmatrix} 1 \\ -3 \end{pmatrix} e^{-2t}$, $\mathbf{X}(t) = \begin{pmatrix} e^{4t} & e^{-2t} \\ 3e^{4t} & -3e^{2t} \end{pmatrix}$

3. $\mathbf{X}(t) = \begin{pmatrix} e^{-2t} & e^{3t} \\ -4e^{-2t} & e^{3t} \end{pmatrix}$ **5.** $\mathbf{X}(t) = \begin{pmatrix} e^{t} & 5e^{-3t} \\ e^{t} & e^{-3t} \end{pmatrix}$

7. $\mathbf{X}(t) = \begin{pmatrix} -7e^{t} & e^{-t} & -e^{-2t} \\ e^{t} & -e^{-t} & e^{-2t} \\ 2e^{t} & 0 & -e^{-2t} \end{pmatrix}$

9. $\mathbf{x}(t) = (5e^{4t}/6 + e^{-2t}/6,\ 15e^{4t}/6 - 3e^{-2t}/6)^{T}$

11. $\mathbf{x}(t) = (\sqrt{2}(-e^{-4t} + e^{-t})/3,\ \sqrt{2}(2e^{-4t} + e^{-t})/3)^{T}$

13. $\mathbf{x}(t) = (\sqrt{2}(-e^{-4(t+1)} + e^{-(t+1)})/3,\ \sqrt{2}(2e^{-4(t+1)} + e^{-(t+1)})/3)^{T}$

15. $\mathbf{x}(t) = \frac{1}{6}(6e^{2t} - 3e^{-t} + 3e^{-3t},\ 6e^{2t} - 12e^{-t} + 6e^{-3t},\ -6e^{2t} + 3e^{-t} + 3e^{-3t})^{T}$

17. $\dfrac{1}{4}\begin{pmatrix} e^{2t} + 3e^{-2t} & 3e^{2t} - 3e^{-2t} \\ e^{2t} - e^{-2t} & 3e^{2t} + e^{-2t} \end{pmatrix}$ **19.** $\dfrac{1}{2}\begin{pmatrix} 3e^{-2t} - e^{-4t} & -3e^{-2t} + 3e^{-4t} \\ e^{-2t} - e^{-4t} & -e^{-2t} + 3e^{-4t} \end{pmatrix}$

21. $\dfrac{1}{6}\begin{pmatrix} -3e^{t} + 3e^{3t} + 6e^{-2t} & 2e^{t} - 2e^{-2t} & -e^{t} + 3e^{3t} - 2e^{-2t} \\ -12e^{t} + 6e^{3t} + 6e^{-2t} & 8e^{t} - 2e^{-2t} & -4e^{t} + 6e^{3t} - 2e^{-2t} \\ 3e^{t} + 3e^{3t} - 6e^{-2t} & -2e^{t} + 2e^{-2t} & e^{t} + 3e^{3t} + 2e^{-2t} \end{pmatrix}$

23. (b) $\begin{pmatrix} \dfrac{e^{2t} + 3e^{-2t}}{4} & \dfrac{3e^{2t} - 3e^{-2t}}{4} & 0 & 0 \\[2mm] \dfrac{e^{2t} - e^{-2t}}{4} & \dfrac{3e^{2t} + e^{-2t}}{4} & 0 & 0 \\[2mm] 0 & 0 & \dfrac{3e^{-t} + 2e^{4t}}{5} & \dfrac{6e^{-t} - 6e^{4t}}{5} \\[2mm] 0 & 0 & \dfrac{e^{-t} - e^{4t}}{5} & \dfrac{2e^{-t} + 3e^{4t}}{5} \end{pmatrix}$

25. (a) $\mathbf{x}_1 = \begin{pmatrix} \lambda_2 - \lambda_1 \\ \lambda_1 \\ \lambda_2 \end{pmatrix} e^{-\lambda_1 t}$, $\mathbf{x}_2 = \begin{pmatrix} 0 \\ 1 \\ -1 \end{pmatrix} e^{-\lambda_2 t}$, $\mathbf{x}_3 = \begin{pmatrix} 0 \\ 0 \\ 1 \end{pmatrix}$

26. (a) $\mathbf{x}_1 = (1, 1)^{T}$, $\mathbf{x}_2 = (V_2,\ -V_1)^{T} \exp(-k/V_1 - k/V_2)t$

27. (a) $y = c_1 e^{t} + c_2 e^{2t}$ (b) $\mathbf{x} = c_1 \begin{pmatrix} 1 \\ 1 \end{pmatrix} e^{t} + c_2 \begin{pmatrix} 1 \\ 2 \end{pmatrix} e^{2t}$ (c) $y(t)$ is the same as $x_1(t)$

Section 7.8   **1.** $\mathbf{X}(t) = \begin{pmatrix} \cos \pi t & \sin \pi t \\ -\sin \pi t & \cos \pi t \end{pmatrix} e^{-2t}$

3. $\mathbf{X}(t) = \begin{pmatrix} 5 \cos 2t & 5 \sin 2t \\ 4 \cos 2t + 2 \sin 2t & 4 \sin 2t - 2 \cos 2t \end{pmatrix}$

5. $\mathbf{X}(t) = \begin{pmatrix} \cos \sqrt{2}t & \sin \sqrt{2}t \\ -\sin \sqrt{2}t & \cos \sqrt{2}t \end{pmatrix} e^{-3t}$

7. $\mathbf{X}(t) = \begin{pmatrix} 3e^{3t} & e^{t} \cos 2t & e^{t} \sin 2t \\ 4e^{3t} & e^{t}(\cos 2t + \sin 2t) & e^{t}(\sin 2t - \cos 2t) \\ 4e^{3t} & 0 & 0 \end{pmatrix}$

9. $\mathbf{x} = (\sqrt{2} \sin \sqrt{2}t,\ -\sqrt{2} \sin \sqrt{2}t - 2 \cos \sqrt{2}t)^{T}$

11. $\mathbf{x} = e^{-t}(2 \cos 2t + \sin 2t,\ -2 \sin 2t + \cos 2t)^{T}$

13. $\mathbf{x} = e^{3t}(2 \cos t + \sin t,\ -\cos t - 3 \sin t)^{T}$

15. $\mathbf{x} = (e^t/2)(1 - 3\cos 2t + 2\sin 2t, 3\sin 2t + 2\cos 2t, 3 - 3\cos 2t + 2\sin 2t)^T$

19. $\mathbf{x} = (\sqrt{2}\sin\sqrt{2}(t + \pi), \sqrt{2}\sin\sqrt{2}(t + \pi) - 2\cos\sqrt{2}(t + \pi))^T$

21. $\mathbf{x} = e^{3(t+5)}(2\cos(t + 5) + \sin(t + 5), -\cos(t + 5) - 3\sin(t + 5))^T$

23. $\mathbf{x} = (e^{t-10}/2)(1 - \cos 2(t - 10), \sin 2(t - 10), 3 - \cos 2(t - 10))^T$

25. (b) $e^{-t}\begin{pmatrix} \cos 2t & \sin 2t \\ -\sin 2t & \cos 2t \end{pmatrix}$

(d) $\dfrac{e^t}{2}\begin{pmatrix} -1 + 3\cos 2t & 2\sin 2t & 1 - \cos 2t \\ -3\sin 2t & 2\cos 2t & \sin 2t \\ -3 + 3\cos 2t & 2\sin 2t & 3 - \cos 2t \end{pmatrix}$

26. $\mathbf{x}_1 = e^{3t}(1, -1, 4, 0, 0)^T$, $\mathbf{x}_2 = e^t(\sin 2t, \cos 2t, 0, 0, 0)^T$,

   $\mathbf{x}_3 = e^t(\cos 2t, -\sin 2t, 0, 0, 0)^T$

$\mathbf{x}_4 = \begin{pmatrix} \cos 2t + 2\sin 2t \\ 2\cos 2t \\ -\cos 2t - 4\sin 2t \\ -14\cos 2t - 5\sin 2t \\ -5\cos 2t + 14\sin 2t \end{pmatrix}$ $\mathbf{x}_5 = \begin{pmatrix} -2\cos 2t + \sin 2t \\ 2\sin 2t \\ 4\cos 2t - \sin 2t \\ 5\cos 2t - 14\sin 2t \\ -14\cos 2t - 5\sin 2t \end{pmatrix}$

28. The eigenvalues are $\lambda_1 = 0$, $\lambda_2 = i\sqrt{w_1^2 + w_2^2 + w_3^2}$, $\lambda_3 = \bar\lambda_2$.

31. (a) $y = c_1\cos 2t + c_2\sin 2t$

(b) $\mathbf{x} = c_1\begin{pmatrix} \cos 2t \\ -2\sin 2t \end{pmatrix} + c_2\begin{pmatrix} \sin 2t \\ 2\cos 2t \end{pmatrix}$

(c) $y(t)$ is the same as $x_1(t)$

Section 7.9

1. $\mathbf{X}(t) = \begin{pmatrix} 1 & 1 + t \\ -1 & -t \end{pmatrix}e^{3t}$

3. $\mathbf{X}(t) = e^{3t}\begin{pmatrix} 1 & t + \frac{1}{4} \\ 1 & t \end{pmatrix}$

5. $\mathbf{X}(t) = e^{-t}\begin{pmatrix} 2 & 2t - 1 \\ 1 & t \end{pmatrix}$

7. $\mathbf{X}(t) = e^{2t}\begin{pmatrix} 1 & 0 & 0 \\ t & 1 & 0 \\ -t & -1 & 1 \end{pmatrix}$

9. $\mathbf{X}(t) = e^{2t}\begin{pmatrix} 1 & t & t^2 \\ 2 & 1 + 2t & 2t^2 + 2t \\ 4 & 4 + 4t & 4t^2 + 8t + 4 \end{pmatrix}$

11. $\mathbf{X}(t) = \begin{pmatrix} \cos 2t & t\cos 2t & \sin 2t & t\sin 2t \\ -2\sin 2t & \cos 2t - 2t\sin 2t & 2\cos 2t & \sin 2t + 2t\cos 2t \\ -4\cos 2t & -4\sin 2t - 4t\cos 2t & -4\sin 2t & 4\cos 2t - 4t\sin 2t \\ 8\sin 2t & -12\cos 2t + 8t\sin 2t & -8\cos 2t & -12\sin 2t - 8t\cos 2t \end{pmatrix}$

13. $\mathbf{x} = e^t(1 + 2t, 1 - 2t)^T$ **15.** $\mathbf{x} = e^{3t}(4t, 4t - 1)^T$ **17.** $\mathbf{x} = e^{2t}(0, 1, 0)^T$

19. $e^{At} = \begin{pmatrix} 1 + 2t & -t \\ 4t & 1 - 2t \end{pmatrix}e^t$

21. $e^{At} = \begin{pmatrix} 1 + t & t \\ -t & 1 - t \end{pmatrix}e^{2t}$

23. $e^{At} = e^{2t}\begin{pmatrix} 1 & t & \frac{t^2}{2} \\ 0 & 1 & t \\ 0 & 0 & 1 \end{pmatrix}$

25. $\mathbf{X}(t) = \begin{pmatrix} e^{-3t} & e^{-3t} & e^{3t} \\ -e^{-3t} & e^{-3t} & e^{3t} \\ 0 & e^{-3t} & -2e^{3t} \end{pmatrix}$

29. $\mathbf{v}_1 = (1, 2)^T, \mathbf{v}_2 = (0, 1)^T$ **30.** (b) $I + \sum_{n=1}^{\infty} (t^n A^n)/n!$

33. (a) $y = (c_1 + c_2 t)e^t$ (b) $\mathbf{x} = c_1 \begin{pmatrix} 1 \\ 1 \end{pmatrix} e^t + c_2 \begin{pmatrix} t \\ t+1 \end{pmatrix} e^t$ (c) $y(t)$ is the **same as** $x_1(t)$

Section 7.10   **1.** $\mathbf{x}_p = (1 - t \sin t - \cos t \log|\cos t|, 2 + t(\cos t - \sin t) - (\sin t + \cos t) \log|\cos t|)^T$

3. $\mathbf{x}_p = e^{4t} \begin{pmatrix} \dfrac{5t}{6} + \dfrac{1}{36} \\ \dfrac{5t}{6} - \dfrac{5}{36} \end{pmatrix} + \begin{pmatrix} -\dfrac{1}{8} \\ \dfrac{3}{8} \end{pmatrix}$ **5.** $\mathbf{x}_p = (e^t/2, e^t/2)^T$

9. $\mathbf{x}_p = \begin{pmatrix} e^{3t} & 1 \\ 2e^{3t} & -1 \end{pmatrix} \begin{pmatrix} \dfrac{3}{4} \\ 1 \end{pmatrix} + \begin{pmatrix} \dfrac{e^{-t}}{4} \\ -e^{2t} - \dfrac{e^{-t}}{2} \end{pmatrix}$

13. $y(t) = \dfrac{-1}{\pi^2 - 1}(\pi \cos \pi t + \sin \pi t - \pi \cos t - \pi \sin t)$

15. $y(t) \to 1$ as $t \to \infty$

Section 7.11   **1.** $\mathbf{x} = (e^{-t} + 2e^{-4t}, e^{-t} - e^{-4t})^T/3$ **3.** $\mathbf{x} = 0$

5. $\mathbf{x} = 6^{-1}(7e^{-t} + 2e^{2t} - 3e^t, 6e^{2t} - 6e^t, 6e^t)^T$

7. $y_1 = e^{2t} - 2e^t + 1, y_2 = 2 - e^t$

9. $\dfrac{1}{6} \begin{pmatrix} -3e^t + 3e^{3t} + 6e^{-2t} & 2e^t - 2e^{-2t} & -e^t + 3e^{3t} - 2e^{-2t} \\ -12e^t + 6e^{3t} + 6e^{-2t} & 8e^t - 2e^{-2t} & -4e^t + 6e^{3t} - 2e^{-2t} \\ 3e^t + 3e^{3t} - 6e^{-2t} & -2e^t + 2e^{-2t} & e^t + 3e^{3t} + 2e^{-2t} \end{pmatrix}$

11. $e^{2t} \begin{pmatrix} 1 + t & t \\ -t & 1 - t \end{pmatrix}$

13. (a) $H(s) = (s + 1)/s^2 + 1$ (b) $h(t) = \cos t + \sin t$

(c) $y(t) = -[\sqrt{2} \cos \sqrt{2} t + \sin \sqrt{2} t - \sqrt{2} \cos t - \sqrt{2} \sin t]$

Review Problems
Chapter 7   **1.** $\mathbf{x} = e^t \begin{pmatrix} 3 \sin t + \cos t & 3 \cos t - \sin t \\ 2 \sin t & 2 \cos t \end{pmatrix} \begin{pmatrix} c_1 \\ c_2 \end{pmatrix}$

$e^{At} = \begin{pmatrix} 3 \sin t + \cos t & -5 \sin t \\ 2 \sin t & -3 \sin t + \cos t \end{pmatrix}$

3. (a) $\mathbf{x}' = \begin{pmatrix} 0 & 1 & 0 \\ 0 & 0 & 1 \\ 3 & 1 & 0 \end{pmatrix} \mathbf{x}, \quad \mathbf{x}(0) = \begin{pmatrix} 1 \\ -1 \\ 0 \end{pmatrix}$

(b) $\mathbf{x}' = \begin{pmatrix} 0 & 1 & 0 & 0 \\ 1 & 0 & 1 & 0 \\ 0 & 0 & 0 & 1 \\ 0 & 1 & 0 & 1 \end{pmatrix} \mathbf{x}, \quad \mathbf{x}(0) = \begin{pmatrix} 0 \\ 0 \\ 1 \\ 1 \end{pmatrix}$

5. $\mathbf{x}(t) = \begin{pmatrix} te^{-2t} \\ e^{-t} - e^{-2t} - te^{-2t} \end{pmatrix}$

Section 8.1

1. For $h = 0.1$, $y(1) \cong 0.10737$, $e \cong 0.02796$
   For $h = 0.05$, $y(1) \cong 0.12158$, $e \cong 0.01376$

3. For $h = 0.1$, $y(1) \cong 0.87842$, $e \cong -0.01376$
   For $h = 0.05$, $y(1) \cong 0.87149$, $e \cong -0.00683$
   For $h = 0.025$ (if you try it) $e \cong -0.00340$

5. For $h = 0.1$, $y(1) = 3$, $e = 0$ and the same at $h = 0.05$

6. For $h = 0.1$, $y(-1) \cong 2.67788$, $e \cong -0.08388$

9. (a) For $h = 0.1$, $y(0.6) \simeq 4.37641$ and $e \simeq -0.95110$
   (b) For $h = 0.025$, $y(0.6) \simeq 5.03446$ and $e \simeq -0.29304$ (this is almost $\frac{1}{4}$!)
   (c) The error must be less than 0.005. Hence, one can use approximately proportional decreases to predict that $h \simeq 0.00043$ will work. Try it! $h = 0.00043$ may or may not actually work—it depends on round-off error.

10. (c) $y(-1) \cong -1.40890$

Section 8.2

1. For $h = 0.1$ the results are
   (a) $y(1) \cong 0.13745$, $e \cong -0.00211$
   (b) $y(1) \cong 1.53289$, $e \cong 0.02451$
   (c) $y(3) \cong -0.85069$, $e \cong 0.001816$

2. For $h = 0.1$ the results are
   (a) $y(1) \cong 0.13745$, $e \cong -0.00211$
   (b) $y(1) \cong 1.55379$, $e \cong 0.00302$
   (c) $y(3) \cong -0.84838$, $e \cong -0.00049$

3. For $h = 0.1$ the results are
   (a) $y(1) \cong 0.13534$, $e \cong -0.4265 \times 10^{-5}$
   (b) $y(1) \cong 1.55741$, $e \cong -0.1281 \times 10^{-5}$
   (c) $y(3) \cong -0.84887$, $e \cong -0.1744 \times 10^{-6}$

5. (a) $h = 0.2$ gives $e \cong -0.40366 \times 10^{-4}$
   $h = 0.1$ gives $e \cong -0.21328 \times 10^{-5}$
   $h = 0.05$ gives $e \cong -0.12299 \times 10^{-6}$
   $h = 0.025$ gives $e \cong -0.75063 \times 10^{-8}$
   (b) The true solution is $\varphi(x) = 1.5 + 0.5e^{-2x}$. The ratios are approximately 18.9, 17.1, and 16.4.
   (c) As h gets small the ratios will tend to 16.

6. $y(-1) \cong -1.42832$ (using $h = 0.1$)

Section 8.3

1. (a) For $h = 0.1$, $y(1) \cong 0.13745$, $e \cong -0.00211$
   (b) For $h = 0.1$, $y(1) \cong 1.55379$, $e \cong 0.00362$
   (c) For $h = 0.1$, $y(1) \cong -0.84838$, $e \cong -0.00049$

2. (a) For $h = 0.1$, $y(1) \cong 0.13549$, $e \cong -0.00016$
   (b) For $h = 0.1$, $y(1) \cong 1.55848$, $e \cong -0.00108$

4. (b) $k = 0, 1, 2, 3, 4$

5. For $y' = 1 + y^2$ and $h = 0.1$, $y(1) \cong 1.57080$, $e \cong -0.01339$
   For $y' = -2y$ and $h = 0.1$, $y(1) \cong 0.13413$, $e \cong 0.00120$

Section 8.4

1. (a) $y_1 = 0.375$, $y_2 = -0.9375$ with error essentially zero when $h = 0.1$ or 0.05
   (b) Same as part (a)

2. (a) $e_1 \cong 0.04788$, $e_2 \cong 0.22524$ at $h = 0.02$
   $e_1 \cong 0.02447$, $e_2 \cong 0.11087$ at $h = 0.01$
   (b) $y_1 = -1.2484$ and $y_2 = -5.4558$. The errors are better than in part (a) as we would expect. At $h = 0.02$, $e_1 \cong 0.00147$, and $e_2 \cong -0.00124$, while $h = 0.01$ gives $e_1 \cong 0.00037$ and $e_2 \cong -0.00032$.

3. (a) At $h = 0.02$ we have $e_1 \cong 0.00681$, $e_2 \cong -0.01302$, and $e_3 \cong 0.02725$.
   At $h = 0.01$ we have $e_1 \cong 0.00340$, $e_2 \cong -0.00679$, and $e_3 \cong 0.01358$.
   Notice that the errors decrease by approximately $\frac{1}{2}$.

(b) At $h = 0.02$ we have $e_1 \cong -9.3 \times 10^{-5}$, $e_2 \cong 1.9 \times 10^{-4}$, $e_3 \cong -3.7 \times 10^{-4}$. At $h = 0.01$ we have $e_1 \cong -2.3 \times 10^{-5}$, $e_2 \cong 4.6 \times 10^{-5}$, $e_3 \cong -9.2 \times 10^{-5}$. Notice that the error decreased by approximately $\frac{1}{4}$.

Section 8.5

1. Here $\Phi(x, y) = 2y - x$, so $L = 2$. Also, $\varphi''(x) = 3e^{2x}$. Thus $|e_n| \le (e^2 - 1)(3e^2/2)h/2$ and $e_n \cong 3x_n e^{2x_n}h/2$. For $h = 0.05$ this gives $|e_n| \le 1.77034$ and $e_N \cong 0.55418$ at $x_n = 1$. The actual error is $\cong 0.49617$.
2. At $x_n = 1$ with $h = 0.0125$, $|e_n| \le 0.88517$, $e_n \cong 0.13854$, and the actual error $\cong 0.13855$.
3. At $x_n = 1$ with $h = 0.05$, $|e_n| \le 0.39932$, $e_n \cong 0.01692$, and the actual error $\cong 0.01720$.
5. What happens depends on your computer and your program. Probably for Euler's method the error will keep halving (approximately) down to $h = (5120)^{-1}$ or even $h = (10,240)^{-1}$. The Runge–Kutta method will show round-off problems at much smaller values of h.

Review Problems
Chapter 8

1. (a) From $y_{n+1} = y_n + h(2y_n + 1)$, $y_0 = 0$ and from induction one gets $y_n = h[1 + (1 + 2h) + \ldots + (1 + 2h)^{n-1}]$, which is equivalent to the answer.
(b) $y = (e^{2x} - 1)/2$
(c) $m = 1$

Section 9.1

1. The equilibria are -1, 0, and 2.
If $y_0 < -1$, then $y(t)$ tends to $-\infty$ as $t \to \infty$ and to -1 as $t \to -\infty$.
If $-1 < y_0 < 0$, then $y(t)$ tends to 0 as $t \to \infty$ and to -1 as $t \to -\infty$.
If $0 < y_0 < 2$, then $y(t)$ tends to 0 as $t \to \infty$ and to 2 as $t \to -\infty$.
If $y_0 > 2$, then $y(t)$ tends to ∞ as $t \to \infty$ and to 2 as $t \to -\infty$.
3. The equilibrium is 0.
If $y_0 > 0$, then $y(t) \to \infty$ as $t \to \infty$. If $y_0 < 0$, then $y(t) \to -\infty$ as $t \to \infty$. For all y_0, $y(t) \to 0$ as $t \to -\infty$.
5. The equilibria are 0, r_1, r_2, and r_3.
For $0 < r_0 < r_2$, $r(t)$ tends to r_1 as $t \to \infty$. For $r_2 < r_0$, $r(t) \to r_3$ as $t \to \infty$.

Section 9.2

1. -2, 0, and 2 are unstable, while -1 and 1 are asymptotically stable.
3. $n\pi$ is unstable if n is even and asymptotically stable if n is odd.
5. r is asymptotically stable.
6. r_1 and r_3 are asymptotically stable while r_2 is unstable.
9. Unstable   11. Asymptotically stable
16. (c) Infinitely many
17. (a) $y_1' = y_2$, $y_2' = -(g/l) \sin y_1$ (b) $(n\pi, 0)$ for $n = 0, \pm 1, \pm 2, \ldots$
(c) $(\pi, 0)$ is unstable

Section 9.3

1. Unstable   2. Critical
3. Unstable   5. Stable
7. The solution is $\mathbf{x} = c_1(1, 1)^T + c_2(t, t + 1)^T$. If $c_1 = 0$ and c_2 is small, then $\mathbf{x}(0) = (0, c_2)^T$ is near $(0, 0)^T$ but $\mathbf{x}(t)$ will become large as t increases.

Section 9.4

1. Unstable   3. Stable
5. Critical matrix—no information   7. Stable
9. Unstable   11. Critical matrix—no information
13. Stable   14. $1 < B < 2$ for asymptotic stability

16. No information

17. $(0, 0)$ is unstable, while $(1, 0)$ and $(-1, 0)$ are asymptotically stable.

19. $(n\pi, 0)$ is unstable if n is odd, while no information is obtained when n is even.

Review Problems
Chapter 9

1. By sign analysis, $y = 1$ is asymptotically stable while $y = 0$ and $y = 2$ are unstable.

3. The origin is unstable.

5. The corresponding linear system is given in Problem 3. The origin is unstable.

Section 10.1

1. $-(4/\pi) \sum_{k=1}^{\infty} (2k - 1)^{-1} \sin (2k - 1)x$

3. $\pi/4 + \sum_{n=1}^{\infty} [(-1)^n - 1]/(n^2\pi) \cos nx + ((-1)^{n+1}/n) \sin nx$

5. $\pi^{-1} + \dfrac{\sin x}{2} + \sum_{n=2}^{\infty} \left[\dfrac{(-1)^n + 1}{n + 1} + \dfrac{(-1)^{n-1} - 1}{n - 1} \right] \dfrac{\cos nx}{2\pi}$

7. $\pi + \sum_{n=1}^{10} n^{-1} \sin nx$, i.e., $a_0 = 2\pi$, $a_n = 0$ for $n \geq 1$, $b_n = n^{-1}$ for $1 \leq n \leq 10$, and $b_n = 0$ for $n > 10$

9. The negative of the answer to Problem 1.

11. Use $x = 0$ to see that the sum is $\pi^2/12$.

14. (b) $\pi - 2 \sum_{n=1}^{\infty} n^{-1} \sin nx$

15. (b) $4\pi^2/3 + \sum_{n=1}^{\infty} (4/n^2) \cos nx - (4\pi/n) \sin nx$

Section 10.2

1. $f(x) = 1$ for all x in $-\infty < x < \infty$

2. (a) $\dfrac{\pi^2}{3} + \sum_{n=1}^{\infty} \dfrac{(-1)^n 4}{n^2} \cos nx$ (c) Use $x = 0$ to compute $\pi^2/12$.

3. $(2/\pi) \sum_{n=2}^{\infty} \dfrac{n}{n^2 - 1} [1 + (-1)^n] \sin nx$

5. (b) $(2/\pi)(\sin x + \sin 2x + \frac{1}{3} \sin 3x + \frac{1}{5} \sin 5x + \frac{1}{3} \sin 6x + \frac{1}{7} \sin 7x + \frac{1}{9} \sin 9x + \ldots)$

6. (b) $\frac{1}{2} - (2/\pi)(\cos x - \frac{1}{3} \cos 3x + \frac{1}{5} \cos 5x - \frac{1}{7} \cos 7x + \ldots)$

9. $\sum_{k=1}^{\infty} \dfrac{-4}{(2k - 1)^2} \cos (2k - 1)x + \left(\dfrac{2\pi}{2k - 1} - \dfrac{8}{(2k - 1)^3 \pi} \right) \sin (2k - 1)x$

10. (c) $n (\sin x) \sim \sum_{k=1}^{\infty} b_k \sin (2k - 1)x$

Section 10.3

1. (a) $(6/\pi) \sum_{n=1}^{\infty} ((-1)^{n+1}/n) \sin (n\pi x/3)$

(b) $1/\sqrt{2} + \sum_{n=1}^{\infty} (2\sqrt{2}[(-1)^n - 1]/n^2\pi^2) \cos (n\pi x/\sqrt{2})$

(c) $\frac{1}{2} + \sum_{n=1}^{\infty} [((-1)^{n+1} + 1)/n\pi] \sin n\pi x$

(e) $2/\pi + (4/\pi) \sum_{n=1}^{\infty} [(-1)^{n+1}/(4n^2 - 1)] \cos 2nx$

(f) $f(x)$ is already a Fourier series

(g) Since $\sin^2 \theta = (1 - \cos 2\theta)/2$, then $\sin^2(\pi x/\sqrt{3}) = \frac{1}{2} - \frac{1}{2} \cos (2\pi x/\sqrt{3})$.

2. (b) $\frac{1}{2} + (2/\pi) \sum_{k=1}^{\infty} [(-1)^k/(2k - 1)] \cos [(2k - 1)\pi x/2]$

8. (a) $\frac{1}{3} + \sum_{n=1}^{\infty} (1/n^2\pi^2) \cos 2n\pi x - (1/n\pi) \sin 2n\pi x$

(c) $1 - (4/\pi) \sum_{n=1}^{\infty} (1/n)[\sin (n\pi/2) \cos (n\pi x/2) + \cos (n\pi/2) \sin (n\pi x/2)]$

Section 10.4

1. (c) $a_0^2/2 + \sum_{n=1}^{\infty} (a_n^2 + b_n^2) = c^{-1} \int_{-c}^{c} f(x)^2 \, dx$. If f is odd, then all $a_n = 0$. If f is even, then all $b_n = 0$.

2. $\sum_{n=1}^{\infty} 1/n^2 = \pi^2/6 = 1.6449341 \ldots$ **3.** $\pi^4/90 = 1.0823 \ldots$

4. (b) $\left(\dfrac{\pi \cos \alpha\pi}{\alpha \sin \alpha\pi} - \dfrac{1}{\alpha^2} \right) \Big/ 2$

(c) $\left(\dfrac{\pi^2}{\alpha^2 \sin^2 \alpha\pi} \left[1 + \dfrac{\sin 2\alpha\pi}{2\alpha\pi} \right] - 2\alpha^{-4} \right) \Big/ 4$

Section 10.5　1. (a) To $f(x)$ for all x in $[0, c]$
　　　　　　　　(b) To $f(x)$ when x is in $(0, c)$ and to zero when $x = 0$ or c
　　　　　　2. (a) To 1.5 when $x = 0$, π, 2π, to 2 on $0 < x < \pi$ and to 1 on $\pi < x < 2\pi$
　　　　　　　　(c) To x^2 when $0 \le x < 3$, to $(x - 4)^2$ when $3 < x \le 4$ and to 5 when $x = 3$
　　　　　　　　(e) To $\sin x$ when $0 < x < 2$ and to $\frac{1}{2}\sin 2$ when $x = 0, 2$

Section 10.6　1. (a) $x^2 \sim \pi^2/3 + 4\sum_{n=1}^{\infty} [(-1)^n/n^2] \cos nx$
　　　　　　　　(b) $x^3 \sim \sum_{n=1}^{\infty} [12(-1)^n/n^3 + 2\pi^2(-1)^{n+1}/n] \sin nx$
　　　　　　　　(c) $x^4 \sim \pi^4/5 + \sum_{n=1}^{\infty} [48(-1)^{n+1}/n^4 + 8\pi^2(-1)^n/n^2] \cos nx$
　　　　　　3. (b) $f'(x) \sim \sum_{n=1}^{\infty} (2[(-1)^n - 1]/(n^2\pi^2)) \cos (n\pi x/2) + [2(-1)^{n+1}/(n\pi)] \sin (n\pi x/2)$
　　　　　　4. (c) $|x| + x \sim \pi/2 + \sum_{n=1}^{\infty} [2((-1)^n - 1)/(n^2\pi)] \cos nx + [2(-1)^{n+1}/n] \sin nx$
　　　　　　5. (a) $\delta(x) \sim 1/(2\pi) + \pi^{-1}\sum_{n=1}^{\infty} \cos nx$
　　　　　　　　(b) $S_8(x) = 1/2\pi + (8/\pi^2)\sum_{n=1}^{7} (1/n) \sin (n\pi/8) \cos nx$
　　　　　　6. $y = 1 + \sum_{n=1}^{\infty} (ca_n/n\pi) \sin (n\pi x/c) - (cb_n/n\pi) (\cos (n\pi x/c) - 1)$

Section 10.7　1. $f(x) \sim \sum_{n \neq 0} [(1 + (-1)^{n+1})/n\pi i]e^{inx}$　　3. $f(x) \sim (1/2i)(e^{in\pi x/c} - e^{-in\pi x/c})$
　　　　　　5. $f(x) \sim \sum_{-\infty}^{\infty} [(e^c - e^{-c})(-1)^n/2(c - in\pi)]e^{in\pi x/c}$
　　　　　　6. (b) $f(x) \sim \sum_{-\infty}^{\infty} [(e^{2\pi} - 1)/2\pi(1 - in)]e^{inx}$
　　　　　　10. $f(x) \sim \sum_{-\infty}^{-1} (-a_n/2i)e^{inx} + \sum_{1}^{\infty} (a_n/2i)e^{inx}$

Section 10.8　1. (a) $(e^{ix} + e^{-ix})/2 + (e^{2ix} - e^{-2ix})/i$
　　　　　　　　(b) $y = c_1 e^{3x} + c_2 e^{-3x} - (e^{ix} + e^{-ix})/20 - (e^{2ix} - e^{-2ix})/13i$
　　　　　　　　　　$= c_1 e^{3x} + c_2 e^{-3x} - (\cos x)/10 - \frac{2}{13} \sin 2x$
　　　　　　　　(c) $y = e^{-x/2}(c_1 \cos (\sqrt{3}x/2) + c_2 \sin (\sqrt{3}x/2)) + (e^{ix} - e^{-ix})/2i$
　　　　　　　　　　$- e^{2ix}/(2 + 3i) + e^{-2ix}/(3i - 2)$
　　　　　　3. $y_p = \sum_{n=1}^{\infty} n^{-3}(n^4 - n^2 + 1)^{-1}[(1 - n^2) \cos nx + n \sin nx]$
　　　　　　5. (b) $y_T = e^{-x/2}[\frac{13}{17} \cos (\sqrt{19}x/2) + (11/17\sqrt{19}) \sin (\sqrt{19}x/2)]$
　　　　　　　　　　$y_p = \mathrm{Re}\,(e^{ix}/(4 + i)) = (1/\sqrt{17}) \sin (x + 1.3258\ldots)$
　　　　　　　　(c) $x > 11.6$ will do
　　　　　　7. (a) $\delta(x) \sim 1/(2\pi) + \sum_{n=1}^{\infty} (e^{inx} + e^{-inx})/2\pi$
　　　　　　　　(b) $y_p = 1/(6\pi) + \sum_{n=1}^{\infty} [(3 - n^2) \cos nx + 2n \sin nx]/\pi(n^4 - 2n^2 + 9)$
　　　　　　8. (a) $y_p = \sum_{n\,\mathrm{odd}} [(10 - (n\pi/c)^2) \sin (n\pi x/c) - (n\pi/10c) \cos (n\pi x/c)]/$
　　　　　　　　　　　　$[(10 - (n\pi/c)^2)^2 + n^2\pi^2/100c^2]n$
　　　　　　　　(c) $y_p \cong 2.9399 \sin (\pi x + 3.0345) + 0.01267 \sin (3\pi x + 3.1535)$
　　　　　　　　　　$+ 0.00422 \sin (5\pi x + 3.1482) + \ldots$

Review Problems
Chapter 10　1. $f(x) \sim \dfrac{1}{2} + \dfrac{3}{\pi} \sum_{n=1}^{\infty} \dfrac{[1 - (-1)^n]}{n} \sin\left(\dfrac{n\pi x}{c}\right)$

　　　　　　3. $y(t) = e^{-x}(c_1 \cos 3x + c_2 \sin 3x) + \sum_{n=1}^{\infty} \{1/2n[(10 - n^2\pi^2) + 2n\pi i]\}e^{in\pi x}$

Section 11.1　2. (a) $\dfrac{\partial}{\partial t}[\rho(u)c(u)u] = \dfrac{\partial}{\partial x}\left[\phantom{\dfrac{\partial u}{\partial x}} \dfrac{\partial u}{\partial x}\right]$　　　3. (a) $\rho(x)c(x)u_t = \kappa(x)u_{xx} + \kappa'(x)u_x$

Section 11.2　1. $u = 3e^{-t} \sin x + 2e^{-4t} \sin 2x$
　　　　　　3. $v = \sum_{n=1}^{\infty} (2/n\pi)(-1)^{n+1}e^{-9n^2\pi^2 t} \sin n\pi x$
　　　　　　5. $w \equiv 0$
　　　　　　6. (b) $u = e^t \sum_{n=1}^{\infty} (2/n\pi)[1 + (-1)^{n+1}]e^{-n^2 t} \sin nx$
　　　　　　　　(c) $u = e^{-t} \sum_{n=1}^{\infty} (2/n\pi)[1 + (-1)^{n+1}]e^{-n^2 t} \sin nx$
　　　　　　8. $u = \sum_{n=1}^{\infty} e^{-n^2 t} \sin (n\pi/2) \sin nx$

11. $u = (2x)/3 + 1 + \sum_{n=1}^{\infty} g_n e^{-n^2\pi^2 t/9} \sin(n\pi x/3)$,
   where $g_n = -(2/n\pi)(1 + (-1)^{n+1}) - (4/n\pi)(-1)^{n+1}$

13. $u = \dfrac{x}{\pi} + \sum_{n=1}^{\infty} \dfrac{2(2\pi - 1)}{n\pi}(-1)^{n+1} e^{-3n^2 t} \sin nx$

15. (a) $U(x) = T_1 \cos x + [(T_2 - T_1 \cos 2)/\sin 2] \sin x$
   $u(t, x) = U(x) + e^t \sum_{n=1}^{\infty} e^{-(n\pi/2)^2 t} g_n \sin(n\pi x/2)$,
   where $g(x) = f(x) - U(x)$, $T_1 = 1$, $T_2 = 0$
   (b) $U(x) = (e^{-2(x-1)} - e^{2(x-1)})/(e^2 - e^{-2})$
   $u(t, x) = U(x) + e^{-4t} \sum_{n=1}^{\infty} g_n e^{-(n\pi)^2 t} \sin(n\pi x)$,
   where $g(x) = h(x) - U(x)$

17. $u(t, x) = 840x + \sum_{n=1}^{\infty} (2/n\pi)[20 + 50(-1)^n]e^{-144n^2\pi^2 k^2 t} \sin 12 n\pi x$
   (a) $k^2 = 3.33, 0.48,$ or 0.06
   (c) Aluminum is fastest and pine is slowest.

Section 11.3 **1.** $u = \sum_{n=1}^{\infty} (2/\pi n^2)[1 + (-1)^{n+1}]e^{-n^2 t} \cos nx + \pi/2$
   3. $v = 2/\pi - (2/\pi) \sum_{n=2}^{\infty} ([1 + (-1)^n]/(n^2 - 1))e^{-2n^2 t} \cos nx$
   5. $R \equiv 0$ **6.** $u = e^{3t}(1 + e^{-t} \cos x)$
   7. $u = e^{-\pi t}(\tfrac{1}{2} + \sum_{n=1}^{\infty} (2/n^2\pi^2)[(-1)^n - 1]e^{-2n^2\pi^2 t} \cos n\pi x)$
   8. (c) Yes, if $\sqrt{cb/k} \neq n\pi$ for any integer n.
   9. (b) $U(x) = [(T_2 - T_1 \cosh 1)/\sinh 1] \cosh x + T_1 \sinh x$
   $u(t, x) = e^{-t}(g_0/2 + \sum_{n=1}^{\infty} g_n e^{-n^2\pi^2 t} \cos n\pi x) + U(x)$,
   where $g(x) = f(x) - U(x)$, $T_1 = 1$, $T_2 = 0$

Section 11.4 **1.** (a) Let λ_n solve $-\lambda_n = \tan \lambda_n \pi$. Then $u = \sum_{n=1}^{\infty} c_n e^{-\lambda_n^2 t} \sin \lambda_n x$,
   where $c_n = \left[\dfrac{\pi}{\lambda_n} - \dfrac{\sin \lambda_n \pi}{\lambda_n^2} \right] \Big/ \left[\dfrac{\pi}{2} + \dfrac{\cos^2 \lambda_n \pi}{2} \right]$.
   (b) Let $-\lambda_n = \tan 2\lambda_n$. Then $u = \sum_{n=1}^{\infty} e^{-3\lambda_n^2 t} \sin \lambda_n x$,
   with $c_n = \left(\dfrac{2 \cos 2\lambda_n}{-\lambda_n} + \dfrac{\sin 2\lambda_n}{\lambda_n^2} \right) \Big/ \left(1 + \dfrac{\cos^2 2\lambda_n}{2} \right)$.
   3. (a) $T' = -k^2\mu T$, $X'' + \mu X = 0$, with $-X'(0) + hX(0) = 0$, $X(b) = 0$
   (b) $X_n(x) = \sin \lambda_n(b - x)$, where $-\lambda_n/h = \tan \lambda_n b$
   (d) $u = \sum_{n=1}^{\infty} c_n e^{-\lambda_n^2 k^2 t} \sin \lambda_n(b - x)$ and $c_n = \displaystyle\int_0^b X_n(x)f(x)\,dx \Big/ \int_0^b X_n(x)^2\,dx$
   5. (a) $T' = -\mu k^2 T$; $X'' + \mu X = 0$ with $X'(0) = X(b) = 0$
   (b) $X_n(x) = \cos((2n+1)\pi x/2)$, $n = 0, 1, 2, 3, \ldots$
   (d) $u = \sum_{n=1}^{\infty} a_n e^{-[(2n+1)\pi k/2]^2 t} \cos((2n+1)\pi x/2)$, where
   $a_n = \displaystyle\int_0^b X_n(x)f(x)\,dx \Big/ \int_0^b X_n(x)^2\,dx$
   6. $T' = -\mu T$; $(\kappa(x)X')' + d(x)X + \mu\rho(x)c(x)X = 0$ with $X(0) = 0$, $X'(b) + hX(b) = 0$
   7. $\lambda_1 = 2.28893 \ldots$, $\lambda_2 = 5.08699 \ldots$, $\lambda_3 = 8.09616 \ldots$ and
   $c_1 = 1.19090 \ldots$, $c_2 = 0.23366 \ldots$, $c_3 = 0.29771 \ldots$

Section 11.5 **1.** $u = \sum_{n=1}^{\infty} (2(-1)^{n+1}/n)[\cosh ny - \coth n \sinh ny] \sin nx$
   2. $u = \sum_{n=1}^{\infty} (2/n\pi)[1 + (-1)^{n+1}] \operatorname{csch}(n\pi^2) \sin n\pi y \sinh n\pi x + (\text{solution of 1})$
   3. $u = \sum_{n=1}^{\infty} (2/n\pi)[1 + (-1)^{n+1}] \left[\cosh \sqrt{2} ny + \dfrac{1 - \cosh 3\sqrt{2} n}{\sinh 3\sqrt{2} n} \sinh \sqrt{2} ny \right] \sin nx$
   5. $u = \sum_{n=1}^{\infty} \dfrac{2[1 + (-1)^{n+1}]}{n\pi(e^{\lambda_n} - e^{\mu_n})} (e^{\lambda_n y} - e^{\mu_n y}) \sin n\pi x$,
   where $\lambda_n = (-3 + \sqrt{9 + 8n^2\pi^2})/4$ and $\mu_n = -(3 + \sqrt{9 + 8n^2\pi^2})/4$

7. $u = \pi/2 - y/2 + \sum_{n=1}^{\infty} (2/n^2\pi)[(-1)^n - 1][\cosh ny - \coth n\pi \sinh ny] \cos nx$

9. $u = 1 + \sum_{n=1}^{\infty} \dfrac{(-1)^n - 1}{n^2\pi^2} \left[\cosh \left(\dfrac{n\pi x}{2} \right) - \coth \left(\dfrac{n\pi^2}{2} \right) \sinh \left(\dfrac{n\pi x}{2} \right) \right] \cos \left(\dfrac{n\pi y}{2} \right)$

12. (b) $X_n(x) = \sin \lambda_n x$, where λ_n solves $-\lambda = \tan \lambda$

    (c) $u = \sum_{n=1}^{\infty} a_n(\cosh \lambda_n y - \coth \lambda_n \sinh \lambda_n y) \sin \lambda_n x$,

       where $a_n = \int_0^1 f(x) \sin \lambda_n x \, dx \Big/ \int_0^1 (\sin \lambda_n x)^2 \, dx$

13. (a) $X_n(x) = \sin (n\pi x/a)$, $\mu_n = -(n\pi/a)^2$ (b) $Y_n(y) = (\text{constant}) \times e^{-n\pi y/a}$

    (c) $u = \sum_{n=1}^{\infty} f_n e^{-n\pi y/a} \sin (n\pi x/a)$, where $f_n = (2/a) \int_0^a f(x) \sin (n\pi x/a) \, dx$

Section 11.6   **1.** $u = 2\pi - 1 - 4 \sum_{n=1}^{\infty} (r^n/n) \sin n\theta$

3. $u = \frac{1}{2} + \pi^{-1} \sum_{n=1}^{\infty} (r/2)^n \dfrac{1 + (-1)^{n+1}}{n} \sin n\theta$

5. $u = 1 + \sum_{n=1}^{\infty} (r/4)^n e^{-n} \sin n\theta$ **6.** $u \equiv 0$

7. $u(r, \theta) = \sum_{n=1}^{\infty} (r/R)^n g_n \sin n\theta$, where $g_n = (2/\pi) \int_0^\pi g(\theta) \sin n\theta \, d\theta$

9. $u = a_0 + A_0 \log r + \sum_{n=1}^{\infty} r^n(a_n \cos n\theta + b_n \sin n\theta)$

    $+ \sum_{n=1}^{\infty} r^{-n}(A_n \cos n\theta + B_n \sin n\theta)$,

    where $a_0 = \dfrac{1}{2\pi} \int_0^{2\pi} g_1(\theta) \, d\theta$, $A_0 = \dfrac{1}{\log 2} \int_0^{2\pi} [g_2(\theta) - g_1(\theta)] \, d\theta$

        $a_n = \dfrac{1}{2\pi} \int_0^{2\pi} \dfrac{[g_2(\theta) - 2^{-n}g_1(\theta)]}{2^n - 2^{-n}} \cos n\theta \, d\theta$

        $A_n = \dfrac{1}{2\pi} \int_0^{2\pi} \dfrac{[-2^n g_1(\theta) + g_2(\theta)]}{2^{-n} - 2^n} \cos n\theta \, d\theta$

    and b_n and B_n satisfy similar formulas with "$\sin n\theta$" instead of "$\cos n\theta$."

Section 11.7   **1.** $u = \sum_{n=1}^{\infty} (2/n)(-1)^{n+1} \cos (\sqrt{2} nt) \sin nx$

2. $u = \sum_{n=1}^{\infty} (12/n^4\pi)[(-1)^n - 1] \sin (nt/3) \sin nx$

3. $u = \sum_{n=1}^{\infty} (2/n\pi)[1 + (-1)^{n+1}] \cos (3n\pi t/2) \sin (n\pi x)$

5. $u = \sum_{n=1}^{\infty} (2/n\pi)[1 + (-1)^{n+1}] \cos \sqrt{(n\pi)^2 - 1} \, t \sin (n\pi x)$

7. $u = \frac{1}{2} + \sum_{n=1}^{\infty} (2/n^2\pi^2)[(-1)^n - 1] \cos (n\pi t) \cos (n\pi x)$

9. $u = \sum_{n=2}^{\infty} e^{-t}[(2/n)(-1)^{n+1} \cos \sqrt{n^2 - 1} \, t$

    $+ (2/n\sqrt{n^2 - 1})(-1)^{n+1} \sin \sqrt{n^2 - 1} \, t] \sin nx + e^{-t}(2 + 2t) \sin x$

11. $u = \sum_{n=1}^{\infty} e^{-t}(1/2^n \sqrt{2n^2 - 1}) \sin \sqrt{2n^2 - 1} \, t \sin nx$

13. $P = f_0 + \sum_{n=1}^{\infty} f_n \cos (n\pi ct/b) \cos (n\pi x/b)$, where the f_n are the Fourier cosine coefficients of $f(x)$

15. $u = \sum_{n=1}^{\infty} (f_n \cos [(n\pi/b)^2 ct] + (g_n/c)(b/n\pi)^2 \sin [(n\pi/b)^2 ct]) \sin (n\pi x/b)$

17. $u = \sum_{n=1}^{\infty} a_n \cos [(2n + 1)\pi ct/(2b)] \sin [(2n + 1)\pi x/(2b)]$,

    where $a_n = \int_0^b f(x) \sin [(2n + 1)\pi x/(2b)] \, dx \Big/ \int_0^b \sin[(2n + 1)\pi x/(2b)]^2 \, dx$

Section 11.8   **1.** $u = [\sin \pi(x + 2t) + \sin \pi(x - 2t)]/2$

3. $u = [\text{sech} (x + 3t) + \text{sech} (x - 3t)]/2 + [\log [(x + 3t)^2 + 1] - \log [(x - 3t)^2 + 1]]/12$

5. $f(x) = \cos \pi x$, $g(x) = -(\sin \pi x)c\pi$

7. (a) $f(x) = -[\log (x^2 + 1)]/(2c)$ (b) $f(x) = [\log (x^2 + 1)]/(2c)$

Section 11.9   **1.** (a) $u = 2e^{-x_3^2 t} J_0(x_3 r) - e^{-x_5^2 t} J_0(x_5 r)$

(b) $u = \sum_{n=1}^{100} n^{-2} e^{-x_n^2 t} J_0(x_n r/2)$

(c) $u = \sum_{n=1}^{N} A_n e^{-(kx_n/a)^2 t} J_0(x_n r/a)$

3. (a) The Fourier–Bessel coefficients are

$$b_n = \frac{a^2}{x_n} J_1(x_n) \Big/ \int_0^a R_n(r)^2 r \, dr = \frac{a^2}{x_n} J_1(x_n) \Big/ \left[\frac{a^2}{2} J_1(x_n)^2 \right] = \frac{2}{x_n J_1(x_n)}$$

Thus $1 \sim \sum_{n=1}^{\infty} \frac{2}{x_n J_1(x_n)} J_0 \left(\frac{x_n r}{a} \right)$

(b) $u = \sum_{n=1}^{\infty} \frac{2}{x_n J_1(x_n)} J_0 \left(\frac{x_n r}{a} \right) e^{-(kx_n/a)^2 t}$

(c) $b_1 \simeq 1.601954$, $b_2 \simeq -1.064799$, $b_3 \simeq 0.851399$
$b_4 \simeq -0.729645$, $b_5 \simeq 0.648524$, $b_6 \simeq -0.589543$
Note that $x_6^2 \simeq 326.5633$, so that the sixth term of this series, $b_6 e^{-x_6^2 t} J_0(x_6 r)$, is smaller than 5×10^{-8} for $t \geq 0.05$ and is smaller than 2.1×10^{-36} for $t \geq 0.25$.

4. (b) $u = \sum_{n=1}^{\infty} (a g_n / x_n c) \sin(x_n ct/a) J_0(x_n r/a)$, where the g_n are the Fourier–Bessel coefficients of $g(x)$.

(c) The solution is

$$u = 2 \cos(x_2 t) J_0(x_2 r) + 4 \cos(x_4 t) J_0(x_4 r) + \frac{1}{x_1} \sin(x_1 t) J_0(x_1 r)$$
$$- \frac{3}{x_3} \sin(x_3 t) J_0(x_3 r).$$

5. (a) Let x_n be the nth zero of $J_0(x)$ and let f_n and g_n be the Fourier–Bessel coefficients of $f(r)$ and $g(r)$. Then

$$u = \sum_{n=1}^{\infty} \left[f_n \cosh \frac{x_n z}{a} + \left(g_n \operatorname{csch} \frac{x_n b}{a} - f_n \coth \frac{x_n b}{a} \right) \sinh \frac{x_n z}{a} \right] J_0 \left(\frac{x_n r}{a} \right)$$

(b) Let y_n be the nth zero of $J_0'(x)$. For $R_n(r) = J_0(y_n r/a)$ let F_n and G_n be the Fourier–Bessel coefficients

$$F_n = \frac{\int_0^a f(r) R_n(r) r \, dr}{\int_0^a R_n(r)^2 r \, dr} \qquad G_n = \frac{\int_0^a g(r) R_n(r) r \, dr}{\int_0^a R_n(r)^2 r \, dr}$$

Then

$$u = \sum_{n=1}^{\infty} \left[F_n \cosh \frac{y_n z}{a} + \left(G_n \operatorname{csch} \frac{y_n b}{a} - F_n \coth \frac{y_n b}{a} \right) \sinh \frac{y_n z}{a} \right] R_n(r).$$

Review Problems   **1.** $u = \frac{1}{2} + \frac{2}{\pi^2} \sum_{n=1}^{\infty} \frac{(-1)^n - 1}{n^2} e^{-2n^2 \pi^2 t} \cos(n\pi x)$
Chapter 11

3. $u = \frac{y}{3} + \sum_{n=1}^{\infty} \frac{4(-1)^n}{n^2 \pi^2 \sinh(n\pi)} \sinh(n\pi y) \cos(n\pi x)$

5. $U = \frac{\pi}{4} + \sum_{n=1}^{\infty} \left(\frac{r}{2} \right)^n \left\{ \frac{(-1)^n - 1}{n^2 \pi} \cos n\theta + \frac{(-1)^{n+1}}{n} \sin n\theta \right\}$

6. (b) $v = Bx + A$

Index

Miscellanea

$$\sinh x = \frac{e^x - e^{-x}}{2}$$

$$\cosh x = \frac{e^x + e^{-x}}{2}$$

$$a^x = e^{x \log a}$$

$$\Gamma(n + 1) = n!, \quad \Gamma(\nu) = \int_0^\infty e^{-t} t^{\nu - 1}\, dt$$

$$e^{ix} = \cos x + i \sin x$$

$$\cos x = \frac{e^{ix} + e^{-ix}}{2}$$

$$\sin x = \frac{e^{ix} - e^{-ix}}{2}$$

Euler Eq.: $\quad x^2 y'' + bxy' + cy = 0$

Bessel Eq.: $\quad x^2 y'' + xy' + (x^2 - \nu^2)y = 0$

Legendre Eq.: $\quad (1 - x^2)y'' - 2xy' + \nu y = 0$

Laplace Eq.: $\quad u_{xx} + u_{yy} = 0 \quad$ (rect. coordinates)
$\qquad\qquad\qquad (rU_r)_r + r^{-1}U_{\theta\theta} = 0 \quad$ (polar coordinates)

Heat Eq.: $\quad u_t = k u_{xx}$

Wave Eq.: $\quad v_{tt} = c^2 v_{xx}$

Table of Laplace Transforms

1	$\dfrac{1}{s}$	$\log t$	$-\dfrac{\gamma + \log s}{s}\ (\gamma = 0.5772156\ldots)$
e^{at}	$\dfrac{1}{s - a}$	$t^\nu \log t,\ \nu > -1$	$\dfrac{\Gamma'(\nu + 1) - \log s\,\Gamma(\nu + 1)}{s^{\nu+1}}$
$u_c(t)$	$\dfrac{e^{-cs}}{s}$	$\sin bt$	$\dfrac{b}{s^2 + b^2}$
t^n	$\dfrac{n!}{s^{n+1}}$	$\cos bt$	$\dfrac{s}{s^2 + b^2}$
$\dfrac{\sin at}{t}$	$\arctan\left(\dfrac{a}{s}\right)$	$e^{at} \sin bt$	$\dfrac{b}{(s - a)^2 + b^2}$
$t^{-1/2}$	$\dfrac{\sqrt{\pi}}{\sqrt{s}}$	$e^{at} \cos bt$	$\dfrac{s - a}{(s - a)^2 + b^2}$
$t^\nu,\ \nu > -1$	$\dfrac{\Gamma(\nu + 1)}{s^{\nu+1}}$	$Si(t) = \displaystyle\int_0^t \dfrac{\sin r}{r}\, dr$	$\dfrac{1}{s} \arctan\left(\dfrac{1}{s}\right)$
$\sinh at$	$\dfrac{a}{s^2 - a^2}$	$J_0(at)$	$\dfrac{1}{\sqrt{s^2 + a^2}}$
$\cosh at$	$\dfrac{s}{s^2 - a^2}$	$\operatorname{erf}(t)$	$\dfrac{1}{s}\, e^{s^2/4} \operatorname{erf}\left(\dfrac{s}{2}\right)$
$t^n e^{at}$	$\dfrac{n!}{(s - a)^{n+1}}$	$\operatorname{erf}(\sqrt{t})$	$\dfrac{1}{s\sqrt{s + 1}}$
		$\delta(t - c)$	e^{-cs}